Violence and the Civilising Process in Cambodia

In 1939, the German sociologist Norbert Elias published his groundbreaking work *The Civilizing Process*, which has come to be regarded as one of the most influential works of sociology today. In this insightful new study tracing the history of violence in Cambodia, the authors evaluate the extent to which Elias's theories can be applied in a non-Western context. Drawing from historical and contemporary archival sources, constabulary statistics, victim surveys, and newspaper reports, Broadhurst, Bouhours, and Bouhours chart trends and forms of violence throughout Cambodia from the mid nineteenth century to the present day. Analysing periods of colonisation, anticolonial wars, independence, civil war, the revolutionary terror of the 1970s, and post-conflict development, the authors assess whether violence has decreased and whether such a decline can be attributed to Elias's civilising process, which identifies a series of universal factors that have historically reduced violence.

RODERIC BROADHURST is Professor of Criminology at the Australian National University.

THIERRY BOUHOURS is Visiting Research Fellow at the Australian National University.

BRIGITTE BOUHOURS is Visiting Scholar at the Australian National University.

Violence and the Civilising Process in Cambodia

Roderic Broadhurst, Thierry Bouhours,
and Brigitte Bouhours
Australian National University

CAMBRIDGE
UNIVERSITY PRESS

CAMBRIDGE
UNIVERSITY PRESS

University Printing House, Cambridge CB2 8BS, United Kingdom

One Liberty Plaza, 20th Floor, New York, NY 10006, USA

477 Williamstown Road, Port Melbourne, VIC 3207, Australia

314-321, 3rd Floor, Plot 3, Splendor Forum, Jasola District Centre, New Delhi-110025, India

79 Anson Road, #06-04/06, Singapore 079906

Cambridge University Press is part of the University of Cambridge.

It furthers the University's mission by disseminating knowledge in the pursuit of education, learning and research at the highest international levels of excellence.

www.cambridge.org
Information on this title: www.cambridge.org/9781107521193

© Roderic Broadhurst, Thierry Bouhours, and Brigitte Bouhours 2015

This publication is in copyright. Subject to statutory exception
and to the provisions of relevant collective licensing agreements,
no reproduction of any part may take place without the written
permission of Cambridge University Press.

First published 2015
First paperback edition 2017

A catalogue record for this publication is available from the British Library

ISBN 978-1-107-10911-7 Hardback
ISBN 978-1-107-52119-3 Paperback

Cambridge University Press has no responsibility for the persistence or accuracy of URLs for external or third-party internet websites referred to in this publication, and does not guarantee that any content on such websites is, or will remain, accurate or appropriate.

Contents

List of illustrations	*page* vi
List of figures	vii
List of tables	viii
Preface	ix
Acknowledgements	xiv
List of abbreviations	xvi
Map of Cambodia	xviii

	Introduction	1
1	Resistance of a peasant society	35
2	Patterns of premodern criminality	54
3	Development of the colonial state: modernisation and control	82
4	The 'golden age' of the Protectorate: 1920–1940	100
5	The anticolonial war: 1940–1955	128
6	The golden years of Sihanoukism: 1955–1966	149
7	Criminal states and civil wars: 1967–1975	166
8	The perfect storm: decivilising state and society: 1975–1979	187
9	Reconstruction in the midst of a civil war: pariahs, bandits, and international accomplices: 1979–1991	226
10	Crime and violence in contemporary Cambodia: 1991–2012	246
11	Civilising processes and violence in contemporary Cambodia	271
12	Discussion	315
	Appendix: Historical data	336
	References	339
	Index	358

Illustrations

1.1 The *Garde Indigène* on manoeuvre near Stung Treng 1903	*page* 39
1.2 Village head and assistants outside the Commissioner's residence Stung Treng, 1903	53
6.1 Mao Zedong, Peng Zhen, Norodom Sihanouk, and Liu Shaoqi, 1956	157
8.1 The killing fields	190
8.2 The killing tree	191
8.3 The killing tools storage shed sign	191
11.1 Antidrugs advert. This billboard explains that those using chemical substances will be liable to criminal charges	307
11.2 Anti-domestic-violence advert. This billboard illustrates that domestic violence can impair child development	308
11.3 Antifirearm advert. An antifirearm billboard encouraging people in possession of an illegal firearm to hand their weapon over to local authorities	309
11.4 Awareness of domestic violence advert. This billboard highlights that domestic violence is a criminal act and can also have a negative impact on child development	311

Figures

0.1	Gurr's distended U curve of criminal violence, 1900–2012	*page* 4
0.2	Estimated rates of homicide victims in Cambodia, 1900–2012	8
2.1	Homicide victims and banditry events, 1909–20 (rates per 100,000 population)	67
4.1	Size of the police forces and *Garde Indigène*, 1915–43 (rates per 100,000 population)	108
4.2	Estimated rates of homicide victims, 1921–40, and homicide cases in court, 1927–40	109
4.3	Estimated rates of banditry events, 1921–40, and banditry cases in court, 1927–40	109
4.4	Rates per 100,000 population of court cases for violent offences, 1927–43	123
4.5	Types of sentences imposed on convicted felons, 1932–8	126
5.1	Rates per 100,000 population of homicide events for which offenders were wanted by the police, 1948–54	144
10.1	Homicide victims, 1992–2012: estimated rates per 100,000 population	251
10.2	Crime events recorded by police, 1992–2012: rate per 100,000 population	254
10.3	One-year rate of victimisation for 10 crimes combined in 28 main cities, UNICVS, 2005	257
11.1	Urban and rural rates of recorded crime events, 1997–2012	272
11.2	Rates of acquisitive and expressive violence in urban and rural areas, 1997–2012	275
11.3	Average number of offenders by type of violent event, urban and rural, 1996–2008	293
12.1	Model of the civilising process and types of violence	319
12.2	Integrated representation of the modernisation and civilising processes	320

Tables

2.1 Court data from Phnom Penh (1890) and three provincial courts (1905)	*page* 65
4.1 Criminal violence in Cambodia, 1936–40	116
4.2 Banditry in five provinces: rates of events per 100,000 population, 1936–9	118
4.3 Homicide victims: rates per 100,000 population by province, 1936–9	121
5.1 *BPC* 1947–55 homicides	142
8.1 The four aims of the CPK and their consequences	198
10.1 Number of crime events recorded by judicial police, 1992–2012	253
10.2 One-year rate of victimisation and reporting to police, UNICVS Phnom Penh, Kandal, and Kampong Cham, 2000 and 2005–6	256
11.1 Weapons and violent criminal events, 1992–2008	283
11.2 Reporting victimisation to police: Cambodia UNICVS, 2001 and 2006–7 (per cent)	290
11.3 Test of Cooney's privatisation of conflict-related violence	296
11.4 Socioeconomic indicators, 1990–2011	301
11.5 Domestic violence against women and attitude to domestic violence from four surveys	310

Preface

This book examines how key transitions in Cambodia's 150 years of modern history have impacted the prevalence and forms of violence in this country. A substantial and mostly unanticipated decline in crime and violence has occurred in Cambodia since the 1991 peace agreement. In the last 20 years, the homicide rate has been reduced by about 90 per cent – an impressive achievement. Our analysis of this contemporary decline in violence does not overrely on the immediate past but is based on a long-term historical review of criminological evidence, and we hope it yields insights into the general characteristics of violence as well as the factors that drive increases and decreases in lethal violence.

The processes of social change unfold gradually, and unevenly, over generations, and inquiries limited to a decade or two cannot grasp their complexities and implications. It is in historical contexts that change in both social institutions and individual behaviours may be discerned. Observing the ebb and flow of the scale and forms of crime and violence over 150 years revealed a gradual shift from collective violence to private acts driven by interpersonal conflicts and pathologies. The overall trend of violence in Cambodia follows sympathetically the general pattern of long-term declines and individualisation of violence in Western Europe as that area underwent the processes of civilisation observed by Norbert Elias (1939/1994) and Steven Pinker (2011). In both cases this trend was subject to aperiodical surges of violence that disturbed the otherwise cascade-like decline in interpersonal violence and homicide.

One of the authors was in Cambodia in 1998 as an election monitor and became associated with the Cambodian Criminal Justice Assistance Project (CCJAP) funded by Australia's overseas aid organisation (AusAid). The need for criminological expertise in crime prevention as well as the need for better forensic science services were evident. The genesis for our book was a simple question about the number of homicides that had occurred in Cambodia in 1998-9 – and what the likely trends in homicide might be in the future. The question arose because CCJAP wanted to estimate the resources needed to better equip and help the judicial police investigation of suspicious deaths. The team assembled by CCJAP included Australian and Cambodian police and other experts in various fields such as law, health, organisational management, anthropology, linguistics, and corrections. They had started tackling the many problems confronting the delivery of effective postconflict national policing, justice, and correction. Studying the rates of homicide was tied to the broader questions of whether the formation of the Kingdom of Cambodia in 1993 had affected crime and violence and what policies might help reduce serious crime. A pressing priority was the need for effective investigation of homicide and armed robbery – the key to improving the standing of a state and policing service tarnished by a brutal past and the lack of transparency and fidelity to human rights.

Homicide cases are the police 'shop-front' and crucial to the reputation of police and crime prevention. So, the failure to preempt and to solve homicides was indicative of underperformance and low trust among Cambodians of their police and courts. At this time there was a large number of unsolved yet often brutally and boldly performed homicides and armed robberies. There were also frequent incidences of vigilante-like or mob executions of alleged offenders sometimes abetted by police and the shooting of alleged offenders by police in the course of an investigation. It was assumed that improved death investigations and police procedures coupled with reforms to the system of justice would help create a climate of security and certainty and reduce the incidence and fear of crime. It should also help improve the legitimacy of the state and register the emergence of the rule of law over the rule of the gun. The investigation and prosecution of everyday abuses of human rights whether by state or nonstate actors (homicide being one example) would help reassure Cambodians and deter offenders. This improved sense of safety would in turn allow for the return of everyday life and stimulate commerce and social cohesion, creating an ever-evolving virtuous circle. In short – attend to the smaller problems and the bigger problems become easier to resolve. However, Cambodia was not yet pacified, and the eventual monopolisers of the means of violence had not been tamed.

However, as with many apparently simple questions, estimating the number of homicides and other serious crimes was, in fact, difficult. The absence of many of the tools of criminological inquiry, such as a standardised and consistent reporting and recording of crime, made the task challenging. To triangulate problematic official police statistics and obtain more reliable data, we turned to large-scale household surveys that helped measure the prevalence and responses to crime, including the extent of theft, robbery, nonlethal assault, and corruption. We implemented two sweeps of the United Nations International Crime Victims Survey (UNICVS) in several provinces: the first in 2001–2 and the second in 2007–8. The methods and findings are described in the chapters of this book.

Among the many unsolved homicides in the 1990s there was a plethora of 'cold cases', including numerous massacre burial sites across Cambodia. Often, victims' families and survivors lived near suspected or known offenders, and faith in legal remedies had been exhausted. A few of the most egregious mass homicides involved surviving leaders of the former Democratic Kampuchea (DK). The cases were eventually prosecuted. Most of these cold cases remain unprosecuted, but many have been documented by the remarkable efforts of the Sluek Rith Institute (Cambodian Documentation Centre) and its chair Youk Chhang.

A quarter of a century ago, in 1979, the newly formed People's Republic of Kampuchea (PRK) placed on trial two of the senior leaders of the DK Khmer Rouge regime – Prime Minister and Brother Number One Pol Pot (deceased in 1998), and Foreign Secretary and Deputy Prime Minister Ieng Sary (deceased in 2013) – and, using the 1948 United Nations Convention on the Prevention and Punishment of the Crime of Genocide, *in absentia* convicted them of genocide. In 1991, except for the PRK's successor (the renamed State of Cambodia), the parties to the Paris Peace Accord had rejected all references to genocide or crimes against humanity. It was only in April 1997 that the United Nations agreed in principle to a trial of the Khmer Rouge leadership. The first trial in 2010 was conducted by a hybrid Cambodian and United Nations mandated international court known as the Extraordinary Chambers in the Courts of Cambodia (ECCC). It sentenced former S-21 prison chief Kaing Guek Eav, alias Duch, to life imprisonment for supervising the murder of over 15,000 men, women, and children. At the time of writing, the ECCC had found Nuon Chea (aged 88), Brother Number Two, and Khieu Samphan (aged 83), the former head of state, guilty of crimes against humanity committed during the DK regime. Twenty-five years after the events and the first trial *in absentia* of Pol Pot and Ieng Sary by the PRK, charges of genocide against Chea and Samphan are still pending before the ECCC for the mass murder of Cham (Cambodian Muslims), ethnic Vietnamese Cambodians, and other minorities. The legal maxim 'justice delayed is justice denied' is apt.

Our world is confronted by frequent 'small wars' and crimes against humanity by states, warlords, and sectarian groups of all stripes. At the time of writing, several brutal wars – in Syria, Iraq, Mali, South Sudan, Gaza, and Ukraine – are under way with the attendant atrocities and cruelties in blatant defiance of international norms and laws about the treatment of combatants and non-combatants. In the wake of the occupation of towns and cities, the inhabitants evacuate, fearing that they will be massacred because of their religion or ethnicity, and the invaders operate with impunity, subject to neither self-restraint nor law. In such conflicts the territorial struggle to monopolise the means of violence manifests in summary massacres of captured troops and others classified as enemies because of religion or ethnicity or service with the vanquished state. It reminds us of the fragility of peace and the ever-present risk of mass bloodletting. In short, humanity has a long prior record of violent conduct, and it is generally accepted evidence in criminology that prior behaviour is often the best predictor of future behaviour (recidivism). Thus, it may seem deeply counterintuitive in this book to expound the notion of a long and steady decline in the risks of lethal violence. We see some cause for optimism in the promise that under certain conditions the likelihood of lethal violence will recede and that, as in everyday life, the 'bloodbaths' of war will, too, diminish over time. Increasingly, mass murders and other crimes of collective violence will be regarded as outliers rather than the norm. They will be subject to the process of law enforcement and investigation as crimes against humanity in much the same way capable states now prosecute perpetrators of homicide who are routinely investigated by competent teams of detectives and scientists.

We anticipate that some readers will find our position about the civilising prospects of our species contentious, overoptimistic, and perhaps overgeneralised from the 'facts' offered by the Cambodian example. To start with, the very term 'civilisation' is so loaded with the myths and atrocities of colonisation that its use is as apt to offend as enlighten. We alternatively use the expressions 'civilising processes' or 'processes of civilisation' in the specific way suggested by Norbert Elias to refer to growing sensitivity towards violence, its monopolisation by tamed states, and the extent of interdependence among individuals and groups in society. We have endeavoured to avoid factual historical errors but also noticed that historians of Cambodia do not always agree on the facts and on their interpretation. We are not historians and had to rely on their accounts, and when they diverged it was not a straightforward matter for us to settle – in the instances where this mattered, we relied on our discipline's investigative traditions that make explicit uncertainty and speculation. Disputes and related controversies among historians of Cambodia are also not free from explicit or implicit ideological and philosophical opinions and differences. In this sense history shares the same challenges as the other human sciences, including sociology, psychology, and criminology.

We therefore do not claim to be unbiased by ideological and philosophical opinions and free from value judgements. To sum them up, ours include and come from pacifism, or the idea that nonviolent ways of solving conflicts are the best ways, which is consistent with our universalistic and humanist worldview but also founded on realism. Like many, we agree that '*la civilisation n'est pas terminée*' and that there is a long way to go before humanity arrives at some truly 'civilised' state of grace, in which by necessity it uses only nonviolent ways of managing conflicts. We are also wary of 'just' causes that justify 'just' wars in great part because their prosecution often has unintended consequences and too easily kills and maims the innocent. We can be seen as hopeless utopian dreamers but, then, of the pacifist and realist kind, not to be confounded with the many past and current murderous utopias that animate history.

We have also encountered problems with our attempt to realise a genuine multidisciplinary approach to our subject. First among these problems has been finding a common language that bridges the conceptual and methodological differences between historians and social scientists. 'Civilisation', 'civilising', and 'civilised' may mean very different things to historians (particularly historians of colonialism and empires) and social scientists (particularly those interested in historical or process sociology and Norbert Elias's perspective). Perhaps a different nomenclature would lessen translation problems? Would it be preferable to call these processes that lead to less-violent human interactions 'the civility process' or the 'processes of civility'? It is better to go into and explore the substance intended by these terms as we do in this book.

We have strived to do no more than look at the evidence in Cambodian history for the presence, levels, development, or regression of three *processes* (state formation and *monopolisation of violence* by the state; the extent of chains of *interdependency*; and *sensitisation* to violence) theoretically associated with varying levels of violence in human societies. We could not and did not intend to present a detailed account of the last 150 years of Cambodian history, and our focus on violence steered our account. We operationalised these three processes so that we would be able to collect concrete information on them, and we measured as best we could the levels and types of violence across the 150 years from the French Protectorate to the present (to grossly summarise, in terms of violent human interactions, 'we counted the dead'). With these data we analysed the patterns between these three independent variables and our dependent variable – violence – and reached the conclusion fully developed in this book that indeed violence has declined and that this decline can be attributed to these processes of civilisation.

Acknowledgements

Our research undertaken in Cambodia, France, and Australia could not have taken place without the help of many individuals. We could not have completed the book without the aid of the Australian Research Council (ARC), the Australian Academy of the Humanities, and the French Embassy in Australia (Humanities Travelling Fellowship), which enabled one of the authors to visit the *Archives Nationales d'Outre-Mer* in Aix-en-Provence. We have also been fortunate that over many years our various employers, the University of Hong Kong, Queensland University of Technology, Griffith University, and the Australian National University, have supported our research in Cambodia. We were fortunate to receive funding in 2006 from the ARC (Grant DP0776057) and later the support of the ARC, Centre of Excellence in Policing and Security. We gratefully acknowledge this assistance and the generous support of many colleagues over a long time.

During our fieldwork in Cambodia, we were enormously helped by many people, including General Teng Savong, General Van Rotha, Colonel Mohn Kahn San, and Colonel Nuon Bophal of the Ministry of Interior, Royal Government of Cambodia. The generous support and friendship of Robert Bradley, CCJAP team leader (1997–2008), as well as CCJAP team members Steve Woodall, Chan Huot Veng, Kevin Maguire, Malcolm Howlett, Meav Siravuth, John Lawrie, Leng Vuthy, Khurt Nary, Ky Bunnal, and Keith Martin made the demanding logistics and work of the UNICVS possible. In addition the skills of forensic pathologist Phillip Beh of Queen Mary Hospital, the University of Hong Kong, made death investigation and our understanding of homicide less stressful than it may have otherwise been. The unfailing assistance following visits to Cambodia of Robert Bradley, Chan Huot Veng, and Kevin Maguire was invaluable to our continued work in assembling and analysing data. We also acknowledge the wonderful work of the three UNICVS field interview teams (2001–2, 2007, and 2008). We are especially grateful to Chenda Keo and Heng Ken for their help in organising and training the UNICVS team for the Kampong Cham sweep in late 2008 and their continued assistance in later visits. Chenda Keo was our doctoral student (2007–11) whose assistance with translation, cultural interpretation, and many practical matters proved invaluable. We thank Kenneth Johnson, who assisted us with the complex regional mapping and analysis of the dynamics of violence during the postwar insurgency (1947–54) and Natasha Bouhours for her assistance with the preparation of photographs and map. We also thank Michèle Levavasseur, a French teacher whom we met in Kampong Cham in 2008 and whose gracious assistance from Paris led to the discovery of an important source of historical criminal data, the *Bulletins de Police Criminelle* (*BPC*), and Florian Brout, who generously shared the *BPC* data he collected in Paris for his work.

We are grateful to Peter Grabosky, John Braithwaite, Mathieu Guérin, and David Chandler as well as the anonymous reviewers of the manuscript for their valuable advice and critical comments. We thank Hilary Charlesworth, Cheryl White, and Susanne Karstedt for their comments on sections of the text and willingness to engage with our research questions. Any errors, of course, remain ours and not these generous and thoughtful readers. We also thank both our families (Irene, Sebastian, Julian, and Natasha) for their forbearance during absences in the field or in the study. We acknowledge the organisers of the 'Human Sciences Encounters in Cambodia' for arranging a presentation on the subject of this book given one stormy June evening at the Royal University of Fine Arts, in Phnom Penh in 2014. Finally, we wish to thank the publishing editor at Cambridge University Press, Lucy Rhymer, for her support from the outset and her advice in helping to bring the manuscript to completion.

Abbreviations

ANOM	*Archives Nationales d'Outre-Mer* (French colonial archives located in Aix-en-Provence, France)
BNF	*Bibliothèque Nationale de France* (France National Library)
BPC	*Bulletins de Police Criminelle*
CCJAP	Cambodia Criminal Justice Assistance Project
CDC	Cambodian Documentation Centre
CDHS	Cambodian Demographic and Health Survey
CEDAW	Convention on the Elimination of Discrimination Against Women
CGDK	Coalition Government of Democratic Kampuchea
CMAC	Cambodian Mine Action Centre
CMVIS	Cambodia Mine Victims Information System
CNRP	Cambodian National Rescue Party
CPI	Corruption Perception Index
CPK	Communist Party of Kampuchea
CPP	Cambodian People's Party
CSES	Cambodian Socio-Economic Survey
CWCC	Cambodian Women's Crisis Center
DK	Democratic Kampuchea
DV	Domestic violence
ECCC	Extraordinary Chambers in the Court of Cambodia
ERW	Explosive remnants of war
FUNCINPEC	*Front Uni National pour un Cambodge Indépendant, Neutre, Pacifique, et Coopératif* (National United Front for an Independent, Neutral, Peaceful, and Cooperative Cambodia) (Sihanoukist)
GGI	*Gouverneur Général de l'Indochine* (Indochina General Governor)
GRUNK	*Gouvernement Royal d'Union Nationale de Kampuchea* (Royal Government of National Union of Kampuchea)
HSDVC	Household Survey on Domestic Violence in Cambodia

List of abbreviations

IAT	Institutional anomie theory
IUF	Issarak United Front
KPNLF	Khmer People's National Liberation Front
KPRC	Kampuchea People's Revolutionary Council
KPRP	Kampuchean People's Revolutionary Party
KR	Khmer Rouge
KUFNS	Kampuchean United Front for National Salvation
LICADHO	Cambodian League for the Promotion and Defense of Human Rights
MoI	Ministry of Interior (Cambodia)
NAC	National Archives of Cambodia (Phnom Penh)
NADK	National Army of Democratic Kampuchea
NGO	Nongovernmental organisation
NIS	National Institute of Statistics
PAVN	People's Army of Vietnam
PDK	Party of Democratic Kampuchea
PG	Provincial governors
PPA	Paris Peace Agreement
PPP	*Phnom Penh Post*
PRK	People's Republic of Kampuchea
PTSD	Posttraumatic stress disorder
RC	*Résident* of circumscription
RAK	Revolutionary Army of Kampuchea
RCAF	Royal Cambodian Armed Forces
RGC	Royal Government of Cambodia
RSC	*Résident Supérieur du Cambodge* (responsible for the colonial administration of Cambodia)
SOC	State of Cambodia
SRP	Sam Rainsy Party
UNCAC	United Nations Convention Against Corruption
UNDP	United Nations Development Program
UNHCR	United Nations High Commissioner for Refugees
UNICVS	United Nations International Crime Victims Survey
UNTAC	United Nations Transitional Authority in Cambodia

Map of Cambodia

Map of Cambodia
Source: Composite of http://d-maps.com/carte.php?num_car=5448&lang=fr (map of provinces) and http://d-maps.com/carte.php?&num_car=26192&lang=fr (rivers, roads & towns)

Introduction

In the past 150 years, humanity has seen both the triumph of modern civilisation and the occurrence of catastrophic violence. Wars and violent conflicts, mass murders and genocides – megacrimes against humanity – have appeared to be on the rise and illustrate the dangerous side effects of modernity. These surges in mass violence have been mostly state-led, and, paradoxically, they happened in the context of a long, gradual decline in homicide and other interpersonal violence in European (Western) societies since the fifteenth century. This decline in the individual propensity for violent behaviour occurred in parallel with a gradual shift away from social approval of blood vengeance and violence in general, such that in the relatively short span of 150 years the resort to violence has become increasingly regarded as repugnant and 'uncivilised'. These shifts in the thresholds of shame and repugnancy have taken place over time and vary with developments in the social structure or organisation of societies. For example, the public spectacle of the execution of criminals, once a matter for celebration and public participation, is now in most places abolished.[1] Criminals who once faced a gruesome death in front of the crowd are now incarcerated, and even in countries that retain the death penalty (e.g. China, Japan, Singapore, some states of the USA), the whole spectacle is hidden away and executions are performed without additional cruelties in front of a limited number of witnesses.[2] What are we to make of this contradiction? On the one hand, customary attitudes, values, and sensibilities towards interpersonal violence have changed. Most of us would say we have become more 'civilised', probably as the outcome of a process we call 'civilisation'. On the other hand, this general civilising movement has been punctuated by wars and massacres on such a significant scale that these catastrophes could be regarded as 'decivilising' moments.

---

[1] For example, public hangings ceased in England in 1868 but much later in some American states; the last took place in 1936 in Kentucky (Garland, 1990; Johnson & Zimring, 2009).
[2] As Elias (1939/2012) observed, 'Characteristic of the whole process that we call civilization is the movement of segregation, this hiding "behind the scenes" of what has become distasteful' (p. 122).

This book documents and analyses the trends and forms of violence and crime in Cambodia from the mid nineteenth century to the present. During 44 months in the mid 1970s, Cambodia underwent an extremely violent social experiment, which, in an attempt to leap to higher levels of modernity, terrorised and cannibalised its own people. Thus, the Cambodian experience of colonisation, decolonisation, civil war, revolutionary terror, and finally postconflict development presents a challenging test bed for the generality of theories that argue that humanity is on a gradual course towards the diminution of violence.

Norbert Elias's (1939/2012) original concept of the 'civilising process' is such a theory, and it informs our work on Cambodia. Elias outlined broad historical movements that iteratively changed our social structures (sociogenesis) and personality structures (psychogenesis) and over time mitigated the scale and scope of violent behaviours. He proposed that the decline in interpersonal violence and the evolution in social manners were driven by ever-increasing interdependence combined with the forming and taming of the state. He called these phenomena *civilising processes*. Steven Pinker's (2011) recent excavation of empirical data documenting the scale and types of violence from preliterate to modern societies supplied further evidence of the overall decline in violence at both the interpersonal and group levels. Drawing from extensive knowledge produced by modern experimental psychology as well as insights from history, sociology, and political sciences, Pinker demonstrated how the emergence of greater capacities for empathy (psychogenesis), the expansion of interdependency through commerce and globalisation, and the pacifying potential of the state (sociogenesis) are intertwined and help evolve social structures and personality structures that transform collective and individual values about the use of violence. Both Elias and Pinker were aware that the particular development of the process of state formation paradoxically also accounted for the risks of mass violence and periods of 'decivilisation'. Neither Elias nor Pinker drew directly on criminological concepts to formulate their theses. However, historical analyses of crime and violence have been undertaken in Western societies, mainly in Europe, but rarely in other parts of the world. Comparing crime rates across time and place helps contextualise contemporary research (Johnson & Monkkonen, 1996; Monkkonen, 2001). Historical analyses are also relevant to contemporary criminology, particularly for research and interventions focusing on crime and policing in developing, transitional, and postconflict countries. We therefore seek to address two major questions, one empirical and one theoretical.

The *empirical* question is whether trends in non-Western societies, particularly in a developing country such as Cambodia, are similar to those found in Western societies, which show an overall progressive decline in interpersonal violence starting as early as the fifteenth century (Spierenburg, 2008). To answer this question, we attempt to bring to light the particular historical trends

Introduction 3

for Cambodia. Drawing from colonial archives collected in Phnom Penh and in France, historical and contemporary secondary sources, official police data, crime victim surveys, and newspaper records, we estimated the trends in homicide in Cambodia between 1900 and 2012.

The *theoretical* question asks whether macrosocial theories of crime and violence developed and applied in the West can also apply in non-Western contexts. We believe that our examination of long-term trends in the prevalence and forms of violence and crime, as well as the history of the state and governance since the mid nineteenth century in Cambodia, are best analysed through the lens of a process-oriented sociohistorical approach such as proposed in 1939 by Elias in his *civilising process*.[3] We have attempted to follow through on Elias's suggestion that such a study be extended to include oriental or non-Western societies, that is, a study of the civilising process in Cambodia. In short, we study the particular interacting sociogenesis and psychogenesis of the development of Cambodian society and how these shaped crime and violence. Before going further into the details of our study, we present the results of the empirical research on long-term trends in crime and violence in Western countries that inspired and informed our work.

Historical approaches to the study of crime and violence

Analyses of historical trends focusing on Western countries for the period of our study (1900–2012) have revealed a general pattern of criminalised violence shaped as a distended U curve (Gurr, 1981); namely, a steady decline until the mid 1950s followed by an increase up to the mid 1990s – but one that never reaches the level observed in the early 1900s – and then a slow decline again (Figure 0.1).

Historical approaches to the study of crime based on the compilation and analysis of long-term trend data, as well as social-structural and cultural evidence over long periods of time, are indispensable to developing and testing macrosocial criminological theories. A number of scholars in this field have focused on European nations. Through theory testing, they significantly contributed to our understanding of the effects of social-structural and cultural change (i.e. civilising processes) on crime trends, particularly homicide, but most of these theories had originally developed in the context of nineteenth-century Europe. Scholars tested a number of hypotheses about the relations among crime trends, the state, and modernisation proposed by the two major

---

[3] Originally titled *Uber den Prozeb der Zivilisation*, or *On the Process of Civilisation*, and first published in 1939 in German but appeared in English as *The Civilizing Process* (e.g. 1994 edition) – the title chosen by Elias. All quotes from Elias's work are drawn from the 2012 University College Dublin Press edition.

4   Violence and the Civilising Process in Cambodia

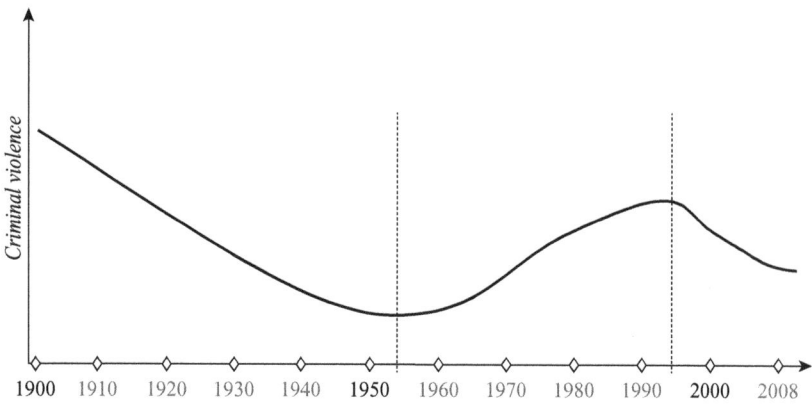

Figure 0.1 Gurr's distended U curve of criminal violence, 1900–2012

Western theoretical schools: Durkheimian functionalism and Marxian conflict perspectives. Well-known examples include Stone's (1983) and Sharpe's (1996) studies of English homicide trends compiled over 700 years, which confirmed functionalist predictions that modernisation was associated with a decline in interpersonal violence. Eisner (2001, 2003) examined other European nations, including Belgium, the Netherlands, Germany, Switzerland, Italy, and Scandinavia, and found a similar long-term decline in homicide in these countries, which he explained by drawing from Elias's notion of the civilising process. Supporting this interpretation was the fact that homicide levels had declined sooner in the most modernised parts of Europe where state formation was well advanced than in regions where states had taken longer to emerge (Eisner, 2001).

Such historical approaches also confirmed Cooney's (1997) thesis that lethal conflicts, whatever their forms (war, rebellion, or mass execution), are more frequent 'when state authority is absent and when it is strong or heavily centralized' (O'Donnell, 2005, p. 683) and generally decline in number between these extremes. For example, O'Donnell (2005) showed how, before 1922, Ireland's colonial status was associated not only with political violence but also with a high level of nonpolitical interpersonal violence, which significantly declined after the Irish Free State in 1922 and reached an all-time low by the time the Republic was declared in 1949.

Stickley and Makinen (2005) examined data from Russia at the end of the Tsarist (1910) and Communist (1989) periods. Their findings showed that violence in non-Russian areas had remained steady or declined, but Russia itself had become more violent. In addition to a number of social-structural theses, they proposed a cultural explanation to account for the differences between non-Russian and Russian areas, in which preexisting cultures of violence were further exacerbated by the role of the state in the Soviet period. Their finding also challenged the belief that the USA was comparatively more violent than Russia. The European empire of Russia in 1910 had a homicide rate of 7.6 per 100,000, that is, similar to the rate in the USA, which had been estimated by Eckberg (1995) at 7.9 per 100,000 during the same year. In 1989, the Russian rate (10.6 per 100,000) was higher than the rate in the USA (8.7 per 100,000). The Russian homicide rate continued to rise and peaked at 19 per 100,000 in 2004 before falling to 10.2 in 2010, but in the USA the rate continued to decline, falling to 4.8 per 100,000 in 2010, suggesting that a sharp anomic period followed the collapse of the Soviet Union.

Archer and Gartner (1976) investigated postwar homicide rates by assembling homicide data from the 1900s to the 1970s in 110 countries. They could therefore examine pre- and postwar homicide rates in relation to World War I, World War II, the Vietnam War, and a number of other conflicts. They found that warfare played a significant role in increasing homicide rates: 'after large and small wars in victorious as well as defeated nations, in nations with improved post-war economies and nations with worsened economies, among both men and women offenders, and among offenders of several age groups [but] post-war increases were more frequent among nations with large numbers of combat deaths' (Archer & Gartner, 1976, p. 960). After testing a number of explanatory models, they concluded that their data fitted best with the notion that the effects of the legitimisation of violence during war carried on during an extended period after the war – the lingering habits of war. Eisner (2008) tried to account for the decline in homicide rates between 1840 and 1950, the rise between 1960 and 1990, and the decline afterwards, using Weber's notion of 'models of conduct of life' and the shifts in culturally transmitted and institutionally embedded ideals of such conduct. Eisner also noted in this explanatory notion of cultural shift[4] that both the 1840–1950 decline and the 1960–90 rise were essentially caused by, first, a decline and then a rise in young male-on-male conflicts in circumstances increasingly defined as public space. Here, it is worth noting, as we shall see later, that Eisner's cultural shift explanation significantly overlaps with Elias's analysis of the psychogenesis of civilising processes.

Crime and violence in Cambodia: a historical perspective

The period of the Khmer Rouge (KR) between 1975 and 1979 has been described as 'year zero', a characterisation borrowed from the title of the book

---

[4] This shift included an emphasis on self-control as a personal ideal, domesticity and familialism as guidelines for private life, and respectability as the yardstick for public appearance, as distinct from premodern standards of honour.

by Ponchaud (1978), *Cambodia: Year Zero*, which described the ideology and policies of the Khmer revolutionaries and how they intended to engineer a radical break from the past.[5] Although the notion of *year zero* is a metaphor for a radical revolutionary agenda aiming to bring a new era and erase everything before it, we should not take it as some kind of reality and relegate the pre-KR Cambodian past to the *oubliettes* of history, particularly if we want to understand crime and violence.

The magnitude of the violence perpetrated during the apocalyptic reign of the KR is certainly unprecedented in Cambodian history, but this does not mean that the preceding epochs were idyllic times of unperturbed Buddhist peace and harmony. With these introductory remarks we do not wish to minimise the horrendous sufferings of the Cambodian people during the KR regime but merely to point out that the terrible crimes committed by the government of Democratic Kampuchea (DK) should not eclipse the past or lead to its romanticisation. In fact, Cambodia's history not only reveals many violent periods prior to the KR but also helps our understanding of the multiple factors that contributed to the murderous years of the KR regime. For example, Chandler (2008) in his *History of Cambodia* described the dire situation in nineteenth-century Cambodia:

> The first sixty years of the nineteenth century form the darkest portion of Cambodia's dark ages before the Armageddon of the 1970s. Invaded and occupied again and again by Thai and Vietnamese forces, the kingdom also endured dynastic crises and demographic dislocations. For a time in the 1840s, it ceased to exist as a recognizable state. Just as Jayavarman VII's totalizing ideology can be compared in some ways to the ideology of Democratic Kampuchea, the first half of the nineteenth century bears some resemblance to the 1970s in terms of foreign intervention, chaos and the sufferings of the Cambodian people. (p. 141)

We do not believe it is possible to link, in any linear fashion, the crimes of the KR regime to some singular historical causal factor. Rather, we argue that cultural, social, economic, and political currents from within and outside Cambodian history have converged towards and precipitated such a tragic outcome, in a process comparable to the build-up of a perfect storm – crystallising as a sudden decivilising event. However, our aim is not just to try and explain the crimes of the KR but rather to present a history of crime and violence in Cambodia since the mid nineteenth century.

---

[5] Ponchaud's title was inspired by the decision of the French revolutionaries to abolish the Gregorian calendar and decree the 22nd of September 1792 as Year One of the Republic. Both the French and the Khmer revolutionaries indeed attempted to eradicate the past through their regimes of terror.

Historical trends in homicide

Our empirical examination of historical and contemporary primary and secondary data on Cambodia shows a pattern punctuated by successive ebbs and flows in the level of homicides: for a decade or so low levels of homicide followed by a spike in homicides, which then recedes but reappears a decade or so later (Figure 0.2). There is such a spike during the first two decades of the twentieth century followed by lower levels of crime and violence in the 1920s and 1930s. From the late 1940s to the mid 1950s a new peak occurs, which peters out until the mid 1960s, when collective violence surges and grows exponentially to reach an unprecedented magnitude during the KR period. After 1989 and particularly in the 1990s, there is again a significant spike, followed from the turn of the new century by a steady decline, with the level of homicides as low as those estimated in the 1920s, late 1930s, and early 1960s. To some extent, these trends mirror the characteristic shape of the distended U curve observed for Western societies if we consider the beginning of the twentieth century, the late 1950s to early 1960s, and the current period. However, given the armed conflicts and the period of revolutionary terror that ravaged Cambodia from the mid 1960s to the mid 1990s, the shape of the Cambodian curve also requires specific interpretations. An important part of this book is devoted to the description, analysis, and discussion of these trends in the context of the socioeconomic and political events that marked Cambodia's history from the end of the nineteenth to the beginning of the twenty-first century. Before we present this historical analysis in the following chapters and the theoretical framework that guides this analysis below, we need to clarify our underlying sociological perspective and associated assumptions as well as our basic definitions of *crime* and *violence*.

Concepts and definitions

'Human nature'

First, we adopt Barnes's (2001) conception of human beings 'as sociable creatures whose interactions are characterised by intelligibility and mutual susceptibility', that is, beings who are 'intrinsically sociable and interdependent' (p. 339). Thus, it is taken for granted that these human interactions include both integrative (e.g. cooperative) and disintegrative (e.g. conflicting) experiences. In our book we focus on disintegrative, or conflicting, events and experiences in Cambodia, but this does not imply that we disregard the other side of human sociability, that is, the role of integrative, or cooperative, experiences. It is only that our focus on conflicts requires us to make such interactions more explicit, as violence and crime are the specific phenomena we study and analyse in Cambodia.

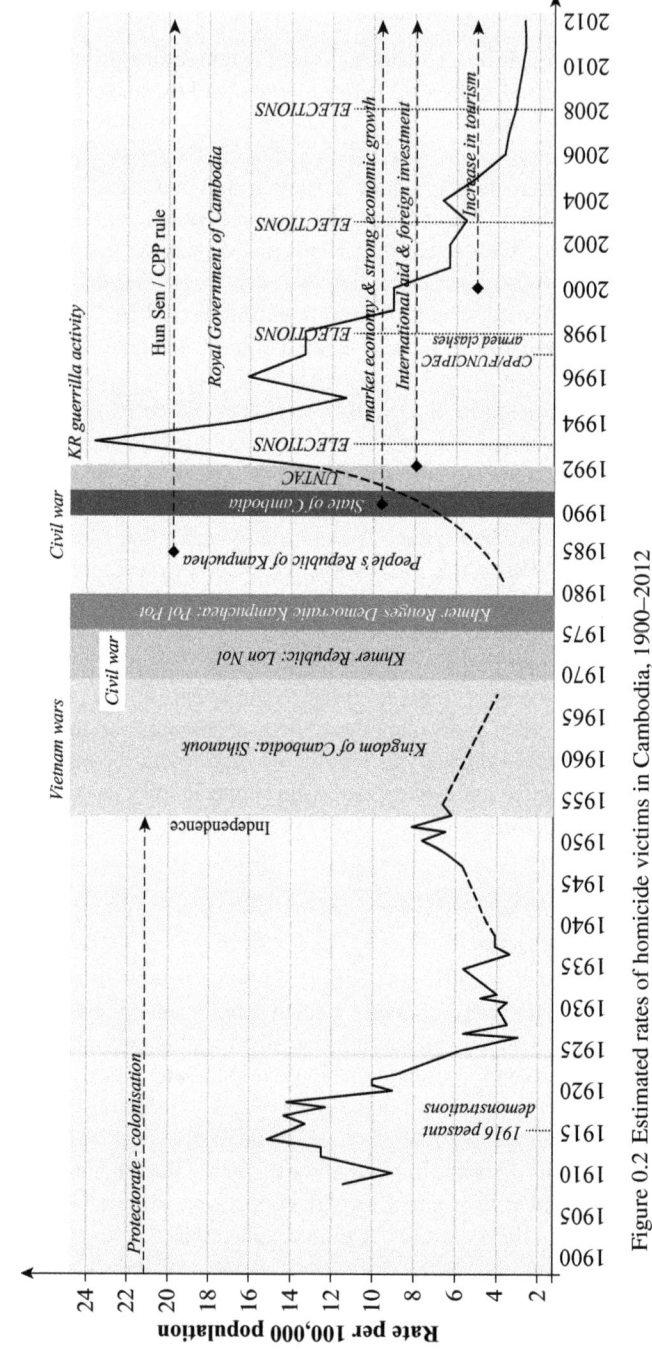

Figure 0.2 Estimated rates of homicide victims in Cambodia, 1900–2012

Violence

For our purpose, we define *violence* as a conscious aggressive behaviour occurring during a conflict between human beings, enacted with at least the awareness, if not the intent, that it will cause physical harm to some other(s), irrespective of whether this behaviour is criminalised or not, and we focus particularly on lethal violence. To further operationalise the main elements of our definition of violence – aggression, harm, and conflict – we make the following propositions:

1. All violent behaviours are aggressive behaviours, but some aggressive behaviours are not violent (e.g. gestures, speeches, and other activities consciously enacted to incur psychological harm). For instance, slander is an aggressive behaviour (consciously enacted to incur psychological harm) but not a violent behaviour because it does not incur physical harm to the victim. However, in the cases of nonviolent behaviours, the perception of aggressiveness may depend also on the subjectivity of the protagonists.
2. To some extent the concept of harm is also subjective. The behaviours that are conceived as harmful change not only along spatial and temporal dimensions but also according to the perspectives of the individual protagonists. Our implicit perspective is that of the modern individualistic rationalist that developed in Western societies with the Enlightenment, in which the expression of pain or displeasure of those who are at the receiving end of particular behaviours, or involved in particular interactions, may be seen as a valid measure of harm.
3. We can also conceive behaviours that cause pain or displeasure to some of the protagonists in terms of conflict (see Christie, 1977). Conflict is a comprehensive concept, ranging on a continuum from minor interindividual nonviolent disputes (verbal disputes or disagreements) to war and genocide and encompassing aggression, harm, and violence, but not limited to any one of them.

Crime

Crime is a value judgement (i.e. a social construction) about particular human behaviours that particular societies prohibit and punish at particular times. Crime can include the following types of behaviours:

1. Some nonaggressive and nonviolent behaviours that are not intended to cause direct harm to others (e.g. drug use and prostitution)
2. Some nonaggressive and nonviolent behaviours performed despite the awareness that they will cause direct harm to others (e.g. theft)
3. Some nonviolent and some violent aggressive behaviours (e.g., respectively, slander and assault)

Although *crime* refers to objectively observable behaviours, it is a normative judgement about these behaviours. It is only when societal norms have determined and institutionalised some rules of appropriation that breaking these rules becomes a crime (e.g. theft or fraud).

Anarchist, Peace-Making, and Republican criminologists have proposed a more principled normative concept of crime, which regards the essence of crime as the exercise of unwanted or unwarranted domination. Tifft and Sullivan (1980), for example, in an early attempt, defined *crime* as 'the suppression of the human spirit', and Braithwaite and Pettit (1990) as 'an invasion of dominion'. These revisions of the notion of crime shift concerns away from conventional definitions of crime based on property rights to wider notions of individual rights and the forms of violence that impinge on the expression of independence or agency.

Even within the restrictive framework of legal positivism, which defines as crimes only behaviours prohibited by the criminal law, modern criminology has broadened its scope. It now includes not only crimes perpetrated by individuals or groups against other individuals or groups – for example, homicide, robbery, rape, assault, theft, and fraud – and crimes against state regulations and general public morality – for example, drug trafficking and corruption – but also, with the evolution of international law, crimes perpetrated by states against individuals or groups – for example, genocide and other crimes against humanity. International and domestic laws generally do not define the mass violence that occurs during foreign and civil wars as criminal, even when many victims are noncombatant civilians. Criminologists, however, are not constrained by legal positivism, particularly when legally defined offences such as crimes against humanity and genocide often occur during wars. More importantly, the boundaries between various crimes perpetrated by and against individuals or states, as well as violence not legally defined as criminal, are often tenuous. These different types of criminality overlap and interact, and one type of criminality may become a factor or a consequence of another type of criminality: for example, corruption may contribute to the onset of mass political violence, which in turn may degenerate into banditry.

In summary, compared to aggression, harm, and crime, violence appears as a more objective concept. We limit our definition of violence to behaviours causing some physical harm to individuals other than the perpetrators and involving the perpetrators' awareness that some physical harm to others is likely to result from the perpetrators' behaviour. We focus on conscious conflicts between humans and, in particular, but not only, on violent conflicts. Those who suffered tangible harm or death in these conflicts we call *victims* and those who caused tangible harm, *perpetrators*. In practice the operationalisation of the main object of this study – the patterns and trends in violence, especially lethal violence – acknowledges the conceptual overlap among aggression, conflict, and violence.

Three sociological concepts that we refer to in this book – modernisation, modernity, and development – have often raised epistemological questions associated with suspicions of Eurocentric, Orientalist, colonialist, or neocolonialist value judgements and discourses. However, for our part, *we* do not use these concepts in a normative sense but as descriptors of observed sociological phenomena. Our terminology is very much informed by Elias's perspective and will therefore become clearer to the reader as we develop our thesis. We use the term *modernisation* to encapsulate a *process* of social change that includes a growing division of labour and the associated development and growth of cities, technology, and industries. This socioeconomic, political, and cultural process of change is associated with an increasing reliance on scientific methods of inquiry rather than religion, faith, and superstition. For us the term *modernity* refers to a state or stage in any given society when the socioeconomic, political, and cultural elements mentioned above prevail. Finally, when we use the term *development* we do not imply more than a movement or change in something observed at different points in time. With these conceptual definitions in mind, we now outline the theoretical framework that informed our study.

Theoretical framework

Our theoretical framework draws from three distinct but overlapping fields of study:
1. A biopsychosociological theory of aggression and violence that integrates analyses at the biological, psychological, and sociological levels. This perspective is useful to understand aggressive and violent human behaviour.
2. Theories of societal change, particularly those focusing on the relation between societal change and human behaviour, including conflicts.
3. Theories of crime, that is, theories attempting to answer the question 'why do people commit crime?'

We now present these theories and discuss the ways that they contribute to our understanding of violence and crime.

Aggression and violence

A large body of theoretical work on aggressive and violent human conflicts generally focuses on distinct levels of analysis: biological, psychological, and sociological. We, therefore, draw from a biopsychosociological theory that manages to integrate and articulate these three levels of analysis (Laborit, 1986). In a nutshell, this theory argues that three types of aggression – defensive/reactive, proactive/predatory, and competitive – common to all animals can be distinguished and in situational terms often overlap and interact.

1. Defensive or reactive aggression occurs when animals (including the human animal) fight to eliminate a noxious or painful stimulus; when the nociceptive stimulus is another animal, the emotions of fear, anger, and hate are generally involved in this type of aggression.
2. Proactive or predatory aggression occurs when animals attack and dominate other animals to obtain some gratification. Although this type of aggression need not be driven by the emotion of fear, anger, or hate on the part of the perpetrator, it often is (e.g. in cases of rape, bullying, sadistic assault).
3. Competitive aggression resembles predatory aggression and is the most common type of aggression in the human animal. It occurs when two or more animals fight for control over gratifying objects (i.e. over things, people, positions in the group hierarchy).

Affective and cognitive memorisations (i.e. learning) of reactive or defensive, proactive or predatory, and competitive experiences and their outcomes affect future behaviours during encounters perceived as similar and, in most social animals, the dynamics and establishment of more or less stable hierarchies of dominance. However, human beings, because of their complex associative cerebral structures that permit symbolic language and imagination, do not need to actually encounter tangible defensive and competitive experiences to resort to aggression and violence. Imagining such experiences is sufficient to trigger aggression and violence; for example, imagined competition socially reinforced by one's community may lead to racism towards another community.

Finally, it is empirically established that there exists a near universal spatial and temporal pattern whereby males are greatly overrepresented as perpetrators in most types of violent aggression, interindividual and collective. As we shall see, this is also the case in Cambodia. Yet females also perpetrate violent actions, and we examine, when the data permit, gendered patterns of violence.

Societal change

Our general thesis draws from theories of societal change, and particularly among them sociological theories focusing on the relations between societal change, human conflicts, and, specifically, aggressive and violent human conflicts. These include the perspectives developed by Weber, Marx, Durkheim, Elias, and Pinker and from criminological empirical studies and theorisation focusing on the same relations as those offered by Gurr, Eisner, Karstedt, Messner, Shelley, Cooney, and others. The scope of the sociological theorists is obviously greater than the scope of the criminological theorists (who are better described as empirical researchers who apply existing sociological theories to explain their data rather than as theorists, per se). For instance, according to van Krieken (2001), Elias 'saw his task as one of drawing on the work of Marx, Weber and Freud, inter alia' and 'elaborating a comprehensive theory of human society, or, more exactly, a theory of the development of humanity, which could provide an integrating framework of reference for the various specialist social sciences' (p. 353, citing Elias's *Reflections on a Life*, 1994, p. 131).

Elias's (1939/2012) oft-cited example (sometimes vulgarised and trivialised) of the changing customs associated with table manners, in particular the knife, perhaps best illustrates the interplay of sociogenesis (the evolution of social structure) and psychogenesis (related changes in individual emotion and behaviour):[6]

When the use of weapons in combat is an everyday occurrence, the small gesture of offering someone a knife at table...has no great importance. As the use of weapons is restricted more and more, as external and internal pressures make the expression of anger by physical attack increasingly difficult, people gradually become more sensitive to anything reminiscent of an attack. The very gesture of attack touches the danger zone; it becomes distressing to see a person passing someone else a knife with the point towards him. And from the most highly sensitized small circles of high court society, for whom this sensitivity also represents a prestige value, a means of distinction cultivated for that very reason, this prohibition gradually spreads throughout the whole civilized society. Thus aggressive associations, infused no doubt with others from the layer of elementary urges, combine with status tensions in arousing anxiety. (p. 462)

We take this broad question of the particular sociogenesis and psychogenesis of societal development and Elias's integrated framework of social evolution as the starting point for further study by specialist social sciences, and in particular criminology. We think it is a pertinent starting point for those criminologists who focus on long-term trends in interindividual violence and biopsychosociologists such as Pinker who focus on long-term trends in all types of violence. As our task involves long-term trends in violence in Cambodia, we also seek to see how such changes in violence reflect societal change in a non-Western society. Indeed, if Elias's prediction that the greater interdependency and sociability of humans that have emerged in modernising societies have also occurred in 'oriental' settings, then violence should decline and follow similar patterns to those in the West.

---

[6] Elias (1939/2012) described the interplay between sociogenesis and psychogenesis: 'Each time the network of dependencies that intersects in the individual has grown larger and changed in structure; and each time, in exact correspondence to this structure, the moulding of behaviour and of the whole emotional life, the personality structure, is also changed. The process of "civilization", seen from the aspects of standards of conduct and drive control, is the same trend which, when seen from the point of view of human relationships, appears as the process of advancing integration, increased differentiation of social functions and interdependence, and the formation of ever larger units of integration on whose fortunes and movements the individuals depend, whether he knows it or not' (p. 288).

Civilising and decivilising processes

Civilising processes

Given empirical evidence that pointed to long-term structural change 'tending to higher levels of differentiation and integration and the formation of nation states', Elias (1939/2012, p. 494) proposed 'a provisional sketch of a theory of civilization' and developed a model

> showing the possible connections between long-term change in human personality structures towards a consolidation and differentiation of affect controls, and the long-term change in the figurations that people form with one another towards a higher level of differentiation and integration – for example, toward a differentiation and prolongation of the chains of interdependence and consolidation of state controls.

Elias (1939/2012) argued that these changes in structure and in individual 'self-steering' arose

> out of the manifold interweaving of human activities, pressure operating in a particular direction, and bringing about shifts in the form of relationships and in the whole social fabric. This rationalization goes hand in hand with a tremendous differentiation of functional chains and a corresponding change in the organization of physical force. Its precondition is a rise in the standard of living and in security, or, in other words, increased protection from physical attack or destruction and thus from the uncontrollable fears which erupt far more powerfully and frequently into the lives of individuals in societies with less stable monopolies of force and lower division of functions. (p. 484)

As Eisner (2008) noted, Elias's theory of the civilising process 'is the idea that increasingly civilized behaviour is brought about by the interplay between two structural forces. The first is the century-long expansion of the state monopoly of power that led to increasing control over behaviour. The second force is the growing "chains of interdependence" brought about by market exchange and capitalism, which put a premium on peaceful interaction guided by self-interest' (p. 290). However, Elias insisted on not only the notions of evolution, of dynamic processes rather than fixed states, but also that this civilising process was not a linear movement implying inevitable 'progress': there were both cohesive (centripetal) and fragmentary (centrifugal) forces at play, and the civilising process was certainly not completed. In the growing expansion of interdependency and monopolisation, sociogenetic processes (changes in the social structures) and psychogenetic processes (changes in collective values, emotions, and behaviours) continued to evolve and interact. Musing about the necessary distinction between interindividual and state violence, Eisner (2008) concluded his study about the decline in homicide between 1840 and 1950 in the Western world by remarking

> that the decline in homicide cut through all the political fault lines and catastrophes of the century; it occurred similarly in democracies, monarchies, and authoritarian regimes;

it continued through dramatic political change in the history of countries like Ireland, Italy, or Spain; and it also cut through the atrocities of the two world wars and the mass killings by the Nazi regime. This observation means – and this is a normative rather than a theoretical thought – that we should probably not equate declines in interpersonal criminal violence with civility in a wider normative sense. Disturbingly, populations in which fighting, feuding, and criminal killing are very unlikely can nonetheless support and engage in denunciation, deportation, and mass killings. (p. 304)

Here we can see why Elias's 'civilising process' had been criticised and why he elaborated on the spurts and counterspurts in these processes and the notion of a 'de-civilising process' (see below) to account for these spikes of state and collective violence and crime. However, on the basis of his observations of an expanding in-group and contracting out-groups and the greater prevalence of the idea of the 'world citizen', had he lived longer, Elias may have answered, contra Eisner, that slowly but surely 'populations in which fighting, feuding, and criminal killing are very unlikely' – in other words, pacified populations – were also becoming less and less likely 'to support and engage in denunciation, deportation, and mass killings'. Elias argued that the civilising process involved a movement towards a democratisation of the state monopoly. Thanks to the increasing interdependency and the associated growth of intermediary structures and civil society, the state monopoly of force shifted from private, that is, controlled by a monarch or a single group or party, to increasingly public, that is, controlled by institutions receiving the input and enjoying the support of the citizenry.

Finally, Elias offered an analysis of the dynamics of colonisation that was more encompassing and explanatory than Marx's. It is not surprising since Elias drew from Marx but also integrated and refined Marx's ideas in his theory of the development of humanity. Through colonisation, the elite or aristocratic top-down civilising process observed in Europe was replicated in the regions coming under the control of Western powers. The now civilised (not in a vulgar normative sense but in the complex and dynamic Eliasian use of the term) masses of the colonising state became the new elite of the colonised. This happened first via the local elites and then expanded to other social strata. However, like in the developmental history of the colonisers, attempts at state monopolisation, at a greater division of labour and resulting interdependency, that is, centripetal (integrative) forces, were resisted (see Marx on colonisation below) by traditional indigenous powers that constituted centrifugal or disintegrative forces. Oppressive and exploitative colonial regimes often maintained and used traditional authoritarian governance that prevented processes of democratisation. This eventually amplified the centrifugal forces of traditional indigenous powers, resulting in generally violent anti-colonial conflicts and independence. However, in most instances, independence was followed by further processes of disintegration leading to civil wars in postcolonial countries that nevertheless had amalgamated some of the colonisers' patterns of conduct with their own (Elias) or, using Lilja and Ojendal's (2009) term, 'hybridised'.[7] For Elias, therefore, the civilising process renders violence more problematic and subject to an intensified criminalisation process with an increasing reliance on bureaucratic surveillance and special policing institutions. This sociogenesis is associated with psychogenetic processes that manifest in increasing self-control of the affects, and particularly a growing sensitisation to violence. The civilising process is reinforced by the role of the state through its monopolisation of violence and welfare functions. By improving health services and literacy, securing livelihood, and suppressing crime, the state legitimates its governance.

It is now important to dispel any misinterpretation about an apparent similarity between Elias's concept of the 'process of civilisation' or 'civilising process' and the colonialist or Orientalist concept of the 'civilising mission' and the 'white man's burden'. Yet, it would be wrong to say that there is no relation at all between the two notions, as the recent concept of 'civilising offensives' (see Powell, 2013, in the discussion) within countries and through international peace missions demonstrates. Whether one argues that the colonialist 'civilising mission' was not a theory but rhetoric to support imperialist goals or that it could be regarded as a theory (as in the Marxist view on the modernising effect of colonialism on premodern societies; see below), one of the colonialists' more or less successful goals was to bring the state monopoly of power and the chains of interdependence of market exchange and capitalism to colonised countries.

Decivilising processes

Mass violence, and in particular state violence, as it occurred in the twentieth century with the two world wars, the Bolshevik revolutions, the Nazi Holocaust, and other late-twentieth-century megacrimes such as occurred in Cambodia, the Balkans, and Rwanda has been levelled as evidence for a refutation of Elias's theory of the civilising process (see, for example, Malešević & Ryan, 2012). To explain the occurrence of such spikes of mass violence during the larger global civilising process, Elias and his followers (e.g. de Swaan, 2001; Fletcher, 1997; Goudsblom, 1992, 1994; Mennell, 1990a, 1990b; van Krieken, 1998,

---

[7] Elias noted that the European states that were the first to form centralized states were also among the first to colonize abroad. In general the civilising processes expand because codes of conduct of a courtly-aristocratic upper class were amalgamated with those of the various bourgeois strata as these rose to the position of upper classes; *civilité* was incorporated and perpetuated – with certain modifications depending on the situation of the new host – in what was now called civilization or, more precisely, 'civilized conduct'. So from the nineteenth century onwards, these civilized forms of conduct spread across the rising lower classes of Western society and over different classes in the colonies, amalgamating with the indigenous patterns of conduct. (Elias, 1939/2012, p. 470; see also Lilja & Ojendal, 2009)

2001; Wacquant, 1999) developed the notion of a *decivilising* process. Elias (1939/2012) was also very alive to the risks of 'counter-spurts' in the civilising process, and writing in 1936 he noted with some prescience the following:

We scarcely realise how quickly what we call our 'reason', this relatively farsighted and differentiated steering of our conduct, with its high degree of affect-control, would crumble or collapse if the anxiety inducing tensions within and around us changed, if the fear affecting our lives suddenly became much stronger or much weaker or, as in many simpler societies both at once, now stronger now weaker. (pp. 484–5)

Malešević and Ryan (2012) have argued that if the same theory can simultaneously explain two opposite processes, as Elias's theory appears to do, then the theory is not falsifiable and therefore is not a proper theory. However, our view is that this criticism is not based on a clear understanding of Elias's dynamic perspective. First, there is the inescapable paradox of the pacifying power of the Leviathan. It is by waging wars – hence, through mass violence – that the Leviathan monopolises violence and therefore pacifies a territory where such a monopoly prevails. Elias's notion of decivilising processes is better understood when associated with his concepts of centripetal and centrifugal forces, or forces and processes that cause a movement towards interdependency, integration, monopolisation, and pacification (i.e. towards civilisation) and those that cause a movement away from interdependency, integration, and monopolisation (i.e. towards autarky, disintegration, war, and brutality – towards decivilisation). These concepts were already included in his original 1939 version of the *Civilising Process*, not as a later response to the mass violence of World War II or to his critics. Although one could be tempted to restrict Elias's civilising process to the Weberian macroperspective about the Leviathan's pacifying role in regard *only* to the decline in interpersonal violence, when properly understood as the effect of centrifugal forces, his notion of decivilising processes is not problematic but actually useful, and there is no reason therefore to restrict his theory only to changes in levels of interpersonal violence. Elias's theory can explain both the decline in interpersonal violence and the aperiodic spikes of mass and interpersonal violence that also occur.

Scholarship on decivilisation has been, advantageously to our purpose, complemented by relatively recent taxonomies and theorisations of genocides and crimes against humanity at both the structural and individual levels (Fein, 1993, 2000; Gerlach, 2006; Hinton, 2002; Kiernan, 2007; Loyle, 2009; Scherrer, 1999; Winton, 2011). Even closer to our topic, historians of Cambodia have debated the nature of the Khmer Rouge movement and argued over different macrotheorisations of the Cambodian revolution (Chandler, 1999; Frieson, 1992; Jackson, 1989; Kiernan, 2008; Lavoix, 2007; Quinn, 1989; Thion, 1993; Vickery, 1984). We draw from these scholars in Chapter 8 when we discuss mass violence in Cambodia and the forms of the revolutionary violence and the crimes perpetuated during the DK regime.

Further empirical support

On the basis of a large set of empirical data, Pinker (2011) argued that Elias's perspective was correct and that in the Western and westernised world all forms of violence and cruelties (interindividual types, intergroup types including wars, and judicial/penal types) have declined in terms of both frequency (in the case of intrastate and interstate wars) and proportion (i.e. rate of victims per population, although not absolute volume). Elias had integrated the insights of Weber, Marx, and Freud into his perspective,[8] and the level of development of the psychological sciences in 1939 of course limited his integration of the psychological dimension. Pinker's more extended empirical data and new insights of biopsychosociological processes not only refined Elias's perspective but also gave it even more explanatory purchase.

Malešević and Ryan (2012) criticised Pinker's argument of a general decline in mass violence. Their criticism rests on the observation that in *absolute* numbers the victims of mass violence in such events have increased. However, Pinker's argument is based on *relative* numbers, that is, the proportion of victims of such violence in the population. Malešević and Ryan, along with Bauman (1989) and Hinton (2002), regarded modernity as a factor in producing mass violence such as genocide. Although there is no argument that modern totalitarian ideologies played an important role in the spikes of mass violence in the twentieth century, those critics appear to underestimate or minimise the mass violence that occurred during the premodern genocides documented by Kiernan (2007) and the pre-state violence summarised by Pinker (2011). In support of Malešević and Ryan's contention that pre-state hunter-gatherer cultures were less violent than the initial state hierarchical systems that followed, it is possible that, at the beginning, the proto-states' monopolisation of violence (hence their use of violence to achieve this monopolisation via elimination contests) increased the levels and types of violence compared to the levels in pre-state hunter-gatherer cultures. However, violence-related evidence pertaining to the Palaeolithic and early Neolithic periods and contemporary remnants of hunter-gatherer cultures is scant and often contrary. Forensic examination of remnants from hunter-gatherer skeletons suggests some individuals suffered violent deaths inflicted by other individuals (i.e. not caused by accidents); however, such investigations are unlikely to specify the type of violence (i.e. interindividual or intergroup) that caused these deaths.

---

[8] Elias mentioned Durkheim only once in *The Civilising Process* but integrated many of his ideas (see Elias, 1939/2012, p. 499, in the 1968 postscript – he also criticised Parson's static depiction of society but even more the tendencies to see individuals and society as separate identities).

Overall, we believe that Malešević and Ryan have not convincingly refuted Pinker's thesis that, as far as relative numbers are concerned and over the long term and so far, all types of violence have declined. Of course, 'we moderns' have the *potential* to annihilate *all* human beings on this planet, which our ancestors did not have, and in addition to technological powers (not to be forgotten) the technologies of management and ideologies realised by social organisations would indeed be determinant in such an outcome.

One may be tempted to hypothesise that, contra to Pinker's evidence of a long peace, interindividual violence and state violence have followed opposite trends; as the former was declining the latter was rising (as in the paradox of the pacifying powers of the Leviathan). However, if in terms of the *absolute* number of harmed individuals, twentieth-century state violence has certainly been greater than during previous centuries, it might not be the case in terms of the *relative* number of harmed individuals or in the frequency of state crimes, which is what Pinker argued. In this case the hypothesis of opposite trends between interindividual and state violence would not be supported. Modern weaponry was clearly an important factor in the huge number of individuals harmed during the twentieth-century states-organised carnage, and it would seem that only modern centralised states could muster the resources to design, produce, and deploy this sophisticated, expanding, and expensive weaponry of mass destruction. On the other hand, given that in 1994 in Rwanda almost one million individuals were slaughtered essentially with machetes, one can see how such large-scale state massacres could happen during premodern times with relatively rudimentary weaponry.[9]

Durkheim's modernisation processes

Although neither Elias nor Pinker mentioned him, Durkheim's modernisation theory is compatible with Elias's theory of the civilising process. The term *modernisation* has often been used in the context of the eighteenth and nineteenth centuries in Europe. This period, particularly the nineteenth century, apart from the transformation wrought by the industrial revolution, coincided with the building of new colonial empires by European states and, for the purpose of this study, by the French in Indochina. The processes of modernisation, at least in the Western world, entailed a shift in economic modes of production from feudal/mercantilist to industrial forms and a greater centralisation and penetration of the state as well as its rationalisation and democratisation. Economic development and rising living standards, urbanisation, the growth of a middle

---

[9] Examples are offered in Kiernan's (2007) comprehensive history of genocide and extermination from ancient to modern times – in particular, his descriptions of the Spanish conquest of the New World under the military 'bandit' adventurers Cortés and Pizarro (see also Heming, 1970).

class, greater individualism, and changes in the nature of relationships from hierarchical to contractual increased the levels of interdependency, weakened communal regulation, and fostered a corollary move from informal to formal social controls and the monopolisation of violence by the state. Theoretically, these modernisation processes would be associated with declines in interpersonal violence. Here, we can see that Durkheim's modernisation perspective had many similarities with Elias's later *civilising process*.

Violence and types of social solidarity

The Durkheimian concepts of 'mechanical social solidarity' prevalent in premodern societies, followed by 'organic solidarity' prevalent in modern societies, the accompanying erosion of 'collectivism', rise of 'moral/cooperative individualism', and, during the transition, 'egoistic individualism' are also helpful for an analysis of long-term crime and violence trends (including in Cambodia). Durkheim referred to two types of societies, each with their norms and values. Mechanical solidarity described the old order of cultural integration and homogeneity characterised by a very low division of labour and level of interdependency (limited or short chains of interdependence, in Eliasian terms) and a faithful observance of unitary religious and customary norms in which deviance was rare and severely punished. Organic societies, on the other hand, were characterised by a complex division of labour, growing levels of interdependency and diversity of outlook, and a premium on the value of the individual. In the Durkheimian sense, collectivism was a way of being and relating in premodern societies whose bonds were based on mechanical social solidarity and 'in which the group – the family, the clan, a professionally defined group, a religious or ethnic community – is valued much more than the individual and his/her well-being' (Messner, Thome, & Rosenfeld, 2008, p. 170). In its normative positive sense, moral or cooperative individualism was the modern, organic way of being and relating in which the individual, following a new universal principle, was more valued than the group; that is, the individual in the group had the same value and enjoyed the same rights as any other individual in the group. In its normative negative sense, egoistic individualism referred to the exploitative attitude of the exclusively self-serving person in modern societies, exemplified through the psychopathic personality or 'maximiser' familiar to criminologists.

But, essentially, Durkheim's concepts of collectivism and individualism were not normative notions implying 'collectivism is good and individualism is bad' but were descriptions of ways of being and relating; he predicted that the movement from collectivistic to individualistic values would be associated with a decline in interpersonal violence relating to intergroup feuding. Premodern mechanical societies were more prone to interpersonal violence than were modern organic ones because the institutional order was shaped by 'honour and a rigidly defined social hierarchy within a society divided into estates'

(Messner, Thome, *et al.*, 2008, p. 170). In contrast, in the organic mode of solidarity typifying modern societies,

> the individual is no longer tied into a closely knit mesh of norms, symbols, and rituals that define his or her own identity primarily in terms of belonging to a collectivity. The fusion of personal and collective identities dissolves. The individual's social standing and reputation are no longer defined by a group-specific code of honor that, for example, makes blood revenge obligatory. Violence that injures, mutilates, or kills another person becomes increasingly repugnant, abominable. (Messner, Thome, *et al.*, 2008, p. 170)

Messner, Liu, and Karstedt (2008) also argued that stagnation or reversion to previous rigid hierarchical orders (in Elias's perspective, a factor of decivilisation) could increase violence in modern societies. However, in their analysis of the relationship between modernisation and crime, Durkheim (1893/1964) and neo-Durkhemian scholars have emphasised the role of anomic processes.

Anomie

Durkheim defined *anomie* as a state of normlessness brought about by sudden and rapid structural changes in society. It is a transitional period when old cultural, social, economic, and political arrangements have been destroyed or seriously weakened by events such as revolutions, wars, economic, or environmental crises. These destabilising events were themselves generating technological, social, and ideological transformations, which, in time, would take over as new values. Developmental anomie, therefore, does not have to be associated uniquely with modernisation in the sense given to the idea of 'progress' during the nineteenth century. However, it is in relation to the transition from premodern mechanical societies to modern organic societies that Durkheim articulated his concept of developmental anomie, when mechanical solidarity was being destroyed but the new order (the new rules of the societal game) was not yet firmly established. During that period of temporary creative chaos, the distinction between legitimate and illegitimate opportunities was blurred, and both recalcitrant and opportunistic behaviours, manifesting as an increase in deviance and crime, abounded. When the new modernised order finally prevailed, the resulting socioeconomic and political progresses fostered the development of 'organic solidarity', namely, a set of new values not based on rigid cultural integration but on human rights, diversity, equality, and cooperation that reduced violence. Here we can see a conceptual overlap between Durkheim's concepts of modernisation as a movement towards organic solidarity – and anomie as a troublesome period of disintegration – and Elias's civilising and decivilising processes.[10]

---

[10] Elias (1939/2012) recognised that during social upheaval the dominant standards of conduct are loosened and an anomic-like 'period of uncertainty preceded the consolidation of a new standard' while the 'social situation itself makes "conduct" an acute problem' (p. 483), and so long-held conventions are tested.

As we shall see later, when discussing empirical tests of Durkheim's modernisation theory, it is important to distinguish between *developmental* or *process-induced* anomie – a temporary condition associated with rapid social change – and *chronic* or *structural* anomie – a stable feature of the institutional order (Messner, Liu, *et al.*, 2008; Messner, Thome, *et al.*, 2008; Thome, 2001, 2007).

Violence and the state

There are many overlaps between Durkheim's (1950) and Elias's visions of the modern state. For Elias (1939/2012), the 'Leviathan state' had initially a Hobbesian purpose: 'Without violent actions, without the motive forces of free competition, there would be no monopoly of force, and thus no pacification, no suppression and control of violence over large areas' (p. 346). According to Elias, the paradox of the civilising process was that the violence required in achieving the monopoly of force (therefore a centripetal or integrative force, in Elias's view) ultimately begot nonviolence. For Durkheim, there was a 'functional primacy of the state over the economy, because the latter [was] immanently amoral' (Messner, Thome, *et al.*, 2008, p. 171). The modern state therefore played a crucial role as both an 'organ of moral discipline' and a 'champion of individualism' in the process of modernisation and the decline in interpersonal violence, as Messner, Thome, *et al.* (2008) commented:

Without the state, the individual could not have been set free from primordial bonds; without the state, there would be no power to protect the individual against the tyrannical claims of the group. Durkheim, on the basis of his reading of history, is led to the conclusion that 'except for the abnormal cases the stronger the state, the more the individual is respected'. (p. 171)

Cooney (2003) made a similar observation: 'As the state evolves, it gradually assumes more and more of the protective and economic functions formerly discharged by corporate groups. The family and locality lose ground; the central authority expands its jurisdiction' (p. 1383). However, good governance was also a useful predictor of lower homicide rates. Cole and Gramajo (2009) reported that the 'quality of government, law enforcement, and political stability appear to be critical factors in understanding the observed variation in homicide rates around the world' (p. 761), while Roth (2009) noted that the best correlates of low homicide rates among unrelated adults in the USA are trust in government and belief in the honesty of public officials.

If we understand Durkheim's idea of a strong state as a democratic state whose legitimacy is based on wide popular recognition and support, we can say that, as far as a general respect for the individual is concerned, such modern states have overall fulfilled his prediction. However, these modern states, like the premodern states studied by Kiernan (2007), have also committed massive crimes against humanity, and Messner, Thome, *et al.* (2008) pointed out that Durkheim's reliance on the state to 'serve as "the guardian, promoter and enforcer of civic morality" can certainly be challenged given subsequent historical development' (p. 171). This is again the paradox of the Leviathan of which Durkheim (and Elias) was aware, because if he believed that 'the stronger the state the more the individual [was] respected', it was also necessary to counterbalance the power of the state with strong secondary social groups (i.e. what is now termed 'civil' society). It is clear that for Durkheim the characteristics of the 'civilised' modern state included a commitment and capacity to greatly respect and protect the individual and the presence of strong democracy, popular legitimacy, and civil society; that is, in Elias's terms, public monopoly had replaced private monopoly. Messner, Thome, *et al.* (2008) noted an important distinction between the two explanatory perspectives on the reduction of violence: 'For Elias, the disciplinary forces of advanced societies hold down individual impulses,' but for Durkheim it is because 'individuals are freed from the closely knit bonds that tied them to the collectivity' (p. 171). For us, these two processes are not antagonistic; on the contrary, they represent the two sides of the same 'modernising/civilising coin': one is freeing individuals from a mechanical form of social control that encourages feuding, and the other is enmeshing them in the new organic form that prevents it. This is confirmed by the fact that Durkheim, like Elias, saw interdependency or 'gentle commerce' (Pinker, 2011) as one of the most important 'disciplinary forces of advanced societies' (pp. 663–4) that would, through constraints borne by longer chains of interdependence, 'hold down individual impulses' (Messner, Thome, *et al.*, 2008, p. 171).

Durkheim on crime

Now that the broad sociohistorical process of societal change from (mechanical) moral collectivism to (organic) moral individualism has been presented, we can discuss Durkheim's understanding of crime. First, for Durkheim, crime is a social construction, and in a normal society (that is, relatively stable and not going through an anomic period) a certain level of crime is normal. Attempting to eradicate crime would be a folly because some level of deviance is necessary not only to permit change but also, through the punishment of the deviant, to buttress the collective conscience and consequent social solidarity. The modernisation processes discussed above not only lessen the forms of violence characteristic of mechanical societies but also change normative beliefs about what should be considered deviant and criminal and how crime should be punished. Organic solidarity goes hand in hand with a collective conscience, forms of social control, processes of criminalisation, and types of punishment based on the new social structures and reflecting the new values of this organic solidarity.

However, the transition from mechanical to organic society and different modes of social solidarity, particularly if rapid and brutal, was likely to be anomic, that is, a difficult process of adaptation fostering a rise in crime and violence. But once the anomic transitional stage had passed, the outcome of modernisation, which promoted economic development and the rationalisation of governance, was a reduction in violent crime. In the Durkhemian model, the transition was a period during which three moral forces were at play: (1) a regressing but still present *moral collectivism* inherited from the mechanical stage of development; (2) a new, emerging *moral/cooperative individualism* based on organic solidarity (complex division of labour and interdependency); and (3) a maladaptive and anomic *egoistic individualism* that increased the level of crime above the normal. The complex division of labour and interdependency (and associated organic solidarity and moral/cooperative individualism), which for Durkheim lessened violence, are the very civilising processes that Elias associated with less violent behaviours. In fact, when Durkheim referred to changes in the division of labour and interdependency, he was referring to changes in the social structure – in Elias's terms, to sociogenesis. When Durkheim referred to changes in the type of social solidarity and morality from mechanical to organic solidarity via moral/cooperative individualism, he was referring to changes in the personality structure – in Elias's terms, to psychogenesis.

Over the years, many have claimed to have empirically tested Durkheim's modernisation theory, but generally only weak and inconsistent findings emerged (e.g. Krohn, 1978; LaFree, 1999; Messner, 1982; Neuman & Berger, 1988; Ortega, Corzine, Burnett, & Poyer, 1992). A problem with many of these studies was the misinterpretation of key theoretical concepts. Another problem confronting theory testing has been the frequent failure to distinguish, and therefore appropriately operationalise, two distinct concepts: modernisation and modernity. Developmental (transitional) or process-induced anomie is associated with the *process of modernisation*, whereas structural or chronic anomie is associated with the *level of modernity*. Cross-sectional designs that examine the relationship between the level of development and crime in a number of countries at a specific point in time measure the impact of levels of *modernity* on crime, not the impact of the *process of modernisation* on crime, including Durkheim's most important concept of developmental anomie. To measure the impact of developmental or process-induced anomie, longitudinal designs, preferably historical long-term trend analyses, are indispensable, whereas cross-sectional analyses are adequate to examine chronic or structural anomie.

More recent theory testing has supported some aspects of Durkheim's thesis. Thome's (2001) analysis of crime data in Germany at the end of the nineteenth century confirmed that a decline in interpersonal violence was associated with the movement from collectivistic to individualistic values. Karstedt (2006) found in a cross-national study of homicide rates in the late twentieth century that an indicator of 'individualism' was negatively associated with levels of homicide. Messner, Liu, *et al.* (2008) pointed out that collectivistic values such as honour and its counterpart defamation could stimulate violent conflicts in a variety of situations.

Criminological theories

Theories of crime abound, but integration, although attempted by some (Braithwaite, 1989; Tittle, 1995), has been difficult, possibly because of a frequent, often unrecognised, confusion between the objective and normative aspects of the behaviours studied by criminologists. When criminologists ask why people commit crimes, they in fact ask why some people violate the social norms and do not respond to social control. Criminological questions ask 'why do some people or groups of people break the rules and norms imposed by the groups and societies they belong to?' 'why and how are these people punished?' and 'why in the first place were these rules and norms made?' Yet, the object of criminological study is more complex. Criminology usually does not directly enquire about the biological, psychological, and sociological mechanisms and drivers of predatory, aggressive, and violent behaviours and why some people or groups are more predatory, aggressive, and violent than others. However, the effect of prohibitions on these behaviours is of criminological interest because such attempts at suppression influence their psychological and sociological mechanisms and their manifestations. We distinguish these two aspects in order to analyse their relationships and interactions, and particularly in order to study the interacting sociogenesis and psychogenesis of the development of a particular human grouping such as Cambodia.

Macrocriminologists who have focused on the pacifying effects of modernisation processes and drawn from Durkheim are often regarded as belonging to the functionalist school of sociology and criminology, and those who have focused on class and group conflicts during the modernisation process and drawn from Marx or Weber, to the conflict school. We would prefer to transcend these rather rigid categorisations and use them here only as a heuristic device to present the particular macrosociological focus of these criminologists.

Functionalism

Gurr (1981) proposed that, on the one hand, long-term declines in interindividual violence in the Western world were generally associated with a growing sensitisation to violence and the development of internal and external controls, particularly modern policing, on aggressive behaviour. On the other hand, factors accounting for temporary deviations from long-term declines included the effect of warfare on the legitimisation of individual violence, the early phases of rapid urbanisation and industrialisation, and periods of economic prosperity or decline. Gatrell (1990) focused on the development of modern policing, Shelley (1981) on the effect of rapid urbanisation, and Archer and Gartner (1976) on war effects on postwar homicide rates.

Cooney's (2003) work on the development of the state and the individualisation (i.e. decline in co-offending) and privatisation (i.e. larger proportion of intimate protagonists) of violence provided an important neo-Durkhemian contribution, and the questions he asked are pertinent to the history of violence in Cambodia:

Historically, the argument implies, for instance, that periods in which the trend toward looser social ties and a stronger state reversed itself should also be periods when violence became less private and more public. Comparatively, it implies that nations with large populations of poor, unemployed undereducated minorities involved in illicit activities (e.g. the United States, South Africa) should have more violence of a public nature than nations with smaller internal, multidimensional status gaps (e.g. Sweden and Japan). (p. 1399)

Drawing from Durkheim, Shelley (1981) focused on specific effects of modernisation at different stages. Because modernisation is a process occurring through time, it involves various phases during which developmental anomic conditions produce different criminological effects. Shelley therefore proposed a version in which modernisation (as a transitional process producing anomie, therefore not modernity conceived as a state of being and relating) was criminogenic but with different effects on trends in violent and property crimes according to the phase of modernisation. An important aspect of Shelley's perspective is also her distinction between rural and urban crime patterns, which, she argued, became more pronounced as modernisation progressed. Here her thesis also had similarities to Elias's notion of the increasing social constraints on and sensitisation to violence during the civilising process. Initially, in rural areas, violent crime was much more frequent than acquisitive crime. As rural populations migrated on a large scale to the cities, both violent and property crimes increased: 'Their tradition of violence accompanied rural migrants to the cities, and their adjustment problems aggravated their usual response to tension. Thus, unprecedented rates of urban violence accompanied new levels of property crime as recent urban arrivals expressed their unfulfilled desire for the fruits of industrialization' (Shelley, 1981, p. 36). As these newly urbanised populations adjusted to city life, violent crimes declined; property crimes, however, continued to grow and eventually represented the largest share in the burden of crime. The remaining urban violence was increasingly motivated by gain, that is, acquisitive violence (e.g. robbery) progressively exceeded expressive violence in the share of violent offending. Neopolitan (1997) combined

Durkheim's and Elias's theories, arguing that violence declined because modernisation increased social equality and organic solidarity and at the same time civilised behaviour.

Taking the concept of developmental anomie further, neo-Durkhemian theorists have introduced the concept of a durable *chronic* or *structural* anomie as a marker of modern globalised societies. They have made important recent contributions to the theoretical literature on anomie and crime in their discussions of the new conditions brought about by globalisation, neoliberal market policies, and, following the collapse of communism, the transition from state-run to market economies (Karstedt, 2003; Messner, Liu, *et al.*, 2008; Pridemore & Kim, 2006). Messner and Rosenfeld (2000) coined the concept of 'institutional anomie'

> to grasp the consequences of neo-liberal market policies in Western democratic countries, but [it] has proven equally pertinent to the analysis of the transitional process from a state-run towards a market economy ... In the process of modernization and transformation, societies need to balance social justice and self-interest, collective and individual interests, welfare institutions, and market forces ... Imbalances between institutions, the dominance of market forces and the erosion of other institutions like the family or the educational system, produce anomic forces that are conducive to crime, both property and violent crime. (Messner, Liu, *et al.*, 2008, pp. 285–6)

Institutional anomie theory (IAT) is relevant to the analysis of crime and violence in Cambodia during the last two decades. Also pertinent to our analysis of the 1990s and previous Cambodian periods (e.g. the 1940s and the 1970s) is Braithwaite, Braithwaite, Cookson, and Dunn's (2010) application, in which the authors link spikes of violence in Indonesia, particularly after the collapse of the Suharto regime, with institutional anomie. Messner, Thome, *et al.* (2008) discussed the differences between IAT and Durkheim's original proposition by contrasting their respective views about two sets of concepts: moral individualism versus egoistic individualism, and developmental anomie versus chronic anomie. They contended that Durkheim would have been 'skeptical about the long term viability [of a] cultural value system' (p. 172) based on egoistic individualism and unregulated and unconstrained markets. They suggested, on the contrary, that 'what Durkheim depicted as a pathological but possibly temporary cultural condition is in fact compatible with an on-going institutional order' (p. 172), that is, developmental anomie can set in and become structural anomie. They argued that the ascendency of moral individualism 'presupposes the effective operation of the restructured agents of social control and moral guidance – the family, the schools, the democratic state, and other entities associated with civil society' (p. 172), and this may not happen, or may take a long time to happen, or may be retarded or destroyed by catastrophes. They suggested, 'The type of individualism that emerges along with the erosion of collectivism as societies become more highly differentiated is thus likely to give increasing weight to the "egoistic" form rather than the "moral" or "cooperative" form... Egoistic or disintegrative individualism provides the cultural foundations for economic dominance in the institutional balance of power and widespread anomie' (p. 172). They concluded that such an institutional order 'is conducive to high levels of violent crime' but specified 'in advanced industrial/post-industrial societies' (p. 172).

Conflict

In conflict perspectives, the core processes linking modernisation and crime are power, domination, oppression, and inequalities, as well as the conflicts to obtain power or resist domination (e.g. class conflicts), which are regarded as both cause and effect of modernisation. Colonialism clearly entails the use of power by one people to subjugate, dominate, and exploit the territorial and human resources of another people. Sooner or later it leads to conflicts between colonisers and colonised. As in the case of the colonisation of Cambodia by the French, the moral justification used by the colonisers is the notion of a 'civilising mission' that will modernise backward societies and propel them towards socioeconomic progress and stability.

Most, if not all, colonial enterprises, including the Vietnamese colonisation of Cambodia in the 1820s (Chandler, 2008), were legitimised, with varying degrees of candour and cynicism, as civilising missions and justified, on the part of the Western powers, as also being part and parcel of the 'White Man's Burden' (Kipling, 1899/1940). The French were no exception, and the rhetoric of the *mission civilisatrice* was couched in terms of the modernisation of both economic and state arrangements (Chandler, 2008; Forest, 1980; Guérin, 2008; Osborne, 1969, 1979; Tully, 1996). The extent of the colonial modernisation of Cambodia, the authenticity of the efforts deployed, and the indigenous resistance to them are addressed in later chapters.

The double edge of colonialism

In the early 1850s, Marx proposed that British colonialism in India would unwittingly fulfil this civilising and modernising mission. Marx obviously endorsed neither the rhetoric nor the real intentions of British colonialism but suggested that, in the final analysis, despite its ruthless exploitative activities, colonialism was a progressive force capable of lifting societies such as India out of the stagnant feudal structures of 'oriental despotism': 'England has to fulfil a double mission in India: one destructive, the other regenerating – the annihilation of old Asiatic society, and the laying of the material foundation of Western society in Asia' (Marx, 1853, cited in Avineri, 1968, p. 125). For Marx the initial conflicts of resistance against the 'regenerative mission' (i.e.

against modernisation) could only be the action of regressive forces, not to be confounded with the progressive forces that would develop once the static and restricting 'Asiatic mode of production' was overthrown. Eventually, colonialism would shake and modernise these societies through capitalistic reforms, which in turn would unleash revolutionary conflicts capable of moving these societies further towards socialism.[11]

Although Marx's optimism about the progressive edge of colonialism later on sobered (Blaney & Inayatullah, 2010), for the purpose of our Cambodian analysis it is an interesting thesis. In fact, Marx's change of mind by the 1870s towards a prototype of dependency theory, or the development of underdevelopment (Wallerstein, 1984, 1989), is equally pertinent for an analysis of the relationship between the political economy and crime and violence in postcolonial Cambodia. As we shall see, under the Protectorate, Cambodia attracted only a small number of French settlers. It remained all along, from 1863 to 1954, a heavily taxed de facto colony with limited economic development.[12] For instance, Slocomb (2010) concluded a chapter on the colonial economy of Cambodia by remarking:

By the end of the Protectorate, therefore, we cannot speak even of incipient capitalism in Cambodia. A very small sector of the economy, that represented by the rubber plantations, was capitalised, but there was almost no local participation in that sector... For all their rhetoric about *mise en valeur*, colonial economic development was reserved for the benefit of French investors and almost deliberately confined to isolated, gated spaces like the rubber plantations of the eastern plateaux. (p. 72)

Contemporary postcolonial perspectives such as Marxian world systems theories link globalisation and market hegemony to crime trends in the postindustrial era (for example, Currie, 1991; Karstedt, 2003, 2006). These approaches to crime in developing nations, particularly their stance on the postindustrial or globalised market 'second-stage modernisation' of such societies, provide a fitting framework for an analysis of the situation in Cambodia after the 1993 United Nations intervention. Messner, Liu, *et al.* (2008) offered a summary of this relatively recent literature:

---

[11] The civilising process and 'civilising missions' past and current in Cambodia converge because, although exploitive, the coloniser also wants to dominate the colonised 'into the web of the hegemonial, the upper-class country' and 'This requires a certain standard of living and 'demands a "civilization" of the colonized. Just as it was not possible in the West itself, from a certain stage of interdependence onwards, to rule people solely by force and physical threats, so it also became necessary... to rule people in part through themselves, through the moulding of their super-egos' and in turn assimilate with varying degree of success their traditions (Elias, 1939/2012, pp. 474–5).

[12] Some authors made a distinction between 'colonies of exploitation' and 'colonies of settlement' with the notion that colonies where it was envisaged that many colonists would settle benefited from comparatively greater socioeconomic development (Tully, 2002).

Criminogenic conditions within lesser-developed nations arise from their subordinate position within larger world economy... The process of urbanisation no longer – as in modernisation theory – reduces violence in the urban environment but to the contrary, elevates it to extraordinary levels... The basic claim is that the expansion of markets and the accompanying triumph of capitalism have unleashed criminogenic forces in developed and developing countries alike. The forces include the spread of rampant individualism... the decline of social reforms that previously mitigated the more deleterious consequences of capitalist societies... and an expansion in the opportunities for organized criminal activities at a transnational level, activities that are often accompanied by violence. (p. 274)

Also relevant to an analysis of Cambodia's historical patterns of criminality are the perspectives reviewed by Neuman and Berger (1988) about the nexus of economic and political factors in the generation of political violence. For instance, they summarised research that suggests economic inequality is more likely to generate political violence when governance is moderately rather than highly repressive or democratic. Moreover, although multinational penetration initially goes hand in hand with antidemocratic governance, it does not increase repression once a regime is securely established (Bollen, 1983; Timberlake & Williams, 1984).[13] Neuman and Berger (1988, p. 299) also suggested that the relations between multinational penetration, level of inequality, and type of regime might influence the prevalence of both conventional and political violence, and we consider these factors in our final chapters from the 1990s to the present.

In summary, our study is also concerned about social control in Cambodia. We look at phenomena such as the monopolisation of violence and the capacity of the state to manage or prevent conflict. In turn we examine the legitimacy of the state (as in the mind of the population) and how this affects conflict resolution (measured as trends in interindividual conflicts and violence). These issues are, in large part, questions about forms of deviance and social control. On the other hand, we see that the dynamic perspective that we borrow from Elias links through an iterative model the development of social structures (sociogenesis) in concert with the development of psychological structures (psychogenesis). In his thesis, a *civilising process* in Europe and by extension in the 'Western world' has been under way, and Elias argued that social processes such as state formation and monopolisation over violence developed simultaneously with increasing self-control (i.e. increasing internalised social control) and increasing sensitisation to violence first among elites and then the population as a whole. If changes in social structures and in particular those structures that exert social control are also interactive with the process of changes in the

---

[13] Since 1993, both growing economic inequality and moderately repressive governance have been observed in Cambodia. Between 1998 and 2012, multinational penetration has increased in Cambodia as well as a more secure and established state.

affective and cognitive 'habitus' (collectively, the culture) of any given population, then our study is also necessarily concerned with psychosociological processes and particularly those involved in predatory, aggressive, and violent behaviours. However, these particular psychosociological processes of aggression and violence concern the habitus, that is, the varying propensity, spatially and temporally, to use aggression and violence, not the fundamental biopsychosociological mechanisms of human aggression and violence, which, inherited through the phylum from prehuman evolution, are universal and in this sense essentially unchanged. We certainly do not assume that Khmer are *essentially* more prone to aggression or violence than any other human grouping.

Informed by the works presented in this introduction, our analyses attempt to answer the following questions. First, what were the trends for different forms of violence over the last 150 years of Cambodian history, including acquisitive and expressive forms manifesting in collective violence (intergroup, political), ordinary violence (interpersonal, intrafamilial/intimate, in revenge, in disputes, and cruel forms), and judicial-penal violence (including extrajudicial executions)? Second, in which way can the processes of civilisation described by Elias and Pinker and the related modernising processes expounded by Durkheim, Shelley, Eisner, and Cooney account for the types of crimes and violence that flourished or not?

The data

In Europe, the preservation of records on crime and justice over many centuries has made historical research possible. In Cambodia, unfortunately, many governmental records were lost or destroyed during the Khmer Rouge period. Yet, historical criminological research is not impossible because most of the colonial records held in Phnom Penh National Archives have been preserved. Also accessible are records compiled by the French during the Protectorate; some were available from the French archives in Paris, but most of them from the *Archives Nationales d'Outre-Mer* (ANOM) in Aix-en-Provence. For the postcolonial period from 1955 to 1965, some patchy criminological records (police, court, and public health data) were kept in Phnom Penh, but from the mid 1960s to the early 1990s we could not find any criminal statistics; perhaps none were compiled, the records have been destroyed, or they have not been made accessible to researchers. For the period from 1992 to 2012, we obtained official crime records from the Ministry of the Interior (MoI) of the Royal Government of Cambodia. We also conducted large household victim surveys in 2001, 2006, and 2008 and collected and analysed newspaper reports of crime events published between 1992 and 2008. The greatest gap in criminological data of any sort, therefore, occurred for the period between the mid 1960s and the early 1990s, and we had to rely on secondary sources and some interviews, which mostly only provided qualitative accounts. This period coincided with high levels of collective violence starting in 1967 with the onset of the guerrilla war and its brutal repression. The violence increased during the first civil war from 1970 to 1975, peaked during the revolutionary terror of the KR regime until 1979, and gradually diminished during the second civil war from 1979 to the late 1990s. We certainly lack quantitative indicators of ordinary crimes during these catastrophic years, but we are able to estimate the types and scale of, as well as the trends in, collective violence.

Over the main period considered in the book (1900–2012), crime data came in many different forms, sometimes as records of numbers of events, victims, or offenders, in police or court statistics, from press reports or victim surveys; at times some of these data overlapped, and at other times they stood alone. The problems associated with gaps in the data and the varieties of measurements are commonly encountered in studies of long-term trends in criminal behaviour but need not preclude such research. Gurr (1981), for example, discussed a number of ways to address these limitations when researching historical trends in violent crime (see also Grabosky, 1974). The types of data used in our study, their limitations, and the strategies adopted to minimise them are presented in the relevant chapters.

Outline of this book

The book contains 12 chapters, in which we chronologically develop our criminological history of Cambodia from the mid nineteenth century to the present and analyse and discuss our findings, guided by the theoretical framework that we presented in our introduction. In addition we offer a general conclusion where we revisit the analysis of our major findings and discuss the broad implications for studies of the relationships between civilising and modernisation processes and trends in crime and violence in Cambodia and in the world at large. The first five chapters are devoted to the period of the French Protectorate.

Chapter 1, 'Resistance of a peasant society', briefly considers the troubled and anomic years of the nineteenth century prior to and during the early stage of the French Protectorate and then examines the movements of violent resistance of a peasant society against the 'civilising mission' of the colonial enterprise.

Chapter 2, 'Patterns of premodern criminality', focuses on crime during the first two decades of the twentieth century, from 1900 to 1920. High levels of crime and violence characterised this period, and frequently rebellions merged with predatory and social banditry. However, at the end of this period, crime and violence started to decline.

Chapter 3, 'Development of the colonial state: Modernisation and control', outlines the administrative and judicial reforms of the Protectorate and analyses the ways in which they influenced crime and violence.

Chapter 4, 'The "golden age" of the Protectorate: 1920–1940', examines the 'golden years' of the colonial period, characterised by the strengthening of the state apparatus and its legitimacy and during which – at least until the Great Depression – levels of crime and violence plummeted.

Chapter 5, 'The anticolonial war: 1940–1955', starts in 1940 and covers the war and postwar period and the struggle for independence until 1954. This was an anomic period associated with the return of a discredited French control and a spike in crime and violence. Once again, insurgents and bandits sometimes coalesced and sometimes confronted each other.

Chapter 6, 'The golden years of Sihanoukism: 1955–1966', focuses on the 12 years that followed independence. These years have often been presented as the golden years of the postcolonial period. However, a peasant rebellion in Battambang in 1967 marked the start of increasing levels of collective violence.

Chapter 7, 'Criminal states and civil wars: 1967–1975', covers the civil war decade during which the levels of collective violence and state crimes overshadowed interindividual criminality. The civil war, closely associated with the Second Indochina War, and the scale of the corruption of the Khmer Republic elites contributed to the acceleration of a wave of collective violence.

Chapter 8, 'The perfect storm: decivilising state and society: 1975–1979', describes the mass violence and terror during Democratic Kampuchea with a focus on the historical, cultural, and internal and external drivers of this violence as well as the types of violence and perpetrators and victims. In this chapter we discuss the relevance and limitations of the traditional criminological paradigm in the study of mass violence and megacrimes such as wars, state crimes, genocides, and crimes against humanity.

Chapter 9, 'Reconstruction in the midst of civil war: pariahs, bandits, and international accomplices: 1979–1991', investigates the decade of state reconstruction from 1980 to 1990 during the second civil war. Although interindividual criminality may have been low, the new regime of the People's Republic of Kampuchea defined many prohibited activities as crimes against the state. The political economy of the armed conflict revived and reinstitutionalised elite corruption.

Chapter 10, 'Crime and violence in contemporary Cambodia: 1991–2012', examines and discusses the trends and patterns in crime and violence during this period. High levels of crime and criminal violence as well as widespread corruption and elite plundering of public assets coincided with the period of transition; however, this was followed by a significant and sustained decline in criminality apart from grand corruption that continued unabated.

Chapter 11, 'Civilising processes and violence in contemporary Cambodia', looks beyond the trends presented in Chapter 10 and analyses them in terms of the mechanisms suggested by modernisation and civilising process theories.

Chapter 12, our last chapter, discusses the main findings of our sociohistorical review of crime and violence in Cambodia by reassessing the utility of civilising processes in understanding the forces driving societal and individual change.

1   Resistance of a peasant society

Historians have described the period from the mid seventeenth to the mid nineteenth centuries as the 'dark ages' of Cambodia. The Vietnamese conquest of the southern Mekong delta heralded the economic isolation of Cambodia. Saveros Pou (1977) described 'a slow degradation of values from the 17th century on' (pp. 48–9). It was a troubled and anomic period marked by frequent invasions from the neighbouring Vietnamese and Siamese kingdoms, civil wars, and recurrent deadly rivalries within the Khmer royal family (Chandler, 2008; Mikaelian, 2009; Sok, 1991). Chandler (1974) summed up the social climate of this period: 'It is difficult to overstress the atmosphere of physical danger and the currents of insecurity and random violence that run through the chronicles and, obviously, through so much of Cambodian life in this period. The chronicles are filled with references to public executions, ambushes, torture, village-burnings and forced emigration' (p. 106).

The rhetoric of the competing colonising powers predated the French's 'civilising mission'. Vietnamese emperor Minh Mang, who reigned from 1820 to 1841, described the Khmers as lazy and uncivilised barbarians, and he made 'turning the barbarians into civilized people' his mission, which included forcing them to speak Vietnamese (Kiernan, 2008, p. 214). In 1837 localised anti-Vietnamese uprisings attempted to fight these impositions. These local rebellions soon turned into a violent national uprising involving 30,000 insurgents – an impressive number given a total population of about 800,000 – killing and uprooting thousands of people and leading to a Thai-Vietnamese conflict waged on Cambodian soil. Eventually, for the sake of peace, King Ang Duong had no choice but to accept the double sovereignty of Annam and Siam[1] over Cambodia. However, during his reign (1848–60) lasting peace and the social, political, administrative, and economic reconstruction of the country improved living conditions. Ang Duong first attempted to build some kind of alliance with France in 1858 against Cochinchina that the French were invading. Sok (1991) concluded his analysis of pre-Protectorate Cambodia by pointing out, 'Only King Ang Duong had enough perspicacity to analyse Cambodia's future

---

[1] The former English names for the Vietnamese empire and the Thai kingdom.

and adopt the measures necessary to ensure its protection and reconstruction. These measures were insufficient, however, when confronted by the murderous synergy of the Siamese [Thai] and Vietnamese suzerainties against Cambodia' (p. 236).

Barely one year after the death of Ang Duong in 1860, two of his sons contested the succession of their brother Norodom and a series of civil wars erupted. Norodom fled to Siam and only regained power in 1862 with the help of the Siamese army. Although French sources of the time may have darkened the picture they painted of this period to justify intervention, Sok (1991, p. 159), referring to Norodom's regaining power, lamented that 'once again a Khmer monarch regained his throne at the cost of an ever growing alienation from his kingdom to a foreign power without benevolence or weakness'. Finally, in 1863, the recently appointed King Norodom signed a treaty of protection with France, making Cambodia an 'independent' French Protectorate. The country had become the poorest in South East Asia, ruined by decades of invasions and civil wars, and ravaged by widespread banditry and frequent raids for slaves in the northeastern region.

The French who discovered Cambodia at the time – explorers, missionaries, administrators, and novelists – agreed on one thing: the great poverty of the country. They generally attributed the utter misery of the people to three 'scourges': the systemic corruption and backwardness[2] of the Cambodian ruling class; the rapacious exploitation of the masses, particularly the peasantry, by Chinese merchants and moneylenders; and the slave trade. Explorer and naturalist Henri Mouhot commented on the corruption of Cambodian custom officials, but noted that

the kings and mandarins get rich through plunder and graft, and other abuses that ruin work and hinder progress... Taxes bear heavily on the producer, the farmer; the more he produces, the more he has to pay; thus, already prone to laziness because of the climate, he has another reason to abandon himself to this vice for the less he produces, the less he will pay, and the less he will need to work. (cited in Bérard, 1989, p. 24)

In 1868, naval officer and explorer Francis Garnier even blamed Chinese ravenousness for pushing debtors into banditry and rebellion: 'The Chinese who are given the exploitation of these monopolies take advantage of it with the greed for gain that characterises their race, and the wretched taxpayer is often so pressured that he has no other alternatives but to seek refuge in the forest and become a thief or even a rebel' (cited in Bérard, 1989, p. 30).

---

[2] The continuation of the institution of slavery obviously contributed to this perception, which would have been buttressed by the knowledge that, as late as 1877, the old capital of Ba Phnom was still used for periodic human sacrifices, sponsored by the Cambodian king (Chandler, 1975, p. 19).

As for the slave trade, it centred on the Laos-Cambodia border and affected particularly the highland villages of the northeast that had not yet been integrated into the kingdom. According to Garnier, 'For a bit of brass or gun powder, for some glass jewellery, the chiefs of the savage tribes from this area agree to provide adolescents, sometimes entire families that the Chinese then sell at the market, nowadays a French one, in Phnom Penh' (cited in Bérard, 1989, p. 31). He also noted that the consequences of the trade were 'almost permanent war between highland villages, armed abductions, and repugnant violence by merchants attracted every year to this lucrative traffic'. The occurrence of raids to capture slaves has been documented, but evidence is lacking to assess how frequent these raids were and how widespread the slave trade was (Guérin, 2008).

In addition to these problems, the influence of the tropical climate and Buddhism was said to contribute to the Khmer people's indolence and fatalism. This Orientalist perspective, however, particularly the gentle and smiling resignation of 'the Khmer', was not universal. For example, anthropologist Paul Mus, thinking of the Angkorian monuments, argued:

Do you really believe that a people who, under an iron rule of one kind or another, built such high splendours, dug these canals, erected these giant temples, conquered and annihilated the kingdom of Champa, dominated the entire peninsula of Indochina, do you really believe that this people could only have known how to smile? Believe me; you have to be violent to build and to conquer. The Khmers are naturally violent, and can be terrible. You shall see one day the explosion occurring. (cited in Bérard, 1989, p. 5)

Articulating the tenets of the *mission civilisatrice*, Mouhot declared 'European domination, abolition of slavery, laws that are protective and wise, loyal and experienced administrators who are scrupulously honest, this is the only way to regenerate this State' (cited in Bérard, 1989, p. 23). In this peasant society, however, the civilising mission of the colonial enterprise encountered much resistance. We describe below the major insurrections and rebellions that punctuated the first 60 years of the Protectorate and belied the idea of peaceful Cambodia.

Early resistance under Norodom's reign: 1863–1904

If the French intervention in Cambodia put an end to Siamese and Vietnamese invasions, it did not stop rebellions and banditry, at least during the remaining years of the nineteenth century. On the contrary, millenarian groups continued to appear who added a new crusade to the struggle for a regenerated kingdom of peace and justice for the peasantry: ridding the country of the European invaders. Many bandits turned 'social', in the sense of primitive peasant rebels given by Hobsbawm (1969); however, if both mercenary and social bandits frequently participated in millenarian rebellions, they need to be distinguished from millenarian leaders. Millenarian rebels generally came from the forest and claimed to possess supernatural powers, but, following a typical Cambodian model, millenarian leaders also claimed to be of royal lineage and fought to take the throne.

Achar Sva (1864–1866)

Hardly a year after the signature of the Protectorate treaty, the first insurrection started. It was led by Achar Sva and directed against Norodom and his French protectors. Achar Sva was a slave and former monk pretending to be Prince Preah Ang-Phim, who, in fact, had died in Bangkok in 1855. The insurrection began in the southwest of the kingdom where Achar Sva – in order to claim his rights to the throne – raised an army, including rebels who believed in his princely status and bandits who saw an opportunity for plunder. The insurgents pillaged Kampot and marched on Phnom Penh but were defeated before reaching their destination. Achar Sva sought refuge in a pagoda, where he was killed in August 1866.

Pou Kombo (1865–1867)

A far more serious insurrection led by Pou Kombo started in 1865 in the northeast and by 1867 had spread to the eastern provinces. Pou Kombo, an ex-monk and possibly an ethnic Kui,[3] also claimed he was from royal lineage. On 23 April 1865, Pou Kombo presented himself before the commander of the French post of Tayninh as a legitimate heir and claimant of the Cambodian throne. The commander, probably alarmed by the popular support that Pou Kombo had already mustered in the eastern provinces, had him arrested and imprisoned in Saigon. In June 1866 Pou Kombo escaped and organised the uprising of Khmer and Cham peasants, as well as Kui and Stieng highlanders, against the king and the French. The uprising was fuelled not only by the unpopularity of Norodom and the attraction of millenarian beliefs but also by the imposition of oppressive taxation policies that Pou Kombo pledged to rescind (Hansen, 2008). On 24 June 1866, 1,000 Vietnamese joined his cause, increasing the total number of partisans to at least 2,000. Pou Kombo's forces killed the governors of Kratie and Sambor, 17 French soldiers, a French priest; ransacked unsupportive villages; and targeted Catholic communities. In October 1866, leading 6,000 men, Pou Kombo defeated the royal forces near Ba Phnom (Batz, 1931) and killed the Cambodian navy minister.

These military successes increased his prestige, and by November 1866, he and 10,000 followers marched on Phnom Penh and Oudong. Pou Kombo

---

[3] One of the highland groups located in the northeast of Cambodia.

Resistance of a peasant society 39

Illustration 1.1 The *Garde Indigène* on manoeuvre near Stung Treng 1903.
Source: Photograph by Albert Tajasque courtesy of Marine Pommereau – photographs of the Pommereau and Tajasque family. (Albert Tajasque served in the French Indo-China administration 1901–1909 reaching the post of Commissioner 1st class. Tajasque, formerly Lieutenant 111th Infantry Regiment was Resident in Stung Treng in 1903 then part of Laos.)

had become a serious threat to King Norodom's power, but a French battalion attacked his headquarters and inflicted serious losses on the insurgents (Guérin, 2008). Pou Kombo narrowly escaped capture, and the insurgents were forced to retreat to the northeastern regions of Kratie and Sambor, although in January 1867 their group pillaged the province of Ba Phnom in the southeast of Cambodia (Guérin, 2008). Pou Kombo was captured in Kampong Thom in November 1867 and beheaded. According to Hansen (2008) 'his severed head was sent to Phnom Penh for display in order to persuade the populace that this supposedly invulnerable leader had been apprehended and decapitated through French military power' (p. 55), but Osborne (1969) suggested that Pou Kombo was put to death by Khmers, not by the French.

Pou Kombo's death coincided with a reduction in the lethality and scope of the insurrection, but it did not stop it. In June 1868, one of Pou Kombo's lieutenants and around 600 mostly Stieng men raided villages around Kratie. In 1870, after they stopped paying taxes, angry villagers killed the governor of Sambor. Several raids followed through the Mekong Valley and against convoys of supplies to the French troops based in Cochinchina. Tully (2002) interpreted these raids as the degeneration of rebellion into banditry, but Guérin (2008) suggested that they were motivated by the need to replenish the rebels' rice supplies. The repression was severe, and the French launched punitive expeditions, occupying and burning down Stieng villages.

Sivotha (1875–1877)

In 1874, Prince Sivotha, Norodom's half-brother who had fought for the throne in 1860, took command of the remnants of Pou Kombo's army, therefore securing the support of the Stiengs and the Mnongs in the northeast (Guérin, 2008). A rebellion occurred in the province of Kampong Svay requiring the mobilisation of 5,000 of the king's Cambodian soldiers and resulting in an exodus of population to Laos (Tully, 2002). This rebellion was soon followed between 1875 and 1877 by an uprising, triggered by Sivotha's claims to the throne and more importantly numerous abuses of power by high dignitaries and mandarins about which the king had turned a blind eye (Batz, 1931). Sivotha had raised a large army at Ba Phnom, but on 23 February 1877 a coalition of French and Cambodian troops and Vietnamese militias attacked the insurgents. Many were killed,[4] but Sivotha managed to escape. He would reappear as a rebel leader less than a decade later.

The Great Insurrection (1885–1887)

The largest and most serious insurrection of the nineteenth century was triggered by the signing of an intrusive convention imposed by French Governor Thomson and his military aide Captain de Jarnowski at 'gunboat point'[5] (Tully, 2002, p. 87). In June 1884 King Norodom was forced to accept administrative, judicial, financial, and commercial reforms, handing over the administration of the kingdom to France. A number of these reforms had previously been part of several royal ordinances signed by Norodom, who, as a master in the art of passive resistance, had made no effort to implement them. The major reform of 1884 was the introduction of private property.[6] Muller (2006), somewhat overstating the point, commented: 'In other words, with the exception of Buddhist temples and royal real estate, all land in the Khmer Kingdom had overnight became French property and was now up for sale... Villagers would have to leave subsistence agriculture for a money economy' (pp. 65,

---

[4] The records did not provide further details about the number of casualties.
[5] French gunboats arrived in Phnom Penh and stationed on the riverfront facing the royal palace, providing the necessary persuasion and thus an example, literally, of 'gunboat diplomacy'.
[6] Very little is known on the question of land ownership in the nineteenth century. Sok (1991, p. 235) remarked that some form of private ownership of land existed prior to the Protectorate. Guérin (2012) suggested a consequence of the reform was that all land in Cambodia was accounted for as either private land (that could be bought) or Crown land (that required a lengthy administrative process before it could be used).

183). Legally speaking, the land did not become French property but the land of the domain upon which the French had control; yet, it is probably true that the instauration of private property had serious economic, fiscal, political, and social consequences. Meyer (1971) quoted Prince Yukanthor, who, in 1899 in his indictment of colonial politics, declared: 'You have established property; you have created poor people' (p. 203). Meyer, however, also reported that in practice the new regime of property did not radically change the situation of the peasants during the Protectorate because 'until 1953, the repartition of property had remained unchanged and the economic life of village communities had not been modified by the new regime. With or without land titles, Khmer peasants continued to directly exploit the lands transmitted to them through inheritance or that they newly cleared' (Meyer, 1971, p. 204).

Thomson's coup was supported by entrepreneurs in Cochinchina impatient with the preservation of precapitalist structures in Cambodia and was intended to pave the way for a straightforward annexation of Cambodia (Brocheux & Hémery, 1995). It led to the Great Insurrection that Muller (2006), with ample justification, does not hesitate to call 'the War'.[7] The main leader was Prince Sivotha, but other 'independent chieftains' were involved, and if there were perhaps four main seats of rebellion, they were coordinated (Tully, 2002, p. 84). The Great Insurrection brought together the diverse classes and segments of Cambodian society, including mandarins, millenarian rebels,[8] social bandits, and ordinary peasants. According to Forest (1980, p. 479), even Chinese financiers and merchants whose interests were threatened by the transfer of fiscal control to the French administration joined the insurrection. During six months of apparent calm following the signing of the convention, the aggrieved groups scoured the country and, with Norodom's quiet approval, roused the population against the French and for the liberation of the kingdom. The insurrection started in the northeast on 7 January 1885 when Sivotha attacked a French military post near Sambor, burning houses, destroying the telegraph, killing two French officers and four infantrymen, and then retreating after suffering heavy losses (Guérin, 2008; Tully, 2002). The brutal and indiscriminate repression that followed only raised the popularity of the insurgents.

While Sivotha was leading more attacks in the northeast, and one of his lieutenants with 600 men reached Kampong Cham province, the insurrection quickly spread east and south to the circumscriptions of Kampong Thom, Pursat, Kampong Speu, Prey Veng, Takeo, Kampot, and Svay Rieng (Tully, 2002).[9]

---

[7] Leclère (1914/1975) also referred to the insurrection as a war.
[8] In 1887, one of them called Nong, 'claimed to be the incarnation of a protector-spirit of Cambodia' and led a rebellion against local authorities in Kampong Svay, while another in Kampot assured his followers that thanks to his holy water they could not be harmed by French bullets (Hansen, 2008, p. 55).
[9] The western provinces of Battambang and Siem Reap, still under Siamese control, were not part of the kingdom.

On 6 May 1885, 5,000 insurgents stormed Phnom Penh but were pushed back after a fierce battle (Collard, 1925/2001).[10] This war against French domination continued for two more years, involved tens of thousands of armed insurgents and 4,000 French and Vietnamese troops, and cost the lives of at least 10,000 people, probably more, according to Tully (2002) and Muller (2006). Muller (2006, p. 195) suggested that by the end of 1885 and apart from Phnom Penh, provincial headquarters, and small forts in strategic locations, the French had lost control over most of the kingdom's territory. It was a brutal and ferocious war on both sides. French-led troops committed atrocities against civilian populations, including rapes, executions, thefts, and assassinations. The insurgents also perpetrated crimes against civilians, particularly Vietnamese Catholics (Osborne, 1969). Today, many of these acts would certainly be considered war crimes and crimes against humanity. Yet, these crimes were condoned and even ordered by French officers such as Captain de Jarnowski:

In Takeo, the chopping off of heads followed Jarnowski's own erratic judgment: 'Around Takeo, the severed heads pegged on pickets, and unfortunately renewed, showed from afar the effects of the terrible justice of the *sous-résident* [Jarnowski]. Nearly everywhere, people arrested without arms, by virtue of the denunciation of some native, or their embarrassed answers, or their bad appearance, sometimes because of phrases wrongly translated by an interpreter, were sent to their death after an interrogation of five minutes.' Jarnowski also acquired a reputation for abducting and raping women, and it appears that at least two reports on his crimes were sent to his superiors in Phnom Penh, one of which was mysteriously lost... A few months later, Jarnowski was nominated for France's most prestigious honorary order, the Légion d'honneur. (Muller, 2006, p. 208)

The conflict stopped in 1887, not because of a military victory by the French but because they decided, at least temporarily, not to impose the hated reforms of the 1884 Convention. They obtained from Norodom a promise that he would use his royal authority to call for the end of the hostilities.[11] Tully (1996) estimated that as a result of killings, famines, and population movements during this large anti-French insurrection, the population had fallen to 750,000, that is, a decrease of 20 per cent compared to that of 1883. In the absence of accurate population statistics, Tully's estimate cannot be considered authoritative, but it is certain that the insurrection was catastrophic for the country. It devastated the countryside, ruined the economy, and caused famines throughout the war and for several years to come.

The remaining years until the beginning of the twentieth century were relatively calm, although small rebellions erupted from time to time. Forerunner of

---

[10] Batz (1931) also reported that Phnom Penh was 'invaded by 5,000 rebels', while Tully (2002) mentioned the figure of 500 – a difference likely due to transcription error.

[11] At the same time as the Great Insurrection, the French were faced with the Can Vuong insurgency in Vietnam and could not fight on two fronts.

more troubles a quarter of a century later, there was an insurrection in April–May 1889 in the northeast in which 800 Stiengs were crushed by a coalition of Khmer and French forces (Guérin, 2008). Seven years later, Achar Prak, the leader of a group of rebels operating in the southeast on both sides of the Cambodian-Vietnamese border, was killed in November during an encounter with French troops (Forest, 1980). In 1898, a man called Ngo Prep and his band of 40 followers were arrested in Takeo for plotting against the state, and Ngo Prep was executed. The same year in Battambang, still under Siamese control, Thai Governor Phya Kathathorn brutally repressed an antitax revolt of 500 cardamom pickers, during which about 50 of them, including women and children, were massacred and a village pillaged (Forest, 1980; Tully, 1996).

Resistance during Sisowath's reign

With the death of the recalcitrant Norodom in 1904 and the crowning of the pliable Sisowath,[12] the early years of the twentieth century promised to be brighter for the French Protectorate. In fact, the first 20 years of the new century were punctuated by frequent rebellions, which, however, never reached the intensity of the Great Insurrection of the 1880s. These rebellions never really threatened the Protectorate, but three of them – the Battambang uprisings between 1907 and 1908 following the retrocession of the western provinces from Siam to Cambodia, the revolt of the highlanders between 1912 and 1918, and the great peasant demonstrations of 1916 – gave the French no rest.

Millenarian nostalgia

The French feared that the death of King Norodom would trigger unrest, but apart from minor disturbances around Kampong Cham, the succession itself did not spark any serious uprisings. Troubles resumed in 1905 when a defrocked monk, who, in the tradition of Khmer millenarianism, called himself Ang Snguon[13] and claimed magical powers, led an uprising in Stung Treng, Kratie, and Kampong Thom. These attacks were easily foiled and his band disappeared into the Dângrêk Mountains. The same year, a former partisan of Sivotha called Neun Srey with about 600 men relit a small pocket of anti-French resistance in the Kratie circumscription, but it was a failure and all the leaders, including Neun Srey, were killed. The next year, another former monk in Kampong Chhnang, then a destitute peasant in Kampong Cham, tried to rally fresh bands

---

[12] Sisowath was a half-brother of Norodom. As a pragmatist, opportunist, or a Francophile, he had fought alongside the French in the 1860s during the Pou Kombo's insurrection, in the 1870s during Sivotha's uprising, and during the Great Insurrection of the 1880s.
[13] Khmer king from 1749 to 1755.

of rebels and start new insurrections, but they did not succeed (Forest, 1980). While these small groups of desperados pushed by nostalgia may have contributed to the endemic rural insecurity associated with banditry, they were not taken too seriously by the French administration. The uprisings of 1908 and 1909 in Battambang and Siem Reap and the related guerrilla activities of Nheou Vises were another matter altogether.

The Battambang uprisings

In March 1907, after years of negotiation, France and Siam signed a retrocession treaty that returned the western territories of Battambang, Siem Reap, and Sisophon to the Protectorate. The treaty granted some of the best agricultural lands back to Cambodia as well as the Angkor complex. Although amply compensated by the French, the Siamese governor of Battambang, Phya Kathathorn, had nevertheless a lot to lose with the retrocession treaty, and he is regarded as the principal instigator of the uprisings. To increase the climate of insecurity associated with the transfer of control from Siamese to French rule, he 'opened the gates of the prisons [so that] bands or robbers were terrorising the population' (Tully, 1996, p. 114). In October 1907 and in January 1908, rebels attacked a military post, wounding several French soldiers (Forest, 1980). In April 1908, 300 rebels stormed the post of Mongkolborey but were driven back by the garrison, and a few days later 28 of them were shot dead (Batz, 1931). The French administration indiscriminately labelled the insurgents 'bandits', claiming that the majority of them were professional thieves seeking to benefit from the unrest; Tully (1996), however, argued that the French exaggerated the importance of the criminal element in the uprising.

One of the most significant leaders of the insurrection was Nheou Vises, a veteran of the 1885 insurrection.[14] During the whole of 1908, the number of ambushes multiplied. The cycle of attacks, counterattacks, arrests, repression, and punitive raids of the Great Insurrection was revisited on a smaller scale. In April, 8 rebels were killed and 126 captured; a Catholic Vietnamese village was pillaged; 5 French soldiers were wounded and 1 was killed in August, followed by 8 deaths among the insurgents. In October, Nheou Vises struck twice at the Moung militia post before retreating to Siam. He returned in February 1909, leading a band of 170 well-armed men. The group destroyed telegraphic installations, attacked numerous military posts from which they restocked their supply of weapons, and killed several French soldiers, always benefiting from the complicity of local populations. As a repressive measure, the entire male population in three villages was arrested and whole villages from the Moung region

---

[14] Sources on the activities of Nheou Vises are Batz (1931), Forest (1980), and Tully (1996).

were deported towards Mongkolborey. This uprising, which had mobilised between 1,300 and 1,500 infantrymen, militiamen, and regional guards (Forest, 1980), officially ended on 29 March 1909 with the capture of Nheou Vises,[15] but, according to Tully (1996), raids – increasingly turning into pure banditry – lasted until 1912.

Troubles in Kampot (1909–1915)

Many communities of ethnic Chinese lived in the Kampot circumscription. As the reports from the *Résidents Supérieurs du Cambodge* (RSCs) to the *Gouverneur Général de l'Indochine* (GGI) showed, the French administration was constantly worrying about their 'independence and unruliness' as well as their politically 'contaminating' influence on the 'docile and apolitical' Khmers (for example, between 1913 and 1915, RSC 430 – for details on sources, see the Appendix). In 1908 and 1909, the major agricultural industry in the region, pepper, was in crisis, resulting in the sudden unemployment of a great number of Chinese agricultural workers (Forest, 1980). The administration looked at the situation with suspicion rather than compassion, reporting 'groups of Chinese, in great part composed of seamy elements, without well-defined means of existence exploit, thanks to an attraction to gambling, the Cambodian population and moreover refuse to acknowledge the authority of the chiefs of the native administration' (p. 405).

Early in 1909, small bands of Chinese attacked the authorities and liberated their compatriots when the police had arrested them for lack of identification papers. During the same period, there were also a few small groups pillaging houses. In addition, some Chinese communities were fighting over the control of the local fisheries. Some Chinese from Kampot were members of a secret society known as 'Heaven and Earth',[16] and Tully (1996) believed that the society organised and launched the rebellion described below. The Khmer community was also protesting against unpopular policies about private property and a new tax on fishing equipment.

On 14 April 1909, a group of around 100 rebels led by a bonze (or Buddhist monk) named Uch and armed with spears, knives, and a few old guns attacked the *résidence* of Kampot. Twenty-three of them were killed or wounded, and Uch was captured. During his interrogation, Uch reportedly confessed that the chief of the rebellion was a Chinese named Bou, who had founded a secret society in Kampot, and Uch was to have transported rifles for Bou from Bangkok to

---

[15] According to Tully (1996, p. 128), after his capture, Nheou Vises was exiled 'to far off Trang on the Malay peninsula' on the order of Thai Prince Damrong, and he probably died there, 'for there are no reports of him returning to Battambang'.

[16] There may have been an outpost of the anti-Manchu or 'Hung Mun', a secret patriotic triad society then associated with the reformer Sun Yet Sen and Chinese republicanism.

be used in a joint attack on Kampot by Chinese and Cambodians. Tully appears to accept Uch's confession to this conspiracy as the truth, but Forest believes that, although Bou's foundation of the secret society was true, the rest was an attempt by Uch to mislead the inquiry and was never corroborated. Still, the fact that the rebellion included not only Khmers but also Chinese and Vietnamese had the French worried.

Uch and three main acolytes, who were also former bonzes from Kampong Chhnang and who had originally come to Kampot to collect medicinal plants, became involved in local problems. Ready to listen to the grievances of the peasants, they quickly gained the peasants' trust and allegiance. Following the traditional pattern of peasant rebellions, the leader Uch claimed some royal blood as well as prior involvement in the 1885 insurrection. He pledged 'to free the kingdom from the French' and managed to recruit a few followers. Preparatory ceremonies were organised during which the plotters were sprinkled with holy water, were given amulets ensuring invulnerability, and were anointed with their future positions in the liberated land. To indicate that they were not criminals but legitimate liberators, Uch launched the attack in full daylight, declaring to his interrogators 'We are not bandits, we have never stolen anything, we wanted to attack during the day, face to face' (Forest, 1980, pp. 406–7).[17] Tully (2002) reported that the *résidence* was again attacked by a large crowd a couple of months later, and the Kampot rebellion 'contributed to the general upsurge of "insubordination" among peasants across Cambodia in 1909' (p. 169).

In January 1915, the Uch rebellion was more or less reenacted in Kampong Trach (Kampot circumscription) by another self-proclaimed veteran of the 1885 insurrection called Ta Khwet, who was leading a band of 40 rebels composed of Cambodian, Vietnamese, and Chinese men. To get a good supply of weapons and ammunitions before 'conquering the kingdom of Cambodia', they first attacked the customs building in Kampong Trach (Forest, 1980). The doomed expedition resulted in three deaths on the side of the authorities and two on the rebel side. Ta Khwet escaped, but many others were arrested, three were executed, and several sentenced to 20 years hard labour.

Sena Ouch (1913–1916)

Between 1913 and 1916, yet another ex-monk – *Sena* (Commander) Ouch – scoured the northeastern regions with 100 followers, including Stiengs and Mnongs. They intensified their attacks on the colonial administration. Portrayed as a common criminal by the French, Ouch 'claimed to be guided by

---

[17] Neither Forest nor Tully, who are the sources on Uch's rebellion, gave any information about his fate after his capture.

supernatural forces, and to have as his aim the seizure of Cambodian independence and the driving out of foreigners' (Tully, 1996, p. 140). Like Nheou Vises 4 years earlier, Ouch was a popular figure among the rural population. He disappeared in 1914 and reappeared in 1915, this time in Kampong Svay, along with similar but smaller gangs operating in the same area. In March 1916, his son was killed in a skirmish, and Ouch vanished for good. However, a bigger problem for the Franco-Khmer coalition in the northeast was the rebellion of the highlanders between 1912 and 1918.

The 'pacification' of the highlands (1912–1918)

Violence between and against highlands people was endemic in northeastern Cambodia and was in great part associated with the slave trade preying upon them and the oppressive and brutal behaviour of Khmer officials. The pacification of the 1910s was aimed at forcing the submission of the remaining highlands villages that were not yet under the control of the state and subject to taxation and *corvée* labour. A movement of resistance against the 'civilising mission' of a Franco-Khmer form of colonialism developed in the northeastern highlands, which were inhabited by independent people derogatively called *Phnongs* ('savages', 'those living in the wild' in Khmer) whose population may be estimated at 30,000 between 1912 and 1918 (Guérin, 2008). The trigger for the rebellion was a crime committed in May 1912 by four men, including two militiamen, who raped the daughter-in-law of the leader of a highland village called Pa Trang Loeung. Compounding the outrage, they refused to offer the customary compensations when invited to do so. By way of reprisals, the villagers killed the four men, and then attacked a military post (Guérin, 2008).

In November 1912, several villages joined Pa Trang Loeung, who led a group of 400 insurgents. Henri Maître, a former explorer appointed in 1909 by the *résidence supérieure* to 'pacify' the region, was after him. Between May 1912 and July 1914, at least 15 clashes occurred during which 35 people were killed and 34 abducted. The worst incident took place in the village of Mdai Dop, which Pa Trang Loeung had accused of working for the French and the Khmers. The village was pillaged and burnt down; 4 men, including the village chief, were killed, and 11 people were abducted to be sold as slaves. Both feared and admired, Pa Trang Loeung eluded all attempts at capture, and his popularity, his legend, and the number of his followers soared:

It is said that bullets ricochet off his body, that the French and the Khmers cannot kill him, that no one can kill him. His status strengthened, Pa Trang Loeung manages to bring together several Mnong villages ready to take arms against the invaders. With time and the multiplication of the columns launched against him, Pa Trang Loeung's prestige increases considerably, and, with it, the support of the undecided for the insurgents. (Guérin, 2008, p. 85)

Of the 7 years of the insurrection, 1914 was the most violent one. In January 1914, a new *balat*,[18] called Neang, came to the region and tyrannised the aborigines, who were flogged, tortured, half-starved, and used like working animals. The people sent several delegations to Kratie to ask the French administration to stop the exactions of the *balat* to no avail. Guérin (2008) remarked:

> The Mnongs from Bu La and Bu Gler witness the occupation of their lands and at the same time they see that Pa Trang Loeung, the man who has rebelled, is still free and more and more powerful. Worse, Pa Trang Loeung destroys the villages that help the French and the Khmers... Despite the risk of a difficult war against the colonial power and the Khmer administration, their choice is made... The burden of the administrative stranglehold that they saw being erected around them, conflicting with their desire for freedom, the fear of being invaded by foreigners and the exactions of the functionaries explains this choice. (pp. 86–9)

On 22 July 1914, hundreds of Mnongs, used as *corvée* labourers in Bu Gler, armed themselves with bamboo spears and killed Neang and four militiamen. Convinced that Henri Maître would launch reprisals when informed of the murder of the *balat*, they led him into a trap and killed him along with his 28-man escort on 3 August 1914.[19] During the remaining months of 1914, violence escalated. Guérin (2008) retraced the bloody mayhem of the last trimester, which also marked the start of World War I and with it the repatriation of military forces to France:

> Aboriginal villages that refuse to join the revolt or were in dispute with the principal leaders are pillaged and destroyed. The Khmer villages on the east side of Kratie and Sambor are also targeted. Not only the Mnongs do not let the authorities regain power in the Yok Laych but they also multiply bloody raids against Cambodian ricefields. Early October, the village of Chbar in the north of Yok Laych is attacked, several people killed, the survivors flee toward the north and find refuge on the right bank of the Seprok. On the 11 October, eight Cambodians are killed, including a *chumtup*:[20] The next day, several hamlets of Sre Chi in the plain northwest of the plateau are stormed by three Mnong bands that kill eight men and destroy the crops. Two days later, nine Cambodians are killed at Sre Kadoy. On 19 November, eight people are killed and two young women are abducted in Neang Lang. On 20 November, the village of Sre Sangke east of Sambor is entirely destroyed: between seventeen and twenty people, men, women, and children are killed, and six are kidnapped... Everywhere, between the Srepok, the Mekong and the Chhlong, and as far as the Darlac and Cochinchina, the Mnong warriors bring terror and devastation to their enemies. (p. 91)

---

[18] First deputy of a provincial governor.
[19] This is the number of deaths, in addition to Maître, reported by Guérin (2008, p. 89), but Forest (1980, p. 429) reported the death of 47 militiamen as well as a Maître's Vietnamese interpreter and domestics. However, Forest wrote that the *balat* Neang was with Maître and killed in the same ambush, which does not fit with Guérin's narration of the events.
[20] The Cambodian term for deputy village or commune chief.

Between August 1914 and August 1916, the archives recorded that more than 60 villages had been targeted, at least 108 Cambodians killed, as well as aborigines who had refused to join the insurgents, and more than 120 people had been abducted. In addition, Chinese, Khmer, and Vietnamese merchants were also regularly robbed and assassinated. In January 1915, another Frenchman, Truffot, the administrator of Kratie, and his escort were killed near Sre Chi. After Truffot's death the Franco-Khmer troops no longer dared to enter too deep into Mnong territories (Guérin, 2008). Although raids were less bloody than those conducted in 1914 and 1915, highlanders continued their attacks until mid 1918. Preoccupied by the war in Europe, the French did not succeed in completely 'pacifying' the highlands, particularly when, in 1916, a formidable peasant protest movement emerged in the kingdom.

The 1916 affair: from active to passive resistance

Left to their own device this people would not prove wrong their reputation of docility to our authority; dominated in their general attitude by the resignation that their Buddhist faith imposes on them, they surrender to the quietude facilitated by the few needs of their existence. To extract them from their indifference, one would need a calculated will coordinating their grudges, rekindling their old pride, making shine in their eyes the mystical and the marvellous, carrying them along in an élan of fanaticism exasperated by unending humiliations and generalised abuses regarding goods and persons. Then, in their naïve faith in the supernatural might of the leader who would have succeeded in arousing them, they would forget their own virtues and become more terrifying and cruel than neighbouring peoples. King Norodom compared Cambodians to the placid buffalo that becomes terrifying once pushed to its limit. While it does not seem that these people have yet discovered the predestined man who could carry them against our domination, we should remain watchful by exerting on them the necessary political surveillance. (*Résident Supérieur du Cambodge*, 1915 [RSC 430])

When *Résident Supérieur Baudoin* wrote these lines in 1915, he did not know that a year later hundreds of thousands of peasants would engage in a large protest movement across almost all the Cambodian provinces. The '1916 affair', as the French administration euphemistically called the peasant protests, was certainly caused by 'unending humiliations and generalised abuses regarding goods and persons', but overall it was relatively nonviolent. For the protectors, a puzzling and worrying feature of the protest was that the peasants' grudges had clearly been coordinated, but nothing indicated that a charismatic leader or predestined man had played this coordinating role. The Cambodian peasantry was apparently able to rely on its own informal networks to protest against oppression and injustice.

On the surface it seemed that the series of demonstrations was essentially motivated by anger at *corvée* labour,[21] taxes, and the corruption of Khmer officials (Forest, 1980; Osborne, 1979; Tully, 1996). Peasant discontent may have run deeper, however, because in a few provinces where most of the lethal violence occurred, such a Prey Veng, no demand for *corvée* labour had been announced (Osborne, 1979, p. 233). Peasants universally hated *corvée* labour and taxes, and already in 1915 a crowd of 100 people in the Battambang circumscription had petitioned the administration about the increasing levels of taxes and *corvée* requisitions. As a result, 93 people were arrested, and 57 were sentenced from 3 to 10 years imprisonment and 3 to 20 years of hard labour. The administration's disproportionate response to the petition may explain why Battambang remained quiet during the '1916 affair'.

The protest started on 5 January 1916 when peasants from Kampong Cham called to perform their *corvée* duty marched on Phnom Penh seeking the king's intervention about the repurchase payment of the *corvée*. This was a legal option, but not a right, and their request was rejected. Unhappy about the outcome, on the way back to their region they invited local populations to join in a large demonstration in the capital. From that moment until the end of January, at least 40,000 peasants came to Phnom Penh to petition the king (see Chandler, 2008, p. 188), expanding their demands to include the abrogation of a number of taxes and putting an end to the corruption and power abuses of Khmer officials. The movement spread rapidly, and many peasants did not turn up to the work sites where they were required to perform their *corvée* obligations. Within a few weeks, 100,000 people were engaged in a general strike against *corvée* labour and numerous demonstrations took place across the country. In Phnom Penh, apart from some looting of Chinese liquor shops, the demonstrations were generally peaceful, but in the provinces, particularly Kampong Cham and Prey Veng, at times the protests turned violent.

In Kampong Chhnang, Chinese homes were robbed by marching demonstrators; in Kampot, a village was ransacked; in Kandal, the protesters attacked a number of Khmer officials and burnt down government buildings; and in Takeo, a village of Vietnamese Catholics was attacked. In the circumscription of Kampong Cham, protesters were said to shout 'death to the *Résident*' (Osborne, 1979) before assaulting Khmer officials and destroying a Chinese-owned plantation. The leaders were arrested, but 400 peasants attacked the prison. Guards, commanded by a French officer, shot randomly at the crowd and killed seven

---

[21] *Corvée* labour (peasants required to perform free labour for the kings and nobles) existed in Cambodia before the Protectorate and in France before the revolution of 1789. In Cambodia the French maintained and extended *corvée* labour, which was mobilised by the state for its infrastructure development, such as the building of roads. Under certain conditions, peasants could repurchase *corvée* labour for a fee corresponding approximately, per day of repurchased *corvée*, to the daily wage of a free labourer.

people (Forest, 1980). The highest level of violence occurred in Prey Veng, where the provincial *Résident* likened the events to an insurrection (Tully, 2002, p. 159). There, too, Chinese shops and fisheries were destroyed and Khmer officials bore the brunt of the protestors' anger when their houses were burnt down. In mid February, more peasants were killed and many others wounded (Osborne, 1979; Tully, 1996). There is no general agreement about the number of people killed during the 1916 demonstrations, but estimates suggest that around 25 individuals possibly lost their lives ('a half-dozen Cambodian lives' is mentioned by Chandler, 2008, p. 188). A Saigon newspaper, *La Voix Libre*, reported that demonstrators had been machine-gunned in Phnom Penh and bodies were floating on the Mekong River for several days afterwards, but Tully (1996) cautioned that this newspaper 'hated Baudoin and was sometimes unscrupulous in the methods it used to discredit him' (p. 195).

It was not so much the level of lethal violence but the scope and apparent coordination of the protest that made the 1916 affair remarkable. The timing of the events during World War I was not fortuitous since it had forced the Protectorate to reduce to a minimum the number of its troops in Cambodia and furthermore coincided with serious unrest in Cochinchina. The French could not imagine that such a coordinated movement had been organised at the grass-roots level by the peasants themselves,[22] and, at first, they entertained the possibility of a German conspiracy. They also saw in it the hand of the son of Norodom, Prince Yukanthor, who during a visit to Paris in 1900 had denounced French colonialism in Cambodia and was exiled in Bangkok. Eventually, they abandoned the hypothesis of an external political influence, and, unwilling to consider or unable to understand the deeper political implications of the colonial enterprise on a peasant society, they concluded that 'the 1916 Affair was not fundamentally a political matter [but caused] by unsatisfactory taxation and *corvée* administration' (Osborne, 1979, p. 231).

Although their certitudes about the loyalty of Cambodian people towards the Protectorate had been somewhat shaken, the French reassured themselves with the idea that this formidable peasant movement had been directed against the abuse of power and exploitative practices of local officials, not against the protectors and their system. Yet, as Osborne (1979) pointed out, not only had the communal reforms brought about by the French

> created the framework in which [the] venality [of Khmer officials] operated, [but] the expansion of French interest in Cambodia and the greater control exercised by the colonial administration over the whole span of governmental activity ensured that few, if

---

[22] Possibly, the coordination and spread of information from place to place was ensured by monks, who had always been and, as we shall see, continued to be an important group in Cambodian grass-roots politics.

any, among the rural population escaped the effects of a process of significant and rapid change. (pp. 239–41)[23]

Being in direct and regular contact with them, the peasants had naturally targeted the Khmer officials who implemented and certainly abused policies developed higher up, but it was simplistic to conclude that the blame lay uniquely with the deficiencies of the Khmer administration. It was simplistic also to characterise the leaders as 'men without occupation, the looters and the bandits', as did the *Résident* of Kampong Cham, even if the 1916 protest very probably increased opportunities for bandits and other criminals. As for petitioning the king – the 'fount of justice' in peasant premodern society (Hobsbawm, 1969) – rather than the *Résident Supérieur du Cambodge*, it might well have been a way for the peasantry to indicate whose authority it trusted and regarded as legitimate and whose it did not.

The legal response was severe: 580 individuals were prosecuted, and the harshest punishments included 13 death sentences and 50 sentences of life with hard labour (Forest, 1980). Perhaps the Khmer elites intended to impress their French protectors or compensate for the accusations of corruption and abuse laid against them by the peasants, and they showed no mercy for their accusers. Strongly influenced by the *Résident Supérieur*, the appeal court commuted all the death sentences and confirmed only 3 of the 50 sentences of life with hard labour. On the other hand, the Protectorate proceeded to undertake a drastic purge of the Khmer administration, followed in 1917 by a comprehensive reform of the indigenous bureaucracy. Because of a shortage of troops, the French were unable to rely on sustained suppression and brutal reprisals, a tactic that anyway had not been effective during half a century of precarious control over the country, and assisted since 1904 by a compliant monarch, the protectors now concentrated on the further modernisation and strengthening of the state apparatus. For instance, while denying that the movement had been politically threatening, they significantly increased the numbers in the *Garde Indigène*, the main policing body, from 1,700 before 'the affair' to 2,400 after the events, representing a jump from 71 to 100 in the rate per 100,000 population.[24] By 1920, numbers had dropped back, and it was only during the turmoil of the 1940s that the rate would reach 100 per 100,000 again.

Reflecting on the French vision of rural unrest, interpreted either as 'nativistic regression' or solely caused by 'economic discontent', Osborne (1979) suggested that

---

[23] As well as its anomic effects and consequences on crime and violence.
[24] The *Annuaire Statistique de l'Indochine* reported a population of 2,403,000 in 1921 (BIB AOM A/1017).

Resistance of a peasant society 53

Illustration 1.2 Village head and assistants outside the Commissioner's residence Stung Treng 1903.
Source: Albert Tajasque; courtesy of Marine Pommereau – photographs of the Pommereau and Tajasque family.

by embracing the monocausal explanations of economic resentment, and failing to recognize that economics are not always dominant in guiding men's actions, French officials in Cambodia, no less than elsewhere in Southeast Asia, deserved Harry Benda's estimation that quite unknown to themselves they were caught in the toils of a crude Marxist view of history. (p. 228)

In the next chapter, our analysis of crime and its control in the first quarter of the twentieth century, therefore, needs to be situated in the context of a peasant society initially resisting the assault of the modernising vision of a colonial power.

2 Patterns of premodern criminality

This chapter focuses on crime during the first two decades of the twentieth century, from 1900 to 1920. High levels of crime and violence characterised this period, and frequently rebellions merged with predatory and social banditry. However, at the end of this period, crime and violence started to decline. This decline was in great part associated with significant processes of state formation, notably important administrative and judicial reforms as well as more efficient policing institutions and practices gradually implemented during these two decades.

We have seen in the preceding chapter that the French intervention in Cambodia in the middle of the nineteenth century put an end to the threat of violence associated with Thai and Vietnamese invasions and also, at least until 1890, to internal wars of succession. On the other hand, the series of insurrections and rebellions, starting in 1864 with the uprising led by Achar Sva and ending in 1916 with nationwide peasant demonstrations, has shown that the colonial enterprise was resisted and at times massively and violently confronted. In this context, and particularly during the first 60 years of the French Protectorate, what were the types, patterns, and trends of crime and violence in Cambodia? Did the modernising project of the colonial power affect them, and if it did, then in what ways? In short, which forms did violence and crime take and how were they understood and responded to in the premodern peasant society of Cambodia under a colonial power whose espoused mission was to bring modernity?

Banditry, crime, and justice before 1910

The data that we were able to gather do not allow us to estimate rates of crime and banditry before 1910. Our description of patterns and trends in criminality during the first decade of the twentieth century draws from both primary and secondary sources; however, primary sources were patchy and most of the description only provides a qualitative account of the violence and crime in Cambodia between 1870 and 1910. First, we examine the characteristics and spread of banditry, which at that time and later was the main crime problem of the Protectorate. Next, we turn to common crime in the capital Phnom Penh and the provinces before discussing the emerging policing and judicial systems the French administration attempted to establish. In this section we use historical works on Cambodia such as Chandler (2008), Forest (1980), Guérin (2008), and Tully (2002) as well as some primary data from French Colonial Archives. These archival data consist of both monthly and yearly reports by the *Résident Supérieur* of Cambodia (RSC) and court data for Phnom Penh and some provincial courts.[1]

Banditry

By the end of the nineteenth century banditry had almost disappeared from most of Europe, but in South East Asia it remained widespread during the nineteenth century and in some places up to the middle of the twentieth century (Bauzon, 1991). Rural banditry was a common phenomenon in most premodern peasant societies, and it flourished when the state was weak and corruption rampant. Cambodia was no exception, and banditry was endemic well before French colonisation (see Chandler, 2008; Forest, 1980; Tully, 1996, 2002). In the 1880s banditry was so widespread that its repression became one of the first preoccupations of the colonial authorities. Hobsbawm (1969, pp. 33–4), drawing on European examples, suggested that bandits emerged essentially from the peasantry, particularly 'from the rural surplus population', but also included ex-soldiers and deserters. As elsewhere, this was the case in Cambodia, where, as we will see, bandits also counted a number of escaped convicts. In addition, the Cambodian landscape, particularly the mountainous and forested areas, the monsoons that transformed the shape and size of rivers and lakes, the porous borders, and the absence of good roads offered an ideal terrain for roaming groups of bandits. This was typical of other premodern societies, and Hobsbawm (1969) remarked: 'It is commonplace that brigands flourish in remote and inaccessible areas such as mountains, trackless plains, fenland, forest, or estuaries with their labyrinth of creeks and waterways, where pre-industrial travel is naturally both slow and cumbrous. The construction of good and fast roads is often enough to diminish banditry notably' (p. 21).

Social and common bandits

Hobsbawm distinguished between two main kinds of banditry: the mercenary type, which comprised common robbers, and the social type, which comprised individuals who robbed the rich and powerful, supported the poor, and sometimes led peasant rebellions. All peasant societies have produced heroic

---

[1] Data in boxes RSC 239, 243, and 257. We also searched the National Archives in Phnom Penh in 2008.

social bandits, some of whom became legendary like Robin Hood in thirteenth-century England, Cartouche and Mandrin in eighteenth-century France, and Mas Dyakaria and Entong Gendut in nineteenth-century Java (Kartodirdjo, in Bauzon, 1991). In Cambodia, we have met Sena Ouch (Chapter 1) and will soon meet A-Chan, who were active in the nineteenth and early twentieth centuries, respectively. Depending on the particular cultural characteristics of these premodern societies, peasants were likely to applaud, even if silently, the targeting by social bandits of moneylenders, merchants, tax collectors, foreigners, 'and others who upset the traditional life of the peasants' (Hobsbawm, 1959, p. 22). However, if these societies 'know rich and poor, powerful and weak, rulers and ruled, they remain profoundly and tenaciously traditional and pre-capitalist in structure... The bandit is a pre-political phenomenon and his strength is in inverse proportion to that of agrarian revolution and socialism or communism' (Hobsbawm, 1959, p. 23). Social banditry also increased when crises, famines, and wars profoundly disrupted the traditional world of the peasantry and during 'moments when the jaws of the dynamic modern world seiz[ed] the static communities in order to destroy or transform them' (Hobsbawm, 1959, p. 24).

In the nineteenth century and the early decades of the twentieth century, Cambodian society was regularly shaken by such crises and upheavals and notably by continual attempts by the colonial power to transform the structure of this society. Widespread and endemic banditry, therefore, was a normal response not only to the structural anomie of a weak, shattered, and corrupt state but also to the developmental anomie brought about by the efforts of the colonisers to transform society. In a context where the peasantry was suffering from state failure not only to ensure security from civil wars but also to resist changes imposed by foreigners, millenarian rebels and social bandits seen as criminals by the state had a very different status in the peasant communities where they came from. They were 'considered by their people as heroes, as champions, avengers, fighters for justice, perhaps even leaders of liberation, and in any case as men to be admired, helped and supported' (Hobsbawm, 1969, p. 18). However, writing about Cambodia, Tully (2002) warned: 'It would be wrong to romanticize the bandits. The results of their raids on Khmer villages were often horrific. When Huy Kanthoul[2] was a young child, he accidentally stumbled on a bloodstained cart, around which were a number of severed heads, the aftermath of a clash between bandits and villagers' (p. 165).

The difference between social and common banditry was often blurred by the fact that 'a man may be a social bandit on his native mountains and a mere robber on the plain' (Hobsbawm, 1969, p. 18). The colonial administration

---

[2] Teacher and politician, he will play a political role as a member of the Democratic Party in the early 1950s and became prime minister in 1951.

also tended to characterise as banditry any type of resistance against it and to consider that peasant support for bandits was motivated by fear of reprisals rather than by genuine sympathy. Whereas in many cases, but not all, fear of reprisals certainly played a role in the peasants' lack of resistance so decried by the administration, the amalgamation of the political with the criminal has always been a distinctive response of ruling powers when confronted with subaltern/paralegal forms of contestation. Forest (1980) also noted the amalgamation of banditry with localised violent popular protest and contestations.

The bandits of Cambodia

Nonetheless, the colonial archives distinguished between professional bandits, who operated in large and well-armed bands and often specialised in rustling livestock on the Siamese and Vietnamese borders, and destitute peasants, who joined their ranks or formed small bands of thieves and robbers during periods of acute hardship. Souyris-Rolland (1950, p. 427) described three types of Cambodian 'brigands' (*chor*). The first type, *chor plan* (bandits), were armed and organised in bands. He likened them to the highway robbers of medieval Europe who 'became the "gangsters" [in English in the French text] of modern times'. The second type, *chor luoch* (professional thieves, burglars), worked alone or in duo and were reluctant to use force; 'their principal weapon was cunning'. The third type, *chor han tayong* (sneak), were the pickpockets who worked in full daylight on the markets. According to Souyris-Rolland, the 'real' bandits and the most feared and dangerous type were the *chor plan*, who in groups 'methodically, professionally, got into the theft of livestock and valuable objects either to sell them or exchange them for a ransom, or even to destroy them ... as an act of revenge'. People talked about *chor plan* 'with mixed feelings of fear, admiration, and respect'. Apparently, peasants welcomed them in their village not only because they could be hired as hit men 'to enact a revenge by proxy ... against a neighbour who had harmed them or of whom they were jealous' but also because local *chor plan* protected the village against other bandits.

Apprentices in banditry were generally recruited from young men who had learnt boxing, wrestling, or stick fighting and who competed in sporting events during festivals. Their teachers (*krou*) were also versed in the art of tattooing and claimed they increased the strength and agility of their students using the magical powers of symbols tattooed on various parts of the body. When these young men joined a group of bandits, they acquired the skills necessary for the preparation and completion of successful robbing expeditions through strenuous training under the supervision of the leader (*me chor*), who punished disobedience or disloyalty with death and whose authority was absolute (Souyris-Rolland, 1950, p. 427).

Before launching an attack, usually at night and rarely in their own area, bandits consulted a kind of astrological calendar, the *yeam krala*, to calculate the most propitious day and time for the expedition. Each bandit was allotted a specific task, and after the performance of a myriad of occult rituals the band was ready for action:

Following the signal of the leader each bandit hurries to fulfil his prearranged mission. Whilst some take hold of the livestock and run away with it, others smash the doors of the house with axes, and, amidst the screams of the women and children, they steal all the valuable goods. Two men hasten to assault the master of the house and get the keys of the trunks and force him to reveal where he hides his money. If he does not respond quickly enough to the bandits' demands, he may be wounded... Other bandits, armed with guns, have been positioned around the targeted house; their job is to fire at anyone approaching... In general, the leader does not directly take part in the action but supervises the operations in order to signal the withdrawal. Sometimes one of the lookouts is wounded by a villager and cannot flee when the time comes. The leader, who brings up the rear, gets to the man and cuts his throat in order to prevent his capture and the risk that he would reveal the names of the band members when questioned by the authorities. (Souyris-Rolland, 1950, p. 434)

Although professional bandits were ready to kill people if necessary, they were essentially robbers rather than murderers, and banditry in the mid nineteenth and early twentieth centuries was seldom lethal for the victims.[3] It is not that most of them were social bandits of the 'noble' type described by Hobsbawm (1969), although some certainly were. For example, in 1918, the peasants had already made the bandit A-Chan legendary during his lifetime, as the *Résident* of Battambang reported:

...a band of well-established evildoers under the command of the notorious A-Chan whom popular imagination represents as operating successively within and outside our borders, depending on circumstances, at time resurrecting him after having persistently spread the rumour of his death, at times representing him as a vagabond hounded everywhere, rejected by society, living in poverty in the mountain, subsisting from herbs and roots, and at other times attributing to him all kinds of riches and delights, living in royal opulence, heeded and feared by all, spreading his authority and his cruelty in many far-away places. (RSC 209)

According to Hobsbawm's (1969) typology of social banditry, A-Chan would have been idealised by the peasantry as both an enlightened rebel, wild and frugal, and as a feared and cruel 'avenger... whose terror actually forms part of their public image... who are heroes not in spite of the fear and horror their actions inspire but in some ways because of them. They are not so much men who right wrongs, but avengers and users of power [whose] appeal

---

[3] From an analysis of the RSC's reports we found that only about 7 per cent of attacks resulted in the death of villagers.

is not that of the agents of justice, but of men who prove that even the poor and weak can be terrible' (p. 58). Among the bandits, A-Chan had earned the title of *Dang-Khao* (the powerful), 'a title that is granted only to professional wrongdoers and band leaders who have gained by their prowess and first class acts of banditry the respect of their men' (*Résident* of Battambang, 1918). 'First class acts of banditry' were unlikely to have targeted poor peasants, particularly given the widespread support he appeared to have enjoyed among them.

Even if we consider only the mercenary type of bandits, a likely reason for the relatively low number of lethal attacks is not only the rudimentary state of their weaponry but mainly that their victims knew they generally risked injuries or death only if they resisted or attempted to capture the bandits. Although the protectors encouraged resistance, they were aware of the reason why many villagers avoided doing so: 'In many areas where looters' attacks occur, the inhabitants run away at the first gunshot and, no doubt, any vague desire on their part to resist would often force us to register not just armed robberies but assassinations followed by pillage and arson' (RSC, 1913 [RSC 430]).

The cowardice of the villagers, who 'fly away at the noise of a firecracker' (RSC, April 1909 [RSC 263]), soon became an integral part of the racial discourse on the 'inherent character of the Khmers'. In 1914, the RSC lamented that the bandits 'are generally not well armed but they use ploys that scare the populations; thus, for instance, they throw crackers when they reach the spot of their operation and the distraught inhabitants run away, leaving them a free hand' (RSC 430). A possible explanation for the reluctance of the peasants to confront the bandits is that the latter belonged to the social type and they targeted village chiefs who had just collected taxes or Chinese merchants and moneylenders. More often, however, and particularly during the frequent periods of distress that pushed many destitute individuals into banditry, the main victims of mercenary banditry were ordinary villagers who gradually took a more active if not completely voluntary role in fighting it.

Trends and patterns in banditry

Rates of banditry were closely associated with periods of political and social unrest, economic downturns, poor harvests, as well as wars and the collapse of administrative systems. Hobsbawm (1969) pointed out that 'all such catastrophes were likely to multiply banditry of one kind or another... all were likely to pass away, [but] political breakdowns and wars were also likely to leave behind bands of marauders or other desperadoes for a considerable period, especially if governments were weak or divided' (pp. 22–3). Archival data from Cambodia certainly support these remarks. Banditry increased in the 1890s in the aftermath of the Great Insurrection of the mid 1880s (Chandler, 2008). In the years 1904 and 1905, rice shortages and famines led to a spike in banditry, particularly in Takeo where they were accompanied by drought, and then flood and typhoon

(Tully, 2002). In 1906 the price of pepper crashed, particularly affecting Kampot, where sacked labourers were reduced to engaging in criminal activities to survive (Forest, 1980). In Battambang, banditry became rife in the shadow of the 1908 antiretrocession insurrection. In this province banditry targeted mainly livestock and was the subject of frequent communication between the *Résident Supérieur* and the Vice Consul of Battambang. For example, it described how in March 1908, in broad daylight, a group of bandits succeeded in robbing a village of 51 buffaloes and 21 oxen. The year after, 65 heads of cattle were taken from another village, and a group of 60 bandits attacked a convoy, stealing all its merchandise and killing one man. The Battambang police commissioner pointed out that such events happened daily (Forest, 1980).

While criminal activity and acts of banditry were reported across Cambodia, it seemed that banditry was more frequent in Pursat, Kampong Cham, Kampong Thom, and Battambang than in Kampong Chhnang, Kandal, and Takeo. However, the 'hot spots' were all located in the east, particularly in the circumscriptions of Kratie, Svay Rieng, and Prey Veng. The RSC described the circumscription of Kratie as 'one of the most unsafe provinces... [where] bandits too often gathered and pillaged indigenous villages. It has become the den of all prison escapees from Phnom Penh and Saigon'. As for Prey Veng, it was 'a haven for all the bandits from Kratie, Kampong Cham, Svay Rieng, and Tayninh... a kind of republic for hardened bandits'. For the RSC, it was 'an undeniable fact' that the entire region of Prey Veng and Svay Rieng 'lived only from banditry', and

it had been going on for years with increasing audacity, due in part to the complicity of the Cochin-Chinese communal authorities and in part from the return in the region of bandits arrested and convicted by us who escaped from Phnom Penh after a few weeks spent in the Cambodian prison. These bandits could walk in Cochin-Chinese villages a gun in their hand, and we cannot obtain their arrest. (1909 [RSC 263])

French authorities were particularly frustrated when bandits attacked officials, as they did in Kratie in 1909 when a group of bandits stopped a Khmer official transporting tax money with his escort and robbed them of 900 piastres, a small fortune at this time. Widespread banditry represented a real drain on the resources that the Protectorate was struggling to accumulate and a poor record in terms of its protective capacity. The administration tried hard to suppress it, but if the protectors sometimes managed to reduce the cost of banditry, they were never able to eliminate it.

Common crime

In the absence of reliable statistical data, we rely for this period on the 'impressions' of crime of French officials and contemporary and modern authors.

According to Edwards (2007), the new capital, Phnom Penh, and its 25,000 inhabitants suffered high crime rates. A French engineer was murdered in 1884, even though no more than 150 French civilians resided in Cambodia in the 1880s, and two others were murdered in Battambang in 1894 and 1903. As a result of famine in 1889, thefts multiplied and banditry even reached Phnom Penh (Meyer, 1985). By the turn of the century, about 40,000 people lived in Phnom Penh; petty thieves and pickpockets were ubiquitous, and even the small number of French, who probably enjoyed the best protection against crime, was targeted (Tully, 1996). Swindlers targeted rural populations. Forest (1980) described how in 1904 a Turk called Mohamed Effendi, presenting himself as a shipbuilder, came to Kandal with the intention of defrauding Cham communities. He collected money from the Cham, telling them that a large ship would be constructed to transport them free of other charges to Mecca. Apparently things turned nasty for him when he also tried to extort money from the local bonzes and threatened to destroy their pagodas. In 1907 several crooks scoured the provinces in search of naive victims who would believe that the French had given Indochina to the Japanese and that they were collecting taxes on their behalf.

Elite crime was not unheard of either, particularly in Phnom Penh. In 1897, *Résident Supérieur* de Verneville was removed from office. It seemed that his 'lack of tact' in trying to implement reforms on the Council of Ministers could have ignited unrest. More importantly, de Verneville cohabited with his Khmer mistress, Neak Ruong, who was accused of crime and corruption. She was charged with receiving stolen jewellery and storing it at the *Résidence*. Worse, it was alleged she was also involved in 'bribery of judges, trafficking in favours, swindling, kidnapping and theft' (Tully, 2002, pp. 108–9). She was sentenced to 5 years imprisonment, but it was suspected that a number of Frenchmen were implicated in these criminal activities.

Rural violence

If petty crime was rife in Phnom Penh, rural violence, particularly in remote areas, was a serious problem. In 1870, shortly after the Pou Kombo insurrection, Father Jeanneau (cited in Forest, 1980, p. 374) reported that the assassination of overbearing governors by the Khmers was a rather common occurrence. Drawing on the Kratie archives between 1890 and 1904, Guérin (2008) counted 10 conflicts recorded among highlanders that resulted in 17 individuals killed and 45 kidnapped. The situation described by Guérin is not representative of the whole of Cambodia because the Kratie hinterland was a frontier area largely outside the control of the state, with a particularly high level of violence and where the slave trade was still active. For instance, in 1891 a group of 40 bandits plundered a village, kidnapped 6 people and killed 2 others. In 1899, 35 highlanders raided several villages, killing 1 person and taking 5 as prisoners, and in 1904 a similar raid ended up with 9 dead, 7 wounded, and 80 taken as slaves. Accusations of sorcery were frequent and often lethal. In 1897, a highlander accused of sorcery was executed and the women in his family taken as slaves. It happened again in 1898 when 2 men killed a so-called sorcerer, and in 1902, when 3 men perished. Two years later, 3 women were murdered in retaliation. More violence flared up in 1909 in the northeast, where in one day, 2 alleged sorcerers were killed, 17 people were kidnapped, and 20 were taken as slaves.

Familial feuds, matters of honour, and revenge attacks – characteristic of collectivistic or premodern societies, according to Durkheim – were reported several times. In one case, in June 1908, a man kidnapped a young woman but was later lynched by her parents. In another case, in November, a man and several accomplices destroyed the property of a couple who had refused to let him marry their daughter. A year later, in Kandal again, a man who had abducted another's cousin was murdered (Forest, 1980).

The Protectorate's response to crime and violence

The concern of the French administration with the repression of crime, particularly banditry, was not so much that the Protectorate was directly threatened by it but, as the official reports repeatedly showed, that its suppression was a matter of both prestige and revenues. As guarantors of public security, the protectors were required to act against banditry or risk losing not only revenues but also legitimacy. At the turn of the century, the policing system was too embryonic to be effective, and the population, through fear of or sympathy for bandits, was uncooperative. Tully (1996) remarked that despite larger numbers of police officers and soldiers, ordinary property crimes and violence were common in Phnom Penh and provincial towns. Ordinary people had an ambiguous attitude towards banditry: in Kampot, a Vietnamese thief was arrested for attempting to rob a junk carrying a load of pepper, and people spontaneously brought him presents and food. In addition, the collusion between Cambodian authorities and criminals was such that in an edict dated 16 April 1890, Norodom lamented:

> Functionaries... sometimes connive with thieves and share the product of their crimes... It is still happening today that wrongdoers apprehended in the provinces are released for money. The envoys of the ministers, responsible for policing the country, frequently arrest thieves and bandits without informing the authorities so that they can secretly set them free after having extracted money from them. (in Forest, 1980, p. 383)

In 1897, for instance, groups of bandits could operate unfettered in Kampong Cham thanks to the complicity of the Khmer authorities, which continued unabated until at least 1910. Chandler (2008) described that at the provincial level (the *sruk*):

French officials found old habits of patronage, dependence, violence, fatalism and corruption largely unchanged from year to year. Offices were still for sale, tax rolls were falsified, rice harvests were underestimated... Banditry was widespread; and there were frequent famines and epidemics of malaria and cholera. The contrast between the capital and the *sruk*, therefore, sharpened in the early twentieth century, without apparently producing audible resentment in the *sruk*, even though peasants in the long run paid with their labor and their rice for all the improvements in Phnom Penh and for the high salaries enjoyed by French officials, fueling the resentment of anti-French guerrillas in the early 1950s and Communist cadres later on. (p. 198)

The colonial administration resorted to collective punishment, and in 1901 two villages in Kampong Cham were fined a hefty 200 piastres[4] each for having harboured escaped prisoners, but this did not have much effect on reducing banditry. The colonial administration also blamed the ineffectiveness of crime control on the inactivity of the Khmer administration, from governors to village chiefs, and demanded more zeal on their part in policing matters. They were ordered to focus all their activity on the repression of thefts and acts of banditry committed in their provincial territories in order to ensure the security of the inhabitants (Sorn, 1995).

In the fight against banditry, some attempts were made to improve cooperation between French and Cambodian authorities in the control of the bands of livestock thieves, robbers, and smugglers who crossed borders to escape justice (Sorn, 1995). The administration encouraged the extrajudicial killing of bandits by the populace and resorted to it regularly. Records suggest that banditry was far more deadly for the bandits than for their victims. For example, in 1909, the famous bandit A-Duong, who operated in the eastern region, was killed, and a few militiamen and a cohort of villagers trying to save their cattle gunned down at least five other bandits in Battambang. There were, nevertheless, some successes at jailing bandits. During the third trimester 1909 in Prey Veng, where armed robberies and acts of banditry had been on the rise, the RSC reported more than 100 arrests and 'amongst the arrested criminals [were] the most dangerous ex-cons who had committed several robberies and murders'. In the year 1909 and for the entire kingdom, we counted from the RSC reports that at least 308 bandits had been arrested. Unfortunately, jail breakouts were also frequent, sometimes aided by the complicity of officials. In April 1909, 14 convicts escaped from Phnom Penh prison. At least three of them were professional bandits who, a month later, were leading a band of between 40 and 50 men and performing armed robberies in the circumscription of Svay Rieng. According

---

[4] A piastre was approximately 24.3 grams of silver in 1895 and was the coinage/banknote introduced by the French colonial powers. Its value fluctuated against the French franc, and by 1920 the value was about 1 piastre to 10 francs. A fine of 200 piastres is the equivalent of 2,000 days of stipend for an unskilled labourer or 5 to 10 days for one household (Guérin, personal communication, 2014).

to the RSC, most of the 31 bandits arrested during the second trimester 1909 were escaped convicts (RSC 263).

Cases in court

From the *Archives Nationales d'Outre-Mer* (ANOM) in Aix-en-Provence, France, we obtained some data from the courts in Phnom Penh for 1890 (GGI 64394) and in Kampot, Kampong Thom, and Kampong Speu for 1905 (RSC 243). These data consisted of court registers listing each case and included the adjudicated offence, the number of defendants involved in the case, and some information such as defendants' nationality, marital status, and level of literacy. Records for Phnom Penh came from the *Tribunal Mixte* and the *Tribunal de France*[5] and included sentences. While these data are patchy and do not represent the whole picture of crime and justice in early-twentieth-century Cambodia, they give an idea of the types of crime that reached the courts under the French administration. More importantly, they show how very early on the French administration had managed to penetrate Cambodian society.

The most complete data came from the *Tribunal Mixte* in Phnom Penh and covered the whole of 1890, while data from the provincial courts covered only a few months in 1905 (Table 2.1). The data give the impression that Kampot province was not only rebellious but also a crime-prone area. During just 3 months of data, 38 cases were indicted, which was proportionally more than in the other jurisdictions. Generally, cases involved more than one offender, the highest being in Kampong Speu with an average of 2.2 offenders per case. The average age of offenders was 30 years. In Phnom Penh, two thirds were married and only three defendants could read and write well.

Apart from Kampong Speu, where half were Cambodian, the bulk of the defendants were Chinese or Vietnamese. The proportion of violent offences was higher in the provincial courts (ranging from 20 per cent to 33 per cent of all cases) than in Phnom Penh (8 per cent), possibly again reflecting Durkheim's suggestion that higher levels of violence occurred in premodern and rural societies. In cases of theft, the stolen objects were sometimes specified. In Kampong Speu, three men had stolen a buffalo. In another case, two Cambodians had stolen a cotton blanket, something that we might interpret as a sign of the level of poverty that existed in this province (and still today one of the poorest provinces). In comparison with the objects stolen in Kampot, which included jewellery, gold, musical instruments, and relatively large sums of money, the theft of a cotton blanket in Kampong Speu appears very minor, but the theft

---

[5] Until 1881, French citizens were judged in Saigon, and Cambodian, Chinese, and Vietnamese defendants were under the jurisdiction of the *Tribunal Mixte*, in Phnom Penh. In 1881, a court of first instance, the *Tribunal de France*, was created in Phnom Penh to deal with French citizens. In 1895, the *Tribunal Mixte* was abolished and all cases involving non-Cambodian Asian defendants or victims were referred to the *Tribunal de France*.

Table 2.1 *Court data from Phnom Penh (1890) and three provincial courts (1905)*

	Court			
	Phnom Penh[a]	Kampot	K. Thom	K. Speu
Data period	1890	July to Sept. 1905	July 1905	June & August 1905
N cases sentenced[b]	51	38	6	5
N offenders convicted	88	57	8	11
Mean N offenders/case	1.7	1.5	1.3	2.2
Type of case % (N)				
Violent	8% (4)	27% (10)	33% (2)	20% (1)
Theft/fraud	47% (24)	57% (3)	50% (3)	80% (4)
Opium-related	41% (21)	–	–	–
Other	4% (2)	16% (6)	17% (1)	–
Offender's ethnicity	$N = 30$	$N = 30$	–	–
Cambodian	26%	7%	–	50%
Chinese	41%	53%	–	–
Vietnamese	33%	33%	–	–
Other	–	7%	–	–
Mean offender's age (years)	30.0	31.6	Not available	29.3

[a] Data are for the *Tribunal Mixte*, a Franco-Cambodian court with jurisdiction over Cambodian, Chinese, and Vietnamese defendants.
[b] Cases include felonies and misdemeanours.
Source: ANOM: Phnom Penh [GGI 64394]; provincial courts [RSC 243].

of a buffalo would have been a significant loss. Opportunity, it seemed, was a greater driver of crime in Kampot province, particularly given its relatively wealthy Chinese community, than in Kampong Speu, where poverty was likely to be a more salient factor.

Sentences were reported only for Phnom Penh. In the *Tribunal Mixte* all convicted offenders received a jail sentence: for over 60 per cent of them, prison terms ranged from less than a month to a year; for 30 per cent, prison terms ranged between 1 and 5 years; and 10 per cent received more than 5 years imprisonment with forced labour. Although not shown in Table 2.1, we also had some data from the *Tribunal de France*, which dealt with French (and other white) citizens. There were 17 cases involving 17 offenders, and over one third of all cases (36 per cent) were violent offences (assault with injury and carelessness causing death). A striking difference from the *Tribunal Mixte* was what appeared to be the greater leniency of the *Tribunal de France* as well as the iniquity of a dual system of justice. Although 36 per cent of the European cases were violent offences compared to just 8 per cent in the *Tribunal Mixte*, and 18 per cent of the offenders were recidivists, more than one third benefited from mitigating circumstances, 30 per cent received a fine rather than a jail sentence, and none were sentenced to hard labour.

The second decade of the twentieth century: more of the same

During the second decade of the new century, a series of famines and economic recessions, the highlanders' rebellion, the large peasant protest of 1916, and the war in Europe fuelled a crime wave and impeded efforts to control banditry and other crime. During this decade, however, the records were sufficiently rich to attempt quantitative estimations of the rates of banditry events and homicide victims.

Data for estimates of banditry and homicide, 1909–1920

Primary data were collected from the National Archives of Cambodia (NAC) in Phnom Penh and from the ANOM in Aix-en-Provence, France. Primary data included monthly, quarterly, and yearly reports circulated within the administrative hierarchy; specialised reports from the Ministry of Justice, police services, and special inspections of provincial residences; and population and justice statistics from the *Annuaire Statistique de l'Indochine* (Statistical Digest of Indochina). The chain of reporting within the indigenous hierarchy started with the village chiefs and reached their provincial governors (PGs), who in turn reported to the French administration via their respective *Résidents* of circumscription (RCs), who reported to the *Résident Supérieur du Cambodge* (RSC), himself accountable to the *Gouverneur Général de l'Indochine* (GGI). Reports written at each level of the administrative hierarchy usually included a section on crime, covering at least banditry and homicide.

Reports within the administrative hierarchy were available for most of the years 1910–20, but the reports' origins varied in terms of the author's rank in the administration and the type of information provided. Reports could include quantitative data, such as number of events during the month, trimester, or year, or qualitative accounts of increasing or declining trends compared to previous periods, or both. Generally, a brief narration of all or some of the cases was presented, including location of the event, circumstances, number of offenders and victims, weapon use, and so forth. When the precise numbers of acts of banditry or homicides were not available for all the provinces, national figures were estimated from the available quantitative data as well as qualitative accounts on trends and secondary sources such as Forest (1980), Guérin (2008), and Tully (1996, 2002). Banditry (called *piraterie* by the French administration) included violent acquisitive crimes (e.g. robberies, house invasions) and acts of rebellion. We calculated rates based on the number of banditry events.

Patterns of premodern criminality 67

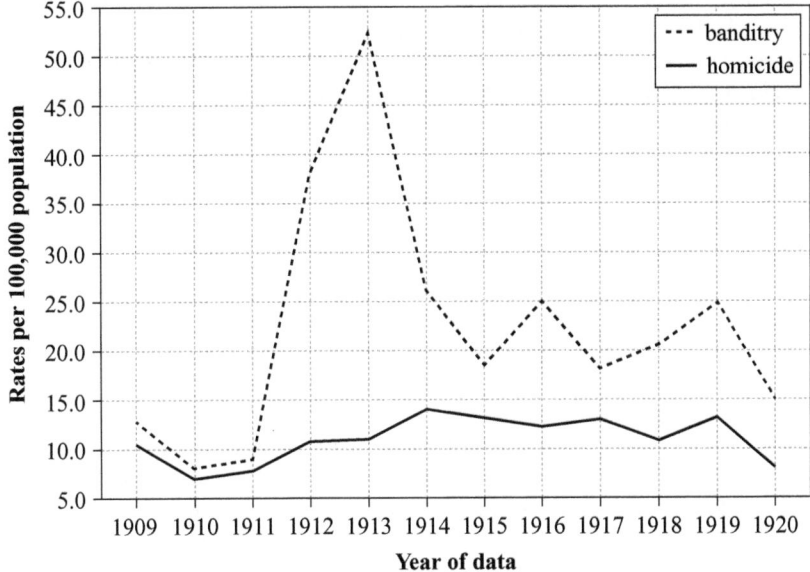

Figure 2.1 Homicide victims and banditry events, 1909–20 (rates per 100,000 population)

For homicides, rates were estimated based on the number of victims, and three types of victims were distinguished:
1. Victims of lethal acts of banditry: these were individuals killed by bandits such as villagers, militiamen, and police officers
2. Victims of homicides, which occurred in incidents other than acts of banditry (labelled 'assassinats' in administrative reports)[6]
3. Extrajudicial killings of offenders by authorities or villagers during the commission of a crime or when being chased; as mentioned earlier, the killing of offenders was openly endorsed and practised by the authorities, who also encouraged villagers to do the same

Trends in banditry events and homicide victims, 1909–1920

Figure 2.1 presents estimated rates of banditry events and homicide victims between 1909 and 1920. These rates both show large variations between some

[6] The French word *assassinat* generally refers to premeditated murder. The reports, written by administrators not lawyers, did not always make it clear if the term covered strictly premeditated murders or if it also included unplanned murders and manslaughter. We assumed data referred to all types of murders but if in practice they referred only to premeditated murders, then our rates of homicide victims are underestimated.

years. The rate of banditry peaked in 1912 and 1913, two years of great hardship marked by periods of famine and economic recessions. Then, it declined between 1914 and 1915 with two smaller peaks afterwards. The first, in 1916, coincided with the great peasant demonstrations discussed in the preceding chapter. The second, in 1918 and 1919, matched a new period of economic recession.

The rate of homicide increased steadily from 1911 to 1914, when it reached its highest level in the decade. It fluctuated during the period of the First World War and only dropped substantially in 1920. Rates of homicide were affected by the conjunction of socioeconomic hardship, political unrest, and increasing occurrence of extrajudicial killings of offenders. The average rate of homicide victims between 1909 and 1920 was close to 11 per 100,000 population. It was significantly higher than the rate of homicide known to police between 1906 and 1910 in England, which was estimated at 0.8 per 100,000, and – although the difference was not so pronounced – than the rate of homicide across 28 large cities in the USA in 1900 and across the entire USA in 1919, estimated, respectively, at 5.1 and 7.5 per 100,000 (Gurr, 1981).[7] In France, the rates declined from an average of 2.1 from 1900 to 1909 to 0.9 from 1920 to 1929 (Eisner, 2008). One must go back to the seventeenth century in Europe to find rates of homicide similar to those in Cambodia at the beginning of the twentieth century.

Drawing from the narratives presented by the *Résidents* and governors in their reports to the French administration, the rest of the chapter paints a broad picture of the criminality and types of violence as well as the response to these events in early-twentieth-century Cambodia. The French administrators were most concerned with banditry and wrote frequently about it. They seemed to have been less concerned with homicides and interindividual violence, as long as it did not target French officials. Because banditry is the most detailed, we first examine the record of these events before turning to homicides and other types of violence and corruption. We conclude this section by discussing the responses to crime encouraged by the administration.

Banditry

By 1910 the number of banditry events had decreased in many provinces, but incidents involving large groups were nevertheless still reported; for example, in January 1910 in the province of Sisophon, '40 bandits killed a woman,

---

[7] Note also Pinker's observation about the USA and Spierenburg's (2006) discussion of the effect of democratisation before pacification on the higher homicide rates in the USA compared with European countries, where pacification (i.e. state monopolisation of violence and disarmament of the citizenry) occurred before democratisation.

burned down four houses and three attics full of paddy before stealing 12 buffalos, 29 oxen and other goods' (Forest, 1980, p. 378). Similar acts of banditry committed by bands of between 6 and 20 individuals were noted by the RSC in Battambang, Svay Rieng, and Mimot. The decline was also short lived because the year 1911 marked the beginning of not only an economic depression that would last until 1914 but also widespread famines and food shortages due to bad harvests in the northwest as well as in the circumscriptions of Kandal, Kampong Chhnang, Kampot, Kratie, and Stung Treng. The *Résident* of Battambang (the source of the greatest amount of rice in the country) reported in 1912 that 'the harvest has been virtually nil, misery is widespread', and as a consequence, he concluded, 'there is no doubt that professional thieves, already numerous in this region, will find it even easier to recruit men' (RSC 237). The RSC (1911) admitted that incursions by armed bands in the northwest were not 'acts of professional banditry; it is the famine experienced in the north that pushes the inhabitants of these Siamese hills to go down through the passes of these mountains to pillage some habitations in the Cambodian plain' (RSC 237). Although he also blamed these 'bad times' on the laziness and improvidence of the Khmer peasantry that refused to diversify its agriculture, he wrote in 1912:

The misery experienced for almost two years in Cambodia has thrown onto the roads and in the forests a part of the population seeking means of existence... The more timid resign themselves to feeding on wild roots and other products from the forest. Others, abandoning their houses, take to the roads toward regions that appear better off and flock like long hordes of scrawny beggars. The most resolute obtain by force what is necessary for their survival or join bands of plunderers who swarm everywhere... Small acts of plunder and brigandage are reported a bit everywhere in all the provinces. The culprits let themselves be arrested without difficulties and cram the prisons where they find what freedom did not bring in these times of famine: the certainty of food and shelter. (RSC 237)

In addition to the 6-year-long highlanders' rebellion we discussed in the preceding chapter, the famine and economic depression worsened in 1912. Despite a ban on rice export and the allocation of emergency funds, misery, epidemics,[8] and crime spread all over the kingdom. In 1912 in the circumscription of Kampong Thom alone, the tribunal prosecuted 53 cases involving 106 offenders; of these, 43 were accused of violent crimes, a rate of 51.1 prosecuted violent offenders per 100,000 population.[9] The cases included four homicides, or a rate of 4.8 homicide events per 100,000 population. Homicide cases had the highest average number of offenders (an average of 4.3), followed by robberies (an average of 3.3). In the notoriously banditry-prone circumscription of

---

[8] For example, in Kampot alone, the number of deaths caused by diseases jumped from 50 in 1911 to 1,000 in 1912 (Reddi, 1970).
[9] Forest (1980) estimated a total population of about 84,200 in Kampong Thom in 1911.

Prey Veng, more than 400 attacks were recorded during the year (RSC 237). The country was engulfed in a massive crime wave, which the RSC acknowledged: 'Not mentioning the simple thefts and the thefts of livestock, which are too many to count, crimes have been committed in all the areas of the country.' The RSC also remarked, 'Not content with having pillaged the inhabitants, the bandits have shown for some times an unprecedented cruelty' (RSC 237). The *délégué*[10] of Svay Rieng described how the region bordering Cochinchina 'offers the sorry spectacle of burnt down houses after the pillage. Inhabitants, even women, are frequently tortured and often prefer to hide during the night in the forest, abandoning their houses' (RSC 237). Illustrating the utter desperation of the populace, several pagodas – places normally highly respected by the Khmers – were plundered.

Banditry peaked in 1913 as the recession and food shortage continued to swell the ranks of the 'criminal elements', with, for example, an average of 290 cases of brigandage in the territory of Battambang in 1913 and 1914 (Forest, 1980). However, the end of the famine and a more vigorous police activity soon led to a decrease in banditry, although some encounters seemed to turn more deadly. The crime reduction in some provinces was matched by a rise in other areas, perhaps reflecting the relative effectiveness of suppression in one place leading to displacement to less protected areas.

A trend characterised by an increase in the lethality of encounters for both victims and aggressors was also noted in the east. Early in 1914, a number of robbery-murders were recorded such as that of a Chinese merchant who was murdered and his commercial house pillaged by seven bandits and a commune chief who was killed by eight offenders. During the second trimester, the RSC reported numerous acts of banditry in the circumscription of Kampong Cham by small groups of between 5 and 7 men, and larger ones with 15 to 20 offenders, which resulted in violent confrontations. As we will see later, it is likely that the increasing violence is related to the villagers' resistance and retaliation against the bandits.

In 1914, banditry was on the decline in most regions, particularly the interior, where policing was easier. The exception was the northwest, which remained a hot spot of crime. 'Attacks against the public security committed in Battambang during the last few months have been far more numerous than in other Cambodian provinces', wrote the RSC (RSC 430). Among the most serious of these attacks the RSC mentioned the assassination of a Cambodian by 8 men armed with sabres and the robbery of a convoy near Mongkolborey by 20 men, during which one traveller was killed, two were injured, and 3,000 piastres were stolen. In the northwest, large armed bands specialising in livestock theft and

---

[10] Administrator with duties similar to the *Résident* but appointed to a lower hierarchical position and occupying a post in a remote location.

sometimes coming from Siam were particularly active. In Kampong Thom a group of 50 armed men pillaged a village and took with them 117 buffaloes and 8 horses. In another attack, 25 bandits tried to rob all the cattle from a village near Sisophon. In May 1915, a well-armed group of 21 (they had 18 guns) killed the former notable of a village and stole 130 oxen and buffaloes. Four days later, also in the Battambang territory, another group managed to take 177 oxen and cows from a village before moving back to Siam. In Oddar Meancheay in 1915, 50 men armed with 40 guns prepared to attack Chongkal, but the governor and a troop of infantry managed to repel the bandits and killed a few of them (RSC 430).

The high level of banditry in the regions bordering Siam and Cochinchina continued through 1916. In Siem Reap alone, 138 cases of banditry were registered for the entire year (Forest, 1980, p. 377), and in Battambang, 300 cases during the first 9 months (RSC, 1916 [RSC 430]).[11] The small rise in banditry was certainly linked to the large peasant protests in the early months of 1916. Although the RSC tended to amalgamate disputes and protest with criminality, he was probably correct when he suggested that 'the incidents that occurred during this first trimester were an opportunity for professional wrongdoers to mix with the demonstrators and to pillage the villages whilst they were absent' (RSC 430). By 1917 banditry had dropped back, and no more than 400 cases of armed robberies were recorded nationally. The *Résident Supérieur* remarked, 'Even in Battambang where the number of acts of banditry has usually been around one hundred per trimester, it has fallen to 41' (RSC 431).

Some regions, such as Kratie, remained hot spots of banditry, with 94 cases recorded there compared to only 16 in Kampong Cham (Forest, 1980).

Bad harvests and a recession exacerbated by protectionist policies that blocked trade with Siam and restricted foreign investments again led to a temporary rise in crime that peaked in 1919. Rice exports were prohibited to try and contain the extent of a threatening famine, which nevertheless worsened through 1919, a year of great hardship. Pauperisation and desperation once again resulted in the plundering of a number of pagodas as in Prey Veng where in August a band even chased the monks from Ba Phnom wat and settled in it (Forest, 1980). Around 320 cases of armed robbery were reported in the first 6 months of 1919, but the *Résident* stressed 'no event of a political nature has been recorded' (RSC 431). In the meantime, and despite the severe economic and financial crisis, the construction of the road to Mount Bokor where the development of a luxurious sanatorium was planned had just started. Building

---

[11] We note in passing that the approximate figure of 400 acts of banditry communicated by the RSC to the GGI for 1916 was a gross underestimation. Using available reports from provincial residents, we counted already 458 cases over 9 months in Battambang, 12 months in Siem Reap, and 6 months in Kandal. Reporting too many problems reflected badly on the French *Administration* (always written with a capital A), and 1916 was already troubled enough.

this road would eventually cost the lives of hundreds of prisoners sentenced to hard labour. In 1920, the economic crisis and famine eventually subsided, and this coincided with declining crime rates. In his report for the second trimester of 1920, a more satisfied RSC declared: 'There still exists, particularly on the borders, marauders who regularly engage in acts of banditry, sometimes even murders, but they are in decline compared to previous years. This is one of the problems that Cambodia has always suffered from, but far more in the past than today' (RSC 431).

But some regions remained more affected than others, as the RSC noted during the third trimester: 'Banditry has continued to ravage the same regions than in the past, those in the border zones of Cochinchina and Siam where a greater number of crimes have always been committed' (RSC 431).

The colonial archives for this period show clearly that banditry was closely linked to economic conditions. During bad times, young peasants left their paddies and joined armed bands. Millenarian leaders and various eccentrics who took up banditry were sometimes mentioned in the reports. For example, in 1913 the RSC mentioned in Preah Vihear 'a bandit named Suon described as one of those "cranks" appearing very frequently in the history of Cambodia who succeed in impressing naïve inhabitants by the prestige of their person and sorcery formulas'. Suon would have gathered 100 men, 'professional thieves and inhabitants recruited by force, or attracted by the promise of some spoils' (RSC 430). Bandits were typically men, but one band active in 1914 included five women:

Worth to report too is the comeback in the province of Soaiteap of the band led by the dreaded chief A-Khleang. This band, after having pillaged the house of an Annamite from the village of Bavet on July 27th, managed to escape and hide in the forest of Svai-Bada (Tayninh). The day after, on the 28th, the same band, with the addition of 5 women, were confronted by the night watch of the same village (Bavet) who ordered them to stop. The bandits immediately fired four times. A bullet killed the night watchman Chau Mau through the chest and another one slightly wounded another watchman in the hip. Only the 5 women were arrested. (RSC, 1914 [RSC 430])

The same year, the RSC reported another 'crank, a defrocked monk, called Chuon, [who] had gathered around him a band of about 15 individuals armed with guns, sabres, and machetes, and started to extort money from the inhabitants of the *Khum* of Baset [circumscription of Kampot]'. The group did not last long, as 'the rebel band, which had several members killed, was entirely destroyed' (RSC 430). Some bandits were escaped prisoners or deserters from the infantry or the militia and were described as 'professional' bandits. For a start, ex-soldiers turned bandits generally deserted with their guns. Those without guns used various edged weapons, while some did not have any weapons. Examination of the reports on banditry from 1918 and 1919 suggests that on average there was one gun for every four or five bandits, one other weapon for every two bandits, and one in three to one in four bandits were unarmed.

Targets of banditry were varied. Large bands were able to ransack whole villages and pillage houses, but also livestock and cattle, particularly in the western regions bordering Siam. Near the Tonle Sap and along the Mekong River, they targeted junks carrying merchandise as well as ferries and travellers' boats. In 1917 the RSC described how 'near Phnom Penh five bandits attacked a Chinese passenger boat, beat the travellers, and tried to rob them but "thanks to the energy of the Chinese boss,"' two bandits were captured and one of them grievously wounded (RSC 431). Smaller gangs of highwaymen roamed the countryside. For example, in his 1917 report the RSC noted, 'The roads from Phnom Penh to Takeo and Kampot have been for some time infested with bandits who robbed isolated travellers' (RSC 431). Khmer officials and functionaries were regular victims of bandits because they were wealthier than ordinary peasants but also because they were carrying and collecting tax and fine money. For example, during the second trimester of 1913 the RSC illustrated the risk of violence faced by officials:

It seems that bandits, chased away from the region of Svay Rieng, found refuge to the north, toward the circumscription of Kampong Cham, or having left to the west of the river in the résidence of Takeo and toward Chau Doc. Livestock thefts are reported to be very frequent on the border, and on May 23rd, a band of thieves led by the Cambodian Uong has even attacked, with an amazing savagery, the house of the *Mekhum* of Pechar and stolen the tax money temporarily under the care of this functionary; about 10 persons were seriously injured during this attack and several of them needed to be evacuated by car to the Phnom Penh hospital; however, the *mekhum* spontaneously volunteered for the search and capture of the chief Uong; he discovered him in his retreat and killed him. (RSC 430)

Forest (1980) has highlighted the high proportion of Chinese victimised by banditry, noting, for example, that during the first 6 months of 1916, out of 20 houses plundered in Kandal, 5 (25 per cent) were owned by Chinese, adding, 'It is about the same in the entire country.' Our data certainly support Forest's observations, and year after year the RSC reported the robberies and murders of ethnic Chinese. Although xenophobia may have played a part in these attacks, it is more likely that because the Chinese were often merchants and businessmen, they were wealthy targets. As an illustration, the Prey Veng *Résident* in 1911 noted an increase in armed robberies whose victims were mostly Chinese merchants targeted for their houses and boats and was sorry to report that 'several of these merchants had been seriously injured during the attacks' (RSC 237). In November 1910, in the circumscription of Kratie, a Chinese man's house had been ransacked by a group of 30 bandits armed with guns and knives who also plundered the neighbouring house of a Cambodian family (RSC 691). The greatest armed robbery of 1911, during which the bandits pocketed no less than 3,000 piastres, involved a Chinese merchant in the Kampot circumscription (RSC 237). However, in an even more costly attack in 1919, 10 Chinese bandits[12] travelled by car from Cochinchina to Takeo and pillaged at night the house of a wealthy Chinese, killed him, and stole all his possessions valued at 50,000 piastres, a huge fortune at the time (RSC 209).

Homicides and other violence

The characteristics of the homicides described in the reports matched Gurr's (1981) description of homicides in England during the thirteenth century when between 80 per cent and 90 per cent were the results of fights among neighbours, and between 10 per cent and 20 per cent were caused by thieves and bandits. Weapons were rather rudimentary and included mainly agricultural implements. Several offenders were generally implicated in each case, which often consisted of brawls between small groups rather than one-on-one attacks. As Durkheim (1893/1964) had suggested, these homicides were typical of a premodern society, and in their frequency, they seemed the result of the structural anomie that existed before and the developmental anomie that accompanied French colonisation. Examples of the lethal violence occurring during this period include the case in October 1911 in the Kampot circumscription of a village chief who killed a woman because he believed she was a witch who had made his child die (Forest, 1980). The year after, the Battambang *Résident* described how in a village eight individuals murdered one man, gagged his wife, and pillaged his house, during what was possibly a crime of passion. In 1913 a 'quadruple assassination' was reported in Kampong Chhnang where, in order to steal 300 piastres, three men working on a junk threw in the water 'their Annamite female boss, her daughter and two children; one of the children survived and reported the authors of the crime'. Ordinary murders were rarely mentioned by the RSC in his reports to the General Governor of Indochina because such events, as opposed to banditry, did not constitute 'attacks against public security' (RSC 237).

The protectors, however, did worry about any violent aggression against French nationals because such events could be motivated by anti-French political sentiments. Three such assaults occurred in early 1913. In March, the bandit Sena Ouch and his gang attacked the Apostolic Mission's plantation in Chhlong and seriously wounded Father R. P. David. Then, Mr. Canavy, a colonist resident in Kampot, was wounded on the head by a man wielding a meat cleaver, but he survived. Captain Castelin, knifed by one of his indigenous servants, was

---

[12] According to the RSC, the attackers consisted of 'a band of about 10 Chinese from Akas'. Most but not all were arrested, but the prosecution was slowed down because those arrested were 'obstinately denying' that they were guilty.

not so lucky and died a few days later from his wound. That these attacks may have been politically motivated was briefly considered, but eventually such fear was interpreted as the result of a worrying state of mind caused by the state of insecurity in the country: 'During this trimester, three attacks have been committed against French citizens, and these events, which in a normal period might have been regarded as isolated incidents, may be linked to the political situation because of a worrying state of mind' (RSC, 1913 [RSC 430]).

These fears reemerged in February 1918 when Thomas, a French settler in Kampong Thom, was killed by his domestic servants because of his 'excessive demands'. Enraged by the despotism and Thomas's apparent brutality, his 20 or so murderers also killed his concubine and then pillaged and burnt down his house. Seventeen of the alleged murderers were later arrested in Siem Reap, and two others were shot dead by the police. The next year, a former Khmer sergeant who had been reduced in rank to corporal, murdered Duclos, the French commander of the *Garde Indigène* of Stung Treng. In this revenge attack, the man had also shot and wounded Duclos's wife and killed a militiaman before committing suicide. In the next section, we see that what we would call today 'white collar' or 'elite' crime was apparently also widespread among Khmer administrators.

Corruption

The monthly extracts from the provincial reports sent to the Second Bureau[13] by the Chef du Cabinet of the RSC included a litany of the bad behaviour of Khmer functionaries. Embezzlement by Khmer public officials was a recurring theme, such as the case of three village chiefs caught red handed in the circumscription of Pursat in 1910 (RSC 691), a commune chief from Koh Kong who fled to Siam with 500 piastres of collected taxes, and a high-level official from Stung Treng accused of fraudulent collection of taxes and embezzlement to the detriment of many inhabitants in 1911. At least 14 cases of corrupt and criminal conduct were recorded in 1911, including the first deputy governor of Snoc-Trou in Kampong Chhnang circumscription, who illicitly profited from illegal gambling houses. In 1912, it was reported that the former governor of Prey Veng 'has left a state of anarchy and the mandarins have taken the habit of looking at the money from the taxes as their personal assets'. In Kampong Chhnang circumscription, a *balat*[14] had gambled the tax money and lost nearly 600 piastres (RSC 237). In the words of the RSC (1912), the 'most resolute' among the populace may have regarded Khmer functionaries, motivated

---

[13] The *Deuxième Bureau de l'État-major général* (Second Bureau of the General Staff) was France's external military intelligence agency from 1871 to 1940.

[14] A Cambodian official who holds the post of a first deputy to the provincial governor.

by greed rather than need and involved in the theft of public funds collected from an impoverished peasantry, as legitimate targets for retaliation. However, these cases of corruption and abuse and many others uncovered every year were also a major contributing factor in the surge of peasant protests in 1916. Indeed, the '1916 affair' gave the French administration an opportunity to crack down on the corruption of the 'native administration' and extend French control by sacking and/or prosecuting hundreds of Khmer functionaries.

Officials were also sometimes complicit with bandits. The provincial governor of Kdol led a band of armed partisans who stole livestock in Siamese territory, but in 1910 he was captured when he returned to Cambodia with 50 head of cattle (Forest, 1980, p. 383). Militiamen and prison guards also helped bandits escape from prisons, as in Kampong Cham when several prisoners escaped from jail with the complicity of the militiamen on guard duty, 'who took this opportunity to desert' (RSC, 1910 [RSC 691]). In 1912, the governor of Svay Rieng was accused of violence against prisoners, one of his associates of connivance with wrongdoers, and the chief warden of the Cambodian prison and 10 of his subordinates were accused of having facilitated the escape of several prisoners (RSC 237).

The conduct of French functionaries, however, was also far from being exemplary. For example, in an incident in Kampong Speu, Husson, a custom official and tax inspector, shot dead an indigenous sergeant during a drunken brawl with militiamen. A forestry guard, Brasier, was accused of brutality and abuse of power in Kratie, and according to the Chief of Cabinet (1911), 'could one day, given that Cambodians are proud and vindictive, become victim of his way of doing things towards the indigenes' (RSC 237). We do not know if Brasier eventually paid for his brutality, but such behaviours were frequent in the northeast and certainly contributed to the rebellion of the highlanders that broke out in 1912.

The French administration regularly attempted to clean the bureaucracy and suppress elite crime. In 1912, the vice president of the Cambodian appeal court was sent before the Council of Ministers to answer charges of corruption, and five province governors were charged with embezzlement (RSC 237). In 1913, the governor of Romduol and the *balat* of Snoc-Trou were suspended for corruption. A year later, an official in Battambang who, according to the RSC, was 'a former Siamese functionary maintained by us and completely worn out by opium', attempted to embezzle 1,000 piastres but failed. Because he paid back 'the deficit' and 'given his great age', he was not prosecuted, but his dismissal was requested before the Council of Ministers (RSC 430).

Policing response to banditry

The French administration tried hard to fight banditry by building up the capacity of the Khmer police forces and also encouraging villagers to resist and report attacks by bandits. In the same way that, according to the French administration, famine was in part the fault of a lazy and improvident population, unpunished banditry was in great part due to the communal authorities, which 'were to be blamed as nothing is able to shake their inertia'. Arrests were sometimes made, but it seemed it was in spite of the Khmer authorities and the victims who apparently waited '8 or 10 days after the passage of the bandits' to make a report. Frustrated, the RSC despondently remarked in his 1913 report to the GGI:

The spirit of the population is good if by 'population' we mean only the honest and working elements. However, next to the majority of the people, who have many times given us proofs of their docility and loyalty, unfortunately we have to witness a recrudescence in the audacity of the criminal elements, bandits and thieves, encouraged in their enterprise, on the one hand, by the insufficient means of repression at the disposal of *Résidents*, and, on the other hand, by the apathy and fear of the indigenous authorities. (RSC 430)

Although the RSC often lamented that 'all these crimes remained unpunished', 'achieved justice', that is, the extrajudicial killing of offenders, became increasingly systematic. In the Battambang region, five bandits were gunned down between April and May 1912, and in other parts of the country at least 25 others met a similar fate (RSC 237). In Kandal circumscription, on 9 January 1913, 'a band of 40 evildoers pillaged several houses in the village of Choeun-Ros and managed to escape all searches', but 3 weeks later in Stung Treng, when 24 bandits attacked a village 'they encountered fierce resistance from the inhabitants who killed one of the aggressors' (RSC 430). These acts of local bravery encouraged by the RSC were apparently becoming more frequent, and when one of the *sophea*[15] of the circumscription of Kampong Thom gunned down a bandit leader called A-Khom in February, it was another occasion for celebration. Banditry was becoming a more hazardous activity, although there were also many casualties among the villagers. For example, in 1916 in Takeo when bandits attacked the house of a notable, his son was murdered, but the villagers managed to also kill one of the bandits (RSC 430). In Kampong Cham, two separate attacks resulted in the death of two villagers. In Pursat, however, villagers counterattacked when seven offenders invaded their village; one bandit was killed and another wounded. In August 1918 Prey Veng saw the end of the band leader A-Meas and three of his men, killed during an encounter with a detachment of the *Garde Indigène* led by French officer Larriu, who was seriously wounded in the engagement (RSC 431).

The repression of those who had targeted French citizens was always pursued with great energy. In December 1909, three of the bandits who had killed the *colon* (colonist) Michelon had been arrested, but the others were still free

---

[15] A Cambodian official who specialised in legal matters and with the rank of deputy governor.

and active (RSC 263). In March 1910 in his report to the GGI, the RSC was glad to announce that when eight of Michelon's murderers, armed with guns and spears, had come to the village of Chomka-Dampril in the Kratie circumscription to organise a complete pillage, the inhabitants let the bandits enter the village, surrounded them, and killed three of them. However, in June, six individuals armed with guns murdered a village chief from the circumscription of Prey Veng, and according to the RSC, it was a case of revenge 'provoked by the energetic attitude of this village chief and his activity during the pursuit of the bandits in the Michelon case' (RSC 691). The police response was often ruthless and not discouraged by the French administration, particularly when they were concerned about potential 'political agitators'. They found two in 1917. In the Pursat region an 'Annamite bonze led a band armed with old guns and spears'. They attacked the police detachment sent against them, which resulted in their leader's death. In February, the RSC mentioned some 'agitation' in Prey Veng when 'a visionary called Meas, a kind of sorcerer very common in Cambodia, gathered 20 peasants in the forest [and] presented himself as the Messiah; when the communal authorities intervened during the ceremony they were somewhat manhandled'. The response was swift and brutal. The *Gardes Indigènes* were sent; they killed three, wounded two, and captured five of these apparently unarmed individuals, but Meas escaped. This response was not considered excessive, and the RSC casually remarked: 'This incident, which did not spread thanks to the swiftness of the measures taken, shows how easy it is for unscrupulous individuals to impose themselves to the timidity and credulity of the Cambodian population in order to lead it into the worst excesses' (RSC 431).

Referring to several acts of banditry that occurred in 1916, the RSC (1916) complimented the good work of the police: 'All these depredations, which cost the lives of two militiamen and 10 inhabitants, have also caused the bandits significant losses with 27 of them killed and 47 captured, which shows the praiseworthy activity of our police detachments' (RSC 430). Among the 47 offenders arrested, 2 of those who murdered the militiamen in a revenge attack were sentenced to death. Five other death sentences were pronounced in relation to the murder of the French curator of Angkor, Commaille. Commaille had been the victim of a robbery-murder committed in Siem Reap by six offenders who stole the 600 piastres reserved for the wages of the coolies at work on the monuments. Nothing could excite more fear and anger than the murder of a French notable by the 'natives'. Fear and anger because 'this scourge of banditry, which found a propitious place in Cambodia, constitutes a real danger not only for the native population but sometimes also for Europeans' (RSC, 1916 [RSC 430]). A disproportionate repression followed. While only six people had been directly involved in the murder, in addition to the five death penalties, 58 persons were sentenced to hard labour or jail, 'the latter group for giving

Patterns of premodern criminality

hospitality to criminals and giving them information' (Tully, 1996, p. 210). Tully (2002) also reported: 'The militia evicted the entire population of a nearby village and burned down their homes in an act of savage overkill that would have drawn gasps of outrage if committed against peasants in Metropolitan France' (p. 165).

Despite the perennial complaints about the many hidden accomplices that restricted the number of arrests, the RSC regularly reported that the police and the *Sûreté*[16] had managed to make arrests in Phnom Penh and the provinces. Records from the tribunal of Kampong Thom for 1918 mentioned, among other things, 12 homicide events involving 14 victims and 84 offenders and that 45 of them had been arrested (RSC 926). We also learned that 10 of the 17 individuals arrested for the murder of Thomas in February had, within 10 months of the murder, all died of beriberi in the Kampong Thom prison (RSC 926). Cambodian jails were clearly primitive and unsanitary, but it is hard not to suspect that the status of the victims (a Frenchman and his concubine) had something to do with the swift end of their suspected aggressors.

Villagers, nevertheless, carried most of the burden of the fight against banditry. The 1918 record of police action indicated that at least 166 banditry events had occurred in the Battambang circumscription (RSC 209). They cost the lives of nine villagers and injured nine others. No casualty was recorded among the police force, but 11 bandits were killed, 2 others wounded, and 77 captured. The weaponry carried by 337 offenders revealed that 61 (18 per cent) had been armed with guns, 175 (52 per cent) with other weapons, and 101 (30 per cent) were unarmed (no detail was provided for 91 events). Police or militia detachments intervened in 67 events; however, across all these events, 7 militiamen and 51 regional guards were engaged, compared to 455 villagers. The record for 1919 indicated that at least 194 events had occurred. Twenty-one villagers were killed and five others injured (RSC 209). Again, no casualty among the police, but 11 bandits killed, 7 wounded, and 90 captured. Among the 387 offenders, 95 (24 per cent) had guns, 196 (51 per cent) had other weapons, and 96 (25 per cent) were unarmed (no detail was provided for 90 events). Police or militia detachments were sent in 94 events in which altogether 23 militiamen, 128 regional guards, and 458 villagers participated. The proportion of events confronted by police or militia detachments had risen as well as the number of police personnel involved, but villagers were still the major front line engaged in antibanditry interventions.[17]

---

[16] A police force involved in criminal investigations, crime prevention, and the surveillance and repression of 'political agitation'. See discussion of the diverse police forces during the protectorate in the next chapter.

[17] Note also that compared to 1918 gun use by the bandits had increased as did the number of banditry events, bandits, and casualties among both bandits and villagers.

Conclusion

Although Pannetier (1921, cited in Forest, 1980, p. 385), relying on the testimony of Cambodians, asserted that banditry had increased between 1900 and 1920, our own research suggests that it drastically increased between 1911 and 1913 but then declined with some lesser spikes in 1916 and 1918–9 (Figure 2.1). We could only present an impressionistic picture for the period between 1900 and 1909, but this picture suggested a general decline rather than an increase, despite spikes during particularly eventful years such as 1905 and 1907–8. Forest (1980) acknowledged that the abolition of slavery by '[putting] back on the labour market a number of people who [could] not straightaway make a living' (p. 385) and the strict regulation of taxes may have contributed to the process of bandit group formation. He also argued that banditry had declined due to the relatively better control exercised by the colonial state:

> Yet, one can be sceptical about the idea that the conditions of the development of the phenomenon were more favourable under colonisation than under the power of a sovereign who did not have any apparatus of police control – apart from some haphazard punitive expeditions – on a country with no central administration and weakened by an arbitrary tax system... The testimony of the peasants must therefore be taken with some caution.

On the basis of data collected before and after 1920, as the next chapter shows, we agree with Forest's (1980, p. 385) discussion of the role of the colonial state in achieving better control over banditry. Forest alluded to the emergence of a particular 'civilising process', that is, from Elias's perspective (Elias, 1939/2012), a new sensitivity to violence among the peasantry after at least three decades of relative peace, associated with the development of the modern state and its monopolisation of violence. This sensitivity to violence would bias popular perception and create the *illusion* of increasing levels of violence, a well-known criminological phenomenon:[18] 'Moreover [we should consider] a change in the rural attitude toward this phenomenon: When the trend in village life is a movement towards stabilisation and equilibrium, would not banditry appear increasingly "abnormal" and threatening?' (Forest, 1980, p. 385).

At the end of the second decade of the twentieth century and after 60 years of precarious and sometimes seriously challenged control, it seemed that the French administration was finally entering the golden years of its 'domination'.[19] In great part it was because during all these years it had worked hard to rationalise and modernise the Cambodian state. Modernisation of the state, however, is not synonymous with modernisation of the society, which

---

[18] The sensitisation to violence is conditional and occurs only when the fear of it abates – as in the pacification of an area. How much of societal change in attitudes to violence was under way by 1920 remains tentative.

[19] The term was used repetitively in the reports of the RSC to the GGI.

can only be achieved through transformations in the economic, educational, and health domains, and importantly through fostering a lively and democratic civil society. Some improvements were made in these areas, but overall they were neglected (Slocomb, 2010). As for the development of a democratic civil society and a pluralistic political consciousness, it was simply suppressed.

The next chapter describes the implementation of the colonial state, and Chapter 4 focuses on the two decades from 1920 to 1940 in Cambodia. We shall see that the violence associated with protopolitical contestations greatly diminished after 1920. Banditry, particularly in the border provinces, remained a concern for the Protectorate, but as we will see, the Protectorate became progressively more effective in the control of banditry. We do not argue that an era of social justice in which banditry had been eliminated began after 1920. Chandler's (2008) observations about immense inequality and the persistence of rural violence in the 1920s is incontestable:

The gap in income between the French and the Cambodians – with the rare exceptions of a few favoured officials and the royal family – was very wide. A French official could earn as much as 12,000 piastres a year; with exemptions for his wife and two children, such an official would pay only 30 piastres in tax... A Cambodian farmer, on the other hand, with no salary other than what he could earn (at 30 cents per day, or 90 piastres a year) or what he could sell his crop for (seldom more than 40 piastres a year) was saddled with a range of taxes that totalled in the 1920s as much as 12 piastres a year. He was taxed individually and in cash payment in lieu of corvée, his rice was taxed at a fixed percentage, and he paid high prices for salt, opium, and alcohol and abattoir taxes when his livestock went to slaughter. What did the peasant receive in exchange? Very little, despite French rhetoric to the contrary. Monthly reports from French residents show widespread rural violence and disorder, which because it made no direct challenge to French control, seldom rose into the political portions of the reports. It is clear, however, that to most villagers the perpetual harassment of bandit gangs, especially in the dry season, was far more real than any benefit brought to them by the French. (pp. 189–90)

We argue (as Elias did in relation to the civilising process in Europe) that the rationalisation of the state apparatus and the greater control it eventually came to exercise through its monopolisation of violence had a beneficial impact on reducing crime and violence between 1920 and 1940 in Cambodia. Next, we examine the purpose and the ways of the colonisers in their attempt at 'modernising' the Cambodian state and its security apparatus.

3 Development of the colonial state: modernisation and control

When the French government established its Protectorate over Cambodia, it considered that the Cambodian state was moribund, and French representatives believed that the corrupt Khmer administration had descended into anarchy (Taboulet, 1956). At least until 1884 not much was done to transform this situation. France considered Cambodia as essentially a buffer zone against Siam and the alleged influence England exercised over it; what mattered most was that the conquest and colonisation of Vietnam remained unhampered by anti-French manoeuvres from the Siamese and 'perfidious Albion' (Osborne, 1969; Taboulet, 1956). In France, there was political unanimity neither about imperialistic ventures nor about colonial policies. Debate and controversy abounded around issues of direct or indirect rule, and establishment of colonies or Protectorates, straightforward annexation, or more subtle systems of control (Osborne, 1969; Taboulet, 1956). The colonial enterprise was motivated by a mixed bag of mercenary, geopolitical, and idealistic interests associated with the diverse positions of the colonial actors as missionaries, explorers, scholars, aristocratic admirals, adventurers, entrepreneurs, and bureaucrats and administrators. Almost all of them were products of the Enlightenment and of the 'Great Principles of 1789'. Most were devoted to the cult of Science, the fetish of Progress, and the morals of the work ethic and were great believers in the superiority of the Christian and European civilisation.[1] For example, missionaries

---

[1] See Elias (1939/2012, p. 15) about the arrogant perspective of 'civilised Europeans':

> The concept of 'civilization' refers to a wide variety of facts: to the level of technology, to the type of manners, to the development of scientific knowledge, to religious ideas and customs. It can refer to the type of dwelling or the manner in which men and women live together, to the form of judicial punishment, or to the way in which food is prepared. Strictly speaking, there is almost nothing which cannot be done in a 'civilized' or an 'uncivilized' way; hence, it always seems somewhat difficult to summarize in a few words everything that can be described as civilization. But when one examines what the general function of the concept of civilization really is, and what common quality causes all these various human attitudes and activities to be described as civilized, one starts with a very simple discovery: this concept expresses the self-consciousness of the West. One could even say: the national consciousness. It sums up everything in which Western society of the last two or three centuries believes itself superior to earlier societies or 'more primitive' contemporary ones. By this term Western society seeks to describe what constitutes its special character and what it is proud of: the level of *its* technology, the nature of *its* manners, the development of *its* scientific knowledge or view of the world, and much more.

and admirals alike were genuinely horrified by the state of misery, the underdevelopment of the country, and the arbitrariness and corruption of a regime reminiscent of the darkest periods of France's *ancien régime*. Informed by Beccarian perspectives on law, justice, and punishment,[2] they were therefore also genuinely shocked by slavery and the cruel and irrational treatment of offenders.

Initially for France, geopolitical interests dominated: Cambodia served to provide a buffer zone against Siamese and British influences so that it could pursue the colonisation of Vietnam unhampered by the expected anti-French manoeuvres of these challengers. That the Protectorate's interest in Cambodia was not at this stage economic but geopolitical is evidenced by the decision of the Ministry of Foreign Affairs in 1867 to leave the western provinces, in particular the richest region of Battambang, under Siamese sovereignty. King Norodom and the military governor of Cochinchina, Admiral de la Grandière, protested this decision to no avail (Taboulet, 1956). Economic interests eventually came to the fore in 1884, but their actualisation was imagined and realised in the context of a Protectorate that attracted few settlers compared to the colony of Cochinchina. Taxation rather than agricultural and industrial development, which required a larger investment, became the means deployed in Cambodia to fulfil economic interests conceived at the level of Indochina as a whole and largely for the benefit of Cochinchina. That Cambodia, the most heavily taxed state in French Indochina (Tully, 2002, p. 310), should become the 'milking cow' of Indochina was not unanimously intended either. Some *Résidents* complained about this state of affairs, but eventually the economic and fiscal policies implemented in Cambodia led to and maintained Cambodia in this position. The colonial enterprise in Cambodia was characterised by a small number of colons, few investments, and little development. In this context, the Protectorate, 'a model of domination *à bon marché* [cheap]' (Brocheux & Hémery, 1995, p. 74), was an adequate option for Cambodia. On the other hand, as Brocheux and Hémery noted, 'The priming and the development of colonial profit, investment, in a word the *mise en valeur*, demand the rapid financial profitability of the colony, putting its budgets in a position of surplus, and this implies a vigorous intervention of the colonial state apparatus in the functioning of the dominated societies' (Brocheux & Hémery, 1995, p. 74).

Under this regime of 'domination *à bon marché*', the intervention of the colonial state in Cambodia vigorously targeted the collection and protection of revenues generated from taxes. The administrative, policing, and legal and judicial

---

[2] Beccaria (1738–94) was an Italian jurist best known for his treatise 'On Crimes and Punishments'. He advocated a rational system of criminal justice that eschewed torture and the death penalty and greatly influenced the development of modern European justice systems.

systems, that is, the political economy of the Protectorate, were geared towards the realisation of this goal, and this would determine the scope and limitation of the modernisation of the country. The repression of banditry and corruption was essentially a strategy to protect revenues, both directly by preventing losses and indirectly by preserving and extending the legitimacy of the protectors who were supposed to provide security. Maintaining the political consciousness of the Khmer population as low as possible through isolation from the potentially subversive influence of the Chinese and Vietnamese was also motivated by the need to ensure the 'docility' of this mass of taxpayers. The construction of roads facilitated not only tax collection but also the repression of banditry and its negative impact on revenues.

This is not to say that the unique preoccupation of the French in Cambodia was fiscal exploitation, and some actors in the colonial enterprise denounced this policy, but in practice it became the dominant characteristic of the Protectorate. We suggest that taking this particular political economy as a background helps us understand the development and reforms of the colonial state apparatus, their scope, and the limitation they imposed on modernisation, with consequences that played out at the end of French rule.

The penetration and control of the colonial state apparatus in and over Cambodian society necessarily followed a top-down process. It originated and was strongest at the central level of governance and in time gradually moved down with reduced strength to the level of provinces and eventually communes and villages. Urban areas, Phnom Penh and the provincial towns, were therefore the first to experience the penetration of the machinery of the colonial state. The surrounding villages and rural areas experienced it later and with greater difficulties, while remote areas often remained untouched. French control was thus more pervasive at the top or centre of society than it was at the periphery and diminished in proportion to the social and geographical distance from those centres of administrative concentration.

This particular pattern of development (i.e. modernisation, rationalisation, penetration) of the state apparatus eventually affected the regional trends and characteristics of criminality and its control. Therefore, before discussing the justice and policing systems of the Protectorate, we examine the development and penetration of the colonial apparatus over time.

Administration of the Protectorate

In the 1870s the French started to push for a number of reforms, including cleansing and reorganising the Khmer administration, a stricter control of the collection and distribution of public revenues, the creation of a council of ministers in which a French administrator would have a seat, reforming the regime of property, and the abolition of slavery (Forest, 1980). On 15 January 1877

Norodom reluctantly proclaimed a series of reforms in the direction desired by the French, including a council of ministers in which he would only have a ratifying role. Administratively, these reforms stipulated a reduction in the number of provinces and functionaries, the remuneration of the mandarins according to their rank, the prohibition for ministers and provincial governors to be involved in commercial activities, and, already planning for a local administration, the election of village chiefs by the inhabitants. These were not implemented, and in July 1878, Admiral Lafont (Governor-General 1877–1879) complained to Norodom that the Ordinances of 1877 had remained a dead letter, in particular pointing out that there were too many provinces and mandarins and insisting on the nexus between unpaid mandarins and corruption (Taboulet, 1956).

This first attempt at rationalisation and control was a failure, and the French resumed their efforts in 1884 but with disastrous consequences. Article 1 of the Convention of 17 June 1884 imposed on the King, stipulated: 'His majesty, the King of Cambodia accepts all the administrative, judicial, financial and commercial reforms which, in the future, the Government of the French Republic will judge it useful to introduce in order to facilitate the accomplishment of his Protectorate' (Taboulet, 1956, p. 671). French *Résidents* were to be appointed to provincial regions to control and supervise the administration of Cambodian officials (Osborne, 1969) and a commune system instituted, 'with a mayor and council of notables, to ease the administrative task of the French' (Osborne, 1969, p. 211). It was an attempt at complete French control over central government and extending to provincial and village levels. The Great Insurrection that followed and the concessions made by the French regarding their program of reforms only slowed down the ineluctable expansion of colonial control, but this growth was often accompanied by unintended negative consequences. For instance, between 1882 and 1886 the governor of Cochinchina, Le Myre de Vilers, not only 'forced the king's agreement to meeting the cost of the Protectorate' but also eliminated his rights to a number of taxes (Osborne, 1969, p. 201). To compensate for the loss of revenues, the king increased his customary rent-seeking practices in the appointment of officials and 'Norodom's increasing alarm over the loss of his wealth made financial gifts for the king the essential qualification for appointment' (Osborne, 1969, pp. 232–3).

French attempts at a rationalisation of the Khmer administration between 1877 and 1884 had failed, but the colonisers had nevertheless consolidated their centralisation of power and extended their control. In 1887 Cambodia was integrated into the *Union Indochinoise*; in 1892 the protectors had control over virtually all the taxes; and between 1888 and 1894 the number of provincial *Résidents* increased from 4 to 10. At the local level, an 1899 Royal Ordinance defined the role and duty of village chiefs and their councils to include 'the reception of royal envoys charged with the census of the population and the perception of taxes; the publication of royal ordinances; the raising of troops for the war; the adjudication of conflicts between villagers; the functions of rural police' (Forest, 1980, p. 30). Village chiefs were not properly remunerated before 1892, but they received a partial tax exemption on their harvested paddy in addition to a proportion of the fines they themselves imposed or helped authorities to impose. Forest (1980) aptly observed, 'A village chief essentially makes a living from his role as gendarme' (p. 30).

The most important and decisive reform initiative occurred in 1897 and achieved complete French control at the centre. The king and even the council of ministers were relegated to the role of rubber stamps for the *Résident Supérieur*, who 'de jure and de facto... is indeed the chief of the Cambodian government [whose] power is only limited by the instructions he receives and the control that the Governor General exerts on him', as the then Governor General Doumer wrote 8 years later in his memoirs (cited in Forest, 1980, p. 63). In 1898 the number of provincial *Résidences* (also called circumscriptions; see Chapter 2) had reached 12, and Forest (1980) argues that their creation and development were at this stage essentially motivated by the need for effective collection of taxes, ensuring law and order, and showing the presence of the colonial power. The reform of the provincial administration also led directly to the dismissal of 14 corrupt governors (from among about 50 such officeholders) during the third trimester of 1897.

Between 1900 and 1920, the main reforms addressed the rationalisation of the Khmer administration through better control, discipline, and training of Khmer functionaries. Starting in 1902, all provincial functionaries had to sit a formal examination of their aptitude to obtain their post. In 1914 a school for *kromokars* (functionaries, from secretaries to governors) opened in Phnom Penh. In 1917, it became the School of Cambodian Administration, where secretaries of the various services were formed and candidates to the positions of functionaries and judges were trained. Students were recruited through a competitive exam and attended for 2 years. The same year, the Protectorate promulgated the *Status of the Personnel of the Cambodian Administration*, which enounced the principle of the separation of administrative and judicial powers, including the creation of two distinct administrative and judicial personnel. The role and duties of the provincial governors were also better defined:

The governor must in fact control, countersign, and keep two copies of all the administrative acts proclaimed in his province among other things... the registries of births, deaths and marriages and the registries of title deeds when the village chiefs transmit them to him. He keeps watch over the establishment of the tax rolls and the collection of the taxes in due course. He stamps the sale certificates of animals established by the village chiefs. He supervises the progress of public works in his circumscription. Finally he is responsible for maintaining order and delivering justice. (Forest, 1980, p. 103)

Concerning this last duty, Forest (1980) remarks that governors devoted much time to it as they also made important profits from it: 'Indeed, judiciary acts, until the creation of the Inspection of the Indigenous Affairs in 1913, are still more or less escaping control and the governor draws substantial financial advantages from them' (p. 103).

Recognising its status of capital city, the municipality of Phnom Penh was created by decree of the General Governor of Indochina (GGI), with a specific urban budget and under the authority of a *Résident*-Mayor, appointed by the GGI. Assisted by a municipal commission of eight members (five French, one Cambodian, one Vietnamese, and one Chinese), the *Résident*-Mayor combined the functions of *Résident* and provincial governor (Forest, 1980). In the provinces also, during the first two decades of the twentieth century, the Protectorate returned several times to the difficult task of the local administration, and 1901 saw 'the first embryo of a communal organisation and the first attempt to make the inhabitants of the *srok* (district) participate in its organisation' (Forest, 1980, p. 118). The ordinance of 21 August 1901 instituted elections of the *mesrok* (village chief) by the inhabitants of the *srok*, through secret ballot; however, the *Résident* provided the list of candidates, and if he judged the elected authorities were incompetent, illiterate or corrupt, he could immediately order new elections. These elections were intended to renew and bring fresh blood into the old local administration regarded by the *Résidents* as staffed by 'the worst functionaries, sometimes conniving with livestock thieves or bandits, and very often with other villagers... to evade taxes' (Forest, 1980, p. 117). Forest argued that the dominant motive behind this local reorganisation was once again fiscal because the *mesrok* and his council now had the duty to collect personal taxes.

The creation in 1908 of the commune (*khum*) as a formal administrative unit encompassing a few villages shifted some of the *mesrok*'s tasks, particularly in relation to taxes and public order, to the *mekhum*, elected every 4 years. This further reorganisation again increased control over the local population. For example, Article 5 of the 1908 Ordinance required all the inhabitants of a *khum* to be registered on the personal tax roll and to communicate to the *mekhum* the names and ages of his wife and children, as well as those of his domestics and their wives and children. Apart from a tighter surveillance of the population, some positive effects in terms of tax collection, and possibly better control of criminality, the commune was a failure as far as democratisation and economic development were concerned. The representative institutions never met, and local finances and economic development were neglected. In 1913, the election terms of the *mekhums* changed from being elected every 4 years to being elected until they reached 55 years of age, a decision apparently motivated by both fiscal considerations[3] and the need to lighten the growing burden of responsibilities carried by the *mekhums*. Until 1901 the *mesrok*'s main duties

---

[3] Forest (1980, p. 121) notes that the reform of 1908 'dangerously multiplied the number of village authorities and elicited some concerns regarding the tax exemptions that could result', as village authorities were partially exempted from taxes. In Kampong Cham, for example, he reports that the number of village authorities increased from 1,800 to 10,000 after the 1908 election.

included recording the sales of cattle, the establishment of tax rolls and the control of tax collection, the gathering of *corvée* labour, and local policing. Starting in 1901, his bureaucratic tasks steadily increased to include the collection of personal taxes as well as agricultural taxes, the registry of births, deaths, and marriages as well as that of lands and crops, and the obligation to attempt free-of-charge mediation of conflicts between villagers prior to referring unresolved matters to the courts. *Mekhums* represented the *khum* in judicial proceedings. They had judiciary police function: they could undertake police investigations and were involved in the questioning and arrest of persons suspected of felonies and misdemeanours. Finally, after the great peasant demonstrations of 1916, the *mekhums* were charged with the surveillance of the monks to whom they had to provide certificates of identity.

Many *mekhums* were denounced and attacked by angry peasants during the demonstrations of 1916, which shows that if these administrative reforms at the grass-roots level permitted greater penetration and control by the colonial state, they also severed the traditional links between the peasants and their local representatives. With his new functions of mediator, policeman, and tax collector under the colonial authority, and remunerated from a percentage of the diverse taxes he collected, the *mekhum* represented less and less the interests of the villagers but increasingly those of the protectors as well as his own. Such functions also offered greater opportunities for abuse. However, *mekhums* found themselves in the unenviable situation of having to be ruthless with the villagers put under their authority to themselves avoid severe punishment by the higher authority who had appointed them. Forest (1980) remarked:

If there was a certain solidarity between inhabitants and *mekhum* regarding taxes, the system of profit sharing in the tax yield severed this solidarity: the *mekhum* became the tax collector and was no longer the representative of his constituents... And the French did not spare the village chiefs-tax collectors. It was not rare for the latter if they did not bring the tax in time, to be accused of embezzlement and incarcerated until full payment of the tax. (p. 125)

In addition, their new role as tax collectors had made *mekhums* prime targets for banditry.

Further reforms were introduced between 1920 and 1940, but the blueprint for the administrative penetration of the colonial state down to the village level was well in place at the beginning of the 1920s. Tully (2002) remarks:

According to Gabriel Maurel, the 1911 decrees [that defined the powers of the *Résident Supérieur* and his consultative body] meant that the *Résident Supérieur*'s powers were 'close to absolute' in matters of law, the police, the fixing and collection of taxes, the drawing up and execution of budgets, public works and so on... While the consolidation of power by the French did help weed out corruption and incompetence in the Khmer bureaucracy, it did not break the pattern of despotic control. (p. 143)

This important observation encapsulates the scope and limitations of the modernising enterprise of French colonialism in Cambodia. It summarises the effect of French policies that focused on revenue collection, which required only minimal modernist efforts at rationalisation in specific domains in order to increase and protect revenues but which maintained premodern authoritarian modes of governance to better accomplish this goal. If this enterprise served to reduce crime and violence, it also reinforced a political pattern of an authoritarian rule by elites that would contribute to tragic developments in the future. However, in light of the Eliasian civilising process, these limited reforms corresponded to the despotic stage of the centralising monarchy, observed in sixteenth- and seventeenth-century Europe, in the achievement of state monopolisation of force, violence, and taxation.

Justice and legal system

Very early the Protectorate had created two separate systems of justice. Cambodians were dealt with by the Cambodian courts; non-Cambodians – French, Europeans, subjects of an American or European power, and all 'foreign Asians', including Vietnamese and Chinese – were under the jurisdiction of French courts and subject to the law as it was applied by the French courts in Indochina. As we have seen in Chapter 2, French courts were more lenient than Cambodian courts. For example, court data for the year 1890 indicated that in Phnom Penh, 36 per cent of non-Cambodian accused were convicted of violent offences and 18 per cent were recidivists; none of them was sentenced to hard labour and one third received only a fine. The remainder of the non-Cambodians were acquitted or served short prison terms. By contrast, all Cambodians were sentenced to prison, including 10 per cent who were sentenced to more than 5 years of hard labour.

The fiscal regime also varied depending on the nationality of the potential taxpayers. The Chinese, for example, paid higher taxes than Cambodians but were under French legal jurisdiction. Sino-Cambodians could opt for one or the other nationality, which led to further inequities. Jurisdictional issues were only one aspect of the colonial influence on the Khmer justice system, which, as Tully (2002) remarked, remained inequitable. Although Ang Duong had revised the code around 1850,

it was still chaotic, arbitrary and in places cruel – even sadistic – and unjust... It was possible for those with money to buy immunity from prosecution or to otherwise pervert the course of justice. The word of a commoner carried less weight than that of a noble. The system encouraged corruption as 'native' magistrates relied on fines levied on real or imagined malefactors for at least part of their income... There were no examinations for judicial officials. (p. 141)

The French therefore saw it as their mission not only to rationalise but also to humanise the 'indigenous' justice system. They were genuinely horrified that 'female adulterers could be partially impaled astride a sharpened bamboo stake' (Tully, 2002, p. 141) or by the frequent use of corporal punishment, spectacular and ghoulish public executions, and the legal and codified use of torture during interrogations, even though they themselves unofficially used some of these methods, particularly in their supervision of the convict colony of Poulo Condor.

As early as 1877 the French had tried to reform the justice system, and ordinances included that the practice of justice be entrusted to specialised mandarins, that justice fees be paid to the Treasury and no longer to the judges, that the latter be remunerated by the state, and that the conditions of the prisoners be improved (Taboulet, 1959). These were not implemented, but similar requirements were restated in the 1884 convention imposed on the king by R. S. Thomson, and French *Résidents* in the provinces were entrusted with strict control over the administration of justice. Felonies and misdemeanours were tried in provincial courts of first instance or in Phnom Penh, in the *sala lukhum*.[4] These courts were composed of one judge, the governor or his deputy, assisted by two notables, one prosecutor, and one clerk. The presence of a defender was not compulsory. The tariff of the fines and court fees were decided arbitrarily, and the functionaries of the justice system pocketed the revenues made from the cases according to the norms of patronage (Forest, 1980). In 1897, the provincial *Résidents* became president-judges of the French courts where all non-Cambodians were judged. In addition the *Résidence* had to examine and stamp all the judgements made by the Cambodian courts in which the governors were the judges (Forest, 1980).[5] In 1904, special examinations for officials with judicial functions were introduced.

This new judicial structure, however, did not stop the illegitimate accumulation of wealth through judicial practice. For example, in 1912 the vice president of the *sala outor*[6] and the deputy-minister of justice were sacked for corrupt conduct (Forest, 1980). Yet, if such cases surfaced and were dealt with, it was because from 1900 onwards the French had put in place a system of control over Khmer functionaries to police and discipline them. The Council of Ministers was entrusted with the centralisation and judgement of all enquiries related to accusations against provincial authorities, including *mekhums*, and the Council ruled on sanctions, demotions, and dismissals. In 1918, a specialised agency was created to deal with these disciplinary issues (Forest, 1980).

---

[4] A Khmer term for a criminal court presided over by Cambodian officials.
[5] However, these judgements were in Khmer, which *Résidents* rarely spoke, and few of them were translated (Mathieu Guérin, personal communication, 7 March 2014).
[6] An appeal court in Phnom Penh created in 1897.

Development of the colonial state: modernisation and control   91

Reforms of the substantive law and matters related to punishment were introduced from 1904 with the beginning of the reign of Sisowath. Corporal punishments, chaining prisoners in their cells, harsh punishment for adultery, and inhumane[7] methods of capital punishment were abolished (Tully, 2002). At the end of 1911, a new criminal code was put in place that 'provided for respect of the ancient principles of Cambodian law, but torture and corporal punishment were "suppressed as incompatible with the principles of humanity and justice"' (Tully, 2002, p. 142). In 1920, this complex and often contradictory criminal code was replaced 'by new legislation attempting to better integrate tradition and the essential principles of French jurisprudence' (Forest, 1980, p. 109). However, it was not until 1922 that the judiciary became formally independent from the executive. From this date the provincial courts were no longer under the control of the governors: professional judges were now adjudicating cases and the judiciary service was placed under the authority of a French magistrate. Felonies such as homicide, robbery, and rape were no longer judged in the provincial courts but in Phnom Penh's criminal court.

Policing

The most direct way of maintaining order while raising and protecting revenues was through policing and the rapid development of an effective police force. The importance of policing for the Protectorate is demonstrated by the relatively large proportion of the total budget allocated to criminal justice expenditures (police, justice, prisons) and, within the criminal justice budget, the share allocated to policing. Forest (1980) calculated that between 1913 and 1920, policing expenditures represented on average 12.3 per cent of the total budget of the Protectorate compared to 4.1 per cent for education, 3.9 per cent for health, and a measly 1 per cent for agricultural development.[8] During the same period, policing consumed around 60 per cent of the total criminal justice system budget compared with 25 per cent for the prisons and 15 per cent for the courts.

At first glance it seems that policing in Cambodia attracted a disproportionate amount of resources and reflected the policing situation in France, about which Karl Marx would have quipped, 'there is not a single rat that is not administered by the police' (cited in Morlat, 1995, p. 9). In fact, if the aim was indeed to attain such a level of control, in terms of resources it was more a case of 'much too little'. The overall government budget in Cambodia was rather light since only a small proportion of the resources raked from Cambodia were reinvested in

---

[7] The 'humane' method was the guillotine.
[8] The share of the total budget allocated to the criminal justice system grew from 12 per cent in 1914 to a peak of 16 per cent in 1919, before decreasing to around 15 per cent in 1920.

Cambodia. Therefore, the police service that evolved also needed to be *à bon marché*. The reports of the provincial *Résidents* and the *Résident Supérieur* alike were full of complaints about the lack of police officers to effectively control banditry, and they constantly asked the GGI to increase the size of the *Garde Indigène*, the indigenous police and major frontline force in Cambodia. In fact the development of the police in Cambodia followed the development of the police in Indochina, and almost all the decisions, including the size of these police forces, came from the GGI.

Early development of the police forces

Initially, the policing of the Protectorate was a military affair. The *tirailleurs* (infantrymen) of the French colonial army, first mainly composed of Vietnamese soldiers and auxiliaries but later on recruiting more and more Khmers, were used early in the colonisation of Cambodia to fight insurrections, rebellions, and banditry and to control borders. Forest (1980) reports that in June 1886, during the Great Insurrection, the colonial army of intervention in Cambodia counted just over 3,500 men: around 40 per cent were Vietnamese, one third were French, and one quarter, Cambodians. Very quickly, the Protectorate created an indigenous police force in charge of day-to-day policing matters as well as more specialised forces dealing with political matters and intelligence.

The Garde Indigène

According to Daufès (1933), the Cambodian *Garde Indigène* was created in June 1893, but Guérin (2008) argued that it already existed in 1885, and Forest (1980) reported that in 1886 it had already enlisted 908 Cambodian militiamen. The earlier date is credible given that the 1884 Convention required Norodom to approve the creation of police posts throughout Cambodia (Osborne, 1969). It seems that 1893 was the date of its official creation but that it had been unofficially formed 10 years before. Although it was organised as a paramilitary police force, it was a civilian police, officially named the *Garde Civile Indigène du Cambodge* but referred to as the *Milice*, the *Gardes*, or the *Miliciens* (Morlat, 1995). Until 1903, it was the only formally constituted police force in Cambodia. Initially, enrolment was for 2 years, and villages were required to provide volunteers in proportion to the number of inhabitants (between 1 and 1.5 per cent). Single men were recruited first, and then married men, and if there were no volunteers, governors drew lots. Recruitment was always difficult, and because it relied on conscription more often than on free consent, desertions were frequent. In 1909 the *Résident Supérieur du Cambodge* (RSC) expressed satisfaction that conscription had not resulted in major troubles: 'The normal tax collection and the ease that has marked the operations of drawing lots for the *Garde Indigène* and the *Bataillon Cambodgien*[9] are an index of the good attitude of the population.' Brigades of the *Garde Indigène* existed in all provinces and were headed by a *Garde Principal*, who was often a French gendarme or a former noncommissioned military officer. Small detachments were dispatched to fight banditry and rebellions, to escort *mekhums* during tax collection, but they were also employed to watch over convict labour in public works and to guard prison convicts. From the start, provincial *Résidents* and RSCs constantly complained about the insufficient number of *Gardes Indigènes* to ensure the effective policing of the country:

> The calm that reigns in Cambodia – given that since February 1st no new acts of banditry have been reported in Svay Rieng – is illusory and will only last if the brigade of the *Garde Indigène* of Prey Veng/Svay Rieng is maintained with its reinforced staff numbers; however, this measure, taken temporarily by drawing staff from the Phnom Penh Brigade can only be made permanent if the size of the *Garde Indigène* is increased as I have requested many times... Prisons overflow with prisoners and the *Garde Indigène* is more than busy with guarding the premises and *corvées* on the working sites open to penal labour; the *Résidents* are unanimous in their request for an increase, even if only a modest one, of their militia brigades which are overworked and discouraged. (RSC, 1913 [RSC 430])

In 1912, the number of *Gardes Indigènes* was reduced from 1,600 to 1,300 (bringing the rate per 100,000 population from 76 down to 62), but the length of service increased from 2 to 3 years. It included 31 Europeans, all in supervisory roles. In 1913 the number was increased to 1,500 (70 per 100,000), and mobile columns were created to exercise a more effective surveillance of the territory. In 1915 its size was increased again; it peaked in 1916 at 2,400 (100 per 100,000 following the 1916 Affair) but dropped to 2,200 (92 per 100,000) in 1917 and 1,900 (79 per 100,000) in 1920.

Gendarmerie

The gendarmes had a military status and participated from day one in the colonisation of Indochina. They were employed for policing purposes as early as 1899 in a joint brigade for Cochinchina and Cambodia (Beaudonnet, 1998). The Gendarmerie, always French, counted only a handful of members in Cambodia (e.g. 27 gendarmes in 1919 up to 50 in 1942), but they had important supervisory and officer roles, for example, in the *Garde Indigène*. Most often a gendarme headed the *Commissariats* (police posts) in provincial towns where the repression of illegal gambling was one of the gendarmes' tasks.[10] Despite

---

[9] The *Bataillon Cambodgien* was dissolved in 1910. Its mission was the repression of insurrections; for example, it was deployed during the Battambang rebellion in 1908–9.

[10] The Gendarmerie also supervised two specialised police forces: the *Police Fluviale* (River police) and the *Brigade des Lacs* (Lake Brigade), which were used to police waterways, including fighting banditry and smuggling.

its small size, the Gendarmerie was an effective as well as very profitable police force. For example, with hardly more than 50 men, in 1940 and 1942 the Gendarmerie collected fines and taxes amounting, respectively, to 518,420 and 580,016 piastres; that is, more than double what it cost to run the force, estimated at between 150,000 and 200,000 piastres (GGI 65902).

The administrative and judiciary police and the municipal police

In 1903, the GGI created the *Police Administrative et Judiciaire*, placed under the authority of the RSC and the *Procureur de la République* (public prosecutor). Its mission was to 'maintain public order, protect property and individual liberty, to ensure the surveillance of public morality and public health, the investigation of crimes and misdemeanours as well as the initiation or facilitation of the repression of infractions'. This new police force was operational mostly in Phnom Penh, but if circumstances demanded it, it could exercise its action over the whole Protectorate. In 1903 it was composed of both European and indigenous personnel (10 and 41, respectively), with, however, a huge pay difference between them: for the same rank the indigenous personnel was paid 14 times less than the European personnel. The Phnom Penh Municipal Police was composed of agents seconded from the administrative and judiciary police and was entrusted with looking after 'public health, public roads, the repression of crimes and misdemeanours against public peace, to ensure that good order was maintained in the city's public spaces, to prevent accidents and calamities such as fires, epidemics, etc.' (GGI 17198).

Police forces under Khmer administration

In addition to the police forces, mentioned above, all under French administration, a number of ill-defined policing bodies were under Khmer administration.
- First mentioned in 1909, the *Gardes Régionaux* (regional guards) were mostly employed to fight banditry in the provinces under the authority of the provincial governors.
- The *Police Rurale* (rural police) was formally created in 1925, but well before that many forms of policing in villages and communes had been attempted. It was part of the mekhums' duties to perform some level of policing in their districts.

These self-help 'community policing' schemes were strongly encouraged by the French. Extensive engagement of villagers in fighting banditry was attempted, and in some instances weapons were provided to the local authorities to fight banditry and help maintain order during specific events. Villagers were frequently called upon between 1912 and 1918, particularly during the highlanders' rebellion, to perform defensive functions. Around 1910 the engagement of villagers against banditry started to have some momentum:

This new attitude from the villagers as well as the police patrols effectively dissipated the last remnant of the band and brought back tranquillity in the province (RSC, 1910 [RSC 691]). Acts of banditry tend to disappear, thanks on the one hand to the ceaseless police patrols deployed to the far away regions, to the creation of militia posts, and on the other hand particularly to the support given to the indigenous authorities away from the main centres looking for the thieves by the inhabitants themselves who are in the end tired of being continually the victims of criminals. (RSC, 1911 [RSC 237])

The turning point: 1916

The year 1916 represented a turning point in the policing of Cambodia. A series of events in Indochina generally and Cambodia in particular led to the reorganisation of the police forces in Indochina. First, there was the suspicion during World War I that Germany supported anti-French revolutionary activities in Indochina and possibly assisted the anticolonial activities of Cambodian Prince Yukanthor and of the Chinese living in Cambodia. Then, the Cambodian peasant demonstrations of January 1916, although not politically linked to it, coincided with a serious insurrection in Cochinchina, and the highlanders' rebellion was still an incipient risk in Cambodia's northeast. These events prompted a reorganisation of the police forces in Indochina, and particularly of political policing in Cambodia. Various reports by inspectors from the Department of Administrative and Political Affairs pointed out that the different police forces in the whole of Indochina lacked cohesion. They said that criminals took advantage of the absence of a central policing body to move to places where the police had no jurisdiction. This lack of cohesion and cooperation between Cambodia and Cochinchina was a recurrent complaint of the RSCs:

Regarding the special situation of the provinces bordering Cochinchina, I have to lament the negative consequences for public security of this border zone because the administrative authorities of Cochinchina do not always conduct on their side sufficient surveillance over elements causing trouble. Brigands, once their misdeed is done, too often find help and protection from cantonal and communal Annamite authorities, and if a police column tries to cross the border to pursue a band, they do not hesitate to complain against a so-called violation of frontier. (RSC, 1913 [RSC 430])

Border policing was an important issue, not only politically but also in the repression of banditry. Some collaboration between the Protectorate and Siam existed in 1910, but in 1913 the relationship deteriorated. However, with the entry of Siam into the war on the Allies' side in 1917 the relationship improved significantly, and in 1919 a convention on the cooperation of the border police of both countries was in the process of being ratified, and a similar type of agreement was being discussed with the government of Cochinchina. Cooperation improved slowly from 1923 to at least the mid 1930s when the relationships between Siam and the Protectorate were regarded as excellent, and the decline in banditry in the border region was in part attributed to the better cooperation between the Siamese and Cambodian police forces.

In Cambodia itself, 1916 saw not only a substantial increase in the size of the *Garde Indigène* (from 1,700 to 2,400) but also the formation of what the RSC called the regional police, indicating that '400 *Gardes Indigènes* have been dispatched between the 51 Cambodian provinces and put at the disposal of the governors for the service of the regional police whose duty is to maintain order and arrest wrongdoers in the province in which they are posted.' But, and this was underlined in the original report, 'in no case whatsoever, will the governors or functionaries of the *salakhets* [provincial centres] employ the *Gardes Indigènes* as domestics or for personal services' (RSC 430).

The extension and rationalisation of the police forces were not without effects on criminality, as the RSC commented in his report of the fourth trimester 1925: 'Order and security having been normally assured in the kingdom, the public attitude has overall remained as satisfactory as possible, a situation to which has certainly contributed the organisation of the rural police, established on bases that our experience allowed us to achieve successfully' (RSC 475).

The greatest development in the policing apparatus of the Protectorate, however, was in the organisation and extension of the service and the *Police de la Sûreté* (security police). In Indochina, like in France, the role of the *Sûreté* included political policing (surveillance, identity, and espionage) but was not limited to it. The official creation of the *Police de la Sûreté* in Cambodia occurred in 1918, but the *Service de la Sûreté* already existed in 1914. In 1916 a section of the RSC's report dedicated to 'Measures of Political Surveillance' already mentioned that the Protectorate was developing,

following the indications of the *Gouverneur Général*, its means of political and administrative surveillance within Cambodia as well as on its maritime and continental borders... The arrests, the resulting inquiries and the information gathered thanks to our new means of surveillance have permitted to identify the opponents of our authority, to foil their activities and plans, and to take the necessary measures to paralyse any of their attempts. (RSC 430)

The RSC reiterated this view in 1917: 'I believe that there remain in the Far East and in Indochina enough factors of local troubles to motivate a constant vigilance and the maintenance, if not the growth, of the administrative police forces upon which the principle of our domination or of our Protectorate rests' (RSC 431).

The two main sections of the *Police de la Sûreté* were the *Service de l'Immigration Asiatique* (Department of Asian Immigration, mainly concerned with the Chinese community) and the *Service d'Identification et de Renseignements* (Department of Identification and Intelligence). Their role was to monitor and control the activities of foreigners in Cambodia. This task included the establishment of files and index cards targeting 'defendants, convicts, suspects, foreigners, workers, sailors, and boys following the Bertillon method'[11] (Brocheux & Hemery, 1995, p. 109).

In Cambodia, because seriously threatening pro-independence political turmoil was almost absent, between 1920 and 1940, the political role of the *Sûreté* was not particularly important and was actually contested. For example, in 1919, the Battambang *Résident* expressed doubts about the usefulness of the *Police de la Sûreté* in his circumscription:

Inspector Crettier, who is full of zeal and enthusiasm, and spends much energy, is doing many rounds, yet without much substantial result, as the service he is managing at the moment includes only indigenous agents of very low quality. For a long time to come, the way it is functioning in the circumscription, the *sûreté* will not do any service from a political point of view and very little in term of investigating crimes and misdemeanours. (RSC 209)

Yet, the *Sûreté* was apparently busy: in 1919, it had made 2,358 arrests in Phnom Penh and the provinces and 1,326 in a 6-month period the following year. During the same 6-month period, the details of 8,347 suspect foreigners were put on cards. These figures increased every year. In 1937, 3,835 'foreigners whose situation was irregular' were arrested, and 1940 saw the creation of 73,776 new records, nearly 10 times as many as in 1920. This huge bureaucratic work was in great part motivated by the politics of isolation of 'the docile Khmer' from the allegedly pernicious influence of the Chinese and Vietnamese and was regarded as valuable by almost everyone in the Administration. Unfortunately, the restrictive surveillance of police and resistance to the development of a modern political consciousness, combined with the maintenance of pre-modern and authoritarian modes of governance and the poverty of educational developments, stunted the development of civil society. These politics of isolation were clearly identified over and over again in the RSC's reports.

The political situation of the country is satisfying; the surveillance of the apathetic and fearful Cambodian race is easy and it is rather on the foreign migrants and travellers of the Annamite race that the vigilance of our surveillance must focus. (RSC, 1913 [RSC 430])

The political situation is therefore satisfying in all Cambodia, the state of mind of the masse of the people is good, but needs to be carefully handled and shielded from all anxieties, which in fact could only come from foreign elements, restless Annamites or greedy Chinese who every year during the harvest spread alarming news intended to

---

[11] Alphonse Bertillon (1853–1914) was a French police officer, who created the criminal identification system known as anthropometry, which included fingerprinting. He was also the inventor of the 'mug shot', and an unreliable expert witness in the Alfred Dreyfus trial of 1894.

confuse peasants and lower the price of paddy for the greatest profit of Chinese commerce. (RSC, 1913 [RSC 430])

For, if on their own and until now Cambodians have not given us any troubles, it remains true that they are worked on/manipulated by foreign elements that are underhandedly hostile to us. These external influences are of two main kinds: first there are the conversations, attitudes, false news or occult excitations of the Sino-Annamite population... there is another important seat of xenophobic influence in the country and particularly in the Battambang territory, no so much through direct calls to insurrection but by the example of its own independence and its affinity of character with Cambodia itself; this is the brother kingdom, the free country of Siam... This is why our vigilance must focus particularly on the recently retroceded territories. Such are the two pernicious influences: Sino-Annamite and Siamese. (RSC, 1915 [RSC 430])

The implementation of the politics of isolation required the investment of energy and resources that competed with the resources needed to fulfil another no less important goal: assuring the legitimacy of the Protectorate in providing security. This, too, was frequently expressed in the reports of the provincial *Résidents* and the RSC:

It is toward a better organisation of the repression of these acts of brigandage that the efforts of the administration of the Protectorate must focus, because we should worry, indeed, that if firm measures are not urgently taken to give to the population the efficacious protection that we engaged ourselves to provide in Cambodia, discouragement may paralyse the best will of peaceful inhabitants and lead them through fear of retaliations to join the ranks of the plunderers. The movement generalising we might even have to dread more serious political preoccupations as our enemies would not miss the opportunity to use our inaction as an argument against us. (RSC, 1913 [RSC 430])

The very critical report against the *Sûreté* by an inspection of the police forces of Cambodia in 1924 appears to have expressed the resource-wise antagonisms between these two goals:

Its sole preoccupation is to please everyone, carefully taking shelter behind someone else. A complete re-organisation of the Service is required. At a lower cost, a well organised *Sûreté* will give far more interesting results that the current service, which produces an enormous quantity of useless wretched papers but does not provide the administration with any useful political information... The *Sûreté* cost around 50,000 piastres in 1914. It will cost over 150,000 piastres in 1924. Its spending has tripled... On the other hand, the *Garde Indigène*, which renders such valuable services, has only doubled its spending. The budgetary crisis allows neither an increase of its size despite its necessity, nor an improvement of the situation of such a deserving personnel... A rigorous reduction of police spending is indispensable now that the Protectorate needs all its resources to give public instruction and social welfare their necessary development; the reduction should, I think, be borne by the *Police de la Sûreté*: the development of the country and the political situation do not justify its current size. (RSC 475)

It should be noted that in the following years, and particularly in the 1930s during the Great Depression, the *Police de la Sûreté* would be increasingly employed in fighting banditry and also developed the more conventional features of the typical judicial police.

Conclusion

As we show in the next chapter, it seems to us that the processes of modernisation and rationalisation of the colonial state and its penetration into Cambodian society from 1884 to 1920 eventually paid off and helped reduce criminality between 1920 and 1930. We will see that the relative economic boom of the 1920s also played a role and how the Great Depression of the 1930s reversed the downward trend in crime. However, these processes were constrained by the imperatives of a Protectorate '*à bon marché*' that maintained premodern and authoritarian modes of governance as cheaper and more convenient ways of collecting revenues. These modes of governance were preserved through the co-option of traditional power so that real power was totally in the hands of the French, but the symbolic power of the king was not only preserved but also usefully reinforced by the French. This is the sense we give to Forest's (1980) remark that 'if there is a papering over the cracks of the administration, there is not the creation of a properly Cambodian state apparatus' (p. 112). However, from the point of view of the protectors, 'The system of Protectorate implemented in Cambodia is a masterpiece, the powers mutually assist each other, each masking or shock-absorbing the imperfections of the other' (Forest, 1980, p. 115).

Another important mechanism generated by the colonial enterprise in Cambodia was the further isolation of the country both economically and politically. We have seen direct means of political isolation from the influence of 'foreign Asians' assisted by the services of the *Sûreté*. Forest (1980) discusses the politics of isolation in broader terms as arising from a colonial enterprise

> that sabotages itself by proclaiming the participation of the people to the modernisation of the institutions, which in fact is ending up in the isolation of these people and the loss of their initiative... however, this isolation carries with it serious negative effects in the long term. The people can no longer express themselves: someone talks for them, thinks for them. They and the state get accustomed to this situation... by the absence of the diffusion, thanks to a lack of schools, of modern culture in the rural world, and by a kind of withdrawal into traditional modes of economic activities. (pp. 140–1)

These paternalistic politics of 'protection' via isolation were aimed at and resulted in the 'infantilisation' and political retardation of Cambodian society with dire consequences in the development and resolution of future conflicts. Next, we turn to the 'golden years' of the Protectorate between 1920 and 1940, when social peace seemed assured, and crime and violence were declining.

4 The 'golden age' of the Protectorate: 1920–1940

The period between the two world wars has been characterised by one historian of Cambodia as the 'golden age' of the Protectorate (Aldrich, 1996) or a kind of *belle époque* (Tully, 2002).[1] This was certainly true for the protectors, the Khmer elites, and sections of the bourgeoisie, but for many ordinary Cambodians the benefits of this golden age were limited, as limited indeed as the 1920s economic boom that contributed to this happy characterisation. Economic development occurred in certain areas such as public works and the booming rubber plantations, but other areas such as industry and agriculture improved little, while social development through better education and health services remained underfunded. Taxes continued to grow in a society increasingly ruled by a repressive colonial state. In 1925, the *belle époque* was momentarily disturbed by the protopolitical murder of Kampong Chhnang *Résident* Felix Bardez, while *Résident Supérieur* Baudoin began squandering a huge amount of public money on the Bokor resort, a project in which he had personal interests and that cost the lives of hundreds of forced labourers. The 'Bardez affair', however, occurred during a time of great social peace and declining crime trends in Cambodia, and such a situation had not been enjoyed since the eighteenth century.

The Great Depression put an abrupt and prolonged brake on economic and social development and coincided with a crime wave, and particularly another surge in banditry. A slow economic recovery started in 1936 and crime receded, but World War II, the French defeat in 1940, the retrocession of the Battambang province to Thailand[2] in 1941, and growing Khmer nationalism undermined French colonial hegemony and changed the patterns of criminal violence.

---

[1] Aldrich (1996, p. 114) described this period as 'the zenith of the French Empire – a veritable golden age'. Tully (2002, p. 191) referred to Huy Kanthoul's (Cambodian teacher, writer, and politician in 2002) recollections: 'If I have stretched out my account of the years between the wars, it is because this period was for me, as for others of my generation, a kind of "*belle époque*", forever gone. Afterwards Cambodia would never again be the same.'
[2] Siam was renamed Thailand in 1939.

The economic boom

Historians of the Protectorate have described and discussed the characteristics and limits of the relative economic boom and associated golden age during the 1920s and 1930s (see Chandler, 2008; Forest, 1980; Osborne, 1969; Slocomb, 2010; Steinberg, 1959; Tully, 1996, 2002). A detailed account is outside the scope of this book, and we only mention here some major features. Some public works were achieved, mainly the construction of roads and the development of communications and economic markets, which also facilitated the collection of a growing number of taxes and the repression of banditry. Rice production increased, but because of a lack of major hydrologic developments, crop yield per hectare did not (Tully, 1996). Trade and industrialisation increased but were limited by protectionist policies that discouraged foreign investments in the country. Rubber plantations became a significant source of economic development and export; however, they employed very few Khmers, and the conditions of the predominantly Vietnamese workforce were often horrendous.[3] Health and education were neglected, resulting in little socioeconomic progress. Vaccination campaigns and sanitation programs were effective in the reduction of epidemics such as smallpox and plague, but many waterborne diseases could not be significantly controlled without major public works in water management. There were no Cambodian doctors and very few French health professionals, and no effort was made to educate and train such a professional indigenous body.

Notwithstanding the resistance of Khmer society to modern medicine and education, as usual the Protectorate was motivated by both bureaucratic and fiscal considerations. Schooling had been made compulsory for boys, and non-compliance was punished with a fine. This bureaucratic decision did not bring many children to school but merely opened a new source of fines and opportunities for abuse and corruption. In any case, the education provided by the reformed pagoda schools that boys attended was of very poor quality, and Tully (1996) mentioned a 1921 inspection report lamenting: 'nothing could be more

---

[3] For instance, in 1927, Emile Desenlis, the *Résident* of Kampong Cham, reported: '[The coolies are] human livestock, terrorized by the overseers, and they don't dare complain for fear of bullying and cruelties' (Tully, 2002, p. 311). Accidents, diseases, malnutrition, and brutality were commonplace: they were 'crammed in ramshackle huts' with hardly any sanitation, and 'because of the general lack of hygiene, outbreaks of cholera, dysentery and other diseases were common', leading to mortality rates which 'ranged from 0.8 to 3.0 per cent, with "spikes" during epidemics'. In 1927, after a demonstration of 330 coolies from the Mimot plantations, labour inspector Delamare 'observed the unhealed scars of whipping on the workers' bodies and learned that they had been denied medical treatment'. Eventually, these conditions 'led early to militant labour action, including strikes, go-slows and work-to-rule protests', and 'the plantations became – and remained – a stronghold of the Indochinese Communist Party' (Tully, 2002, pp. 314–22). However, in some plantations and after 1936, working conditions were not inferior to the European standard at the time (Guérin, 2008).

distressing than the contrast between the wide-awake air of the pupils and the stupid expression of the teacher' (p. 242). He also remarked, 'When the French decided that the best – or possibly the cheapest – option for the establishment of a public education system lay via the Buddhist *sangha*, they were trusting to an order whose members were medieval in outlook' (Tully, 2002, p. 224). The schooling of girls was simply nonexistent except for the few among the elite and the bourgeoisie who could join their 'brothers' in the French high schools of Phnom Penh, Saigon, and Hanoi, where not only a handful of current and future monarchist administrators were educated but also the future right-wing republican and left-wing communist cliques. Such constraints on the socio-economic and political development of Cambodia formed part of a deleterious legacy with dire, albeit lagged effects on the future; however, from 1920 to 1930, the relative economic boom coincided with a significant decline in criminal violence.

Criminological data

We had access to rich sources of criminological data for the period 1920 to 1940, and we also draw from secondary sources, particularly Tully (1996, 2002) and Sorn (1995), who were among the few historians to provide some sources on crime and violence. Four types of primary data were available: reports from the administration, police data, judicial and court data, and prison data. We describe these data and how they were coded below.

Administrative reports

Reports from the *Résidents Supérieurs* and the *Résidents* of circumscription continued to provide information about banditry and homicide trends and patterns between 1920 and 1940.[4] They were complemented between 1936 and 1939 by the monthly reports from the provincial governors of Kampot (RSC 266), Siem Reap (RSC 409), Kampong Speu (RSC 329), and Kampong Chhnang (RSC 270).

Police data

Administrative and police reports,[5] and the *Annuaire Statistique de l'Indochine* [BIB AOM A/1017 and A/1048] provided information about the size of the police forces and their activities, and occasionally some crime data. However,

---

[4] These documents were found in boxes RSC 338, 343, 346, 347, 350, 352, 354, 421, 427, 460, 647, 674, 675, and 676.
[5] Found in RSC GGI10202, 64280, 64281, 65850, and 65855 and RSC 230, 336, 289, and 688.

the bulk of our crime data came from the *Bulletins de Police Criminelle* (*BPC*) published monthly by the *Section de l'Identité Judiciaire* of the *Sûreté* (see Chapter 3). For this chapter we drew from the series published between 1936 and 1940.[6] The *BPC* recorded all the individuals wanted by the police for an alleged felony or misdemeanour, including the name, age, sex, and residence of the wanted person, the province where the alleged offence had been committed, and the legal definition of this offence. The structure of the *BPC* allowed also for the measurement of co-offending by listing all the alleged offenders wanted for the same *event* (a *case* in court data). Finally, the *BPC* also provided a monthly record of those who were no longer wanted and the reason for this decision (e.g. arrested, killed, acquitted, amnestied, or case dismissed).

The same wanted individuals often appeared repeatedly in successive issues. This reflected the judicial procedure involved in putting an individual under a police search warrant. Typically, the initial step, rarely recorded, was the *avis de recherche* (literally, a search notice). Most cases, however, started with the *mandat d'amener* (warrant to bring), followed by a *mandat d'arrêt* (arrest warrant), and, finally, an *ordonnance de prise de corps* (literally, an order to take the body). On average, 13 months passed between the *mandat d'amener* and the *ordonnance de prise de corps*. The *ordonnance de prise de corps* was issued by the Phnom Penh Supreme Court, and when a case reached this stage it was submitted for instruction to the *Chambre d'Accusation*, which could dismiss it or send it to court for trial. If the individuals involved in this case were still at large and wanted by the police, then a decision to send the case to court for trial meant that the alleged offenders were judged and possibly sentenced *in abstentia*.

Collecting and coding information from the *BPC* to determine how many criminal events had occurred each year between 1936 and 1940, how many alleged offenders had been involved in these cases, and for how many the search had ended due to arrest or other reasons was a painstaking task. The analysis of the *BPC* permitted the compilation of a statistic of criminal events for which the alleged offenders were 'at large', hence wanted by the police, therefore excluding events for which offenders had been arrested *in flagrante delicto* or soon after the crime. However, by combining information from the *BPC* with court data, it was possible to estimate how many cases of homicide *flagrante delicto* had occurred.

---

[6] The *BPC* data (BNF cote 4 JO774, Paris) was collected in 2011 by Florian Brout. He was pursuing a master's degree under the supervision of Mathieu Guérin, and we exchanged data with him. The series extended to 1945, but he was unable to photocopy the records and had no time to examine the five remaining years, nor did we have funds to extend the series.

Judicial and court data

Court data could come from two different sources: the Ministry of Justice (National Archives of Cambodia [NAC]) and the *Annuaire Statistique de l'Indochine*. These data were available from 1927 to 1947 (missing for 1944–6) and recorded the number of cases and defendants.[7] They distinguished between felonies and misdemeanours. Felonies consisted of homicide, rape/sexual assault, kidnapping, violence against parents, *vol qualifié* (robbery, burglary, livestock theft), arson, organised crime, illegal possession of firearms, graft of public money, and counterfeiting. Misdemeanours included serious and minor assaults; theft; fraud; corruption; gambling; use of fake identity cards and official documents; destruction of livestock, cultures, and harvests; resisting arrest; offences against public morality (e.g. adultery); slander; vagrancy; and public drunkenness. Finally, sentencing data were available between 1929 and 1947 and permitted the measurement of the patterns of punishment and their severity (from fines, to imprisonment, time determined hard labour, life hard labour, and death penalty) during this period.[8]

Prison data

We only found a consistent series of quantitative penal data between 1929 and 1947 in the *Annuaire Statistique de l'Indochine*. Before 1929, the administrative reports mainly provided qualitative information and some quantitative data for a small number of provinces.[9] The 1929–47 series allowed for the measurement of the rates of the prison population, deaths in custody, and entry and exit from prison.

Before turning to the trends and patterns of violent crime during the period, we briefly examine the role of the police in ensuring the subservience of the Khmer population.

The colonial state

Tully (2002) described the Protectorate as 'a dictatorship of civil servants and police [with]... no tradition, either of an independent judiciary, [in which] a free press was largely absent' (p. 288). None of the civil and political rights enjoyed by the citizens of France existed in Cambodia. The mail service was

---

[7] They provided the number of accused and acquitted defendants, in respect to their categorisation as either felony or misdemeanour, but not the specific crime type.
[8] General primary judicial and court data were found in boxes GGI65789, 65840, and 65841.
[9] Some data were found in boxes RSC 321, 336, and 468.

under surveillance, and any politically suspicious letters and packets were confiscated. The new penal code of 1924 punished with imprisonment any criticisms of the actions of the French or Cambodian administrations. Following the spread of a new syncretic religious movement, the 'Cao Dai' starting in 1926 and spreading rapidly throughout Cochinchina, religious freedoms were curtailed. The Pantheist features of the sect gave it a panethnic appeal, which worried the Khmer monarchy and the Buddhist religious establishment. The French regarded Cao Dai and its panethnic promise as an anti-French, potentially anticolonial movement. In 1931, new articles were added to prevent religious activities not recognised by the government, and a systematic and brutal suppression of the sect by the police was unleashed.[10]

Ennis (1936, cited in Tully, 2002, p. 304) characterised the government established by the French in Indochina as a kind of 'occidental despotism'.[11] The policies of extortion, isolation, and infantilising practised by the Protectorate relied on a police state, which at time of 'indocility' could become brutal. Denied freedom of speech and assembly, recalcitrant individuals risked severe beatings and torture by the *Sûreté*. The cruelty of the physical abuses performed some 45 years later by the Khmer Rouges in S-21 under Comrade Duch was not unprecedented but already allegedly practiced, according to Tully (2002) by the officers of the *Police de la Sûreté* in the 1930s:

Beatings, canings, the suspension of prisoners on their toes, and the insertion of needles under fingers and toenails were common. The inquisitors denied food and water to prisoners under interrogation. They put young female political offenders into the same cells as rapists. They used pincers to spring eyeballs from their sockets and funnelled gasoline into prisoners' stomachs. They slashed the skin of prisoners' legs into long shreds plaited with cotton, and set it alight. Perhaps most ghastly of all was the insertion of a corkscrew into the urinary tract, followed by its sharp removal. (p. 293)

Although Tully's quotation drew from Andrée Viollis, a journalist for *SOS Indochine*, and referred to the 'work' of the *Sûreté* in Vietnam rather than in Cambodia, it is likely that the *Sûreté* did brutalise suspects to obtain information.

An important task of the *Sûreté* was to establish a comprehensive *cordon sanitaire* around the Khmer population to prevent the spread of subversive ideas from foreign Asians, particularly politically active workers. In 1921, the French ruthlessly repressed the first recorded workers' strike and the colony's first trade union. When 200 Phnom Penh Chinese builders went on strike after a failed attempt at negotiation with their employers, the police raided the union headquarters and arrested the leaders, who were deported to China after spending

---

[10] American Protestant missionaries were also targeted.
[11] Akin to the stage of absolute monarchy in seventeenth-century Europe described by Elias.

6 months in jail. A court ruled that the union was illegal and it was dissolved, and, according to Tully (2002), in 1923 'the Phnom Penh police chief noted with some satisfaction that there were no Cambodian associations other than an authorised friendly society' (p. 237).

A source of concern for the Protectorate was the 16,000 (mostly) Vietnamese workers on eight major rubber plantations. Most of these workers were ruthlessly exploited to extract the maximum profit, and many absconded. The horrendous working conditions, however, led to several labour actions (strikes), and plantations soon became a stronghold of the Indochinese Communist Party (Tully, 2002). This was a new factor in the 'contaminating' potential of Vietnamese workers. In 1935, the *Résident* of Strung Treng was concerned that the construction of the colonial road was bringing many Annamites to the province, and he reported 'a close surveillance has been exercised from day one on the more or less suspicious looking elements' (RSC 422). He expounded his prophylactic methods against political contamination:

For some months now and due to the increasing immigration of Annamites in the province, particularly in the town of Stung Treng, it is required that as soon as they arrive these Asians present themselves to the bureaux of the *Résidence* for verification of their documents and administrative situation. The Secretary of the *Identité* entrusted with this work maintains a register in which he records the description of the Annamites whether newly arrived or just passing by. This information is communicated to the *Sûreté* of Phnom Penh. Similar information is also communicated to the Chief of Police Services about Europeans, natives, and others 'in transit' through Siempang-Veunsai. (RSC 422)

The monthly reports from the first section (political) of the *Service de la Sûreté* for 1936 – a turbulent period marked by massive strikes and demonstrations in Vietnam and the leftist government of the *Front Populaire* in France – focused on the surveillance of the potential revolutionary activities of plantation workers, Annamites, and students (GGI 65448). In 1937, the same section in a paragraph on the 'Surveillance of the plantations' reported:

The *Service de la Sûreté* had discovered in the plantation of Peam-Cheang (K. Cham) the existence of a newly constituted group called 'Dong-Tem,' which includes 21 members, all recently arrived in the province. Thirteen workers have been arrested and put at the disposal of the *Résident*-Judge of K. Cham. The service is busy trying to determine the exact aim of this association. (GGI 65449)

The same year the report remarked that 'the Cambodian Heng Pheng deported back to Poipet after serving time in a Thai prison informed the Chief of the post of Poipet that ideas of independence were inculcated by the Siamese to Cambodian and Lao prisoners, inciting them to shake off the yoke of the French' (GGI 65449). Even tourists visiting Angkor were put under surveillance. From 1936 to 1942, over 1,000 'foreign Asians' and other foreigners had been expelled from Indochina, and 1,768 Annamites from Cambodia.

Combined with the lack of rural development and an emancipating education and the absence of unions, a free press, and books and newspapers in the Khmer language, and compounded by xenophobic sentiments towards the Vietnamese, the *cordon sanitaire* was effective. Khmers indeed appeared indifferent to the development of revolutionary ideas and communism. The first Khmer-language newspaper, *Nagarawatta*,[12] was first printed only in 1936 (Tully, 2002, p. 241). Although nationalist and embracing modernity and notwithstanding the fact that censorship prevented the expression of anticolonial sentiments, it was not anti-French but anti-Vietnamese and to a lesser extent anti-Siamese (see Chandler, 2008; Edwards, 2007; Tully, 2002). After all, the Protectorate had officially been established to protect Cambodia from the annexationist proclivities of these two neighbours. As Edwards (2007) has argued, Khmer nationalism developed as a coconstruction of the Khmer elites and the French. The French scholars, with their work on Angkor and on Khmer Buddhism and their promotion of traditional handicrafts, fostered 'a sense of pride in Khmer culture, or *Khmérité* as it was later known' (Tully, 2002, p. 217). Tully (2002) argued: 'From its inception Cambodian nationalism contained a thick strand of envy. The French historian Daniel Hemery has described Khmer nationalism as reactive nationalism' (p. 242). A glorious past was revered, but about which the French and the Cambodian intellectual elites were telling Khmers they had fallen from and should strive to regain. This 'cult of antiquity' (Kiernan, 2007) contributed to the development of a form of xenophobic and paranoid ethnonationalism, which from the late 1960s to 1979 would become increasingly virulent and murderous and whose violence would linger until the present.

Given all these measures of political surveillance and recurring waves of banditry, the Protectorate could not, even during the Great Depression and despite the desire for a police *à bon marché*, restrict the budget of the police forces too drastically. In the early 1930s, there was a slump of about 30 per cent in police expenditure, but the budget of the police as a proportion of the total budget actually increased from 11 per cent in 1930 to 16.5 per cent in 1935 but later reduced to 13 per cent of all budget outlays in 1941.

Following a peak during the large protest movements of 1916, the size of the *Garde Indigène* (calculated as the rate per 100,000 population) stabilised around 90 per 100,000 in the 1920s (Figure 4.1). It decreased between 1930 until 1935 but increased again steeply from the outbreak of war in 1939 and under the new Vichy regime. The rates per 100,000 of all the police forces

---

[12] One of its cofounders, Son Ngoc Thanh, would later become a prominent figure of Khmer nationalism and anticolonialism in the 1940s.

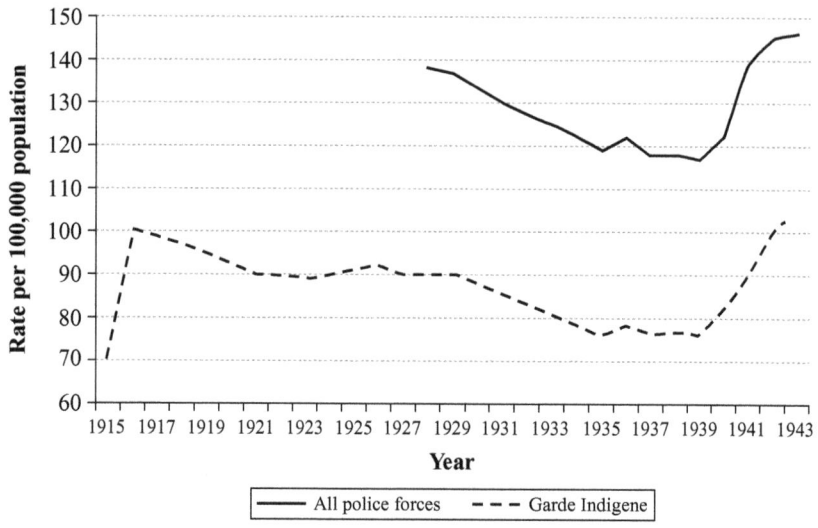

Figure 4.1 Size of the police forces and *Garde Indigène*, 1915–43 (rates per 100,000 population)

between 1928 and 1943 showed a similar pattern, and over this period the *Garde Indigène* forces represented about two thirds of all police.

Trends and patterns in violent crimes: 1920–1940

Figure 4.2 presents the estimated rate of homicide victims in the country between 1921 and 1940 and the rate of homicide cases in court between 1927 and 1940. Figure 4.3 presents the estimated rate of banditry events and the rate of *vol qualifié* (core banditry events, including robbery, burglary, and livestock thefts) in court. Both figures show a decline in homicide and banditry in the early and mid 1920s. From 1927, these figures and court data for assault, rape, and kidnap (not shown) point to a rise in violence, particularly in the early 1930s and peaking between 1933 and 1935, the worse years of the Great Depression in Cambodia. Rates then decline until 1940, although both the estimated and court rates of homicide suggest a new increase after the steep post-Depression decline of 1936.

The fall in crime: 1920–1927

The decline in violent crime started in 1922 for banditry and 1924 for homicide (Figures 4.1 and 4.2). In 1920 and 1921, the rapid pace of fiscal and

The 'golden age' of the Protectorate 1920–1940

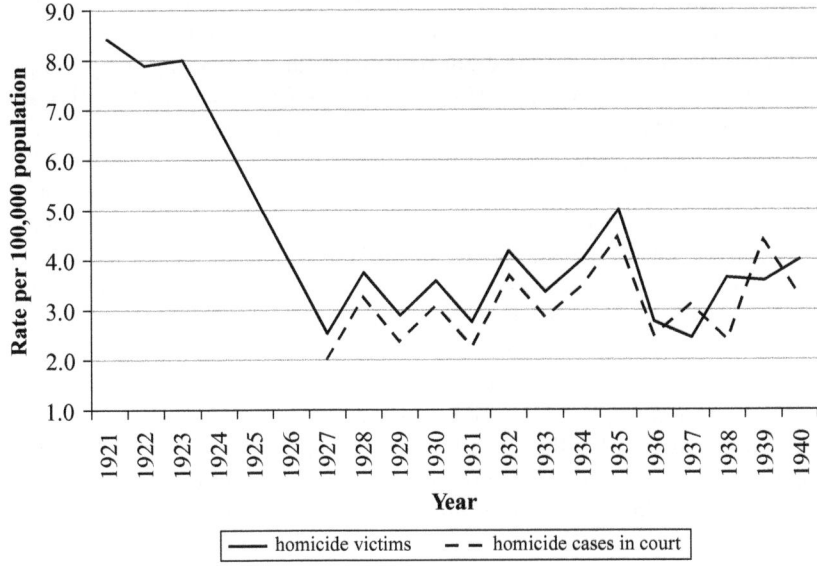

Figure 4.2 Estimated rates of homicide victims, 1921–40, and homicide cases in court, 1927–40

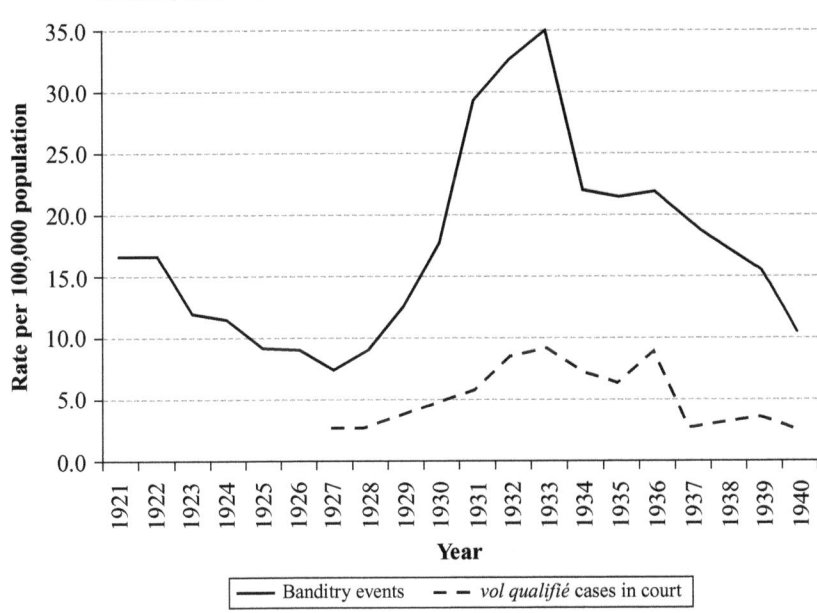

Figure 4.3 Estimated rates of banditry events, 1921–40, and banditry cases in court, 1927–40

religious administration reforms had reignited popular discontent and the *Résident Supérieur du Cambodge* (RSC) reported an increase in banditry and related gun use everywhere but particularly in Battambang, Prey Veng, Kampong Thom, and Kampot. However, the second semester of 1921 was marked by a significant decline. According to the RSC, only one incident was worth reporting: a mini rebellion in Kampong Speu where a 'hundred individuals, enrolled willingly or by force and grouped under the command of a dangerous ex-convict claiming invulnerability, had decided to go and plunder Kampong Speu, the administrative centre of the *Résidence*' (RSC 475). During the police operation launched against them, eight bandits were killed and many arrested, and the French officer commanding the detachment of the *Garde Indigène* was wounded. In encounters with bandits (who increasingly targeted the Chinese), police often resorted to lethal force, and such actions were routinely reported. Foreshadowing the second highland rebellion, which took place during the Great Depression, a pro-French Stieng *balat* and a number of his relatives were ambushed and murdered in Kratie in October 1922.[13] In 1923, acts of banditry dropped significantly and mainly occurred on the western and eastern borders. More than a dozen offenders were killed and others seriously injured by the police. The RSC was very pleased and waxed lyrical about the 'favourable attitude of our protégés, which is due to the greater understanding that they start to form about the benefits of our civilising work in this country and our fair administration' (RSC 475). The RSC causally associated this 'favourable attitude' with the decline in banditry because

if they don't know how to publicly manifest their appreciation for our paternal politics, at least they want to show us their gratitude for the peace and prosperity they are enjoying through a moral conduct about which no doubt is possible; thus they are less and less disposed to listen to the incitements of some wrongdoers who make a living out of theft. (RSC 475)

The declining trend in criminality continued until 1925 and homicide fell to a very low rate of 2.5 per 100,000. Yet, in this seemingly peaceful period, two events occurred with the potential to disrupt the colonial 'golden age': the murder of the Kampong Chhnang *Résident* Felix Bardez and the Bokor scandal.

---

[13] The RSC wondered in his report for the fourth trimester 1922 whether revenge for the brutality of the *balat* had led to his murder. Guérin (2008, p. 271), however, citing the Kratie *Résident*, suggested that the murder may have been a response to the strong pro-French action of the *balat*, who was very efficient at rallying highlanders to submit to the administration but was disliked by the Khmers.

Troubles in a colonial 'paradise'

Bardez was 43 years old in 1925 and had already spent 15 years as a civil servant in Cambodia although he was still unable to speak Khmer.[14] As the acting *Résident* in Prey Veng in 1923 and 1924, he had managed through vigorous tax collection procedures to increase revenues in all 18 categories of tax. For this feat he was rewarded with the position of *Résident* of Kampong Chhnang, where tax revenues were considered too low. In fact, and despite mediocre harvests, revenues from paddy taxes in Kampong Chhnang had increased 17 per cent between 1921 and 1922 from 37,500 to 41,500 piastres. Poiret, Bardez's predecessor, had also warned, 'The Cambodian of Kampong Chhnang appears to be taxed almost to the limit of his means' (Tully, 2002, p. 297). Bardez's arrival in Kampong Chhnang coincided with a new tax to pay for the luxury resort of Bokor (see below). In 1925 a better harvest and Bardez's forceful tax collection methods since late 1924 paid off. Compared to 1923, revenues from paddy taxes had increased nearly 75 per cent and brought in over 77,000 piastres. However, all was not well in the province. Early in 1925 a Cambodian tax collector was severely beaten by villagers from Kraang Leav and, according to Tully (2002), on two occasions 'several hundred of the poorest people marched in from Kraang Leav district to present their grievances to Bardez in the provincial capital' (p. 298).

In April 1925, many villagers from Kraang Leav had still not paid their taxes, and Bardez decided to visit the village accompanied by his interpreter and a militiaman. Bardez was a good friend of RSC Baudoin, but he was also renowned as a tactless, arrogant, and abusive individual. His distasteful nature combined with the fact that he did not speak or understand Khmer when interacting with villagers was a precipitating factor in his murder. As soon as he arrived in Kraang Leav, 'he lined them [villagers] up in the centre of the village and delivered an insulting harangue... demanding to know how the village could have afforded a new pagoda if they were destitute as they claimed... and even suggest[ed] that the women should prostitute themselves to raise the outstanding money' (Tully, 2002, p. 298). He had several villagers handcuffed and threatened with imprisonment.

While he went for his lunch he prevented the handcuffed men from having theirs. More and more onlookers had gathered, drinking palm wine in the hot sun and becoming increasingly angry. When Bardez resumed his harangue after lunch, sensing the growing anger in the crowd, he sent for reinforcements. At this moment, 'his escort, the Cambodian militiaman, Leach, nervously cocked his rifle and a ripple of rage spread through the crowd. The villagers wrestled the man's rifle from his hands, someone hit him over the head

---

[14] Information in this section is essentially from Chandler (2008) and Tully (2002).

with a wooden stool (some accounts say an axe was used) and he fell dead' (Tully, 2002, p. 299). As Bardez was trying to come to the rescue of the militiaman, 'the crowd surged at him... trampling and bludgeoning him to death' (p. 299), using everything they could put their hands on, 'chairs, fence palings, axe handles, and the militiaman's rifle butt' (Chandler, 2008, p. 209). His interpreter, who had found refuge in a pagoda, was dragged outside and beaten to death. According to Chandler (2008), 'The corpses were then mutilated... the murderers danced around them' (p. 192). The tax money that Bardez had collected disappeared.

After the murders, the crowd started marching on the *Résidence* asking for the return of their taxes. However, the adrenaline rush and the effects of palm wine wearing off, they realised the gravity of their act. The march broke up and when the militiamen Bardez had called for confronted them they did not resist arrest. The French response was brutal: 1 death sentence, 4 sentences of hard labour for life, and 18 sentences of between 15 and 5 years hard labour as well as the collective punishment of the village. By Royal ordinance, for 10 years the village would be called *derachan* (bestiality). Villagers were forced to attend 'expiation' ceremonies where they confessed their guilt, a memorial paid for by the villagers was erected, and villagers were no longer able to move freely.

For the Protectorate, the murder of Bardez was shocking not only because it was the first time that a high-ranking French official had been killed collecting tax but also because it occurred, socially and criminally speaking, during a very quiet period. The crime was portrayed as an apolitical robbery-murder,[15] but few believed it was, particularly Baudoin's enemies. The defence lawyers, the radical French press in Saigon, the League for the Rights of Man and the Citizen in France, and other political leaders stated that the murders had to be blamed on the '"exasperation and despair" caused by the rise in paddy taxes', thus placing the event in a political context where 'to an extent it was colonialism itself which was on trial in the Phnom Penh court' (Tully, 1996, pp. 281–4).

The same year as Bardez's murder, in the province of Kampot, Baudoin presided over the opening of the Bokor luxury resort for which a supplementary tax had been levied. The Bokor scandal again exemplifies the ruthlessness of the colonisers. According to Tully (2002):

Baudoin had a villa built for his own use, replete with a private electrical power plant, out of public funds. In 1925, a new ten-room extension to the hotel was built at a cost of 335,000 piastres, accounting for some 20 per cent of the annual public works budget. In comparison, the total public expenditure on education throughout the kingdom for 1925 amounted to slightly more than 630,000 piastres. (p. 295)

---

[15] The tax money he had managed to collect disappeared, but the roll of banknotes he had on him was not stolen. Clearly, the motives of the murder were not mercenary.

The whole project was said to have cost 900 million francs (Tully, 2002).[16] If the colossal waste of revenues drawn from a mass of impoverished taxpayers made a mockery of the French 'fair administration', the treatment of the convict labourers and the cost of life associated with the construction of the road leading to the resort was criminal and, in kind if not in scope, no different from the horrific conditions of the Khmer Rouge (KR) worksites 50 years later. Between 900 and 2,000 labourers were estimated to have perished, and a journalist from *La Libre Cochinchine* claimed that the road to Bokor was 'reinforced with human bones' (Tully, 2002, p. 296). Marguerite Duras,[17] recalling 'her mother's horrors at the treatment of the convict labourers at Bokor', supported this claim: 'The whole road was like the Way of the Cross... Every kilometre, every two kilometres, you could see holes filled up with people who'd been put there to force them to work, to punish them; they were put in the ground up to their necks, under the sun, as an example' (cited in Tully, 2002, p. 296). According to Tully, many of the labourers were convicts imprisoned for their inability to pay taxes. Tully notes the cruel irony, given that a special Bokor tax was levied at the time, that 'it was possible to end up in a chain gang on the Bokor road for one's inability to meet the taxes levied to build it!' (p. 296).

Why did so much oppression and injustice as revealed in the Bardez affair and Bokor scandal not lead to widespread unrest when all the peasantry in Cambodia was suffering under the burden of heavy taxation? A combination of factors may explain the absence of popular reaction: the economic boom, the growing penetration of the colonial state apparatus in Khmer society, the politics of isolation discussed in the previous chapter (see below also), the subservient collaboration of the Khmer elites with the French administration, and, particularly, the support given to this administration by the king whose prestige was reinforced by it. In any case, ordinary crime and violence continued to decline until the end of the 1920s. But this would change dramatically when the Great Depression hit Cambodia.

The Great Depression and the crime wave: 1929–1935

The impact of the Great Depression on the socioeconomic situation of Cambodia can be judged by the sharp drop in the level of spending during the crisis. The total spending budget of the Protectorate had nearly tripled from 1913 to 1930, but between 1930 and 1935 it was slashed by more than half, falling from 14,000,000 piastres in 1930 down to 6,000,000 in 1935, a level similar to that

---

[16] Applying the 1925 exchange rate, this was the very large expense of 75.3 million piastres.
[17] Writer and film director born in Saigon, she spent part of her childhood in Prey Nop in Kampot province west of Bokor.

of 1920. The economic slump from 1929 to 1935 was dramatic, and Figures 4.1 and 4.2 show that criminal violence in the form of both homicide and banditry soared in inverse proportion. The situation was so bad and the police so overwhelmed that from April 1930 authorities trialled allocating a monetary reward or an honorific distinction to people who actively contributed to fight acts of banditry (Samnang, 1995).

To make matters worse, a second highlanders' rebellion triggered by the progressive encroachment of rubber plantations on their traditional lands started in 1931 (Tully, 2002).[18] In 1935 the rebellion peaked in intensity and bloodiness after around 150 rebels attacked a French military camp. Determined to crash the insurrection, the French were now using the most modern means of warfare at their disposal, and a brutal campaign of repression descended on the highland villages. Planes started bombing villages and machine-gunning their livestock. Villagers sought refuge in the forest, and human casualties were fortunately limited, but all the abandoned villages, including livestock, were destroyed. The worst blow for the insurgents, however, came in May 1935, when Pa Trang Loeung, the great leader of the highlanders' rebellion since 1912, his wife, and his son-in-law were killed. By 1938 the 'pacification' of the highlands had been achieved and had cost the life of about 50 rebels. Thirty years later, different groups of highlanders from Rattanakiri would rebel to protect their land against similar encroachments, and the region under their control would become the first refuge and training ground for future KR leaders such as Pol Pot, Ieng Sary, and Khieu Samphan.

Crime in the 1930s

The Great Depression certainly was a socioeconomic factor that contributed to the resurgence of banditry and homicide, which once again became widespread. The rate of banditry tripled between 1928 and 1931 to peak at 35 events per 100,000 population in 1933 (Figure 4.2). Across the country bands of 20 or 30 individuals rustled livestock, stormed government offices, and ransacked shops. There were many more occasional bandits pushed by utter poverty than professional ones. Tully (2002) relates the story in July 1933 of such a case of strain-induced criminality:

Fifty Cambodians stormed aboard a junk at the Truong Khanh market in Soctrang, just over the border in Cochinchina. Each took a sack of rice in what an inquiry labeled a *jacquerie*,[19] akin to 'requisitions' organised by Communists in northern Annam. The miscreants were arraigned at an extraordinary court session, and sentenced to long jail terms. In their defense, they simply said they were hungry. (p. 268)

---

[18] Most of the information in this section comes from Guérin (2008).
[19] The French word for a peasant revolt or rebellion.

Poverty pushed many women into prostitution. Prostitution increased in Phnom Penh as well as embezzlement of public funds by officials and illegal gambling. Also noted was a worrying trend for the future ethnic conflicts: 'One perennial feature of the city was interracial brawls, in which Khmers and Vietnamese – who dismissed each other, respectively, as *Yuon* or "barbarians from the north" and *Thô*, or "men of the earth" – would bash each other senseless on the river banks and other common territory' (Tully, 2002, p. 265).

The crest of the crime wave was reached in 1933 with 1,035 acts of banditry recorded in the kingdom, followed by a sharp drop until 1940, when the rate of banditry was again at the level of the late 1920s. In 1936, the protectors declared a fiscal amnesty for those 'tax-delinquents' who had fled their villages to escape prosecution and imprisonment. Although a slow recovery had started, the French possibly feared other 'Bardez affairs' in this period of economic crisis, compounded by increasing food shortages in Siem Reap, Kampong Speu, and Kampot from 1934 to 1938 (annual reports from Siem Reap, Kampong Speu, and Kampot *Résidents* [RSC 676]; see also Tully, 2002; Chandler, 2008).

Post-Depression: 1936–1940

During the post-Depression years from 1936 to 1940, our criminal data were richer than in the previous periods. We used the *BPC*; the monthly reports of the provincial governors[20] of Kampot, Siem Reap, Kampong Speu, and Kampong Chhnang; and the annual provincial *Résident* reports for the financial year 1939–40. From the *BPC* 1936–40, we were able to calculate the number of violent criminal events in five categories of crime as well as the number of wanted offenders per event, their sex, and their average age (Table 4.1). The five categories of criminal violence were (based on the most serious offence):

1. *Expressive lethal violence:* homicide, murder, assassination, attempted murder or assassination, infanticide, and manslaughter
2. *Acquisitive lethal violence*: robbery-murder
3. *Expressive nonlethal violence (excluding sexual offences):* assault with injury, violence against parents, kidnapping, resist arrest, and threats of violence
4. *Sexual violence:* rape, incest, and indecent assault
5. *Acquisitive nonlethal violence*: robbery and extortion

During these 5 years, 1,112 individuals were wanted for their alleged participation in 615 violent criminal events, half of which were lethal (50.6 per cent).

---

[20] Provincial governors were Khmer, and the content of their reports may be somewhat more reliable than the French *Résident*'s because they were closer to the people and the *mekhum* reported to them.

Table 4.1 *Criminal violence in Cambodia, 1936–40*

Type of offence	Type of violence	Offenders	Mean N offenders per event	Offenders' age (years)[a]	
				Mean	Median
All violence	N = 615	N = 1,112	1.8	29.1	28
Expressive	82.1%	71.9%	1.6	28.6	27
Acquisitive	17.9%	28.1%	2.8	30.3	30
All lethal violence	N = 311	N = 535	1.7	29.8	30
Expressive	93.2%	85.0%	1.6	29.3	28
Acquisitive	6.8%	15.0%	3.8	32.5	32
All nonlethal violence	N = 304	N = 577	1.9	28.3	28
Expressive nonsexual	38.8%	35.9%	1.8	27.8	27
Acquisitive	29.3%	40.0%	2.6	29.4	29
Sexual	31.9%	24.1%	1.4	26.1	25

Source: *Bulletins de Police Criminelle* (*BPC*), 1936–40 (BNF cote 4-JO-774).
[a] Mean age based on N = 349 offenders with age recorded.

The overwhelming majority of these offenders were male, females representing less than 1 per cent. Most of the violence was expressive rather than acquisitive, but more so for lethal violence: acquisitive violence represented 6.8 per cent of all lethal violence but 29.3 per cent of all nonlethal violence (Table 4.1). The relatively low proportion of acquisitive violence reflected the decline in banditry post-Depression.

Sexual offenders were the youngest (26.1 years) and were most likely to act alone (in 73 per cent of sexual cases only one offender was wanted, and cases involved 1.4 offenders per event on average). Violent acquisitive offenders tended to be older (30.3 years) than expressive offenders (28.6 years).[21] Acquisitive violence was the most collective form of offending: on average 1.6 offenders were involved in expressive events, but 2.8 for acquisitive events and reaching 3.8 for lethal acquisitive events (robbery-murders), reflecting the characteristically collective feature of banditry. These were the bands of 'dangerous *pirates*' often invoked in the administrative reports, but higher levels of co-offending in acquisitive violence was not a specific Cambodian feature. Cooney (2003), for instance, noted that in general 'predatory homicides...tend to be more collective' (p. 1385). However, this level varies across space and time, in great part as a function of the degree of modernisation and state strength. For example, the number of offenders involved on average in each banditry event

---

[21] This specific age pattern reverted during the modern period. See later chapters reporting age and other offender details derived from the 1992–2008 newspaper data.

in Cambodia at the beginning of the century was far greater than indicated by the *BPC* records for the period 1936–40.[22]

Rural and urban crime patterns

The *BPC* 1936–40 permitted us to examine regional patterns and differences between Phnom Penh and rural areas. During this period, Phnom Penh was still a small city with 103,000 to 110, 000 inhabitants and was the most urbanised of any provincial town. If the *BPC* data of wanted offenders were representative of the actual regional patterns of violent crimes in Cambodia during this period, then the rates of violent events per 100,000 population were higher in Phnom Penh than in rural areas; however, they were declining in Phnom Penh, from 19 per 100,000 in 1936 to 8 per 100,000 in 1940, and rising in rural areas, from 3 in 1936 to 6 per 100,000 in 1940. The trend reversal was clearest for acquisitive violence, and in 1940 the rural rate for such crimes became higher than the rate in Phnom Penh. Although here we focus on violent crime, it is worth mentioning that an analysis of all criminal events for which offenders were wanted between 1936 and 1938 indicates that there were almost 10 times more nonviolent acquisitive crime events in Phnom Penh than in rural areas. Another regional difference was the mean age of violent offenders, who were younger in Phnom Penh (27.2 years) than in rural areas (29.3 years).[23]

Overall, the regional crime patterns revealed by the *BPC* data fit with Shelley's (1981) modernisation hypothesis regarding the first stages of urbanisation during which 'cities experienced an increase in commission rates for both violent and property offences while rural areas continued to suffer primarily from the consequences of personal violence' (p. 36). Both violent and particularly property crimes were higher in Phnom Penh than in rural areas. To a certain extent, in rural areas, violent crimes had a more dominant position relative to property crimes, while the reverse was indicated in Phnom Penh. In addition, in rural areas violent crime was rising while it was declining in Phnom Penh. The declining trend in violent crime in Phnom Penh suggests the beginning of the second phase of urbanisation, when, according to Shelley (1981, p. 36), violent crime starts to decline in urban areas as 'the recently arrived urban inhabitants [have] adjusted to city life' and the policing of cities improved. Shelley's thesis did not predict an increase in violent crime in rural areas during either the first or second phase of modernisation, but in Cambodia at the beginning of the 1940s a new conflict was building momentum, namely,

---

[22] The number of offenders per event may be underestimated because the *BPC* listed only those whose identity was known and the data include crimes other than banditry. The analysis of the provincial governors reports, presented in the next section, however, confirms a reduction in the size of the groups engaged in crime.

[23] This age pattern between rural and Phnom Penh offenders has continued during the modern period. See newspaper data 1992–2008 at page 263.

Table 4.2 *Banditry in five provinces: rates of events per 100,000 population, 1936–9*

Province	1936	1937	1938	1939
Battambang[a]	45.1	18.3	12.5	5.1
K. Chhnang[b]	20.3	21.7	11.3	28.7
K. Speu[c]	21.4	21.6	22.4	19.3
Kampot[d]	30.6	53.1	93.1	79.5
Siem Reap	40.4	13.5	24.7	29.6
5 provinces	32.8	26.4	34.2	32.1

[a] Rates for Battambang are from the Battambang *Résident*'s annual report to the *Résident Supérieur* for 1939–40 (ANOM RSC 692).
[b] The *Rapport d'Inspection* (June 1939) reported 33 acts of banditry in 1937 and 14 in 1938 (ANOM RSC 343).
[c] The *Rapport d'Inspection* (March 1940) reported 38 acts of banditry in 1937, 37 in 1938, and 38 in 1939 (ANOM RSC 350).
[d] The annual report of the Kampot *Résident* to the *Résident Supérieur* for 1939–40 (ANOM RSC 692) reported 176 acts of banditry in 1939.

the beginning of the violent proindependence and anticolonial struggle of the postwar period between 1947 and 1954.

Patterns of violent crimes in the provinces

The monthly reports of the provincial governors (PGs) of Kampot, Kampong Chhnang, Kampong Speu, Siem Reap, and Battambang provided detailed information on the patterns and characteristics of banditry and homicides between 1936 and 1939. Except for Battambang, PGs reported the number of acts of banditry but also generally described what happened, how many bandits were involved, whether fatalities or injuries occurred, and what was stolen. Governors also reported non-banditry-related homicides and described the victim(s), perpetrator(s) when known, as well as the circumstances and motivation for the homicide.

Banditry

Overall, 1,258 acts of banditry were recorded in the five provinces. While the rate of banditry across the provinces remained relatively stable between 1936 (32.8 per 100,000) and 1939 (32.1 per 100,000), there were large fluctuations in some provinces (Table 4.2). As in the past, in Battambang and Siem Reap, banditry continued to mainly target livestock, which was often moved and sold in Thailand. However, in both provinces, rates of banditry dropped from 1936 to 1939, particularly in Battambang, where they reduced dramatically (i.e. nine-fold, from 45.1 to 5.1 per 100,000). This sharp decline in banditry was the result of increased control by and cooperation between Cambodian and Siamese police as well as the implementation of measures such as cattle registration and branding (Forest, 1980). For example, in August 1936 the governor of Siem Reap remarked, 'Livestock theft is diminishing since orders have been given to apply fire-heated marks to all cattle, according to the Royal Decree of 30 March 1922' (RSC 409). Given the high value of cattle and cattle's importance to agricultural work and transportation, the net loss to banditry was greater in Siem Reap than in other provinces, and this explains the sustained antibanditry effort in this province.

Across the provinces, the size of bandit groups ranged between 2 and 40 individuals, with an average of 5.8 bandits per event. Bandit groups were the largest (that is, most collective) in Kampong Speu (average of 6.9 bandits per event), but Kampot was characterised by a large number of acts of banditry committed by smaller bands (3.8 bandits per event).[24] From 1936 to 1939, banditry tended to become less collective, with the average number of bandits involved in attacks decreasing from 6.5 in 1936 to 5.2 in 1939. The slow decline from 1936 in the size of the bandit groups corresponded to the start of the economic recovery following the Great Depression.

Bandits were armed with a variety of weapons, including locally made and European guns, swords, machetes, coupe-coupes, cleavers, axes, and knives. According to the PGs, the presence of guns, particularly European ones, suggested a higher level of sophistication, organisation, and criminality. They noted that gangs without guns often became active in periods of famine and acted out of poverty and desperation rather than entrenched criminality. For example, the Kampot governor reported in August 1937 '35 acts of banditry this month. They have been perpetrated by small gangs of between 3 to 5 individuals armed with machetes, cleavers and knives, among which we find destitute people, motivated more by hunger than their criminal instinct' (RSC 266). In Siem Reap, three quarters of all attacks involved guns, and bandits had the largest number of guns (one gun for every 2.2 bandits), reflecting a more professional type of banditry in this province; by contrast, in Kampong Chhnang guns were present in only half the attacks, and bandits shared one gun between four individuals.

---

[24] Kampot was the only province where rates of banditry soared from 30.6 per 100,000 in 1936 to 79.5 in 1939. As we noted in Chapter 2 when reporting on the 1905 court data in Kampot, this province counted many wealthy Chinese merchants. The economic recovery generated opportunities for 'professional robbery' that had reduced during the Depression. The distinction between banditry pushed by strain and the more professional type driven by opportunity should be kept in mind.

Villages and houses were the main targets of banditry. During village raids, large bands were able to rob every house in the village; smaller bands, particularly in Siem Reap, stole the cattle. About one in five events targeted travellers, for example, single villagers coming back from the market after selling their harvest or convoys of carts carrying goods to the market. The number of victims in each event ranged from a single individual to over 30 during village raids. Not all the attacks involved direct physical violence. If villagers were able to run away or handed over their possessions to the bandits, they were generally unharmed. Most victims were injured or killed when they resisted or fought back. Attacks in Kampong Speu were particularly violent, with over half the events resulting in victims seriously injured or killed. While bandits in Siem Reap were the most likely to use guns, only 21 per cent of events in this province resulted in injuries or death, probably because attacks tended to target livestock, kept in paddocks and fields, rather than individuals.[25] Governors often noted in their reports the presence of Chinese victims. The proportion of banditry events targeting Chinese victims was generally between 5 and 7 per cent, but in Kampot over one quarter of events had Chinese victims, who were mostly merchants and shopkeepers. It had been a recurring pattern in Kampot because the province was home to a large Chinese population since at least the early 1900s, and Chinese in general had increasingly been the targets of banditry since the 1920s (Forest, 1980; Sorn, 1995; Tully, 2002).

Banditry was a dangerous occupation and bandits were often killed during the attacks, when villagers fought back or chased bandits, particularly if *mekhums* were armed or police were involved. The number of bandits killed and arrested peaked in 1936 ($N = 65$) but numbered 40 in 1939. The monetary reward awarded to those who fought banditry seemed to have some effect. In January 1936, the Siem Reap PG wrote: 'I have noticed that villagers resist bandits more since the provincial authority has made the beneficial decision to reward those who manage to arrest bandits or take their guns away' (RSC 409). In May 1940, however, the Kampot *Résident* in his summary of the banditry situation in 1939 remarked, 'We often wonder what the best way to curb rural banditry is: is it to encourage with a bounty the resistance by villagers, whose cowardly passivity is notorious?' (RSC 692). Kampot inhabitants' lack of interest in fighting banditry and the governor's scepticism about the effect of the monetary reward may explain the lower rate of arrest in this province compared to the others in 1939.[26] As we will see in the next section,

---

[25] The use of firearms in robbery events is also more likely to deter victims' resistance than the use of sticks or knives, hence reducing the likelihood of homicide, as we found later on in our examination of the 1992–2008 newspaper data in rural areas.

[26] It is also probable, as we saw in Chapter 1, that Khmer peasants looked at the robbery of Chinese merchants and moneylenders with some sympathy for the 'avenging' offenders who may have been considered as social bandits.

Table 4.3 *Homicide victims: rates per 100,000 population by province, 1936–9*

Province	1936	1937	1938	1939	All years
K. Chhnang	4.9	2.4^a	4.8	6.4	4.6
K. Speu	4.1	2.9	1.7^b	3.9	3.2
Kampot^c	2.3	3.2	1.3	1.3	2.0
Siem Reap	19.3	3.7	14.4	8.3	11.4
4 provinces	7.1	3.0	5.2	4.7	5.0

^{a} Only homicides associated with banditry were reported in 1937.
^{b} Only homicides associated with banditry were reported in 1938.
^{c} Rates for Kampot are underestimated because the Provincial Governor did not report expressive homicides.

villagers who denounced bandits to the authorities were also at risk of revenge attacks.

Homicides

This section focuses on the total number of homicide victims, that is, expressive homicides reported by the PGs as well as all banditry-related deaths, that is, of villagers, police, and bandits. Across the four provinces, rates of homicide tended to decrease from 1936 (7.1 per 100,000) to 1939 (4.7 per 100,000) (Table 4.3). Although rates also declined in Siem Reap, they remained consistently higher than in the other provinces, which was due to the high number of expressive homicides since the number of banditry-related deaths was comparable or lower to that of other provinces. The high number of homicides in Siem Reap prompted the Khmer PG to comment in March 1937: 'I have noticed that the inhabitants of this province are incredibly vicious. For the smallest grudge or to avenge the slightest insult, they kill each other without any fear of punishment. This is because they are still too primitive... too savage' (ANOM RSC 409). In a way, the PG's remark illustrates Shelley's theory of modernisation, which suggested that expressive violence in rural areas is usually high, following a premodern pattern, but decreased in urban areas, where it becomes supplanted by acquisitive violence. It is also an illustration of how Elias's civilising process evolved in colonised countries where the local elites were the first to adopt the language and sensibilities of the colonisers, as the Khmer governor of Siem Reap showed by characterising peasants in his province as 'too primitive, too savage'.

Motives for expressive homicides consisted of fights and disputes (40 per cent), revenge killings including sorcery (38 per cent), and family violence, crimes of passion, and madness-related killings (22 per cent). Fights and disputes leading to death sometimes occurred during festivals or celebrations, when people were drinking. For example, in May 1938 in the province of Siem Reap 'a group of friends shared a "cheery" meal; however, after the meal one man, Tit-Prim, followed his friend to the kitchen and killed him. The others gathered immediately and tried to arrest Tit-Prim, but the latter was armed with a long machete and no one dared to approach him. They ended up grabbing wooden sticks and bludgeoned him to death' (RSC 409). Revenge killings, by contrast, were often committed in cold blood. In January 1936, the Siem Reap provincial governor reported the murder of a man believed to be a sorcerer and who had been accused of teaching magic to two others. One of his 'students' had supposedly cast a spell on a child and was wounded, while the 'teacher' was killed (RSC 409).

While the last category of family violence included many crimes of passion motivated by jealousy, they also involved disputes between family members, such as the following case in March 1936, in Kampong Chhnang. In the evening, a discussion over petty matters between two brothers-in-law got increasingly heated, and one man, Kol, hit the other, Ming, with a piece of wood. Ming was seriously injured and died soon after. Kol, realising the gravity of what he had done, fled.

The great majority of expressive homicides (91 per cent) involved a single victim, and most of the victims (88 per cent) were male. In two thirds of cases, victims and offenders knew each other prior to the homicide as friends or acquaintances, 10 per cent were intimate partners or family members, and 23 per cent were strangers. Crimes of passion, domestic homicides, those related to madness, and two thirds of homicides due to fights and disputes/quarrels involved only one offender; however, 64 per cent of revenge killings involved more than one offender.

Offences in court, 1927–1943

It is also worth looking at the court data for violent offences between 1927 and 1943 and the overall movement of cases and patterns of conviction and acquittal. We include in this analysis all categories of violent offences, that is, homicide, assault with injury and violence against parents (combined), robbery, and rape and kidnap (combined).

During this period, violent cases represented, on average, 14 per cent of all cases. Between 1927 and the mid to late 1930s, the volume of cases increased, reflecting both the activity of the police and the significant increase in criminality during the Great Depression (Figure 4.4). The rates of cases heard in court rose more slowly than the rates of crime commission because of the typical lagged effect (between crime commission, arrest, and judgement) that

Figure 4.4 Rates per 100,000 of court cases for violent offences, 1927–43

became even more pronounced as the number of prosecution cases increased. The decline in the volume of violent cases after 1938 was also in great part due to the end of the Depression. However, the steep fall of violent cases between 1939 and 1941 is exaggerated because, in 1940 and 1941, most assaults were not recorded. The increase in violent crime between 1941 and 1943 may have been associated with the beginning of the insurrectional period.

In 1933, in the middle of the Great Depression, correspondence between the RSC and the Ministry of Justice stressed both the rise in violence and the alarming situation created by the crowding of prisons. In 1932 the rate of imprisonment had reached a peak of 172 per 100,000, the highest level between 1929 and 1938 (see penal data below). The RSC requested measures of clemency to reduce the penal population, not only because of the crowding and associated risks of epidemics but also, of course, to reduce financial costs. The RSC requested more lenient sentencing policies for petty offences but far more punitive attitudes in regard to serious violence. Requests by the RSC were in fact orders that could not be challenged, and we will see later in the movement of cases and the penal data that they had been obeyed to the letter. It is therefore quite possible that the decline in 1934 and 1935 in the rates of court cases for violent crimes, shown in Figure 4.3, was also in part the result of the RSC's requests.

The reasons for the second peak in the rates of court cases for violent offending in 1937 are not so clear. Was it a return to the practices that the RSC had criticised in 1933 or an actual increase in crime? The *BPC* rates of violent crime events in rural Cambodia between 1936 and 1940 were increasing. Given that 96.5 per cent of the Cambodian population resided in the provinces during this period, it is likely that the national court data reflected a rural rather than an urban pattern and that the increase in the rates of court cases for violent crimes between 1936 and 1939 and 1942 and 1943 were in part caused by an increase in rural violence. In 1939, *La Presse Indochinoise* noted that banditry was still widespread in Cambodia and 'the product of social conditions in the countryside' (Tully, 2002, p. 163).

In 1932 there were some signs of rationalisation in the court process, reflected in the diminishing number of cases sent for appeal or annulation, as the Ministry of Justice noted: '[there is a] recorded fall in the number of cases sent for appeal and annulation in all judicial matters. A satisfying observation that shows that a real improvement is taking place in the way justice is delivered by First Instance tribunals' [NAC]. From 1936 onward, the justice system was streamlined. Both the number of accused and acquitted persons diminished, but the proportion of convicted persons increased. From 1940 to 1943, a particularly repressive period under the Vichy regime (see next chapter), the number of accused persons significantly increased, but not the number of acquittals.

The general impression conveyed by the court data, independently of the actual volume of crimes and infractions committed in the population, is one of growing state penetration and formal social control where Cambodians were increasingly involved in a modernising justice system. Between 1924 and 1942, the rate of all categories of cases altogether at first instance grew from 288 to 867 per 100,000 and the rate of persons involved in these cases from approximately 464 to 1,023 per 100,000. This growth was concomitant with a decline in criminal violence, except of course during the specific circumstances of the Great Depression. We can also see in this pattern a civilising process, in the sense of the monopolisation of violence by the state, and with it dispute settlement that Durkheim, as well as Elias and more recently Cooney among others, proposed should reduce the need for 'personal justice' and therefore feuding, honour contests, and interpersonal violence.[27] This very notion was evoked by

---

[27] The organising principles of premodern European societies highlighted by Durkheim are in essence no different from the organising principle of nineteenth-century Cambodia, and, if

the *Résident* of Kampong Cham in 1934: 'Thanks to the development of roads and means of communication, people are eager to come from any parts of the province, to present their case to the court, instead of seeking justice themselves' (RSC 242). The volume of civil cases also greatly increased, from an average of 100 per 100,000 between 1924 and 1934, to close to 200 per 100,000 in 1937, and jumping to 400/500 per 100,000 between 1937 and 1944. This is another indication of the growing trust in the state system of conflict resolution during this period.

Sentencing

Sentencing data were available from 1932 to 1947 and provided the number of convicted individuals punished with fines, prison sentences, time-limited hard labour, life hard labour, and the death penalty. Data were not disaggregated by sex, age groups, provinces, or type of offending, but through a comparison of the penal and court data (the latter provided the number of accused individuals convicted of felony and misdemeanour) it was possible to measure the severity of the punishments meted out on individuals sentenced for a felony (Figure 4.5). In 1932, 67 per cent of convicted felons were sentenced to the most severe sentences (hard labour and death), and this percentage increased to over 90 per cent between 1933 and 1935. The declining proportion of felons sentenced to prison followed the RSC's recommendations to address the prison overcrowding crisis by imposing less severe sentences for petty offenders and more severe ones on 'dangerous criminals', including capital punishment. No death sentence was imposed in 1932, but 12 were in 1933, 2 in 1934, and 1 in 1935. Many of those sentenced to hard labour would be sent to the convict colony of Poulo Condor on the coast of South Vietnam, thereby not crowding further the Cambodian prisons.[28] From 1936 to 1938, reflecting both the end of the Depression and the somewhat more humane/benign influence of the

---

somewhat eroding, they were still quite salient during the twentieth century and into this current century. (See, for instance, Hinton [2005] on face, honour, and hierarchy in contemporary Cambodia, and later our newspaper analyses, which show the importance of face and honour in both homicides and suicides in Cambodia.) From 1927 to 1947, cases of defamation in Cambodian tribunals represented on average 5.5 per cent of all misdemeanour cases, and it is possible that their formal adjudication by the institution of justice was a process of modernisation/pacification likely to reduce violence. However, correlations between proportions (out of all court cases) of defamation, homicide, and assault cases between 1927 and 1947 produced inconclusive results. So this finding does not support the hypothesis that the formal adjudication of face and honour conflicts lessened the reliance on violence but rather suggests that when the volume of serious cases increased the courts reduced their prosecution of less serious cases.

[28] It was a brutal policy of incapacitation via executions and exile, which nevertheless must have been effective in eradicating hardened criminals who, thanks to complicity from Cambodian prison personnel, could have otherwise easily escaped and resumed their criminal activities.

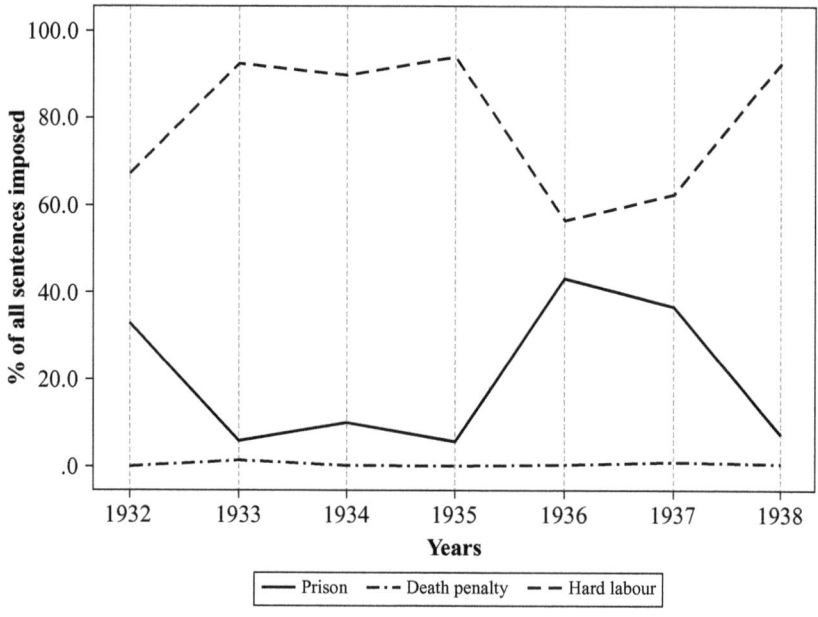

Figure 4.5 Types of sentences imposed on convicted felons, 1932–8

leftist coalition in the French government of the *Front Populaire*, the number of sentenced felons diminished, and a smaller proportion of them were sentenced to the harshest punishments (about 62 per cent hard labour and death penalty, but the number of capital sentences handed down remained low, with 2 in 1936, 3 in 1937, and 1 in 1938). The sentencing patterns of misdemeanours tended to reflect the movement of judicial rationalisation whereby declining numbers of sentenced individuals corresponded to a greater proportion of harsh sentences (in this case, prison rather than fines).

Prison population

The penal data provided a further means of exploring the working of the colonial state between the two world wars. The rise in crime during the Great Depression led to a significant increase in rates of imprisonment, which doubled from 84 per 100,000 in 1929 to a crisis point of 174 per 100,000 in 1932. At that point the RSC decided to address prison overcrowding and the associated risks of epidemics and mounting maintenance costs, and the fall in rates to 116 per 100,000 in 1938 shows that his requests had been obeyed. The policy and pattern of 'decarceration' of petty criminals helped reduce the number of deaths in custody, which were mostly caused by illnesses, from 7 per cent of the prison population in 1932 to 2.5 per cent in 1938.

By the end of the 1920–40 period – the first half regarded by the French and Cambodian elites as a *belle époque*, the golden age of the Protectorate – French rule in Cambodia had only 14 years left. In the next chapter we discuss the patterns of criminality between 1940 and 1954.

5 The anticolonial war: 1940–1955

In 1940, France was defeated by Nazi Germany and signed an armistice that ratified the occupation of France by the victors. The event profoundly shocked King Monivong, who 'must have mused [how] this "tiger with broken teeth" could protect Cambodia' (Tully, 2002, p. 329). But the most distressing blow came 13 months later when the western territories were returned to (now) Thailand on 11 August 1941. If before World War II the French protective mission in Cambodia had retained some credibility, it certainly lost it all during the war. Although France regained some control over Cambodia in 1945, the way was paved for independence, which was finally granted in 1953 to the young King Norodom Sihanouk. The period from 1940 to independence was an anomic period (Durkheim), a period of disintegration (Elias), associated with a discredited French administration. The spike in crime and violence was intrinsically linked with the war and the political struggle for independence. Once again, insurgents and bandits alternately coalesced and confronted each other.

Our primary data for this period consist of a series of *Bulletins de Police Criminelle* (*BPC*) spanning 1948 to 1955, from which we recorded all homicides. We examine these rich data in the second section of the chapter and analyse how patterns of homicide paralleled the independence struggle. In the first section, we draw mainly from secondary sources and highlight the ways in which patterns of criminality and violence, as well as policing, were greatly influenced by the external political events of this period: the Second World War, the French defeat and the fascist Vichy regime, the loss of Battambang and much of Siem Reap to Thailand in 1941 and their return in November 1946, the Japanese de facto occupation of Cambodia and in March 1945 their forceful overthrow of the French administration followed by the declaration of a short-lived Cambodian independence sponsored and protected by the Japanese, the return of the French in October 1945, and finally the 9-year-long war of independence.

Cambodia under the Vichy government

Following the surrender of France to Germany on 22 June 1940, World War I hero Marshal Pétain and other right-wing politicians set up the Vichy regime, a reactionary government, which actively collaborated with Nazi Germany. The newly formed government signed friendship treaties with Japan, which allowed Japanese troops to transit through and station in Cambodia and to use military facilities in Indochina. Soon Japan occupied the key strategic sites in Cambodia but allowed France to remain nominally in charge. King Monivong died in April 1941. His successor, 19-year-old Prince Norodom Sihanouk, was chosen by the French, who expected him to be very compliant.

The Vichy regime was particularly repressive in Cambodia. Tully (2002, p. 365) noted 'the police were omnipresent' and cited Huy Kanthoul, who remarked, 'They poked their noses into everything.' After reaching the lowest point in 1939, the size of the *Garde Indigène* increased steeply between 1939 and 1943, from less than 80 to more than 100 per 100,000 population. Other police forces followed the same pattern, and the police budget, which had dipped during the years of the economic depression, also rose after 1940. Between 1940 and 1942, the gendarmerie reported that they had arrested 4,267 individuals, 'transferred'[1] 13,919, and put 9,508 'at the disposal of the Administrative Authority'. In the same period, the *Sûreté* made 1,550 arrests, and in 1942 alone, the Harbour Police arrested 3,319 people. The specialist *Section de l'Identité Judiciaire*, whose task was to identify perpetrators of crime but also to keep an eye on suspected opponents, made nearly 30,000 photographic plates and established files on 150,327 individuals. Also reflecting the attitudes of the Vichy regime, the number of sentenced felons and the severity of punishment increased greatly. The penal data introduced in the preceding chapter indicate that the proportion of felons sentenced to *life* with hard labour doubled after 1940 and reached 15 per cent in 1944. A new peak in the number of sentenced felons was recorded in 1947, coinciding with the beginning of the armed anticolonial struggle.

Rates of imprisonment increased significantly between 1941 and 1946, with a peak of 263 per 100,000 population in 1946 followed by a substantial fall to 114 per 100,000 in 1947. The new surge in the rates of imprisonment between 1941 and 1946 coincided with the period of the Vichy regime, including its suppression of the growing nationalist movement, as well as the chaotic time between the near-end of World War II and the return of the French after the brief period of independence supported by the Japanese. In the 1930s, in addition to the central prison in Phnom Penh and the provincial prisons, there was only one penitentiary in Cambodia, located in the Haut-Chlong. With a great surge in imprisonment, how was a new prison population crisis apparently avoided? To avoid the risky crowding of existing prisons, internment camps were built. One of these camps was built in 1940 'at Pich Nil on Route Locale 7, in a malarial

---

[1] We did not find any definition of this administrative practice; it may have been a screening process of some sort.

area of Kampong Speu province' to incarcerate any suspected opponents and was described by the 'police boss Truc himself as a concentration camp' (Tully, 2002, p. 365). Not surprisingly, the growing incarceration trend between 1941 and 1946 was matched by a significant increase in the proportion of deaths in custody, reaching a peak of 6.5 per cent of the prison population in 1943. The *Annuaire Statistique de l'Indochine* for 1945 counted nine penitentiaries, but in 1947, there was no mention of penitentiaries in Cambodia, suggesting that these makeshift prison camps had been closed down and their population released. This is consistent with the near halving of the prison population from 1946 to 1947.

The Franco-Thai war

Encouraged by the defeat of France in Europe and the presence of the Japanese in Cambodia, the pro-Japanese government of Thailand revived its claims on Cambodia's western territories lost in 1907. The Franco-Thai war started in September 1940 with small-scale incursions over the border, but by the end of the year the conflict had escalated to open war 'with artillery fire, aviation attacks and infantry raids in both directions across the borders [and] tanks and armoured personnel vehicles... on flatter terrain'. The towns of Stung Treng, Battambang, Siem Reap, Sisophon, Ream, and Mongkolborey were bombed (Tully, 2002, pp. 335–7). Casualties in the land war can be estimated at 1,500 on the Franco-Khmer side and as many if not more on the Thai side:

Over one hundred European casualties were admitted to hospitals in Phnom Penh in both November and December, with the figure rising to almost 350 in January and declining thereafter. The surgical team at Battambang, closer to the fluid front lines, operated on almost 200 casualties. *Time* magazine, however, reported that there were 600 casualties in one battle in January and one French document claimed that around 1000 Thais had been killed and wounded in the Sisophon region, compared with 200 legionnaires. (Tully, 2002, p. 336)

The land war reached a stalemate, but in January 1941 the French defeated the Thais in the naval battle of Koh Chang. According to Tully (2002), 'of the 860 officers and men on the destroyed Thai ships, only 82 survived... in contrast, the French suffered few, if any casualties' (p. 338). The French had won a battle, but not the war, because the decisive power in the region at that time was no longer France but Japan, and Tully (2002) pointed out, 'the French [were] allowed to rule only by Tokyo's grace' (p. 339). Japan mediated a truce at the end of January but ruled that Cambodia had to hand over to Thailand all of the province of Battambang and parts of the provinces of Siem Reap (but not Angkor), Stung Treng, and Pursat. It was a great loss not only for King Monivong, who from January until his death on 23 April 1941 was inconsolable and refused to meet any French officials (Tully, 2002, p. 342), but also economically. The lost territories were inhabited by around half a million people[2] and yielded large quantities of high-quality rice and corn. The Pailin gem mines and part of the Tonle Sap fisheries were also lost (Tully, 2002). The economic restrictions resulting from the loss of the richest Cambodian regions increased drivers of criminality. These were compounded by the anomic conditions associated with the Protectorate's loss of legitimacy at not being able to safeguard its own territory against Germany or ultimately its administration in Cambodia against the Japanese. No doubt many Cambodians shared the king's fear that the Protectorate was impotent to protect their country, but many 'others must have sensed that the road to their own liberation lay in France's powerlessness' (Tully, 2002, p. 329). The *baraing*,[3] after all, were not invincible.

Monks in revolt

Despite their idealisation of Angkorian past and their promotion of *Khmérité* as a national cultural identity, the administration under the Vichy regime attempted to impose the romanisation of Khmer writing and the adoption of the Gregorian calendar in a move towards the modernisation of Khmer education and administration.[4] Although some Cambodians may have supported these reforms on the ground that they could help improve literacy, the entire monkhood and traditional Buddhist educators were incensed by such a move. In Cambodia, monks had a great deal of influence on the population, and the population had many reasons to be unhappy with its situation. The loss of the rich western regions and the restrictions imposed by the war had brought increased austerity as well as heavier taxation (Tully, 2002). It was in this atmosphere that the commonly called 'revolt of the parasols' occurred in July 1942.

It started when Achar Hem Chieu, a monk and teacher of Pali at the Buddhist Institute

called on all the monks to boycott romanization of the Khmer script and the introduction of the Gregorian calendar... condemned the French administration as arbitrary and dictatorial and asked the soldiers if they would serve Cambodia or the foreign masters, and denounced 'the abuse of power by our self-styled French protectors who are themselves today under Japanese domination'. (Tully, 2002, p. 373)

He was swiftly arrested along with his friend Nuon Duong, a graduate of the school. News of their arrest spread rapidly, and the founders of the now clearly anti-French *Nagaravatta* Khmer newspaper, Son Ngoc Tanh and Pach Chhuon,

---

[2] Tully (2002) estimated the loss of population as one million, but we think this was an overestimation. The *Annuaire Statistique de L'Indochine* reported a total population for Cambodia, excluding the western provinces, of 3 million in 1943. Thomas (1978) proposed 3,485,000 in 1940, and on the basis of several estimates we suggest 3,277,000.
[3] Khmer word for French people and by extension all Westerners.
[4] Such a move had already been adopted in Vietnam, where in 1910 the French colonists established the romanised script.

called for a demonstration near the *Résidence Supérieure* to demand the release of the two men. More than a thousand people, half of them monks but also lay nationalists, joined the march. There are different accounts of what triggered the violence, but in a short time the once peaceful demonstration turned into a mêlée where monks fought several hundred baton-wielding police with their traditional sunshades.[5] The Japanese authorities had shown some sympathy for the organisers, but they did not intervene to stop the French repression. Yet, Tully (2002) argued that Son Ngoc Than's contention that the Japanese presence on the scene 'prevented the French police from opening fire on the demonstrators' is credible, and 'given the ruthless intolerance of the French for the slightest criticism of their rule, it is likely that the Japanese presence prevented a bloodbath' (p. 374).

Pach Chhuon and a number of demonstrators were arrested on the spot.[6] Others were arrested later after the police developed the photographs they had taken during the demonstration (Chandler, 1991; Tully, 2002). Hem Chieu, Pach Chhuon, and Nuon Dong were sentenced to death, others to long years of hard labour. Death sentences were commuted to life hard labour at Poulo Condor,[7] possibly to avoid further unrest or because the Japanese had interceded on behalf of the condemned (Tully, 2002). Son Ngoc Than avoided arrest with the help of the Japanese, and from exile in Tokyo he founded the Khmer Nationalist Party for the Independence of Cambodia. Another demonstrator, Achar Mean, took refuge in the countryside and would become in 1951 under the alias Son Ngoc Minh the first president of the Khmer People's Revolutionary Party (KPRP) and predecessor of the Communist Party of Kampuchea. Hem Chieu died at the end of 1943, but Pach Chhuon, Nuon Dong, Bunchan Mul, and many others, politically educated by Viet Minh prisoners during their detention, were freed in 1945 after the Japanese takeover. Although it was a relatively minor event, for many the Revolt of the Parasols was an early manifestation of Khmer nationalism and the first step towards independence.

Cambodian Petainism and Khmer nationalism

The form of nationalism and the type of independence movement that developed in Cambodia in the 1940s were influenced by both global and local factors.

---

[5] Hence the name 'Revolt of the Parasols'.

[6] Estimates of the number of arrests range from 30 to 200 (Tully, 2002).

[7] An unintended consequence for the French was that incarceration in the 'ill-disciplined' Poulo Condor put a dent in their politics of isolation (Zinoman, 2001). As Bunchan Mul, who had been sent to Poulo Condor, later related, Khmer inmates in Poulo Condor were befriended, protected, and trained in revolutionary ideology and discipline by Vietnamese prisoners, who represented the majority of the penal colony. The French could not forecast that when the Japanese disbanded the French administration in Indochina in 1945, they would also free the prisoners from Poulo Condor.

Globally, there was the rise of worldwide anticolonial struggles and the growing influence of communist parties within these struggles. Locally, the arrival of the Japanese – seen by some as invaders and by others as liberators from colonialism – a very young and unpredictable king,[8] and, despite undermined legitimacy, the cultural and ideological influence of the Protectorate also influenced the characteristics of the movement. Transposed to Cambodia, the fascist dictatorship of France, which itself had also become a nation fallen from a glorious past and wrapped in a cult of antiquity, not only brought an increasing level of political repression but also contributed its own concerns with past grandeur and purity into the development of Khmer nationalism. Like most authoritarian states – and this will be repeated with increasing salience during the Sihanouk and Lon Nol regimes, the civil war, and the Khmer Rouge (KR) regime – the regimentation and indoctrination of youth were important features of the Vichy regime both in France and in Indochina. In 1941, mass organisations for Khmer youths were developed. The major one, the Yuvan, was presided by King Sihanouk, who 'asked youth "to help remake the greatness of the homeland..." Sihanouk continued by stressing their responsibility to serve their family, Cambodia, France, and the empire as part of their "duty"' (Raffin, 2005, p. 126). The main ideological diet was a 'cult of antiquity' (Kiernan, 2007) that idealised Angkorian times and Jayavarman VII. Such promotion of *Khmérité* was a somewhat subtle attempt by the Petainists of Phnom Penh to mobilise the youth behind the regime. Paradoxically, while these organisations aimed at indoctrinating rather than liberating young people, they also played an emancipating role that was influential in the development of Khmer nationalism: 'Ironically, these organizations were to provide the Khmers with their first taste of mass politics... The organizers of these movements were able to mobilize tens of thousands of Khmer youths in a variety of activities. The experience of the Yuvan in particular was invaluable for the growing nationalist movement' (Tully, 2002, p. 369). In addition, as Chandler (2008) pointed out, for many young Khmers this was 'their first taste, outside the sangha, of membership in an extrafamilial group' (p. 203).

The Japanese coup and short-lived independence

In 1945 it became clear to the representatives of the Vichy *collaborateurs* in Phnom Penh that the allies had won the war and the Japanese would soon be defeated and expelled from Indochina. The French administrators in Cambodia

---

[8] All the kings of the Protectorate, Norodom, Sisowath, and Monivong, were middle-aged men when they ascended the throne; the French could therefore predict their attitudes easily. They could not with Sihanouk but expected that his young age would make him very malleable to their desires.

would soon 'turn coat', and confirmation of the 'betrayal' of the Japanese came on 7 February 1945 when the US air force bombed Phnom Penh but the French antiaircraft crews did not respond. The bombing may have caused the death of around 100 people,[9] and 250 were wounded in the Khmer districts (Tully, 2002). On 9 March 1945, the Japanese turned against the French Indochina administration in a coup, and in Cambodia five Khmer militiamen lost their lives and all the French soldiers were incarcerated in the very concentration camps the French had opened for the so-called *indésirables*. Two weeks later, all French citizens were arrested and detained:

> Men, women and children were imprisoned in what one French writer later described as 'camps of slow death,' where abused by brutal guards, they suffered from lack of food and water and endured vermin and disease. A number of Frenchmen were murdered after or soon before the Japanese surrender... Afterwards their killers paraded with bloody swords and clothing to advertise the event. (Tully, 2002, p. 389)

Encouraged by the Japanese and the Khmer nationalists, Sihanouk declared the independence of Cambodia as 'the Kingdom of Cambodia no longer feels the need for French protection and hereby declares that the treaty of Protectorate is null and void' (cited in Tully, 2002, p. 387). The new government quickly annulled the romanisation of Cambodian script and the Gregorian calendar, both hated features of the French administration. Explaining this, Sihanouk argued that under the French, Cambodians had remained 'asleep' and the reversion to the traditions of Cambodia was because: 'The French laws would make us devoid of customs, and devoid of history' (Chandler, 1991, p. 82).

Sihanouk was well aware that Japanese protection was illusory and would end very soon with their defeat. The nationalists, heroes of the Revolt of the Parasols, were freed from Poulo Condor by the Japanese and returned to Phnom Penh. Son Ngoc Than also returned from Japan in May 1945 and received a hero's welcome, not from Sihanouk but from his fellow nationalists. Again prompted by the Japanese, Sihanouk appointed him as foreign minister. Following a palace coup by seven young Khmers who stormed the royal palace, Son Ngoc Thanh became prime minister on 10 August. However, he had the plotters arrested 'perhaps... to smooth Sihanouk's ruffled feathers, for he also included a number of old guards royalists in his cabinet alongside more predictable choices from his own political current' (Tully, 2002, p. 395). From that moment, although he had not yet publicly declared himself a republican, Son Ngoc Thanh and Sihanouk hated each other. Thanh's followers started hunting pro-French opponents and used the Pich Nil concentration camp to detain them without trial (Tully, 2002). Some were assassinated; one of the killers was allegedly the future Marshal Lon Nol (Tully, 2002, p. 396). Independence

---

[9] Reddi (1970) estimated the death toll at 600.

lasted barely 6 months. In August, the Japanese surrendered, and in October, the French returned to Cambodia, hoping to resume their colonial administration.

A taste of democracy and a war of independence

On their return, the French arrested Son Ngoc Thanh, following an arrangement – if not with Sihanouk himself – with his defence minister Kim Thit, Prince Monireth, and the Queen Mother (Tully, 2002). The arrest sealed the deep hatred between Sihanouk, his monarchy, and Son Ngoc Thanh, who from then on proclaimed his fierce republicanism. Thanh was deported to France and would return in 1951. The Khmer people had enjoyed the short period of independence, and a *modus vivendi* giving a modicum of autonomy to the Cambodian government was signed between the French and the monarchy. Sihanouk declared: 'The Cambodian people had always loved France and pro-French feelings of his [Sihanouk's] people were evident to all' (Tully, 2002, p. 400).

But the war years, the Japanese occupation, and the chaos of 1945 had seriously damaged the Cambodian economy. The period was anomic and marked by a rise in criminality. Chandler (2008) suggested an increase in banditry in the countryside following the disappearance of French control. Tully (2002) echoed these remarks: 'There are reports of the countryside falling into disorder, with "theft and banditry on a grand scale" and "frequent collusion between the thieves and the police forces" in Kampong Thom province for instance' (p. 401). In addition to the patriotic fervour, anti-Vietnamese sentiments resurfaced: 'Another strand of post-war nationalism consisted of officially sponsored antipathy to the Vietnamese, and clashes apparently took place in this stirring disorderly summer between Khmer and Vietnamese inhabitants of southern Vietnam' (Chandler, 2008, p. 209).

Political awakening and experiment with democracy

The period was also a time of political awakening. The French were hoping that if they could grant a modicum of autonomy to the kingdom and some kind of democratic system to the competing Khmer elites, and regain the provinces lost to Thailand, perhaps they could also regain control of Cambodia. To achieve the first aim, they decided to hold popular elections to elect a Consultative Assembly, which would advise the king on drafting a constitution. Elections were set for September 1946 with 'universal' male-only suffrage, and for the first time, Cambodians were allowed to join political parties. It was the beginning of an experiment in democratic governance that would eventually utterly fail.

Many parties were formed before the Consultative Assembly elections, but only two of them stood out: the Liberal Party and the Democratic Party. Tully (2002) described the Liberals as 'a conservative, royalist, pro-French grouping based on elite layers of functionaries, landed proprietors, Sino-Cambodian merchants and some religious milieux' (p. 415). It was, of course, favoured by the French and for the time being by Sihanouk. The Democrats, on the other hand, 'were a more radical grouping under the leadership of Prince Yuthevong, a genuine intellectual who had recently arrived back from studying at Montpellier, Vichy and Paris, where he studied mathematics and astronomy, and married a Frenchwoman' (p. 415). Yuthevong was anticolonialist but aimed at achieving independence incrementally and peacefully. For the French and Sihanouk, the Democrats were enemies to defeat, but the party had the sympathy of most nationalists.

More than 60 per cent of the electorate went to the polls and the Democrats won an incontestable victory with 50 of the 67 seats. The new constitution, which was adopted in 1947, was very similar to the constitution of the recent French Fourth Republic, except it did not create a republic but a constitutional monarchy, which reduced the power of the king and was sure to attract Sihanouk's wrath. Soon after, Yuthevong died from tuberculosis. The party had lost its best leader, and Cambodia the first and perhaps only true democrat leader so far in its history.

Despite opposition from the French, the Democrats again won a majority of seats during the National Assembly elections of December 1947, but the party became caught up by factionalism. In early 1949, an influential member of the Democrats, Yem Sambaur, and 12 of his colleagues created a dissident faction that went into coalition with the Liberals. The move effectively robbed the Democrats of their majority and resulted in a new government led by Sambaur. In 1950, Ieu Koeus, the leader of the Democrats, was assassinated in a grenade attack. An illiterate peasant was charged with the murder, but the real culprit – or culprits – was never uncovered. Later that year, two other Democrats were targeted for assassination; Khuon Nay escaped death, but Nget Hiem did not (Reddi, 1970; Tully, 2002).

Yet, the 1951 National Assembly elections again delivered a majority of seats (54 out of 78) to the Democrats. In October, Son Ngoc Thanh was welcomed in Phnom Penh by a crowd of 100,000 people. He had promised Sihanouk and the French to abstain from anti-French politics and had been allowed to return. However, he did not keep his promise, and in March 1952, he and his deputy joined the Issaraks of the northwest. 'Thereafter', wrote Tully (2002), 'paranoia sprouted on all sides and the provinces were swept away by a wave of lawlessness' (p. 447). In June 1952 and with the tacit support of the French, Sihanouk sacked the democratically elected government of the Democrats and assumed the position of Prime Minister.[10] He banned all demonstrations and

---

[10] He took as pretext the arrest a few weeks earlier of Dap Chhuon, Yem Sambaur, and Lon Nol, who had openly called for a coup against the government and were suspected, particularly Sambaur, of having been implicated in the murder of Ieu Koeus in 1950.

political meetings. In Paris, Khmer students who had received scholarships to study in France from the Democrat government published an antimonarchist manifesto signed by, among others, Saloth Sar, better known later as Pol Pot. The experiment with parliamentary democracy had ended.

The struggle for independence

The second aim of the returning French was achieved in November 1946 when, backed by the British and the Americans since Thailand had been Japan's ally during the war, the western provinces were finally returned to Cambodia. This was not an easy matter for the French because Battambang had always been a hotbed of bandits and anti-French rebels (see Chapters 1 and 2), and between 1941 and 1946, the Thai had, of course, intensified their anti-French propaganda in the region. In fact, the war of independence had already started. As early as 1941, in Thailand-occupied Battambang, exiled Cambodians had set up a Khmer Issarak (Free Khmer) committee 'dedicated to driving the French from their home land' (Tully, 2002, p 378). Even before the retrocession of the western regions to Cambodia, Issaraks were mounting guerrilla attacks against the French and their Khmer supporters. For example, on 7 August 1946, a group of 300 to 500 of them raided and occupied Siem Reap for 6 days. Seven French officers were killed, but the Issaraks lost 30 men in the fighting and there were dozens of casualties on both sides (Jennar, 1995; Reddi, 1970; Tully, 2002). The French estimated the western Issarak forces at 3,500, but Tully (2002) reports that they were about 5,000 in late 1946. In October, more than 100 French and Cambodian Christians were massacred in Battambang, and in December, two French officers were killed (Reddi, 1970; Tully, 2002). The anticolonial struggle had also started in the east, where Issarak groups claimed to have 5,600 under arms. Between late 1946 and early 1947, 3,000 guerrillas were 'marauding through the [eastern] countryside before their defeat by superior French firepower' (Tully, 2002, p. 463).

The Issaraks did not form a unified movement, and very early on two major groupings could be distinguished: the relatively united groups in the east that started to make common cause with the Viet Minh, hence often referred to as 'Viet Minh Issaraks', and those initially more numerous in the west that we refer to as 'traditional Issaraks'. The latter were without a single centralised command, often Vietnamophobic, and included large numbers of former and active social and predatory bandits. At least in the beginning, both traditional and Viet Minh groups were fighting a common enemy, the French and the Royal Khmer Army, and both were accused by the French and the Khmer administration of acting like bandits, which many of the traditional Issaraks certainly did. Hobsbawm (1969) remarked that bandits were more likely to play a part in national liberation movements than other types of revolutions:

It does not take much sophistication to recognize the conflict between 'our people' and 'foreigners', between the colonized and the colonizers... National liberation bandits are therefore common enough, though commoner in situations where the national liberation movement can be derived from traditional social organization or resistance to foreigners... It is harder for bandits to be integrated into the modern movements of social and political revolution, which are not primarily against foreigners. (pp. 103–4)

From 1947 until independence in 1954, Cambodia fell into social and economic decay (a decivilising period) caused by post–World War II conditions, the Franco-Vietnamese war, the Issarak insurrection, corruption,[11] and the absence of tax collection, or more exactly, the redirection of tax money to the insurgents rather than to the Franco-Khmer administration. It seems that the country was on the verge of famine, and crime was on the rise (Reddi, 1970; Tully, 2002). The level of violent criminality can be gauged by the rate of court cases for robbery reaching 11.1 per 100,000 in 1947, the highest rate since 1927, even exceeding the peak of 1933 at 9.6 per 100,000. There were also reports that in retaliation for supporting the French against the Viet Minh in 1945, the latter, in February 1947, massacred several hundreds of Khmer Krom in Cochinchina.

According to Chandler (2008), the traditional Issaraks' armed struggle against the French was at its most intense in 1946 and 1947, thereafter declining, when the Viet Minh Issarak groups began to emerge in the field. In May 1947 alone, the French reported 500 Issaraks were killed in the west (Kiernan, 2004). In February 1948, a force of 800 men led by Dap Chhuon in Battambang created the Khmer People Liberation Committee (KPLC) and formed an alliance with the Viet Minh (Jennar, 1995). In 1949, the French were counting 10,600 'Khmer rebels' throughout Cambodia. However, intra-Issaraks conflicts were increasing, particularly after the arrival of the new Sambaur government, which imprisoned many extraparliamentary opponents but also offered an amnesty to potential Issarak defectors and a new treaty between Sihanouk and the French extending Cambodia's autonomy. These two events led to the defection to the government of 'several thousand Issarak, particularly those opposed to the Viet Minh' (Chandler, 2008, p. 215). From then on, the Viet Minh Issaraks became the growing wing of the movement, aided also by geopolitical events such as the communist victory in China, which provided the Viet Minh with an 'arsenal, an ally, and a sanctuary' (Chandler, 2008, p. 217). On the other hand, the French were receiving increasing military aid from the USA on

---

[11] Widespread corruption had resurfaced in 1948 'when a number of deputies, including Sam Nhean, the vice-president of the National Assembly, were implicated in the illegal sale of rationed cotton thread'. In 1946, reports of illegal gambling operations 'run by members of the elite, including the politician Sim Var [Democrats] and members of the royal family... enjoyed the protection and active participation of Lon Nol, the chief of the Cambodian police' (Tully, 2002, pp. 438–9).

the pretext that they were no longer fighting Indochinese nationalists but Communists. To fight them, the military budget grew from 75 million piastres in 1950 to 200 million in 1951. The police budget also soared, reaching 40 million piastres in 1951 (from about 6.5 million in 1948). The 'hot Indochinese manifestation' of the Cold War had started.

By 1950, Issaraks controlled one third of the country (Tully, 2002, p. 458). In September 1951, the former monk Achar Mean, better known as Son Ngoc Minh, helped establish the first Cambodian communist party called the Khmer People's Revolutionary Party. In the countryside, insurrectional and counterinsurgency operations multiplied. Showing the growing ascendancy of the Viet Minh, important strikes occurred against the Chhup rubber plantations (Kampong Cham), a bastion of the Indochinese Communist Party (ICP). In 1951, Khmer Viet Minh (as Viet Minh Issaraks became increasingly called) accentuated their operations. However, traditional Issarak groups – half-rebel, half-bandits – had not all disappeared, and in April 1951, a group of 600 to 1,000 men massacred an entire village south of Phnom Penh (Tully, 2002). By 1952, French intelligence estimated that 'almost two-thirds of the kingdom was no longer under the day to day control of the Phnom Penh government' (Chandler, 2008, p. 242). In 1951, Khmer Viet Minh were thought to control more than 15 per cent of Cambodian territory and up to half in 1954 (Chandler, 2008). More and more men joined in the fighting, and the Australian Department of External Affairs considered that 3,000 Issaraks and 9,000 Viet Minh[12] were fighting in Cambodia in late 1952, and a British diplomat suggested Issaraks numbered 4,000 in 1953 (Tully, 2002). The French authorities also believed that 'taxes and contributions levied by the revolutionaries among the population amounted to the equivalent of half the national budget' (Chandler, 2008, p. 239). However, in September 1952, Sihanouk proclaimed another amnesty, and small groups of traditional Issaraks, generally anti-Vietnamese and anticommunist, defected to the government.[13] Early in the next year, as the Assembly refused to approve his budget, Sihanouk gave the *coup de grace* to parliamentary democracy by dissolving the Assembly and declaring martial law, 'declaring the nation to be in danger' (Chandler, 2008, p. 242).

The conflict was a brutal affair and atrocities, such as the massacre of entire villages, were committed by both sides. Even Sihanouk 'lamented that French soldiers were not always able to distinguish between peaceful peasants and

---

[12] Kiernan (2004) has argued that by this stage many of them were not Vietnamese but Khmer Viet Minh. French intelligence estimated the number of Khmer Viet Minh at 5,000, but Chandler argues that this was an underestimate.

[13] We will see later on that a similar scenario reoccurred in the mid 1990s when the bicephalous Ranariddh-Hun Sen government wooed/paid remnants of the KR movement to rally to their cause and granted amnesty to top leaders responsible for the hecatomb of Democratic Kampuchea (DK).

insurgents' (Tully, 2002, p. 459). Some Issaraks, including future KR such as Nuon Chea and Ta Mok, were brutal. One of them had 'his prisoners chained up beneath the house without food and water and then executed on his own firing range a few hundred yards beyond the back yard'. Another used the '*srangae pen*, literally "a field crab crawling round in circles"', which involved the close encirclement of the victim by the soldiers and the victim's beheading (Tully, 2002, p. 460). In May 1953 a bomb exploded at the *lycée* Sisowath, and Puth Chhay, the warlord who had led the massacre of an entire village south of Phnom Penh in April 1951, rallied the government and was assigned the defence of Phnom Penh, where his band resorted to terrorist methods to control the population (Steinberg, 1959; Tully, 2002). Puth Chay's men were probably responsible for the 'bomb attack in the capital in August 1953, which killed one European and seriously injured several others' as well as the brawls and murders between ex-Issaraks and French troops (Tully, 2002, pp. 450–1).

The royal crusade for independence

Seizing the opportunity provided by the mayhem, and warning the French of the risk of a communist takeover[14] if independence was not granted very soon, Sihanouk launched his famous 'royal crusade for independence'. He journeyed to Paris in March 1953, but the French still refused to respond to his claim for independence. He then embarked on a political tour in Europe, Japan, and America, and his anticommunist warnings 'scored [him] a propaganda triumph' (Tully, 2002, p. 477). He returned to Phnom Penh in May and in June called for a general mobilisation for independence. This call won him immense popularity, and 200,000 people responded to it, leading to widespread desertions in the army and the police (Jennar, 1995). In October the French yielded to his demands, and virtual independence was granted, with all police, judicial, military, and foreign affairs functions handed over to the Cambodian government.

Most of the remaining traditional Issarak fighters decided to lay down arms (except Son Ngoc Thanh), but not the Khmer Viet Minh, who were fighting not just for independence but also for a communist revolution. Late in December 1953, a military operation supported by the French air force was deployed against the Khmer Viet Minh in Battambang. But in April 1954 the Khmer Viet Minh mounted attacks on Stung Treng and then on the railway between Phnom Penh and Battambang, causing a few hundred deaths and followed by other attacks in Kampot, Takeo, Svay Rieng, and Prey Veng (Reddi, 1970). According to Jennar (1995), in early May, the communist Issarak United Front (IUF)

---

[14] It may well have happened, and Sihanouk of course was also worried about the survival of his monarchy and personal power.

had about 3,500 fighters and still controlled one third of the country, possibly half, according to Chandler (2008).

In May 1954, the French were defeated decisively at Dien Bien Phu in Vietnam, and Cambodia participated in the Geneva Conference 3 weeks later as a fully independent nation. French rule in Indochina had finally ended. The Cambodian delegation opposed the participation of any Khmer Viet Minh at the conference. First concerned by their own national and revolutionary interests, the Vietnamese did not insist on the inclusion of their Khmer comrades.[15] Thereafter, and until the elections of September 1955, the Cambodian Left became the victim of a brutal Sihanoukist repression (Jennar, 1995). Over a thousand Khmer Viet Minh went to exile in Hanoi, 'not to return to Cambodia until the early 1970s, when most of them were killed by US bombing, Lon Nol's army, and particularly by internal Communists purges at the instigation of Pol Pot, who by then was the leader of the Cambodian Communist Party' (Chandler, 2008, p. 228).

Homicides during the anticolonial war

The number of homicides committed during the anticolonial struggle, from 1946 to 1955, including those not regarded as criminal but as casualties of the anticolonial war, has never been measured. Our series of *BPC* published between 1948 and 1955 provides a measure of criminalised homicides for which alleged offenders were wanted by the police, their characteristics, as well as an estimation of the total number of such homicides in the population.

BPC *data 1947–1955*

With limited time and resources, we analysed only homicide and attempted homicide events for this period.[16] Because of the lag in the publication of the warrants[17] and missing issues of the *BPC* from October to December 1955, data for 1947 and 1955 were incomplete. Offences associated with the homicides allowed us to code the cases into two main categories: acquisitive and expressive (nonacquisitive) homicides/attempted homicides. Acquisitive homicides

---

[15] This was seen by Khmer communists, particularly the Pol Pot faction, as the first betrayal by the Vietnamese communist party, the second one occurring, according to them, in 1973 when the Vietnamese signed the 'Paris agreement' with the USA. For discussions of the geopolitical interests, factors, and negotiations that determined the outcomes of the conference, see Chandler (2008), Heder (1980), and Kiernan (2008).

[16] For example, in 1948, the *BPC* recorded 5,856 cases of wanted persons for any crime; 8 per cent ($N = 480$) were homicide cases.

[17] For example, out of the 5,856 cases published in the *BPC* for 1948, 39 per cent referred to warrants issued in 1948, 57.2 per cent in 1947, 3.4 per cent in 1946, and 0.4 per cent in 1945.

Table 5.1 BPC *1947–55 homicides*

Type of homicide	Type of homicide (%)	Offenders male (%)	Offenders female (%)	Mean N offender by event	Mean age (years)
Acquisitive homicides	12.4	16.5	7.0	2.9	29.6**
Ordinary homicides	60.8	49.7	65.1	1.8	31.0
Planned homicides	19.9	20.7	20.9	2.3	31.1
Political homicides	6.9	13.1	7.0	4.2	30.5
All expressive homicides[a]	87.6	83.5	93.0	2.1	31.0
All homicides	100	99	1	2.4	30.8
Total N	1,929	4,211	43	–	–

[a] Expressive homicides combine ordinary, planned, and political homicides.
** $p < 0.01$.

were associated with offences such as robbery and theft. Among the expressive homicides, *assassinats* (homicides with premeditation) were coded as *planned* homicides, while homicides associated with political actions or people were coded as *political* homicides. Others were coded as *ordinary* (i.e. intimate and other interpersonal disputes) homicides.

Demographic patterns

From 1947 to 1955 the *BPC* recorded 4,254 offenders wanted for their involvement in 1929 homicidal events (Table 5.1). There were only 43 females (1 per cent), and two thirds of them were wanted for ordinary homicide. On average, offenders were 31 years old, but acquisitive offenders were significantly younger (29.6 years).[18] Of all homicidal events, ordinary homicides were the most frequent (60.8 per cent) and political homicides, the least frequent (6.9 per cent). It is likely that a proportion of ordinary homicides were, in fact, directly associated with the insurrection and that the proportion of political homicides is underestimated. On the other hand, the anomic situation created by the insurrection also provided opportunities for an increase in ordinary homicides.

As would be expected, given the disruptions of an anticolonial insurrection, political homicides were the most collective (4.2 offenders per event), followed by acquisitive and planned homicides and finally ordinary homicides, which still involved almost two offenders per event. Nearly 10 per cent of homicides were accompanied by kidnap, 7.4 per cent by grievous bodily harm of other

[18] While the gender pattern was the same, there was an opposite age pattern compared to the period 1936–40 but similar to the pattern observed in the modern period 1992–2008 in our analysis of the newspaper data.

victims, and around 4 per cent by arson and escape, which was in keeping with the typical activities of armed gangs during such contested situations.

There are a number of differences in the pattern of homicide events between this period, 1947–55, and the earlier period, 1936–40. First, the number of acquisitive homicides as a proportion of all homicide events nearly doubled, from 6.8 per cent in the period 1936–40 to 12.4 per cent for the period 1947–55. Second, in both periods acquisitive homicides involved more offenders than expressive homicides did. However, the size of groups involved (average number of wanted offenders per event) had increased from 1.6 in the earlier period to 2.1 in the later period for expressive homicides but decreased for acquisitive homicides, from 3.8 in the period 1936–40 to 2.9 in the later period.

One factor contributing to the increase in the size of the groups (average number of offenders) involved in expressive homicide events is the greater proportion of planned homicides between 1947 and 1955 (22.7 per cent of all expressive homicide events compared to 18.9 per cent between 1936 and 1940). The mean number of offenders involved in planned homicides increased from 1.8 in 1936–40 to 2.3 in 1947–55. The greater proportion of planned homicides, their more collective character, and the emergence of politically motivated homicides reflect the insurrectional/incipient civil war and the broader impact of the anticolonial First Indochina War (i.e. both a disintegrating and decivilising moment). It is likely that the decrease in the number of offenders in acquisitive homicides is spurious and caused by the averaging of more years during the later than during the earlier period and by large yearly fluctuations.

Rates of homicide, 1947–1955

While rates of homicide soared during the insurrectional years, there were also variations in the types of homicides. Figure 5.1 shows the total rate per 100,000 of homicide events for which offenders were wanted and the rates per type of homicide for the years 1948 to 1954. The two years 1947 and 1955 are omitted because of missing data. These incomplete data, however, suggest that the rates in 1947 were probably similar if not higher than in 1948 and that rates in 1955 had probably fallen below the 1954 rates. For example, drawing from a memo by the security services of the French High Commissioner for Indochina, Chandler (1991) suggested that although by October 1945 the French had reestablished their authority in Cambodia, 'in 1946–47, an increase in rural banditry and violence, a lapse in police protection, and the revolution in neighbouring Vietnam encouraged Cambodian peasant resistance to the French and exposed many Cambodians to revolutionary ideas' (p. 5).

Figure 5.1 shows a progressive decline in the rates of acquisitive homicide events (i.e. banditry), between 1948 and 1954, and a rise in the rates of expressive homicides, with two marked peaks in 1950 and 1952. Striking features are the decline in ordinary homicide events between 1950 and 1953 and the rise in

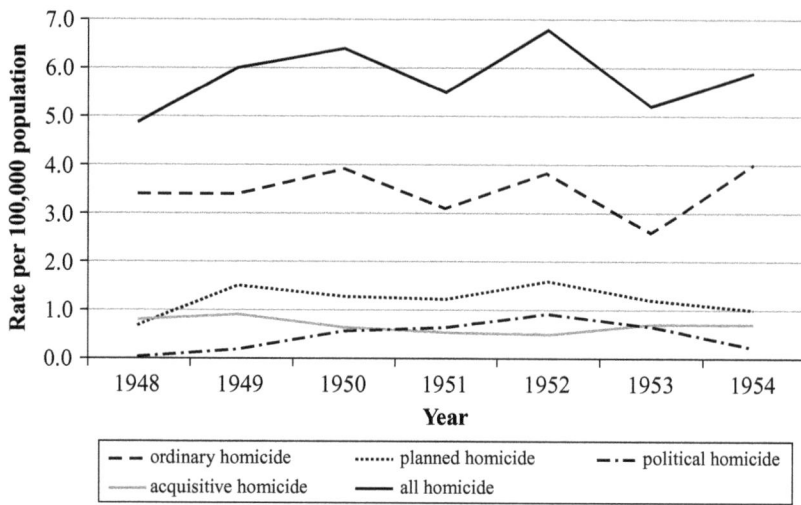

Figure 5.1 Rates per 100,000 population of homicide events for which offenders were wanted by the police, 1948–54

political homicide events between 1948 and 1953. Thereafter, rates of ordinary homicides picked up and rates of political homicides declined. The rates of planned homicides events also declined after 1949, but there was peak in 1952. The period from 1947 to 1955 was a complex anomic and insurrectional period during which banditry and insurrection overlapped. As some bandits joined and lent their skills to the insurrection, some insurgents used banditry as a means to provide resources to the anticolonial war, and others simply took advantage of the prevalent disorder and anomie.

Regional patterns

We suggest that the variations between the four types of homicide rates reflect the dynamics of the insurrection at regional and national levels, particularly in terms of the ascendency or decline of the two types of insurgents, the traditional and the Viet Minh Issaraks. For this demonstration, we analysed and coded Kiernan's (2004) detailed narratives of the Issarak anticolonial struggle, in terms of regional control and inter-Issarak conflicts. The 15 provinces were therefore coded each year from 1947 to 1954 (8 years) in terms of five alternative territorial control conditions: (1) by the government, (2) by the traditional Issaraks, (3) by the Viet Minh Issaraks, (4) by both the traditional and Viet Minh Issaraks in coalition, and (5) by conflicts between the two Issarak groups. Here, the concept of 'regional control' is only a shorthand to specify in which provinces the insurgents were active and to which Issarak group they predominantly belonged. Of course, both groups, separately, in a coalition or in a situation where they were fighting each other, were also fighting the Franco-Khmer governmental forces, and although the latter were in total control of some provinces, for instance, Phnom Penh, 'control of other provinces' by Issarak groups did not mean that Franco-Khmer governmental forces had no control over these areas. In some of these provinces they had much and in others little control.

The rates of (1) ordinary, (2) planned, (3) acquisitive, and (4) political homicides from the *BPC* were calculated for every province each year from 1947 to 1954. The result was therefore a mapping of both the type of regional control and the corresponding rates of the four types of homicide between 1947 and 1954. Our analysis shows that rates of homicide events were significantly higher outside Phnom Penh, a reverse of the pattern of the 1936–40 period.[19] Violence arising from the anticolonial 'troubles' occurred in rural areas, and homicide rates were consequently concentrated in rural areas. As Kiernan (2004) remarks, 'Even by 1954 the Khmer communist movement was so negligible in the capital that it was open to a relatively easy takeover by a small outside group [Pol Pot's Khmer Rouges] more at home there' (p. 118). In 1954, there seemed to have been a reverting pattern in the urban and rural homicide rates, the former increasing, and the latter declining. The end of the militant independence movement indicated by the fall in political homicides (see Figure 5.1) led to a return to the urban/rural patterns of the 1936–40 period, that is, eventually, to the higher urban crime rates associated with the early phase of urbanisation. In fact, if we look only at ordinary and acquisitive homicides, by 1954 the declining trend in the provinces and the rising one in Phnom Penh were the most pronounced.

Insurrection, crime, and social control

The political and crime mapping of regional developments during the insurrectional years starting in 1945 shows that the anomic and criminogenic characteristics were associated not only with this insurrection and the frequent challenges to the Franco-Khmer state's authority but also with the divisions and the fratricide violence within the Issarak movement. Although the *BPC* data included homicides that were clearly associated with the insurrection, these data were not exclusively 'insurrectional'; they also included not only individuals wanted for ordinary homicides but also many individuals wanted for

---

[19] Details of these patterns are on file with the authors.

nonlethal offences.[20] Yet, the trends in the national rates of homicide from the *BPC* between 1948 and 1954 matched the developmental stages of the insurrection based on Kiernan's data for the same period. The increase and decline in these homicide rates paralleled the increase and decline in the strength of the anticolonial insurrection. In these trends, we therefore see both the direct homicidal effects of the insurrection and the indirect lethal effects resulting from the anomic situation of the period. At the regional level, these rates were associated with insurrectional developments in corresponding provinces. Provinces with high homicide rates, such as Battambang, were generally also 'hot insurrectional spots'. It is equally important to distinguish between the various Issarak factions and fluctuations in their relative strength in particular provinces between 1948 and 1954, because this factor appears to be associated with varying homicide rates, including varying rates of acquisitive homicides. Vickery (in Kiernan & Boua, 1982, p. 103) wrote:

Throughout the nineteenth century Cambodia had been plagued by warfare, and the colonial period had seen whole regions ridden by endemic large-scale banditry, that is, outlaw bands who would raid, rob and burn entire villages with impunity. In the years following the Second World War, these bands turned themselves into 'Issaraks' and fought for independence against the French.

Not all Issaraks, however, used banditry and pillage as a means to a revolutionary end or just as an end in itself. There was a clear difference in this regard, illustrated by Kiernan's data, between the communist and noncommunist factions. The communist/Viet Minh–trained Issaraks generally opposed and repressed banditry and exactions against peasant populations. They were far better organised and disciplined than traditional Issarak factions. In their areas of influence, they exerted a relatively benign type of social control that worked against anomie, and this is reflected in lower rates of homicides, including lower rates of acquisitive (banditry-related) homicides in the provinces they controlled, such as Kampong Cham. On the other hand, the data suggest that in the provinces where inter-Issarak conflicts (between communist and noncommunist factions, and within noncommunist factions) were important and/or on going, such as Battambang, Kampong Speu, and Kandal, homicide rates, including planned and acquisitive homicide rates, were comparatively higher. In Kampong Cham, where unchallenged communist control appears to have been achieved very early and maintained throughout the period,[21] the rates of

---

[20] Recall that our analysis of the *BPC* 1948 suggested that crimes other than homicide represented 92 per cent of the cases. Recall also that, as data of wanted offenders, the *BPC* do not include *flagrant delicto* cases that we estimated to represent between 40 per cent and 50 per cent of all homicides. *Flagrant delicto* homicides were far more likely to be ordinary rather than political, planned, and acquisitive homicides.

[21] Kiernan (2004), for instance, noted: 'In 1952 intelligence sources even reported evidence of "several autarchic agricultural enterprises, like kolkhozes" in Kampong Cham' (pp. 92–3).

homicides significantly declined after 1949, including the rates of acquisitive homicides, which then were among the lowest compared to other provinces. In Prey Veng, where complete communist control was only achieved later (many factions were still present in 1949), the rates of acquisitive homicides were generally higher than in Kampong Cham but lower than in Battambang, where such hegemonic control was never achieved. Yet, traditionally, both Battambang and Prey Veng were hot spots of banditry. It is also interesting to see that in 1953, when only the communist Issaraks continued to struggle and maintain their territorial control, and the traditional factions had abandoned the struggle, the rates of all the types of homicide dropped, except for the political type, which increased. However, in 1954 when the struggle ended and communist control therefore lapsed the rates of ordinary and acquisitive homicides increased.

The colonial legacy

By 1955, Cambodia was an independent nation, but what was the legacy of 90 years of French rule? If their colonial mission was only to protect Cambodia against annexation by its neighbours, then the French had fulfilled their part of the contract. In 1954, Cambodia was returned to Cambodians with more territories (i.e. the northern and northwestern provinces) than it controlled in 1863, and most historians (see, for instance, Chandler, Forest, Osborne, and Tully) agree that had France not established its Protectorate, Cambodia might well have disappeared as a nation. The French not only provided peace and stability but also restored and protected Angkor and preserved and promoted Khmer arts and crafts. They 'built'[22] the major towns, including Phnom Penh, and a modern and substantial road system.

However, if the colonial mission was also supposed to be *civilisatrice*, in the sense of bringing economic and social development and democratisation, then it failed utterly. The politics of a colony of exploitation had hindered genuine economic development such as industrialisation and in social terms the development of a sizeable proletariat and middle class. Mass education had been profoundly neglected and modern education reserved to a very small urban elite. The politics of isolation from education, political awareness, a modern civil society, and governance and the politics of division between the 'natives' and their 'hereditary enemy' were infantilising and they retarded and stunted social emancipation. To this was added the maintenance, protection, and even sublimation of archaic systems, including the monarchy, as well as a cult of antiquity that strongly informed the reactive form of Cambodian ethnonationalism. The modernisation of the state apparatus did not challenge 'the traditions

---

[22] That is, they had these things built by Cambodians and often by *corvée* and convict labour.

of absolutist rules' (Tully, 1996, p. 309); on the contrary, it supported these traditions thanks to the modernisation of the bureaucracy and its associated police state. As Tully (1996) wrote:

Cambodia was left with a seemingly bottomless reservoir of ignorance, credulity, and superstition, which, along with acceptance of absolutism, made the Cambodian people prey for a variety of political quacks, charlatans and demagogues. Lon Nol the leader of the ill-fated Khmer Republic of 1970–75, consulted sorcerers, and in Pol Pot we can see the direct descendent of the *illuminés* who terrorised the countryside. (p. 310)

Referring to Marx's concept of the double edge of colonialism, Tully (1996) concluded: 'Despite some considerable successes, France did not leave post-independence Cambodia with the kind of infrastructure Marx predicted colonialism would bring to Asia' but 'an economically backward state' a precapitalist peasant society with no proletariat and 'a tiny indigenous middle class' (p. 311). Both nationalism and Marxism-Lenino-Stalinism were products of modernity that colonisation willingly for the first and unwittingly for the second introduced to Cambodia's tiny indigenous middle class. But even these potentially dangerous ideologies were developed very late in Cambodia, limiting the capacity for these ideas to evolve into more mature philosophies.

Easterly, Gatti, and Kurlat (2006) examined an international data set spanning from 1820 to 1998 for any relationship 'between the occurrence and cruelty of episodes of mass killing and the levels of development and democracy across countries and over time' (p. 129). Countries with both low levels of development and democracy were more likely to experience particularly cruel occurrences of mass killing. Other factors were necessary to create such a murderous climate, but particularly low levels of development and democracy were the main legacy of French colonialism in Cambodia.

In the next chapter we examine the first 13 years of independence under the Sihanouk regime of the *Sangkum Reastr Niyum* (Popular Socialist Community), a period still today regarded, somewhat romantically by Cambodians old enough to remember, as the golden years of independent Cambodia.

6   The golden years of Sihanoukism: 1955–1966

According to Chandler (1991), 'Compared with what came later and what had gone before, the years 1955–1965 constituted a kind of golden age' (p. 89). The Geneva Accords signed in mid 1954 consecrated Cambodia's independence, and general elections were scheduled for the following year. In February 1955, Sihanouk founded his political movement, the *Sangkum Reastr Niyum*, or Popular Socialist Community. In March he abdicated in favour of his father, Summarit, and moved openly into the political fray as the leader of the *Sangkum*. Sihanouk's movement, however,

> despite its name ... ruled in the interests of the rich and powerful. In the first issue of its newspaper, which began in June [1955], it sets forth an authoritarian philosophy according to which natural leaders should rule and those less fortunate should not envy them. The natural leaders were the rich and powerful who enjoyed such a situation in the present because of virtuous conduct in previous lives (a common belief in popular Southeast Asian Buddhism). The poor and unfortunate should accept their lot and try for an improved situation in the next through virtuous conduct in the present. (Tully, 2002, p. 481)

With Sihanouk as both de facto revered king and de jure popular head of state, Cambodia, according to Meyer (1971), was to 'come back to a monarchy not very different from the one that existed before the French conquest' (p. 74). The general elections set for 11 September 1955 were to be supervised by the International Commission of Supervision and Control (ICSC).[1] Yet, on the day, voters were intimidated and threatened if they did not vote for the *Sangkum*. Observers 'had some reservations about certain aspects of the voting process: unusual deployment of police forces, absence of opposition voting slips and arrests of left-wing leaders ... Ballot boxes were tampered after the vote to eliminate candidates of the left' (Kiernan, 2004, p. 160). The *Sangkum* achieved total victory, winning every one of the 91 Assembly seats with 82 per cent of the vote. The Democrats received 12 per cent, the *Pracheachon* (communist organisation) 4 per cent, and various small right-wing parties

---

[1] The ICSC was a United Nations international force charged with overseeing the implementation of the Geneva Accords.

the remaining 2 per cent. Given Sihanouk's charisma, the *Sangkum* would still have obtained many votes through free and fair elections, but Kiernan (2004) on limited evidence argues that the *Pracheachon* could have won six or seven seats and possibly hold the balance of power between the Democrats and the *Sangkum*.[2]

Shortly after the elections, the small right-wing parties dissolved into the *Sangkum* and many Democrats also joined in. Sihanouk had reached his political goal: the disappearance of political parties and the gathering of their members within a large movement in which the doctrine was personal loyalty to the former king who had become the national leader (Meyer, 1971). Sihanouk had all the power and could almost do as he pleased. Almost, because his 'reign' occurred in the context of the Cold War, and soon the Second Indochina War would put the independence and territorial integrity of the Kingdom and Sihanouk's neutralist politics in a precarious situation.

Independence and the *Sangkum*

The neutralist waltz

In 1955, Cambodia remained a small underdeveloped nation with a hybrid state,[3] 'part-modern and part-feudal' (Pomonti & Thion, 1971, p. 21), surrounded by more powerful neighbours whose allegiances in the Cold War were clear but opposite. On the western side, Thailand leaned towards the USA; on the northern side, a civil war between communists and pro-Western politicians was gaining momentum in Laos (Smith, 1961); on the northeastern side, communist North Vietnam was supported by China and the Soviet Union; and on the southeastern side, South Vietnam remained dependent on the USA. Sihanouk confided that 'as a result of his meetings with Nehru [in 1956] he adopted his special brand of "neutrality"' (Gordon, 1965, p. 443). To preserve the Kingdom from war, protect its territories, but still benefit from international development aid, Sihanouk was dancing a delicate neutralist waltz, which was playing on the friendly and not so friendly relations between the various contenders. For example, in May 1955 when he signed an agreement with the USA for military assistance, Sihanouk was seemingly waltzing with America; he had nevertheless refused to join the anticommunist and US-controlled Southeast Asia Treaty Organisation (SEATO) in February, and he stood by his decision (Jennar, 1995; Meyer, 1971; Szaz, 1955), which pleased China, the Soviet Union, and

---

[2] In many districts of Kampong Cham and Takeo provinces and despite the repression, the *Pracheachon* obtained between 25 per cent and 50 per cent of the votes.

[3] We argue in our final chapter that it is still the case today, although the current hybridisation is more complex than it was in 1955.

North Vietnam. In March 1956 Cambodia accepted the first grant-in-aid ($22.4 million) given by the Chinese People's Republic to a noncommunist country, and this alarmed the USA and its allies (Kiernan, 2004, p. 170).

Fearful of annexation, Sihanouk endeavoured to have an international conference recognise Cambodia's borders, as they existed at the time. The proposal, endorsed by France and the communist countries but resisted by the USA, failed. Finally, in 1963, Sihanouk rejected all US military and economic aid. This decision was at this stage[4] a political success on the domestic front. It pulled the rug from under the feet of the *Pracheachon* and wedged the Democratic Party's support for Sihanouk into acquiescence for his anti-US imperialist stance. Sihanouk thus appeared to have realised political unity in the Kingdom.

L'Oeuvre du Sangkum

At his zenith, Sihanouk could now embark in his experiment with 'guided democracy' (Meyer, 1971, p. 137) in the role of a benign dictator, a populist and/or illiberal democrat, or simply as the 'citizen king' who, like Saint Louis, listened to and rendered justice in the open among his subjects, whom Sihanouk called his 'children'.[5] According to Meyer (1971), as early as 1960 'personal power had started to transform popular consultation in the systematic approbation of the decisions taken by Prince Sihanouk who now had become the head of State'. In September 1955 women were given the right to vote, and the principle of elected provincial assemblies was adopted. Although these assemblies may have been an original and genuine attempt by Sihanouk to engage ordinary Cambodians in public affairs, they were doomed from the start short of a profound transformation of Cambodian society. By 1959, the lack of political maturity in the peasantry, which led to the elections of 'notables who alone had the sufficient education and only defended their class interests', combined with the opposition of the mandarins and functionaries who were to be controlled by these assemblies brought an end to this experiment in regional self-governance (Meyer, 1971).

Yet, the *Sangkum* also engaged in important socioeconomic developments, but too often the programs were badly planned, mismanaged, and increasingly riddled with corruption. The greatest effort was put towards improving education, but this effort was quantitative rather than qualitative. While the number of schools at all levels more than doubled between 1953 and 1968, it was not matched by the formation of competent teachers or the implementation

---

[4] It would be a factor of his downfall in 1970.
[5] The phrase *L'Oeuvre du Sangkum* can be translated as *The Work of the Sangkum*. It was the title of a Sihanoukist publication series, and a special issue, 'Summary from December 1962 to June 1963', was presented at the 15th National Congress of the *Sangkum Reastr Niyum* (in French, *oeuvre* can be alternately translated as 'work', 'achievement', or 'showpiece').

of an indigenous curriculum (Pomonti & Thion, 1971). The main pedagogy remained rote learning rather than critical thinking, and the pursuit of scientific and technical education was not encouraged despite the country's urgent need of such professionals. In Cambodian culture, positions in the civil service were most valued, but around 1966 the bulk of these students who expected a job in the administration found themselves unemployed because of budget cuts. This would eventually greatly disenchant the youth and turn many of them against the regime (see also Chandler, 1991).

There were some achievements in other socioeconomic domains such as health, communication, light-industry, recreation, and financial schemes to reduce peasant dependence on extortionist moneylenders. There were also many failures caused by mismanagement and corruption.[6] Pomonti and Thion (1971, p. 71) have argued that formal independence did not shake up the legacy of the past. France remained the major supplier to Cambodia. The competition for cultural, economic, political, and military influence between the former protectors and the new contenders from the USA was apparent, but French neocolonialism in Cambodia was not ready to abdicate in favour of the American alternative. Whether motivated by neocolonial interests or genuine support for Cambodian independence, the inauguration in April 1960 of the port of Sihanoukville financed by the French freed Cambodian trade from its control by pro-American Saigon. Eventually, it would also help trade with and supply routes to China, North Vietnam, and the South Vietnamese communists.

'Social Sihanoukism'

On 3 April 1960 Sihanouk's father, King Suramarit, died. Sihanouk refused the crown and instead organised a referendum that confirmed him as head of state, the supreme ruler of Cambodia. From now on, personal power would be the norm and, as Meyer (1971) argued, 'the Sangkumian doctrine became "Sihanoukism" and to be Sihanoukist was to give carte blanche to a man whose politics were arrived at through inspiration' (p. 151). As in the 1958 election, Sihanouk handpicked the candidates of the June 1962 ballot and included leftist intellectuals such as Khieu Samphan, Hou Youn, and Hu Nim. In July they became members of the eighteenth government of the *Sangkum*, but incorruptible Samphan and Youn did not stay long as government ministers; by July 1963 the right wing of the *Sangkum* had them ejected. Like in other recently decolonised countries, Sihanouk favoured a political economy based on socialism, which included the nationalisation of foreign trade and banks. But as Vickery (1986) remarked, 'The economic reforms of 1963–4, albeit

---

[6] A number of authors such as Meyer (1971), Osborne (1979), Pomonti and Thion (1971), and Slocomb (2010) have examined the successes and failures of this period.

superficially leftist, did not lead to "socialist" results' (p. 18). The nationalised enterprises became the personal fiefs of the royals and mandarins forming the Cambodian ruling elites. To try and remedy the economic ills of the country, particularly foreign debt, low rural development, and corruption, Sihanouk drew from the economic strategy proposed by Khieu Samphan in his doctoral thesis of 1959 (*Cambodia's Economy and Industrial Development*). This strategy resembled a form of moderate Marxian socialism and included government investment in productive enterprises, increased taxing of luxury items, and a politic of austerity combined with reforms to reduce the impact on the poor. These reforms were not radical, but nevertheless radical enough to be despised and fought by the venal and increasingly corrupted elites (Osborne, 1979).

Rumours of a planned invasion supported by the USA, and the overthrow and assassination in South Vietnam of president Ngo Dinh Diem and his brother – supported by the USA searching for a more acceptable 'strongman' – precipitated not only Sihanouk's program of nationalisation but also his decision to renounce US military and economic aid in November 1963. In a meeting with businessmen, Sihanouk declared

the reforms were not undertaken to cause them trouble but rather to avoid the revolution which will surely break out one day if we are complacent in capitalism or even semi-capitalism...as American aid...is only conceived to consolidate capitalism in Cambodia [and] has enriched the wealthy class and not the nation...We will practise a policy of autarchy[7] and protectionism but appeal to the private sector to get the cadres needed for [the] state or mixed-economy enterprises as experience has already amply demonstrated that our bureaucrats are absolutely incapable of becoming good managers of commercial or industrial enterprises. (cited in Slocomb, 2010, p. 112)

For the pro-American right, it was a shock and Sihanouk would eventually pay a heavy political price for these decisions, but in the short term, they reduced the trade deficit, and French and Chinese aid contributions significantly increased.

By the time of the 1966 elections, the economic situation had turned disastrous (Leifer, 1967; Slocomb, 2010). To make the situation worse, the 'rice war', that is, the smuggling of Cambodian rice across the border to both sides of the Vietnam conflict,[8] bankrupted the government by depriving it of its main source of revenues, export duties (Kiernan, 2004). Then Sihanouk took a decision that many historians found baffling: this time he did not handpick the *Sangkum* candidates and 415 of them competed for the assembly's 82 seats. Given the level of corruption, the vote buying and intimidation that could be

---

[7] Whether inspired or not by Samphan, the desire for autarchy, radically established during DK, was already evoked by Sihanouk.

[8] Kiernan (2004, p. 228) estimated that in 1966 up to 40 per cent of the rice crop had been smuggled out of Cambodia.

organised by the wealthy helped ensure the success of the conservative forces. Meyer (1971) described this decision as a 'veritable demission of the Cambodian head of State, leaving the field free to the traditional right pushed by a clearly fascistic faction' and a government 'that brought together the most reactionary personalities of the Kingdom' (p. 154).

Sihanouk returned to his hobby of filmmaking as a dilettante film director, an interest that Chandler (1991) noted might have been 'the result of or a symptom of his disenchantment with politics' (p. 153). Meyer, however, pointed out that 'a progressive leader one day confided that the movies of the head of State were incomparable tools of propaganda to "show the rottenness of the regime"'.

> All his movies screened in the countryside show the head of State and the main dignitaries living in a level of luxury that the poor peasants had never imagined. They'll understand that the large American cars, the galas, the fancy-dress balls, the roulette and the baccarat, the games of love are the sole and entire universe of the ruling classes and this *joie de vivre* that Prince Sihanouk often evokes. (Meyer, 1971, p. 157)

Sihanouk's political miscalculations during this period would have serious repercussions (see next chapter). We now turn to what is known about the extent of crime and violence, starting with ordinary crime, and then following with war violence and state crime.

The fall in crime

Although we found very little reliable or quantifiable information about crime during this period, the primary data we were able to unearth and secondary sources converge to suggest that crime and violence declined substantially between 1955 and 1966. By late 1954, the anticolonial war had ended, and although the 1955 *Bulletins de Police Criminelle* (*BPC*; National Archives of Cambodia [NAC]) data were incomplete they pointed to a fall in lethal violence. Hospital morbidity records reveal a sharp fall in deaths due to homicide and war wounds from 147 in 1958 to 1 in 1965.[9]

Patchy crime figures published in the *Cahiers du Sangkum* (NLC)[10] permit some estimation of the level of crime. Between 1 January and 30 April 1959, 29 people were arrested for robbery and 2 for kidnapping.[11] Using an average number of offenders per event of 2.44 (as recorded in the court data between 1928 and 1947), it is possible that these arrests would have amounted to only 12 cases of robbery in that 4-month period, and by extension about 36 cases for the year.

---

[9] Between 1958 and 1965 Cambodia was not at war, and it seems unlikely that cases of war injuries occurring between 1947 and 1954 would have been treated in hospitals between 1958 and 1965. One can therefore assume that the number reported refers to homicidal violence.

[10] This was a monthly publication that described the achievements of the *Sangkum*, the political movement created by Sihanouk in 1955 (NLC).

[11] In addition, during the same period, 616 functionaries were fired or prosecuted for incompetence and/or corruption.

Even if we accept the extreme and unlikely scenario that a single offender was involved in each event, no more than 87 cases would have been recorded, that is, a rate of 1.8 per 100,000. This would be a lower rate than any rates for robbery recorded between 1927 and 1940. The same source recorded 183 arrests for felony and misdemeanour during January and February 1961. If we use this figure as an index for the year 1961, the total number of arrested individuals for felony and misdemeanour would have been 1,098. Between 1928 and 1943 the average number of people accused in court of felony and misdemeanour per year was 14,202. Another piece of evidence suggesting a general decline in criminality appeared in another *Sangkum* publication (NLC). Between 1 May 1962 and 30 April 1963, 12,826 cases of felony and misdemeanour had been adjudicated, which represented a rate of 223.9 per 100,000 population. For example, the 1930s registered significantly higher rates of such cases, averaging 350 per 100,000 population, than in 1962–3.

It is very likely that the crime figures published by the *Sangkum* were grossly underestimated for propaganda purposes. However, secondary sources also suggest a decline in criminality. Steinberg (1959), for instance, commented about the crime situation after 1955:

Cambodia has few of the more violent social problems that plague most industrialised nations today. Murder and sexual crimes are at a minimum. Petty thievery is common (in spite of the Buddhist prohibition), in part because the Cambodian's concept of private property is not a strict one. Habitual drunkenness and alcoholism are almost unknown, though a large amount of wine is consumed, mostly during festivals and other social occasions... Juvenile delinquency has been virtually nonexistent in Cambodia. (p. 250)

Vickery (in Kiernan & Boua, 1982, p. 103) remarked that banditry had seriously abated during the postindependence years:

Another return from the system was a few years of complete peace and internal security, something which the country had not known within living memory. Throughout the nineteenth century Cambodia had been plagued by warfare, and the colonial period had seen whole regions ridden by endemic large-scale banditry, that is, outlaw bands who would raid, rob and burn entire villages with impunity. In the years following the Second World War, these bands turned themselves into *Issaraks* and fought for independence against the French and the last of this activity wasn't ended until 1958–59. By 1960, when I first arrived, one could travel anywhere without danger from outlaws or hindrance from the authorities, and the Sangkum government, in the eyes of the people, received credit for this.

His comment also suggests that the lingering violence between 1954 and 1960 may be interpreted as a temporary postconflict effect of the armed struggle for independence as well as the settling of political accounts between Sihanouk and his opponents. Finally, the suggested decline in crime between 1955 and 1966 is theoretically consistent with the immense popularity and legitimacy enjoyed by Sihanouk and his regime, particularly as the latter was associated with a

Political unrest and repression: crimes of the state

Fraudulent and violent elections

Up to the day of the elections of 11 September 1955, Sihanouk directed a campaign of repression against the left. Even Son Ngoc Thanh, who in September 1954 had wanted to 'pledge his loyalty to the government' was turned down by Sihanouk, and by February 1955, he was the leader of 2,000 Khmer Serei, an anti-Sihanoukist extreme right group based in Thailand (Jennar, 1995, p. 57). Thanhist and communist newspapers were banned and their editors jailed. The offices of the Democratic Party were ransacked or occupied, one of its candidates was jailed, and its deputy general-secretary Keng Vannsak was shot at, arrested, and incarcerated before the voting (Kiernan, 2004).

In late 1954, about 30 former members and cadres of the United Issarak Front (UIF; communist) were killed in several Prey Veng villages. In November 1954, '36 inhabitants of a village in Krakor district, Pursat, who had been members of the IUF forces were all imprisoned for "forming an association of malefactors, offences against the King, and the spreading of false news"' (Kiernan, 2004, p. 156). Finally, in February 1955 another IUF cadre was executed by Dap Chhuon, a former traditional Issarak and one of Sihanouk's henchmen who had defected to the government. In Kampong Cham and Kampot, the authorities targeted former members by shooting at them to prevent them from taking part in the electoral process. Many ended up in Kampong Cham gaol for most of the campaign (Kiernan, 2004, p. 159).

The newly created aboveground communist organisation *Pracheachon* ('the people') attempted to contest the elections, but 20 party members were arrested during this period and 3 of its candidates spent most of the campaign in gaol. There were also several political killings targeting members of the *Pracheachon*. In Kampot, six *Pracheachon* members were arrested by government troops and two were shot dead. In Battambang, two campaigners were gunned down by soldiers and another was shot at but was unhurt. In Kampong Speu, in October following their success in the elections, another two *Pracheachon* members were also killed by local authorities (Kiernan, 2004, p. 159).

Plots and counterplots

Kiernan (2004) argues that between 1956 and 1966 the Sihanouk regime 'was *not* characterised by severe and brutal repression of dissidents' (p. 176).

Illustration 6.1 Mao Zedong, Peng Zhen, Norodom Sihanouk, and Liu Shaoqi, 1956

Kiernan's is a relative statement, and if it is true that the forceful methods of repression used during the period leading up to the 1955 elections were used less frequently after the elections, the silencing of Sihanouk's political opponents through arrests, incarcerations, and sometimes assassinations was nevertheless not an infrequent occurrence.

For example, in August 1957, leaders of the Democratic Party invited to the palace for a friendly meeting with Sihanouk were beaten up by Lon Nol's soldiers on departure (Kiernan, 2004). The Democratic Party dissolved shortly after, but supporters and their associates and families continued to be persecuted. Political opponents mostly from the left were beaten up, arrested, jailed, sometimes tortured and a few, such as the editor of *Pracheachon*, were killed (Jennar, 1995; Kiernan, 2004).

In 1959 three plots against Sihanouk were discovered.[12] The first one involved Sam Sary, then ambassador in London, was relatively benign. Recalled to Phnom Penh after mistreating a Khmer maid, he rebelled against Sihanouk and created an opposition party, allegedly supported by the USA and Thailand. His wife was arrested, but Sary managed to flee. According to some reports, Lon Nol's hired killers tried to eliminate him, and in 1963 Sary was mysteriously murdered in Laos (Meyer, 1971), although Chandler (1991) noted that he disappeared in 1962, 'probably assassinated by one of his foreign patrons' (p. 101).

---

[12] Most of this section is drawn from Chandler (1991, 2008) and Meyer (1971).

The second was more serious. It involved Dap Chhuon, a former traditional Issarak who had rallied to Sihanouk in 1949. This quasi-illiterate warlord had been appointed governor of Siem Reap, which he ruthlessly ruled for 10 years. In 1956 he became a general of the Royal Army and minister of national security. Fiercely anticommunist, he openly disapproved of Sihanouk's foreign policy, and in 1959 he took the lead in a complot planning the secession of the provinces of Siem Reap and Kampong Thom that would be immediately recognised by the USA and its allies as 'free states' (Meyer, 1971). The French and then the Chinese intelligence services informed Sihanouk of the treasonous conspiracy, which was promptly crushed. Chhuon was shot, two South Vietnamese army officers involved in the complot were captured and executed, and a parliamentarian, Slat Peou, was sentenced to death.

The closest attempt against Sihanouk occurred on 31 August 1959, when a parcel bomb coming from Hong Kong exploded in the royal palace and killed Prince Vakravan and two domestics. The authors were never apprehended, but the attempt was imputed according to Jennar (1995) to the Khmer Serei or Sam Sary. However, the involvement of the South Vietnamese was more likely given the damage to the Khmer Serei influence after the failed Chhuon plot (Chandler, 1991, pp. 101–7).

The *Cahiers du Sangkum* for the period January to April 1959 recorded these events 'as an achievement of the Sangkum':

During the last four months the National Security has carried a remarkably efficient action against the group of traitors in the pay of foreign powers... The capital and the provinces have never ceased to enjoy the most complete calm. The number of arrests shows plainly how little following the Sam Sary's complot has received. Twenty-nine individuals have been arrested for complot against the interior security of the State. Eighty of the traitors' accomplices have been jailed. It should be noted that the majority of these individuals are ex-convicts, without a permanent domicile, who cannot justify of any means of subsistence. The defendants have made the most damning confessions for the instigators of the rebellion. (NLC)

In April 1961, Sihanouk delivered a speech at the Royal Police Academy, reproduced in the *Cahiers du Sangkum*, that nevertheless recommended also using education and prevention in dealing with ordinary crimes:

It is the duty of the chiefs to set a good example and to rigorously combat incompetence and corruption, but the final success of your task will not solely be measured by the degree of success in this cleansing job but also by the way you will have served public interest and contributed to the movement of your country towards the path of progress. **You will only make this contribution if you assign yourself not only a repressive role but also an educative and preventive one** [boldface in the original]. The latter, ungrateful because difficult, will demand that you become interested in the masses, study their problems and their penchants, and redress the wrongs done against them. Contraventions, arrests, etc. will remain indispensable, and the question is not to abolish them, but there are more and better things to do. Through your patient and judicious action amongst the masses you will succeed better in cleansing[13] [or cleaning up] the society, which in our country includes a number of unoccupied people whose idleness and laziness push into vices and crimes, and thus in eliminating factors that are hampering progress and social order. What I am asking you is to break the habitual framework of your functions that might make you think that you are above all a body of *sévices* [literally physical abuse or maltreatment] that must be feared by the public, and to **understand that your true role is to obtain the confidence and the collaboration of the public to serve it better.** (NLC)

It is ironical and also revealing that Sihanouk used the word *sévices* about police practices when it is likely that he only meant repression in general.

In February 1963 in Siem Reap a schoolboy was found beaten to death. Students accused the police of brutality and murder, but the local authorities defended the officer. These events led to violent demonstrations and the death of several students and policemen (Becker, 1986, p. 113). Student solidarity strikes and demonstrations spread in Phnom Penh and most provincial towns. In June 1963, underground communists, until then based in Phnom Penh, decided it was safer to go to the provinces, although some of them were hunted down by the security forces and pushed into the *maquis*. In November it was on the radical right that Sihanouk's repression fell, a Khmer Serei named Preap In and his comrade Saing San were arrested, but unlike San, Preap In failed to implicate the USA in support for Son Ngoc Thanh. Preap In was sentenced to death by a military court and executed on 20 January 1964. On Sihanouk's orders, the execution was filmed in minute detail, including up-close shots of Preap In's agony. The movie was then shown over a month in all the cinemas at every screening (Jennar, 1995; Meyer, 1971), and posters of the execution were sent to Cambodian schools (Chandler, 1991, p. 134).

The rampant repression of the left continued in 1965 with arrests, beatings, and the death of dissidents, such as that in March of 'a youth who had been arrested in Kampong Cham after being discovered distributing leaflets and putting up posters, [who] was found dead, hanging by the neck in the bathroom of the local police station' (Kiernan, 2004, p. 217). The youth, interrogated by the police for distributing leaflets, 'would answer only with the following tight-lipped formulation: it is useless to ask us questions, just deal with us as you see fit, since from now on it is obvious that the small, the weak and the poor must lead their lives in neglect and silently endure what is imposed on them by the big, the strong and the rich'.

---

[13] In the context of the speech, the French words *assainir* and *assainissement* did not have the radical meaning of the modern expression 'social cleansing'.

From the French, Sihanouk had inherited a police state where police brutality and torture were commonplace, and these practices continued during his rule and increased after 1966. Pomonti and Thion (1971) remarked:

> There was (and still is) a badly known political police that arrested suspects and kept them for long periods in jail without trial. There is, in the premises of the security, a large common room that the detainees call the 'grille' where all kinds of people were crammed: petty thieves, Vietnamese deserters from the governmental army, Vietcong, Khmer professors, former politicians, functionaries accused of corruption. Some stayed there a few days, others several months. The common characteristic was that they were not prosecuted. Every evening, around 7 o'clock, some detainees were taken away and interminably beaten or tortured in an adjoining room... Amongst the political detainees there were disappearances. They were several hundred detained in cells. Opponents from the right, from the left, simple suspects; they were somewhat forgotten by the world. Nobody from abroad claimed them. In Phnom Penh nobody talked about it and in fact we did not always know what happened to those the police had arrested. (pp. 95–6)

At least seven leftists were assassinated in 1966, of whom six 'members of a mobile traditional orchestra in a former Pracheachon stronghold near Oudong were arrested by soldiers, disembowelled and their livers exhibited outside the local military post' (Kiernan, 2004, p. 231).

War on the borders

As early as 1957 South Vietnamese troops conducted raids in Svay Rieng and Stung Treng provinces. The Second Indochina War spilled over into Cambodia when Vietcong fighters established sanctuaries in Cambodian border territories and South Vietnam started bombing Cambodian villages. In 1964, the war on the borders intensified. At least five deadly attacks occurred on the Vietnamese-Cambodian border between March and October 1964 (Jennar, 1995). South Vietnamese planes and tanks often led by American officers plundered and destroyed villages in Svay Rieng, killing and wounding many villagers. American planes and helicopters attacked villages as far as Kampong Cham and Mondolkiri.

On 27 October 1964, Sihanouk threatened to break diplomatic relations with the USA if the latter persisted with its border attacks. The attacks continued killing more villagers, and the rupture occurred on 3 May 1965. However, in November 1965, in Beijing, Lon Nol signed a secret military treaty with the Chinese in which Cambodia agreed to protect the communist Vietnamese fighters in border regions and to help the transport of supplies to them from China. Sihanouk also entered into a secret agreement with the Vietnamese communists according to which the Cambodian army could take 10 per cent of the military aid transiting through the port of Sihanoukville. These treaties de facto ended Cambodia's neutrality, and on 21 December the US government officially authorised military attacks in Cambodia. In April 1966, for the first time, a US military spokesman acknowledged deliberately firing upon Cambodian soil, and these attacks multiplied throughout 1966 (Jennar, 1995; Leifer, 1967).

On both the Thai and Vietnamese borders, incursions by the dissident Khmer Serei, equipped and trained by the CIA and supported by Thailand, became more frequent. At the beginning of 1966, the clandestine Khmer Serei radio declared war on Cambodia and claimed responsibility for incursions across the Thai border. Around the same time, Thai irredentist attitudes led to a crisis over control of the ancient Prasat Preah Vihear temple, which is located adjacent the Thai province of Sisaket on the Cambodian border in the northern province of Preah Vihear. Thai troops occupied the area, which was retaken 3 days later by the Cambodian army. Leifer (1967) reported: 'Conflict along the border with Thailand was also a prominent feature of the first half of 1966 in the North Western province of Oddor Meanchey and in the South Western province of Koh Kong' (p. 72). While border clashes continued, an early sign of the growing risk of civil war occurred when on 12 June 1966 a passenger train between Battambang and the western border town of Poipet was attacked by an armed group of Khmer communists led by Muol Sambath (Jennar, 1995).

A fatal crime: corruption

Meyer (1971) argued that 'in 1953 Cambodia had inherited an administration with little experience and a small number of superior managers; but it was *healthy*' (italics in original). The preceding chapters made it clear that the protectorate had prevented Cambodians developing managerial experience, but that it left an overall uncorrupted administration is debatable. However, it is credible given that the Protectorate, to protect its revenue, tried to minimise corruption, at least by Cambodians. What is not credible is the declaration of a functionary of the Phnom Penh Post Office published in one of Sihanouk-sponsored newspapers that 'corruption was this social scourge we had the misfortune to inherit from the regime of the protectorate' (Slocomb, 2010, p. 83). In any case corruption became widespread and incomparably greater than what it might have been under French rule. For example, Meyer (1971) remarked,

During the first few years after independence corruption had been 'reasonable.' Ministers and Chiefs of the national services limited their ambitions to the construction of a villa and the purchase of a car... but appetite came with eating and it soon spread to all the agents of the State with a bit of power, starting from the rank of orderly. Corruption became an institution. (p. 171)

According to Chandler (1991) and Meyer (1971), Sihanouk himself was honest, but he did little to discourage corruption within his entourage. For example, in 1956, Prince Monireth, who according to Meyer (1971) was renowned for his integrity, was appointed Minister of *Assainissement*[14] and decided to indict 10 notoriously corrupt individuals. He presented his project to the Council of Ministers, but the latter, panic stricken, rejected it and Sihanouk asked Monireth to resign. The top culprits were never threatened, and when damning reports against them were sometimes transmitted to the cabinet of the head of state, they were quickly filed away. In 1962 Sihanouk delivered a lofty lecture to the students of the Royal School of Administration:

> To be a civil servant is to be dedicated body and soul to the service of the nation and its people, and not to consider oneself a privileged person exclusively preoccupied with the material and moral advantages of one's position... The task awaiting you is gruelling. Your pay will be too low; I know it. But I am asking you to accept these sacrifices until the time our country has achieved the prosperity we are working toward. You will have to resist the temptation of easily and dishonestly obtained money, of sumptuous cars, villas, and jewellery for your wives. You will be tempted – and this is human – by the example of some who enjoy inexplicable luxury and who temporarily have escaped sanctions. I am asking you to opt for a more modest existence, rather than all these things, to value the respect granted to those who can hold their head high. Admittedly, the corrupt are far from being the majority of our civil servants, but few as they may be, their action is nevertheless harmful to our honour and the national interest and we have an obligation to regard this issue as a particularly important one. (reproduced in the *Cahiers du Sangkum*, May 1962, pp. 142–3 [NLC])

At the same time, laws that could only increase the scope of rent seeking and encourage capture by organised criminals were passed. The most damaging was the total prohibition in 1961 of prostitution and brothels, until then licensed and regulated (Keo, Bouhours, Broadhurst, & Bouhours, 2014; Sandy, 2006).[15]

Half-hearted attempts at reforming the legal system were never actually implemented. Such failed attempts included the separation of administrative and judiciary roles, particularly the executive and the judiciary, the creation of administrative jurisdictions to deal with complaints against the administration, the publication of court decisions, and anticorruption judicial bodies. Corruption spread to all the strata of the power hierarchy, where anyone with a modicum of authority had to be bribed. The police, the army, and the customs service were 'unassailable bastions' of corruption 'where the occupants easily and in a very short time ma[d]e colossal fortunes' through grand contraband (Meyer, 1971, p. 173). Police extortion on the roads, in shops, restaurants, bars, and cinemas, and in the issuing of identification documents, permits, and so forth became common practice. Police chiefs made considerable benefits from

---

[14] Department charged with cleaning up and restoring confidence in the public service.
[15] After wasting over 2 million riels to create a reeducation centre for girls debauched by prostitution (*Cahiers du Sangkum*, 1962, p. 128 [NAT LIB CAMBODIA]), by 1963 the regime reverted to the old regulation, and the brothel licensing system was reinstated.

the protection of gambling and prostitution and the traffic of opium (Meyer, 1971; Pomonti & Thion, 1971; Steinberg, 1959).

The embezzlement of state enterprises such as the beer factory of Kampong-Som, the textile industry, and the cement works; the disappearance of pharmaceutical products obtained for public health services; the diversion of funds for maintenance works; and the use of bogus supply orders for public works became endemic. The gulf between the city and countryside grew and 'endemic, unpunished corruption affected nearly all official decisions. For any kind of government service money changed hands' (Chandler, 1991, p. 181). A middle management civil servant earning about 5,000 riels in salary could acquire a villa up to 2 million riels and a small car; a top civil servant, minister, or general earning between 10,000 and 25,000 riels a month would own several luxurious villas and two or three cars (Meyer, 1971). Slocomb (2010) remarked that although it dominated industry, the private sector paid very little tax, and tax evasion represented a serious loss to the state budget. By 1970, Cambodia's government had turned into a vulnerable kleptocracy, and during the Lon Nol regime the capacity for corruption would become a fatally bottomless one. Like the proverbial phoenix, in the late 1980s, the kleptocracy would eventually rise from the ashes of the Khmer Rouge apocalypse, but in the late 1960s the only elites showing an absolute integrity had been the three co-opted and short-time communist ministers Khieu Samphan, Hou Youn, and Hu Nim. The scholar Philippe Preschez (in Pomomti & Thion, 1971) was already warning 'the risk is to witness the formation in Cambodian minds of a kind of equation: communism = honesty' (p. 124).

The communists: *purs et durs*

Cambodian communism was born during the anticolonial war between 1947 and 1954 and, in its infancy, was influenced by the more mature and experienced Vietnamese communist movement. After the Geneva Convention of 1954 and Sihanouk's anticommunist repression, about 1,000 of the Khmer Viet Minh fled to Hanoi. At the same time, between 1947 and 1954, young intellectual supporters and sympathisers of the Democratic Party were given scholarships to pursue tertiary studies in France. There they met and got acquainted with revolutionary theories, in particular Marxism-Leninism with a good tinge of Stalinism, that they, for better or worse, incorporated into their strong nationalist ideals.[16] Most, but not all of them, would become the leaders of the

---

[16] The English translation of the phrase *purs et durs* as 'hardliners' does not capture the French puritanical connotation. For detailed histories of the Cambodian communist movement, see the works of Becker (1986), Chandler (2008), Heder (1980), Kiernan (2004), and Vickery (1982, 1986), from which most of this section was drawn.

murderous regime of Democratic Kampuchea. For example, Pol Pot came back to Cambodia in 1953, Son Sen in 1956, Ieng Sary in 1957, and Khieu Samphan in 1959. As Becker (1986) wrote, 'The Cambodians studying in Paris came back to a political monstrosity, in their terms – an independent Cambodia ruled by a "democratically" elected god-king [who] called himself a socialist and enjoyed the friendship of the communist states of Asia' (p. 99). Some of this new French-educated vanguard set to work aboveground as the *Pracheachon*, still supporting Sihanouk's foreign relation policies, and underground as the Kampuchean People's Revolutionary Party (KPRP), with its new urban intellectuals who hated the monarchy and whose nationalism and phobia over the Vietnamese blended increasingly with Maoist ideology.

Sihanouk favoured the French-trained urban radicals and hunted down the old rural vanguard. As Kiernan (2004) argued, the outcome was significant:

By pinning down that section of the left most inclined towards political moderation, and promoting the section more prone to be hot-headed, he eventually effected a transformation of the local communist movement from a Vietnamese-oriented group led by former peasants, displaying patience and caution in both political and social demands, to a Chinese-oriented group led by intellectuals, advocating social and political upheaval. (p. 183)

The lack of professional prospects for the young educated class was another opportunity for the new urban vanguard. Disenchanted students were becoming increasingly receptive to the republican and communist views of their teachers, among them Pol Pot, Ieng Sary, Vorn Vet, Son Sen, Hou Youn, Hu Nim, Khieu Samphan, Duch, and others.

As the new urban middle class was developing, the agricultural sector seemed stubbornly resistant to growth of the kind needed to support a modern economy (Slocomb, 2010, p. 93). While authors have argued and disagreed about the importance of landlessness in the Cambodian agrarian problem,[17] most of them agree on the growing level of peasant indebtedness[18] compounded by the lack of rural and agricultural development and the associated low productivity. The divide between an unfettered and conspicuous urban consumerism, corruption, and waste and the deepening of peasant pauperisation was growing. The 'rice war' had a seriously detrimental effect on peasants, particularly in Battambang. In 1963 the government lowered the price paid to peasants for rice. Peasants tried to withhold their harvest, but they were forced, sometimes at gunpoint, to surrender their paddy to the state at the lowered official price. Slocomb (2010) argued that 'it is fair to say that the peasant's living standard

---

[17] See Delvert (1961) about agricultural land ownership in Cambodia. On the basis of Delvert's study, many authors have argued that landlessness was rare in the 1960s but was increasing. However, Guérin (2012) found it already existed in the 1930s.

[18] Slocomb (2010) estimated that 75 per cent of them already had significant debts in 1952.

in 1966 was not higher than it had been in 1958... Those employed in the non-agricultural sectors of the economy represented 20 per cent of the economically active population, but... enjoyed 60 per cent of the national income' (p. 89).

As Vickery (1986) remarked, it was not surprising that 'ultra-leftists statements [calling for] a renewal of armed struggle began to find favour with increasing numbers of the peasantry' (p. 18). This is supported by the electoral victories of Hou Youn, Khieu Samphan, and Hu Nim despite Sihanouk's campaign against them. Economically and politically, in 1969, Cambodia remained a precapitalist society ruled by a populist but repressive authoritarian regime that could not bear any opposition. As Chandler (1991) wrote, one of its legacies was that 'the Khmer Republic and the CPK [Pol Pot's Communist Party of Kampuchea] were in a sense both children of the Democratic party and products of this repression' (p. 94). Another legacy was 'his [Sihanouk] rejection of foreign models and emphasis on past glories, [foreshadowing] policies espoused by the Khmer Republic and DK' (Chandler, 1991, p. 87). According to Chandler, Sihanouk would have declared: 'Our socialism is national. We Cambodians will never accept the tearing down of the barrier which preserves the originality of our race, of our traditions, of our religious faith, and which safeguards our independence vis-à-vis certain of our neighbours (particularly Vietnamese).'

This potentially autarkic, disintegrative, and decivilising 'national socialism' would eventually haunt and devour him, as it would his successors Lon Nol and Pol Pot later on. When Sihanouk reached the apogee of his popularity in 1962, Leifer (1963) wrote: 'The only organised group with the capacity to seize power is the army, which appears to be loyal to the Prince and suspicious of the young intellectual class. If Prince Sihanouk was suddenly removed from the political scene, General Lon Nol, the 47-year-old Chief of the General Staff, appears to be a promising candidate for succession' (p. 57). The next chapter shows how this prediction was realised in March 1970.

7   Criminal states and civil wars: 1967–1975

The year 1967 marked the beginning of exponential levels of mass and state violence foreshadowing that perpetrated by the Khmer Rouge after 1975. Kiernan (2004) called the period from 1967 until the 1970 coup against Sihanouk 'the first civil war' and the postcoup period between 1970 and 1975 'the second civil war'. The first was waged by Sihanouk and Lon Nol against those Sihanouk called the *Khmers rouges*. However, it led to the massacres of many peasants who were angry about their plight but little acquainted with the Khmer communists. The second was waged by the 'unholy' alliance of Sihanouk and his supporters with the Khmer and Vietnamese communists against Lon Nol's Khmer Republic 'supported'[1] by South Vietnam and the USA. During the first civil war, the number of homicides caused by the conflict can be estimated at nine per day and escalated to between 313 and 522 during the second. While the carnage of the civil wars raged in the provinces, paranoia, repression, waste, corruption, and ordinary crime soared in Phnom Penh in the late 1960s. We found little quantitative data on ordinary crime, and this chapter deals for the most part with the mass violence created by the civil wars and the violence inflicted not only by Cambodian governments but also by the USA and its allies, the Viet Minh and Vietcong combatants, and Khmer Rouge revolutionaries.

Crime wave and corruption

We do not have primary sources that allow us to estimate the level of 'street crime' during this period, but secondary sources all point to a rise in crime in Phnom Penh and the provinces. Although somewhat romanticising the past, Meyer (1971) described how a crime wave hit urban Cambodia:

The noble traditions of Cambodian banditry are almost gone today, but because of the hooliganism that is developing in the cities and the exactions committed in the countryside by armed 'people' in uniform we will end up missing them [the bandits]... The *natural* honesty of the past has disappeared from all classes. In parallel to the great corruption of the administration we find all kinds of thefts, and villainous crimes and rapes,

---

[1] We will see later that the term 'supported' in reality meant, 'exploited by ... for their own ends'.

increasingly committed by young delinquents belonging to the new bourgeoisie... All classes have become engaged in an artificial consumer society in which the imported goods on display exceed even the financial means of the privileged classes. The inherent honesty of the Cambodians did not resist the open temptations but was replaced by an unbridled corruption spreading to all the levels of the administration, from fraud in the business world, to pick pocketing and burglary, and since 1970, to armed robbery. Yesteryear the safest and most peaceful city in Asia, the Cambodian capital of 1970 is rather similar to Bangkok or Manila. (pp. 37–9)

Meyer looked at the anomic times in Durkhemian terms of brutal modernisation:

The worshipping of money associated with the temptations of the city has deeply transformed the traditional behaviour of urban Khmers... in general the adaptation to the materialist civilisation of the twentieth century has traumatised the entire urban population. Brutally, without any preparation, Cambodians went from ox carts to cars and jet aircrafts, from a world in slow motion to a world in fast forward. All the moral values and human relations have been affected. Social interactions, yesterday courteous and relaxed have become nasty and aggressive and, in their relationships with the peasants, the workers, and the small shopkeepers, the nouveau riche mandarins behave ruthlessly displaying an 'aristocratic' superiority even unknown to the royal family. This class attitude sparked the cynical reflection of an anti-conformist Cambodian intellectual who regretted that 'Cambodia had fallen under the colonialist domination of the Phnom Penh people!'

Indeed, 'a rift had occurred between the capital and the countryside, between a small urban society getting richer and richer, and the mass of the peasants becoming poorer and poorer; between those who frenetically grasped the gadgets of western civilisation and those who remained attached to traditional values' (Meyer, 1971, pp. 42–3). Criminal statistics were not available in Cambodia because the authorities imposed a total blackout on this topic. Meyer, however, suggested that murders were quite frequent in rural areas and described them as:

Rarely villainous and premeditated, they are committed during a fit of madness, which is not too different from the Malaysian *amok*. The triggers for these explosions can be an unbearable insult, a blatant injustice or a romantic rivalry. Two strokes of a hatchet or machete and that's it. The culprit is taken and put into the hands of justice, which alone can impose the price of blood, but when judgement comes six months or a year later, 9 times out of 10 the killer has forgotten the reasons for his deed and even the deed itself!

As the war progressed, a growing number of refugees fled to the capital, and by mid 1970 the population in Phnom Penh had doubled[2] and crime flourished:

As Cambodia's Communists-occupied territories grew larger, much of their population fled to Phnom Penh in the hope of finding safety from the fighting, above all from the

---

[2] By 1971 it had grown from 600,000 to 2 million (Shawcross, 1979).

most destructive American bombing. The capital also offered hope of shelter and the bare necessities of life. Quickly Phnom Penh, the once remarkably well-tended capital, became pockmarked by jerry built slums. Entire families lived on sidewalks or public patches of grass. The outstretched hands of begging children tugged at one's trouser legs or pinched one's arm. Cambodian women and girls took over from the banished Vietnamese the sad métier of prostitution. Petty crime flourished. (Kamm, 2011, pp. 87–8)

In parallel to street crime, grand corruption was also growing and would reach its apogee during Lon Nol's regime. In December 1968 Sihanouk took the ill-conceived decision to open casinos in Phnom Penh and Sihanoukville (Meyer, 1971; Osborne, 1979; Pomonti & Thion, 1971). The aim was to try and fill up the empty state coffers but also to fund Sihanouk's private charity. A group of Chinese swindlers from Macao associated with royals and top mandarins controlled the Phnom Penh casino in exchange of a daily royalty of USD 25,000 when in fact the profits during the first few months were between USD 150,000 and 200,000 per day, and then settled at USD 80,000 (Meyer, 1971). Pomonti and Thion (1971) recall the ruinous madness of this decision for the greater benefit of Chinese organised crime and corrupt Cambodian elites:

It was unbelievable. From the first day people rushed in. Thousands of people, shopkeepers, functionaries, high-school students, peasants were eager to loose their small savings on the tables of Chinese games. The casino was open day and night; the city seemed caught up in a frenzy... Some sold their car on the spot, others committed suicide; a circular prohibited entrance to the casino to any functionary with financial responsibilities, thefts multiplied... (p. 94)

The proceeds of the corruption were divided in two: the biggest share ended up overseas and the smallest one was put back into circulation as a 'voluntary contribution' to Sihanouk's private charity. The co-option of the 'gift-giving tradition' noted by Hughes (2006) in the Kingdom today is not a new phenomenon in Cambodia. Sihanouk did it well before Hun Sen when he liberally used this charity to fund various public works in the provinces that should have been the responsibility of the state. Here we can see how the process of state monopolisation discussed by Elias first arose as the private monopoly of despotic monarchs and later evolved with the taming of the state as a public monopoly that even today has yet to become genuinely public in Cambodia.

Shortly before the coup, Sihanouk's brother-in-law and secretary of state, Colonel Manorine, was caught red-handed in the smuggling of fabric from Hong Kong. Manorine was in charge of the national police and had been able to oversee and profit from the smuggling of rice coordinated by Chinese merchants and Vietnamese communists (Kirk, 1975). Meyer (1971) reported that Manorine 'had been known for a long time as the organiser and beneficiary of a network of traffickers and large-scale smuggling, and owner of most of the illegal gambling and prostitution dens, and responsible for hundreds of murders and disappearances' (p. 314). The case was discussed at the Assembly and was used as a pretext for the coup.

Lon Nol's Republic not only quickly turned dictatorial but surpassed Sihanouk's *Sangkum* in its appetite for corruption. Under the Khmer Republic, corruption in the army reached unprecedented levels, which amounted to high treason. It included using ghost soldiers to gain funds to pay rapidly promoted and corrupt officers, drafting children to inflate the membership, and siphoning large amounts of military aid from the USA so the generals could sell equipment to the enemy, build mansions, buy imported limousines, and open Swiss bank accounts. At the same time many soldiers did not even receive their meagre food rations and were reduced to engage in plundering or to the forced requisition of food and supplies from an already exhausted peasantry (Becker, 1986; Chandler, 1991; Meyer, 1971; Osborne, 1979; Ros, 1993; Shawcross, 1979). Already by 1967 the anger of the peasantry over their extreme exploitation prompted the start of the civil war.

The first civil war: 1967–1970

Most authors agree that the first civil war began in April 1967[3] with the Samlaut rebellion in Battambang province (Chandler, 1991; Kiernan, 2004; Kirk, 1975; Shawcross, 1979; Vickery, 1986). Kiernan and Boua (1982) described the Samlaut rebellion as 'the most extensive outbreak of violence since the 1946–54 uprising against the French'. From the events Kiernan related, we counted 1,200 homicides committed mainly against the insurgents. Douc Rasy, law lecturer and parliamentarian, reported, 'Sihanouk claimed in August 1968 that he had put to death 1500 Khmer Rouge during the rebellion in 67–68' (in Kiernan, 1982, p. 166).[4]

The Samlaut rebellion: 1967

The principal causes of the rebellion included Lon Nol's (by then Prime Minister) violent rice war, which had been brutal and costly to peasants, who had sometimes resisted and attacked soldiers (Chandler, 1991; Jennar, 1995, Kiernan, 2004; Kirk, 1971). In addition, recently arrived Khmer Krom refugees

---

[3] Most authors (Becker, 1986; Debré, 1976; Kiernan, 2004; Smith, 1968) date the start of the rebellion in April, but Meyer (1971, p. 158) puts it in February.
[4] According to Chandler (1991), Sihanouk remarked, 'I have read somewhere that the fighting resulted in ten thousand deaths' (p. 166). Rummel (1994, p. 165) conservatively estimated the democide toll during the *Sangkum* at 12,000 deaths and for the Lon Nol regime, 15,000, a grave underestimate given the attacks on the Vietnamese immediately following the coup of March 1970.

from South Vietnam had been given good common lands by the provincial governor of Battambang, displacing in the process the local peasants who were farming them (Becker, 1986; Debré, 1976). Finally, a number of farmers had their lands expropriated without compensation to make way for a sugar refinery (Shawcross, 1979). Confronted by increasing pauperisation, landlessness, and brutal authorities, the peasants were angry and had had enough. Meyer (1971) affirmed, 'Sihanouk had in his hand a very detailed report showing that the Samlaut peasants had been pushed to the brink by the exactions of the provincial authorities, the police and regional guards' (p. 158).

The rebellion ignited when two soldiers collecting rice were murdered in the Samlaut district of Battambang province and several people were killed during the ensuing riot (Debré, 1976, p. 110). Becker (1986) recounted:

> The villagers responsible for the killing boldly stole the weapons off the soldiers' corpses and returned to the same spot that afternoon brandishing more arms and waving sophisticated banners opposing the Nol government and US imperialism. They were joined by other peasants, and when the crowd reached 200 they marched on a youth agricultural settlement nearby and burned it to the ground. Unmolested they continued their protest and attacked the provincial guard post. (p. 104)

Sihanouk was abroad, but Prime Minister Lon Nol responded swiftly, and the repression quickly escalated from the police beating of a village chief to the army clubbing to death, then machine-gunning and bombing villagers. Many escaped to the forest, and Kiernan (1982) reported that in June 1967 'over 4000 villagers fled their home in southern Battambang Province for over a month' (p. 166). Battambang students visited the villagers in the forest and read pamphlets about a necessary revolution to illiterate peasants, but 'the peasants did not really understand: capitalism, feudalism, socialism... for them, there were the rich, the powerful and the poor, it was the order of the world... they had simply wanted to defend their villages' (Debré, 1976, p. 111).

Was the Samlaut rebellion spontaneous or premeditated? For Vickery (1986) and Shawcross (1979) it was spontaneous, but for Smith (1968) and Kiernan (2004) it had been planned by the Cambodian communists, and for Kirk (1971), by 'leftists financed in part by the Chinese embassy' (p. 241). However, all agree that declining socioeconomic conditions and brutalities were important factors. If Becker is correct in her recounting of the events, then 'waving sophisticated banners opposing the Nol government and US imperialism' suggests that it was somewhat organised. Communist radicalisation of some of the peasants could have easily led to the spontaneous murder of the two soldiers, while the subsequent riot was a more organised event. Officially over in June 1967, in fact the rebellion spread not only through Battambang province but also to Pursat, Kompong Speu, Kampong Thom, Kampong Chhnang, and Kampot. Chandler (1991, p. 166) observed that the rebellion mostly arose from local grievances and did not need 'orders from the CPK', but the CPK, according to their later accounts, was unable to capitalise on the nascent 'armed struggle' for lack of preparation.

Violence and repression followed in Phnom Penh, too. Blamed for the rebellion, Khieu Samphan, Hou Youn, and, later, Hu Nim disappeared. Those who were not quick enough to flee, such as Phouk Chhay, were arrested and sentenced to death.[5] Six days after Samphan's and Youn's disappearance, 15,000 students demonstrated in Phnom Penh to protest against what they believed to be an assassination; in fact, the two 'ghosts'[6] had taken to the hills of the northeast. On 28 June 1967, youths and students ransacked the offices of a right-wing newspaper and tore down a portrait of Sihanouk. As a result, the national student union, all private newspapers, and foreign friendship associations were banned. Freedom of expression had been given the *coup de grace*. Later in the year teachers from Phnom Penh accused of being 'reds' were executed by the police in Kampong Speu (Kiernan, 1982).

The spread of the insurrection and the highlanders' rebellion: 1968

Starting again in Battambang on 17 January 1968 with the attack by members of the Communist Party of Kampuchea (CPK) on a government post that killed a dozen provincial guards, the insurrection spread to many parts of the country. Jennar (1995) reported that on 25 February simultaneous attacks occurred in Battambang, Kampong Chhnang, Kampong Speu, Takeo, Kampot, and Koh Kong, and more than 10,000 villagers joined the insurgents, who lost 76 men during the campaign. In Koh Kong the attack targeted local authorities, and 10 subdistrict chiefs were assassinated. In the east, however, the revolutionaries were still reluctant[7] and only became engaged in August 1968, with a limited military campaign, killing 10 militiamen in Prey Veng (Kiernan, 2004). As the insurrection spread, defence and national police spending reached 30 per cent of the total budget, and in August, the National Assembly allowed arrests and detention of anyone merely suspected of involvement in the insurgency (Kirk, 1971; Slocomb, 2010).

Highlanders, victims of more land grabbing – now in part by colonies of retired soldiers and refugees – and racist policies, also took up their sabres, spears, and crossbows to fight what they regarded as the Phnom Penh colonialists. Once again, the trigger for their revolt had been the brutal response to

---

[5] Sihanouk eventually commuted his sentence to imprisonment.
[6] Hu Nim will join them in October and the three would thereafter often be referred to as the 'three ghosts'.
[7] See Kiernan (2004, 2008) and Heder (1980) for discussions of CPK attitudes and strategies in the east and the influence of the Vietnamese, whose geopolitical and revolutionary interests demanded that the CPK refrain from engaging in armed insurrection against Sihanouk.

their protest against the land grab. Beaten and chased away by the police, they came back to their villages to find Cambodian soldiers driving away inhabitants and plundering and destroying their homes. The first soldiers sent to squash the rebellion, unaccustomed to the terrain and weakened by tropical diseases, were massacred. The army sent planes and armoured vehicles in an extremely brutal repression that included bombing villages with napalm; yet, two thirds of Ratanakiri still escaped government control, perhaps because the highlanders in August and September 1968 had started using modern weaponry that the Vietnamese had given them (Debré, 1976; Meyer, 1971). Sihanouk admitted that 180 highlanders had been 'annihilated' and 30 ringleaders captured and subsequently executed (Becker, 1986).

Jungle revolutionaries: 1969

By 1969 Sihanouk was no longer in control of the *Sangkum* that openly rejected his wishes on important matters. The Vietnamese communists were also making more frequent use of their bases inside Cambodian territory, indeed launching the Tet offensive in January 1968 from them. While the number of armed insurgents was between 2,000 and 3,000, their Vietnamese supporters were estimated at 30,000 or 50,000 (Gordon & Young, 1970). Battambang and Pursat in the west, Kampot in the south, Svay Rieng in the east, and Rattanakiri in the northeast were hotbeds of insurgents. The first semester of 1969 'saw over 130 rebels killed, 100 wounded and 60 captured or forced to surrender', but, again, the east preferred to concentrate on political work rather than armed actions (Kiernan, 2004, p. 283). However, it did not prevent government massacres of eastern province civilians that predated those committed later by the Polpotists. Kiernan's (2004) informants claimed that

in 1968 or 1969 troops in Kampong Cham arrested over a hundred people, mostly students from the province capital, and took them in four trucks to May Sak forest in Sralap subdistrict of Tbaung Khmum, where they were executed and their bodies buried in two large pits... and another fifteen women, villagers and intellectuals were executed at O korum. (p. 293)

Yet, according to Becker (1986), by the end of 1969 these revolutionary groups had already recruited an army of more than 5,000 soldiers. They were sufficiently assured of popular support to punish in some regions village chiefs or notables collaborating with provincial authorities. The Cambodian revolutionaries, however, were far from unified. Debré (1976) distinguished those in the centre and towards Kratie who, like Khieu Samphan, Hou Youn, and Hu Nim, had fled from Phnom Penh; those from the northeast composed of highlanders and former Viet Minh Issaraks supported by the North Vietnamese; and elsewhere, rebel peasants who roamed the countryside, living from banditry.

The Pol Pot's group had grown resentful of Hanoi communists, who were primarily concerned with their own struggle. If the latter supported the political work of the eastern group, they were still reluctant to provide weapons for an armed insurrection against Sihanouk because his foreign policies, if increasingly ambiguous, were still to their advantage. The relative nonengagement of the east in armed combat since 1967 reinforced the resentment and isolation of Pot Pol's faction, by then the leading group in the CPK. This imposed physical and political isolation was turned into a revolutionary ideology of autarchy and purity:

They had to throw out the old ideas – 'international communism' had been of no help when they needed their allies – since concentrating on the Indochina-wide war, mostly the Vietnam War, had made them weak and cautious in their own country... Thus, in their isolation, Sar and the party emphasized the nobility of fighting on meagre resources, the purity of 'self-sufficiency.' Being pure became Sar's chief idea. It was an angry concept that easily fostered cruelty when that narrow idea of revolution nourished in the mountains was enlarged to include the whole nation. (Becker, 1986, p. 121)

Meyer (1971), who unlike Becker did not have the benefit of hindsight, also mentioned their isolation, but he argued that it was also their strength 'because through it they gained a total political freedom that allowed them to better adapt to the psychology of the Khmer peasant, which had not been the case during the Cambodian resistance of 1951–1953 dominated by the Viet-minh' (p. 201).

The second civil war: 1970–1975

In December 1969 Sihanouk realised that something was seriously wrong and his prestige and control threatened by the right. Twice Sihanouk tried to get the populace to show its support and loyalty to 'the father of the nation' and demand the resignation of the government and the dismissal of the assembly and new elections. However, the government counterattacked in late December by gathering 2,000 soldiers in civilian clothes 'ready for any eventuality' (Meyer, 1971). Sihanouk admitted defeat and shortly after left for France. Economic collapse, repression, authoritarianism, the unsustainable neutralist waltz with the Cold War giants, xenophobia, and corruption were among the main factors that undermined support for Sihanouk and led to the coup of 18 March 1970. The coup was in fact a bloodless coup of *chef d'état*, which left the government and the assembly intact (Becker, 1986; Slocomb, 2010).

Using the pretext of a case of grand corruption involving Sihanouk's brother-in-law but also more or less 'persuaded' by the presence of the army outside, the Assembly unanimously withdrew its confidence from Sihanouk as chief of state (Becker, 1986; Jennar, 1995). Historians have debated and disagreed about the likelihood of US involvement in the coup. For Meyer (1971), the

Central Intelligence Agency (CIA) was involved. Becker (1986) is noncommittal, saying that circumstantial evidence abounds, which may have 'led Cambodians and foreigners alike to believe that the US was behind it' (p. 127). Vickery (1986), however, like Frieson (1992), not only points to the lack of hard evidence but also contends that 'given Sihanouk's shift during 1969, the American government would have seen little reason to remove him' (p. 20).

Postcoup demonstrations

Peasant loyalists

Between 26 and 28 March 1970, large-scale pro-Sihanouk demonstrations, involving altogether about 56,600 peasants,[8] were organised in Kampong Cham, Takeo, Kampot, Prey Veng, and even Siem Reap. They were brutally repressed with heavy military weaponry – tanks, heavy machine guns, antiaircraft and big guns, and armed speedboats – and marked by new atrocities that we discuss below. Many authors have written detailed accounts of these demonstrations and their savage repression, and we refer the interested reader to them (see Becker, 1986; Frieson, 1992; Kiernan, 1982; Meyer, 1971; Pomonti & Thion, 1971; and Shawcross, 1979). In 3 days, over 500 people were slaughtered, including a few on the government side such as two parliamentarians and Lon Nol's brother, Lon Nil, whose livers were eaten by demonstrators in Kampong Cham. If the rate of 170 homicides per day during the postcoup demonstrations had been maintained until April 1975, the second civil war would have killed 326,000 people. However, as we will see, the violence escalated, and most estimates of the number of people killed on all sides between 1970 and 1975 are around 600,000.[9]

Were the demonstrations spontaneous or organised, by whom, and were they essentially Sihanoukist? Accounts of peasants brandishing Sihanouk's portraits, offering their chest to the bullets, and shouting 'long live Samdech Euv' (Kiernan, 2004; Pomonti & Thion, 1971) are certainly evidence that Sihanouk remained popular in rural Cambodia and that some of these peasants may have risen up spontaneously. However, Meyer (1971) remarked that 'spontaneous demonstrations being unconceivable in Cambodia, it is certain that the peasants, little aware of the events, had been mobilised in Sihanouk's name. But it seems plausible that this gamble had been organised by the Cambodian revolutionaries to gain power and not improvised by the Vietnamese' (p. 333).[10] This

---

[8] This figure was estimated from a count of the number of demonstrators reported by Kiernan and Boua (1982) in diverse localities during these 3 days. Jennar (1995) estimates more than 10,000 in the first demonstration organised in Kampong Cham, and Frieson (1992), quoting Ponchaud, 50,000 overall.

[9] Rummel (1994, p. 165) estimated the civil war deaths caused *by the KR* until April 1975 at 211,000.

[10] Lon Nol blamed the demonstrations on the Vietnamese communists.

is also the view of Kiernan (1982, 2004), who provided evidence that most of the localities involved in the demonstrations had been electoral strongholds of the *Pracheachon* and the 'three ghosts' – Kieu Samphan, Hou Youn, and Hu Nim – at a time when Sihanouk was publicly and sometimes violently campaigning against them.

As we have described several times in this book, there had also been a long history of manifestations of peasant anger and rioting, targeting local administrations and destroying their documents. The riots of 1970 followed in that tradition.

Never since the Samlaut revolt in 1967 had the resentment of the peasantry manifested in such an explosion... The demonstrations first and foremost targeted the administration and all that it represented... The letting of steam against the functionaries and administrative buildings had a meaning. Instinctively they turned their sight towards the capital... indeed what is more natural but to march on the place that most directly represented power? (Pomonti & Thion, 1971, p. 177)

For the peasants, 'the place that most directly represented power' was the hated and corrupt city that devoured the taxes imposed on the peasants. Vickery (1986) echoed this view: 'Even if Cambodian society was not "feudal", and the peasantry's enemy was urban business men rather than landlords, this did not make the revolutionary potential any less. It simply meant that if the Cambodian peasantry became revolutionary, they would direct their wrath against the towns' (p. 19).

Joy and disappointments

In Phnom Penh, by contrast, not only business and military elites but also the middle class and many young people, mostly republican idealists, applauded the coup. Their joy would be short lived. Utterly disappointed by the authoritarianism and corruption of the Sihanouk regime, they could not foresee that the republic led by Marshal Lon Nol would soon become one ruled by martial law and even more corrupt than the *Sangkum*. However, for now and as proof of the liberal times to come, all the 486 political prisoners of the *Sangkum*, from right to left, were released, and some of them quickly fled Phnom Penh to join Sihanouk's newly created National United Front of Kampuchea (NUFK) (Frieson, 1992; Meyer, 1971; Shawcross, 1979) or the CPK (Chandler, 1991). Fed with romantic notions of the founding of the French Republic, to which the coup was likened, and promises of *liberté*, *égalité*, and *fraternité*, they could now enlist in the army to fight the 'enemies of freedom': the feudalists, the communists, and the Vietnamese forces occupying large swaths of Cambodia. From a force of 35,000 and almost entirely as a result of voluntary enlistment, Lon Nol's army by the end of the year had grown to 150,000 young, inexperienced, and badly trained, equipped, and led soldiers who would prove no match for the Vietnamese forces (Jennar, 1995; Kiernan, 2004; Osborne, 1973).

Prelude of a perfect storm

There is no single explanation of how the Khmer Rouge hemoclysm or bloodbath came to be; rather, we argue that a number of factors coalesced and intersected to create a 'perfect storm'. We discuss some of these factors below, but our list is not exhaustive and the next chapter discusses these and other factors. Among the converging factors already evident was the anti-Vietnamese genocidal xenophobia that grew under the Lon Nol regime but that had already started under Sihanouk. All sides in the conflict committed acts of extreme violence and perpetrated cruelties, and this included the terror and destruction of the American bombing of Cambodia. The Khmer communist movement became more concerned about their relationship with the Vietnamese communists and their putative threat to Cambodia's territorial integrity. The eastern zone adjacent to Vietnam differed from the west and southwest zones in their pragmatic response to the growing tensions between these supposedly fraternal revolutionary movements. Finally, Sihanouk entered into an alliance with the Khmer Rouge, which would prove to have drastic consequences up to the present day.

Xenophobia: en route for genocidal massacres

Priming

Since the early nineteenth century, Vietnamophobia has been an enduring characteristic of many Khmers. We have seen how Cambodian history had shaped this antagonism and created the notion of a 'hereditary enemy' that could be exploited for demagogic reasons of state by successive regimes until 1979. However, from 1970 onward Vietnamophobia turned into genocidal massacres. Meyer (1971) noted that since the mid 1960s the condition of the Vietnamese living in Cambodia had deteriorated because of professional interdictions, discriminatory decisions by the administration and the justice system, and an increasing number of exactions against them by the police. In 1967 there were 250,000 Vietnamese in Cambodia (Slocomb, 2010), but with the many refugees fleeing the war in Vietnam their number may have reached 300,000 in 1970 (Meyer, 1971). As early as 1968, confronted by the rural rebellions, Sihanouk and his right-wing government used the old xenophobic tactic to try and re-create a 'national consensus' (Debré, 1976; Meyer, 1971), and beginning in 1969, 'raids were organised, hundreds of Vietnamese were cooped up, sometimes for days, in some kinds of camps outside the city without any official reason given to them. The fallacious pretext of a particularly high level of criminality in the Vietnamese district, dubbed catholic village, allowed all kinds of police exactions' (Pomonti & Thion 1971, p. 185).

The 'priming phase'[11] of genocidal massacres had started. On 8 March 1970, the first series of 'spontaneous' anti-Vietcong demonstrations of 200–300 people, organised by local authorities on government orders, broke out simultaneously in Svay Rieng and four other localities close to the border (Jennar, 1995; Meyer, 1971). On 11 March 1970, several thousands of demonstrators ransacked the embassies of the Democratic Republic of Vietnam and of the Provisional Revolutionary Government of the Republic of South Vietnam in Phnom Penh and pillaged neighbouring Vietnamese shops. Although they were presented as the expression of popular feelings, these demonstrations, Meyer (1971) argued, had in fact been planned a month earlier by Sihanouk to justify his request for the withdrawal of Vietnamese communist troops from Cambodia. The authorities' lack of interest in this Vietnamophobic wave of violence supports Meyer's (1971) suggestion:

[On March 12th and 13th] bands of young hooligans spread into the Russey Keo district where the population [was] in majority Catholic Vietnamese. Habitants were beaten, girls raped, houses pillaged, and the church desecrated. The police remained indifferent, when they did not compete with the plunderers for the loot. A personal intervention from the queen mother to the president of the National Assembly, to general Lon Nol, and the principal people responsible for the security, was necessary for a military unit to be sent and bring back order. (p. 313)

Genocide and revenge

The Vietnamophobic wave did not stop after the coup or after the postcoup demonstrations, which were blamed by Lon Nol on Vietnamese communists, but transformed into what Debré (1976, p. 133) called 'a genocide'. On 10 April 1970, when some insurgents shot at a Cambodian navy gunboat cruising on the Tonle Sap and wounded an officer, the army and the police had found a pretext for the systematic massacre of thousands of Vietnamese civilians. The shots had been fired near a fishing village close to the Vietnamese and Catholic community of Chrui Changvar, which faced Phnom Penh across the Tonle Sap and was inhabited by 3,000 people. The next day the fishing village was razed by the Cambodian air force. On 12 April, soldiers came to Chrui Changvar at night, arrested 800 men aged between 14 and 65 years old, carried them on boats to a close-by island, and slaughtered them: 'Their bodies will be found some days later floating on the river, sometimes ten of them tied up together, sometimes decapitated, most of the time riddled with bullets. One of the authors of the

---

[11] See Hinton's (1998, 2005) discussion of the various stages in the development of genocidal massacres as well as Kiernan's (2007). They provide examples of how the demonisation and dehumanisation of a particular class or ethnic group is the basic preparation or priming necessary to incite violence against the dehumanised group.

massacre will recall that at the end "we cut their throat to save ammunition"' (Pomonti & Thion 1971, p. 184).

Similar massacres took place in other localities. In the town of Prasaut (Svay Rieng) numerous Vietnamese were also killed by soldiers; elsewhere they were detained in camps, while in other Vietnamese communities the army engaged in pillage and rape (Becker, 1986; Pomonti & Thion, 1971). The government admitted to the arrest of 30,000 Vietnamese and the incarceration of 7,000 of them, and it transformed warehouses, factory floors, and sport grounds into concentration camps where the victims, crammed in horrific conditions without water, food, and medicine were 'turned over to the army and agitators who after pillaging their houses, massacred them with machine guns, cut their throat and drowned them in the river' (Debré, 1976, p. 133). For the police, the pillaging of Vietnamese communities became a source of profit, and it seemed that xenophobia, nationalism, and greed had turned banditry into a patriotic duty. The Buddhist, Catholic, and lay emergency services independently estimated that between 20,000 and 30,000 Vietnamese had been killed in Cambodia after the coup of 18 March 1970 (Pomonti & Thion, 1971, p. 187).

Whereas the army and the police were actively engaged in the genocide, there are diverging accounts of the attitude of the Cambodian populace. For Pomonti and Thion (1971), the populace almost never associated with the massacres, and there were many instances when Cambodians helped and protected the Vietnamese, hiding them in their houses or providing those in the detention camps with food at cheap prices. Thus, the government brought in martial law in June 1970 to intimidate Cambodians who did not follow the genocidal movement and protected Vietnamese friends. For Debré (1976), however, the xenophobic harangues found an echo in the population, and if Cambodians did not actively join in the murders, they let them happen and rushed to the abandoned houses to loot them. Whatever was the actual scale and degree of popular participation in this particular genocide, we will see in the next chapter that criminologists who focus on the phenomenon in general argue that it is never a simple top-down process where the state commands and perpetrators merely follow orders (Dumont, 2006; Felices-Luna, 2012; Leman-Langlois, 2006; Liwerant, 2012; Tanner, 2006, 2012).

The genocide of the Vietnamese communities in Cambodia would not be forgotten. The international community, including the USA, protested against the genocide. In Saigon, the populace and the government had been incensed by the Vietnamophobic massacres and exactions perpetrated against their compatriots by their so-called allies in the war against communism. During the repatriation of the victims, which had been negotiated between the two governments, young Vietnamese deportees immediately enrolled in the South Vietnamese army with the promise that they would be deployed in Cambodia and, therefore, be given an opportunity for revenge (Debré, 1976; Meyer, 1971). The US and the South Vietnamese governments did not wait for an official invitation from their ally to enter Cambodia and chase the communists, but invaded on 29 April. While US soldiers razed Memot and Snuol (Kampong Cham), South Vietnamese soldiers took a brutal revenge, killing, robbing, and raping Khmer peasants everywhere they marched (Becker, 1987; Debré, 1976; Gordon & Young, 1971; Jennar, 1995; Kiernan, 2004, 2008; Meyer, 1971; Shawcross, 1979). Debré (1976) recalls that the radio in Phnom Penh warned its listeners: 'An operation by the south Vietnamese ally's troops is scheduled tomorrow in the region of Neak Luong; leave your houses, hide your money, send your daughters to the city' (p. 136).

Extreme violence and cruelty

From the time of the Samlaut rebellion in 1967, not only the lethality of the conflict but also the number of atrocities increased. Government forces fighting 'the reds' committed most of these atrocities. Kiernan remarked that prisoners taken by the army were usually shot, while Meyer (1971) reported: 'Small groups coming down to the plain were often captured by the detachments of the regular army and the prisoners beheaded or massacred with all the niceties in use. Following superior orders, the "reds" had to be clubbed down "to save cartridges"' (pp. 193–4). According to Debré (1976), soldiers 'were forced to club the condemned men three times: first against communism, second for the throne, and third for religion, until death' (p. 122).

In 1968, Sihanouk described the fate of captured 'reds' and claimed: 'I... had them roasted. When you roast a duck you normally eat it. But when we roasted these fellows, we had to feed them to the vultures' (Kiernan, 1982, p. 195). He might very well have meant it literally rather than metaphorically. For example, in 1968 and on Sihanouk's orders, 40 schoolteachers accused of subversive activities were tied up by groups of two or three, thrown from a cliff at Bokor, and left there agonising for several days while students in Kampot were beaten to death (Debré, 1976; Kiernan, 2004; Meyer, 1971). Then Sihanouk offered rewards to governmental units for victorious 'combat'. To get the bounty, soldiers had to bring the head of an insurgent. As a result, patrols came up with imaginary clashes and started bringing back the heads of unlucky individuals who could pass for rebels. Quickly, they were required to also 'bring back a weapon because to get the bounty a number of soldiers killed and beheaded highlanders who had nothing to do with the insurrection' (Debré, 1976, p. 115). Khmer newspapers published photos showing a rifle and a severed head next to each other on a mat; in Kampot severed heads were displayed in the market, and Becker (1986) mentioned 'enemies heads stuck on poles' (p. 120).

The use of extreme violence occurred throughout the pre- and postcoup period. Occasionally, some victims were disembowelled alive and their liver eaten, a practice that was rare but that had occurred throughout Cambodia's history (Hinton, 2005; Kiernan, 2008). In Battambang province, 'two young children accused of being messengers for the guerrillas had their head sawn off with palm fronds' and in Kampong Cham local authorities 'were ordered to take part in beating innocent peasants to death' (Kiernan, 1982, p. 195). Communist troops would generally execute local authorities that carried out repressive government policies, but not peasants, although some exceptions were noted particularly in regions controlled by Polpotist factions.[12] Finally, during the March 1970 postcoup demonstrations in support of Sihanouk in Takeo, tanks rolled over the demonstrators; however, 'some people were not yet dead but lying there, waving flags in their hand and saying "... long Live Samdech Euv" [so] soldiers brought back the tanks and flattened them all again' (Kiernan, 2004, p. 302). Other atrocities would be perpetrated against Vietnamese civilians during the genocidal massacres of April 1970. Atrocities will multiply, in the metaphorical and literal sense of the expression 'with a vengeance', during the second civil war and the DK regime.

Several authors have wondered about the alchemy of Khmer violence. Contemporary observers such as Meyer (1971) and Pomonti and Thion (1971) remarked that the bloody parades described above were popular, a view echoed by Debré (1976): 'The crowd, it is true, enjoyed these strong spectacles; the exposition of the tortured bodies of thieves or the severed heads of bandits on the markets aroused curiosity rather than reprobation; public executions with a sabre were very popular like in all the countries where traditional banditry leads to repressive, expeditious and brutal habits' (p. 122).

Becker (1986) pointed out that the Polpotists' obsession with purity was 'an angry concept that easily fostered cruelty' (p. 121). However, the Khmer Rouge were not alone in their relishment of cruelty. Cruelties had been perpetrated many times in Cambodian history, including by the French protectors and of course during the first and second civil wars between 1967 and 1975. As criminologists, we put aside extreme forms of cultural relativism and consider cruelties and atrocities that an Orientalist perspective may label barbarity or savagery as dimensions of violence worth studying not only as ordinary and mass or state crimes but also as particular forms of cultural expression. Meyer (1971) rejected the myth of 'the gentle Khmer' popularised during the French Protectorate:

---

[12] Kiernan (2004) described two incidents in mid 1968 when five civilians were robbed and killed in Koh Kong and seven peasants were killed in Kampong Thom. Kiernan suggested that the infamous Polpotist warlord Ke Pauk, as cruel and bloody as Ta Mok, may have organised these attacks.

Suffice to read in the Cambodian Codes the list of the various tortures that were still in use during the last century to entertain some doubts about the gentleness of the Khmers. In reality, a deep-seated inclination for cruelty is ready to surface at the first occasion, as we have observed with the tortures and methods of execution inflicted on the Khmers 'rouge' prisoners or peasant revolts of 1968 and 1969. Cambodian leaders are actually surprised that we could qualify as barbarous the publication of photos of severed heads or the projection of a movie showing close ups of the last breath of an executed man. (pp. 37–9)

He also warned of the sociocultural factors that could fuel mass violence and atrocities:

We can actually fear that the current events [the coup against Sihanouk, the civil war, the bad treatment of the peasantry] may provoke a dangerous awakening of the 'quiet and peaceful' Khmer peasant. Unpredictable in his daily behaviour, he is even more so in his emotional reactions. He may lose his patience and prudence without warning signs and then be capable of all types of excess... There is not a country in the world when a raging mob is not capable of committing the worst atrocities. However, in Cambodia, collective violence to a certain extent takes the form of a ritual festival in which one destroys, burns, and kills with great bursts of laughter!

Pomonti and Thion (1971), however, found these brutalities difficult to understand:

Generally Cambodians are gentle and peaceful people endowed with great patience. But it seems that when they are removed from their village environment and its customary constraints and confronted to the issue of life in war or banditry, all constraints are removed in one swipe, as if the absence of intermediary bodies in their society was paralleled in their individual psychology: the absence of a gradual code of behaviour allowing to react to the confrontation at different levels. Depending on the degree of pressure, one could then move from extreme docility to the most implacable cruelty. One therefore would have to attribute to the Khmer culture this absence of faculty of adaptation, at least and as far as the history of the kingdom and its institution bear witness. However, it is only a hypothesis, and for all that of a gratuitous nature, that many facts could possibly contradict. (p. 184)

But Chandler (1991) took a similar stand to Meyer: 'the potential for violent behaviour was always there, supported by abundant evidence from nineteenth-century wars, bandit depredations in colonial times, the Issaraks, and more recently the anti-Communist commandos mobilized in the 1960s' (p. 241). A more encompassing analysis, however, is Elias's psychogenetic mechanism of growing sensitisation to violence and emotional control that develop during the civilising process as the state monopolisation of force and interdependency increase. The musings and illustrations provided by the authors above show that this psychogenetic mechanism of sensitisation to extreme violence and cruelty had not really developed in Cambodia, and the poorly developed sociogenetic processes of state monopolisation and interdependency were probably associated with this state of affairs.

We will see in the next chapter that some anthropologists, particularly Hinton (2005), have addressed the dimension of history and culture with some focus on keeping face and revenge in Khmer culture to account for the atrocities committed during the Democratic Kampuchea (DK) regime. So, was there anything new in the violence of the 1970s? What was new, said Chandler (1991), 'was the increase in its occurrence, on the one hand, and the absence or erosion of legal or community sanctions against it, on the other' (p. 241). The violence was widely deployed not only by the Cambodian state and Khmer Rouge but also by the United States and its allies.

Democide from the air: the US aerial bombardment

Since the early 1960s teams from the US Special Forces had conducted secret reconnaissance missions and mine-laying incursions in Cambodia. From 4 October 1965, the Johnson and then the Nixon administrations engaged in increasingly deadly terror bombing of Cambodia. Justified by 'reasons of state', the number of deaths and large-scale devastation they caused would probably today be regarded as a crime against humanity. The American bombing did not generate the atrocities of the revolutionary violence or cause Cambodian people to become violent. It was nevertheless criminal, at least in a humanistic sense. It certainly brutalised Cambodian people further and fostered deep hatred against those who were regarded as responsible, and this included, rightly or wrongly, Lon Nol soldiers and city dwellers.

It was just the beginning, and from mid March 1969 to May 1970 the US administration embarked on a secret bombing mission (known under the code name *Menu*) of Vietcong sanctuaries. These bombing operations were hidden from the US Congress and public opinion (Becker, 1986; Jennar, 1995; Kiernan, 2004; Shawcross, 1979). Sihanouk's attitude had been particularly ambiguous on this topic. In March 1969 he had started a virulent campaign against Vietcong and North Vietnamese infiltrations in Cambodian territories and, according to Meyer (1971), unofficially told the USA that he would not protest if they only bombed the known sanctuaries. The bombings were more extensive than that, and later on Sihanouk eventually protested half-heartedly. In the meantime, and despite serious air-raid damage to Kampong Cham rubber plantations by the American air force, diplomatic relations with the USA were reestablished in July 1969.

Kiernan (2004) estimated that between March 1969 and March 1970, over 3,600 US bombing operations took place, and 'night after night through the summer, fall and winter of 1969 and into the early months of 1970... peasants were killed [but] no one knows how many' (p. 285). Napalm and the defoliant Agent Orange were also used. In April and May 1969, Agent Orange was spread over 85,000 hectares; by 1970 the majority of rubber plantations had been destroyed (Gordon & Young, 1971). These crimes, perpetrated by one of the most powerful states, were followed by several massacres when on 29 April 1970 the USA and their South Vietnamese allies secretly invaded Cambodia to destroy Viet Cong supply bases. As murderous as these excursions were, they pale in comparison to the massive carpet-bombing campaign conducted all over Cambodia in 1973. Following the declassification of the US Air Force archives in 2000, we now know that between 4 October 1965 and 15 August 1973, the USA dropped 2,756,941 tons of munitions on Cambodia, in the course of 230,516 operations destroying 113,716 targets (Kiernan & Owen, 2006).[13] In comparison, the Allies during all of World War II dropped 2 million tons of munitions, including those on Hiroshima and Nagasaki. One of the most intensive campaigns against a nation since World War II, it ravaged villages; terrorised, killed, and maimed thousands of Cambodian peasants; and destroyed livestock and crops. Nevertheless, the very same year, Kissinger was awarded and accepted the Nobel Peace Prize.

Fraternal rivalries: reds against reds

The Cambodian communist movement was far from being united.[14] There was a growing split between CPK leaders in the east influenced by the Vietnamese style of Marxism-Lenino-Stalinism and others, particularly in the southwest, following Pol Pot's ultra Maoism. In fact, the black-clad Polpotists and the green-fatigue-clad eastern communists were deeply suspicious of each other. The Vietnamese communists and the Cambodian communists who adhered to an internationalist and pragmatic form of communist revolution also adhered to strict revolutionary discipline, not only avoiding harm to peasants but protecting and helping them in this phase of 'winning over the peasants' (Kiernan, 2004; Meyer, 1971; Pomonti & Thion, 1971; Shawcross, 1979). Unsurprisingly, they enjoyed growing support from the peasantry and by the end of 1970 controlled already two thirds of Cambodia's territory, but mostly the east and northeast (Gordon & Young, 1971).

However, in the regions controlled by the ethnonationalist and Vietnamophobic Polpotists (broadly, the southwest, the west, and the northeast) tyrannical rules were imposed and xenophobic attacks and the massacre of peasants had

---

[13] Rummel (1994, p. 165) estimated the US democide (i.e. the killing of noncombatants) in Cambodia between March 1970 and August 1973 at 60,000 deaths. Since the declassified archives have revealed a fivefold increase in the tonnage of bombs dropped on Cambodia, it is possible that the number of casualties is much higher.

[14] For a detailed and in-depth analysis of CPK factions, see Heder (1980) and Kiernan (2004, 2008).

started. In fact, already in 1968 clashes between Polpotists and Vietnamese communists had occurred in the northeast (Kiernan, 2004). The first recorded massacre by Polpotists occurred in the town of Baray (Kampong Thom) in August 1971, where they slaughtered at least 180 villagers who had previously sheltered Vietnamese communists (Jennar, 1995; Kiernan, 2004). Then they started to physically eliminate the *Hanoi Khmer*, that is, the Khmer communists of the 1950s who had returned from their exile in North Vietnam to fight for the Cambodian revolution and had the misfortune to end up in regions controlled by the xenophobic 'national-communists'.[15] The black-clad 'cormorants' systematically executed captured Lon Nol soldiers, but the Vietnamese communists and their eastern Cambodian allies seldom executed common soldiers, preferring to indoctrinate them to turncoat. By mid 1972, in the regions they controlled, Polpotists were driving out not only Vietnamese communist troops but also Vietnamese civilians who had managed to escape the Lon Nol's genocide of 1970 (Kiernan, 2004). In these regions the totalitarian and murderous policies, which were installed by the Polpotists after April 1975, were already in place. In August 1974, news from the village of Sarsar Sdam in Siem Reap, captured by the Polpotists, provided an atrocious glimpse of things to come when they would rule the country:

The whole village had been burned down... over 60 peasants had been brutally killed: old women had been nailed to the walls of their houses before they were burned alive, children had been torn apart by hand. In another incident in January 1975, about 40 civilians were reported to have been massacred and mutilated at Ang Snuol on Route 4. (Shawcross, 1979, p. 353)

Revengeful alliances

On 23 March 1970, coup de theatre in Beijing: Sihanouk announced he was entering into a coalition with the very people he had for 3 years brutally hunted down, imprisoned, and vowed to exterminate. The National United Front of Kampuchea, including communists and Sihanoukists, was established and Sihanouk called for an armed insurrection against the new regime in Phnom Penh. The second civil war had started. However, this time Vietnamese communists had no longer any reasons to restrain their Cambodian counterpart, and Sihanouk's engagement would allow the Cambodian communists on the ground to rally many more combatants. Why would Sihanouk, who knew and publicly acknowledged that he would never regain the power he had lost, enter into such an unholy alliance? In his own words, revenge:

Indeed in the struggle that I am determined to carry until the end, or at least until my death in the *maquis* that I will join soon, I also seek a personal goal, which is

---

[15] In orthodox Marxist terms it is of course a perfect oxymoron.

revenge... Regarding my personal revenge, it will be fully satisfied in our left and extreme left taking power and the elimination of a right and extreme right which is particularly execrable as they had the cowardice and baseness to attribute to myself their own 'sins of Israel' and all the responsibilities for the socio-economic failures of which they were the main architects. (Meyer, 1971, p. 381)

Accused of corrupt behaviour and venality by the plotters, he declared to a correspondent of the Agence France Press on 16 April:

If I should ascribe a personal motive to my struggle I would say that I want to avenge myself for having been so cowardly, so despicably, so viciously slandered, insulted and humiliated by my enemies from the far right... Had they only removed me from power without dragging my name through the mud I would probably have been content with a peaceful exile in France. (in Meyer, 1971, p. 372)

We will see that the extreme, all-or-nothing politics of revenge that Hinton (2005, p. 45) called 'disproportionate revenge' or 'a head for an eye', already visited in the reports of the Siem Reap governor in the 1930s, continued to leave a bloody trail in Cambodian history up to the present time.

Fascist brother enemies

If, as Meyer argued (1971), Sihanouk's behaviour became incoherent when he abdicated his responsibilities and turned to movie making in 1966, Lon Nol did not bring any level-headedness to the regime. Following the genocide of the Vietnamese, Lon Nol proposed to put into concentration camps the 400,000 or so Chinese living in Cambodia. This time the ministers, most of them Sino-Khmer like Lon Nol himself (Meyer, 1971, p. 338), stopped the madness, but many Chinese, alerted by the start of a Sinophobic newspaper campaign, sent their families and their capital to Hong Kong and Singapore (Becker, 1986; Debré, 1976; Meyer, 1971). This did not stop the 'mad marshal' from advocating his fascistic brand of ethnonationalism, called *Neo-Khmerism*. In the army, instead of providing training and equipment, he promoted the practice of all sorts of witchcraft supposed to confer invincibility to the soldiers in their holy war against the infidels:

Lon Nol now believes himself possessed of the power of divination and, consequently, saw his military orders as holy writ or *khuon*, the unchallengeable wisdom gleaned from magical formulae and sacred scriptures. He believes he was the leader prophesied by Lord Buddha himself to lead a war for the survival of Buddhism in Cambodia against the *thmils*, or foreign infidels. (Becker, 1986, pp. 138–9)

Lon Nol resembled the millenarian cranks of the nineteenth and early twentieth centuries, called *illuminés* by the French, but unlike them, he had the state power of a Caligula and was sending to a carnage several hundred thousands of people.[16]

Much has been written about the nature of the DK regime established by the Pol Pot–led communists. Was it Marxist-Leninist, Stalinist, Maoist, a new form of Asiatic despotism, a premodern peasant revolution, or straightforward fascism? (See Becker, 1986; Chandler, 1992; Frieson, 1992; Kiernan, 2008; Thion, 1993; Vickery, 1986.) Becker (1986) argued that despite apparent differences Lon Nol and Pol Pot were 'fascist brother enemies'. Brother Number One, Pol Pot, was simply 'Lon Nol without sorcery', and they were both 'heading toward the same goal of turning Cambodia into a fascist state': 'Their goals were fascist in the strict definition of the phenomenon: a regime that exalts nation and race, stands for a centralized autocratic government headed by a dictatorial leader, imposes severe economic and social regimentation, and forcibly suppresses the opposition. Both leaders also encouraged fascism's by-products – racism and xenophobia' (p. 136). But in the final analysis, from our criminological standpoint, these various ideological appellations do not matter much. They all refer to totalitarian-prone regimes that, independently of their specific ideological brand, believe in and use similar forms of collective violence to gain and maintain power.

Next, we shall see how Pol Pot with his clique of followers and his army of poor indoctrinated teenage peasant-soldiers would bring the perfect storm to its horrific conclusion.

---

[16] On 25 June 1970, general mobilisation was proclaimed for both men and women aged between 18 and 60 years (Jennar, 1995).

8 The perfect storm: decivilising state and society: 1975–1979

For nearly 4 years, from April 1975 to January 1979, *Angkar*, the 'organisation', ruled Cambodia by fear. Perhaps up to a quarter of the population perished, of whom large numbers were summarily murdered, beaten, and deliberately starved. Terror, autarky, collectivisation, ethnic purity, forced mobilisation of the masses in state building, and deliberate isolation were the hallmarks of the new state. Despite controversy about the scale of the lethal violence due to the policies and practices of the regime, there is ample evidence to situate the form, sequence, and proximate causes of mass murder in Democratic Kampuchea (DK). Our thesis is that DK, realised by the secret state and opaque instrument of the Communist Party of Kampuchea (CPK) known as Angkar, set about the further and complete decivilisation of Cambodia via a rapid and deliberate process of disintegration of the old society. Brought into being by terror, the new one was to be a pure communist society. Civil war, and with it the domination of warrior values and the widespread performance of authorised murder, had been the prelude to DK, and these murderous habits came to be played out in the CPK's radical social transformation of Cambodia. The strategies and decivilising shocks administered to Cambodian society by Angkar overwhelmed customary restraints against violence. The reversion of the state to archaic barbarism has occurred throughout history, and Cambodia is a compelling modern-day example. In this chapter we focus on the types of violence that were perpetrated in this period and examine through a criminological lens the extraordinary scale of lethality that occurred.

The story of the Cambodian hemoclysm,[1] its causes and evolution, have been documented and accounted for by a sustained and critical scholarship. We draw on this literature to account for the extreme lethality of the DK regime led by the Communist Party of Kampuchea.[2] First, we briefly outline the scale of the

---

[1] We use the term *hemoclysm*, which encompasses all forms of mass killing, including the death of war combatants, rather than the term *genocide*, which is too narrow to account for the varieties of victims of the mass murders that took place during DK. Under the 1948 Convention, only the killing of the Muslim Cham and Vietnamese minorities qualifies as genocide.

[2] The Cambodian Documentation Centre (CDC) and its director Youk Chhang, as well as Ben Kiernan, Chantou Boua, David Chandler, Michael Vickery, Stephen Heder, Elisabeth Becker, Alex

violence during DK and then describe the phases, patterns, and surges of violence against different 'classes' of victims that occurred with the implementation of the DK's nation-building plans, and in doing so offer a sketch of the DK's short-lived attempt to create a communist utopia. Then we situate our criminological analysis in terms of the struggle to define megacrime and mass violence and the limitations of current criminological theories. Next, we outline the explanatory contribution of both macrolevel and microlevel criminological theories about the causes of extreme violence and how these aid us in understanding how individuals and the DK regime were able to implement terror and repeatedly perform acts of murder. We conclude by reexamining the likely causes of this catastrophic surge in mass violence and argue that although ample precursors of such violence are evident in Cambodia's history, the convergence of a multitude of adverse external and internal factors combined with the particular form of radical Maoist policies imbued with indigenous overconfidence produced a perfect storm of violence.

Accounts of the unfolding of the revolution help us both contextualise the extraordinary or exceptional 'boom' in homicide that occurred during DK and, in later chapters, the apparent rapid 'bust' or decline in homicide that seems to follow the pattern we have already seen in Cambodia's past. Using the term 'boom' to refer to the atrocities inflicted during the Cambodian terror is in fact absurdly inadequate as the scale of homicidal violence far exceeded anything before or after. The scale of homicide (including neglect of the necessities of life) was the result of a generalised practice of rule by terror and is to be measured in fractions of the population rather than in conventional rates per 100,000; indeed, it is estimated that, depending on estimation of fatalities and total population, between one fifth and one quarter of the population perished in a period of less than 4 years. Most scholars place the loss of life at about 1.7 million, although lower and higher estimates have been made. For example, an early estimate by Vickery (1984) placed the death toll at 740,000, or about 10–12 per cent of the estimated population of approximately 7.1 million.[3] A thorough review by Kiernan (2008, pp. 456–62), based on an estimated population of 7.89 million in 1975, produced a death toll of 1,671,000, or 21 per cent of the population. Kiernan estimated that about 29 per cent of the 'new' people perished, with a higher proportion among the Chinese, and 16 per cent of the 'base' people, with a higher proportion among the Cham.[4] The proportion

---

Hinton, Karl Jackson, Khamboly Dy, and many others, have laboured to describe, document, and understand the lethal catastrophe that was DK.

[3] Rummel (1994, p. 192) noted that one of the highest estimates – 3,315,000 deaths – was based on a household census in 1982–3 conducted by the PRK.

[4] The term 'new' people referred to those who had been expelled from the cities and towns, and 'base' people were those in the KR rural support areas during the civil war. In a 1977 speech, Ieng Sary, deputy prime minister, estimated one million casualties, or 13 per cent of the population,

of the deaths that can be regarded as murderous (i.e. with the intention to kill)[5] was substantial, and Kiernan estimated that 800,000 were murdered. The Cambodian Documentation Centre (CDC) has identified 196 prisons and execution centres of varying size and significance and as many as 388 'genocide' sites, containing 19,733 mass burials, across Cambodia related to the KR period (Dy, 2007, p. 4). The numbers interned in all these sites are not known but vary considerably (as few as 4 victims to over 1,000) from site to site. Given the scale of homicide inflicted on the population, although varying by place and in intensity, an organised, systematic, and sustained effort of suppression by the regime was necessary. Estimates of fatalities are inevitably imprecise given the limited census data available to demographers but also because of the CPK's emphasis on secrecy and deception. In a 1978 speech, Brother Number Two Nuon Chea explained:

Secret work is fundamental in all that we do. For example, the elections of comrades to leading work are secret. The places where our leaders work are secret. We keep meeting times and places secret, and so on... Only through secrecy can we be masters of the situation and win victory over the enemy, who cannot find out who is who... We base everything on secrecy. (cited in Ciorciari & Chhang, 2005, p. 225)

There was frequent resort to deception by the DK security apparatus in their rooting out of potential enemies. One example was the ruse of calling on any remaining Vietnamese (or any other class or ethnic groups) to assemble for repatriation to Vietnam or back to their home villages. When the trucks arrived to take them, they only drove a short distance to a killing field (Kiernan, 2008). An apparent version of the Maoist tactic of 'let a hundred flowers bloom' was also commonplace in the frequent workers meetings and 'struggle sessions' involving self-criticism, which were required by Angkar. These demanding meetings were aptly described by Bizot (2000/2004) throughout his imprisonment in a camp commanded by Duch (see below) during the civil war

---

occurred during the civil war (in his speech, 17 January 1968 is the commencement of the war of liberation).

[5] We refer to homicidal events as those deaths directly committed by an individual or group, whether 'authorised' or not, that take place outside the immediate conditions of armed conflict or between armed combatants. We include conventional homicides that arise from disputes, quarrels, contests of honour, jealousy, and property and that in the situation of revolutionary terror may be masked as acts of the revolution or war communism. We also include political murders because of the victims' class, occupation, religion, or ethnicity, which constitute crimes against humanity. Thus, Cambodians summarily 'executed' for stealing the property of DK (in a state where all private property was abolished), for failing to work, or after denunciation for incorrect political attitudes and beliefs are included as murder. Deaths caused by starvation and neglect as a result of the policies of DK can also be included, but responsibility is diffused, and they form a class of crime that is state led or sponsored, which may be also said of the murders justified by war communism. The latter were (extrajudicial) arbitrary executions of former combatants (and often included the family of the targets) undertaken without benefit of law, and therefore they gravely offend conventions for the treatment of such persons.

190   Violence and the Civilising Process in Cambodia

Illustration 8.1 The killing fields

(see also Locard, 2013; Picq, 1989; Sikoeun, 2013). Those who ventured more than self-criticism were targeted for murder. Another method was blandishments and reassurance, often playing to the victim's hopes and desperation. The soothing talk, reminiscent of the 'showers' offered in Nazi concentration camps, was designed to subdue the victim and freeze resistance.[6] There was a notable use of crude means of execution, and stabbing and blunt force traumas were common. Participation in these forms of execution appeared to reinforce obedience and loyalty among the supervising militia, cadre, and CPK candidates. Elements of the Revolutionary Army of Kampuchea (RAK) had also become highly specialised execution squads.

The murders and disappearances were often hidden and seldom made a public spectacle (exceptions appeared to be the massacre of some Cham and Vietnamese villages), yet everyone knew the likely fate of the victims. Survivors report instances of exemplary public punishments of individuals; however, these frequently cruel and lethal events did not proceed according to a systematic pattern. The very unpredictability of these murders increased their terror.

---

[6] Here one can see the influence of the pedagogical practices of former educators – realised in Mao and Pol Pot, both successful and well-regarded teachers.

Illustration 8.2 The killing tree

Illustration 8.3 The killing tools storage shed sign

In the well-documented case of S-21 prison, commanded by Comrade Duch,[7] which allegedly handled high-security cases of the *Santebal* (the internal security arm of the CPK) under the direct command of the Minister of Defence Son Sen and the CPK leadership, as many as 21,000 were murdered at the prison and nearby 'killing field', among them many children (see Chandler, 1999). The S-21 prison operation highlights the bureaucratisation of the terror but may have been exceptional in this respect, since its priority role was not the performance of executions but intelligence gathering, the production of confessional statements (required to implicate others), and reports for the consumption of senior leaders.

During the course of our work in Cambodia, we spoke with survivors and perpetrators of the DK hemoclysm. Our conversations with older Cambodians were sometimes punctuated by remarks about 'Pol Pot time' and the fear, hardships, and losses endured. Details were seldom offered, and events themselves often described as if they had occurred like a sudden storm or inexplicable disease, and recalled like a vivid nightmare. Explanations and reasons for the murderous extremes were elemental: Pol Pot people were very cruel, killed freely, and hated anyone connected with the towns, the bonzes, Vietnamese, the King or Lon Nol: they even killed their own cadres. These anecdotes reveal the all-pervasive fear and uncertainty Cambodians experienced as well as the variability in the experience of terror of both the 'liberated base' peasants and the deported city people. Although the latter suffered the worst extremes, much depended on where, when, and with whom they became 'depositees' or so-called new people. The nominal class that one belonged to (i.e. 'old', 'candidate', or 'new' people) was also crucial; all but poor peasants were at risk of being classed as enemies of the revolution. So, supporters of the old regime, feudalists (members of the royal family and high officials), capitalists, bourgeoisie, rich and middle peasants, and even urban workers were targets for elimination and exploitation along with teachers, monks, intellectuals, and professionals (Carney, 1989, p. 99).

The Cambodian bloodbath, or hemoclysm

The revolutionary violence of DK, described below, followed a pattern similar to other state murders or megacrimes undertaken with Bolshevik-inspired ideology and tactics, and it relied on the same methods of killing. The purges of traditional nationalists and orthodox communist elements of the revolutionary

---

[7] The case of Duch, or Kang Khek Iev, has become the leitmotif for the many murders undertaken by DK (see Dunlop, 2005). His failure to destroy the documents relating to the torture of 14,000 victims at S-21, as instructed by DK's Number Two, Nuon Chea, has provided valuable evidence of the regime's brutality.

movement account for a substantial share of the deaths; however, the emphasis on racial purity ('Khmerness') and the particular conceptualisation of the class struggle, as primarily directed at the people of the cities and towns (urbanites) by the peasant classes, greatly amplified the death toll. Forms of violence included mass murders and selective killing by military forces and 'shock troops'; mass deportation of whole classes, towns, and villages; forced marches; work brigades; temporary camps and concentration areas; deprivation of food and medical security; and special security (elimination) prisons.

There was an element of collusion between Angkar and base people against the city or new people and the ethnic Vietnamese. City people had been demonised and dehumanised as both an exploiting class and 'white' Khmer, that is, not pure Khmer. The degree to which Cambodia's masses directly participated in the murders and control of the new people varied, but this collusion was seldom realised by interpersonal violence of the Rwanda kind, where Hutu murdered their Tutsi neighbours (Kiernan, 2007).[8] Although the collusion took the form of peasant or 'subaltern revenge', it was often directed and soon replaced by surges of revolutionary terror against base people and party members that arose from the precarious standing and utopian ambitions of DK throughout the 44 months it functioned. The CPK's fear of counterrevolution was apparent, and this determined the elimination of all putative rivals during the civil war and in the immediate months after the fall of the Lon Nol government.

We view DK as a weak state locked in war communism and unable to govern without recourse to terror while constantly facing an existential crisis from forces within and outside. The CPK 'fell under the spell of the counterespionage myth consuming itself', and changed 'from reduction of opposition by seduction and surgical violence, to threat, terror and coercion' (Carney, 1989, p. 97).

The revolution

By 1972, most of Cambodia had fallen to anti–Lon Nol forces, and by late 1974 only the larger towns and cities remained in Republican hands. Under siege, Phnom Penh, Battambang, and Kampong Cham battled on precariously supplied aid and were dependent on US air strikes to keep the Khmer Rouge (KR) forces at bay. The civil war ended on 17 April 1975 with the capitulation of the

---

[8] Kiernan (2007) drew interesting parallels between the Rwandan and Cambodian hemoclysms: 'the catastrophes in Cambodia and Rwanda span the spectrum of the twentieth-century ideologies of mass murder. From opposite horizons of the political imagination... in many ways the Khmer Rouge replicated Stalin and Mao, while Hutu Power echoed Enver Pasha and Adolf Hitler. Yet they all shared virulent racism, a bitter sense of lost ethnic dominance, inchoate cults of agriculture and ambitions of territorial expansion' (p. 569).

wholly corrupt Khmer Republic and the capture of Phnom Penh by a united front, the *Gouvernement Royal d'Union Nationale de Kampuchèa* (GRUNK). Marshal Lon Nol had fled Phnom Penh a few days earlier on a US helicopter. The occupying Khmer Rouge–led forces, like an ancient conqueror, promptly and forcefully emptied the city of its population of nearly two million, including hospital patients and medical staff. Phnom Penh's population had been enlarged by hundreds of thousands of war refugees displaced by the devastating bombing and the severity of the fighting, and many were in no condition for the rigours of a forced march to precarious transit camps, villages, and communes. There, the new people would have to fend for themselves and grow the rice crops essential for survival, as Cambodia then faced an acute food shortage.[9] Those incapable or resistant were summarily executed or abandoned en route to their destinations, the open prisons of a rapidly implemented totalitarian authority. The exact death toll from the exodus is unknown but counted in the thousands. Kiernan (2008) estimated about 10,000 died on the march and the same number was killed in the city itself.[10] In addition, Quinn (1989) mentioned a deadly outbreak of cholera following the exodus that killed about 100,000 individuals. The march out of the cities enabled the initial screening of the deported population for class enemies (identified and often immediately executed). Throughout the countryside, the rounding up and execution of the old hierarchy and functionaries of the short-lived republic had started. The evacuation of the cities was the opening phase of 'year zero', the beginning of the formation of the state of Democratic Kampuchea and a radical transformation of Cambodian society in the image of its 'original Khmer'[11] communist leaders.

The exodus of the city dwellers to the countryside was the first decisive act of the revolutionary leaders and signalled the eclipse of the loose united front of nationalist, monarchist, and communist of many stripes. In hindsight we can see that this was the pivotal moment when the pragmatic and moderate elements of the 'liberation' forces (nominally a coalition of forces under Sihanouk) and of the CPK (represented by some of the Eastern Zone commanders whose loyalty soon wavered) were deceived by the radical Maoist elements led by Pol Pot, Ieng Sary, Son Sen, and Ta Mok.[12] The victors sought to realise a pure Khmer

---

[9] USAID estimated that 250,000 tons of rice was urgently needed in the immediate months following the fall of the Lon Nol regime (Kiernan, 2008). Although Chinese rice shipments and purchases in border areas occurred, these made up less than half the required food needed and were soon replaced by military equipment from China in exchange for rubber, pepper, and forest products for Chinese medicine.

[10] Kiernan's (2008) estimate was based on interviews with a small sample of families who made the exodus via the three main routes out of Phnom Penh. Their accounts also show that the treatment of the city dwellers varied, with eastward routes faring better than routes to the centre, southwest, and north, and some KR units providing food and assistance to the evacuees.

[11] The name Saloth Sar, alias Pol Pot, used to describe himself in one of his early essays critical of the monarchy during his days as a student in Paris.

[12] Ta Mok, leader of the Southwest Zone, became the enforcer of the will of the revolutionary leaders and murdered all that might oppose the party centre.

communist state through the supremacy of the CPK and its dictatorial inner circle headed by Pol Pot and Nuon Chea (Brothers Number One and Number Two). There was no room for moderation, pragmatism, or conventional Marxist-Leninist ideas;[13] history was to be made regardless of the material circumstances. There was only one path: the neomillenarian path of an idealised autarchic restored Khmer state as brilliant as the Angkor Empire and the most pure communist of all.

Building DK

The basic policies of DK were foreshadowed in the 'liberated' zones prior to the fall of the Republic and at first featured programmes of collectivisation and persuasion rather than murder and terror, although from 1973 forced collectivisation, purges, and atrocities were already occurring (Quinn, 1989). On 20 May 1975, CPK leaders and thousands of military and civilian cadres from all over Cambodia attended a meeting to learn the Centre's plans and to implement them. The creation of an autarkic agrarian utopia based on collectivisation and, therefore, entailing the banning of money and private ownership and the closure of markets was one of the principal aims of the new state. Another aim was to modernise agriculture and industry and achieve 'scientific socialism'. This required the need to screen (code for killing) for disloyalty among CPK cadres and the masses to ensure they remained pure. The Centre, in effect the CPK leaders, was to be the ultimate arbiter of revolutionary purity, and thus the process of centralisation began. Two classes were created: 'full rights people' from the base areas and 'candidates' or 'depositees' from among the new people.[14] According to sources cited by Kiernan (2008, pp. 55–8), in particular an aide to the Eastern Zone's 1st Division commander Chhouk, and Chea Sim, the eight-point plan announced by the party secretary Pol Pot and deputy secretary Nuon Chea was brutally simple:

    Evacuate people from all towns (and this was to be permanent).
    Abolish all markets.
    Abolish republican currency (and do not issue revolutionary currency).
    Defrock all Buddhist monks and put them to work in the rice field (this also meant the banning of festivals).

---

[13] Pol Pot's eulogy for Mao at a party meeting after Mao's death was one of the few occasions when the regime acknowledged its intellectual legacy; however, in China the death of Mao ended the ultraradicalism of the Cultural Revolution, which had devastated the country's economy and killed many of its citizen. For Pol Pot, on the other hand, the Cultural Revolution in China failed not because of an excess of radicalism but too little.

[14] Base areas were defined as the villages and districts that supported the liberation army during the civil war. Class background could be redeemed through a 'good political attitude' (Heder, 1980).

> Execute all leaders of the Lon Nol regime, beginning with the top leaders.
>
> Establish high-level agricultural cooperatives throughout the country (i.e. village-level collectivisation with communal eating; the latter being implemented a year later in 1976).
>
> Expel the entire Vietnamese population.
>
> Dispatch troops to the borders, particularly the Vietnamese border.

The sources also mentioned opposition to schools and hospitals and orders to close them. The list was not definitive, and lower-rank informants who heard about the plans via senior cadres simplified the plans to more basic orders to kill Lon Nol soldiers and monks, expel the Vietnamese, and 'uproot spies root and branch'. The interpretation of these orders inevitably varied according to local circumstances. Many accounts by new people showed that the attitudes of local CPK cadres could mollify or worsen the impact of these orders. Some of the characteristics that may have mitigated the frequency of homicidal terror, such as checks and balances on the authority to execute people, literacy of the cadres, and the presence of a rudimentary tribunal (as required by the DK constitution), were mostly absent. The combination of the oral transmission of orders and the intense secrecy of the CPK also account for the increasing swiftness, the arbitrary and summary nature of the murders of officials of the former government and other class and ethnic enemies.

Constitution and law

The constitution[15] of DK was promulgated on 5 January 1976 and based on CPK leadership meetings during May and December 1975. It abolished the monarchy, ended Buddhism as state religion, and established the appropriation by the state of all private property while forming a ruling proletariat of peasants, workers, and soldiers (Quinn, 1978). As stated in the preamble, the constitution purported to express the 'fundamental desires of the people, workers, peasants, and other labourers as well as ... the Kampuchean Revolutionary Army', and it extolled the role of the 'peasants, the lower middle peasantry, and other strata of labourers in the countryside and cities, who account for more than ninety-five per cent of the entire Kampuchean nation' in the liberation of Cambodia and who could now hope for (but not realise as, for the most part, individuals were relegated to the role of worker-slaves serving the collective) 'a national society informed by genuine happiness, equality, justice, and democracy without rich or poor and without exploiters or exploited, a society in which all live harmoniously in great national solidarity and join forces to do manual labour together and increase production for the construction and defence of the country'.

---

[15] Translation is from Etcheson (1984).

Article 1 set out DK's revolutionary credentials as a nonaligned democratic state 'of the people, workers, peasants, and all other Kampuchean labourers' where 'all important general means of production are the collective property of the people's State and the common property of the people's collectives' (article 2).[16] It is governed by 'the collective principle in leadership and work' (article 4) and 'absolutely opposed to the corrupt, reactionary culture of the various oppressive classes and that of colonialism and imperialism in Kampuchea' (article 3). Chapter 9 of the constitution outlined 'The Rights and Duties of the Individual', which required 'the duty of all to defend and build the country together in accordance with individual ability and potential' and guaranteed a living, equal rights for men and women, the prohibition of polygamy and 'complete equality among all Kampuchean people'. Article 20 established the right to religious freedom but specified that 'reactionary religions which are detrimental... are absolutely forbidden'. The description of 'actions violating the laws of the people's State' was short and vague: 'dangerous activities in opposition to the people's State must be condemned to the highest degree. Other cases are subject to constructive re-education' (article 10).[17] Although the Kampuchean People's Representative Assembly (with most seats allocated to peasants and the RAK) was created to make laws and appoint the executive and judges of the people's court, it never functioned, as most of its representatives soon perished in the purges that followed.

The phases of violence

Quinn (1989) described how Pol Pot, imbued with righteousness and uncanny military and political success, planned to remake Cambodian society and preserve the revolution through the systematic use of mass violence and terror as well as purges of the impure and achieve four aims: (1) breaking the ancient regime, (2) initiating social transformation, (3) protecting the revolution, and (4) defending it from outsiders. Table 8.1 summarises these four aims and their consequences. Each of these aims and their associated methods identified different targets for terror. The deliberate emptying of the cities led to mass deaths among deported urbanites, the identification and elimination of the former enemy from the top down led to countless executions, and the suppression of cultural workers and technical experts to both widespread starvation and execution. Vietnamese were murdered along with the thousand or so 'Hanoi-trained Khmer' and those perceived to be collaborators. The collectivisation of agriculture and imposition of communal living and the mobilisation of

---

[16] Yet allowing 'property for everyday use [to] remain[s] in private hands', although this was also eventually denied to the population.

[17] Eventually, Khieu Samphan claimed that crime had been eliminated from Cambodia.

Table 8.1 *The four aims of the CPK and their consequences*

Aim	Actions	Consequences
• Destroying social, political, economic, and cultural infrastructure of the old society	1. *BREAKING THE SYSTEM* • April–September 1975: killing of old regime officials and army officers • Urban centres emptied; city dwellers enslaved; intellectual, professional, and religious classes eliminated • From September 1977: purges of remaining old enemies; from mid 1978, deportation of rebellious Eastern Zone base people	• Disintegration • Decapitation (elimination of the old elites) • Anomie • Moral inversion • Strategic and subaltern revenge
• Implementing agrarian autarky for a great leap forward to a workers' paradise • Forcing society into communist-inspired socioeconomic patterns • Instilling new collectivist values	2. *SOCIOECONOMIC TRANSFORMATION* • Collectivisation of agriculture • Deportations to scale up collectives, mobile work brigades • Regimentation of village and commune life through forced communal eating and family separation • New 'crimes' against the state, such as keeping individual property, theft from the collective, failure to meet collective targets	• Disintegration • Destruction of village and household production patterns • Famine and mass deaths • Anomie • Flight-freeze behaviour • Moral inversion • Hyperconformity
• Eliminating revisionism and the risk of coup d'état	3. *POLITICAL PROPHYLAXIS* • Mid 1976 and mid 1978, two waves of executions of unreliable or soft party cadres and their families and associates • Purges of CPK in 1977 and replacement of old cadres with new cadres from another zone • Mass execution and deportation of rebellious Eastern Zone population from mid 1978	• Greater party and state centralisation • Many deaths of cadres and their 'strings' • Solidifying the dictatorship by the vanguard
• Eliminating threats posed by Vietnam and alleged Khmer collaborators	4. *DEFENDING AGAINST EXTERNAL THREATS* • Massacre of ethnic Vietnamese and other minorities in 1975; second wave targeting survivors in 1977 • Elimination of all Hanoi-trained cadres in 1975 • Military incursions into Vietnam and border massacres of villages	• Militarisation • Mass surveillance and paranoia (real or imagined) • Constant mobilisation of the masses and deportations of entire suspect communes and districts • Retaliation by the Vietnamese in early 1978 • Widespread defections of anti–Pol Pot elements to Vietnam

Source: Adapted from Quinn's (1989, p. 180) four aims of the CPK.

labour brigades combined with food ration discipline led to further starvation and 'crimes against the state'.

Breaking the old: decivilising

For the CPK, the rise of the new society necessitated the destruction of the old; therefore, in the months following the fall of Phnom Penh, senior officials, army officers, and noncommissioned officers (NCOs) of the former Republic were systematically murdered,[18] often en masse, in a policy of 'war communism' designed to smash all enemies and to break the old system. Belated efforts by the Centre in September 1975 to restrain the executions of surviving officials, professionals, and soldiers of the Republic (i.e. attempts to suppress subaltern massacres) were temporary, and such executions renewed in subsequent phases of violence. No seeds of counterrevolution were to be left and all challenges answered by death. The scale, thoroughness (ruthlessness), and timing of the executions of these groups varied from zone to zone with the most extant reported in the Southwest (under Ta Mok's clannish control) and Centre Zones. These areas were closely allied to the Pol Pot group and soon evolved into 'model' collectives, expelling all the new people and minority ethnic groups. The CPK cadres in these zones became the revolutionary vanguard, often replacing purged cadres from other zones.

The CPK, like other Bolshevik-inspired revolutionary organisations, was deeply hostile to religion; yet, the influence of Buddhism[19] was apparent in the transcendental purpose of the revolution and the ascetic, sect-like certainties of the vanguard, engaged in the epic and apocalyptic[20] struggle for communism and who made real the cosmic fate that befell unbelievers. Nevertheless, the regime targeted monks and religious leaders as well as intellectuals and teachers. Like Mao, Pol Pot saw individualism as the basis for attachment to private property, and so a threat to communism. Eradication of individualism would allow the correct collective values to flourish, so from this perspective 'it was necessary to kill the professional or well-educated persons, the wives of military officers and government officials and their children, as well as rich landholders and merchants. All of them possessed the ethical and philosophical heritage by which the individualist system operated' (Quinn, 1989, pp. 193–4). The 'smashing' of enemies become an all-consuming task; once external and class enemies were eliminated, it became necessary to find enemies from within.

---

[18] Despite repeated assurances that only several of the leading figures of the Republic were to be executed and the remaining granted amnesty and reeducation (Dy, 2007).

[19] The point is applicable generally to religious and philosophical systems that propound the transcendence of the self via merging with God or some other absolute all-knowing abstraction.

[20] In most religions, the apocalypse refers to both the total destruction of the 'evil world' and the advent of paradise (see Pearson, 2006).

Provoked by fears of espionage, paranoia about Vietnamese hegemony, and the failure of agrarian 'leap forwards' (attributed to sabotage and low revolutionary spirit), lower-rank Lon Nol soldiers, teachers, monks, and then peasants with relatives from the old regime, and finally the disobedient even among the base people were eliminated. Within a year of April 17, purges of 'soft' party cadres (and their 'strings' of associates and family) had begun, and these would continue in growing intensity and absurdity until the mass deportations and purges of the Eastern Zone in 1978 when DK was completely at war with itself.

Preserving Khmer purity

In addition to class enemies, the non-Khmer Cham, the Vietnamese, the Khmer Viet Minh or Issaraks – the Khmer 'who were Vietnamese at heart' – and other ethnic minorities were targeted for elimination, and here the term of *genocide* as defined by the 1948 convention is overall appropriate. The loss of life among the Muslim Cham was estimated by Kiernan to be about a third (around 90,000 deaths of an estimated population of 250,000) of this minority; the forced consumption of pork, the banning of Cham language (as were all foreign languages), and the prohibition of religious practice were at first resisted by the tight-knit Cham communities with dire consequences. Even though a number of Cham villages had been classed as base people, they were 'scattered' and treated like new people, and the hostility of the CPK to their religious practices resulted in a high proportion of murders, including most of the religious leadership. According to Kiernan (2008), of 339 community leaders, only 45 survived.

Seen as an external threat, the entire resident population of ethnic Vietnamese of about 20,000 was massacred during the forced exodus to Vietnam in mid 1975. Later, from late 1977, the CPK began to murder ethnic Vietnamese spouses of Khmer and their children, the speaking of Vietnamese was banned, and those of mixed ethnic backgrounds were also targeted for murder. Another group that also fared badly were Kampuchea Krom (Khmer located in Vietnam who spoke Khmer with a distinctive accent), many of whom had resettled in Cambodia as a result of the Second Indochina War.

The ethnic Chinese population counted around 413,000 and their fate was also severe, with perhaps half perishing, mostly due to starvation rather than murder. The Chinese, whose merchant occupations and urban status placed them firmly as class enemies and new people, were highly vulnerable to the rigours of forced labour and food shortages. It has been speculated that DK's close alliance with China may have quelled deliberate murder of the Chinese en masse. Other minorities such as the small Thai, Lao, and Malay populations probably also fared badly, although the evidence about what happened is limited; nevertheless, whole communities disappeared.

The war on the people

The CPK's assault on customary life, especially the prohibition of home meals and the separation of parents from children, the relentless work quota, food shortages, and the loss of cherished festivals, was so drastic that even base people and 'full rights' people deeply resented Angkar and its cadre. The arbitrary form of the terror and its indiscriminate murder of significant leaders (moderates and extremists) combined with the reduction of subsistence proved fatal to support for DK.

> The Center spearheaded its systematic assaults on peasant ties to land, family and religion with punishing search-and-destroy missions into the economic, personal and spiritual provinces of peasant life. But these areas were heavily contested, and required aggressive, indefinite state patrolling... Along with massacres that threatened peasant life itself, it was the CPK's attack on the family that alienated peasant supporters. (Kiernan, 2008, p. 215)

While food shortages occurred through 1975–6, the seizure of most of the 1976 rice paddy by the Centre and further relocations of new people created disastrous conditions in 1977 through to early 1978. Many survivors reported that young children, the old, the weak, and the frail began to perish in large numbers during the latter half of 1977. Some reported cases of cannibalism, similar to what happened during Mao's Great Leap Forward (Yang, 2012). Rations of gruel and compulsory communal meals, combined with prohibitions on foraging, also led to the stealing of food, complaining, and other forms of resistance, which were frequently met with summary executions. Again, the intensity of the resistance and subsequent executions of those lacking revolutionary zeal varied from locality to locality (Beang & Cougill, 2006; Dy, 2007; Kiernan, 2008).

The creation of a totalitarian society of open prisons required the full weight of a weak state (i.e. without popular legitimacy) to enforce and maintain surveillance over its inhabitants, reducing them to 'digging in, bending low and cursing inwardly' (Frieson, 1992, cited in Kiernan, 2008, p. 13). This 'freeze' alternative to the normal response to danger and fear – flight or fight – was the natural response of the new people, but in time it became more commonplace among base people, as peasant support waned when the regime's more radical programmes, combined with economic hardship, conspired to delegitimate the revolutionary order that those peasants had supported. Evidence suggests that although flight was an option for the more able individuals (failure was certain death), it became increasingly difficult to undertake. Fighting back was seldom an option. Long-practiced peasant strategies of avoidance, dissimulation, and 'stubborn and sporadic acts of petty resistance' (see Scott, 1985) were observed, but wilful and mass noncompliance also occurred. Examples are recorded of

Western Zone cadres fighting and fleeing to Thailand and, as noted, of resistance of Cham villagers who killed CPK cadres. Vickery (1984) reported a peasant revolt in the district of Chikreng in 1977 provoked by the introduction of communal meals and the separation of families that resulted in the death of 8,000–10,000 peasants in the subsequent suppression. Resistance to the intrusive and radical restructuring of peasant life began to shape DK's response to the worsening conditions in the countryside.[21]

A new phase of murderous activity emerged as CPK leaders shifted their focus from war communism and non-Khmer 'cleansing' to agrarian collectivisation and irrigation projects, which in turn required the relocation and reclassification of peasant classes; for example, the definition of 'full rights people' gradually narrowed. The inevitable failures to achieve the impossible production quotas imposed on the populace were blamed on internal enemies among the masses as well as the party (Jackson, 1989; Kiernan, 2008; Quinn, 1989). The urgency of party purification and purges of 'soft' cadres became a constant, while the enforcement of communal discipline and work quotas from 1977 onwards required frequent resort to mass terror. From 1978 there was the constant fear of Vietnamese military activity and intentions, addressed by increasingly irrational military provocations of their powerful former ally. These murderous phases varied in intensity and duration depending on the locality or zone, the relative scarcity of food, especially in 1977, and the interpretation by the local CPK and RAK leaders of the orders from the Centre. The evidence points to an increase in the frequency of murders of all not classified as full rights people in localities where food was scarce and where purges of less zealous cadres had occurred. Thus 1977–8 may have been the peak period for lethal violence following a relatively short respite after the initial mass murders of those connected with the Lon Nol regime and others who had been deemed expendable.

The fall of Democratic Kampuchea

Despite its apparent dominance over the means of violence, in April 1976 the new state experienced attempts to overthrow the DK and CPK leadership. This set the stage for the perpetual purges that accompanied increasing centralisation and ultimately another round of deportations and mass murders in the wake of

---

[21] Penologist Mathieson (1984) argued that the use of moral censoriousness by prisoners to challenge the guards has some purchase in moderating behaviour and limiting abuse (i.e. appealing to the rulers to obey their own rules). In a society like DK, where rules were vague and ambiguous and rights unknown, this was also likely to be fatal. As we shall see, the interpretative tools of criminology fail to fully explain these forms of state crime and a specific study of the sociogenesis and psychogenesis of totalitarian societies is required.

the rebellion in the Eastern Zone in 1978,[22] prelude to the invasion by Vietnam. Pol Pot's solution to the inevitable 'contradictions'[23] that arose was to crush them with violence, and so in September 1977 he renewed the elimination of the old society because of the continued differences (contradictions) between the peasants and the old urban rulers. The party would then be purged of its revisionist, rightist, and internal rivals. The broad sequence of Central CPK 'screening' of cadres began with the Western Zone in March 1977 and continued with the Northeast Zone in September 1977, the Eastern and Northeast Zones in June 1978, and the Northern Zone in August 1978.

By early 1978, supported by the Vietnamese, an incipient 'people's war' against the 'Pol Pot–Ieng Sary Clique' was developing among a growing number of disaffected cadres in the Eastern Zone (Kiernan, 2008; Quinn, 1989). A failed second coup d'état in mid 1978 was the likely proximate cause of a second purge of the party and mass deportations of Eastern Zone old or former base people. This was the most significant challenge to the CPK thus far and was notable for the scale of defections. Thereafter, the RAK and masses were placed on a full war footing, relying on substantial war materiel from China. During the latter half of 1978, the Centre turned its attention to the further purification of the CPK and the conflict with the rebellious Eastern Zone. An all-pervasive fear of the hated external enemy made the war with Vietnam inevitable. Territorial clashes had occurred immediately in 1975 after 'liberation' (the consequence of the decision to reinforce the borders, especially in the east facing Vietnam). Skirmishes between KR and Vietnamese forces had occurred during the civil war, and these continued in the southwestern and eastern border areas throughout 1976 and 1977 but were contained as both sides exercised some restraint over border claims. However, large-scale incursions by the RAK in late 1977 heightened border tension. The mass atrocities that accompanied these border attacks by the RAK were notable for their brutality and included the massacre of entire villages inside Vietnam. The tit-for-tat response to these attacks by the People's Army of Vietnam (PAVN), in the hope of forcing negotiations, failed but heightened the war tensions and the already visceral anti-Vietnamese stance of the Centre.[24]

The Eastern Zone, with its 'contaminated' population, was soon perceived by Pol Pot as a 'nest of traitors' and deported after the apparent second coup.

---

[22] Carney (1989) reported that the CPK was less in control than assumed, and he cites Ieng Sary's claims (in October 1978) that less than half of all cooperatives were in the hands of loyal cadres, with some under the control of cadres of unreliable backgrounds and associated with former united front and nationalist movements.

[23] The term was borrowed but vulgarised from Marx's principles of 'scientific socialism' and 'dialectical materialism' and was used by both Mao and Pol Pot as justification for murder.

[24] Divisional-scale counterattacks by the PAVN in January 1978, despite reaching as close as 38 km from Phnom Penh, failed to deter continued RAK efforts to cross the border.

The regime's fragility manifested in an extreme purge of the Eastern Zone, and the forced relocations of thousands of peasants pushed many to seek refuge in Vietnam from mid 1978 onwards. As rebel cadres and the communes they controlled were attacked by their zealous enemies from the party Centre and Southwest Zone, they crossed the border en masse; Hun Sen, the future prime minister, had been among the first to defect in June 1977. The suicide in June 1978 of So Phim, first vice president of DK and leading member of the CPK Standing Committee of the Central Committee and Eastern Zone secretary, and the defection of his deputy Heng Samrin to Vietnam brought to an end the old and fragile alliances between moderates, pragmatists, and revolutionaries.[25] As a result of this turmoil and the perennially imagined external threat, now regarded as imminent, violence against the masses in other zones somewhat abated, in part to prepare the population for the pending conflict with Vietnam.

Revolutionary terror: transforming state and society through authorised crime

The form and revolutionary purpose of the new state of Democratic Kampuchea help account for the nature and targets of its lethal violence. However, the type or character of the CPK-led revolutionary movement has eluded easy classification: was it primarily a peasant rebellion, vulgar Marxist-Leninist or Bolshevik dictatorship, a Khmer adaptation of Maoism, an extreme and fascist form of ethnonationalism, or indeed a unique hybrid of all these elements? Quinn (1989) and Jackson (1989) describe the close ties between DK leaders and Mao's China and the frequent approving references by Pol Pot, Ieng Sary, and Khieu Samphan of the Cultural Revolution and the collectivisation of the Great Leap Forward. Not easily reduced to a basic core, the regime manifested as an amalgam of radical Maoist-inspired ideology, nationalism, racism, archaism, and millenarianism, grafted on a premodern (preliterate) society whose rural manners and sentiments (Elias, 1939/2012; Shelley, 1981) made it vulnerable to more extreme expressions of violence that were seldom 'simply' strategic and instrumental.

We have noted in earlier chapters an undercurrent of millenarianism in previous periods of rebellion and banditry in rural Cambodia that was often associated with extreme acts of collective brutality. Such acts when undertaken on the scale of the civil war and revolutionary terror share some of the characteristics of 'subaltern genocide' when the 'oppressed and disempowered adopt genocidal strategies to vanquish their oppressors' (Robins & Jones, 2009, p. 3). In these mass or megacrimes, the harnessing of the state apparatus for violence

---

[25] Heng Samrin was to hold leading positions in the PRK formed after the occupation of Cambodia by the PAVN.

is not essential; rather, a humiliated and dominated group (as in the case of the rural Cambodian 'black' peasants) overcomes its previous masters and dominators (the rich and 'white' city dwellers) and proceeds to turn the tables, invert the normal social relations of class and social superiority (Chandler, 1999, 2008).[26] The circumstances prevailing at the close of the civil war with massive US air bombardments of the Cambodian countryside helped create a 'potent ideology of class revenge' against the Lon Nol regime and the city dwellers who had escaped from the terror of the war raging in the countryside (Robins & Jones, 2009, p. 5).

The leaders of the CPK and DK, the Pol Pot faction, departed from the practices of the Vietnamese communists, who did not abolish markets, education, and currency or push for radical collectivisation and communalism. The orthodox Marxist-Leninist class struggle against capitalism and the owners of the means of production was broadened to encompass all city dwellers inclusive of the urban working class and reified the poorest peasants as model 'workers'. The pursuit of ethno-Khmer purity added a racial and nationalistic motive that was contrary to the usual strictures of international communism. However, like other ideological fanatics, they chose the Bolshevik 'blood and soil' route to socialism and communism (Kiernan, 2007). And, like Stalin and Mao, they were prepared to sacrifice the people to 'leap forward' and forge a new utopia – a hypercultural revolution. Yet, it was not an espoused retreat from modernity but a leap towards it. As Jackson (1989) observed:

The Khmer Rouge sought not to turn back the pages of time to an earlier era of Khmer greatness but to rush forward at a dizzying pace regardless of the consequences. By combining the idealism and heroic virtue extolled by Maoism with a Fanonist or Stalinist reliance on wholesale terror, the Khmer Rouge sought to stimulate the Khmer people to participate in a forced march toward a vision of communist modernity. (p. 59)

They envisaged a state that would rapidly outperform China and North Korea in both revolutionary ardour and modern industrial achievements. The revolutionary song *Long Live 17th of April*, urging elimination of enemies, and the national anthem (*Glorious Seventeenth of April*) reifying blood sacrifice as the means of surpassing the brilliance of Angkor, captured these ambitions, while the constitution, albeit a façade of legalism, set the tone for the formation of an ideal peasant worker state.

Who was responsible for directing the military personnel to carry out murders and whether DK's policies were 'genocidal' in respect to the mass murder of Cham, Vietnamese, and other non-Khmer groups are still the subjects of legal interest and debate. Our proposition, drawn from the literature, is that the

---

[26] See Braithwaite's (1991) notion of 'structures of humiliation' in the genesis of violent subaltern crimes.

scale of mass murder occurred because of the deliberate policies of Angkar and the goals of the principal leaders of the CPK. Further, the failure to provide food security for the new collectives, the work brigades, and other mass mobilisations and deportations constituted the crime of denying the necessities of life and greatly aggravated the death toll. The evidence prepared by the CDC, including the telling records of S-21 and other survivors' accounts, shows that DK and its leaders advocated policies of genocide against minorities but also and independently of their ethnic or religious background authorised summary executions of whole classes of 'enemies' people, deviants to the new order, and people relegated to the lowest castes of the revolutionary order.

For DK, the ends perfectly justified the means: communism could not be achieved unless the lessons of the Russian and Chinese revolutions were learned – ruthless use of the available human capital and elimination of all opposition. Many perpetrators claimed that they acted from fear of Angkar and had no choice but to murder the so-called enemies of the revolution. The defence of duress (kill or be killed), which may diminish culpability among many low-ranked cadres, is somewhat more compelling than the so-called Nuremberg defence of 'acting on orders'. Here, disentangling the effects of brutalisation, the capacity to exercise volition, and the habits of obedience to authority is relevant. The broader evidence is that many functionaries of the CPK were indeed believers in the use of violence to purify and renew Cambodia. For the CPK upper echelon, the application of murder was a matter of policy, and for the most part they avoided having blood literally on their hands. The frequent recourse to excessive violence and the presence of cruelties by brutalised shock troops suggest that the disintegrative process designed to break the old society unleashed anomie and a return to archaism, in short a deep decivilising epoch. This aspect of organised serial mass murder, especially when authorised by the state, poses special moral and legal problems for the assignment of culpability but is nevertheless without recourse to pathology, understandable in criminological terms. This is the focus of the next section; from a criminological perspective, what can we say about DK that has not already been said?

DK's revolutionary terror and criminological perspectives

Beyond recounting and describing the unprecedented wave of violence that engulfed Cambodia during the short reign of the KR, this chapter seeks to make sense of the mass murders that accompanied the creation and fall of DK as part of our longer picture of the descending cascades of violence that have been observed in the previous chapters. The relatively short-lived surge in mass violence that occurred during DK appears exceptional and extreme, but not unprecedented. In this section, we apply the theoretical and empirical tools of criminology to account for the scale and forms of mass violence. Before doing so, we discuss the problem of definitions and the limitations of criminological theory.

Megacrime and the limitations of criminological theory

Macrotheoretical approaches that explain conflict and social change are helpful but poorly account for divergent levels and types of violence across time and place. We eschew legalistic definitions and look beyond the legal and normative template of the international crime of genocide. Hinton (2012) redefined genocide broadly to focus on process and context that capture its variety as 'the more or less coordinated attempt to destroy a dehumanized and excluded group because of who they are' (p. 10). Among the many terms employed to define different forms of mass violence, we find *politicide*, the murder of adherents of a particular ideological position or political class; *democide*, state mass murders of any civilian grouping and captured soldiers; *genocide*; *megacrime*; *mass murder*; *mass violence*; and *crime against humanity*. The variety of terms, all applicable to the Cambodian situation, suggests an overlapping and unsettled field of inquiry to account for the variety of victims and serial nature of many mass murder events. Leman-Langlois (2006) reviewed a number of criminological theories in relation to megacrime and refrained from making the object of his study dependent on definitions found in international criminal law.[27] A nonlegalistic approach widens the object to include mass murders other than state-sponsored planned events (such as the Holocaust) and invites a fuller examination of the field of genocide (Tanner, 2006). So far, criminology has not contributed significantly to our understanding of mass violence and this is because of the limited reach of conventional criminology. 'Hence, notions of war-crime, crime against humanity and crime against peace ... and of State crime, in general are ignored' (Leman-Langlois, 2006, p. 23). Thus, despite criminology's voluminous studies of violence and homicide, the problem of 'authorised crime', genocide, and mass violence remains largely unexplored.

We argue that understanding megacrime in the context of DK poses special challenges for the explanatory frameworks of traditional criminology. For Leman-Langlois (2006), criminology is incapable of explaining megacrimes not because these acts are outside of its field of study but because the explanation is 'rather to be found in its narrow persistent focus on purely individual

---

[27] See the definitions adopted in the 1948 UN Genocide Convention, which places the elimination of ethnic groups as the crime against humanity par excellence. Not surprisingly, it drew on the experience of the mass crimes committed by the Nazi regime of Adolf Hitler. Although the Jewish Holocaust accounted for most of the civilian deaths, other ethnic groups such as the Gypsy, persons with mental illness, homosexuals, and political opponents were also targets of the Nazi extermination camps.

conduct' (p. 23; see also Cohen, 1993; Hagan & Rymond-Richmond, 2009; Hagan, Rymond-Richmond, & Parker, 2005; Liwerant, 2007; Loyle, 2009; Rhodes, 2002). Others, such as Winton (2011) and Rhodes (2002), have made similar observations but applied microlevel and cultural explanations to address the question of why perpetrators participate in megacrimes. For example, Winton's (2011) adaptation of Athens's (1992) 'process of violentization' is essentially a microlevel explanation of individual pathways to extreme violence scaled up to address collective violence and crimes against humanity. The adaptation draws on the perspective of symbolic interactionism by using Athens's map of the psychic processes that create and release actors capable of extreme violence (see below).

Another challenge for criminology in developing a coherent theoretical approach to mass violence is the classical conception of the state (Dumont, 2006). Dumont argued that the idea of the state carries the contradiction of the state as both protector and perpetrator. The state successfully monopolises the means of violence to end the 'war of all against all', but this is combined with the politically potent notion that the state is the ultimate legitimate force (of last resort) and that 'reasons of State' justify all forms of mass violence whether occurring internally or in respect to other states. For criminologists wedded to the notion that the state strives for constant improvement in crime reduction and control, the paradox of a criminal state, or a state captured by criminals, renders conventional criminology based on social contract theory irrelevant; only macroconflict theories are then available and, as noted, these have little to say about the relationships between the individual and the 'criminal state'. Liwerant (2012, p. 11) argued that this crucial limitation (the legitimacy of the state based on social contract) in the sociopolitical settings usually envisaged by conventional criminology is also bounded by the normative discourses of international human rights and penal justice, which assume a privileged place in the social reaction to mass murder and its excessive horror. In short, moral repugnancy also reveals our 'lack of interpretative tools for such violence, including criminological ones'. Outrage replaces analysis.

Despite these constraints we see criminological studies as an untapped reservoir of empirical knowledge about violence yet to be applied fully to the question of the nature and form of megacrimes, including genocide. Hagan et al. (2005) asserted that: 'modern criminology possesses the theory and methods to document, describe, analyse, and explain "the crime of crimes" and other important violations of international criminal law. The denial and neglect of these crimes in modern criminology itself needs explanation' (p. 556). While neglect of the topic of megacrimes in criminology can be related to the limitations of existing research and theories, we would argue that 'political' topics have also been outside of the preoccupations of mainstream criminology, dominated by concerns about the reform of individuals and domestic criminal justice systems. Yet reengagement with the political in crime, especially the integration of both individual and collective violent behaviour, could offer a source for the renewal of criminology's traditional paradigms (Liwerant, 2012). For Liwerant (2012, p. 22) 'murderous normativity' appears in these megacrimes as a mode of political management such that traditional criminologists no longer see grave breaches of norms but the construction of a new (dominant) normative worldview; therefore, the transformation of the transgression of murder into an institution requires the construction of new interpretative tools (Liwerant, 2012, pp. 12–13). The poverty of interpretative tools, including those offered by criminology, suggests a deep ambivalence towards violence and its meaning, especially given our near universal taboo against extreme cruelty and our repugnancy towards perpetrators. This ambiguity is apparent in the normalised behaviour of executioners and in the consequential but privileged juridical discussion of these crimes rather than a focus on the warlike behaviour that creates the conditions for barbarity (Liwerant, 2012).

Criminological explanations of megacrime

Can megacrime be interpreted using traditional crime theories such as strain, differential association, social control, and techniques of neutralisation? We draw on the work of Hélène Dumont (2006) and Stéphane Leman-Langlois (2006), who discussed the applicability of these theories and explored their limits in the case of mass violence and genocide. Dumont (2006) introduced a special issue of the journal *Criminologie* on genocide and remarked, 'The study of genocides causes paradigmatic breaks and raises epistemological difficulties to these fields of study [criminology, law, philosophy] which have to revise their classic modes of thinking' (p. 3).

In the same issue, Leman-Langlois (2006) examined the reality of the recent genocides in Bosnia-Herzegovina and Rwanda using three criminological approaches (rational choice, differential association, and techniques of neutralisation) for conceptualising individual, organised, and collective criminality. He suggested that criminological theories are not yet capable of providing an analytical framework to understand the crime of genocide. Using a similar approach, we now examine whether and in which way a range of criminological theories can help us understand and account for the megaviolence under DK. But first it is necessary to have a critical look at the notion that megacrimes generally rely on a strict pyramidal structure of authority where the goals and orders of all-powerful deciders are blindly executed by an army of overobedient executioners. This notion is often based on simplified accounts of both the Holocaust and the structure of organised crime.

Dumont (2006) noted that Holocaust studies have 'highlighted the authoritarian and organised structure of the genocidal operation and, in a similar way, studies of organised crime take into account the pyramidal structure of authority and the authoritarian culture to explain the scale of the criminal activities of many participants' (p. 5). Yet, she warned against generalising from these studies as they may 'tend to categorically separate the participants in a genocide between rational order-givers on the one hand and obedient, constrained, or strongly manipulated and irrational perpetrators on the other hand' (p. 5). Other limitations are apparent with any analogy to organised crime, especially given the role of loose macrocriminal networks in the morphology of organised crime. Our review of the phases and patterns of the Cambodian hemoclysm and the following theoretical perspectives show the limitations of a conventional top-down analysis of megacrimes.

Rational choice

Leman-Langlois concluded that the opportunistic economic calculus of maximising gain for hedonistic actors envisaged by rational choice (or classical deterrence theory) cannot 'account for the scale of the criminal massacres, the number of participants in a genocide and the motivation behind genocidal actions'. It is not that individual opportunistic motivations for power and gain are absent in megacrimes of any form (genocides, mass terror, civil wars, and the like) but that 'where he 1) chooses certain actions, 2) with a goal in mind, and 3) within a context, the perpetrator of mega-crime is *rational* per definition. However, this helps little to understand what and how he is thinking and even less why he chooses certain means rather than others' (Leman-Langlois, 2006, p. 27). At best it fits with the observed evidence that both organisers and perpetrators of megacrimes are rational (i.e. not affected by pathology), and it shows that they are not rigorously split between rational authorisers on one side and perpetrating automatons on the other side. The problem with rational choice is that it 'explains' so much that it ends up explaining little. Unless profoundly brain damaged, all individuals choose to escape pain and seek pleasure (as they experience it). Fear and duress (kill or be killed) can then be framed into a rational choice, albeit one bounded by the circumstances found by the actor. However, rationality is also bounded or limited (i.e. dependent on the knowledge, content, skills, and actual resources brought to play), especially if exercised via a closed or fixed set of ideas or ideologies. With these limitations in mind, we look to social psychological perspectives, which suggest interactions between actors at the 'top and bottom' are critical in the implementation of mass violence.

Differential association and neutralisation

Leman-Langlois found in the general criminological theories of 'differential association' (e.g. Akers, 2009) and 'techniques of neutralisation' (Sykes & Matza, 1957) a more helpful approach for addressing group or collective crime.

This is because differential association theories propose that individuals learn to see reality in accordance with the collective ideology of the dominant group, and they apply techniques of neutralisation, which are not post hoc justifications or excuses but authorised departures from the customary prohibitions. The 'techniques' formulated by Matza and Sykes were originally postulated to explain illicit acts by juveniles that were undertaken despite the juveniles' recognition and endorsement of general social and moral codes of conduct. These techniques are instrumental in forming the belief system of the individual as well as the group or collective. Deviance, however, does not require the creation of new moral codes of conduct; rather, offenders can 'drift' between a deviant and a legitimate lifestyle as circumstances require and justify their deviant actions by using these techniques of neutralisation (Matza, 1964). Five techniques were identified: denial of responsibility, denial of injury, denial of the victim, condemnation of the condemners, and appeal to higher loyalties. These techniques allow violent actors to perceive their collective criminal acts as dissociated from the general morality of society.

Participation in actions previously judged immoral requires that the actor be situated in a relatively particular system of beliefs, and above all beliefs that favour obedience to orders and general deference to authority. The formation of this belief is far more effective in the closed environment of a totalitarian bureaucracy, relatively isolated from the outside world. It is the same socio-psychological dynamic that spreads in extremist sects... In a nutshell the *authorised crime* is the result of power games within a group where a culture of neutralisation of certain acts commonly considered as crimes (immoral and punished) by the members has established itself. (Leman-Langlois, 2006, pp. 28–30)

In the learning processes that lead to the preemptive use of violence, effective efforts to reduce the humanity and worthiness of the victim in the mind of the perpetrator are paramount. Thus the use of techniques such as the denial and blaming of the victim, constructed as 'enemy', and the appeal to the moral force of socialism, communism, fascism, or any other higher fealties can be both preparatory and consistent with a new and more persuasive morality. Techniques of neutralisation draw together micro-individual processes that help provide grounds or justifications for violent action but that arise from an interactive process between the individual and the salient groups and associations that enmesh the actor; in short, groups that are predisposed towards violence create a climate for its use and compel the individual to use violence as a prerequisite for joining and participating in the group. In the Cambodian situation, all five techniques are relevant, but 'denial of responsibility' may apply both as an enabler and post hoc rationalisation. The frequent use of dehumanising language about enemies of DK shows the utility of 'denial of the victim', while the barbarity of the enemy, especially the USA and Lon Nol republicans, offered a compelling opportunity for 'condemning the condemners' (i.e. the condemners were just as bad). 'Appeal to higher loyalties' such as the revolution, patriotism, or one's 'race' is common to many persistent acts of violence (Sykes & Matza, 1957). 'Denial of injury' is the least useful, particularly for frontline soldiers, but often used by the authorisers to deny the extent of injury caused.[28]

Anomie and strain

'Anomie', a state of uncertainty, anxiety, and disengagement, which arises when the 'rules of the game' undergo abrupt change, for instance, when social norms and customary hierarchies of age and class invert as in DK, often leads to normlessness or drift among individuals and groups (Durkheim, 1893/1964; Merton, 1938/1949). Anomie offers a midrange theory that accounts for the impact of sudden transition and change and the strain or tension that arises when traditional – or in the DK case newly minted social goals – norms and values clash with the means available to realise them. This tension produces individual or collective adaptations that include deviance, rebellion, retreatism, ritualism, and conformity (Merton, 1938/1949). The DK period was certainly a period of rapid social change when not only the monarchy, village life, and religion were abolished but also the names of ancient provinces were renamed 'zones' and a new language (reminiscent of Orwell's newspeak) was also invented (Hinton, 1998, 2002; Picq, 1989). It was duly amplified by revolutionary zeal and the radical reorientation of the ('archaic') individual to new collective socialist norms. Anomie thus arose from the disruption and disintegration of relations between individuals and familial groups, villages/neighbourhoods, the wider society, and the state and from the uncertainties and ambiguities that occur when the social order (power centres) disintegrates and re-forms. Given that terror was the main tool of DK to change the rules of the game, ritualism may have been the only adaptation available: most knew the goals were unattainable, but hyperconformity to the required social behaviour could ensure survival.

The social psychology of violence

A few celebrated laboratory studies that appear to show shallow inhibitions of human capacities for violence have been widely quoted in the genocide literature as compelling illustrations of how ordinary people may do 'evil'. These studies from the 'golden age of social psychology' showed that 'people take their cues on how to behave from other people' (Pinker, 2011, p. 558). They also attempted to unlock the sort of circumstances that would allow 'group

---

[28] The techniques were formulated with minor juvenile delinquency in mind, not serious acts of violence and homicides. Bandura's (1999) psychological theory of moral disengagement may be more appropriate in cases of serious violence.

think' to flourish. Two such studies have been highly influential: one focused on the prison or custodial environment and the other probed how an authoritative setting would test the 'obedience' of subjects in administering pain to others when ordered to by an experimental researcher. Given the research ethics standards of today, these experiments cannot be fully replicated and thus give grounds for scepticism regarding the 'conditions' and generalisation to real-world situations. For Pinker, the overall findings of laboratory studies of this type showed that 'a majority of people will still hurt a stranger against their own inclinations if they see it as part of a legitimate project in their society' (Pinker, 2011, p. 560).

The prison simulation at Stanford University created a basic custodial environment populated by naive subjects randomly assigned to roles of guards or prisoners. Within 6 days, violence between guards and inmates had become so frequent and the trauma of the inmates so serious that the experiment was ended. The researchers, Haney, Banks, and Zimbardo (1973), concluded that the environment and structural conditions of prisons generated the violence rather than the disposition or personalities of the experiment's participants. A lesser-known replication of the Stanford prison simulation by Lovibond and colleagues at the University of New South Wales introduced three conditions: the first was a replication of the Stanford experiment; in the second 'individualised' condition, guards were given instructions to follow the rules of conduct of the New South Wales Corrective Service; the third was a 'participatory' condition, which encouraged a consultative approach and fostered constructive and responsible behaviour. While the strict replication produced similar results to the original experiment, the 'individualised' and 'participatory' versions were substantially less traumatic and violent than the crude simulation at Stanford. The researchers also concluded that the results provided support for 'further evidence that hostile affrontive relations in prison are a function of the social organization of prison rather than the personal characteristics of the participants' (Lovibond, Mithiran, & Adams, 1979, p. 273).

In the well-known laboratory studies of obedience conducted by Yale psychologist Stanley Milgram, naive subjects were paid an hourly fee to act as 'teachers' and were compelled by a supervising scientist to administer (fake) electric shocks to 'learners' in an experiment designed to test compliance to authority but disguised as studying the impact of punishment on learning (Milgram, 1963, 1974). Two thirds of the subjects (65 per cent) administered the maximum voltage (a supposedly near fatal 450 volts) to the 'learners', who were usually out of sight in another room and who carefully faked distress and pain. Greater proximity to victims and the physical absence of the supervising scientist weakened compliance to the orders to continue the experiment. Milgram was surprised by the willingness of his subjects to respond to the stern commands of an authoritative source; although not entirely able to shake off the possibility that his very willing subjects sensed the experiment was a hoax, he nevertheless concluded,

> Ordinary people, simply doing their jobs, and without any particular hostility on their part, can become agents in a terrible destructive process. Moreover, even when the destructive effects of their work become patently clear, and they are asked to carry out actions incompatible with fundamental standards of morality, relatively few people have the resources needed to resist authority. (Milgram, 1974, p. 76)

The Milgram studies were partially replicated – at least to the initial 150 volts shock threshold – by Burger (2009) 40 years later, and Burger predicted that many of his subjects would be likely to proceed to higher levels of harm, hence confirming the nexus between a compelling authority and the performance of otherwise taboo conduct, such as hurting another under the compulsion of a command. Yet, a larger proportion of Burger's subjects declined to obey the experimenter than had those who participated in Milgram's studies (about 30 per cent compared to 17.5 per cent). While these studies are indicative of the influence of authority on obedience, they are nevertheless limited by the experimental conditions, particularly the context of a scientific experiment administered by an institution of repute, which claimed that the subjects were not harmed.[29] The legitimacy of the authority ordering the violence is thus highly relevant. Shifting the context to a real event of torture or killing requires a different order of compliance and circumstances where a 'legitimate' ideology and government authorise such extremes. Obedience in the context of a totalitarian regime, as Pinker (2011) noted, depends on 'pluralistic ignorance' that requires individuals 'to cultivate thoroughgoing thought control lest their true feelings betray them' (p. 562). Their sincerity must be demonstrated, and techniques of neutralisation (in Pinker's terms, euphemisms, gradualism, displacement and diffusion of responsibility, distancing from and derogation of the victim) allow the 'moralisation gap' or cognitive dissonance to be moderated and help manage the inherent stress of breaking taboos. In the Cambodian setting under the DK regime, the transformation of society through organised violence provided an extreme ideological authorising condition, one where terror was employed and participation in such terror demonstrated loyalty. Deliberate techniques of brutalisation of the torturers undermined moderators such as empathy, and the fear wrought by terror (kill or be killed) subdued potential acts of collective disobedience.

---

[29] Goldhagen (2009) argued that the notion of 'crimes of obedience', which suggests moral judgments are incapacitated by a strong state is contradicted by the evidence. His account of the actions and recollections of men serving in German police battalions, some drawn specifically from the German Order Police as well as SS Einsatzgruppen, shows widespread support among these soldiers (and more generally in the armed forces and population) for the elimination of Jews.

Violentisation

Winton (2011) adapted Athens's (1992) individual microlevel 'process of violentization' to the crime of genocide in an attempt to integrate individual pathways to excessive violence with collective manifestations of extreme violence. Athens's original theory described four stages of the process of violentisation: during the first *brutalisation* stage,[30] individuals are taught how to engage in violence; the *defiance* stage provides a belief system supportive of the use of violence; in the third stage, *the violent dominance engagements* stage, individuals engage in acts of violence – they may be punished for failing to do so and rewarded for successfully becoming violent; ultimately, in the final *virulency* stage, individuals adopt a violent and dangerous self. Winton added the final stage of *extreme virulency* to account for the capacity of brutalised groups to perform extreme violence such as torture. In the process, the brutalised subjects become incapable of empathy. The process of brutalisation and desensitisation applied to Angkar's Revolutionary Army (RAK) was achieved through the habits of war, but it was more fully realised by the conscription of boy (and some girl) soldiers (*chlomb/chlorbs*). These very young peasant recruits were trained as shock troops who together went through the violentisation process of priming for the murder of class enemies, often practising on animals various methods of killing (Quinn, 1989, pp. 237–9, citing Sihanouk, 1980, and others). The result was an obedient shock force indoctrinated by Bolshevised reeducators and led by warlords.

The phenomenological process of 'violentisation' is underpinned by demonstration and imitation by significant others who hold the idea of the generalised violent 'other' (cf. Becker, 1963). Athens developed the idea of the generalised 'other' to the broader notion of a 'phantom other' or 'phantom community', which allows the offenders to legitimate their violence and reflects the essential fluidity of the self, similar to the notion of drift (Winton, 2011, p. 366). In short, an imagined other or community serves to mobilise an oppositional posture that also enables neutralisation to take place. The RAK was the incubator for the conversion of peasant boys to revolutionary instruments and murderers through the suppression of dehumanised (phantom others) class enemies. In the final stage of 'virulency', the actor aware of his notoriety becomes 'overly impressed with his violent performances and ultimately with himself in general' (Athens, 1992, p. 75). Winton's additional stage of 'extreme virulency' carries the same risks of overconfidence due to the unrestrained performance of previously taboo behaviour such that perpetrators may feel they transcend

---

[30] This stage was itself divided into 'violent subjugation' (being assaulted), 'personal horrification' (observe others being assaulted), and 'violent coaching' (taught how to carry out violent behaviour). Athens (1992) suggested that although all three experiences are necessary they may occur over a long period of time but are usually completed by adolescence.

the normal; a new state of being arises – indeed, a new persona emerges, and in Cambodia, by extension, a new society.[31] The creation of an army of actors capable of breaking all taboos and customary sociability required such a violentisation process. This training in violence was undertaken via the educative zeal of the vanguard, the party zealots and former teachers who formed the leadership of Ankgar and the CPK. Violentisation processes were aided by the dominance of radical preferences for violence in the resolution of conflict and 'contradictions', the archaic preliterate communal nature of Cambodian society, the legacy of absolutism, and the transcendental fatalism of Buddhism that rendered violentisation possible once impressionable youths were separated from the customary social order and traditional hierarchies.

Disproportionate revenge

According to Hinton (1998, 2002), cultural traditions in Cambodia require that bad deeds, like good deeds, must be repaid, and the obligation to do so links or ties the parties concerned; thus, 'revenge is the inverse of gratitude'. He further referred to the Cambodian cultural trope of disproportionate revenge ('a head for an eye'), or *kum*, which, in his view, provided a context for the excess of violence by shock troops and their leaders. Hinton argued that the epic poem *Tum Teav* illustrates the resort to excessive violence that forms this cultural trait. It tells the story of the thwarted love of two sweethearts and the awful revenge of decapitation by plow and harrow visited by King Rama on the family and seven generations removed of the Governor Archoun, whose conduct caused the death of the two lovers. For Hinton (1998), the disproportionate use of violence during DK was in part the result of these 'salient cultural models' (p. 353). Recruits to the CPK and RAK learned the anger needed to 'smash' the rich capitalist class and transform Cambodia, the underlying notion being that violence must be paid back and be used perforce to suppress rather than resolve conflict. The build-up of grudges based on class resentment proved 'lethal during the DK when Khmer Rouge ideology encouraged the poor to take revenge upon the rich for past abuse' and 'provided a legitimizing and highly motivating basis for much violence during DK' (Hinton, 1998, pp. 356, 360). The cultivation of hate and the dehumanisation of class enemies descended on city dwellers, who once were the dominating and superior rich but who were reduced to the inferior status of 'new people'.

---

[31] For more about the transcendent quality of violent crime, see Katz (1988). Baumeister (1997), in support of Athens's violentisation thesis, suggested that sadism is learnt by repeated acts of cruelty followed by reassurance (partly resulting from the absence of a negative response), which reinforces the performance of authorised crime as vital to the assertion of domination. Eventually, the revulsion to visceral violence, often at first a panic response, abates and becomes normalised by its repetition.

In an intensely hierarchical social order, honour may be fragile, and frequently tested loss of face and perceived slights can only be resolved by payback, which reasserts face. Homicide studies refer to such violent contests, often lethal once commenced and usually between males, as honour contests.[32] These cycles of payback ultimately end only with the destruction of the entire familial line of the challenger. The killing of all those associated with the Lon Nol regime, class enemies, and disloyal cadres, including their families and children – the so-called strings of association and patronage that included subordinates – was an example of such spirals of revenge. This was a reversion to the ancient penal codes of collective and clan punishment that had been practiced in the precolonial era and in premodern times elsewhere. Ponchaud's (1989) observations that this form of archaism was not out of place in DK pre-dated Hinton's and drew on the same cultural tropes:

> They therefore did not hesitate, in certain sectors, to execute the wives and children of the condemned, especially those of former officers in 1975, and even those of Khmer Rouge cadres after 1977. In fact it was 'the application in attenuated form of the 1877 Cambodian penal code which stipulated that sudden death could be meted out to the entire family of the culprit as well' ... The novel *Tum Teav*... echoes a certain tradition as concerns forms of punishment: the relatives 'to the seventh degree' of the culprits were buried alive, their heads raked off with an iron harrow. (p. 165)

However, we do not subscribe entirely to Hinton's ethnocultural explanation. Durkheim, Elias, and others have argued, and we shall ourselves contend later on, that disproportionate revenge and associated affective and cognitive processes have been observed almost everywhere in the history of humanity and are more likely associated with sociogenetic and psychogenetic development than any particular ethnic culture.

Criminology and megacrime

Traditional criminological theories can be applied to account for the crimes committed during DK, but they fail to fully explain the varied forms and apocalyptic levels of the violence. Yet, phenomenological approaches, based on the idea that 'crime' is socially constructed and what constitutes crime and who are regarded as deviants are essentially learned through a process of domination and social construction (including neutralisations), remain relevant and potent.[33] These theories are pertinent to show how repeated and powerful

---

[32] Many homicide studies refer to such events, often arising from apparently trivial disputes, and 'face' and status or class differences may have increased the risk of violent conflict in the new communes and among the mobile brigades.

[33] Becker (1963), drawing on the symbolic interaction perspective, proposed that, via a process of labelling driven by moral entrepreneurs, 'Social groups create deviance by making rules

exposure to hostility towards those 'others' deemed outsiders, that is, warlike conduct and violentisation, tie individual and collective learned dispositions to violence with events of mass violence authorised by the state. The scale of the violence suggests a new phylum or division in the 'kingdom' of violence, and criminological theory offers assistance in understanding how extreme violence unfolds in circumstances of drastic change.[34] While extreme forms of violence occur in all societies, they are generally rare. Here we are thinking of occasional, brutal, often expressive murders that are often associated with the pathology of the offender and involve the extreme violation of deeply held taboos such as the murder of children, sexual murders, and the torture and post-mortem mutilation of victims. The repugnancy of these events is such that social outrage appears universal and the response of the state swift and substantial.

These extraordinary crimes thus have the function of reaffirming social solidarity and social values (cf. Durkheim) and allow the state to assert moral legitimacy. In a situation where the scale of extraordinary murder is prevalent and unchecked – indeed, authorised, as in DK – is a new order or division of crime required? In this situation new normative definitions must be considered, and the subject of crime must be redefined. Indeed, theoretical argument about the definition of crime, usually forming around narrower legalistic or broader sociological definitions, is crucial to the project of criminology. The 'essential crime' in these extreme megacrimes might be conceived as *domination*, which is the key element in the struggles within and between hierarchies of dominance and therefore is seen as intractable as long as the exercise of power remains fundamental and unchanging. Anarchist and associated peace-making or constitutive criminology redefine crime broadly as 'the suppression of the human spirit' (Tift & Sullivan, 1980) or in republican criminology as 'an invasion of dominion' (Braithwaite & Petit, 1990).

Conclusion: the perfect storm

Applying a macrotheoretical approach based on conflict generally accounts for the dynamics that led to the 'perfect storm' of mass violence in Cambodia.

---

whose infraction creates deviance, and by applying those rules to particular people and labeling them as outsiders. From this point of view, deviance is *not* a quality of the act the person commits, but rather a consequence of the application by others of rules and sanctions to an "offender". The deviant is one to whom that label has been successfully applied; deviant behavior is behavior that people so label' (p. 8). Erikson (1966) provides an illustration of this labelling process in his analysis of the witchcraft trials in colonial New England in the seventeenth century.

[34] Maier-Katkin, Mears, and Bernard (2009) also offer a nonlinear, multicausal, and multilevel theorisation of mass crimes that overlaps with ours but that focuses on the nonbureaucratic type of mass violence, which, in the case of Cambodia, could include the genocidal massacres of Vietnamese that took place after the 1970 coup, the 1975 killings of Lon-Nol soldiers and officials, and generally the activities of the KR shock troops. Olusanya (2013) also attempted an integration (articulated around the concept of cognitive dissonance) of multidisciplinary macro-meso-microlevel theories to more fully explain participation in megacrimes.

The analysis of factors leading to that perfect storm can be understood through a criminological perspective that combines historical, cultural, and situational/proximate factors. The Second Indochina War in tandem with civil war converged with peasant revenge, revolution, and racist nationalism, which in turn coalesced with state policies of economic, political, and cultural autarky and literal social reengineering of state and society. All these factors combined as disintegrating forces of decivilisation, but the scale of violence became magnified by the unique amalgam of Cambodian communism and the impact of Cold War externalities. These broad drivers help contextualise the relevance of criminological theories such as neutralisation and violentisation, which are usually applied to individual-level explanations, and show how their principles can be extended to group and collective violence; in doing so, the types of violence, perpetrators, and victims found in mass violence can be more easily distinguished and analysed.

As far as violence is concerned, 1975 was certainly not 'year zero': Cambodian history has exposed many examples of ordinary violence, mass violence, and atrocities. Since the mid 1960s violence had become commonplace, and the revolutionary terror and totalitarian regime of the KR had been established as early as 1970 in certain regions. As Jackson (1989) observed: 'The fact that massive amounts of blood were shed by the Khmer Rouge diverged from the Khmer norms in scope rather than in kind' (p. 72). Rummel's (1994, pp. 4–5) comparative research on megamurders or 'democides' placed Cambodia as the highest of all democides that occurred between 1900 and 1987 when measuring the proportion of those who perished as an annual rate of the total population. DK was the most lethal of the twentieth century's most lethal regimes that he compared.[35] The civil war, combined with the destructiveness of the Vietnamese war of liberation, produced a surfeit of war victims and war psychosis. War terror was etched into everyday existence. As Becker (1986) remarked, the Cambodians had become conditioned to the habits of war.

The Cambodian legacy of unending authoritarianism and, particularly during the French Protectorate, the politics of isolation and infantilisation ensured a political consciousness that was limited by ethnic and nationalist interests. Political organisation of the masses in the years after decolonisation was undeveloped and participation remained very low. The economy, dependent on rice production and only partially linked to regional trade, was vulnerable, while the division of labour and interdependency were not developed, and so the promise of autarkic communism and liberation from the burdens of both the city

---

[35] Besides DK, Rummel included in the comparison in chronological order: Mexico (1900–20), USSR (1917–87), Turkey (1919–23), Mao's China (1926–76), Mongolia (1926–87), Romania (1938–48), Czechoslovakia (1945–48), Poland (1945–48), North Korea (1948–87), Uganda (1971–79), and Angola (1975–87). In terms of absolute total numbers of deaths, Rummel ranked DK among the 'lesser mega-murderers', estimating a death toll of 2 million or 2.4 million inclusive of the civil war periods (1968–87).

and money promised enough to mobilise the vanguard, especially the RAK and its young shock troops of poor peasants. The metaphor of the perfect storm describes the rapid convergence of critical conditions that cascade into a decivilising episode. Gerlach (2006) stressed: 'Societies are not extremely violent in principle or by character; rather societies turn extremely violent in what is a temporary process. Under conditions mostly perceived within as a crisis, longer-term negative attitudes and prejudices are radicalised' (p. 461). The violent pattern of a Bolshevik-like revolution emerged from the civil war, and an amalgam of the Jacobins, Mao and Stalin, Fanon and Samir Amin mixed with indigenous sources offered ideological justifications for violence; they reinforced one another and coalesced to form 'the main features of modern genocidal ideology that emerged then, from combinations of religious or racial hatred with territorial expansionism and cults of antiquity and agriculture' (Kiernan, 2007, p. 3).[36]

The incipient violence that followed the ruthless practice of war communism was seldom restrained or moderated by the Centre. Although attempts were made to curtail the arbitrary murders by local authorities (Kiernan, 2008; Vickery, 1984), the Centre itself was captured by fear of rebellion and sabotage. Indeed, the vast majority of Cambodians were traditional, undereducated peasants, infantilised and overtaxed by the colonial and postcolonial state, and often exposed to harsh, cruel, and arbitrary punishment. Premodern peasant sensibilities thoroughly brutalised by corrupt and authoritarian rulers and civil war and informed by revolutionary intolerance were fully exercised by permanently generalising the traditional capacities for individualised acts of cruelty, which occasionally rose to periodic collective violence. In this sense they were primed for retaliation in kind.

The 'moral inversion' discussed by Chandler (1999), which played a role through undoing hierarchies of age, status, and religious and social order (but not hierarchies of dominance per se, on the contrary), manifested in the sudden change in the 'rules of the game' that accompanied 'liberation day' and induced 'lawlessness' and normlessness (as in anomie). The most vulnerable to this inversion was the revolutionary vanguard, the young shock troops that formed the bulk of the revolutionary army and became dominant after the purges of the Issarak, the Hanoi Khmer, and the Eastern Zone officer corps. In a process of violentisation reinforced by constant performance of violent acts, these youthful agents of terror came to relish their power, and acts of violence became 'virulent'. It was as if bandits and murderers now ruled and

---

[36] Given the central importance of the French Revolution in the education of some of the CPK leaders, we add Jacobinism to the amalgam. Jackson (1989, p. 241) saw these influences as constituting an amalgam eclectically drawn upon by the CPK rather than copied – an amalgam of radical ideas that urged the necessity of violence to change society.

thoughtlessly implemented grand abstract policies upon a fearful population of slaves – an oriental Sparta in the making. The image of an adolescent KR soldier wielding a pistol during the evacuation of Phnom Penh on the cover of *Time* in April 1975 illustrated the effectiveness of the civil war on hardening the youthful vanguard capable of conducting the murders made necessary by the revolution.[37] DK's decivilising practices were the means to achieve the goals of a new socialist Cambodia, free of all vestiges of the old regime.

These young shock troops, often younger than fifteen and from 'old' or base villages, implemented the violence and terror necessary to create DK because, as Quinn (1989) explained:

a small group of alienated intellectuals, enraged by their perception of a totally corrupt society and imbued with a Maoist plan to create a pure socialist order in the shortest possible time, recruited extremely young, poor, and envious cadres, instructed them in harsh and brutal methods learnt from Stalinist mentors, and used them to destroy physically the cultural underpinnings of the Khmer civilisation and to impose a new society through purges, executions and violence. (p. 240)

First, former rivals and enemies were eliminated, followed by the suppression and elimination of Vietnamese, students, monks, and teachers. Later, those idle or unproductive, especially among the 'new people' (who carried urban, class, and foreign contamination), and those imbued with the old values and all who deviated from the strictures of the new order became lethal targets. For DK, 'the academic world posed an inherent threat: if it had produced them, it could also produce a new dissident group to overthrow them'. Religious leaders and teachers blinded the masses to their exploitation and the necessity of class struggle and were targeted as an 'essential part of breaking up the old system' (Quinn, 1989, pp. 188–9). The CPK also set to undermine the family and sequestered the young for ideological training that turned them into active agents against parental authority and the 'old' ways. The object of these new communes was to affirm the power of Angkar and to reduce and eventually eliminate individualism. Cambodia was to become a giant agricultural society with each person filing a distinct, specific function. As in Mao's vision, true communism was only realised as collective action (Quinn, 1989, p. 193). The radical changes wrought by terror and the new communes were designed to undermine Cambodia's institutions – religion, family, property, monarchy, money, cities, and home villages – all ultimately destroyed, and with this overturn, any customary constraints on violence. The extreme reduction of interdependency through the destruction of relationships

---

[37] A short description of the role of these soldiers can be found in an interview by Martin (1989/1994, pp. 165–7).

that were normally formed via these institutions brutally unleashed the processes of decivilisation.

The CPK was thus aiming to remodel the very inner thoughts and behaviours of its citizens. Reminiscent of Foucault's (1977) thesis that the microphysics of control in total institutions (such as prisons and asylums) changed when the aim of the rehabilitators or reeducators of the modern prison turned from the discipline or taming of the body to the taming of the mind, DK also sought to rearrange and tame the minds of its captive population. So, with collectivisation, violence, surveillance, and self-abnegation, old individualist values and habits would be eliminated. The Khmer had been reduced to slaves, but they had yet to be transformed into the perfect collective tools of the state. The ultimate goal of the regime's reeducators was a reconfigured ardent and compliant Khmer subject re-created as model worker and peasant so beloved by revolutionary propaganda. The educators themselves, the self-proclaimed 'society of secular saints' driven by the Jacobin obsession with purity and unanimity, were filled with an 'excess of morality'. Armed with the means of the state and primed with ideological justification for extreme violence, they planned first to destroy a corrupt ancient regime and then to rebuild a model communist state by cannibalising the population and exerting absolute control.

Postface

In the final days of December 1978, during a rare brief official visit, the journalists Elizabeth Becker (*Washington Post*) and Richard Dudman (*St. Louis Post-Dispatch*), as well as Dr Malcolm Caldwell, a Marxist UK academic (School of Oriental and African Studies, University of London), interviewed – or rather, were lectured by – Pol Pot. They were allowed an escorted visit outside Phnom Penh to see a model collective. Becker observed a surreal world of confected agrarian bounty, poorly mechanised production brigades, and industries populated by rigid figurants without a single smile – faces of apprehension overseen by young armed soldiers. Before they departed for Beijing on 23 December 1978, Caldwell obtained another meeting with Pol Pot, which apparently went well. Caldwell returned affirmed in his positive support for Pol Pot's vision. Later that night he was killed in their Phnom Penh guesthouse. Awakened by gunshots, Becker was confronted by a pistol-bearing young man, and she fled back into her room. Gunfire erupted and armed men were seen on the street; all was confusion. The minders reappeared and Becker and Dudman were shown the body of Caldwell, who had been shot, along with a young Cambodian man. They left Cambodia no wiser about who killed Caldwell and why. Becker suspected that Caldwell was unlikely to have offended Pol Pot because of his

The perfect storm: decivilising state and society: 1975–1979   223

support and sympathy for the CPK's programme, but the motives for his killing and the identity of the real attackers are still unknown.[38]

Four of the visitors' guards were arrested and, after interrogation at S-21, two confessed that Caldwell was killed to undermine the regime and 'to prevent the party from gathering friends from around the world'. Another explanation was that Caldwell was killed by a Vietnamese commando unit as part of the essential 'psych-ops' that precede a military invasion, a propaganda coup to illustrate the instability and brutality of the Pol Pot clique (Short, 2004). For Becker (1986) and Osborne (1994), this 'murder' was illustrative of the madness, anarchy, and weakness of the regime as the last days unfolded and the state was unravelling as rapidly as it began.[39] A recent, more prosaic version reported by both Sikoeun (2013) and Locard (2013) drew on an account by Phi Phuon, who was in charge of security at B1 (DK Foreign Ministry), including the security of those invited by the regime.[40] In his version, one of the young guards charged with the security of the three foreign guests was in love with a young female revolutionary; this was reciprocal, but, of course, during DK, prohibited. She had rejected the advances of another suitor and, to show her love to the young guard, the girl had given him a *krama* (a cotton scarf, one of the few personal items permitted). Seeking revenge, the rival denounced the young guard, and, as was common, his arrest for this 'sexual crime' happened at night. The young guard, knowing what such an arrest meant for him, defended himself, and in the resulting shooting, Caldwell, rather than hiding like his two friends, went out his bedroom and in the confusion was accidentally killed. The young guard was also killed, intentionally or perhaps in self-defence, by his arresters. This version places the motives of common jealousy in the hands of a thwarted suitor, who, to get revenge, manipulates the system of puritanical terror endorsed by DK. Such an account, as plausible as the others, does not need conspiracy theories to illustrate the madness of the regime. Three days later Vietnamese forces invaded Cambodia with 'overpowering force to wipe out the enemy'.[41] Hollowed out by impossible ideas and terror and as incompetent as the old corrupt regime it had replaced, Democratic Kampuchea collapsed in 2 weeks.[42]

---

[38] Caldwell's family and William Burchett have suggested that while Caldwell may have felt the interview went well Pol Pot's demeanour was famously warm even when greatly angered. Pol Pot later claimed the murder was authorised by Son Sen the Minister for Defence.

[39] A thorough account of the event is given by Kiernan (2008) based on Becker's and Dudman's accounts as well as the *Santebal* S-21 records, and these reports undermine the role of a Vietnamese commando raid (although such attacks took place – see Chandler, 1991, p. 310) but do not report the interviews with Phuon, the head of security at the Foreign Ministry.

[40] Both Locard and Sikoeun interviewed Phuon in 2001.

[41] General Vo Nguyen Giap cited in Kiernan (2008, p. 450).

[42] The delusion of military prowess bolstered by China and by the CPK's fantasy that they alone had defeated US imperialism encouraged fatal triumphalism and adventurism (Burchett, cited

On 7 January 1979, the People's Army of Vietnam, supported by a small indigenous force led by former Eastern Zone officers under the banner of the Kampuchean United Front for National Salvation (KUFNS), occupied a hastily deserted Phnom Penh, and the People's Republic of Kampuchea (PRK) was proclaimed the following day. The PAVN quickly moved to occupy all the major towns and strategic locations.[43] The remnants of the RAK were scattered to the west and the north, and the CPK leadership survived diminished but still with powerful allies. In their retreat, further forced marches of base people, destruction of granaries, and massacres occurred in an apparent policy of scorched earth (Kiernan, 2008).

The Cold War politics of the time allowed the remaining DK forces to find refuge in Thailand and to receive the support of China and the USA, which saw in the Khmer Rouge an enemy of Vietnam – a case of 'the enemy of my enemy is my friend' – despite the shameful atrocities that had occurred. The lifeline offered to the remaining DK forces under Pol Pot enabled an insurgency and civil war to linger for another 20 years, compounding the disaster of the revolution. The leaders returned to the forests and mountains and to the guerrilla tactics they had practised in the past.

Vietnam's invasion and occupation ended DK and was welcomed by many Cambodians. It allowed them to begin to return to a more normal life, no longer subjected to arbitrary punishment or forced to work in collectives. Finally they were able to return to familial rather than communal meals, as they had been compelled by the ambitious form of collectivisation attempted by DK. The Vietnamese intervention may have been required by the realpolitik of the border wars and hegemonic aspirations for Indochina, but it was also fundamentally an act of humanitarian assistance – a costly exercise in what today would be called 'the responsibility to protect'. The military defeat of DK provoked the Chinese, already then concerned to contain the Vietnamese, into further support of a regime that it yet recognised as deviant from the normal path of communist development. By then, the pragmatists led by Deng Xiaoping had returned to power, ending the Cultural Revolution and left radicalism. In January 1979, the Chinese launched a divisional-scale excursion across the northern borders of Vietnam in response to the invasion of Cambodia but were repulsed, with heavy losses. The Cambodian-Vietnam war was not just another proxy conflict

---

in Kiernan & Boua, 1982, pp. v–viii). RAK suffered disastrous battlefield losses within days and was soon unable to manoeuvre or counterattack. The purge of the Eastern Zone damaged the more effective units and eliminated a large proportion of the experienced officer corps (as Stalin had done to the Red Army in the 1930s).

[43] The rapid advance of PAVN had been unexpected and caught the Centre unprepared and so quickly that the commander of S-21, Duch, failed to destroy what would amount to irrefutable evidence of the regime's savagery.

for the Cold War (Regaud, 1992), but it was played out in the context of Russian-Chinese rivalry. The tone was set for the extension of hostilities in Cambodia. The desperate need for reconstruction and the creation of a sustainable form of government was to be delayed by the formation of a new united front against the PRK and the Vietnamese occupation.

9 Reconstruction in the midst of a civil war: pariahs, bandits, and international accomplices: 1979–1991

In late December 1978, People's Army of Vietnam (PAVN) troops entered Cambodia; by the end of April 1979, they had liberated the entire country from the Democratic Kampuchea (DK) regime. In January, a new government, the People's Republic of Kampuchea (PRK), was formed by returned anti-Polpotist Cambodian communists and supported by the Vietnamese. They were faced with the huge task of reconstructing a country devastated by years of civil war and a genocidal regime. However, peace did not return because most of the international community continued to prop up the Khmer Rouge (KR)[1] and ordered an arms and economic embargo that prevented reconstruction and development aid to be sent to Cambodia. Sporadic fighting continued even after the Vietnamese troops left Cambodia in 1989. Hundreds of thousands of Cambodians had been uprooted, and many were living in precarious and dangerous conditions in refugee camps on the Thai border. This chapter investigates the decade of state reconstruction after the catastrophic years of the regime of DK. The levels of interindividual 'ordinary' criminality may have been low, but the new regime of the People's Republic of Kampuchea defined many prohibited activities as crimes against the state, and the political economy of the armed conflict revived and reinstitutionalised clientelism and elite corruption.

On 25 December 1978, 150,000 PAVN troops and between 20,000 and 30,000 anti-Polpotist Cambodian fighters invaded Cambodia (Jennar, 2010).[2] Two weeks later, on 7 January 1979, they liberated Phnom Penh and, by the end of April, the entire country from the Pol Pot regime, which managed to keep control of only small enclaves bordering Thailand. Months before the invasion, several anti–Pol Pot DK cadres from the Eastern Zone had defected to Vietnam

---

[1] The United Nations (UN) imposed economic sanctions on the new regime, and Cambodia's UN seat was retained by the KR under a revised Coalition Government of Democratic Kampuchea: a united front comprising pro-Sihanouk and nationalist groups as well as the self-reformed KR.
[2] Kampuchean United Front for National Salvation (KUFNS) forces may have been as few as 15,000 (see Kiernan, 2008, p. 450) and, according to Thayer (1994), PAVN troop numbers peaked at about 200,000 in 1979 before winding back in 1982. The PAVN assault was based on rapid encircling movement of troop-led armoured units supported by air and artillery attack with the prime aim of incapacitating command and control. The Revolutionary Army of Kampuchea (RAK), perhaps about 70,000, was no match for the PAVN.

with some of their troops and had asked for Vietnamese military support. One of the first to do so, on 20 June 1977, was a 25-year-old commander named Hun Sen. Three weeks before the intervention, on 2 December 1978, he and other former DK cadres, some Cambodian communists who had not been in Cambodia during DK but had remained in exile in Vietnam, and a few non-communists had formed the Kampuchean United Front for National Salvation (KUFNS), presided by Heng Samrin. About a month later, communists within the KUFNS re-created the Kampuchean People's Revolutionary Party (KPRP). They formed the Revolutionary Council and, on 12 January, proclaimed the People's Republic of Kampuchea (PRK). The task awaiting these eight men[3] with no previous governmental experience was gigantic. They had to lead the reconstruction of a country ruined by 5 years of civil war and intense US bombing and followed by 4 years of violent revolutionary politics during which all state and social institutions had been destroyed and perhaps a fifth of the population, including almost all skilled individuals, decimated.

The resistance front of the warlords

In 1980, the Polpotists officially repudiated communism in a press conference for Western journalists, when Khieu Samphan 'acknowledg[ed] that the Khmer Rouge experience was "a murderous utopia" [and] explain[ed] that Communism was dead and that to reject Communism once and for all [was] undoubtedly the best way of uniting all Kampucheans in the anti-Vietnamese crusade as part of a national front' (Leifer, 1981, p. 98). Many saw in it only a tactic to be able to form an anti-Vietnamese front that the KR would control and through which they could regain state power and possibly reimpose DK practices; but others considered it was the only opportunity to preserve national independence. In 1982, the national front the KR desired was created and included themselves, Sihanoukists, and former supporters of the Lon Nol Khmer Republic. The new Coalition Government of Democratic Kampuchea (CGDK) was once again nominally presided by Sihanouk, but, on the ground, militarily dominated by the Polpotists. It had many features reminiscent of the anticolonial front of the late 1940s, early 1950s, between traditional Issaraks and Khmer Viet Minh communist Issaraks. First, the front had a common foe, Vietnam: the foreign invader, the 'hereditary brother enemy' (Chanda, 1986), feared and demonised by successive regimes. Second, in the anticolonial front, Sihanouk and his de facto rule had been protected by the French invaders against the Issarak front for independence, which had been fighting against this foreign

---

[3] Heng Samrin, Pen Sovann, Chea Sim, Hun Sen, Chan Ven, Nou Beng, Mok Sokun, and Keo Chanda.

power as well as for its own political ambition. In 1982, the future prime minister Hun Sen was protected by the Vietnamese invaders against a neo-Issarak front, which was also fighting for independence from this foreign power as well as its own political ambitions, albeit Sihanouk now belonged to the 'liberation' front. Finally, the noncommunist factions of the CGDK were disunited, given to in-fighting, prone to banditry, and in conflict with the far more disciplined Polpotists, in a similar way as the traditional Issaraks and the Khmer Viet Minh communist Issaraks had been 40 years previously.

Another similarity with the independence struggle of the 1940s and 1950s was the tendency of guerrilla fighters to turn to banditry. By mid 1979, 'several camps had been established along the border with Thailand. They hosted a variety of forces, mostly loosely organised bands of self-appointed "nationalist" commanders, many of them little more than smugglers operating under various pretences and flags. A few were genuine patriots who later became the leaders of the non-communist resistance' (Bekaert, 1997, p. 12). In 1986, Sihanouk contended that 'many of the fighters in the Khmer People's National Liberation Front (KPNLF) have become pirates, smugglers and bandits who were reportedly selling arms' (cited in Chanda, 1986, p. 117). The next year, a report revealed the involvement in banditry and violations of human rights by KPNLF troops, and Amnesty International uncovered 'executions, beatings, and rape by troops in camps under KPNLF control' (Chanda, 1988, p. 106). However, it seemed that the forces of the Polpotists did not readily engage in warlord banditry before 1991, although by 1985, with the growing factionalism among them, and Pol Pot's warlords Ta Mok and Ke Pauk, more or less capable of independent action, banditry may have become more frequent after 1987 (Chanda, 1988). But, according to Brown (1992), by late 1991 'some "land-grabbing" by all factions [including PRK forces] was evident' and '"banditry" – non-ideological plundering by the armed forces of all factions – plagued many rural areas' (p. 93).

In August 1979, the Revolutionary Tribunal of the PRK conducted the trial *in abstentia* of Pol Pot and Ieng Sary for the crime of genocide during which numerous witnesses testified to the horrors they had endured under DK. The fledging government of the PRK probably believed that the international community, now fully aware of the cataclysm engineered by the ousted DK regime, would assist them in rebuilding their society. They could not have been more wrong. The United Nations (UN) continued to recognise the legitimacy of the KR government, and most of the world supported the megamurderers of two millions of their compatriots. It treated the liberators as pariahs and regarded the assassins as legitimate representatives of the survivors. Such was the reason of state during this stage of the Cold War.[4]

---

[4] To compound the situation for Cambodia, the Western nations, China, and the Association of Southeast Asian Nations (ASEAN) states refused to provide reconstruction assistance directly

Return of Cold War politics

Vietnam's military intervention in Cambodia occurred after repeated DK attacks of Vietnamese border villages in which '25 communes and 93 villages had been destroyed, between 250,000 and 300,000 Vietnamese had lost their houses, 100,000 hectares of cultivable lands had to be abandoned, and thousands of civilians had been massacred' (Jennar, 2010, pp. 26–7). Vietnam had attempted to negotiate with DK at the end of 1977 without success. Repeated calls for UN mediation in 1978 had fallen on deaf ears. It seemed that direct intervention to remove their belligerent neighbours was the last option. In the 1980s, the major power that prolonged the misery of the Cambodian people by supplying military equipment to the defeated and moribund KR army in 1979 and again in 1985 was not the USA but China (Jennar, 2010, p. 50). However, a broad coalition of nation states was involved, which directly included China, the USA, Britain, Thailand, Singapore, and Malaysia, and indirectly, West Germany, Belgium, South Korea, France, Sweden, and Taiwan. Had this Sino-Western coalition denied financial, political, and military support to those responsible for the Cambodian bloodbath and instead provided economic and developmental aid to the new PRK, it is possible that mass violence could have stopped as early as 1980. A decade of civil war may have been avoided, and the Vietnamese army could have withdrawn after the defeat of the KR. But the superpowers' imperatives of the final decade of the Cold War, such as the Sino-Soviet conflict and the US need for revenge after their defeat in Vietnam in 1975, prevailed over a political resolution and the need to provide urgent humanitarian assistance.

Instead, Vietnam occupied Cambodia until 1989 to prevent the return of the resurrected KR. This led to the formation of noncommunist anti-Vietnamese armed factions that formed an alliance with the KR, and an international embargo was implemented against the PRK. The PRK, therefore, could rely only on the Soviet bloc for assistance, creating a vicious cycle that punished the victims even further. For example, the civil war generated a mass flow of refugees fleeing to the Thai border. Although humanitarian aid was provided, a great part of it went to support the Polpotist guerrillas and their allies. Direct military training was also provided, as in 1983 when the British Special Air Service (SAS) trained anti-Vietnamese factions, which included the KR, in the use of explosives for terrorist missions in Cambodia (Bekaert, 1997, p. 214; Kane, 2007, p. 38). We argue that the failure of the international community to bring to justice the principal authors of the revolutionary terror and the conduct of the Sino-Western coalition were the most important factors that led to further mass crimes between 1979 and 1991. It is this context of hyperrivalry

to the new regime, and the UN relief agencies were not allowed to operate within Cambodia. The bulk of international aid from Western nations would be diverted to refugee camps along the Thai border.

that influenced much of the violence and crimes committed during and after this period. We first examine violence and criminal behaviour directly resulting from the civil war. Then we turn to the reemergence of corruption and the development of an enduring kleptocracy. Finally, we focus on ordinary crime, which was certainly influenced by the war, but not directly linked to it.

Types and patterns of violence

War-related violence

The death toll

We have not found any comprehensive records of the total number of casualties on both sides during the 1979–91 civil war, but in addition to the ousting of the KR in 1979 and the direct fighting between Polpotists and Vietnamese troops, the ensuing period of civil war occasioned much violence against non-combatant civilians. Bekaert (1997) estimated that by the end of 1981 the death toll among Vietnamese soldiers could have reached 25 a day, and in 1983, 2,500 Vietnamese soldiers had been killed. According to Jennar (2010), PAVN casualties reached 55,300 in Cambodia between 1979 and 1989, while Regaud (1992, p. 148) reported that 55,000 Vietnamese soldiers died and as many were wounded between 1977 and 1987. Regaud included the China-Vietnam border war of February 1979, but he noted that at least a third of the Vietnamese death toll could have been caused by malaria and the lack of medicine. On the KR side, from late December 1978 to 1987, 80,000 soldiers could have been killed or wounded (Regaud, 1992, p. 33). Rummel (1994) estimated the 'democide' between 1979 and 1987 killed 461,000 noncombatants, but the reliability of his figures is debatable.[5] Thayer (1994), based on interviews with PAVN commanders, put Vietnamese battle casualties at around 25,000, but this figure excludes combat in 1977 and 1978 before the invasion and combat after the significant clashes with KR forces in 1984–5.

Scorched earth

During their retreat towards the western regions, the KR carried out a scorched earth policy, destroying rice and other supplies they could not carry. Slocomb

---

[5] Rummel's figures (1994, p. 243, table 11.1) include 461,000 civilian deaths caused by the Vietnamese army between 1970 and 1987 (hence, not estimating separately such casualties during the 1970–5 civil war and the period of occupation between 1979 and 1989). We did not find any reliable reports of widespread attacks against civilians by the PAVN during these two periods. Rummel (1994, p. 202) estimated about 850,000 deaths from all sides, including famine, between 1979 and 1987: according to him, the Samrin regime was responsible for 230,000 deaths and the KR united front about 150,000–160,000 (p. 165, table 9.1). Rummel (1994, p. 192) noted an upper limit for the KR period estimated at 3,315,000 for the period 1967–79 and based on a household census in 1982–3 conducted by the PRK.

(2010) wrote about the forced deportations of populations, the destruction of infrastructure, and the plunder during the Polpotists' retreat that not only terrorised villagers but also increased the risk of famine: 'The scorched earth retreat of the Khmer Rouge as the PAVN [People's Army of Vietnam] and the Salvation Front invaded in late December 1978 destroyed many of the gains that may have been made in the industrial reconstruction of the country' (p. 214). Locard (2013) reported the mass execution of prisoners in many of the 150 prisons and S-21-like district-level centres.

The bamboo wall

The most controversial policy of the PRK during the civil war was the forced conscription of peasants to build, as part of the K5 plan,[6] a bamboo wall on the mine-infested and malaria-prone western border between 1982 and 1987. Some authors (e.g. Luciolli, 1988) described this policy, which resulted in thousands of death and amputees, as similar to the labour camps of DK. The aim was to seal the Thai border to prevent incursions by armed resistance factions. There is disagreement about the necessity of this policy in terms of national defence and the number of people who were conscripted and died during the construction of this PRK 'Maginot line'. According to Luciolli (1988, p. 68), one million people could have participated in its construction between September 1984 and December 1986, and between 50,000 and 59,000 may have perished. Jennar (2010, p. 74) has argued that these figures were grossly exaggerated and that, at most, 288,000 people were involved during the above-mentioned period, the examination of the figures provided by the relevant ministries amounting to no more than 150,000 people.[7] Jennar also suggested that K5 prevented more civilian deaths by KR guerrilla action than it caused during its construction; on the other hand, as Slocomb (2002) demonstrated, it provided PRK commanders with significant opportunities for increased power and corrupt wealth accumulation. The forced conscription created resentment against the new government as peasants were forced to leave their farms to perform what they perceived as useless and dangerous labour, and many fell sick. The area became one of the most densely mined regions in Cambodia with repercussions up to this day.

Refugees

During the DK regime, an estimated 26,000 Khmer refugees arrived in Thailand, and by the end of 1978, 20,000 of them had been resettled. From 1979, a flow of refugees poured out of Cambodia, and makeshift refugee camps

---

[6] The K5 plan was a border defence programme to stop KR incursions by building trenches, fences, and minefields along the entire Thai-Cambodia border.
[7] Jennar did not provide an estimate of the casualties.

sprouted on the Thai border. Referring to the 1979 movement of refugees, Vickery (1984) explained:

The principal reasons for the new movement, without making any attempt to assess their relative order of importance, were (1) to make contact with the outside world for the purpose of either going abroad or contacting friends or relatives already abroad; (2) to trade across the border for commercial purpose; (3) to join, or organise, one of the para-military or bandit groups loosely called Khmer Serei, 'Free Khmer.' (p. 29)

Gottesman (2003) described how

Cambodians became aware of humanitarian assistance being distributed at the border. In some parts of Cambodia this push-and-pull effect led to the complete breakdown of local authority. Newly appointed village chiefs not only left for Thailand but permitted entire villages to flee. Village militias abandoned defence tasks, sometimes to form bandit groups to steal rice. A web of paths and trails soon twisted through the forests along the Thai-Cambodian border as refugees and smugglers attempted to avoid bandits, the Khmer Rouge, and Vietnamese and Thai soldiers. (pp. 41–2)

Similarly Bekaert (1997) related: 'Anyone who was at the border in 1979 must have vivid memories of the extreme chaos that was then the rule. Warlords were struggling for a piece of the meagre black market pie much more than attempting to liberate Cambodia' (p. 54). In June 1979, over 42,000 Cambodians crossed into Thailand to escape fighting between the Khmer Rouge and PAVN and PRK troops. The Thai government, fearing it would have to carry alone the burden of the refugees, rounded them up and took them to Preah Vihear. There, they were forced to climb down a steep cliff and return to the Cambodian plains below. Those who resisted were shot or pushed over the cliff, and soldiers threw rocks down the cliff to prevent them climbing back (Thompson, 2010). When they reached the bottom, they had to walk through minefields. The UNHCR estimated that 3,000 had died and 7,000 were unaccounted for (Thompson, 2010), but 'a death toll of 10,000 [was] considered conservative by some' (Mysliwiec, 1988, p. 96). The UN, the Red Cross, and other organisations responded to the need for a massive humanitarian aid campaign on the border, but very little aid reached Cambodia's interior since the UN still considered the KR and their allies to be the legitimate government.

By 1983 there were 250,000 refugees in border camps in Thailand. Life was not easy because the camps also served as sanctuary for the remaining KR and Khmer Serei fighters, and some camps were under their direct control. One of the camps was even administered by Ta Mok, a cruel KR warlord known as 'the butcher of Kampuchea' (Mysliwiec, 1988). Most of these refugees 'lived in makeshift camps at the mercy of warlords and hooligans or under the iron thumb of the Khmer Rouge' (Chanda, 1988, p. 110). There were reports of political executions and forced recruitment by the various armed factions (Terry, 2002). Only a portion of the humanitarian aid reached refugees who were suffering from malnutrition and poor health as food and medical supplies were diverted by the Thai military (Terry, 2002). In addition to the ordinary hardship experienced by refugees everywhere, Cambodian refugees were victims of violence, including rape, robbery, and murder, by Thai soldiers and police, Thai and Khmer criminal groups, and the diverse armed factions of the Coalition Government of Democratic Kampuchea, as well as ordinary predatory crime, corruption, and racketeering (Chanda, 1986; Gottesman, 2003; Mysliwiec, 1988; van der Kroef, 1979, 1984). Writing about the early 1980s, Gottesman (2003) reported: 'Refugees attempting to cross the border into Thailand faced threats of extortion and violence from newly formed village militias, bandit groups, the Khmer Rouge, and, as they arrived at the border, Thai soldiers' (pp. 41–2). In 1989, the crime situation in the camps was so bad that, according to Khatharya Um (1990), 'the UN [had] also attempted to superimpose a Western-style judicial system, aimed not so much at reducing the rising crime rate, especially prevalent in the two non-communist camps, as to "re-inculcate" a sense of rule of law that the repatriates can carry back with them to their home areas' (p. 104). Finally, because of their military value and their role as havens for military training and resupply, the camps controlled by the anti-PRK factions, and civilians living in them, became targets of the Vietnamese and PRK forces. The first such attack occurred in June 1980, killing 400 refugees and wounding 900, and many others followed (Terry, 2002).

Other types of violence

Banditry
Banditry resumed as soon as the DK dissolved and the Revolutionary Army of Kampuchea (RAK) retreated in disorder in January 1979, driving with them the forced or fear-motivated population exodus towards the Thai border.[8] The retreat and the general chaos that followed provided many opportunities for banditry. As we have seen, throughout Cambodian history, rebellions, insurrections, and civil wars offered ideal situations for banditry. The stories of many refugees, such as Chanrithy Him (2000), Laurence Picq (1989), and Y Phandara (1982), show how isolated groups of refugees were targeted by bandits: 'After Svay Sisophon, we had to take the circuitous way of the smugglers because we could not take the National road to the borders. There we had to take the risk of falling into the hands of bandits (Vietnamese, Thai, Cambodians) who were waiting for smugglers to rob them' (Phandara, 1982, p. 272). Vickery (1984) reported their stories:

---

[8] Polpotists provoked fear among the villagers by playing on their anti-Vietnamese sentiments and by claiming that the Vietnamese army would massacre them all.

It soon became clear, most of the Khmer Serei were less rather than more eager to fight, could not in any case agree on leaders or organization, and found their true vocation in the control of cross-border trade and refugee traffic – activities in which most of them degenerated to the level of bandits and racketeers... The peasants were unanimous, though, until late September 1980, that force was not used by Vietnamese soldiers, and that once they had reached Non Chan and loaded up with rice they were not bothered by the authorities on their return. The real physical danger was from bandits, Thai or Khmer, both on the way to the border and on return. (pp. 30, 212)

Blood debts and revenge

Mysliwiec (1988, p. 48) suggested that Buddhist values might have lessened the likelihood of revenge attacks; yet, the killing of DK cadres and supporters by mobs of survivors of the KR terror was probably quite frequent in 1979 and 1980. Gottesman (2003, pp. 37–8) described instances of survivors' revenge. Luguern (in Scalabrino, 1989, p. 86) recalled the account of Vandy Kaonn, a witness of such settling of blood debts:

Then we went to Kampong Cham. It was around January 10 1979. Despite the defections and the soldiers who were laying down their arms, there were still some combats. That's how I saw the Pol Pot regime collapse. I say 'collapse' because the cadres were in majority against Pol Pot. The Khmer Rouge were taking flight but many were killed by the villagers. In 1979–1980, many Polpotists were killed by their victims. But not all the Khmer Rouge had been fanatics. The most moderate were forgiven. We even hid a few. We were telling them: 'first hide and run away from this region as quick as possible'.

Smugglers and black marketers: towards 'free-market socialism'

The chaotic beginning of the PRK was marked more by laissez-faire and the revival of free markets than the strict rules of a communist command economy (Frings, 1994; Mysliwiec, 1988; Vickery, 1984). 'By the middle of 1981', wrote Slocomb (2010, p. 214) '... foreign journalists were describing "booming markets" in Phnom Penh and Battambang, stocked with a wide variety of goods smuggled from Thailand... This private trade... had already allowed hundreds of Chinese or Sino-Khmers to dominate the business scene. Economic disparity between the low-paid government workers and the newly rich merchants in the market was already apparent.' In 1981, prostitution reappeared in Phnom Penh as well as the smuggling of goods and related bribery of guards at checkpoints (Boua, 1983, pp. 276–7). Vickery (1984) warned that the laissez-faire situation in 1982 could have negative consequences:

Surplus food does come into Phnom Penh, as the well-stocked numerous small restaurants testify; but the prices indicate that most of it is not being consumed by people on salary, but by those with an income from trade. There is thus a danger of Phnom Penh regressing to the pre-war situation in which an urban trading community accumulated the country's surplus agricultural wealth to sell abroad, importing luxuries which most people, especially government employees, could not honestly afford, and leading to a downward spiral of corruption. (p. 240)

In November 1982, an import tax was imposed. According to Slocomb (2010), 'within two months of its implementation, it had earned 11 million riels for the state [but] collecting this tax was a dangerous exercise. In Kompong Som and Koh Kong, highly organised smugglers were skilled in tax evasion and used bribery and armed threats against officials. Minister for Finance, Chan Phin, estimated that in one month alone the state lost at least 10 million riels on cigarette smuggling by rail' (p. 222).

The unofficial but tolerated free markets, particularly the cross-border trade with Thailand and Vietnam, were eventually officially recognised in the 1986 constitutional change (Frings, 1994; Mysliwiec, 1988; Vickery, 1984). Pragmatist Hun Sen became prime minister in 1985, and in 1987 he said, 'What we should be afraid of is not that we have a free market economy. What we should fear is the poverty of the population' (Chanda, 1988, p. 108). Slocomb (2010) argued, 'surrender to the free market and recognition of private property in 1989 was simply official acknowledgement of a state of affairs that had already existed for several years' (p. 223). Her conclusion was bleak but realist, and after asking whether the Cambodian economy was changed by the years of revolution, she answered:

While there were significant political changes, it cannot be denied that the nature and structure of the economy remained fundamentally unaltered. Even the usual 20 or so big capitalists who now undoubtedly included those wealthy, gun-wielding smugglers from Koh Kong were ready to exert their influence over the new rulers once the Vietnamese made their final withdrawal. Most Cambodians responded to the new State of Cambodia [SOC] with practised cynicism, summed up in the often-heard remark, 'same bus, new driver.' They never seriously questioned the route the bus was going to take. (p. 225)

The year 1989 was indeed the consecration, via a new constitution and state appellation (SOC), of the rule of the new pragmatic 'rebel' Eastern Zone survivors and their kleptocracy, which coincided with a peak in the levels of corruption.

The political economy of the civil war: cultivating the emerging kleptocracy

The political economy imposed on the PRK by this second civil war not only facilitated the reemergence but also new developments in the historical scourges that plagued Cambodia, namely, the patron-client system, corruption, and the predatory militarism of warlords. DK had not put an end to clientelism but merely replaced the traditional patrons. Although during the DK regime 'familialism' (personal attachment to family members) was a mortal sin against Angkar and the revolution, in practice the DK elites were notoriously 'politically incestuous' and put their relatives at the head of the political, administrative, and military structures (see Jennar, 2010; Locard, 2013; Picq, 1989; Suong, 2013). During DK, the advantage of belonging to such strings was not the accumulation of wealth but that of power, although it did provide some material advantages such as better food rations and accommodations. It is trite, yet perhaps necessary to repeat that war is the lifeblood of warlords and their warriors (Tilly, 1985). DK had not managed to unify regional warlords who had emerged from the successive armed conflicts since the 1940s but had used purges and extermination as the main tools to control them. The open civil war that started in 1979 offered opportunities for commanders *cum* patrons on both sides of the conflict to strengthen their politico-military power. Given the de facto gradual return to market economy and private wealth accumulation, they were also able to sell their services to the most generous buyers. The dynamics of this political economy of civil war eventually led to the institutionalisation of plunder and asset stripping by the military elites and their clientele.

The new regime was weak, insecure, and at war; loyal military and police forces were essential to its survival. However, referring to the situation in 1983, Bekaert (1997) stated: 'Problems within the rank of the PRKAF are nothing new. Just read reports from 1979 and later. There have been mutinies, defections, contact with the "enemy" and a score of disturbing problems from the very beginning' (p. 54). The regime needed to buy the commanders' loyalty and, therefore, gave the police and the military economic advantages in, and even some control over, the informal and formal free markets, de facto legitimising corrupt and extortionist practices. For example, the police were allowed to take a percentage of the fines they collected, and according to Gottesman (2003), in 1981 the leadership

> decided that the police could take 20% of all fines... [a] decade later, with the police extorting bribes from private motorists and the regime starved for revenues... Finance Minister Chhay Than... proposed that the police receive 10% of all fines. [However] Interior Minister Sing Song, looking out for the police, was more generous, suggesting a take of 50 percent. (p. 323)

Slocomb (2002) pointed out:

> The remoteness of forestry bases made them excellent targets [for the KR], so the militia forces, and support from the KPRAF (Kampuchea People's Revolutionary Armed Forces) were necessary. Their support, however, had to be paid for. For example, in May 1987, the Council of Ministers allowed the army and state authorities in the state forest regions an extra 3% to 5% bonus over the stipulated amount of timber that they were permitted to extract. (p. 789)

During the French Protectorate, raising revenues for the state had been an all-important police function, distinct from state security; during the PRK and for the sake of its security, the state allowed the police to raise revenues not for the state but for themselves.

During the early years of the PRK, the development of what was to become a fully fledged military kleptocracy, and the associated corruption and abuse of power, was not the result of a top-down process. In fact, the central government of the PRK initially denounced the corrupt practices and abuses of power occurring in the provinces. As early as 1979, there was evidence that predatory and corrupt behaviour by regional cadres was indeed occurring, but it was denounced by the central government.

In a KPRC[9] report on the condition of the country issued in mid-March 1979, party cadres from the provincial committee level on down were upbraided for their inefficiency, their 'lack of spirit' to learn from the masses, and for behaving instead like 'Mandarins' and in a 'scornful' manner towards the people. They were charged with selecting their own friends and favourites to fill positions ('using worldly goods such as shirts and pants to encourage them'), and of becoming greedy and 'blinded' by material gain ('they collect all kinds of property for their own use and for the use of their families'). While some cadres, according to this report, 'evidently have given themselves over to despair, other have abandoned themselves to lives of pleasure (raping the daughters of the people' and keeping concubines in the collectives). (van der Kroef, 1979, p. 741)

In 1980, life at the top was still frugal. The top salary was only three times the average one: 'The highest salary was 260 riels per month, and was given to three people, Heng Samrin, Penn Sovann, and Sae Pouthang, the Director General of Cadres. The lowest salary, that of an ordinary worker, was 65 riels, with the average around 90... Minister 230 riels, school teachers from 90 to 120,... university instructors with doctorates, pharmacists, and doctors starting at 135' (Vickery, 1984, p. 230).

In August 1980, Heng Samrin denounced 'embezzlement, theft, graft, and bribery by government officials' (Leifer, 1981, p. 101). The first allegations of corrupt behaviour by a minister, namely, Keo Chenda, the Minister of Industry, surfaced in 1981 (Boua, in Chandler & Kiernan, 1983, p. 285). In 1984 and 1985 the first corruption peak occurred, coinciding with the second resurrection of the KR and their allies by the Sino-Western coalition. Slocomb (2010) illustrated the level of corruption in 1984–5 in relation to primary production:

According to official figures, output dropped in 1983 and even further in 1984 when only 56,000 tons [of fish] were produced... It seems far more likely that production remained very high but that illegal sales and exports were flourishing... The transportation of logs within and across provincial boundaries was regulated by official permits. There were,

---

[9] Kampuchea People's Revolutionary Council.

however, many abuses of the system either by provincial authorities acting alone or by Vietnamese military units that stole logs and defied the government monitors. Large-scale abuse and theft began during the 1984–85 dry season when the PRK government implemented the K5 Plan to seal the border against incursions by resistance troops. (pp. 210–11)

It was also the time when 'ghosting', as it had been the practice during the Lon Nol regime, reappeared in the military, as Eiland (1985) described in 1985: 'Press reports citing Phnom Penh sources made note of an ironic echo of earlier days – PRK officers collecting payrolls for Phantom soldiers' (p. 122). But even as late as 1986, there were still some signs that the central government did not condone these abusive and corrupt practices. Chanda (1987), for instance, reported:

[The] rapid expansion of the party ranks brought some immediate problems of discipline and abuse of power. *Pracheachon* (the official PRK bulletin) noted in September that 'a number of cadres and party members... have misused their own rights and powers to oppress and exploit the masses. They are bureaucratic, arrogant, aloof from the masses, extravagant and wasteful; they misappropriate collective property for their own interests and create misunderstanding among the people, thus reducing the party's prestige.' (pp. 119–20)

However, by the late 1980s corruption had become rampant. Slocomb (2010) estimated that in 1988 as much as one third of all exports, mostly in gems, timber, and fish, may have 'disappeared' into the informal market. In 1989 corruption pervaded all spheres of government and re-created the dangerous urban/rural gap of the late 1960s, as Um (1990) noted:

Recently, moreover, there has been increasingly vocal criticism of the rampant corruption that is said to pervade the Hun Sen government, purportedly traceable to the Hun Sen family itself. Typical of the entrenched 'new class,' it has been observed that the People's Revolutionary Party of Cambodia is basically a kind of exclusive club whose membership often guarantees a certain number of privileges. It is the kind of privilege that generates the gap between town and country that was exploited in the past by the Khmer Rouge. To observers of the Khmer political scene, this poses the same problem that contributed to the overthrow of the monarchy and an ignominious defeat in war. (p. 104)

Brown (1992) remarked that 'the disparity between Phnom Penh's glitter and the countryside's extreme poverty clearly spelled future political turbulence' (p. 94) and even talked of a second Khmer Rouge revolution: 'the disastrous condition of Cambodia's economy and social structure – and the rampant corruption – once again provided the breeding ground for a neo-Khmer Rouge radicalism' (p. 96). It did not happen, and we shall see why later in the book.

From bloody revolution to conventional communist dictatorship

The PRK may have put an end to the cataclysmic revolution of DK and its crimes and horrendous violence, but it did not establish a democratic state. Even if at the beginning it could not avoid a certain degree of laissez-faire and free markets, the regime was a conventional Vietnamese-style communist dictatorship. The Sino-Western coalition's support for the Khmer Rouge and economic embargo against the new regime prevented any chance of a democratic alternative. Because, in the absurd logic of the Cold War, if the only substantial help could come from communist dictatorships, it was unlikely to influence the PRK and Cambodian society towards democratic reforms. So, while the PRK reconstructed the state and the country, through necessity, habit, and the need for loyalty, it did so with many of the cadres and resources inherited from the previous regime. For example, many KR with blood on their hands during DK were recruited in the new PRK state security apparatus (e.g. the police) (Gottesman, 2003).

As in most communist dictatorships, deviant political thoughts and behaviours were criminalised and defined as *betrayal of the revolution* (Gottesman, 2003). Political prisoners, disappearances, and executions were, therefore, not uncommon. The Kampuchean United Front for National Salvation was riddled with factions, soon resulting in political violence and purges in 1983, although mainly manifesting in incarcerations rather than assassinations and executions (Becker, 1984, p. 44). Shawcross (1984) remarked that by the end of 1983,

> there were reports of several thousand political prisoners under Heng Samrin, almost all non-Communists, not Khmer Rouge. Indeed some political prisoners who had escaped or been released testified that their jailers were former Khmer Rouge and that the conditions under which they had been held, while not like Tuol Sleng, had been execrable. One former official of the Heng Samrin regime, who had been imprisoned for quarrelling with a Vietnamese adviser in his ministry, later said that there were Vietnamese officers in the prison system – this was welcome, because they exercised some restraint over the former Khmer Rouge guards. (p. 404)

In 1986, Amnesty International reported 'arbitrary arrests of suspected political opponents, torture, and imprisonment, and... death sentences being handed down without right of appeal' (Chanda, 1988, p. 110). According to Chanda (1988), there was 'a tightening of security and harsher measures against political dissidence [resulting from] continuing insecurity, and particularly propaganda activities by the resistance [i.e. the Polpotists and their non-communist allies] through leaflets, radio broadcasts, and word-of-mouth, which seemed to exacerbate the general unpopularity of the Vietnamese' (p. 119). While we did not find any reliable reports of widespread exactions and criminal behaviours by the Vietnamese army, Slocomb (2002, pp. 783–4) noted the involvement of some Vietnamese units in illegal logging and smuggling of timber, and Bekaert (1997, p. 51) mentioned rapes by Vietnamese soldiers in 1983.

Ordinary criminals

Primary data on ordinary criminality during the PRK/SOC regime were unavailable, but it is possible at least to suggest some crime trends and patterns based on qualitative accounts and some theoretical considerations. But first we need to briefly present the way in which crime and policing were conceptualised at that time.

Resurrecting the police to reeducate betrayers of the revolution

Although a modicum of crime control and order maintenance policing was gradually reintroduced, the civil war situation and communist habitus meant that state security remained the main function of the new police force. The activities of the latter were not only arbitrary and brutal but, within the resurging patron-client system, also increasingly corrupt. In 1979 Vietnamese police units operated in Phnom Penh, and then police forces were created in provinces, districts, and communes. Recruitment in these police forces was barred to 'police, soldiers, or officials from the prerevolutionary regimes [or] any ethnic Chinese or Sino-Khmer' but open to former Khmer Rouge security police as long as they had reformed (Gottesman, 2003, p. 75). Most offences, political or not, constituted cases of 'betraying the revolution'. Vickery (1986) described two such cases:

[In June 1980] the case of Hem Krisna and 15 accomplices, given sentences of 3 to 20 years imprisonment for active subversion in the service of the non-communist anti-PRK forces on the Thai border; [in October 1981] a group of five men and a woman were tried for subversion and sabotage as 'Pol Pot mercenaries.' The five men had all been DK soldiers and cadres since the period 1970–3, and had fled in January 1979 to DK bases in western Cambodia or the Thai border where they accepted assignments to carry out sabotage in Phnom Penh. They were given sentences of eleven years to, in one case, life. The woman, who had no political background or, in contrast to the men, education, and who was only guilty of knowingly giving shelter to the saboteurs, was let off with a two-year suspended sentence. (pp. 119–20)

However, 'counterrevolutionary culture', 'social vices', and prostitution, that is, behaviours that offended 'revolutionary morality', were also targets for policing (Gottesman, 2003, p. 77). A report from the Ministry of Interior showed:

Between 1983 and 1985 the Phnom Penh police arrested 532 'betrayers of the revolution,' 3203 people engaged in undefined 'criminal cases,' 1377 people accused of 'theft, rape, gambling, etc.,' and 1842 people who had allegedly engaged in 'social offenses from the old regime, such as drugs, prostitution etc.,' or 'activities that have a strong effect on the youth, such as pornographic videos.' (Gottesman, 2003, pp. 254–5)

Using Gottesman's figures and excluding the 532 cases of 'betrayers of the revolution', we find an average annual arrest rate of 28.3 per 100,000 between 1983 and 1985.[10] Rates of arrest, of course, say little about actual crime prevalence and the above data provide only a gross categorisation of the types of crime. There was also petty crime arising from destitution. For example, Mysliwiek (1988) reported the case of a 'restaurant owner in Phnom Penh [who] claims that anywhere from 200 to 300 amputees a day come in threatening to damage the premises if they are not given a few riels' (p. 58). As for violent crime, Vickery (1986) cited the case of a robbery-murder and commented: 'one non-political trial which was reported involved five men accused in May 1982 of robbery and in one case murder, who were sentenced to prison for terms of 18 years up to life for the murderer' (p. 120).

In 2007 and 2008, we interviewed villagers and police officers old enough to remember and reflect about crime during the 14 years of the PRK/SOC regime and gathered anecdotal data. The general recollection was of very little crime occurring during this period. At the beginning, corruption was not a problem because 'there was so little to be corrupt about'. Slocomb (2002) indeed wrote: 'For most of the decade of the PRK [that is until about 1987], however, the opportunity level for corruption and evasion remained low because of barriers to economic development, especially the international embargo on credit and trade that Cambodia shared with Vietnam' (p. 775). According to police officers, the few violent crimes that occurred were essentially lethal robberies of gold jewellery, as the case cited by Vickery probably illustrates. If caught by citizens or police, such offenders were often summarily executed.

Ordinary crime can only be conceived when a modicum of normality, especially in respect to interindividual relationships, exists. With the reestablishment of this normality during the PRK regime, that a certain level of ordinary crime returned was normal. Durkheim had argued that in any society crime is normal, and he warned against the folly of attempting to eliminate crime. Attempts at achieving a perfect society, 'a society of saints', as DK endeavoured, must not only eliminate creativity but also, for the sake of maintaining a collective conscience (social cohesion), invent new forms of deviance to be disapproved and punished.

---

[10] There would have been 6,422 arrests, an average of 2,141 per year for a population estimated between 7.2 million and 7.9 million.

Contexts that would limit ordinary criminality

After the horrors of DK, the state, which was in the process of reconstruction, could probably, at least early on, count on a strong collective conscience encouraging social cohesion, and therefore limiting ordinary criminality. We have seen also that at the beginning of the PRK there was little economic inequality in the country. Criminological studies have suggested that it is not so much poverty per se but inequality that is associated with varying levels of violent crimes in societies (see Hagan & Pederson, 1995). A high level of equality in the initial stages of the PRK may have fostered social cohesion and lessened ordinary criminality.

Hinton (2002) observed that in 1984 the PRK instituted

an annual observance called The Day of Hate, in which people were gathered at various locales to hear invectives heaped on the Khmer Rouge. State propaganda played on this theme with such slogans as 'We must absolutely prevent the return of this former black darkness' and 'We must struggle ceaselessly to protect against the return of the Pol Pot, Ieng Sary, Khieu Samphan genocidal clique.' (pp. 282–3)

He also pointed out that these 'formulaic and state-sanctioned expressions were genuine and often expressed in conversations among ordinary folk' (see also Ebihara, 2002, p. 104, and Frings, 1997, p. 834). It was certainly an Orwellian tool (uncannily having the same name 'Day of Hatred' and date '1984' as in Orwell's famous book), but it could also have been an effective one for reinforcing the collective conscience and social cohesion. On the other hand, what sort of effect might the Day of Hatred have had on revenge killings of former low-ranking KR, particularly when they were living in the same villages as former victims? It could be that such an event might increase the desire for revenge and subsequent killings; however, the slogans focused on three characters – Pol Pot, Ieng Sary, and Khieu Samphan – 'a clique of monsters' presented as solely responsible for the DK nightmare. The process may have had cathartic outcomes, lessening the desire for revenge on a broad scale and instead channelling it towards the three cited 'monsters'? Hinton (2002, p. 288) also remarked that Buddhist morality may have lessened revenge killings and led only to scorn and ostracism of the former oppressors.

In the country, a system of voluntary cooperative solidarity groups called *Krom Samaki* (see Mysliwiec, 1988, pp. 27–8) put in place by the PRK may have, at the beginning, helped maintain cohesion in villages and limited predatory crimes. Finally, the 1986 Decree-Law 27, which gave some legitimacy to police, may have contributed to a degree of social cohesion. Mysliwiec (1988) explained that this law regulated 'arrest, detention, temporary imprisonment, release, and search of domicile, property or person' and it defined responsibility and procedures, what constitute a crime, who can carry out an arrest, under what circumstances, the length of detention, and through what procedures. It defin[ed] the penalties for those who abuse their authority by false arrest or detention, illegal search and entry, as well as for use of torture during interrogation. It also defin[ed] the rights of the individual including the right to defence, notification of the family, visiting and other rights. (p. 49)

In addition, Ledgerwood and Vijghen (2002, pp. 122–3) remarked that police control was generally closely exercised at the local level during PRK/SOC, and this would have reduced opportunities for ordinary crimes.

Contexts that would increase ordinary criminality

Paradoxically, the DK regime had been characterised by a violent form of social engineering based on absolute collectivism but ultimately produced the profound atomisation of relationships because previous attachments had been replaced by the compulsory and dedicated love of the godlike Angkar. What level of social cohesion remained in the aftermath of DK has been keenly debated. Some have argued that the destruction of the traditional fabric of society by the KR had profoundly damaged social cohesion.

Children who had been separated from their parents and taught to report on them, today [1988] no longer have the traditional respect for them. Women complain of increasing problems of marital infidelity from their husbands caused by the disproportionate ratio of women to men and the high numbers of widows. Relationships have changed and families are no longer intact and supportive. (Mysliwiec, 1988, p. 11)

These behaviours illustrate anomic conditions when old norms have been destroyed, leaving a moral vacuum during which crime is likely to grow, and Mysliwiec (1988) reported on the incidence of crime within families and between neighbours, although she focused more on the crowded situation of people in refugee camps. The DK experience would also have affected social norms, such as the willingness to perform mutual aid. Ovesen, Trankell, and Ojendal (1996) argued that social norms had been destroyed and people had become atomised, greedy, and selfish – therefore, hypothetically increasing ordinary criminality. For Frings (1994), the DK experience did not really change these social norms, because individualism had always been the norm. To the contrary, Ledgerwood (1998) and Marston (1997) argued that the DK experience did not manage to destroy these social norms but may have (through shared adversity) reinforced them – therefore, hypothetically lessening ordinary criminality, which seems to be the case, although our evidence is flimsy. Hinton (2002), who summarised this debate, pointed out that Frings's and Ovesen *et al.*'s views were based on 'a romanticized notion that mutual aid in Khmer social networks before the DK was based on purely altruistic generosity and kindness' (pp. 277–8) when it was, in fact, a system of reciprocity. Moreover, the rhythms and requirements of wet rice cultivation demanded a certain degree of cooperation between villages, hamlets, and households, as they do today (see Broadhurst, 2002).

Vickery (1984) pondered about the effect of the radical demographic change in Phnom Penh in 1982, not in terms of population numbers, which he estimated similar to the prewar level of 600,000, but in terms of its very different social background:

> It is soon clear, however, that very few of the present population are of the pre-war 600,000. Most of those people either perished or have fled abroad since 1979, and Phnom Penh has been resettled by former villagers who have rushed into the city and squatted in the new freedom of the past 2 years. They live in flats and shop houses with their chickens and pigs, cook in the street, and try to make an urban life for themselves by petty trade. Phnom Penh has thus already become the non-productive, consumer city, which it was before, although on a much less lavish scale, but with the same inherent dangers for national development, or more accurately at present, national recovery. (p. 239)

It is difficult to predict what would have been the effect of such a predominantly rural population on crime and its development in Phnom Penh. If we follow Shelley's hypotheses about early urbanisation, crime would have been higher in Phnom Penh than in rural areas, as a result of both the transfer of more violent rural behaviours and the increased opportunities for property crimes. The data that we present in the next chapter, from 1992 to 2012, support this hypothesis.

Archer and Gartner's (1976) seminal study of postwar effects on homicide trends has showed that the rates of homicide were significantly but temporarily higher postwar compared to the prewar situation. However, even if we had empirical data for Cambodia, deciding which periods to be operationalised as prewar and postwar would be problematic. While, by 1980, Cambodia was seeing the end of the worst murderous nightmare that had started in 1970, or at the earliest 1967, it was still a country at war. Therefore, the question remains about the valid postwar period: should it be 1980, 1993, or even 1998 since the Polpotists were still active, albeit significantly less and less, up to this date?

Conclusion

On the balance of probability, that is, considering both sides of the argument about the risk and protective factors for ordinary criminality during the PRK/SOC period and given that our qualitative accounts point to low rather than high levels, we suggest that the rates of ordinary crimes, including ordinary homicides, were probably initially low but started to increase in the late

1980s. From qualitative accounts, given the absence of criminal statistics, it is plausible they may have been at a similar low level as in the early 1960s. If the criminal records kept by the *Sangkhum* and the Khmer Republic are perhaps lost forever, there might be records that were kept by the PRK/SOC that may someday become available to historians, and their analysis may contribute to a better understanding of this important but underdocumented period.

10 Crime and violence in contemporary Cambodia: 1991–2012

Historical background

The developments and repercussions of the political events of the last two decades, from 1991 to 2012, have been widely recounted by historians and political scientists (e.g. Chandler, 2008; Jennar, 2010; Suong, 2013; Widyono, 2008). In brief, the remaining Vietnamese troops withdrew from Cambodia in September 1989. A new constitution created the State of Cambodia (SOC), and later, in October 1991, the Cambodian People's Party (CPP) was established; both were direct avatars of the previous People's Republic of Kampuchea (PRK) and Kampuchean People's Revolutionary Party (KPRP), respectively. The years 1989 and 1990 represented a geopolitical turning point in the ending of the Cold War, marked by the serious economic bankruptcy of the Soviet bloc, including Vietnam. The antagonisms between the USA and the USSR-Vietnam alliance and between China and the USSR-Vietnam alliance were no longer perceived as irreducible by these countries (Regaud, 1992). The three superpowers, the nations of the Association of Southeast Asian Nations (ASEAN), and Vietnam started to realise that their long-term interests were better served through trade, that is, through interdependent competition in a global market, rather than through violent elimination contests such as wars. This is a manifestation of the processes of pacification and interdependency proposed by Elias to which we return later. Historically and unlike the old capitalist countries, socialist dictatorships had neither the need nor the opportunity to develop institutions and regulatory systems that could contain the most predatory forms of capitalism. Therefore, in this new context of global capitalism, many of them, including Cambodia, adopted a form of *capitalism sauvage*, which was anomic and criminogenic. In this and the following chapters, we examine how and why these developments, which include the international effort to normalise relations among the combatants, impacted on crime and violence in Cambodia.

In October 1991, encouraged and pressured by the international community and a new world order, the four warring factions – SOC, Khmer Rouge (KR), Khmer People's National Liberation Front (KPNLF), and FUNCINPEC (Sihanoukist) – signed a peace agreement in Paris (Paris Peace Agreement

[PPA]), which established a large UN mission, the United Nations Transitional Authority in Cambodia (UNTAC). UNTAC's ambitious programme included disarmament and peacekeeping, the conduct of general elections, and the establishment of a constitution that mandated political pluralism and democracy. It was enforced by a large foreign military (15,900) and police (3,400) deployment combined with a significant civil component (2,000 personnel to run the election, media, and other services) of altogether over 20,000 people from 45 contributing states.

The UNTAC mission began in February 1992, the same year the KR faction broke from the Paris Peace Agreement, resumed warfare, and decided to boycott the elections, which were nevertheless conducted in May 1993. The FUNCINPEC obtained 45.5 per cent of the votes, and the CPP, 38.2 per cent, with 23 minor parties sharing the remaining votes. However, the CPP was not ready to relinquish power without a fight. The constitutional arrangement stipulated that, to be appointed, the government required a two-thirds majority. Sihanouk, as recently restored King,[1] managed to broker an agreement between Hun Sen, the leader of the CPP, and Prince Ranariddh, Sihanouk's son and leader of the FUNCINPEC. Ranariddh and Hun Sen were, respectively, appointed 'First Prime Minister' and 'Second Prime Minister', and all other ministries were also bicephalous CPP and FUNCINPEC power-sharing arrangements, down to staff and other clientele whose loyalty the two parties could afford to buy. The UNTAC mission ended in September 1993, and by the end of the year most of its personnel had left Cambodia.

The inherently unstable governmental coalition of archenemies lasted 4 years. These years were marked by the continuation of the Polpotists' guerrilla campaign that increasingly relied on terrorism, sometimes turning into banditry, while their movement gradually disintegrated with, for example, Ieng Sary's defection in 1996. The political conflict within the FUNCINPEC/CPP coalition involved a competition to harness the support of potential Polpotist defectors, former 'friends' of both the CPP (from 1970 to 1979) and FUNCINPEC (from 1979 to 1991) leaders. In July 1997, the depth of the political conflict reached a crisis with the two parties reverting to limited but open armed clashes, particularly in the capital. Many regarded the clashes as a CPP coup (see Adams, 2007),[2] but others saw the events as a FUNCINPEC attempted

---

[1] Under the new constitution, Cambodia was a constitutional monarchy where the King 'will reign but not rule'.

[2] Adams (2007), who was a member of the UN Human Rights mission in 1997, argued that Hun Sen engineered the coup despite opposition from CPP president Chea Sim, Sar Kheng (Ministry of Interior), and CPP defence minister Tea Banh. According to Adams, the confusion about the coup was also compounded by Ranariddh's attempts to shore up his weak military situation vis-à-vis co-prime minister Hun Sen.

coup preempted by a CPP countercoup (Jennar, 2010;[3] Roberts, 2001), in which First Prime Minister Ranarriddh was ousted and exiled for nearly 9 months. After further political violence, general elections were held in July 1998. The CPP's share of the votes increased from 38.2 per cent in 1993 to 41.4 per cent in 1998, an important gain, but not substantial enough to give it an absolute majority. Almost 60 per cent of Cambodians continued to favour other parties, which, nevertheless, were paying for their factionalism: the FUNCINPEC's vote declined from 45.5 per cent in 1993 to 31.7 per cent in 1998, a significant loss of popularity, and many voters shifted to the Sam Rainsy Party (SRP) led by a former FUNCINPEC finance minister and dissident who obtained 14.3 per cent of the vote, with the remaining 13 per cent distributed among 36 other parties.

With the death of Pol Pot and the final implosion of the KR, 1998 saw the end of armed conflict and the start of a dramatic decline in crime and violence. For the decade that followed up to 2008, in elections after elections the CPP consolidated its vote, getting 47.3 per cent in 2003 and 58.1 per cent in 2008, while the FUNCINPEC declined to near extinction (20 per cent in 2003 and 5 per cent in 2008). The SRP, however, progressed to become the main opposition and obtained 22 per cent of the vote in 2003 and 2008. The commune elections of 2002, 2007, and 2012 showed a similar pattern, with the CPP mustering over 60 per cent of votes at each election. It seems that the electoral ascendency of the CPP in general elections peaked in 2008, from which it dramatically fell in 2013, although it still garnered 48.8 per cent of the vote, but with an opposition party, the Cambodian National Rescue Party (CNRP),[4] that obtained 44.5 per cent. A low turnout of 68 per cent of eligible voters at the polls may have affected the CPP vote, as it seemed that many among those who abstained were former CPP voters. The loss of votes and seats occurred not only in Phnom Penh but also in the countryside where the CPP had long dominated. The subsequent political uncertainty is briefly discussed in our concluding chapter.

It was only in 2005 that the Extraordinary Chambers in the Court of Cambodia (ECCC) commenced operation with the trial of Duch, the former KR commander of the infamous S-21 torture and elimination centre. He was eventually convicted for crimes against humanity in 2010. Ieng Sary, the former foreign minister, died in 2013, and his wife, Ieng Thirith, was considered unfit for judgement on medical ground (suffering from dementia) and released. In August 2014, Brother Number Two Nuon Chea (88), considered chief ideologist, and Khieu Samphan (83), the former head of state, were sentenced to life following conviction of crimes against humanity committed during the Khmer

---

[3] Jennar (2010, pp. 140–1) also presents evidence of an assassination plot against Hun Sen, involving Nhiek Bun Chhay (FUNCINPEC commander), Ho Sok (interior state secretary), and Ly Tuch (Ranariddh's cabinet director).

[4] A coalition of the former Sam Rainsy Party (SRP) and Human Rights parties.

Rouge regime.[5] At the time of writing, indictments of genocide are proceeding against Nuon Chea and Khieu Samphan.

This chapter examines and discusses the trends and patterns in crime and violence in contemporary Cambodia from 1991 to 2012. We have conducted extensive field research in Cambodia for many years and have access to a wealth of primary and secondary data. We start our analysis of trends and patterns in crime and violence by looking at homicide, but first we briefly describe our data.

The data

Our data from various sources allowed effective triangulation for most of the period. These data included official crime statistics, crime victim surveys, and media reports, as described below:
- Official police statistics: Official crime statistics spanning 1992 to 2012 were provided by the Ministry of Interior (MoI) and translated from Khmer. Data were incomplete for a number of years between 1992 and 1996, when some remote provinces still more or less under KR control did not provide any, but particularly in 1997, when police work was seriously impaired by the CPP/FUNCINPEC armed clashes.
- Crime victim surveys: We conducted three sweeps of the United Nations International Crime Victims Survey (UNICVS). In 2001 the UNICVS household survey included Phnom Penh, Kandal, Kampong Cham, Kampong Speu, Kampong Chhnang, and Kampot; in 2006, Phnom Penh and Kandal; and in 2007, Kampong Cham.[6] Follow-up interviews with villagers and police officials were done in 2008. We also examined the results of other large national repeated surveys that included a section on criminal victimisation (Cambodian Socio-Economic Survey [CSES 2003/4–2008/9] and Cambodian Demographic and Health Survey [CDHS 2005–10]).
- Media reports: *Phnom Penh Post: The Phnom Penh Post* (*PPP*) is an English-language newspaper published since 1992. The *PPP* has a regular column called the Police Blotter, which has been reporting a relatively large number of criminal events. The reports provide a brief summary of each event, as in the following example:

---

[5] In 1979, the PRK, drawing upon the International Convention of 1948 on the crime of genocide, had organised a trial of the KR, in fact indicting only Pol Pot and Ieng Sary, which was criticised by many as a Vietnamese propaganda ploy. In 1991, any references to 'genocide, massacres, crimes against humanity' requested by the SOC during the Paris Agreement had been successfully rejected by all the other parties to the agreement. It was only in April 1997 that the UN agreed in principle to a trial of the KR leadership. For further information on the ECCC, see www.eccc.gov.kh/en.

[6] The communes and villages sampled in the first survey were sampled again in the second survey of Phnom Penh, Kandal, and Kampong Cham.

5 January 2001: Mang Man, 57, was chopped to death in a robbery at 6 pm in a ricefield in Kap Prich village, Koas Kralor district, Battambang. Police said the victim was chopped three times in the head and face with an axe by a group wearing military uniforms who attempted to steal his cows and cow cart. The robbers escaped empty-handed into a forest after authorities arrived.

We collected and coded 5,937 crime events, including 2,719 homicide cases spanning 17 years from 1992 to 2008. It was possible to code more or less consistently about 15 variables, including the date and location of the criminal event; the type of crime; some details on the victim(s), offender(s), and their relationship; whether a weapon was used; and so forth.[7] On average, the Police Blotter column reported 350 crime events, including 160 homicides every year (i.e. around 45 per cent of all reports were about homicide). These journalistic reports were biased towards the most serious and violent crimes; however, the number of homicide stories in the *PPP* varies in parallel with the official numbers, suggesting that over the years, the *PPP* captured a relatively stable share of all homicides. Generally, the *PPP* tended to report more crime stories from Phnom Penh compared to the provinces. For example, across the 10 years between 1997 and 2008, the *PPP* reported, on average, 75 per cent of the Phnom Penh lethal events recorded by the police but about one third of those recorded in the provinces. Nevertheless, if we cannot rely on the *PPP* to assess trends in crime, we can use the Police Blotter as a source of qualitative data on crime in Cambodia, which the official data did not provide.

Trends in homicide victimisation

Figure 10.1 plots the estimated rate of homicide victims since 1992. It includes victims of ordinary crimes reported by the MoI as well as victims of political homicides and extrajudicial killings (from *PPP* and/or MoI sources). The media reports were used to estimate the number of victims by type of homicide (e.g. murder, grenade attack) and weight the number of cases accordingly. The striking feature in these trends is the significant fall in rates after 1998. The year 1993, with a rate of 23.5 per 100,000, represented the peak in homicide. Since 1992, the Polpotists had resumed terror attacks and in 1993 increased their hostilities, particularly against Cambodian villages inhabited by Vietnamese (the available data show that *at least* 67 Vietnamese were killed or injured by the KR in 1992 and *at least* 282 in 1993). KR violence against Khmers had also dramatically increased from *at least* 25 victims in 1992 to a *minimum* of 347 victims in 1993. In addition, the May 1993 elections generated a wave of political violence between competing factions (again intensifying from *at least* 34 victims in 1992 to *at least* 264 in 1993). In 1994, the rate of homicide victimisation dropped to 14.8 per 100,000, but in 1994 as well as 1996, showed

---

[7] Details about the *PPP* estimation procedure are on file with the authors.

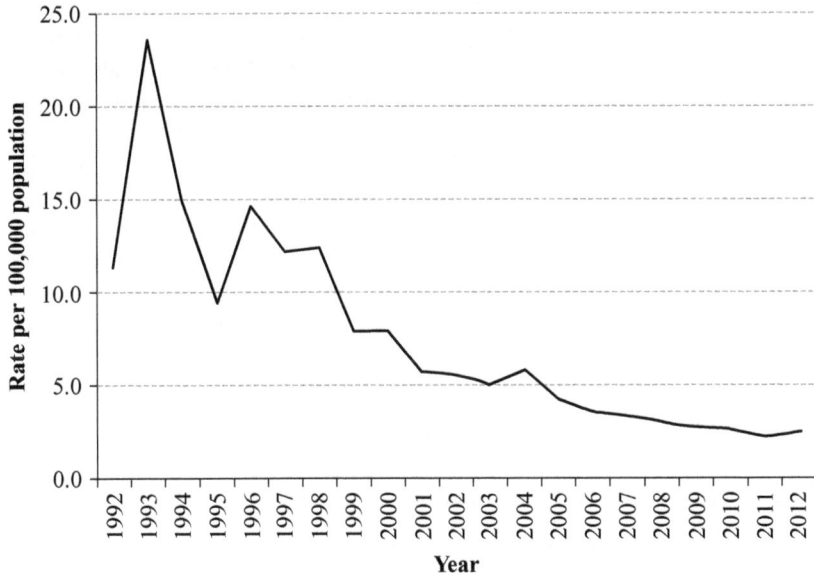

Figure 10.1 Homicide victims, 1992–2012: estimated rates per 100,000 population
Sources: MoI and *PPP*.
Note: Includes ordinary homicides and political and extrajudicial killings.

the second highest rate of homicide. The year 1994 was marked by the security vacuum that followed the end of the UNTAC mission and the shaky establishment of the bicephalous system of government, which encouraged a surge in banditry and predatory crime as well as political assassinations. The number of victims of the KR (dead and injured) in 1994 was *at least* 171, and 44 per cent of them were Vietnamese. The homicide rate dropped to 9.4 per 100,000 in 1995, which suggested a degree of stabilisation and also corresponded to a decline in the number of victims killed by the KR. However, from 1996 to 1998, political and common violence increased again as the conditions leading to the armed clashes of 1997 worsened and the second general election was scheduled for 1998 (we estimated a mean rate of homicide of about 13 per 100,000 across these 3 years).

The significant and consistent decline from 1999 to 2012 appears to have occurred in three stages. First, an important fall to around 8 per 100,000 in 1999 and 2000, followed by a second fall stabilising at 5.5 between 2001 and 2004, and a third but more gradual decline from about 4 per 100,000 in 2005 to 2.4 in 2012. Before describing our analysis, we should note that among the numerous factors (political, socioeconomic, and police effectiveness), which may account for the declining crime rates, particularly for homicides and armed robberies as we will see later, one causal variable might be the increasing rate of incarceration. Between 1995 and 2008, the estimated rates of imprisonment had escalated significantly from 24.2 to 83.6 per 100,000 (Keo, Broadhurst, & Bouhours, 2011). Greater incapacitation of violent offenders (and possibly greater deterrence of potential violent offenders) may have played a direct role in the declining rates of criminal violence. As we will also see later, it is equally possible that growing rates of imprisonment had an indirect influence on the declining rates of criminal violence, particularly on private or mob justice. The high rate of offender death in the 1990s along with the rapid expansion of imprisonment may have served to reduce the impact of the more serious, desperate, and pathological behaviours evident among some offenders in the 1990s (Broadhurst, Keo, & Bouhours 2013). As Black's (1976, 1983; see also Cooney, 2003) thesis would predict, when the state becomes more efficient in its repression of offenders, citizens are less likely to seek private justice.

Trends in crime and violence

We now broaden our examination to three categories of crime and violence: (1) 'ordinary' violent crime (generally referred to as 'street crime'); (2) political violence, which we subdivide further into 'militarised political violence' or 'military hostilities', as in the continuation until 1998 of the civil war between the Royal Government of Cambodia (RGC) and the KR, and 'civilian political violence', manifesting, for example, in political assassinations; and (3) elite predatory violence and crime. The types of crime distinguished here often overlap, and ordinary crime may sometimes blend with the other types. We draw from primary data to discuss ordinary crime and violence and mostly from secondary sources to discuss the two other types of crime.

Ordinary crime

This section draws from two sets of primary data: official police statistics of recorded crime and a series of crime victimisation surveys (UNICVS) that we conducted in 2001 and 2006–7. Police statistics should be read with the understanding that

- They report *crime events*, not the number of victims or offenders (i.e. an event may involve several victims and offenders).
- They represent the number of crime events *recorded* by police. Most crimes, especially if they are not serious, are not reported to the police, and police record only a fraction of reported crime. Criminologists refer to this unreported and unrecorded crime as the 'dark figure of crime'. A comparison between the police and UNICVS household survey data suggests that the rates of both violent and nonviolent victimisation were probably and respectively 50 and 6,000 times higher (varying according to the type of crime

Table 10.1 *Number of crime events recorded by judicial police, 1992–2012*

Year	Murder and attempted	Armed robbery[a]	Grenade attack	Rape[a]	Assault with injuries	Kidnap	All theft[b]	Other offences	All crime events
1992	443	1,414	40	106	515	9	1,451	136	4,114
1993	646	1,613	157	43	267	93	915	514	4,248
1994	345	905	79	39	353	133	1,018	255	3,127
1995	420	832	27	84	423	24	1,122	310	3,242
1996	566	1,345	54	122	1,050	44	1,710	747	5,638
1997	338	887	46	46	445	23	965	208	2,958
1998	793	1,822	68	130	1,114	130	2,115	905	7,077
1999	601	1,396	42	165	1,058	91	2,037	639	6,029
2000	653	1,252	39	209	1,130	63	2,049	432	5,827
2001	560	1,296	21	218	1,131	51	1,970	295	5,542
2002	527	1,419	10	279	1,141	38	2,048	283	5,745
2003	602	1,175	23	331	1,301	25	1,901	335	5,693
2004	511	1,320	33	281	1,024	7	1,616	204	4,996
2005	517	868	20	254	1,010	10	1,565	230	4,474
2006	526	657	17	250	1,218	1	1,566	221	4,456
2007	493	572	14	238	1,017	10	1,260	137	3,741
2008	408	466	13	198	830	0	847	119	2,881
2009	436	428	11	241	978	1	1,181	180	3,456
2010	386	276	2	310	947	6	976	170	3,073
2011	318	183	4	340	888	14	1,001	116	2,864
2012	378	212	7	279	879	11	875	127	2,768

[a] From 1992 to 2002, the data provided did not specify whether robbery-murders and rape-murders were recorded, respectively, as robbery and rape or as murder.
[b] Includes personal theft, fraud, pickpocketing, and theft of cultural heritage.
Source: Cambodia Ministry of Interior, Judicial Police Centre.

reported by survey respondents) than what was recorded by the police. These representative surveys revealed that only 11 per cent to 14 per cent of victims of nonviolent crimes reported these events to the police compared to 34 per cent of victims of violent events. While the nonreporting of crime is widespread in all countries, it is particularly so in developing countries such as Cambodia where effective police services are only emerging and people rely on local dispute settlement mechanisms at the level of the village and the commune for dealing with minor and mostly nonviolent crime.[8] In short, the judicial police record only serious crimes.

Table 10.1 presents selected official crime statistics provided by the Ministry of Interior (MoI) since 1992, and Figure 10.2, the rates of recorded crime

---

[8] The average international reporting rate for the nine violent and nonviolent crimes measured by the UNICVS was 51 per cent in 2005 (31 countries) but tended to be lower in developing than in developed countries (van Dijk *et al.*, 2007, pp. 263–8).

Figure 10.2 Crime events recorded by police, 1992–2012: rate per 100,000 population
Source: Cambodia Ministry of Interior, Judicial Police Centre.
Note: In 1997 police record keeping was disrupted and MoI data for this year are unreliable.

for the same period.[9] In 1992–3 not only elite crime but also ordinary criminality were directly and indirectly fuelled by the UNTAC mission. The sudden pouring of wealth into a poor country added to the existing problems of the repatriation of refugees and the demobilisation of soldiers, and the shortage of mine-cleared land and employment led to lawlessness and violence. It also exacerbated social resentment. For example, as the construction sector was dominated by Vietnamese settlers, the boom 'further pitted the haves and have-nots along ethnic lines' (Um, 1994, p. 77). With the import of 22,000 UN personnel, mostly young men with more money than they could spend, prostitution boomed (Heder & Ledgerwood, 1996, p. 154). Boua (1994) estimated that between 1991 and 1992, the number of prostitutes had increased from 6,000 to 20,000, and Jordens (1996) reported a threefold growth between 1992 and 1993. From these estimates, the number of prostitutes could have reached more than 60,000 in 1993. Between 1992 and 1998, rates of crime fluctuated but remained relatively high; however, following the elections of 1998, rates of both violent and nonviolent crime started to fall dramatically.

As discussed above, apart from homicide rates, official police statistics are not a reliable measure of the true prevalence of crime, particularly for minor offences, which are the least likely to be reported. However, it is important to distinguish between the reliability of the *rates* and the reliability of the *trends*. The declining trends indicated by the police statistics are credible, at least from 2000. This declining trend is supported by the analysis of our repeated crime victim surveys (UNICVS) between 2000 and 2006 in the three most populated provinces of Phnom Penh, Kandal, and Kampong Cham (altogether 32.2 per cent of the Cambodian population in 1998 and 31.9 per cent in 2008). Table 10.2 reveals this dramatic decline in both violent and nonviolent victimisation, including corruption, particularly in Phnom Penh and Kampong Cham; the decline was less pronounced in Kandal, and we will explore why in the next chapter.

Two large household surveys conducted independently – the Cambodian Socio-Economic Survey (CSES) and the Cambodian Demographic and Health Survey (CDHS) – that included a section on criminal victimisation produced results that confirmed the fall in crime indicated by the UNICVS. These large surveys included all Cambodian provinces, not just the three sampled in the UNICVS. The CSES found that the percentage of victims of violence causing injury and of property crime had respectively declined from 1.1 per cent to 0.6 per cent and 3.9 per cent to 2.6 per cent between 2003/4 and 2008/9 (National Institute of Statistics [NIS], 2004, 2009). The CDHS showed a decline in reports of violent victimisation from 3.8 per cent to 3.1 per cent

---

[9] Extrajudicial killings of offenders and lethal and nonlethal political violence are not reported because such data were not provided in the police statistics.

Table 10.2 *One-year rate of victimisation and reporting to police, UNICVS, Phnom Penh, Kandal, and Kampong Cham, 2000 and 2005–6*

Crimes	Phnom Penh				Kandal				Kampong Cham			
	2000		2005		2000		2005		2000		2006	
	% vic	% rep[a]	% vic	% rep[a]	% vic	% rep[a]	% vic	% rep[a]	% vic	% rep[a]	% vic	% rep[a]
Robbery	1.9	45.5	1.5	62.5	0.3	100.0	0.6	50.0	0.9	100.0	0.1	0.0
Assault/threat	7.8	27.2	2.0	27.3	4.4	28.0	2.8	27.8	6.2	29.4	2.3	44.4
Sexual assault[b]	1.8	8.3	0.2	50.0	0.3	0.0	0.0	0.0	0.3	0.0	0.0	0.0
Burglary and attempted	23.9	21.3	10.2	15.3	15.7	13.0	9.6	16.4	20.3	24.1	3.7	6.9
Car-related offence[c]	24.3	8.9	6.0	7.1	18.0	8.3	7.2	16.6	8.3	0.0	5.7	0.0
Moto theft[c]	7.7	61.5	2.4	69.6	4.5	46.7	4.2	66.7	5.4	46.7	1.0	50.0
Bicycle theft[c]	9.9	10.9	5.8	2.4	6.7	8.7	7.6	5.3	14.7	13.8	3.1	0.0
Personal theft	13.8	8.6	6.5	9.9	5.2	3.3	3.1	0.0	7.3	10.0	2.3	5.6
Livestock[c]	20.0	5.3	8.2	0.0	19.1	1.8	13.6	0.0	24.8	8.9	11.1	1.3
Consumer fraud	39.6	5.7	25.4	6.5	31.8	5.5	18.7	1.7	29.8	2.4	22.0	4.6
Corruption	27.8	1.2	18.2	1.0	18.5	1.9	18.3	3.4	15.6	1.2	12.9	5.9

[a] % reported to police calculated on number of victims.
[b] % victimised calculated on number of female respondents.
[c] % victimised calculated on number of owners; includes car theft, theft from car, and vandalism on car.

Source: Broadhurst and Bouhours (2009).

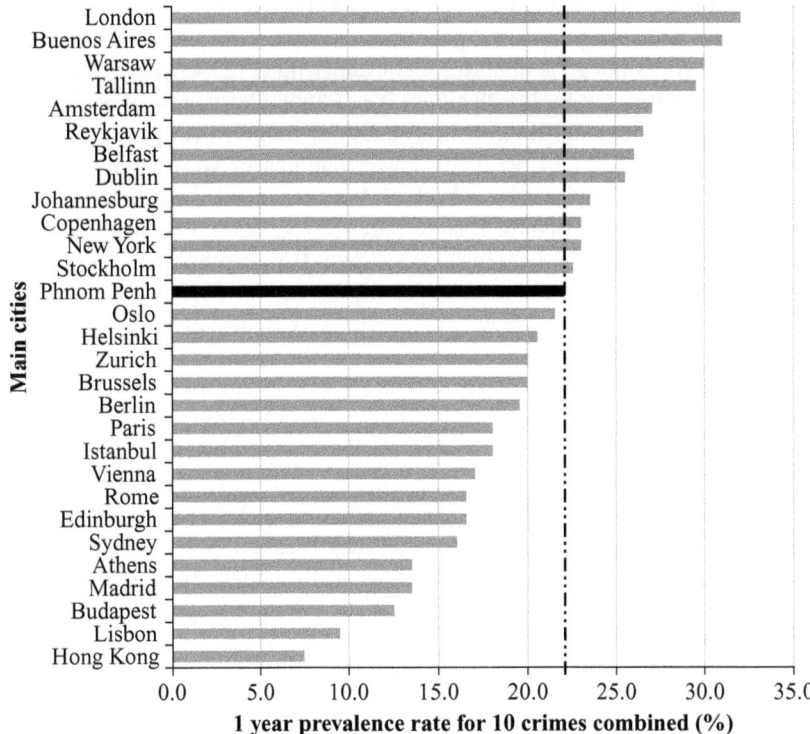

Figure 10.3 One-year rate of victimisation for 10 crimes combined in 28 main cities, UNICVS, 2005
Source: Van Dijk, van Kesteren, & Smit (2007).

between 2005 and 2010 (National Institute of Public Health, NIS, & ORC Macro, 2006; NIS, Directorate General for Health, & ICF Macro, 2011).

While the UNICVS in Cambodia produced prevalence rates of violent and nonviolent crime that were much higher than indicated by police statistics – a classic phenomenon in criminology – these rates were not higher than those measured by the UNICVS in many other countries. It was possible to compare Phnom Penh with 28 other main cities for 10 crimes (i.e. excluding car vandalism, livestock theft, fraud, and corruption) during 2005. The average annual rate of crime reported by survey respondents for these cities was 21.5 per cent, similar to that of Phnom Penh, at 22 per cent (van Dijk, van Kesteren, & Smit, 2007, pp. 241–2). As Figure 10.3 shows, 12 main cities had a higher overall prevalence of crime than Phnom Penh (ranging from 22.5 per cent for Stockholm to 32 per cent for London). Among the cities compared, Phnom Penh had the highest risk of burglary (7.5 per cent, and over twice the average of

3.2 per cent), motorcycle theft (2.4 per cent, nearly five times the average of 0.5 per cent), and corruption (18.2 per cent, compared to an average of 4.7 per cent). It was also among the highest for consumer fraud (25.4 per cent with an average of 14.8 per cent for the 28 cities). Yet, Phnom Penh's rate of nonlethal violent crime was among the lowest. The risk of robbery (1.5 per cent) was lower than the average (2.4 per cent), lower than that of Western cities such as London (2.6 per cent) and New York (2.3 per cent) and about one sixth of the highest estimate reported for Buenos Aires (10 per cent). Phnom Penh also recorded among the lowest rates of sexual assault (0.2 per cent) and assault and threats (2 per cent) compared to averages of, respectively, 1.9 per cent and 4 per cent. Cities such as Johannesburg (11.2 per cent), Belfast (9.2 per cent), and London (8.6 per cent) experienced more assaults than Phnom Penh.

Political violence

Military hostilities

We cannot present figures of combatant casualties on the KR or the government side during the remaining years of the civil war between 1991 and 1998. We could estimate the number of civilian victims who were directly targeted by the KR, but not of civilians killed or maimed during military clashes initiated by either of the two sides. Relying on secondary sources, press reports, UN and nongovernmental organisation (NGO) reports, we calculated that a minimum of 1,050 victims had been targeted by the KR between 1992 and 1998, ranging from fewer than 100 in 1992 to a peak of 630 in 1993 and tapering off to just 11 in 1998. Brown (1992), for example, reported that in September and October 1991, the Khmer Rouge 'engaged in forced movement of population under their control along the Thai border into so-called liberated zones inside Cambodia' (p. 93). Massacres of Vietnamese residents by the KR in the great lake region during 1992 resulted in 'at least three dozen Vietnamese... murdered in separate incidents' (Brown, 1992, p. 89). Brown (1993) pointed out that 'the possibility of another pogrom (like that of 1970 stimulated by the Lon Nol government) cannot be excluded' (p. 89), and his assessment was accurate even if the series of KR's pogroms were not as deadly as Lon Nol's.

Indirect victims of military hostilities, most of them civilians, include those killed and maimed by land mines. Human Rights Watch estimated that as of October 1995 at least 10 million landmines (i.e. about 55 landmines per square kilometre) had been laid across Cambodia by the various warring factions.[10] In addition, 30 years of war and massive US aerial bombings had left a lethal legacy of various unexploded armaments or explosive remnants of war (ERW). The Cambodia Mine Victims Information System (CMVIS) estimated that

---

[10] www.unicef.org/sowc96pk/hidekill.htm (citing Human Rights Watch, the Arms Project).

from 1979 to 2011 at least 64,017 casualties from landmines or ERWs were recorded, including 16,619 deaths. Cambodia consequently has one of the highest rates of amputees in the world at around 344 per 100,000 population in 2010. Despite a consistent demining effort since 1992, deaths and casualties due to landmines and ERWs are still occurring today. From a peak of 4,320 people killed or injured in 1998, the numbers declined to an average of 2,000 persons per year between 1992 and 2000 (Jennar, 2010), and then 850 per year between 1999 and 2005. The rate of mine clearance nearly doubled in 2005,[11] which helped reduce casualties in subsequent years to 286 in 2010 (including 71 deaths) and 211 (including 43 deaths) in 2011 (Cambodian Mine Action Centre [CMAC], 2010; Landmine & Cluster Munition Monitor, 2014). One third of victims of ERWs are children, mostly boys, and 87 per cent of survivors are males, with an average age of 28 years. In a country with a limited health system and no disability benefits, the social and economic consequences of landmine injuries are far reaching. The high number of male victims of working age places strain on many rural families' livelihood. Although large areas have been cleared of mines, the Landmine Monitor estimated that, in 2013, 1,915 km^2 remained contaminated, predominantly in the northwestern regions.[12] The presence of mines on agricultural land prevents farmers cultivating this land, which in turn leads to a loss of income, food scarcity, and higher risks of associated malnutrition. The Cambodian Mine Action Centre (CMAC) estimated that at the current rate of funding for mine clearing (USD 30 million/year), it would take another 10 to 20 years to rid the whole country of the threat of landmines and ERWs.

Civilian political violence

It is difficult to present a comprehensive measure of the number of individuals killed and injured in events of civilian political violence. Relying on a range of sources,[13] we computed what could be described as 'celebrated cases' reported by the media and international agencies. Between 1992 and 2012, the number of killed and injured victims of civilian political violence in such cases was *at least* 920, with peaks in 1993 (264 victims) and 1997 (320 victims). Most of the victims were opponents of the SOC regime or the KPRP/CPP. For example,

---

[11] The Cambodian Mine Action Centre has coordinated demining. A large part of its funding comes from foreign aid. From 1992 to 2004, an average 12 km^2 per year were cleared, but through the use of machinery and improved methods, clearance rates doubled in 2005 and have continued to increase (CMAC, 2010).

[12] www.the-monitor.org/index.php/cp/display/region_profiles/theme/3324.

[13] Albritton (2004), Beresford (2005), Brinkley (2009, 2011), Coates (2005), Heder and Ledgerwood (1996), Hughes (2003b), Jennar (1995, 2010), Langran (2000, 2001), Ledgerwood and Un (2002), Lizee (1996, 1997), Moorthy and Saroeun (1998), Peou (1998, 1999, 2000, 2006), Saroeun and Chaumeau (1998), Saroeun and Eckardt (1998), Saroeun and Grainger (1998), Springer (2011), Un and Ledgerwood (2002, 2003).

the SOC regime allegedly set up a secret death squad (the so-called S91 unit) that tortured and assassinated opponents and committed numerous robberies and rapes (Heder & Ledgerwood, 1996; Jennar, 1995).

However, in addition to celebrated cases it is necessary to add the other cases reported by the *PPP* that mention a political aspect (e.g. assassination of a SRP activist) and ambiguous cases of 'revenge' such as assassinations that are not accounted for by nonpolitical motives. We coded the 912 cases of planned successful and attempted expressive homicides that were reported by the *PPP* between 1992 and 2008 in terms of their likelihood of being politically motivated. Sixty were coded as definitely or probably politically motivated. Of these 60 cases, 57 per cent occurred between 1992 and 1994, 12 per cent between 1995 and 2002, 17 per cent in 2003, 8 per cent in 2004, and 6 per cent between 2005 and 2007. The declining proportion of politically motivated homicides confirms that political violence has significantly abated in Cambodia, in sharp contrast to the next type of crime we examine.

Elite predatory crime and violence

As we have shown in the previous chapter, by 1990 the corruption and plunder perpetrated by the ruling military, business, and political elites had reached the stage of a kleptocratic system. The dramatic social and economic repercussions of the UNTAC mission, the massive international financial assistance that supported it, and the competition between the two factions of the bicephalous government brought corruption and plunder to new heights, which often involved violent strategies. In 1990, the economy was stagnating and the population was becoming increasingly dissatisfied with the rampant corruption. Many allegations of misuse of aid funding were made, and several countries such as Czechoslovakia, Poland, Hungary, Bulgaria, and the Soviet Union ceased further assistance (van der Kroef, 1991).[14] Slocomb (2002) reported major corruption in the forestry industry in 1991–2 and concluded: 'The rate and extent of logging, illegal and abusive practices, and the undisguised collusion of leading political and military officials . . . amounted to major theft of the country's forestry resources' (p. 772). Le Billon (2002) characterised these political and economic arrangements as 'shadow state politics'.

The Polpotists had also turned into warlord-businessmen, building fortunes through the timber and gem trades in western Cambodia with the help of Thai business and the Thai military (Brown, 1993). Abuza (1993) considered that this wealth accumulation partly explained why the KR had retained some popular support in the regions they controlled and that 'commerce within PDK

---

[14] They essentially stopped because of their own frail economies, but they also made these allegations about corruption in respect to their aid to Cambodia.

[Party of Democratic Kampuchea] zones tends to be quite adequate, as they have the best roads, few mines, and no banditry... They champion the peasantry and they don't tolerate corruption' (p. 1021).

According to a report in the Thai newspaper, *The Nation*, each refugee in the KR-controlled camps was promised 24 *rai* (nearly four hectares) of land in Battambang Province, one of Cambodia's most fertile regions, and many people thus went to the KR's zone because they didn't believe that the UNHCR [United Nations High Commissioner for Refugees] would provide as much land... The NADK [National Army of Democratic Kampuchea] soldiers are well organized, disciplined, respectful of the peasantry, and there is a lack of corruption at every level of their organization. They do not rape, pillage, or conduct forced conscription although there have been many reports of forced conscription of support people such as porters – in stark contrast to the unpaid SOC troops who often turn to banditry. (Abuza, 1993, pp. 1013–14)

The combination of the UNTAC mission with further extensive privatisation of property was a potent mix that fuelled corruption to a more extensive and systemic level. Um (1994) explained the negative impact of the UNTAC's presence on the development of crime, violence, and corruption:

One of the immediate negative consequences of UNTAC's presence was the effect of some 22,000 UN personnel with a hardship per diem that equalled the annual per capita income of the country. The economy almost spun out of control. Monthly rent for a small apartment in Phnom Penh could cost as much as $2,000 generating widespread real estate speculation and incentives for evictions, some with casualties. (pp. 79–80)

Grand theft preempted UNTAC's attempts at controlling public assets, and high-ranking SOC officials rushed to sell or steal state property, which resulted in an estimated monthly loss of around $10 million to the revenues of the RGC. A growing shady banking sector provided a conduit for laundering the proceeds of heroin and other drug trafficking, originally orchestrated by military commanders from Koh Kong in the mid 1980s (Um, 1994).

Studies of elite corruption in Cambodia since 1992 have been abundant, and we cannot review them all here. A few examples are sufficient to illustrate the extent of corruption and how it is supported by violence. In 1994, Um (1995) pointed out that one of the pressing issues facing Cambodia was the regulation of land ownership and that 'without a valid legal framework and its enforcement, land speculation will continue unabated, with evictions and physical dislocation becoming progressively more common' (p. 82). Her prediction has been fulfilled as evictions have indeed increased in recent years and often resulted in violent clashes between police (as well as armed private security) and evictees in Phnom Penh and the provinces.

Another widespread corrupt practice in Cambodia's military and civil service was that of 'ghosting'. In 2000, the Ministry of Defence discovered it had on its payroll 12,868 'ghost' soldiers and 105,234 'ghost' dependants, costing nearly $400,000 per month (Langran, 2000, p. 30). Waste and diversion of government funds occurred in other areas. In 1999, while landmines were killing and maiming around 100 people per month, financial improprieties and frauds dating back at least 5 years were discovered at the Cambodian Mine Action Centre (Fuller, 1999; Kyne, 1999). Inadequate accounting practices made the CMAC's financial structure particularly sensitive to dubious purchases, manipulations, and lack of accountability. The allegations led to the temporary suspension of funding by international donors pending an external audit. Allegations of mismanagement and wasteful spending were again raised in 2000 (Kyne, 2000). Another case reported by Un and Ledgerwood (2003) involved 'one anti-smuggling officer who had stopped his investigations because of death threats, [and] estimated the losses in government revenues on imported cars alone at $100 million annually' (pp. 117–19). A UN investigation found that 'about 4000 tonnes, about 44 per cent of the rice intended for distribution to poor participants in its work-for-food program, had been stolen or "diverted" by government officials from January 2003 to February 2004' (cited in Beresford, 2005, p. 138).

Langran (2001) cited several independent reports mentioning 'the involvement of government, military, and police officials in illegal activities, including human trafficking, poaching, and smuggling' (p. 158). She also remarked that torture in prison was common and pointed out that the judicial system lacked independence from the government, which resulted in the 'widespread practice of vigilante justice' that reflected 'the lack of confidence Cambodians place in the judicial system and a history in which the rule of law is weak' (Langran, 2001, p. 159). We analyse and discuss vigilante justice in the next chapter.

Elite crime has continued unabated until today. Since it was first included in Transparency International's Corruption Perception Index (CPI) in 2005, Cambodia has ranked among the most corrupt states and its score has remained low (ranging between 1.8 in 2008 and 2.3 in 2005).[15] In 2005 it ranked 130th out of 158 countries; it obtained a similar ranking in 2012, 157th out of 174 countries. A law against corruption was eventually enacted in 2011 and, based on its impact since then, as well as the impact of many other Cambodian laws, appears to be inadequately or corruptibly enforced, and there is little evidence to suggest that the political will to enforce these laws has overcome entrenched patron-client practices. Starr (2007) argued that in view of the considerable

---

[15] The CPI does not directly measure the prevalence of corrupt practices but provides an indication of the extent of corruption in the public and political sectors using the experiences and perceptions of a range of business people and country analysts. A country's score indicates the perceived level of corruption on a scale from 0 to 10, where 0 means a country is perceived as highly corrupt and 10 as very clean. The rank indicates the country's position relative to the other countries included in the index; the lower the rank, the greater the perception of corruption. See www.transparency.org/research/cpi/overview.

negative and durable impact persistent grand corruption[16] has on the overall wellbeing of a population it should be considered a crime against humanity.

In the final section of this chapter on contemporary Cambodia, we complement the MoI data with the *Phnom Penh Post* (*PPP*) crime reports and the UNICVS data to examine the characteristics of offenders and victims as well as the types of violence.

Offenders, victims, and types of violence

Offenders

In Cambodia, as universally observed elsewhere, males represent almost the totality of the violent offender population. Between 1992 and 2008, 94 per cent of offenders involved in the 5,238 violent criminal events reported by the *Phnom Penh Post* were male. The youngest was 5 and the oldest 86 years.[17] This population of offenders was relatively young: the mean age was 28.4 years, and half were 25 years or younger.[18] Urban offenders were significantly younger (mean = 27 years) than those in rural areas (mean = 30.2 years) overall and for each type of crime. This pattern is explained by the structure of the Cambodian population in which, according to the CDHS, the age group of 15- to 24-year-olds represented 23.5 per cent of the urban population in 2005 and 23.4 per cent in 2010 but only 19.2 per cent of the rural population in 2005 and 18.6 per cent in 2010 (NIS, Directorate General for Health, & ICF Macro, 2011). This explains the older age of both offenders and victims in rural areas. There might also be cultural factors behind the apparent later onset of offending in rural areas, as *Bulletins de Police Criminelle* (*BPC*) offender data for the period 1936–40 also showed relatively older male offenders in rural areas than in Phnom Penh, and it was also the case in the *BPC* (homicide-only) data for the period 1947–55. The proportion of offenders aged 20 years and younger, however, climbed slightly post-2005, particularly in rural areas. If this recent pattern is not an artefact of the *PPP* data, it might suggest that youth crime is rising, and the rise in rural areas could be associated with socioeconomic (i.e.

---

[16] A more toxic form of government corruption occurs when corruption is so systematic that a kleptocracy (rule by thieves) arises which in effect disarms law enforcement capacity to investigate and indict. In Cambodia, there may not be sufficient formal evidence of capital flight, embezzlement, or misuse of state treasury for personal expenses and the like. However, several unambiguous examples are known of the ruling elite accumulating wealth on a rapid and grand scale.

[17] The *PPP* reports tallied 7,740 violent offenders and age was available for only 40 per cent of them.

[18] This matches the general population in which 53.8 per cent of individuals were 24 years and younger in 2012 (*World Fact Book*, https://www.cia.gov/library/publications/the-world-factbook/geos/cb.html).

rural unemployment) and cultural (i.e. modernisation) factors. Female violent offenders tended to be older than male (mean age of 33.1 years and 28.6 years, respectively), and acquisitive offenders were generally younger than expressive offenders (25.6 years compared to 30.5 years).[19] Those who had killed someone, whether as a consequence of acquisitive or expressive violence, were also significantly older (30.2 years on average) than nonlethal perpetrators (28.2 years on average). In addition, as the relational closeness between offender and victim increased, so did the age of offenders: extracommunal offenders (i.e. those offending against strangers) were on average 25.7 years, but intrafamilial offenders (i.e. those who offended against family members and relatives) were the oldest (35.3 years).[20]

There were differences in the types of offences perpetrated by male and female offenders, although we need to keep in mind that the reporting of crime by the *PPP* is biased towards serious and violent offences and may not reflect typical male or female offending, the bulk of which is minor and nonviolent.[21] The majority of violent female offenders reported in the *PPP* had committed acts of expressive violence, with only 13 per cent involved in acquisitive violence. Their crimes occurred mostly within the family (52 per cent compared to 11 per cent of male violent offenders). In contrast, just over half the male offenders (52 per cent) had offended against strangers compared to only 13 per cent of female offenders.

Victims

Just over 60 per cent of victims of violent crime in the *PPP* data were male, and 39 per cent were female. Nearly three quarters (72 per cent) of deaths resulting from criminal incidents were of male victims.[22] The average victim of violence was 30.7 years old, but like offenders, and for the same regional demographic reasons, victims from Phnom Penh were significantly younger than those from the provinces (29.5 and 31.6 years, respectively). Victims of expressive violence were also significantly younger than victims of acquisitive violence. Across the whole period a similar proportion of males and females (57 per cent) were the victims of extracommunal violence; however, if we

---

[19] The older age of female violent offenders is associated with the expressive and intrafamilial types of violence females committed. Most of them were married women involved in domestic violence (see below).

[20] The latter were generally husbands and fathers, therefore, likely to be older individuals.

[21] For instance, the Cambodian UNICVS incidence statistics for years 2000 and 2005 showed that violent victimisation represented, respectively, only 8 per cent and 6 per cent of all victimisation incidents (because incidence statistics compute the number of different types of victimisations suffered by each respondent multiplied by the number of occurrences for each type of victimisation during the given year, they produce an estimate of the total volume of offending).

[22] The number of deaths is underestimated because among the injured male and female victims at least 42 per cent had been seriously injured and some may have later died of their injuries.

exclude cases involving KR violence, which typically killed and injured a large number of unassociated individuals, we find that males were predominantly the victims of extracommunal violence (54 per cent), with only 8 per cent of victims of intrafamilial violence, while females were more likely to be the victims of people known to them (intracommunal violence, 40 per cent, and intrafamilial violence, 26 per cent). The Cambodia Socio-Economic Survey (NIS, 2009) found that in 90 per cent of cases of violence with injury, the victim knew the perpetrator, and more so when victims were female. The general pattern of sex differences in the crime victimisation situations reported by the *PPP* is similar to many other countries (i.e. females are more at risk of victimisation in the home than are males), but the proportions may not be the same because of the *PPP* bias in reporting serious cases.

Trends in violent multiple victimisation
From the *PPP* crime reports between 1992 and 2008, we estimated the number of victims by violent event using the 'ecological' approach; that is, we took into account *all* the victims in a given violent event, including those who were not physically harmed, and offenders who were victims of extrajudicial violence. For example, consider the case of three individuals robbed by five offenders: one victim is killed, another is injured, and the third one is not physically harmed; as the police intervene, two of the robbers are killed. In such a case we count *five* victims.

The average number of victims of violent crime events reduced substantially from 1992 (6.9 victims) to 2008 (1.6 victims). The proportion of violent crime events involving a single victim increased in reverse proportion, from 55 per cent in 1992 to 74 per cent in 2008. The year 1993 saw the return of full-scale KR attacks, the assassinations of Vietnamese civilians, and the increasing political violence associated with the election. Attacks by KR typically killed and injured large numbers of people.[23] The average number of victims generally tended to be higher in rural areas (2.4 victims) than in Phnom Penh (1.8 victims), but the difference was particularly marked pre-1999 when the average number of rural victims was nearly three times that of Phnom Penh (7.3 and 2.6 victims, respectively). In addition to postconflict effects and their eventual decline, and regional variations in modernisation processes (including policing), this pattern is likely to also be associated with differences in the use and control of weapons, as we will see in the next chapter.

Until 2009, MoI data on victims of crime were incomplete, patchy, and sometimes undecipherable; however, for the 3 years 2010–12, they confirm

---

[23] The average number of victims of violent events was 4.1 between 1992 and 1998 but subsequently dropped to 1.6; events of lethal violence claimed on average 3.4 victims between 1992 and 1998, with a drop to 1.1 victims post-1998, illustrating, among other factors (e.g. weapon collection; see next chapter), the strong impact of KR attacks on rates of victimisation.

PPP data: during these 3 years, the average numbers of victims killed or injured through homicide, robbery, serious assault, and domestic violence never exceeded 1.2 individuals per event.[24] Also in line with the *PPP* results, these averages tend to be higher in rural areas than in Phnom Penh.

Types of violence

Acquisitive violence: robbery

The *PPP* reported two types of robberies: street robbery and house robbery. Across the 17 years of the *PPP* data, house robberies represented 17 per cent of all robberies[25] but a larger share of all robberies in the countryside (23 per cent) than in Phnom Penh (12 per cent). In 2003 and 2010, the police data provided situational information on robbery, which also revealed that a larger proportion of residential robberies occurred in the countryside (for these 2 respective years, 59 per cent and 66 per cent of all rural robberies compared to 7 per cent and 41 per cent in Phnom Penh). Many of these residential robberies were home invasions by armed offender(s), and the greater likelihood of residential robbery in rural areas is reminiscent of the traditional rural banditry that targeted villagers and pillaged their homes. Situational factors are also important. Dwellings are more likely to be isolated and poorly protected in the countryside than in the city, and populous urban areas offer greater opportunities for street robberies, although better street policing in recent years, particularly in the city, is likely to have had affected street robberies more than house robberies. Both the *PPP* and the UNICVS show that motorcycles tended to be the main target of violent acquisitive crimes (in 65 per cent of robberies reported by the *PPP*).[26] While motorcycles were more likely to be targeted in Phnom Penh than in rural areas, money and gold were more often reported as targets of acquisitive crimes in rural areas, and this is attributable to the larger proportion of residential robberies in rural areas. Two thirds of robberies involved firearms.

About two thirds of all victims of robberies were male,[27] with some gender differences between the types of robbery: while nearly three quarters of the victims of street robberies were males, females represented the majority (55 per cent) of residential robberies. Street robberies often targeted moto-taxi drivers (all males), who were the victims in 27 per cent of robbery-murders and 47 per

---

[24] Averages based on the *PPP* crime reports are slightly higher because they include rape victims and noninjured victims.
[25] In Australia between 1995 and 2001, 7.5 per cent of all recorded robberies occurred in a residential setting (Mouzos, 2003).
[26] However, between 2001 and 2010, the number of robberies and thefts of motorcycles recorded by the MoI steadily declined from 1,495 to 513 per annum.
[27] This is similar to the situation in Australia from 1995 to 2001 where 65 per cent of victims of robberies were male (Mouzos, 2003).

cent of robberies that occurred on the street. As expected, our analyses indicated that acquisitive violence was significantly more likely to be extracommunal (i.e. between strangers) than internecine (i.e. between people who know each other): from the *PPP* we estimated that 83 per cent of all lethal robberies and 95 per cent of all nonlethal robberies involved strangers. The small proportion of internecine acquisitive violence was more likely to occur in rural areas than in the city.

Expressive violence

Expressive violence by males overwhelmingly victimised friends or acquaintances (65 per cent) and family members and relatives (21 per cent).[28] Of cases of intracommunal lethal expressive violence, over half (55 per cent) involved revenge, which often followed arguments over relatively petty matters. Over one quarter (28 per cent) of cases involved disputes (sometimes over land) and arguments, and at least one in four perpetrators in these cases were drunk. Another 6 per cent of cases were rape-murders. The rest of the cases were 'crimes of passion', simple fights, or not readily classifiable. As in cases of lethal violence, revenge, disputes, drunken brawls, and sexual jealousy or rivalry were behind about two thirds of cases of nonlethal expressive violence between friends and acquaintances, but one third were cases of rape.

The most frequent victims of men's intrafamilial homicides were their wives (44 per cent), and the most frequent reasons were jealousy and domestic arguments.[29] In at least 13 per cent of cases, the husband was drunk. The other intrafamilial homicides involved all sorts of family relationships[30] and at least 12 per cent of perpetrators were drunk at the time of the homicide. These 'other-than-spousal' homicidal relationships appear to be associated with a traditional pattern of close-knit extended-family life that increases the risk of disputes. The majority of these homicides were caused by disputes over petty matters or involved emotionally and mentally disturbed individuals. About 7 per cent involved revenge, 6 per cent, land disputes, and 2 per cent were rape-murders. Nonlethal intrafamilial violence by males was perpetrated against wives in about one third of cases, and another third against parents or sons or daughters. Five per cent of cases of marital violence included rape compared to half the cases of 'nonspousal' violence. In about one third of rape cases, the male perpetrator was drunk.

---

[28] These figures exclude cases where the relationship was unknown.
[29] For theoretical purposes, trends in gendered violence (e.g. domestic violence against women) are examined in the next chapter.
[30] In 21 per cent of cases, the perpetrators killed in-laws; in 20 per cent of cases, the relationship was parental or filial; 8 per cent of cases involved siblings; and the rest, other relatives.

For female offenders, the majority of intrafamilial violence occurred in the context of domestic violence when women injured or killed abusive partners in self-defence or retaliation. Disputes and revenge attacks as well as a few infanticides accounted for about one quarter of intrafamilial events involving female offenders, and 'crimes of passion' accounted for another 17 per cent. In these crimes of passion, jealous wives killed or injured unfaithful husbands, or unfaithful wives killed their husbands or had them killed to be with their lover.

Weapons were present in the majority of cases of expressive violence: 32 per cent involved a firearm, and over 50 per cent a knife or an implement such as a sickle, an axe, or a hammer. Male and female offenders used different weapons: just 5 per cent of female offenders had used a firearm compared to 34 per cent of males, but over half the female offenders had used a knife or a sickle compared to a quarter of male offenders. Over 13 per cent of female perpetrators had used poison and acid. Acid throwing is particularly prevalent in South Asia (e.g. also reported in Pakistan and Bangladesh), where it is often committed by men against women as a type of domestic violence or in honour-related crimes. In Cambodia it is committed against both men and women, and particularly by women in 'crimes of passion' when thrown in the face of rivals or cheating husbands to disfigure them (Cambodia Acid Survivors Charity, 2010).

Sexual victimisation

All the victims of rape reported in the *PPP* were female, but about one third of the 54 victims of illicit sex with male foreign nationals were young boys, around 13 years old. Jennar (2010) also reported that during the UNTAC mission some UN soldiers perpetrated a number of rapes of young Cambodian boys. Overall, rapes occurred more frequently between people who knew each other (70 per cent) than between strangers, but in the city nearly half (47 per cent) involved strangers. Rape victims were on average 18.1 years, but about half of them were 16 years or younger.[31] Those murdered after the rape were significantly older (20.5 years) than the victims of nonlethal rape (17.5 years).[32] Surtees's (2003) qualitative research provided insightful reflections about the cultural context in understanding rape in Cambodian society. She also noted that sexual violence

---

[31] This is consistent with statistics on sexual assault in Australia, which show that girls aged 10 to 14 years have the highest rate of sexual assault (Australian Institute of Criminology, 2012, p. 25).

[32] Respondents who had reported sexual victimisation in the UNICVS were older (mean age 27.3 years) than the victims in the *PPP*. A limitation of the UNICVS is that respondents must be at least 16 years old to participate in the survey; yet, half the victims of rape events reported in the *PPP* were 16 years and younger. Therefore, it is probable that the UNICVS considerably underestimates the prevalence of rape and the age of victims. Exceptionally, in 2004 the police records specified the number of rapes involving child victims (younger than 15 years). None were recorded in Phnom Penh but this type of rape comprised over one quarter of rapes in the provinces.

was widespread under the KR and widely recalled. From the *BPC* (1947–54), we observed that the prevalence of rape was exacerbated by banditry, war, and mass-violence conflicts.

In a household survey conducted between 2012 and 2013 in Phnom Penh and four Cambodian provinces with a representative sample of 1,812 men aged 18 to 49 years, 20.8 per cent of respondents said that they had raped their female partner, 8.3 per cent had raped a nonpartner, and 5.2 per cent admitted participating in gang rape (Fulu *et al.*, 2013). Of the 369 men who said that they had ever raped a woman, half had done so more than once and one in five had raped more than one victim. The major reason given by respondents for raping a female partner was a sense of sexual entitlement. Rape was also used in anger or as punishment for women not following cultural gender norms. One quarter of the men said that rape provided them entertainment, particularly after drinking. Half of the men who had raped suffered no legal consequences, but half were arrested and 28 per cent were jailed. Over half, however, were punished, assaulted, or threatened in response by the family or friends of the victim.

Sex trade victimisation

A number of studies have discussed the postconflict conditions of Cambodian women in relation to prostitution, trafficking, rape, and domestic violence (e.g. Frieson, 2011). Gilboa (1998) provided an impressionistic account of the 'decadent' lifestyle of some of the Western expatriates in relation to prostitution and drugs and the general 'Wild West' atmosphere (anomie) in Phnom Penh between August 1996 and April 1998. For the contemporary period, Coates (2005) wrote about forced prostitution, violence against sex workers, and human trafficking and argued that the number of victims could be counted by the thousands: 'Her mother sold her to a pimp, who sold her virginity and her innocence for several years ... she is one of hundreds, thousands, sold into this dismal trade in human life, day after day, in Phnom Penh's sex shacks' (p. 165). Sex work is widespread in Cambodia; for example, 49 per cent of male respondents in Fulu *et al.*'s (2013) survey said that they were regularly visiting sex workers. However, it is important to be aware that the conflation of sex trafficking with uncoerced commercial sex and the criminalisation and corrupt repression of the latter further victimise poor Cambodian women. Statistics of female prisoners from 18 prisons compiled by the Cambodian League for the Promotion and Defense of Human Rights (LICADHO, 2009) show that women were most likely to be incarcerated for human trafficking (32 per cent of female prisoners in 2008).[33] Keo *et al.* (2014) and others (e.g. Steinfatt, 2011; Weitzer,

---

[33] Women were much more likely to be incarcerated for human trafficking than men to the extent that, among all those incarcerated for human trafficking in Cambodia, 80 per cent in 2007 and 77 per cent in 2008 were female (Keo, 2014).

2011; Zhang, 2009) have discussed the moral panic related to trafficking and provided evidence suggesting the estimates of its prevalence reported in some literature are grossly exaggerated.

In the next chapter we examine how our data between 1992 and 2012 fit with the hypotheses and predictions of the theories of modernisation and civilising processes included in our theoretical framework.

11 Civilising processes and violence in contemporary Cambodia

We saw in the previous chapter that a dramatic decline in crime and violence occurred in Cambodia since the 1991 peace agreement. In 20 years, the rate of homicide in Cambodia fell from 23.5 per 100,000 in 1993 to 2.4 per 100,000 in 2012. Although this rate is still higher than that in most Western countries (the mean for 19 Western and Northern European countries in 2010 was 1.3 per 100,000 [United Nations Office on Drugs and Crime, 2011]), the decline is impressive. Which circumstances and factors may account for this significant decline is the focus of the present chapter. We look beyond simple questions of prevalence and analyse whether the mechanisms suggested by modernisation and civilising process theories are useful to explain these trends. In short, we examine whether the theoretical framework outlined in the Introduction can explain the contemporary data, and in the next chapter we will discuss how this framework accounts for the trends and patterns observed during our 150-year historical survey. First, we disentangle provincial differences in crime trends, drawing mainly from Shelley's predictions regarding changes in urban and rural crime during modernisation. Then, we consider how the three major civilising processes proposed by Elias – the monopolisation of violence by the state, increasing economic and social interdependence, and sensitisation to violence – can explain the evolution of public and private violence. Our analysis draws on official crime data and media reports as well as economic data and household and other surveys conducted in Cambodia described in the previous chapter.

Urban and rural trends and patterns of crime

Considering only the overall decline in crime in Cambodia over the last 20 years masks important differences in the patterns of crime between Phnom Penh and the provinces. A major element of modernisation theories is the development of cities along with industrialisation and with it, large-scale migrations from rural to urban areas. Durkheim (1893/1964) suggested that violence was preeminent in collectivist societies because of the settling of feuds and honour-related disputes. As societies modernise, such violence tends to decline in the cities, where individualistic rather than collectivistic values first emerge. Shelley (1981)

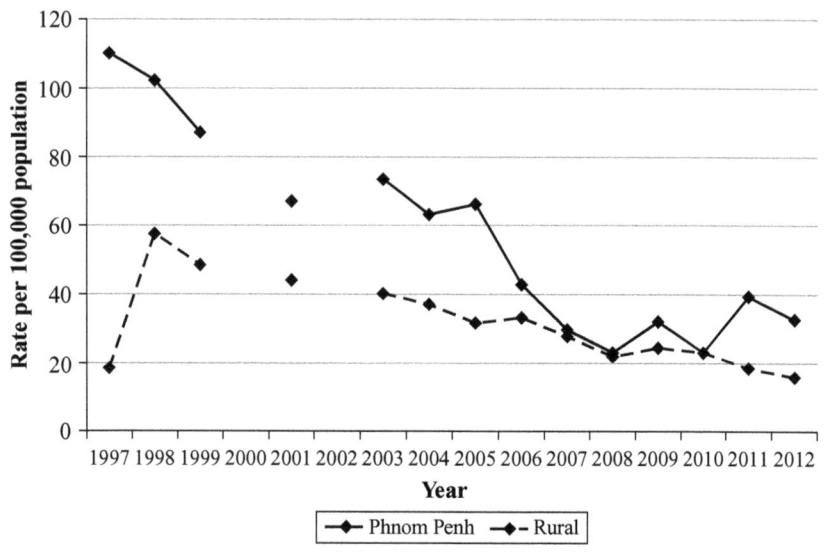

Figure 11.1 Urban and rural rates of recorded crime events, 1997–2012

theorised fluctuations in crime and in the types of violence depending on the stages of urbanisation. In this section, we explore these regional differences in crime and violence in contemporary Cambodia. First, a few methodological remarks are necessary:

- The Ministry of Interior (MoI) started providing data disaggregated by province in 1997, and, apart from 2000 and 2002, these disaggregated data were available up to 2012.
- However, provincial data were not disaggregated further into urban (provincial capital) and rural areas. We therefore only coded Phnom Penh as an urban area, and all the other provinces were coded as rural areas. The province of Kandal surrounds Phnom Penh and is fast urbanising; however, several analyses indicated that Kandal's rates and trends in crime were far more similar to provincial ones than to Phnom Penh's, so we decided to retain Kandal as a rural area.
- In analysing rural and urban crime trends, we assume that the problems discussed earlier about the poor level of crime recording by police, and its consequences on rates and proportion of violent crime compared to nonviolent crime, have affected rural and urban areas equally. This is a reasonable assumption because victim surveys generally support the urban/rural differences indicated by the MoI data that we discuss below.

Figure 11.1 shows that between 1997 and 2005, the rates of recorded crime events in Phnom Penh greatly exceeded those in rural areas, but from 2006 a significant drop in the Phnom Penh rates brought them to the same low level as the rural rates.[1] Between 2011 and 2013, however, rates started to moderately increase in Phnom Penh while they continued to decline in the provinces. A large national survey, the Cambodia Socio-Economic Survey (CSES), also revealed a sharper decline in criminal victimisation in urban areas (from 6.9 per cent of individuals and households per annum in 2004 to 2.9 per cent in 2009) than in rural areas (from 4.7 per cent of individuals and households in 2004 to 3.8 per cent in 2009) (NIS, 2009).[2] Finally, our United Nations International Crime Victims Survey (UNICVS) indicated similar regional trends as the CSES for property crime victimisation. The decline was more pronounced in Phnom Penh (from 42.4 per cent in 2000 to 23.3 per cent in 2005–6) than in rural areas (from 35.5 per cent in 2000 to 20.5 per cent in 2005–6 in Kandal and Kampong Cham).[3]

According to Shelley's (1981) modernisation theory, the pattern of higher crime rates in Phnom Penh compared to rural areas, which we may assume was already present from 1992 to 1997, and which lasted until 2005, is characteristic of the early phase of urbanisation. After the fall of Democratic Kampuchea (DK) in 1979, Phnom Penh repopulated rapidly, and the population growth was in great part due to rural migration. Characteristic of the early phase of urbanisation, crime rates peaked in the city. The subsequent decline in offending from 2006 to 2012, which was relatively modest in rural areas but dramatic in Phnom Penh, is a sign of the later stage of modernisation, when the anomic factors associated with migrant rural population start to recede and the former rural migrants settle into an urban lifestyle.

Acquisitive and expressive violence

Shelley's modernisation theory further posits that during the early stage of urbanisation, *acquisitive* violence (i.e. violence motivated by gain, such as robbery) is more frequent in cities than in rural areas, where *expressive* violence (i.e. violence not motivated by gain) is higher. However, expressive violence is also likely to increase in urban areas during the early stage of urbanisation because rural migrants bring their rural manners towards violence to the city.

---

[1] Trends were similar for violent and non-violent crime, except that non-violent crime started to fall earlier in Phnom Penh (2001) than violent crime (2006).
[2] The operationalisation of urban and rural areas in the CSES was more precise than we could achieve in our analysis of the MoI data. The crimes surveyed in the CSES included: rape, assault, burglary, theft, and robbery.
[3] We could not compare prevalence between the CSES and the UNICVS because questions were more precise and covered more crime types in the UNICVS. As a result, UNICVS rates are about 10 times higher than those estimated by the CSES; however, what matters here are the trends rather that the prevalence rates *per se* and in this regard the UNICVS shows the same trends as the CSES.

By the later stage of urbanisation, expressive violence has declined in cities because rural migrants have adapted to the urban setting (Shelley) and have started to respond to its civilising environment, particularly to the greater levels of interdependency (Durkheim, Elias), but it remains the main form of violence in rural areas. The main type of violence that occurs in the city is acquisitive.

For expressive violence, we combined five types recorded in the police data: murder and attempted murder (but excluding robbery-murder), rape, assault with injury, kidnapping, and grenade attack; and for acquisitive violence, lethal and nonlethal robbery and, since 2010, kidnapping for ransom.[4] Figure 11.2 indicates support for the elements of modernisation theory discussed above: rates of acquisitive violence were significantly higher in Phnom Penh than in rural areas until 2006. Although rates of acquisitive violence fell dramatically in Phnom Penh in 2006 and got closer to the rural rates, they have so far remained higher than the latter (Figure 11.2a). In contrast, rates of expressive violence have consistently been higher in rural areas than in Phnom Penh (Figure 11.2b). Consistent with the hypothesis for the early stage of urbanisation, the level of expressive violence in Phnom Penh from 1998 to 2005 was only slightly lower than in rural areas. In 2006, expressive violence dropped significantly in Phnom Penh, which, regardless of a slight fall in rural areas, widened the gap between urban and rural rates. This pattern supports the hypothesis for the later stage of urbanisation, despite a short spike in expressive violence in Phnom Penh in the last 2 years.

Looking at patterns of acquisitive and expressive violence within Phnom Penh and across the provinces, we also found that they are mostly consistent with the hypotheses of modernisation theory. In Phnom Penh (solid line in Figure 11.2), until 2005, rates of acquisitive violence were significantly higher than rates of expressive violence, which supports the early-urbanisation-stage hypothesis. Consistent with the later-stage-urbanisation hypothesis, expressive violence from 2005 to 2009 declined in Phnom Penh; however, acquisitive violence also fell and more steeply than expressive violence. By 2009, acquisitive violence had dropped to the same level as expressive violence (around 8 per 100,000) and in 2010 fell lower than expressive violence (around 5 per 100,000). This specific pattern does not fit the hypothesis of the later urbanisation stage: if rates should fall for both crime types, because of a general decline in violence, in the urban setting, acquisitive violence should nevertheless remain higher than expressive violence. In rural areas (dashed line in Figure 11.2), from 1998 to 2012 both expressive and acquisitive violence have been declining, but expressive violence has remained significantly higher than

---

[4] Since 2010, kidnapping for ransom has been distinguished from other types of kidnapping, and we therefore coded the former as acquisitive violence, like robbery.

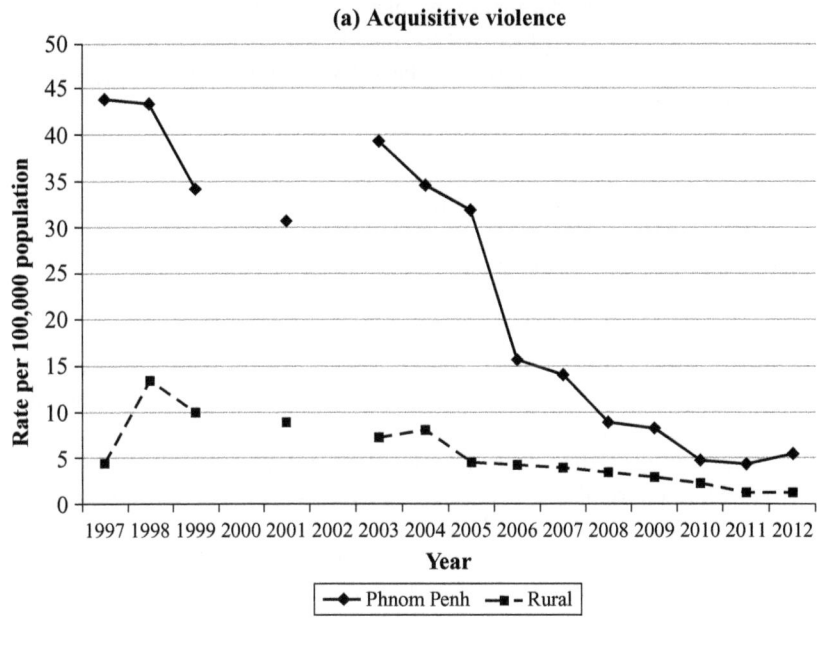
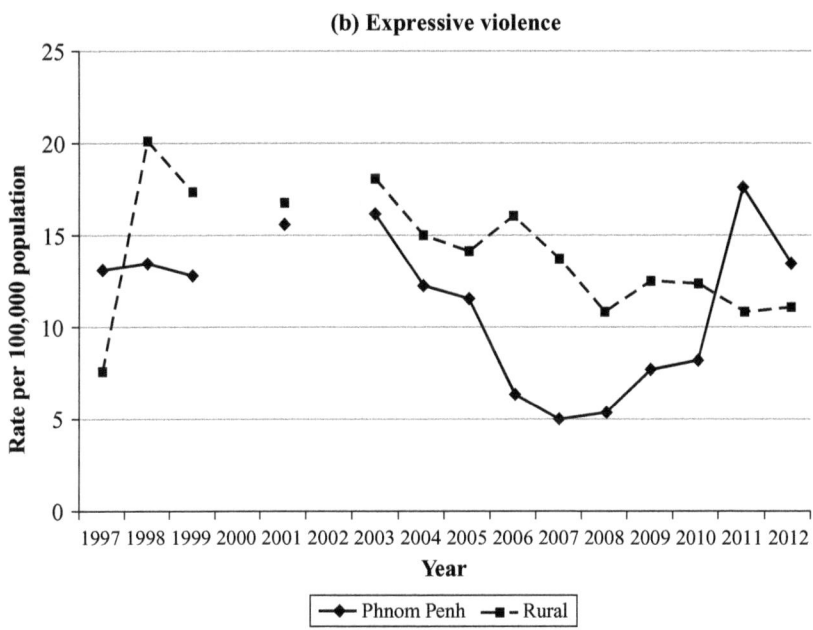

Figure 11.2 Rates of acquisitive and expressive violence in urban and rural areas, 1997–2012
Source: Cambodian Ministry of Interior, Judicial Police Centre.

acquisitive violence and the main type of rural violence. At the start of the observed period, it is likely that postwar effects had revived the characteristically Cambodian phenomenon of rural banditry, therefore contributing to the higher rates of both types of violence.

Types of expressive violence
Expressive violence was overall more frequent in rural than in urban areas, and here we analyse whether this pattern holds true for all types of expressive violence and examine other characteristics of these violent events.

Murder and attempted murder
Official data show that since 2001 rates of expressive successful and attempted murder[5] have declined in equal measure in Phnom Penh and in rural areas and have remained at a similar level until 2010 (2.4 per 100,000). In the last 2 years of the available data, the rate in Phnom Penh increased to 3.2 per 100,000 in 2012, while the rural rate decreased to 2.2. The *PPP* reports showed that one quarter of expressive homicides targeted strangers in Phnom Penh but only 16 per cent in the provinces; however, 24 per cent of victims of rural homicide were family members compared to just 12 per cent in Phnom Penh.[6]

Rape
Until 2009, rates of recorded rape events were considerably higher in the provinces (mean rate of 1.8 per 100,000) than in Phnom Penh (0.3 per 100,000), but in 2010 the urban rate soared to 2.5 per 100,000, that is, to the same level as the rural rate. Official rates of rape are not a reliable measure of prevalence because they also reflect increases in reporting fostered by changing attitudes and greater confidence in the police. The sharp increase in Phnom Penh since 2010 could therefore indicate a growing prevalence as much as an increase in the willingness to report to police. Nevertheless, higher rural rates are consistent with Shelley's hypotheses about rural and urban crime patterns. The *PPP* reports also showed that in the countryside intrafamilial and intracommunal rapes were more frequent (respectively, 21 per cent and 71 per cent) than in Phnom Penh (respectively, 16 per cent and 52 per cent).

Serious assault
Rates of serious assault (i.e. those occasioning injury) peaked at a similar level in Phnom Penh and the provinces in 2001–3 (10 per 100,000) but then fell

---

[5] Including murder, attempted murder, rape-murder, poisoning, but excluding robbery-murder.
[6] Here and in subsequent analyses, percentages are based on the number of events in the *PPP* data where we could determine the relationship between victim(s) and offender(s), but in 8 per cent of cases of expressive violence the relationship was unknown.

dramatically in Phnom Penh while remaining stable in the countryside. In 2011, however, the rate peaked again in Phnom Penh (11 per 100,000), becoming higher than the rural rate (5.8 per 100,000). In 2012 it declined to 7.3 in Phnom Penh, which was still higher than in rural areas (6.1). The *PPP* from 1992 to 2008 reported a higher proportion of internecine assaults in rural areas (92 per cent) than in the city (73 per cent). There was also a noticeable increase in the proportion of assaults between strangers reported by the *PPP* in the city after 2004, which may be associated with the growth of youth gangs. The presence of youth gangs may also explain the growing rates of assaults recorded by the MoI in the city since 2008 (see Gender and Development for Cambodia, 2003).

Archaic rural violence: the killing of sorcerers

Before we conclude our exploration of urban and rural crime, it is important to mention a typically rural type of violence, the killing of so-called sorcerers. The following two excerpts are from the *PPP* in 1999:

Kampong Speu: one male victim (59) believed to be a sorcerer has been killed with an AK 47 by another man.

Battambang: one male victim (46) regarded as a sorcerer, was killed with an AK 47 by four men (one was 33 years old) who cooked his liver and ate it.

Between 1994 and 2008, the *PPP* reported 48 violent, and often lethal, incidents in which sorcery was invoked (on average, over 3 cases per year) and involving 79 individuals who had been killed or injured. All but one case occurred in the provinces, and half the cases occurred in the province of Kampong Speu. This archaic form of violence, therefore, appeared to have its epicentre in one of the poorest provinces of Cambodia, which was also a Polpotist bastion. The majority of targeted 'sorcerers' were older males, with a mean age of 52.4 years. In over half the cases, however, this archaic type of violence was carried out using modern weapons, including automatic rifles and handguns. The fact that the victims on average were middle aged may be associated with the 'craft' (i.e. sorcery requires an occult knowledge that can only be acquired with age); yet, the context of the stories suggests that it is also possible that the attacks reflected the settling of blood debts with people old enough to have been politically involved in the DK regime or who still served with the Khmer Rouge (KR) during the People's Republic of Kampuchea (PRK) regime (given the very young age of KR soldiers).[7] Accusations of sorcery may also have been

---

[7] Zucker (2011, p. 92) observed the phenomenon in the highlands of the southwest (former KR stronghold of Ta Mok) and reported that in 2002 she was told by villagers that 'accusations [of sorcery] were similar to an accusation of being Khmer Rouge or working for the government and that people were using this new label to kill people they did not like'.

a pretext for revenge for other wrongs: for example, a man targeted for sorcery in Kampong Speu in 2005 was also accused of having axed another man to death; again in Kampong Speu in 2008, a so-called sorcerer was a village chief accused of stealing money that villagers had entrusted to him to repay a loan from the Farmers' Families Association. In four cases the alleged sorcerers were activists of the Sam Rainsy Party (SRP) and *Front Uni National pour un Cambodge Indépendant, Neutre, Pacifique, et Coopératif* (FUNCINPEC).

Others have remarked that archaism and modernity often seemed to merge in the violence perpetrated in Cambodia since the mid twentieth century (Hinton, 2002; Marston, 2002; Vickery, 1984). Zucker (2011) argued that local discourses about sorcery provide a logic to the 'destabilising forces of modernity and globalisation' and the 'invisible machinations of capitalism' as in the Western world the resurgence of cults is often associated with crises and anomic periods:

> In such an atmosphere of flux and chaos, categories were being restored and social order buttressed by labelling people as traitors or sorcerers. These accusations echo other societies where strong links between charges of sorcery and radical social change have been identified... accusations of traitorous activity and sorcery seem to provide a logic to the chaos of war and to the often mystifying sources of modern globalised products and ideas. (p. 92)

Summary

Our analyses mostly, but not completely, support Shelley's (1981) theory of urbanisation and crime. As the theory predicts, in the early stage of urbanisation (up to the mid 2000s) rates of crime were high in Phnom Penh but then dropped dramatically, narrowing the urban-rural gap. During the whole period, acquisitive violence was higher in Phnom Penh than in the provinces, and expressive violence higher in rural areas. In support of Shelley's hypothesis, as Cambodia entered the later stage of urbanisation post 2000, both acquisitive and expressive violence declined in Phnom Penh. The accelerated migration of rural populations to the city that started between the late 1980s and early 1990s transported the more violent culture, tradition, and historical experience of rural areas to the urban setting. As rural migrants settled in the urban environment and the city modernised, both in terms of economic and policing developments, violent crime declined in urban areas and what lingered was predominantly acquisitive. Also supporting modernisation theories, which suggest that expressive violence between acquaintances predominates in the more personalised rural environment while violence between strangers is more likely in the impersonal urban setting, the proportion of internecine violence in Cambodia, particularly intrafamilial violence, even in cases of acquisitive violence, was higher in the provinces than in Phnom Penh. In addition, archaic forms of violence, like the killing of alleged sorcerers, were found only in the countryside. Expressive violence in Phnom Penh, however, initially remained at a similar level as acquisitive violence, and then acquisitive violence dropped further than expressive violence in contradiction to Shelley's hypothesis, which predicted that acquisitive violence would remain the main type of violence in the later stage of urbanisation.[8] However, we found in the previous chapter that offenders were becoming younger, suggesting a rise in youth crime. Other evidence, which we explore later in this chapter, also points to an increase in youth crime, particularly gang violence. The emergence of intergang violence may partly explain why expressive violence has recently been higher in Phnom Penh than in the countryside. Our comparison of urban and rural crime suggests that Cambodia is no longer in the early stage of modernisation, as conceptualised by Shelley, but perhaps still is at an earlier stage than most Western countries.

The state's monopolisation of violence

In this section we examine the role of the state in the significant decline in crime and violence during the 20 years of the Royal Government of Cambodia (RGC) from its creation in 1993 until 2012. As our theoretical perspective proposed, the monopolisation of violence by the state was a major sociostructural element of the civilising processes. The main process of state formation was a series of violent elimination contests between rival warlords and the resulting ascendancy of a winner who increasingly extended and concentrated his power and resources. Through this process, the nascent state came to represent a centripetal force necessarily engaged for its survival in the elimination or co-option of the centrifugal forces represented by the remaining independent warlords. It extended a domain within which only the state developed a legitimate monopoly over the use of force and consequently was able to deliver peace and stability. This is what we described in our theoretical framework as the paradoxical pacifying process of the Leviathan. However, in the context of a weak state or power vacuum where protection itself is the commodity or service provided, then organised or hierarchical crime groups may act as de facto states in the resolution of conflicts (Gambetta, 1996; Varese, 2011).

In a similar vein, Tilly (1985) saw state and war making as analogous to the protection offered by organised crime, albeit with the advantage of legitimacy.[9]

---

[8] We shall see shortly, however, that this pattern can be accounted for by the process of state monopolisation of violence proposed by Elias and its specific effect on public rather than private violence.

[9] Tilly (1985) proposed: 'If protection rackets represent organised crime at its smoothest, then war risking and state making – quintessential protection rackets with the advantage of legitimacy – qualify as our largest examples of organised crime' (p. 169).

His argument 'stresses the interdependence of war making and state making and the analogy between both of these processes and what, when less successful and smaller in scale, we call organised crime. War makes states I shall claim. Banditry, piracy, gangland rivalry, policing and war making all belong on the same continuum' (Tilly, 1985, p. 170). State capture by organised crime groups through violence and intimidation has given rise to the idea of the 'mafia state' or criminal state (UNODC, 2010), which is primarily predatory and hedonistic rather than a commonwealth. Mafia-like operations and structures may be seen as analogous to some forms of the authoritarian state in the sense that they are both predatory and merge criminal enterprise with the legitimacy of the state. In the Cambodian setting, it was the political and military defectors from the DK rather than an organised crime group that established the PRK/State of Cambodia (SOC), but they similarly governed by relying on the mobilisation of the rural poor and a reputation for violent rule. In their case, the analogy with organised crime is limited. However, unlike DK leaders during their regime, not all of those who created the PRK were or remained zealous believers in communism; for many, their aims turned rather quickly from utopian to pragmatic, and the resulting kleptocratic rule may be likened to the protection rackets of organised crime mentioned by Tilly. As a consequence, rent seeking by state officials and elite corruption (through private rather than a fully public monopolisation of violence) emerged during the PRK/SOC period and led to institutionalised predation. Furthermore, at the beginning, armed groups excluded from the spoils of peace competed for control over illicit markets, as we shall see later in our discussion of rogue security forces.

Pacification starts with the disarmament of subdued rivals, then of the population at large, and the establishment of formal systems of social control, including laws and police to resolve conflicts and stop disorder from escalating. By necessity, the pacification process essentially targets collective and public violence, such as rioting, banditry, feuding, and honour contests, not private or intimate violence, or what we call today 'domestic violence'. We have seen that during the formative years of the Protectorate only public violence (rebellions and banditry) was of real concern for the French administration: public violence threatens the state; it can lead to civil war and political overthrow, but it also threatens the state's legitimacy by tarnishing its pacifying image. In addition, public violence retards economic growth and the development of markets which otherwise also contribute to the legitimacy of the state.

Von Clausewitz (1832/1968) asserted, 'War is the continuation of politics by other means' (p. 119): in Cambodia, the political settlement that led to the creation in 1993 of the RGC represented the phase of state formation and monopolisation of violence when politics was the continuation of war by other means. The coalition government of the rivals Cambodian People's Party (CPP) and FUNCINPEC was a pacifying step, but it could not provide political stability, nor could it stop the guerrilla war still being waged by the remaining KR. The elimination contests of the 1990s (i.e. war by other means) manifested, as we have seen in the previous chapter, in high levels of political violence, which, in 1997, briefly reverted to a military clash that led to the full ascendancy of the CPP. Political stability was finally achieved after the 1998 elections, which marked the consolidation of the CPP's power over the country. The year 1998 also saw the end of all armed conflicts after the mass defection, capture, or surrender of the remaining KR, and, within a year, Cambodia experienced a spectacular decline in violence.

One of the first initiatives of the new government, and a concrete illustration of the state monopolisation of violence and its effect on public violence, was a program of weapon collection starting in Phnom Penh and then spreading to all the provinces. The aim was to control the proliferation of weapons and bring remaining war weapons held by civilians under government control. It reduced violence and disorder by removing weapons from the hands of the populace and, at the same time, minimised the risks of armed insurrections. Another initiative was the implementation of the Beautification Plan, an ambitious agenda of modernisation and infrastructure redevelopment of the capital, which, as we will see, also contributed to the further decline in violence in Phnom Penh.

Disarming and cleaning up the city

Hughes (2003b) has offered a pertinent analysis of the campaigns of securitisation and beautification that were organised by the CPP-led government after 1998. She remarked that after 'the military victory over FUNCINPEC [in July 1997], security in the city much improved, particularly in response to a security drive launched by Hun Sen in August 1997'. While this security drive may have

> also represented a consolidation of power in the hands of those who had been victorious in July [through] the disarming of opponents, ... the drive was successful in reducing the prevalence of weapons carried openly on the streets, and was accompanied by a weapons amnesty which saw the collection of millions of weapons, which were destroyed at a ceremony presided over by Hun Sen at the Olympic Stadium.

Security improved, too, because 'to an extent, the military and electoral defeats of FUNCINPEC in 1997 and 1998 also made further violence in the service of intra-elite struggle unnecessary. With FUNCINPEC in decline and the SRP largely excluded from rural areas, there was no further need on the part of the CPP to pursue intra-elite violence on this scale' (Hughes, 2003b, pp. 182–3).[10]

---

[10] Morris and Graycar (2011) have discussed the high homicide rates in Jamaica, which increased from 17 per 100,000 in 1976 to 60 per 100,000 in 2008, and the connection with partisan politics

In short, the phase of elimination contests had ended with the victory of the CPP, which now monopolised the use of force and could achieve optimum pacification.[11]

In 1998, the RGC passed a decree severely restricting weapon ownership, followed by a countrywide weapon collection and confiscation, and ceremonies in which weapons were publicly destroyed.[12] Prior to the weapon collection, some attempts were made during the 1990s at gathering the weapons of militia fighters by bringing these groups and their armoury into the Royal Cambodian Armed Forces (RCAF) and the police. Wille (2006b) estimated that up to 70 per cent of the weapons held by the factions in the coalition government fell under central government control, but very little of the Khmer Rouge stockpiles did. An effective incentive for surrendering weapons was the 'Weapons for Development' strategy, in which villages where a quota of weapons had been handed in were rewarded through the construction of community-owned infrastructure such as wells.[13] This strategy probably encouraged local CPP leaders to actively promote weapon collection. The weapon stockpile outside government control precollection was estimated at between 153,600 and 216,250 weapons. Over 130,000 military firearms as well as ammunition and explosives were collected and integrated in the government stockpiles. Subsequently, 180,000 weapons from the government stockpiles were destroyed. In 2006, the program had achieved its targets and was deemed successful, leaving an estimated number of weapons outside of government control ranging between 22,000 and 85,000 (Wille, 2006b).[14]

Ours and other independent data show that the weapon collection had a significant impact on reducing violence and crime in Cambodia. For example, while 69 per cent of assault victims admitted to hospital in 1993 had bullet wounds, by 2004 the proportion had fallen to 2.6 per cent (Wille, 2006a). In

and neighbourhood social organisation (i.e. what they call 'garrison neighbourhoods'). Comparisons can be made with Cambodia today, particularly about the role of clientelist political practices in both countries and the different impact their particular evolution had on homicide given that, contrary to Jamaica, in Cambodia political competition and multiparty clientelism quickly ended with the CPP supremacy. In Cambodia, at least since 1998, there are no garrison neighbourhoods or 'virtual stateless locations' (Cooney, 1997) to fuel homicide rates.

[11] UNTAC had launched a weapon collection initiative in 1992, but it was not successful, which suggests that the monopolisation of violence by the CPP was an important factor in the success of the latter initiative.

[12] The Protectorate implemented similar laws to control gun ownership among the population in the 1920s and 1930s (Wille, 2006b). The reasons also were similar; for example, providing weapons to village chiefs and civilians to fight banditry was curtailed because of the risk of these weapons falling into bandits' hands or being used by their owners to commit acts of banditry.

[13] For instance, the quota in one programme in Preah Vihear province was a well for 15 weapons (European Union's Assistance on Curbing Small Arms and Light Weapons in the Kingdom of Cambodia, 2003).

[14] In 2006 the UNICVS asked respondents whether anyone in their household owned a firearm. Only 1.2 per cent of 2,741 respondents said yes (and most of them were policemen).

Table 11.1 *Weapons and violent criminal events, 1992–2008*

Time period	% cases with firearm[a]			Mean N dead or injured per event
	Violent cases	Robberies	Homicides	
1992–6	79	86	83	2.3
1997–2000	56	65	60	1.3
2001–4	38	57	40	1.2
2005–8	31	59	28	1

[a] Includes automatic weapons, handguns, and explosives.
Source: Phnom Penh Post crime reports.

less than 10 per cent of the 5,000 cases of violent crime reported by the *PPP* from 1992 to 2008 were weapons absent (i.e. only threats and hitting with fists, feet, etc.). Among cases with a weapon present, 53 per cent involved firearms or explosives, and the rest, knives, machetes, axes, sickles, hoes, hammers, sticks, ropes, poisons, and acid. The choice of weapon varied with the type of violence: firearms were used more frequently during events of acquisitive violence than expressive violence but also in premeditated murders and attempted murders. Violence between family members and acquaintances often involved objects at hand (e.g. kitchen and farm implements). Handguns were used more frequently in Phnom Penh than in the provinces. The proportion of reports of violent crimes in which explosives and firearms were used steadily and significantly reduced from 1992 to 2008, and along with it the number of dead or injured during such events (Table 11.1).[15] The decline in the use of firearms in great part explains the decline in the average number of victims: events in which explosives were used on average killed or injured 8 individuals, those with automatic weapons, 2.3, and those with handguns or weapons other than firearms, 1.1. Therefore, even if handguns and weapons such as knives were still used during criminal events, they resulted in fewer casualties than those involving military weapons.

Urban beautification
Referring to the urban beautification plan, Hughes (2003a) remarked: 'The twin practices of beautification and corruption, pursued by the city authorities, serve

[15] Bear in mind that the *PPP* is biased towards reporting serious violent offences, which tend to be lethal or incur serious injuries. It is only in the early 2000s that the *PPP* started to report more rapes in which firearms were less commonly used than in other serious violent offences. By the late 2000s the *PPP* had begun to report more minor violent incidents. The increase in reports of minor violence, however, is not sufficient to account for the substantial reduction in the use of firearms.

a complementary purpose: the strengthening of the state, and the disruption of efforts by the poor to gain official recognition as citizens of the city' (p. 13). If this plan further entrenched the system of patronage by providing opportunities to the commercial elites through access to land in the heart of Phnom Penh, it also, as we show below, had some impact on the reduction of ordinary street violence and crime, albeit incurring another form of violence associated with the uncompensated and forced evictions of the urban poor, and some displacement of crime and violence at the periphery, particularly towards the surrounding province of Kandal. An analysis of crime trends based on MoI records for Phnom Penh and Kandal showed that, while crime was declining in Phnom Penh from the mid 2000s, it increased in Kandal during the same period, forming an inverted mirror image of the Phnom Penh trends (the UNICVS showed similar results between 2001 and 2006). This suggests that the forced removal of the poorest towards the periphery during the campaign of beautification in Phnom Penh produced also some crime displacement.

Related to the securitisation goals, the campaigns of urban beautification, particularly in Phnom Penh, not only improved the city's image by removing the slums but also gave developers the chance to realise high profits and state officials to request lavish bribes. It was also an opportunity to engage in the 'social cleansing' of the 'dangerous, unsightly, and (potentially) criminal class': the urban poor. As Hughes (2003b) further argued, this 'reorganization of political space...include[d] both the exiling of unruly elements of the population from the city altogether, and the replacement of unregulated areas of squatter development with monuments to CPP power' (p. 208). Hughes reported that in August 2001 'Chea Sophara [then CPP municipal governor] stated that his aim was to manage urbanization so as "to keep a high standard of living...by not encouraging the poor to live in the city"'. Chea Sophara had claimed that the relocation of squatters 'would contribute to raising living standards by improving the city environment as an aid to attracting tourists and foreign investors and to promoting public health. It would also contribute to a reduction in crime.' Such claims are difficult to assess, yet these measures probably did contribute to the achievements sought by Chea Sophara, including crime reduction. These mechanisms of urban gentrification form part of the process of modernisation and are not unique to Phnom Penh or other cities in Cambodia. They have been used in many other cities and to a certain extent produce the aforementioned results. Our results show a steeper decline in crime in Phnom Penh than in the provinces, and this supports the thesis that modernisation and urban redevelopment transformed urban crime patterns in Cambodia through processes similar to those observed by the social disorganisation criminologists of the Chicago School (e.g. Shaw & McKay, 1942) and related theories of the geography of crime (e.g. Wilson & Kelling, 1982).

The development of modern policing

The ability of the state to monopolise violence within the territory under its control entails the creation and development of a specialised security apparatus with the exclusive power to use force to maintain public law and order, which includes the prevention and control of crime and violent conflicts between citizens. During state formation, the military, tasked therefore with the control of both external and internal threats, generally exercises this exclusive power. As the state develops, a specialised service or police force is created that focuses on internal civil disorder and crime prevention. It is initially modelled on military organisations, and then it evolves its own structure and codes of conduct. We have seen such developments in Cambodia during the protectorate and the PRK/SOC regime. The effectiveness of legal and policing institutions in maintaining stability and order is therefore an essential test of the state's ability to monopolise violence and establish legitimate governance. Consequently, the extent that police serve a general order and provide civil protection is a measure of state strength, and the level of violence, particularly public violence (i.e. what the police failed to control), may provide a measure of that strength. High levels of violence, particularly originating from private and vigilante 'justice', are indicative of state weakness (Broadhurst, 2002; Broadhurst, 2006; Júnior & Muniz, 2006). Referring to the late 1990s in Cambodia, Hughes (2003b), for example, remarked, 'Revenge attacks continue to be a common means of dealing with private conflicts in the absence of an effective state apparatus maintaining public law and order' (p. 57). But a high level of extrajudicial killing or wounding of *flagrante delicto* or alleged offenders by the security forces is also a sign of state weakness, not of state strength, not only because it shows that these forces are unable to keep the peace and maintain law and order (i.e. without adding to the disorder they are tasked to control) but also because in these cases they supplant lawful authorities, for example, prosecutors, judges, and penal officers. These two factors militate against state legitimacy and indeed create a climate of immunity from the legal process. The extent of criminal acts by 'rogue' security forces is another sign of state weakness that undermines the state's legitimacy.

We now examine the trends between 1993 and 2012 of three markers of the weakness or strength of the state in its monopolisation of violence. We start with what we call 'achieved justice', that is, the private and mob killing or maiming of offenders caught in criminal acts or simply suspected of such acts. We follow with cases of extrajudicial justice, that is, 'achieved justice' but perpetrated by the security forces, and we finish with events involving rogue security forces (i.e. police, gendarme militaire, militia, and the RCAF). Our results suggest that although these three types of behaviour still occur they have become significantly less frequent. The police seem to have become better at maintaining order without having recourse to lethal force, and this fledging professionalism is to some extent reflected in increased confidence in the police, as surveys of the population revealed.

'Achieved justice': mob killings and self-defence

Between 1992 and 2008, the *Phnom Penh Post* (*PPP*) reported 232 incidents of extrajudicial killings of offenders, such as this case on 18 January 2002:

> A mob of 300 beat to death three robbery and rape suspects after taking them from a Kampong Speu police station on January 15. The mob arrived in a convoy of ten trucks after hearing the suspects were to be transferred. Deputy police inspector Chea Vuth apologized for the killings. No arrests have been made.

Of these 'achieved justice' events, 70 per cent were mob killing or wounding of alleged offenders by villagers or bystanders, and the rest, acts of victim self-defence during the crime. The great majority of these events occurred during the course of acquisitive crimes. The reported numbers of casualties from mob justice and self-defence were the highest between 1997 and 2000 (an average of 24 per year) but then declined to an average of 15 episodes in 2005, then only 7 episodes, none of them fatal, in 2008. In the early period (pre-2000), the largest share of 'achieved justice' events occurred in Phnom Penh, but in the recent period (from 2004), most occurred in the provinces. The absolute number of events and casualties was also higher in the provinces, which may suggest that rural residents are more inclined to seek 'personal justice' than city dwellers or they often do not have access to the same level of policing. The Ministry of Interior and local authorities have taken measures to curb the trend. For example, in February 2000, Phnom Penh Governor Chea Sophara instructed police to control mob violence and make sure offenders were dealt with through legal means. Whereas there were earlier reports of instances when the police delivered the offenders to mobs of angry villagers or the latter snatched offenders from the police to beat and kill them, in the early 2000s the police started intervening to protect suspects (United Nations Special Representative of the Secretary General for Human Rights in Cambodia, 2002). The overall decline in 'achieved justice' since 2000 also reflects the significant fall in property crime, which would have lessened the drive for mob justice and self-defence; in addition, improvement in policing and the climate of increasing security may have helped pacify violent impulses, as we will discuss later.

Extrajudicial killing of offenders by security forces

Police and other members of security forces have also been involved in the extrajudicial killing or wounding of alleged offenders. Between 1992 and 2008, the *PPP* reported 241 events in which 294 alleged offenders were killed, and a further 88 were wounded by security forces. Most occurred during robberies, but nearly one third during nonviolent criminal events. Police were involved in 86 per cent of events; the rest involved private security contractors (6 per cent), the military (5 per cent), rural militia (2 per cent), and prison officers (1 per cent). The proportion of individuals killed in these events was higher in Phnom Penh than in the provinces, because both violent property crime and police capabilities were greater in Phnom Penh than in the provinces. Patchy data from the MoI showed the highest number ($N = 214$) of recorded extrajudicial killings occurred in 1993 at the time of the United Nations Transitional Authority in Cambodia (UNTAC) mission and the first election. A relatively high number ($N = 108$) was again recorded in 1996. Data for 1997 and 1998 are missing; however, the *PPP* reported the largest numbers of such killings in 1997 ($N = 30$) and 1998 ($N = 48$). In addition, the nongovernmental organisation (NGO) Danish Centre for Human Rights (2001) reported,

Police, military, gendarmerie, militia members, or local officials allegedly killed at least 263 people during a twenty-two-month period from January 1997 through October 1998. While many of these murders appeared to have been deliberate executions, few of the perpetrators had been brought to justice by the end of 1999. In addition, an estimated 130 crimes with political connotations, including assassinations and disappearances, were documented by the Cambodia Office of the High Commissioner for Human Rights (COHCHR) between August 1997 and October 1998. (p. 31)

Again, this high number of extrajudicial killings occurred in the pre- and post-election period. Both MoI and *PPP* subsequently showed a steep decline in the number of extrajudicial fatalities, particularly from 2007 to 2012, when an average of three to four episodes per year were recorded. The conjunction of declining crime trends and improvement in the professionalism of the police forces is likely to have played a role in this pattern. Another trend suggesting improvement in policing is the decline in the number of crimes perpetrated by police and military.

Rogue security forces

The transformation of the governance of state security from a military to civil form was one of the key goals of the first national development plan. Under the 1993 UNTAC demobilisation plan, large numbers of former soldiers were placed in policing roles on below-subsistence wages. Consequently, the management and discipline of such a large body of armed and ill-trained 'police' were a major problem and source of impunity. The planned progressive reductions in the number of underemployed, untrained police and military personnel required that by 2001 their numbers reduce from 137,000 to 67,000. In 2001 this had not occurred; there was doubt about the effectiveness of the demobilisation plan, and donors such as the World Bank identified misuse of funds

(Adams, 2001). Reductions in the size of the security forces had been hampered by factional CPP-FUNCINPEC differences in the key Ministries of Interior and Defence until 2001–3, when CPP domination was completed. The Cambodia Criminal Justice Assistance Project (CCJAP) estimated the Cambodian National Police had only reduced from 65,000 in 1996 to 64,000 in 2001 (AusAID, 2001). By 2000, the national plan to reduce the 1996 staffing levels by 24,000 in 5 years had achieved only half the original target with a reduction of 11,630. In 2001, the Judicial Police alone had between 8,000 and 9,000 officers, of whom only 800 were female. A report by the National Police Commissariat (January 2009) indicated that as of December 2008 the total number of national law enforcement officers was 55,277 (2,325 females), of which 41,015 (1,428 females) were based in 24 municipal/provincial police commissariats (National Police Commissariat, 2009). If the reduction of about 10,000–15,000 police officers between 1996 and 2008 did not reach the initial target, it was still significant enough to remove from the force many of its most dangerous and undisciplined elements.

From 1992 to 2008, the *PPP* reported 372 events in which 471 police officers and 737 RCAF members had been involved in criminal behaviour. The peak for criminal activity by security forces was 1994, when the *PPP* reported 53 cases involving a total of 458 security personnel, reflecting the organised and banditry-like nature of these offences. This coincided with the departure of the UNTAC forces, leaving a security vacuum and a range of imported goods, such as UN vehicles, that rogue security forces targeted. The *PPP* reports suggest that the situation gradually improved, and by the early 2000s the number of crimes involving security personnel had significantly reduced.[16] Until 1996, groups of rogue police officers or RCAF were mostly involved in acquisitive crime, but disputes between security forces (e.g. police against military), which may have been associated with competing political allegiance (e.g. CPP versus FUNCINPEC), also occurred and were often lethal. Increasingly, the types of crime by security forces still reported by the *PPP* in the mid 2000s were mostly expressive crimes such as rapes, domestic violence, and other assaults committed by individual police officers or soldiers, often drunk and carrying firearms which frequently resulted in fatal incidents.[17]

---

[16] There was a slight increase in 2008 compared to the period 2002–7, but it is too early to define this as a trend.

[17] We note that as well as the criminal activities of elements of the security forces, 146 (91 police, 15 security guards, and 40 military) were killed or injured in the course of their operational duties, often when confronting robbery and in the aid of victims. Another 388 security personnel (203 police, 45 security guards, and 140 military) were either victims of accidents/misadventures, robberies, and revenge attacks or, sometimes, of their own involvement in crime. However, over half of the fatalities were recorded between 1992 and 1998. Thereafter, their numbers progressively diminished, reflecting not only the general decline in crime but also improved screening and training of security personnel.

The repeated UNICVS sweeps in 2001 and 2006–7 showed that victimisation through corrupt behaviour by police (i.e. demanding bribes) had declined. The estimated rates of rent seeking by any official, including police, reported by survey respondents had reduced from 27.8 per cent to 18.2 per cent in Phnom Penh, and from 15.6 per cent to 12.9 per cent in Kampong Cham. In the third province, Kandal, the rates (18.3 per cent) had not changed. Apart from Kandal, the actual experience of bribe seeking by police had also decreased: in Phnom Penh, the proportion of respondents who were victims of police corruption nearly halved between 2000 and 2005 (10.1 per cent and 5.7 per cent, respectively); in Kampong Cham the proportion reduced from 4.5 per cent in 2000 to 2.5 per cent in 2006. In Kandal, however, the experience of corruption by police officers increased slightly from 3.5 per cent in 2000 to 4.4 per cent in 2005. In the three provinces the bribe seekers most frequently cited by victims of corruption both in the first and second sweeps were not police but elected commune officials followed by teachers and health workers (Broadhurst & Bouhours, 2009). The proportion of respondents who believed that police officers were likely to be corrupt had also significantly reduced in Phnom Penh, from 28.9 per cent of respondents in 2001 to 14 per cent in 2006. However, in Kandal and Kampong Cham, respondents' negative perceptions about the conduct of police officers had increased from 16.7 per cent in 2001 to 19.8 per cent in 2006 in Kandal and from 31 per cent to 60.6 per cent in Kampong Cham. Such perceptions, particularly in Kampong Cham where the corrupt conduct of police officers had reduced, may indicate that processes of sensitisation regarding abuses of power (raised expectations) have made villagers more demanding of their institutions. As part of its regular monitoring of prison conditions in Cambodia, the Cambodian League for the Promotion and Defense of Human Rights (LICADHO, 2009) conducted interviews with prisoners in 18 prisons and found that the number of inmates reporting being tortured while in police custody fell from 450 in 1999 to 78 in 2008. More importantly, in 1999, 13.7 per cent of surveyed respondents reported torture, with numbers steadily falling to 2.1 per cent in 2006, 1.3 per cent in 2007, and 0.7 per cent in 2008.

Extrajudicial killings by police forces and vigilante groups were also common and strongly encouraged by the French administration in Cambodia from the end of the nineteenth century to the mid 1920s, particularly in areas where banditry was widespread. However, as early as World War I firearm owners needed a licence, and in the 1930s further policies restricting gun ownership showed that the administration not only had started to worry about the risk of vigilantism getting out of control and aiding banditry rather than repressing it but also felt confident that the monopolisation of force by its police (the *Garde Civile Indigène*) was now sufficient to maintain law and order. From 1993 to the early 2000s, extrajudicial killings by security forces and vigilante groups were also frequent and sometimes encouraged by senior officers, but these events

Table 11.2 *Reporting victimisation to police: Cambodia UNICVS, 2001 and 2006–7*

	2001[a]		2006–7[b]		Average UNICVS[c]
	N events	% reported	N events	% reported	
Burglary and attempted burglary	1,109	19.4	821	13.4	56[d]
Motorcycle theft	365	63.3	249	57.4	78
Personal theft	544	9.0	370	8.9	46
Robbery	120	53.3	90	52.2	46
Assault and threats	285	30.2	253	26.9	33
Corruption	518	1.4	416	2.9	–

[a] We combine results for Phnom Penh, Kandal, and Kampong Cham in 2001 ($N = 2,383$).
[b] We combine results for Phnom Penh and Kandal in 2006 and Kampong Cham in 2007 ($N = 2,741$).
[c] Includes 31 countries from the developed and developing worlds (van Dijk *et al.*, 2007, table 11).
[d] Figure for burglary and attempted burglary estimated.
Source: UNICVS.

declined from the mid 2000s onwards. In both periods, the 1920s to the 1930s and the mid 2000s, the change of policy marked a moment when the state realised its monopoly over violence, albeit frequently stretched in remote areas. How all this has influenced trends in the attitude of the population towards the police and feelings of security or insecurity is not straightforward.

Confidence in the police and feelings of safety

Reporting criminal victimisation to the police is one way of gauging the degree of confidence the population holds for its police forces (and its judicial institutions). The repeated sweeps of the UNICVS in Cambodia allow us to observe these trends in crime reporting. Table 11.2 shows relatively low rates of reporting crime to the police and little difference between 2000 and 2005–6. Motorcycle theft was the crime most likely to be reported by around 60 per cent of victims, followed by robbery, reported by just over half the victims. Reporting rates were much lower for personal theft and the lowest for corruption. Compared with global results among the 31 countries surveyed by the UNICVS in 2005 (Table 11.2, far right column), reporting rates in Cambodia were lower than the global average for property crimes but similar for violent crimes (robbery and assault).

The Cambodian Socio-Economic Survey (CSES, 2009) also indicated that only a fraction of victims of violence that resulted in injuries reported the incident to the authorities (police or commune officials). In 2004, 16.6 per cent of victims reported to some authority, and although the proportion increased in

2009 (24.2 per cent), it was still only one quarter of the victims. Of those who reported the crime in both sweeps, most did not report to the police (about one third) but to the village leader (two thirds). The relatively low level of reporting discussed above would suggest low confidence in the police. However, this may relate to the crime-solving ability of the police, not their ability to protect the population against crime or their response to accidents and emergencies. On the one hand, the UNICVS had shown that respondents were slightly less positive in 2006–7 than in 2001 regarding the police 'doing a good job at controlling crime' (from an average of 66 per cent in 2001 to 60 per cent in 2006–7). On the other hand, the CSES suggested that confidence in police appeared to have increased between 2004 and 2009 in regard to whether respondents 'trust[ed] the local police for protection' (50.3 per cent of heads of households trusted police in 2004, increasing to 60.9 per cent in 2009).[18]

Finally, and probably reflecting both the decline in victimisation and some improvement in the professionalism of the police, the CSES showed that feelings of safety increased between 2004 and 2009. Respondents were asked whether the whole household felt safe from crime and violence in the neighbourhood: in 2004, 57 per cent of respondents said they did, and this increased to 67 per cent in 2009. Feelings of safety had improved in both urban and rural areas but remained slightly higher in urban (70.6 per cent) than in rural areas (66.4 per cent). This regional difference is consistent with the findings that violence remained relatively more prevalent in rural areas. An increase in 'feeling safe' was also noted in the two sweeps of the UNICVS in 2001 and 2006–7 in Phnom Penh, Kandal, and Kampong Cham.

As the state develops its policing agencies and increases its control and monopoly over violence, and legal and judicial systems gain legitimacy with the population, personal and collective revenge, feuds, and vendettas tend to disappear. Durkheim and more recently Cooney have hypothesised that over time violence increasingly becomes a one-on-one rather than a collective affair. At the same time, proportionally the trend is towards private rather than public violence, that is, violence between intimates rather than rivals or strangers (Cooney, 2003). We analyse this trend below and examine whether our data fit with Cooney's hypotheses.

Individualisation and privatisation of crime

The previous chapters have documented how violence and crime perpetrated by large groups of bandits have been recurring phenomena in Cambodia. A major hypothesis of modernisation theories is that the collective offending associated

---

[18] The similarities between the CSES and UNICVS rates of trust in police were striking for urban areas (CSES urban 2004 = 55 per cent trust in police, and UNICVS Phnom Penh 2006 = 56 per cent).

with banditry but also feuding and political violence has declined over time in parallel with the ascendancy of modern states. From the *PPP* crime reports, we were able to estimate the number of offenders involved in crime events between 1992 and 2008, and our results suggest that the traditional collective pattern of offending no longer holds in contemporary Cambodia.

Until 1996, while remnants of KR groups were still active and increasingly turning to banditry, the average number of offenders involved in crime events was high and reflected these activities. For the entire period 1992 to 2008, nonlethal acquisitive violence tended to be collective with a stable number of offenders per event (mean of 3.3); however, during the 4 years prior to 1996, other types of violence were also collective events, particularly those relating to KR activity, which, on average, involved between 30 and 35 offenders per event. Violence unrelated to KR activity involved fewer individuals but was still much more collective than it would become post-1996: events of lethal *expressive* violence counted an average of 3.9 offenders, lethal *acquisitive* violence involved 3.3 offenders per event, and nonlethal *expressive* violence, an average of 3 individuals per event.

Post-1996, KR attacks had become less common and were seldom reported in the *PPP*; the number of offenders engaged in crime events dropped dramatically. Between 1996 and 2008, lethal and nonlethal expressive violence involved around two perpetrators on average per event, while lethal acquisitive violence became more like its nonlethal form and involved 3.5 offenders on average per event.[19] As can be expected, when KR attacks were still occurring, the level of collective violence was significantly higher in rural areas where these attacks took place. During the period 1992 to 1996, *expressive* violence in rural areas involved an average of 18.5 offenders compared to only 3.3 in Phnom Penh, and *acquisitive* violence in rural areas nearly 8 offenders per event compared to 3.2 in Phnom Penh. After 1996, the reduction in the number of perpetrators involved in these events was not uniform, and to understand these patterns, we now focus on the period from 1996 to 2008. Figure 11.3 plots the average number of offenders per event in Phnom Penh and the provinces by type of violence.

Overall, greater numbers of offenders were involved in each event of *expressive* violence in Phnom Penh than in rural areas. However, both patterns, but particularly rural, follow a U-curve shape. From the mid 2000s, lethal *expressive* violence became more collective, and this is probably associated with the increasing number of violent incidents involving youth gangs reported by

---

[19] This pattern of higher numbers of offenders in acquisitive violence is similar to the 1936–40 and 1947–55 periods, when more offenders were involved in acquisitive compared to expressive homicides and suggests the more collective, banditry-like characteristic of acquisitive violence. This pattern also supports Cooney's (2003) argument about the universality of co-offending in acquisitive violence compared to expressive violence.

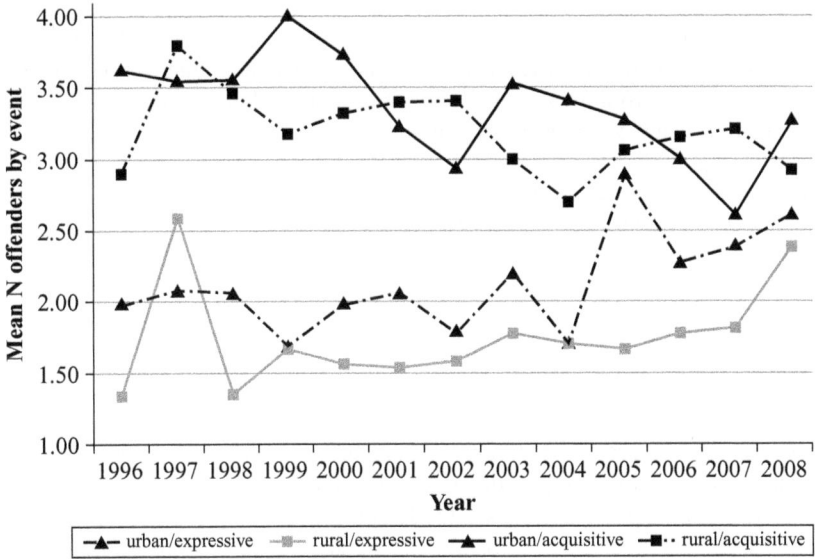

Figure 11.3 Average number of offenders by type of violence, urban and rural, 1996–2008
Source: *Phnom Penh Post* crime reports.

the *PPP* and other sources. For *acquisitive* violence, the comparison pattern between Phnom Penh and the provinces is not as clear-cut; greater numbers of offenders in rural areas are observed during some years and lower numbers during other years. The trend towards a return to more collective offending from the mid 2000s is also far less marked for acquisitive violence than for expressive violence. This finding points to the association of the relative recollectivisation of expressive violence with the modern rise of youth gangs and the likelihood of honour contests between young males, which result in homicide and assault rather than in robbery or theft (Broadhurst & Keo, 2011). In short, this modest recollectivisation of expressive violence is not the same as in the 1990s when postconflict disorder and political elimination contests were major factors. In Chapter 10, we noted that the overall reduction in collective offending has happened in parallel with a sharp reduction in multiple victimisations, which also supports a general trend towards the modernisation of criminality marked by the individualisation and the privatisation of violence.

The privatisation of violence: a test of Cooney's hypotheses
Considering long-term trends in violence, Cooney (2003) argued, 'Over the past several centuries, non-political violence (i.e. violence within societies

between nonstate actors) has become less public, more private' (p. 1378). This privatisation of violence combined two related dimensions: violence increasingly occurred between individuals rather than groups (individualisation), and it increasingly occurred between intimates (i.e. spouses, family members) rather than nonintimates. With regard to individualisation, Cooney (2003) suggested:

Violence varies in the degree to which it is individualized. The most individualized violence is found in conflicts between two people; the least individualized – the most collective – is found in conflicts between large organized groups. Between these extremes lies violence involving attacks by groups on individuals or between unorganised collections of people (e.g. brawls). Over the centuries, as premodern societies have given way to modern societies, collective conflicts have declined substantially in frequency and violence has individualized. (p. 1382)

Cooney (2003) also proposed: 'The privatization of violence is a long-term trend that is least pronounced in premodern societies and most pronounced in modern societies. Intermediate degrees of privatisation are found in what might be called "modernizing societies"' (p. 1381). Modernising societies are those 'having comparatively strong social ties and small legal systems serving culturally diverse and highly unequal populations'. In Durkheim's terms, these societies are moving from mechanical to organic ways of being and relating, a transition that also produces a temporary period of developmental anomie and an increase in crime. Finally, the extent of the privatisation of violence is not uniform but may vary across time and space, remaining 'more collective where modernity was less advanced' (p. 1385) with 'pockets of residual public violence . . . still . . . found within modern state societies' (p. 1377). A Durkheimian analysis of 'these pockets of residual public violence' would include remnants of mechanical forms of solidarity and its collectivist informal social control to which some of the populace remain tied. It would also include crimes associated with developmental anomie mentioned above. Overall, present-day Cambodia fits Cooney's definition of a modernising society. A manifestation of the unevenness of the privatisation of violence is that conflict-related or, as Cooney labels it, 'moralistic violence' should be a more collective behaviour in rural than in urban areas. Cooney also proposed that Black's (1976) theory about the extent of self-help in conflict resolution provided an alternative theory, which helped understand the privatisation of violence in terms of the weakening of social ties (Durkheim) and the strengthening of the state (Elias).

Cooney's argument referred only to violence by and against nonstate actors and therefore excluded political, war, and revolutionary violence. It also focused on 'conflict-related or moralistic' violence, that is, 'force used in the course of a conflict . . . such as barroom brawls, domestic homicides, schoolyard fights, honour killings, and gang pay-backs' (Cooney, 2003, p. 1380), therefore excluding acquisitive violence and violence not related to a dispute but to pathologies, such as some rapes or serial killings. To test whether Cooney's theory of privatisation of violence can be applied to Cambodia, we have matched our data on crime and violence in Cambodia since the mid twentieth century to Cooney's empirical evidence. Following Cooney's operationalisation of conflict-related violence, we have excluded robbery, rape, infanticide, involuntary manslaughters (e.g. traffic-related), Khmer Rouge attacks, and political murders. Since the bulk of Cooney's historical data consisted of homicide, we have also excluded nonlethal violence. We test the concept of individualisation of violence by examining the proportion of lone offenders involved in homicides at various periods of time and by examining the proportion of all homicides that occurred between intimates, that is, those we classified as intrafamilial.[20] Table 11.3A presents our findings for the periods 1936–40, 1947–55, and 1992–2008 in relation to the proportion of homicides involving lone offenders.

Apart from Phnom Penh between 1947 and 1955, the results fit within Cooney's category of 'modernising societies'. During the same period, conflict-related violence was more collective in rural areas than in Phnom Penh, following Cooney's suggestion that 'moralistic violence' should be more collective in rural than in urban areas. It might be that during this period Phnom Penh had reached a level of modernisation characterised by a weakening of social ties and the strengthening of the state, hence the apparent privatisation of violence. However, because this period was marked by the anticolonial armed struggle in the provinces, most wanted offenders, including those involved in conflict-related/moralistic violence, were from the provinces. Only a decade earlier, between 1936 and 1940, conflict-related violence was significantly more collective in Phnom Penh. Yet, if we consider the proportion of lone offenders in conflict-related violence in Cambodia as a whole, the period 1936–40 stands out as the least collective and most individualised of the three periods (71 per cent of lone offenders compared to 62 per cent in the two subsequent time periods). Compared to the insurrectional period of 1947–55 and the state reorganisation period of 1992–2008, the period between 1936 and 1940 was probably a time when the state was relatively strong since it was preceded by two decades of peaceful state modernisation, particularly of the justice system. In fact, in

---

[20] Cooney (2003) specified that 'the movement from premodern to modern societies has brought with it an increase in the proportion of violent conflict between intimates. This is not to imply that there is no intimate violence in premodern societies or that the prevalence of intimate violence has increased. In some societies, the beating of spouses and children, for example, is common. But intimate violence tends to be correlated with non-intimate violence so that high rates do not necessarily mean high proportions' (p. 1386). Greenberg (2003) noted certain limitations in the historical data relied upon by Cooney, namely, in the domestic setting where step relations and servants would be missing.

Table 11.3 *Test of Cooney's privatisation of conflict-related violence*

A: Percentage of lone offenders in conflict-related homicide events: 1936–40, 1947–55, 1992–2008

Cambodia's data	Phnom Penh	Rural areas	Cambodia	Cooney's evidence: % lone offenders
1936–40 BPC	52	74	71	*Modernising societies* • England, thirteenth century: 40% of accused homicide offenders
1947–55 BPC	78	62	62	• England, fourteenth century: 65% of accused homicide offenders
1992–2008 PPP	56	64	62	• Louisiana, 1866–84: 60% rural; 80% urban
				Modern societies • Philadelphia, 1948–52: 85% of solved homicides • Canada, 1961–90: 87% murders • USA, 1980–4: 89% homicides • Australia, 1989–99: 81% homicides

B: Percentage of intimate victims of conflict-related homicide: 1992–2008

Cambodia's data[a]	Phnom Penh	Rural areas	Cambodia	Cooney's evidence: % intimate homicide victims
				Premodern societies • Premodern Bokondini Dani of New Guinea: 10% of deaths involve killers and victims of same parish • Premodern Ju/'hoansi of Kalahari Desert: 20-year period, 9%
				Modernising societies • England, thirteenth century: 6.5% • Northampton, fourteenth century: 8% • Kent County, 1560–9: 9% (adult) • Amsterdam, 1651–1700: 11% (trials) • Kent County, 1770–90: 11% (adult) • Sri Lanka, 1796–1948: 20%
1992–2008 PPP	37	38	38	*Modern societies* • Amsterdam, 1751–1810: 47% (trials) • Iceland, 1900–79: 34% • Kent County, 1950–9: 33% (adult) • Canada, 1961–90: 44% (murder) • USA, 1976–99: 19% • Japan, 1984–95: 65% • Australia, 1989–99: 35%

[a] Data exclude cases where relationship is unknown and cases of political violence.

Cambodia as a whole, the periods 1947–55 and 1992–2008 are rather similar with their high levels of conflict-related/moralistic collective violence.

Results for the period 1992–2008 do not show a more collective pattern of conflict-related violence in rural areas compared to Phnom Penh but the opposite, which may be associated with the greater level of social control exercised by the CPP in the villages. However, they do suggest that if violence in general has significantly reduced, particularly predatory violence in Phnom Penh, the violence that remains is still somewhat collective, when not only predatory violence is concerned but also expressive conflict-related violence, but the modern rise of youth gangs needs also to be accounted for. Cooney drew from Black's perspective on partisanship, and implicitly from Durkheim, to explain the individualisation of violence: 'Much partisanship withered away with the extended family, the tightly-knit community, the patron-client relationship, and more generally with intimacy beyond the household. The web of support has loosened, and self-reliance has proliferated. People are ever more rarely drawn wholeheartedly into the conflicts of their associates. Conflict has individualized' (Black, 1993, cited in Cooney, 2003, p. 1394). In Cambodia, where the extended family remains strong and clientelism is extensive through all spheres of society, it is not surprising that in terms of individualisation of violence, our analysis shows that Cambodia is still at a modernising rather than a modern stage.

Table 11.3B examines where Cambodia fits in Cooney's hypothesis in terms of the intimacy of conflict-related violence between 1992 and 2008. If, for the same period, the results of the analysis of the individualisation of violence placed Cambodia in the 'modernising societies' category, because such violence has remained relatively collective, the analysis of the second dimension of the privatisation of violence – intimacy – places Cambodia at the cusp of the modernising and modern categories, and, at least since 2004, in the modern category. Cooney (2003) remarked:

Homicide between intimate is less variable than homicide between nonintimate. Perhaps the reason is that intimacy is itself less variable than the other factors known to be associated with elevated rates of homicides. Income inequality, unemployment, cultural heterogeneity, and the scale of illegal markets, and so forth [e.g. postconflict effects] all vary considerably over time and from place to place. Intimacy is more constant. The size of intimate groups may fluctuate but the fact of intimate association does not... Hence, the amount of violence fluctuates less among intimates than among nonintimates... What appears to have happened over the centuries... is that although the rate of intimate homicide declined slowly, the rate of nonintimate homicide declined steadily. (pp. 1390–1)

From our data we can conclude that in Cambodia from 1992 to 2008 the proportion of reported lethal family violence had increased, and therefore, the proportion of lethal public violence, such as brawls, had decreased. We cannot ascertain whether rates of intimate homicide have declined more slowly than the rates of nonintimate homicide. We are even less able to ascertain what happened in Cambodia over the centuries regarding either the rates or proportions of intimate and nonintimate conflict-related homicide. Cooney (2003), drawing from Black, suggested that 'as social ties weaken over the centuries, informal social control [was] gradually replaced by law, the presence of which slowly undermine[d] the culture of honour and reduce[d] honour conflicts, with the result that violence, when it occurs, acquires an increasingly intimate character' (p. 1395). In other words, the development of law has reduced violence between unrelated men vying in disputes occurring outside of the family. The violence that remains springs mostly from conflicts between intimates.

Summary

Our results on crime and violence in Cambodia in the contemporary period support the theoretical associations between the development and expansion of the state and a reduction in violence. By the end of 1998, the CPP had in great part succeeded in eliminating political rivals and pacifying the kingdom: with Pol Pot's death, the last of the KR had defected or given up fighting, and after the 1998 elections, the opposition had been marginalised. From 1998 to 2003–4, the CPP consolidated and completed the pacifying process. The government could then focus on disarming the population, and evidence suggests that the firearms collection program contributed to the significant reduction in the prevalence of lethal violence in Cambodia between 1993 and 2008 as well as the reduction in the number of victims in such events. Our results show that both co-offending and multiple victimisation have declined significantly since the 1990s in contemporary Cambodia, which supports the predictions of modernisation and civilising process theories regarding the monopolisation of public violence by the state and the privatisation and individualisation of violence. Cooney (2003) has argued that this phenomenon reflects the ascendancy of law as the modern way to solve conflict and replace the traditional collective forms of feuding. The reduction in extrajudicial killings by security personnel and private and mob justice suggests an association with the greater mobilisation of the law and an improvement in the state's policing capacity. Yet, while reductions in police violence and police corruption are clearly observed, Cambodians seemed less positive and showed less confidence in police in 2006–7 than in 2001, when both crime and socioeconomic conditions were worse. Changing attitudes towards crime and higher expectations about what the state should deliver in response to new challenges to social control may have raised the standards expected of police and accordingly of public confidence in the police, that is, raised the levels of sensitisation to abuse of power and violence in the population. Despite the absence of an established rule of law culture, underresourcing, and rampant corruption, Cambodia is not lawless and its policing institutions have become more capable and are gaining legitimacy.

Elias built his thesis of the civilising process around three interacting processes: the first, which we have discussed above, is the state monopolisation of violence and its apparatus of formal social control, which suppresses public violence. The second, discussed below, is the growth of interdependencies brought about by market exchange and economic development. The pursuit of this 'gentle commerce' (cf. Pinker, 2011), characterised by a multiplicity of interactions and the need to exchange and cooperate with others, combined with the monopolisation of violence requires and leads to growing peace, stability, and predictability. In time, interdependency fosters the growth of civil society, encourages democratisation, and inspires a movement away from the state as a privately to a publicly controlled monopoly over the use of force and other matters of public interest. This second process is also a factor in decreasing public violence because trade and other social interactions flourish in and require secure and predictable environments. While these two processes refer to sociogenetic forces, the third process, sensitisation to violence, is a psychogenetic force that we address in the final section of this chapter.

The chains of interdependency

During the civilising process, in parallel to the state's concentration of power and monopolisation of violence, social processes diversify and individuals start to specialise in specific areas of production or trade and increasingly rely on each other for producing and exchanging resources, goods, and services. Trade and commerce grow, increasing wealth and multiplying interactions between individuals and groups, forming what Elias called 'chains of interdependency'. Through positive feedbacks, this development is associated with population growth, urban expansion, higher skills and educational needs, and a general improvement in wellbeing as the state now focuses on its role in service provision and resource allocation for the population. Chains of interdependency are largely but not only economic; they also involve patterns of association, communication, and cooperation that go beyond economic growth. As the chains of interdependency grow longer and denser, violence becomes increasingly problematic because it threatens this network of interactions and, therefore, the livelihood and income of individuals and states. Pinker (2011, pp. 77–8) has argued that the interdependence that springs from this 'gentle commerce' and centralisation of state are mutually reinforcing. Commerce is one of the important 'disciplinary forces holding down individual impulses', or in Durkhemian terms 'freeing the individual from closely knit bondages that kept him tied into the collectivity', and leads to a reduction in violence (Thome, 2001, p. 75). As socioeconomic conditions improve, individuals, groups, social classes, organisations, and the state increasingly rely on each other and have a vested interest in keeping the peace and protecting their relationships through nonviolent means of conflict management.

From the autarchy of the DK period, contemporary Cambodia has gone a long way towards economic and social integration in Asia and the world. The pacification of the 1990s has brought the stability and security necessary to boost economic and social development. As we noted in Chapter 9, a considerable amount of social and economic restructuring by the SOC, for instance, the dismantlement of collective agriculture and the opening of the country to a market economy, had already occurred prior to UNTAC. After the Paris Peace Accords, and strengthening the chains of interdependency, foreign aid, soon followed by foreign direct investment (FDI), flowed into Cambodia. The net annual amount of foreign aid has consistently increased since 1991, but relative to GDP it peaked in 1995 (over 15 per cent of GDP), and then, as GDP grew, foreign aid slowly declined to around 6 per cent of GDP in 2011 (Table 11.4). FDIs have fluctuated partly in relation to the political situation but have been highest since the early 2000s (USD 600–800 million) (Hill & Menon, 2013; International Monetary Fund, 2013). The RGC began with a solid macroeconomic performance, and GDP growth was estimated at about 7 per cent in 1995, largely due to gains in rice production. Imports increased as a result of the availability of external financing, as did exports of timber. Cambodia's economy slowed dramatically in 1997–8 due to the compounded impact of the political crisis in Cambodia and the Asian fiscal crisis. Illustrating the importance of maintaining peace and stability to protect the chains of interdependency, periods of intense political violence, instability, and widespread corruption brought investment and tourism down. In 1998, the second, after 1993, peak in violence in contemporary times, the harvest was hit by drought, inflation spiked at 14 per cent per annum, and the state treasury was depleted, which contributed to the increase in acquisitive crime. Donor aid fell, and the IMF pressured for further reforms of government finances.

In 1999, the first full year of peace for over 30 years, economic reforms helped the resumption of growth. Once pacification and stability appeared to be sustainable post-1998, economic growth accelerated. Overall growth exceeded 10 per cent per annum until the global financial crisis (GFC) in 2009 but rebounded to about 7 per cent per annum a year later. Although still low compared to neighbouring countries, GDP per capita (adjusted by purchasing parity power) nearly tripled between 1993 and 2012 (Table 11.4).[21] The rapid

---

[21] Using purchasing parity power (PPP) is more useful for comparison than GDP because PPP takes into account the relative cost of living and the difference in the inflation rate between countries. GDP per capita (PPP) was estimated for 2012 at USD 2,150 in Cambodia and for comparison at USD 2,521 in Laos; USD 3,133 in Vietnam; USD 3,277 in India; USD 4,071 in Indonesia; USD 7,957 in China; USD 8,458 in Thailand; and USD 14,774 in Malaysia (data .worldbank.org/indicator/NY.GD:PCA:CD).

Table 11.4 *Socioeconomic indicators, 1990–2011*

Years		1993	1997	2002	2007	2011
ECONOMY						
Foreign aid (% of GDP)[a]		12	10	11	7.5	6.5
Foreign direct investment (% of GDP)		2.1	5.9	3.4	10	7
GDP growth (%)		9.1[b]	5.3	6.7	10.2	7.1
GDP per capita PPP (USD)		773	884	1,116	1,788	2,150[c]
Export of goods and services (% of GDP)		16	33.6	55.4	65.3	54.1
Tourism (N arrivals in thousands)		n/a	219	787	2,015	2,882
% population in poverty[d]		47[b]	36.1	n.d.	30.1	20.5
GINI index[e]		38.3[b]	n.d.	n.d.	44.4	36.0
HEALTH						
Life expectancy at birth (years)		55.3	59.3	63.9	68.8	71.1
Under 5 mortality (per 1,000 live births)		119	123	89	53	42
AMENITIES						
Sanitation (% population)[f]	Rural	3	7	12	18	22
	Urban	36	43	55	67	76
Drinking water (% population)[g]	Rural	28	34	44	54	62
	Urban	48	55	68	80	90
Electricity (% of households)[h]	Rural	n.d.	n.d.	9	13	19
	Urban	n.d.	n.d.	61	67	91
EDUCATION						
School enrolment (% of children of the relevant school age)[i]	Primary	n.d.	83	92	98	98
	Secondary	n.d.	16	22	36	n.d.
	Tertiary	1	2	3	6	15
Literacy (% of people aged 15–24 years)[j]		n.d.	76	83	87	n.d.
COMMUNICATION						
Mobile phone subscription (per 100 people)		0.1	0.3	2.9	18.9	94[c]
Internet users (per 100 people)		0	0.1	0.2	0.5	4.5[c]

[a] Estimated from Hill and Menon (2013).
[b] 1994 data.
[c] 2013 data reports 134 mobile phones per 100.
[d] Proportion of population living below national poverty line of USD 0.93.
[e] The Gini index is a measure of equality that varies from 0 to 100. Numbers close to 0 indicate countries with smaller income disparity. Most recent measure is for 2009.
[f] People with access to improved facilities such as toilets connected to sewer or septic tank, or covered pit latrines.
[g] People with access to improved drinking water source, e.g. piped water, protected well, or spring, rainwater collection.
[h] Data from CDHS for 2000, 2005, and 2010.
[i] Data from UNESCO Institute for Statistics (stats.uis.unesco.org). Enrolment of female students is lower than of male students but increasing at a similar rate.
[j] Data are for 1996, 2004, and 2009. Literacy rates are lower for females than for males but increasing at a similar rate.

Note: n.d. = no data available.
Source: Unless otherwise indicated, data are from the World Bank at data.worldbank.org/indicator/.

economic growth has created employment and contributed to the decline in poverty from nearly half the population living under the poverty line in 1994 to one in five in 2011.[22] Table 11.4 presents a range of socioeconomic indicators from the early 1990s to the present. All economic indicators as well as those related to health, education, and communication show a significant improvement since the 1990s.[23] Hill and Menon (2013) summed up Cambodia's development:

> Looking backward, Cambodia has achieved much more rapid economic development over the past two decades than even the most optimistic forecasts could have projected at the time of the 1991 Paris peace settlement. This has been a period of prosperity and peace almost without precedence in the country's history. The Cambodian people are now better educated and fed, they live longer, they have greater social and occupational choice than ever before, and they have a limited measure of democratic space. At this rate of progress, the country will very shortly graduate from the 'least developed' group of countries, and within a decade or so, it would enter the middle-income developing group. (p. 64)

This suggests that on the one hand, stability and economic growth have begun to accelerate the capacity to improve basic services. On the other hand, improved wellbeing has contributed to curbing aggressive behaviours, as shown by the fall in crime and violence during the same period. For a growing proportion of the population, rising living standards directly diminish the need to commit crime and in turn raise the 'stakes in conformity' (Toby, 1957) of an expanding middle class for which the protection and extension of their socioeconomic gain are closely dependent on political stability and social peace.

Most households still depend on agriculture, and extreme poverty and slower rates of development are concentrated in rural areas, where the majority (80 per cent) of the population resides. Although the manufacturing output has diversified, it remains mostly small scale, and the largest share consists of the garment industry, financed by FDI and geared towards export. Tourism is the other major industry: in 2012, tourism's direct and indirect contribution to GDP reached 25.8 per cent (forecasted to rise by 11.5 per cent in 2013) and employed 22.3 per cent of the total workforce (forecasted to rise to 29 per cent in 2013) (World Travel and Tourism Council, 2013). The gambling industry, particularly near the Thai border, also contributes to tourism, and the construction sector benefited from tourism and helped sustain Phnom Penh's construction boom.

---

[22] The national poverty line for Cambodia is set at an austere USD 0.9 per person per day.
[23] The World Bank estimated that Cambodia was able to reach the Millennium Development Goal of halving poverty by 2009. More stringent loan conditions required by the World Bank in 2005 also helped direct more government services into clearly defined poverty reduction efforts. These increases in overall wealth may also have assisted in the significant improvement in life expectancy from an estimated 55 years in 1993 and 59 years in 2004 to 71 years in 2011.

Cambodia's economy reliance on a steady stream of FDI and an influx of tourists is another example of the lengthening and thickening of the chains of interdependency. The state and its elites also have a 'stake in conformity' (i.e. in preserving and furthering their interests within the constitutional order and without bloodshed) because they have much to lose if investment and tourism revenues dry up, as they certainly would if, for instance, a repeat of the 1997 crisis were to occur. As the economy diversifies and both material and social benefits (e.g. better income and more educational opportunities) reach, however unequally, other social groups, the state becomes increasingly dependent on not only large sections of the growing middle class but also the peasantry and the nascent working class for support and legitimacy of its governance. In time, the development of these chains of interdependency facilitates and becomes increasingly dependent on further processes of democratisation.

As two examples demonstrate, this development is not limited to the economic realm. At the state level, within a short time after the creation of the RGC, Cambodia entered into various bi- and multilateral engagements within and outside of the region (e.g. World Trade Organization in 2004) and implemented a number of United Nations (UN) conventions.[24] The formation of such connections with global partners led to greater openness and increased interdependency. Since 1999, Cambodia has been a member of the Association of Southeast Asian Nations (ASEAN) and hosted the 2002 and 2012 annual summits.[25] The population has also embraced new forms of communication such as the Internet and social media. While Internet usage remains low at just 5 per cent of the population,[26] it is growing exponentially (notably use via mobile phones), particularly relative to the large rural population. During the 2013 elections, social media such as Facebook became an alternative medium for young people to exchange political views and spread information, particularly after the government banned foreign media sources (Soung, 2013). In addition, mobile wireless services phones are now widely available, and the number of mobile phone subscriptions is rapidly increasing.

Socioeconomic improvements have not followed a linear progression; most of them occurred in the second decade of the RGC from the early 2000s and paralleled the decline in violence. The transition from pacification to a focus

---

[24] The fact that some of them are not fully implemented does not completely reduce their symbolic power.

[25] Mirroring the process of pacification and growing interdependency at the national level, at the regional level ASEAN includes in its mission statement 'the protection of regional peace and stability, and opportunities for member countries to discuss differences peacefully' (www.asean.org).

[26] By comparison, Internet usage is estimated at 8 per cent in Laos, 22 per cent in Indonesia, and 27 per cent in Thailand. It is likely to be underestimated in Cambodia because figures are based on Internet subscriptions and do not include a large number of occasional users in Internet cafes (Titthara & Channyda, 2008).

on social development in the wake of economic improvements is a significant 'civilising spurt'. However, the shift from elite to public control of the state's resources is far from being completed; for example, tax revenue still represents a small share of GDP (10 per cent in 2011). A substantial proportion of public service funding is provided by foreign aid and NGOs, or, for instance, in the case of school funding, and reminiscent of similar practices during Sihanouk's rule, directly by Prime Minister Hun Sen (Ear, 2009). Income inequality remains high, although it is improving after the global financial crisis. Measured by the GINI index (where 0 is complete equality and 100 complete inequality), inequality peaked above 40 in the mid 2000s but improved to 36 in 2009. Although positive socioeconomic developments have been recorded in Cambodia, much remains to be done, particularly about the access to and ownership of land, the justice system, and the control of corruption. Elias linked economic diversification and socioeconomic improvements (i.e. changes in the social structure) to changes in affects and behaviours (i.e. changes in the personality structure): changes in behaviour and affects are linked to changes in living conditions. But the process is not instantaneous; there is often a lag between changes in the social structure and changes in the personality structure (van Krieken, 2001, 2005). The growing interdependency inherent in the process of social differentiation and the instrumental interest in conserving and protecting these relational networks force people to control their aggression and violent impulses. In time, as Elias observed (1939/2012), aggression is bound

> even in directly war-like actions, by the advanced state of the divisions of functions, and by the resulting greater dependence of individuals on each other and on the technical apparatus. It is confined and tamed by innumerable rules and prohibitions that have become self-constraints. It is as much transformed, 'refined,' 'civilized,' as all the other forms of pleasure, and it is only in dreams or isolated outbursts – which we label 'pathological' – that something of its immediate and unregulated force appears. (p. 187)

Through socialisation, formal and informal types of social control are increasingly internalised and superseded by self-control, and in turn sensibilities are refined and violence becomes increasingly repugnant. It is to these psychogenetic processes that we now turn.[27]

Sensitisation to violence

In this section we again assess how well the data on crime and violence in contemporary Cambodia match the hypotheses of the theories we have reviewed. To do this we first observe trends in homicides since the 1990s and whether they support Archer and Gartner's (1976) observation of high levels of residual

[27] See Pinker (2011) for a detailed discussion of psychogenetic (sociopsychological) processes.

violence following war and large-scale conflicts. We also argue that the sociogenetic processes that we have discussed above have had most impact on public and collective violence.[28] This is consistent with what Cooney proposed, which the Cambodian data support: while all violence had decreased, nonintimate (i.e. public) violence had decreased more than intimate (i.e. private) violence.[29] By contrast, because they are internalised at the deepest level, the psychogenetic processes of sensitisation to violence impact directly on private violence and indirectly on public violence. We test this later hypothesis by examining trends in domestic violence and attitudes to domestic violence.

Postconflict legitimation of violence

Our analysis of trends in homicide showed a dramatic fall in the rates of victimisation; however, it took almost 10 years following the 1991 Paris peace agreement before the start of a sharp decline in 1999: homicide victimisation peaked in 1993 with a rate of 23.5 per 100,000, dropped to 13 per 100,000 in 1998, and continued declining until 2012 (2.4 per 100,000; Figure 10.1). Trends for other violent crimes followed a similar pattern. In their review of the effects of war on homicide rates, Archer and Gartner (1976) found substantially higher rates of homicide in the immediate postwar compared to the prewar period. They also observed that, irrespective of the outcome of the conflict, high combat losses predicted higher levels of postwar homicides. The best model to explain that phenomenon was one of 'legitimation of violence', which 'suggests that the presence of authorised or sanctioned killing during war has a residual effect on the level of homicide in peacetime society' (Archer & Gartner, 1976, p. 961). They argued that the state's condoning of war violence – killing enemies is not only justified but commendable – leads to the 'wartime reversal of the customary peacetime prohibition against killing [which] may somehow influence the threshold for using homicide as a means of settling conflict in everyday life' (Archer & Gartner, 1976, p. 960). Archer and Gartner's 'legitimation of violence model' is consistent with and can be integrated into Elias's (1939/2012) notion of decivilising processes during which the psychogenetic process of sensitisation to violence is reversed. As peace settles and life slowly returns to normality, homicide rates also return to their prewar levels. The lag suggests that (re-)sensitisation to violence, particularly for some combatants, takes some time to resurface.

---

[28] This is not to say that the state monopolisation of force and the growing chains of interdependency have no effect on private violence but that their effects on private violence are indirect (mediated through psychogenetic processes).

[29] Eisner (2008) similarly suggested that a large part of the decline in homicide in the world consisted of a decline in violence between young men in public spaces.

If we consider that the prewar period spans 15 years from independence in 1953 to the start of the first civil war in 1967, we have only a scant picture of prewar crime, but as we have discussed in Chapter 6, from the mid 1950s to the mid 1960s during Sihanouk's regime, Cambodia was at peace and apparently enjoyed low levels of ordinary criminal violence. If we go back to the period preceding World War II and the anticolonial struggle, we estimated homicide rates from the *BPC* and found that in the 1930s, the rates oscillated between 2.5 and 3.5 per 100,000 (Figure 4.2), that is, a level similar to that of 2012. Our data on homicide victimisation in Cambodia, therefore, fit with Archer and Gartner's (1976) prediction of a residual high level of homicidal violence immediately postwar (1991 to 1998) followed by a gradual return to the prewar level (mid 2000s onwards). Cambodia's history also supports the suggested model. Cambodia has been exposed to an extended period of 'legitimation of violence' during the anticolonial struggle (1947–54), the civil wars (1967–75), the revolutionary period (1975–9), and the post-DK period (1979–89). We described in the preceding chapters how individual and mass killings, bombings, and atrocities were perpetrated by all sides and against both combatants and civilians, culminating in the murderous regime of DK. The long and intense brutalisation of the Khmer population is probably one factor explaining the high level of homicidal victimisation in the early years following the peace agreement. The effects of developmental anomie associated with rapid changes in the 1990s is another relevant factor. For example, violence rather than negotiation was used to settle political conflicts, the remaining KR increasingly turned to banditry, and nonlethal crime was also high. The UNTAC (civilising) mission, the belated condemnation of the KR by the international community, the slow economic recovery through the provision of foreign aid, and other pacifying interventions took some time to reestablish the prohibition against killing and the use of violence.

Awareness and educational programs by government and NGOs, such as those related to the weapon collection scheme, have helped towards reestablishing the previous prohibition. For example, the success of weapon collection depended on a wide-reaching publicity campaign making the population aware of the new law restricting weapon ownership and encouraging people to hand in their weapons. This was achieved through community meetings, posters, billboards, handouts, and public presentations that highlighted the danger presented by guns not only because they had become illegal but because they contributed to high level of violence in the community. The collection was accompanied by 'Flame of Peace' televised public ceremonies attended by ministers and senior members of the police and army, during which the weapons were burned or crushed. Their symbolic power was important because, as de Beer (2005), the campaign coordinator, commented: 'Weapons destruction, while being an end in itself as part of the weapons management programme, also plays an important educational role. The destruction ceremonies are a reminder to the

Illustration 11.1 Antidrugs advert. This billboard explains that those using chemical substances will be liable to criminal charges

public that disarmament is an on-going process and contributed to the growing feeling of security in the country' (p. 5). De Beer concluded that the campaign had been successful not only in regard to the collection but also more broadly in what we call a 'sensitisation tool':

A small, but remarkable success has been the distribution of 'No Gun' stickers throughout the country. In their tens of thousands, these stickers are to be found on motor bikes, taxis, police vehicles, boats, office doors, cupboard doors and in many other places. At times it has been almost impossible to keep up with the demand for them and in 2005 over 50,000 have been distributed. The sticker has virtually become the unofficial symbol of Cambodia's desire to leave its SALW [small arms and light weapons] problem behind and to look towards a future where the old Culture of Violence is replaced by a new Culture of Peace. (de Beer, 2005, p. 6)

Similar campaigns have addressed the problem of domestic violence (DV) and have had some success in reducing its acceptance and perpetration.

Domestic violence

Starting about two decades ago,[30] services and programmes aimed at reducing domestic violence (DV) have operated in Cambodian communes. In 2005 the

---

[30] In 1992 Cambodia signed the Convention on the Elimination of Discrimination Against Women (CEDAW), which prompted the development of victim services and educational programs. A leading NGO for women's rights, the Cambodian Women's Crisis Center (CWCC), was founded

308 Violence and the Civilising Process in Cambodia

Illustration 11.2 Anti–domestic violence advert. This billboard illustrates that domestic violence can impair child development

government passed the Law on Prevention of Domestic Violence and the Protection of Victims, and since 2010 the MoI has recorded what are probably only the most serious incidents of domestic violence. The MoI records show 183 in 2010 (75 per cent injured), 106 in 2011 (92 per cent injured), and 136 in 2012 (85 per cent injured). While enforcement of the 2005 law is limited (the law does not specify which authorities are responsible for intervening), it provides a basis for awareness of and education about DV. Between 1992 and 2008, the *PPP* reported just over 180 homicides when husbands murdered their wives (average of 10 each year), and many more women were seriously injured. It is difficult to assess trends in DV because much of it goes unreported (as indeed is also the case in many other countries). For example, LICADHO (Cambodian League for the Promotion and Defense of Human Rights, 2007) showed an increase in the number of DV cases reported to them from 75 in 2000 to 220 in 2006 but pointed out that this increase may reflect a rise in reporting rather than a rise in prevalence. By contrast, the Cambodian Women's Crisis Center

in 1997. The centre collaborates with the Ministry of Interior and Ministry of Women's Affairs to provide training and education to police and local authorities.

Illustration 11.3 Antifirearm advert. An antifirearm billboard encouraging people in possession of an illegal firearm to hand their weapon over to local authorities

(CWCC)[31] has dealt with a decreasing number of cases: 443 in 2001, 635 in 2002 (Coates, 2005), and 363 in 2011.

Since 1996, several surveys on violence against women have been conducted in Cambodia and used comparable methodology and questions. Table 11.5 presents prevalence results for domestic violence and attitudes towards wife beating reported by these surveys. The findings suggest that physical and sexual violence against women by their partner is declining, particularly if we consider prevalence as measured during the 12 months prior to the survey (Table 11.5A).[32] In 2000, the Cambodian Demographic and Health Survey (CDHS) found that 15 per cent of respondents said their husband had abused them in the last 12 months, but this proportion had dropped to 9 per cent in 2005. The most recent survey conducted by the United Nations Development Program (UNDP)

---

[31] www.cwcc.org.kh.

[32] Lifetime prevalence is not a reliable measure of trends over time as the violence reported by the respondents may have occurred many years previously and also depends on the age of the respondent. For example, the CDHS interviewed women younger than 50 years, whereas the most recent UNDP survey did not set an upper age limit.

Table 11.5 *Domestic violence against women and attitude to domestic violence from four surveys*

	HSDVC[a]	CDHS[b]	Baseline Survey[c]	UNDP[d]

(A) Domestic violence by current or previous partner (% victimised)[e]

Survey year	Type of violence measured Survey period	Physical	Physical + sexual	Physical	Physical + sexual
1996	Since age 15	16			
	Last 12 months				
2000	Since age 15		17		
	Last 12 months		15		
2005	Since age 15		14	23	
	Last 12 months		9		
2009	Since age 15			decrease[f]	
2012	Since age 15				25
	Last 12 months				3

(B) Attitude to wife beating (% agreed)[e,g]

	Sex of respondent				
2000	Women		35		
2005	Women		55	79	
	Men		Not asked	69	
2009	Women			50	
	Men			41	
2010	Women		46		
	Men		22		
2012	Women				33
	Men				28

[a] Household Survey on Domestic Violence in Cambodia sampled $N = 1,374$ married women and measured physical violence (Nelson & Zimmerman, 1996).
[b] Women aged 15–49 years; $N = 2,403$ in 2000 and $N = 2,037$ in 2005 (NIS, Directorate General for Health, & ORC Macro, 2001; National Institute of Public Health, NIS, & ORC Macro, 2006; NIS, Directorate General for Health, & ICF Macro, 2011).
[c] Women aged 15 years and older; $N = 1,576$ in 2005 and $N = 2,029$ in 2009 (Indochina Research Limited, 2005, 2009).
[d] $N = 417$ women aged 18–49 years (Fulu et al., 2013).
[e] All figures rounded to the closest number.
[f] The report shows falls of between −1 per cent and −12 per cent for each specific type of violence, but it does not provide an overall figure for all types combined.
[g] Questions were: CDHS, 'Is a husband justified in beating his wife under a number of circumstances?'; Baseline Survey, 'Is it ever acceptable for a husband to push, shove or throw something at his wife?'; UNDP Survey, 'Do you agree that there are times when a woman deserves to be beaten?'

Illustration 11.4 Awareness of domestic violence advert. This billboard highlights that domestic violence is a criminal act and can also have a negative impact on child development

in 2012 found that 3 per cent of women reported marital abuse. In the same survey, 4 per cent of men admitted having used violence towards their wife in the previous 12 months (Fulu et al., 2013).

Psychosocial interpretations of Cambodia's expressive violence have linked DV to post-traumatic stress disorder (PTSD) associated with the DK regime. A national survey in 2007 found that more than one in ten (11.2 per cent) of the Cambodian population might be affected by PTSD (Sonis et al., 2009).[33] According to Hinton, Hinton, Pich, Loeum, and Pollack (2009), PTSD has affected and continues to affect many survivors of the KR regime and, according to Brinkley (2011), is often transmitted to their children through dysfunctional familial and socialisation processes.[34] It is likely that PTSD has been

---

[33] A study in Kampong Cham found that 7.3 per cent of respondents may have been affected by PTSD (Dubois et al., 2004), but a higher rate of 20.6 per cent was found in Siem Reap (Cardozo et al., 2012; Mollica, Brooks, Tor, Lopes-Cardozo, & Silove, 2014). Yet, these studies suggest a decrease in the prevalence of PTSD compared to an earlier rate of 28 per cent estimated by de Jong et al. (2001).

[34] Brinkley (2011) also linked PTSD to an increasing level of DV in Cambodia: 'In 2004, Cambodian officials estimated that one-quarter of the nation's men frequently beat their wives and

more prevalent in rural areas, not only because of the longer exposure but also because after 1979 many former KR perpetrators of violence continued to live in the same villages as their victims. In addition, rural sufferers of PTSD were less likely to receive assistance than their urban counterparts.

The studies cited above also examined respondents' attitudes towards wife beating. The questions were worded differently in the three surveys, but all measured the degree to which male and female respondents thought the use of violence towards a wife was ever justified or acceptable.[35] Surprisingly, lower proportions of men than women condoned the use of violence towards wives (Table 11.5B). The proportions of respondents varied, but all showed decreasing levels of acceptance of spousal violence over time, for both men and women. The most recent survey conducted in 2012 suggested that 33 per cent of women and 28 per cent of men thought violence towards a wife was acceptable (Fulu *et al.*, 2013). The 2009 follow-up of the Baseline Survey noted a rise in the reported instances of less-abusive interactions (e.g. yelling rather than hitting) towards women perceived by their husbands as failing in their assumed gender roles, which suggests a modernisation of attitudes towards using dialogue and negotiation rather than violence. The CDHS revealed significant regional and associated sociodemographic differences. Women from rural areas, with little schooling, and with the least wealth were the most likely to condone wife beating.[36] The same regional and sociodemographic differences applied to men. The improvement in attitudes between 2005 and 2010 was essentially due to a change of attitude for women in urban areas: in 2005, over half (52 per cent) of urban women agreed with wife beating for at least one reason, but in 2010 this had fallen to only one quarter (27 per cent); in rural areas, however, only a small decline of 5 per cent was observed, from 56 per cent agreeing with wife beating in 2005 to 51 per cent in 2010.[37] This decline in both the

---

children – one of the highest rates in the world. By the end of the decade, as more of the Khmer Rouge victims' children married and had children of their own, the rate had actually increased to about one-third of the nation's families' (p. 139). Our data, however, show a decrease rather than an increase in the level of DV in Cambodia. In addition, assuming the rate Brinkley reported is the lifetime rate, it is comparable to rates of intimate partner violence in Australia (27 per cent) and Denmark (22 per cent) and is lower than, for example, Mozambique (40 per cent), the Czech Republic (37 per cent), and Costa Rica (36 per cent) (see Johnson, Ollus, & Nevala, 2008).

[35] The CDHS asked respondents whether a husband was ever justified in beating his wife under a number of circumstances such as the wife argues with him, neglects the children, goes out without telling him, refuses to have sex, asks to use a condom. The Baseline Survey asked if respondents thought it was ever acceptable for the husband to use a series of violent behaviours towards his wife. Finally, the UNDP survey asked whether respondents agree with the statement 'There are times when a woman deserves to be beaten.'

[36] Greater literacy and general education of women (more likely in urban areas) free them from the constraints of mechanical collectivistic values and extend their participation in the chains of interdependency.

[37] The question was not asked of men in 2005.

Civilising processes and violence in contemporary Cambodia 313

prevalence of DV and attitudes favourable to wife beating is linked to a more general sensitisation to violence. In the case of family violence, it is probably also due to the educational role of the new law on domestic violence as well as educational programs run by NGOs and supported by many commune chiefs. For example, the UNDP survey (2013) showed that 93 per cent of the men they interviewed were aware of the laws against violence against women. The Baseline Survey in 2009 also indicated that for 55 per cent of the men and 52 per cent of the women the lack of enforcement of the DV law negatively affected their attitude towards domestic violence, that is, they were less likely to consider DV a serious matter. This suggests that sociogenetic processes (here, state monopolisation of violence) may also have some indirect effects on intimate violence.

Conclusion

This chapter has shown that the data since 1992 on crime and violence in contemporary Cambodia overall support the general hypotheses of modernisation and civilising process theories regarding trends in violence. Indeed, we see Elias's civilising processes at work. The state's eventual monopolisation of force through the ascendency of the CPP has been crucial in the significant decline of ordinary crime and violence. Improvements in socioeconomic conditions, particularly in urban areas, and a growing sensitisation to violence have further reduced both public and private violence. However, strong social inequalities, particularly between the cities and the provinces, the absence of genuine justice, and unabated corruption remain important criminogenic factors, and particularly factors that can drive both individual and mass violence. Indeed, Springer (2011) has suggested that these growing inequalities are re-creating the very socioeconomic and political conditions that led to the upheavals of the 1970s and may be sowing the seeds of another violent eruption. If Chandler's (2010) prognostic that 'unchecked land alienation to foreign investors and agribusinesses will continue on a massive scale, and the gap between Cambodia's rich and poor will widen' (p. 234) is correct, then outbreaks of collective violence may occur more frequently. For example, resistance against land evictions often turning into riots has increased during the last decade. Finally, the CPP electoral ascendancy has been seriously challenged by the results of the 2013 elections, when it lost seats in both urban and rural areas. On the one hand, postelectoral demonstrations contesting the results of the 2013 elections, the strikes, and violent opposition between garment factory workers and the police, during which police fired at the crowd and killed at least four in early 2014, are outbreaks of collective violence. On the other hand, the fact that compared to previous eras these outbreaks did not degenerate further may signal the shaky beginnings of 'a new era of political maturity for a country all too familiar with political violence' (Quinlan, Boyle, & Street, 2013). From a criminological perspective, what are the prognostics for the future? What would the theoretical interpretations of our historical and contemporary data suggest? This is the object of our next and final chapter.

12 Discussion

History and processes of social change

We have taken the long historical view of our subject because in understanding the nature of violence in contemporary Cambodia we wanted to know how the key transitions in the 150 years of Cambodia's modern history impacted on the scale or prevalence of violence and how the forms of such violence may have changed or not through time. Albeit reduced to a cliché, George Santayana's oft-quoted observation: 'Those who cannot remember the past are condemned to repeat it,' reminds us that the trap of 'presentism', as Elias put it, confines the researcher focused on a few decades to an incomplete picture of social change. The complexities of social change (largely unplanned) unfold gradually, but not evenly, over generations, and inquiries limited to a decade or two cannot grasp these processes and their implications. It is in historical observations that change in both social institutions and individual behaviours may be discerned. Hence from this perspective we can see, by observing the ebb and flow of the scale and forms of violence and crime, how processes of 'civilisation' unfold. Following the historical 'process' sociology advocated by Elias, we have focused on 'change' over a longer time scale and observed the gradual shift from frequent surges of collective violence to private acts driven by interpersonal conflicts and sometimes pathologies rather than in response to collective sentiments or existential threats.

The late twentieth and early twenty-first centuries are notable for the decline in violent superstate rivalry and, consequently, the further expansion of trade that led to the increasing interdependence of states, communities, and individuals. This deepening and widening of the chains of interdependency manifesting as globalisation and cosmopolitanism, and sustained by the rapid expansion of the information/digital revolution, drive the civilising processes we have seen unfold in Cambodia. Cambodia, once isolated from the world and infantilised, and for a time reduced to a 'failed state', is now more connected than ever to the outside, and its premodern autarkic traditions, forms of governance, and subsistence economy have changed forever.

Our historical survey of violence from the beginning of the French Protectorate in 1863 to the contemporary Kingdom of Cambodia suggests that, despite catastrophic decivilising periods, there has been a gradual and overall decline in lethal violence. Admittedly, we lack a complete record for the entire 150 years, and this is an important limitation of our study. Despite many 'missing gaps', we believe there are sufficient primary data from 1900 onwards and reliable contemporary sources, both quantitative and qualitative (e.g. *Résidents* reports and chronicles of events such as the Great Insurrection), to illustrate the broad trends of an uneven decline. The overall trend of violence in Cambodia follows sympathetically the general patterns of similar but earlier long-term declines in violence in Western Europe. In both Western Europe and Cambodia, this trend was subject to aperiodical surges of violence that disturbed the otherwise cascade-like decline in interpersonal violence and homicide.

Cambodia has undergone broadly similar, if delayed, processes of civilisation as those undergone in Europe, but in Cambodia these processes were also in part mediated by the extended impact of colonisation and later via a briefer internationally sponsored intervention by the transitional 'state' of the United Nations Transitional Authority in Cambodia (UNTAC), which inserted democratic elections (as a means of resolving political conflicts peacefully) to end over two decades of violent armed conflict. Notable achievements of this pacification process were the reduction in firearms, especially military small arms, and a consequential decline in lethal crimes, such as robbery-murder. In short, we have seen a reassertion of order, first among the police and armed forces and then by the elimination of armed groups of demobilised combatants and 'desperados' who contested the spoils of peace and/or failed to adapt to the rapid transition from war to exchange-driven means of existence.

From the UNTAC intervention onwards, this decline in violence also engendered a sensitisation to violence that further reinforced the decline in most forms of interpersonal violence. Given the general suppression of the more 'public' and predatory forms of crime that state monopolisation over violence directly produces, it is difficult to measure *how much* sensitisation to violence has contributed to this decline. Here, changes in the 'affects' or sensibilities and attitudes to violence and the capacities of self-restraint are opaque processes that follow a general return to security, which in turn allows for the development and expansion of 'gentle commerce': these combine as multipliers for furthering the chains of interdependence, which also deepen both an instrumental and a moral repugnance to violence. The underlying tendency, predicted by Durkheim, for further individualisation, as the social structure shifts from mechanical to organic forms, is also evident, and through these civilising processes Cambodian customary collective values are gradually replaced by individualistic values that include both consumerism (and associated risks of structural anomie and egoistic individualism) and moral/cooperative individualism associated, for instance, with the development of human rights concerns. As we noted in our general introduction, in this evolving modernising society, the individual is no longer tied into a closely knit mesh of norms, symbols, and rituals that define his or her own identity primarily in terms of belonging to a collectivity. The fusion of personal and collective identities dissolves. The individual's social standing and reputation are no longer defined by a group-specific code of honor that, for example, makes blood revenge obligatory. Violence that injures, mutilates, or kills another person becomes increasingly repugnant, abominable. (Messner, Thome, *et al.*, 2008, p. 170)

This is why we argue that the salience of face, honour, hierarchy, and blood revenge in Cambodia, about which Hinton and others have written, is not so much a question of national Khmer culture – a view that could be regarded as essentialist or Orientalist – but the lingering features of a premodern stage of societal evolution through which all current modern societies have passed. However, following Durkheim, Messner, Thome, *et al.* (2008) observe that the weakening of collectivist values does not mean the disappearance of a 'collective conscience' because

there is a 'collective conscience' even in the individualized societies but the highest-ranking value is the individual 'in general'; not just the individual 'self' but also the individual 'other'. This 'moral' or 'cooperative' individualism respects the individual as the carrier of universal rights and obligations' ... Cooperative individualism thus implies a principled readiness to invest in collective goods (like having a democratic government or preserving the natural environment) even without calculating individual payoffs or losses. (p. 171)

Here it is possible to contend, as the work of Hinton, Brinkley, and others might suggest, that, on the evidence, Cambodia has not yet reached or has just entered this stage of cooperative individualism. Indeed, 'hybridisation', as we argue later, is a useful metaphor for this transitional or partial evolution to modernity, where both old and new customs and sensibilities coexist. Messner, Thome, *et al.* (2008) further note, 'Cooperative individualism seeks to secure justice and to balance personal freedom and equality, mainly by combining social welfare provisions and parliamentary democracy' (p. 171). This is something many Cambodians clearly aspire to and increasingly struggle for but have not yet achieved. However, our reading of contemporary Cambodia shows also evidence that moral individualism is growing among middle-class urbanites and the working class (via unionism, community advocacy, and consumer cooperatives). A civil society espousing moral individualist values is emerging and with it further interdependency and sensitisation to violence but conditioned by the form of governance and the depth of the pacification and civilising processes under way. Because it is a complex, nonlinear, iterative process between evolving social structures and personality structures, and this evolution is not immune to reversals, the shifting relationship to outsiders (strangers) towards more cooperative relations is also nonlinear and subject to reversals. But, over time, social relations become less and less dependent on customary or formal social control to ensure order and compliance – and, ultimately, social control becomes internalised self-constraints.

As the interrupted graph in our general introduction shows, fluctuating levels of homicide and periodic hemoclysms or blood floods punctuated this general decline in violence. The short periods of decline as well as the spikes or surges in violence reflected the inconsistent monopolisation of violence and the slow and weak development of the dominion of democratic and juridical institutions. The pattern of violence was closely associated with the capacity of the Cambodian state to monopolise violence *and* achieve a modicum of legitimacy necessary for the further pacification and economic and cultural development of the country. With these developments came associated changes of 'affects', which in turn interacted with structural forces. But these processes were hampered and slowed down in Cambodia, where not only all the governments that have claimed sovereignty at one time over the past 150 years have resorted to coercion, authoritarianism, or autocracy but also where the superstates' rivalries were waged and, during DK, further decivilisation organised in the name of social revolution.

A model of civilising processes and crime

We represent our visualisation of these complex interactions that drive social change (Figures 12.1 and 12.2) by the image of recurring cycles where widening networks of interdependency lead to state formations (i.e. in Elias's terms – survival groups via elimination contests) that variously pacify and change the nature of social and individual relations and in turn shape the interior thoughts and sensibilities of generations of individuals. This allows us to use concepts of 'individual' (and the process of psychogenesis) and 'society' (the process of sociogenesis) not as independent objects but as 'different yet inseparable aspects of the same human beings' (Elias, 1939/2012, p. 499). These changes in individual sensibilities (as well as the growing capacity to reason and to anticipate) and social organisation are usually sympathetic and create the conditions for further pacification. This process may be disturbed by countervailing decivilising spurts such as war and revolution as well as the disturbances to social order that accompany rapid change – that is, sudden changes in the 'rules' of social life, which engender anomie (initially developmental and in later phases structural forms of normlessness or anomie).

Our model integrates social control perspectives and articulates them as processes of moral development occurring through the interplay of the ever-growing state monopolisation of violence, chains of interdependency, and sensitisation to violence. Monopolisation is achieved through the formal social control of the legal and security apparatus; chains of interdependency are maintained through the informal social control of cooperating individuals and groups; and sensitisation is internalised via self-control. In Elias's terms, the

Discussion

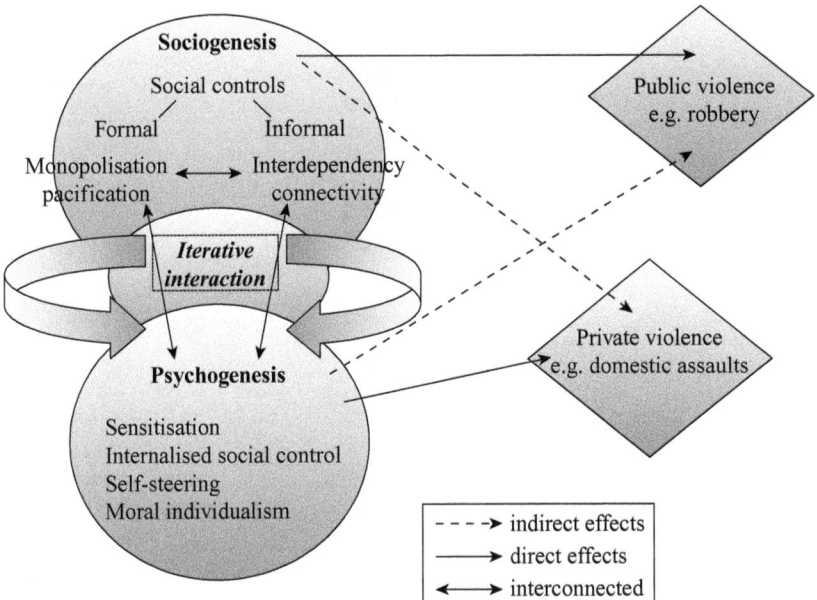

Figure 12.1 Model of the civilising process and types of violence

iterative process of sociogenesis strengthens, through positive feedbacks, the formal and informal forms of social restraint, which in turn acts on the sensibilities of the individual in a sympathetic and reinforcing way – these changes in the content or character of the psychogenetic process in turn interact with the pacifying and evolving state such that violence becomes anachronistic and indeed an increasingly inefficient form of social and individual action. The integration of wider and longer chains of interdependence, more division of functions (labour), and the presence of greater (psychological or internalised) self-constraint, combined with sensitisation towards violence, new sensibilities of empathy, and tolerance of difference, impact on the frequency and lethality of both private and public forms of violence and account for the gradual decline in their prevalence.

Our model, therefore, permits a view of not only the overall civilising (and decivilising) processes and the interaction of the key integrating components put in play by pacification, interdependency, individualisation, and self-constraint but also how these processes differentially affect trends in specific types of violence (see Figure 12.2). For instance, we have noted in the previous chapter that the proliferation of programs ('*civilizing* offensives' cf. Powell, 2013) that aim to reduce violence against women and children is generally a manifestation of this heightened sensitisation to violence. There is also some apparent decline in domestic violence since it was first measured in the 1990s.

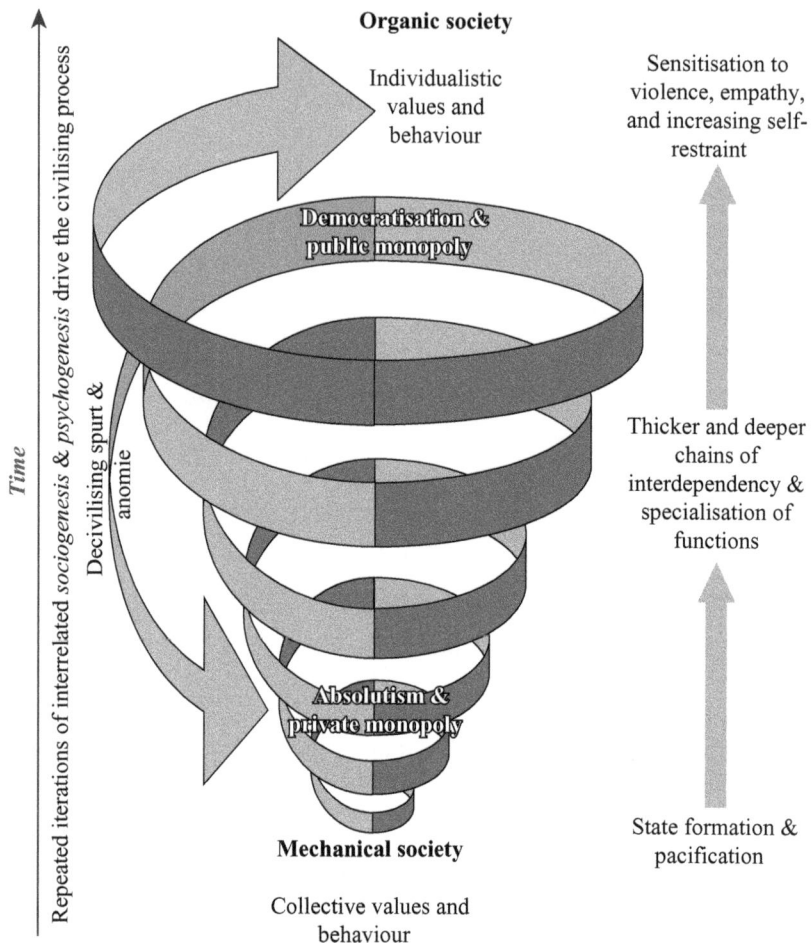

Figure 12.2 Integrated representation of the modernisation and civilising processes

Other trends, such as the increases in suicide,[1] road fatalities,[2] youth gangs, and consumer and other frauds testify to further shifts in social relations and in

---

[1] Official rates of suicide have increased from 2.9 per 100,000 in 2005 to 4.14 in 2012, but since 2010 rates in the provinces have been higher than in Phnom Penh (e.g. in 2012, 4.29 against 2.81) (source: MoI). The World Health Organization (WHO) estimated that one million people worldwide had committed suicide in 2012, with an overall age-adjusted rate of 16 per 100,000 in the general population.

[2] Official rates of fatal victims of transport accidents have increased from 7.44 in 2006 to 13.34 per 100,000 in 2012, but in the same period the rates of injured victims increased from 49.83 in 2006 to 82.61 per 100,000 in 2008 and then gradually fell to 52.59 per 100,000 in 2012 (source: MoI).

the types of crime and violence now relevant to the social conditions and values prevailing in Cambodia. Nevertheless, the increasing potency of the state to both rationalise and centralise its influence upon the forms of relationship between individuals (socialisation processes) and to directly attempt to suppress uncivilised behaviours or amorality, as defined by the 'authorities', can also be observed.

Let us summarise these intertwined social and psychological processes (see Figure 12.2): *sociogenesis* is founded upon the state's (survival unit) monopolisation of force, which leads directly to the suppression of nonstate and predatory crimes of violence (e.g. collective violence, banditry, and extralegal violence), but other crimes such as corruption and fraud may arise. Interdependency, both in the broad sense of the impact of foreign aid and trade (commerce) as well as the connections that bind individuals to expanding social networks, coexists with remnants of archaism, autarchy, and customary (premodern) practice. More broadly, socioeconomic changes and the development of education also influence the types of violence (e.g. instrumental, ideological, xenophobic) that may be present or in ascendancy as modes of conduct. *Psychogenesis* captures the interior processes of human emotions, thoughts, and actions, which shape and are shaped by the individual's interaction with family, neighbours, state, and society. Thus, in a pacified society, sensitisation to violence leads to changes in the 'threshold of repugnancy', with an increasing remit to bar ever-milder forms of violence. Hence, which types of violence remain 'acceptable' or not (e.g. cruelties, excessive violence, and violence against women and children) will partly depend on the changes in values that occur with pacification and the extent that heightened sensibilities of empathy and self-awareness spread through groups and wider society.

Civilising offensives and civilising processes

Powell (2013) noted that the recent concept of the *civilising offensive* addresses attempts by elite groups to reframe conduct and steer 'civilisation' in a particular direction. Civilising offensives are similar in vein to the 'civilising missions' of the colonial powers of the nineteenth century and the moral crusades and moral panics familiar to criminologists that focus on undesirable behaviours and seek through laws and social and media campaigns to change attitudes and behaviour. Civilising offensives such as those directed at disarmament, the development of the rule of law, the control of corruption, the awareness of violence in the family, the beautification of social spaces, or the promotion of public hygiene are conscious, planned events that may reflect changes in sensibilities, especially among the elite and educated middle classes, as well as short-term changes in response to contemporary conditions (e.g. as in the 'civilising' demands of the tourist industry). Civilising offensives, however, may yield superficial compliance with new standards, whereas the long-term role of psychogenesis leads to the internalisation of social constraints and a self-steering actor able to control appetites and impulses. Elias (1939/2012, p. 17) argued that the civilising process experienced by the West became, among the middle classes, a particular 'self-consciousness of the west', and its benefits disseminated to the lower classes and less developed countries (cited in Powell, 2013).

The Kingdom has been subject to two 'civilising offensives'. The first was the French Protectorate, which we have discussed at length, and we noted how relatively transitory and shallow had been the impact of the French on the modernisation of Cambodia. As we observed, the 'golden age' of French Colonial rule and that of the successor king-head of state Sihanouk were too brief to consolidate effective state institutions. Both become enmeshed in and then engulfed by war and then caught up as part of the geopolitical struggles that characterised the global ideological rivalry of the Cold War. Notwithstanding the Protectorate's achievement of pacifying and preserving, for the most part, the territory of Cambodia, the country was only destined to be a colony of exploitation. As such, it underwent a nonintensive process of colonial settlement and modernisation, which produced, as Elias, Marx, and others predicted, the seeds of its demise and the emergence of 'fragile' nations under the thrall of partially 'Westernised' indigenous elites with varying capacities to rule.[3] Cambodia thus experienced the dual effect of colonisation bringing modernisation and civilisation that first undermined traditional elites (and also used them) and partially transformed social and economic relations, especially in urban areas and administrative centres. It was this gap between urban (qua modern) and rural (archaic) Cambodian society that ultimately created the hostile and demonised view of the urban Khmer as exploitative in contrast to the lowly 'black' Khmer of the countryside so cleverly manipulated by the KR.

Nevertheless, French colonisation brought Cambodia into the modern world and saw its partial transformation from a largely feudal and mechanical world (in the Durkheimian sense) to that of a gradually evolving organic society – driven by urbanisation and trade. The transformation of Phnom Penh in the 1860s from an important if small port of a few thousand people into a city of some 330,000 people in 1950 illustrates the impact of colonisation and the importance of the city in the modernisation of Cambodia. The city, built largely by the French and home of the king and the French administration, was considered a charming provincial town. The city has grown at least fourfold since 1970, and in 2013–14 its population was about 2.3 million. Phnom Penh

---

[3] Marx's predictions are only partially relevant here because industrialisation and the growth of a proletariat was not achieved in Cambodia, and the KR revolution did not follow Marx's model – rather following the route of a peasant or subaltern revolt against the exploitative city, modernity, and cosmopolitanism.

Discussion

population was estimated at 450,000 in 1970, although during the civil war, swelled by refugees, it grew to about 2 million, but during Democratic Kampuchea (DK) it may have declined to less than 50,000 (Doyle, 2012). Due to the impact of DK policies, in 1979 Phnom Penh was for the most part reoccupied by people from rural areas and the few survivors of the city's evacuation in 1975. The increase in population has been very rapid, with over 1 million residents added since 2000. Despite this influx of rural workers that we associate in part with the initially high rates of urban violence, since the early 2000s the city has been relatively free from crime and violence, although there are now signs in more recent data of a resurgence of petty theft and the crimes related to the presence of youth gangs. Generally, this is consistent with Shelley's (1981) thesis about the surge of urban violence at first associated with the early phase of modernity (1980 through to the mid to late 1990s) as rural migrants adjust to urban lifestyles. In the later stages, chronic or structural anomie can impact on some types of crime such as youth gangs, which are associated with the late urbanisation phase, as discussed in the previous chapter. Here the notion of anomie is relevant since the shift from rural to urban lifestyles changes the rules of the game and social relationships are redefined. We should also keep in mind that modernisation and urbanisation processes were occurring up to the mid 1960s and were delayed and undermined by the 1967–79 decivilising period.

The second civilising offensive was the peacemaking intervention (i.e. the pacifying mission) of the United Nations Transitional Authority in Cambodia (UNTAC), which, like the French Protectorate, also attempted to insert modern systems, values, and behaviours in Cambodia. This relatively short-term international peacemaking intervention may also be considered a civilising spurt in its own right since it enabled consolidation of the pacification process through the mechanism of multiparty elections. The symbolic legitimacy of multiparty elections conducted under UNTAC also enabled the return of Cambodia to the international community, and this was crucial in opening up Cambodia to greater levels of trade, foreign aid, and interconnectedness. UNTAC's role in the reformation of the Kingdom of Cambodia has also been the source of controversies about its long-term impact and, in particular, its contribution to the creation of viable political institutions. UNTAC's failure to effectively democratise these key institutions may have contributed through the 1990s to the institutionalisation of developmental anomie (in accord with the broad proposition offered by Messner's institutional anomie theory) and consequently reinforced the current elite forms of crime, which are a manifestation of structural anomie.[4]

---

[4] Messner, Thome, and Rosenfeld's (2008) institutional anomie theory (IAT) proposes that when the market is the dominant force in society, that is, when there is an imbalance between the values

So, a civilising offensive drawing on the values of Western neoliberalism was a concomitant function of UNTAC, but this also informed the role of international society in both providing and developing the spurt of interconnectedness in subsequent donor and civil society engagement with the RGC. Following long negotiations between the RGC and the United Nations (UN), this international engagement led to the eventual formation in 2005 of the Extraordinary Chambers of the Court of Cambodia (ECCC), which comprises both Cambodian (majority) and foreign judges within the Cambodian court system and is representative of the hybridisation noted below. The purported 'civilising' role of the ECCC, apart from the prosecution of a handful of DK regime leaders, is to improve fidelity to the 'rule of law' and reinforce the values associated with an independent judiciary among the elites and masses. This is an effort to rekindle rule of law and human rights values via a legalist attempt at closure of the KR period. In 1999, Hun Sen, voicing the concerns of the pacifying Leviathan, hoped the ECCC would help 'close the chapter' and put the dark past behind them. Most valued, he declared, was 'the paramount need for continued national reconciliation and the safeguard of the hard gained peace as well as national independence and sovereignty' (cited in McGrew, 2009, p. 285) rather than an expansive 'civilising' ECCC.[5]

Despite all the shortcoming (see Boreham & Hobbes, 2011; Hughes, 2009; McGrew, 2009), the ECCC may help reduce the amnesia in Cambodian education about the circumstances that led to the DK and post-DK periods and dispel misinformation about the past that has encouraged many Khmer to believe 'foreign hands' were behind Pol Pot's deadly regime (McGrew, 2009, p. 283). This understandable resentment of the international support for the KR after the DK period may be the basis for the avoidance of a broad-based understanding of the causes of the DK state's extraordinary violence and therefore undermines further sensitisation to violence. Despite these underlying sentiments, there are serious efforts by civil society (see Youk Chhang and the Cambodian Documentation Centre) to combat through education the resurgence of the forms of xenophobia that underpinned the violence of the past. McGrew suggests that Buddhist ethics among Cambodians support a cultural preference for amnesty and truth over Western ideas of justice and retribution, so effective conflict

---

associated with market institutions and the values associated with other institutions (e.g. family, welfare) and consequently an unbalanced use of state resources, crime and violence are likely to grow. In Cambodia, these conditions have prevailed and even worsened since at least 1990. IAT would be consistent with the level of elite crime since the late 1980s, but not with the pattern of ordinary property and violent crime, which significantly declined after 1998. IAT may not adequately explain crime in developing societies because it was designed to explain crime in for advanced societies (Messner, Thome, *et al.*, 2008).

[5] Extending the ECCC prosecutions beyond a handful of the most senior KR officials still alive has concerned CPP leaders, who fear that such trials could expose the responsibility of current political leaders for atrocities committed during DK and revive revenge attacks.

resolution must resolve both demands. The ECCC could therefore serve as a partial mechanism for reconciliation, which is also desired by the ruling elites. However, whether or not the ECCC example will also 'trickle down' and enhance the professionalism[6] and legitimacy of Cambodia's courts is a moot point and depends in great part on the political will of the ruling elites. We have stressed the success of the RGC in pacification and with it a concomitant reduction in public violence, but the state has not yet established or demonstrated a strong commitment for a court and arbitration institution that is both capable and independent. Of course, clean, effective, and fair governance upon which the modern state draws its legitimacy cannot emerge in a short span by political will alone, and stalwart independent judges do not prevail in a climate of patronage and fear. The establishment of an effective and reliable arbitration and judicial system embedded in a constitutional multiparty state free of violence is now the step the elites must take to ensure the benefits of peace and security continue to develop and open Cambodia to its full potential.

In response to these external and internal forces, the RGC adapted its security and political institutions, and the result are hybrid forms of governance that combine modernist approaches with traditional patrimonial forms of rule to establish a degree of internal and external political legitimacy. Similarly, the French Protectorate also attempted to create legitimacy through effective governance and initially adapted customary practices of social control (see Hasselskog, 2009). New civilising missions and new protectorates (e.g. UNTAC, ECCC, international donors, nongovernmental organisations, and civil society generally) also seek to legitimate political and social change according to their normative values. But in both cases we find a plurality of actors and motives among the 'protectors' and the 'protected', which contribute to the hybrid forms of governance discussed below and in turn shape the underlying civilising processes that reveal objective changes in social and personality structures.

Cambodia and the future: prognostics from the perspective of civilising processes

The hybrid state

We have seen that the very rapid decline in lethal violence since the formation of the current Kingdom of Cambodia in 1993 is in great part associated with the state monopolisation of violence through the dominance of the CPP

---

[6] The ECCC tribunal deputy co-prosecutor saw the legacy of the court as confronting immunity and building the rule of law and also as deepening connections '... all the knowledge sharing that has passed on from the internationals that have worked on other courts to Cambodians, and those Cambodian professionals... will take those skills and apply them in the local courts to assist in increasing the quality of the trials' (quoted in the *PPP* see Cheang Sokha, 2013).

and its long-serving leader Hun Sen. It was in the new 'court' of Hun Sen, the ruling elite of former communists, survivors of the original warrior/military elite, that wealth accumulated and the benefits of peace and pacification first fell. But these elites were soon bound to the longer and more diverse chains of commercial and geopolitical interdependence and, pushed and pulled by these forces, began to succumb to the civilising influence of the formalities of the bureaucratic-like state. Postconflict Cambodia therefore emerged as a hybrid state, one that endorsed multiparty elections as a legitimatising process but that retained its autocratic and neopatrimonial patterns of power.

The most recent elections in 2013, however, signal that the exclusive power of the CPP is on the wane and that political uncertainty and instability (and with them the risk of violence) may come to characterise the next decade. The new generation aspires for changes that challenge the rule of an ageing and authoritarian prime minister, but in the absence of strong democratic institutions and an independent judiciary the transition from a private to a genuinely public monopolisation of the functions of the state may provoke further spikes in violence. Thus, as in the past, recurring conflicts may arise and manifest as problems of governmental legitimacy, inviting yet another round of elimination contests. However, this assumes that the vexed problem of leadership succession inherent in authoritarian states combined with an overreliance on centralised and coercive means of control is essentially destabilising of states that are unable to adopt the neoliberal governance 'toolkit' (Nathan, 2003). As we discuss below, the hybridisation process operates in a way that underpins 'authoritarian resilience' but may also lay the ground for further evolution of state institutions towards greater accountability and transparency.

Because of the gradual impact of the civilising process we experience as modernity, globalisation, and cosmopolitanism, elimination contests should be less deadly, embedded as they are in evolving political processes and conventions. These structural changes should be reinforced by the evolution of greater intolerance towards violence and higher thresholds of repugnancy in the affects of individuals (psychogenesis) and in turn bring further structural changes towards greater public rather than private distribution of resources (such as the demand for a clean and responsive state). More broadly, the ever-lengthening chains of interdependence associated with a heightened sensitivity to violence, greater civility (tolerance), and capacities for empathy combined with an open economy and trade offer the prospect for sustained reductions in the rate of violence.

During the last two decades, the benefits of pacification have flowed with the development of commerce, growing levels of interdependence and civility, and higher levels of education and increasing wealth, albeit the latter corralled by the ruling elites. The continuation of the RGC as a stable and consolidating force in the political reorganisation of Cambodia since 1993 has been paralleled by sustained economic growth, which has been a contributing factor in the rapid decline in both collective and acquisitive crimes, such as political violence and banditry. The familiar barometer of Cambodian pacification is the prevalence of predatory crimes such as robbery. The current level of 'banditry' in rural Cambodia is so diminished that, since the late 1990s, it has almost vanished – an achievement seldom even realised by the vigilant French. Despite these substantial declines in all forms of collective violence and the relative reduction in expressive violence in both city and country, we have seen since the late 1980s the reemergence and spread of grand fraud and corruption, reminiscent of the Sihanouk and Lon Nol regimes and resulting in a hybrid/oligarchic form of kleptocracy that combines the resilience of traditional and neopatrimonial systems with contemporary neoliberal institutions and ideology.

The general well-being of the population and economic prosperity are strongly linked to the emergence of either autocracies or democracies *that are capable of reliably solving conflicts and establishing legitimacy*. As we noted in the previous chapter, Cambodia's economy accelerated once pacification and stability in 1999 appeared to be sustainable and has grown rapidly over the last decade. Yet, the combination of low living standards and great inequality, along with the demand for democratic forms of governance that seek to make public the private monopolies of the ruling elites, pose great challenges to the continued development of Cambodia.

The RGC is a 'hybrid' state that combines authoritarianism and procedural democracy. It is built on tradition (embodied in the monarchy and the patrimonial system), democratic processes (UNTAC inserted multiparty elections), and modernist institutions, behaviours, and interrelationships. The state in this unplanned process of hybridisation 'emerges as a blend between politically authoritarian and democratic systems carrying hallmarks of both, but the full features of neither' (Ojendal & Ou, 2013, p. 6). The subsequent success of these imported electoral mechanisms in the further legitimation of the RGC and indirectly in the legitimation of the CPP's domination of the government is acknowledged. The latest national election results also help legitimate the role of the political process by reasserting the notion of a loyal opposition. This hybrid form of governance has not readily democratised beyond the plebiscite but has been relatively successful at postconflict reconstruction, and 'the general situation in the country is better and more politically stable ... the constitution is not under threat and no violent outbreaks can be predicted within the foreseeable future' (Ojendal & Lilja, 2009, p. 307).

The 2013 national elections are indicative of this trend as the general level of violence in both the lead-up and the contested aftermath of this election have been, so far, subdued. The gains of the Cambodian National Rescue Party (CNRP) have reversed the dominance of the CPP. However, given the new circumstances brought about by the civilising processes we have discussed in this book, the prospect of a return to full-scale political violence would require an 'immense social upheaval and urgency, heightened by carefully concerted propaganda, ... to reawaken and legitimize in large masses of people the socially outlawed instincts, the joy of killing and destruction that have been repressed from every day civilized life' (Elias, 1939/2012, p. 196). According to the tropes of Khmer culture, such an upheaval would be a return to the *prey* (the forest, the wild, the untamed or savage) and a rejection of the *srok*, signifier of the orderly civilised life of town and market. Nothing indicates that any group in Cambodia today is ready to chance another decivilising spurt. As Elias (1939/2012) observed, the place for the 'pleasures' of violence rapidly diminishes in the pacification process and is further inhibited by the integration and differentiation of function and diversity of population and beliefs:

> Cruelty and joy in the destruction and torment of others, like the proof of physical superiority, are placed under an increasingly strong social control anchored in the state organisation. All these forms of pleasure, limited by threats of displeasure, gradually come to express themselves only indirectly in a 'refined' form. And only at times of social upheaval or where social control is looser (e.g. in colonial regions) do they break out more directly, uninhibitedly, less impeded by shame and repugnance. (p. 187)

Lilja and Ojendal see hybridity as a mutual influencing process and not just democratic processes bolstering an autocratic state. Decentralisation at the commune level (local democracy) works to strengthen the autocracy of Hun Sen, but it also strengthens local grass-roots influence on a government dependent on electoral support. Hybrid governance allows neopatrimonial practices to operate through the formal democratic structure and to be used for elitist purposes such that the distinction between public and private is blurred. These ambiguities, dual roles, and complexities explain 'why advocates of the new order in Cambodia may interpret Cambodia as a successful case of intervention, change and transformation, while critics may equally describe Cambodia as a black hole of corruption and despotic power abuse' (Lilja & Ojendal, 2009, p. 300).

Postconflict reconstruction

As Ojendal and Lilja (2009) observed:

> Post conflict reconstruction deals with deep distrust of politics and leadership. Hence, conflict experienced in civil wars implies, by definition, that the ruler's moral right to rule is contested. The re-establishment of a legitimate political system that includes legitimate government and exercises legitimate governance from a position of strength may be the most central and pressing need in the context of post-conflict reconstruction. (p. 6)

In short, political 'reconstruction' is as pressing as economic reconstruction, and pacification provides the security, predictability, and certainty that encourage investments, which in turn provide the impetus for economic and social development. In the exercise of legitimate and effective governance, the RGC has yet to achieve consistent and certain regulatory regimes, and the probity of officials, including the judiciary, is notably unreliable. Cambodia has yet to implement international standards in the control of corruption and budget transparency (Peou, 2006).[7]

Ear (2009, p. 153) argued that Cambodia's former status as a pariah state and the desperate state of the economy through 1993–8 that required major donor help cemented RGC's dependence on aid. Donor contributions distorted economic recovery but enabled the RGC to transform the 'normalization of international relations and aid into external and internal legitimacy'. Such aid, he noted, draws off the best and brightest persons, who might normally serve the state, to more lucrative positions in the NGO and donor sector.[8] This is the equivalent of a foreign aid version of the 'Dutch disease' (i.e. oil wealth undermined other entrepreneurial activity, reducing economic diversity) captured by the sentiment 'they pretend to pay us and we pretend to work' (Ear, 2009, p. 155). 'First state capacity is weakened when the best and the brightest are neither entrepreneurs nor government policy wonks. Talent is siphoned from the private and public sectors to work for donor agencies, which pay salaries that can fetch more than US$2000 per month' (Ear, 2009, p. 174). Aid is fungible, and because in the Cambodian context it is used to reinforce large-scale patronage networks, it also allowed the state to delay pressing reforms, especially of the tax system. It further encouraged the building of patronage chains rather than broad popular support and undermined the values of the decentralisation scheme (Ear, 2009, p. 161). Ear (2009) notes the disruptive impact of uncoordinated donor efforts:

Aid has *de facto* allowed the RGC to *not* reform and to *not* improve tax revenue collection, but it has allowed the authorities to 'buy' through patronage the loyalty of middle level government civil servants, necessary but not sufficient for real internal legitimacy to be achieved. Aid alone cannot substitute for a true democratic process. (p. 175)

---

[7] Cambodia ranked 157th out of 176 countries surveyed in the 2012 Transparency International Corruption Perception Index (which 'reflects perceptions of the extent to which public power is exercised for private gain'). It has also been ranked poorly on the Open Budget Index (which assesses the availability of budget documents and the extent of effective independent oversight and public participation in national budget decision making; see www.transparency.org/country#KHM) and the World Bank's Doing Business indicators (see www.doingbusiness.org/data/exploreeconomies/cambodia/#). In 2007 Cambodia ascended to the United Nations Convention Against Corruption (UNCAC) and passed a weak anticorruption law in 2011, but little apparent progress has been made in curbing either petty or elite corruption.

[8] Ear provided a telling example by noting that in 2002 an estimated USD 50–70 million was paid to international consultants by foreign donors and NGOs operating various development projects, enough to pay 160,000 Cambodian civil servants for a year.

The overall development outcomes produced by this greater prosperity has had less impact in many social and human development indices than was hoped. Nor have improvements followed a linear trend – most of them have occurred in the last decade, from the early 2000s, rather than in the first decade of the new RGC. In short, the transition from pacification to a focus on economic development appears to have provided a civilising spurt in social development. However, there remains persistent underlying poverty and poor human capital, especially in rural areas, and high levels of inequality have been reported by the periodic household expenditure surveys. The furthering of inequalities (growing gap between rich and poor, rural and urban areas, and ongoing land issues and evictions), lingering reactive nationalism and xenophobia, and continuation of bad governance (clientelism and corruption) remain vectors for conflict and disorder.

Hill, Menon, and Sophal (2010; see also Hill & Menon, 2013) argued that to achieve responsible growth, institutions, however basic in their development, need to be 'effective, trusted and clean'. They pointed to the lack of confidence in the courts ('legal judgements are routinely for sale'), poor revenue protection, and the low salaries of officials (although some live lavishly). The advent of poorly supervised banks also raises the risks of a credit crisis, and the costs of doing business are uncompetitive compared to the region in general (due to widespread 'facilitation' costs). They argue that these economic problems, if not addressed, will risk undoing the gains through economic crisis and civil unrest driven by poor governance and corruption.

As our history of violence in Cambodia has shown, economic crisis and civil unrest driven by poor governance and corruption have been recurring factors in both mass and ordinary violence, but, as we have also seen in our analysis of the KR period, the *hemoclysms* required the addition of antagonistic geopolitical contexts. In the far more congenial contemporary geopolitical context, creating 'everyday peace' (pacification), adapting pragmatically to specific problems, and including the local may be 'good enough' for most Cambodians and allow the gradual processes of interdependence, reason, and empathy to continue to evolve and gently civilise the customary and emerging patterns of violence. Prognostics for such a 'gentle path' are supported by a more enduring sense of security, the influence of the human rights revolution, and significant socioeconomic development.

The majority of Cambodians now are younger than age 25 years, and their perceptions will increasingly bear on the kinds of governance that will be tolerated. Thus the old vanguard will retire and new institutional formations and forms of interdependence will emerge, perhaps more or less faithful to the ideals of the liberal state or at least to a constitutional 'rule of law' state. Other factors in the likely consolidation of the peace will be the continued growth of the economy (albeit as a dollar economy vulnerable to external shocks in world trade – as in the Asian financial crisis of 1997 and the global financial crisis of 2008) and the growing interconnectedness of a better-educated and increasingly cosmopolitan population.

Conclusion

As we noted in our general introduction, Elias's synthesis of the leading sociological theories of the first half of the twentieth century sought to outline a *theory of the development of humanity*. In short, he sought to outline fundamental laws about this development applicable to our entire species. However, his notion of civilising processes – even defanged of confused associations with Eurocentrism, material progress, and racism – has been criticised by some as unduly optimistic, tautological (or teleological), and essentialist (see, for example, Arquilla, 2009; Goldhagen, 2009; Malešević, 2013). Objections have ranged from a critique of Elias's depiction of medieval sensibilities (subject to intense emotional shifts and violent bloodletting)[9] to a rejection of the predictions that, contrary to the evidence of a warlike species (what we criminologists would call humanity's 'prior record or antecedents'), humans are evolving towards more cooperative and less violent modes of conduct. We will address some of them shortly, but above all, the (apparently) simple grand theoretical sweep of the civilising process offends some modern and particularly 'postmodern' sociological notions of development and ideas about the reach of theoretical speculations (Bauman, 1989, 1993; Hughes, 2012). In his 1968 postscript to the English edition of the *Civilizing Process*, Elias explained the problem in these terms:

The rejection of the nineteenth-century ideological understanding of these dynamic aspects of society that has taken place can therefore be seen not only as a criticism of these ideological aspects in the name of a scientific concern with fact, but above all criticism of earlier ideals that no longer correspond to present social conditions and experience and have therefore been rejected in the name of later ideals. The replacement of one ideology by another explains the fact that it is not simply the ideological elements in the nineteenth century sociological concept of development that have been called into question, but the concept of development itself, the very consideration of problems of long-term social development, of sociogenesis and psychogenesis. In a word the baby has been thrown out with the bath water. (Elias, 1939/2012, pp. 511–12)

Elias also suggested that his theory of the development of humanity 'could provide an integrating framework of reference for the various specialist social

---

[9] Tuchman, Foss, Rosenwein, and Cantor and other popular scholars of the Middle Ages noted a similar lack of self-restraint (or 'self-compulsion'; cf. van Krieken's [2005] preferred translation) among nobles, knights, and peasants. Contemporary historians such as Matthew Paris, the Benedictine monk and English chronicler, also provided similar examples; see Bartlett (2000), Whittock (2009), and, generally, Mennell and Goudsblom (1997).

sciences' (cf. Elias, *Reflections on a Life*, 1994, p. 131). We have integrated our criminological methods with that of process sociology and, focusing on the relation between the development of Cambodian society and trends in crime and violence since the mid nineteenth century, tested major premises of Elias's civilising process theory.

Our work has shown that long-term trends in the prevalence and patterns of crime and violence in Cambodia, like those observed in Europe by Gurr, Spierenburg, Eisner, and others, were associated with the modernising and civilising processes studied by Elias in the European context, and before him by the thinkers he had explicitly or implicitly integrated in his theoretical framework (Weber, Marx, Durkheim, Freud) and those after him who continued with the methods of process sociology (Shelley, Pinker). Three major interconnected processes – state formation and monopolisation of force, growing interdependency, and sensitisation to violence – and their degree of development accounted in both Europe and Cambodia for temporal variations in crime and violence. Like in Europe, in Cambodia these civilising processes were subject to counterspurts or decivilising events brought about by anomic and centrifugal forces. Cambodia offered an example of how the theory, in general, accounted for both the aperiodic surges of violence associated with decivilising processes and the decline in violence that followed pacification and state reformation. Although the Cambodian experience is not the same in its particulars as the West, its history of violence nevertheless follows modernising and civilising (including decivilising) processes and outcomes.

Is this sufficient enough or is it too early to suggest that Elias's civilising process theory and our own theoretical framework have universal purchase and constitute a theory of the development of humanity? To answer this question, it is critical to replicate the method of historical sociology in other non-Western societies. They may differ in the way the processes of change unfold, and explorations in other non-Western societies of the kind we undertook in Cambodia would be fruitful. Other important examples might be Buddhist societies such as Thailand and Japan, particularly because they escaped colonisation and display different trajectories in their rates of homicide.[10] At the moment we can only assert with some certainty that the Cambodian case offers an empirical test and shows results that conform to the expectations of the model proposed by Elias. However, because major processes in the theory, such as the growing division of labour (interdependency) and state formation and monopolisation of violence, have been widely observed almost everywhere, and because of

---

[10] Japan underwent industrialisation earlier than most Asian states and achieved low rates of homicide by the mid twentieth century, whereas Thailand recorded extremely high rates of homicide that also began to decline in the late twentieth century. A larger comparative study of non-Western states could include societies based on different religious traditions and colonial encounters.

contemporary global developments, we hypothesise that the model has universal purchase. If not, are there alternative testable theoretical frameworks to explain the long-term decline in violence?

Prophets of doomsday and the end of time have peddled dystopia for millennia and see no future for the human species. The choice of apocalyptic endings has been consistent for hundreds of generations – the Four Horsemen of the Apocalypse – gripped Western imaginations from the Book of Revelations onwards.[11] Notwithstanding the risk of astrophysical events beyond our control, we have the capacity through atomic warfare and human-made ecological disaster to eradicate our species (and many others with us). We recognise that, since 1945, this has been made possible with the invention, spread, and use of nuclear weapons. But the fear of mutually assured destruction (MAD, the collective 'murder-suicide') has injected fresh demands for foresight and restraint between nation states. Worldwide, a profoundly different collective consciousness (a psychogenesis towards species consciousness) is arising, spreading, and increasingly demanding global solutions to global problems and threats.

Linklater (2011, 2012) considers the potentially pacifying roles of nascent regional and global formations and processes (and eventually the emergence of more effective global forms of governance) that developed in response to the MAD threat. His argument is that the balance of terror performed by nuclear-capable states operated as the 'functional equivalent' of a monopoly of power because it placed major external restraints on strategic competition and demanded greater self-restraint and foresight in order to avoid nuclear war. In short, the pressure of necessity to which human beings have always been subjected, in this instance acted as a powerful spurt in the civilising process. What must be overcome, therefore, is the 'gulf between the social standards of self-restraint that generally apply to relations within the group and the more permissive attitudes to the use of force that pervade relations with external competitors and adversaries' (Linklater, 2012). But with the processes of globalisation, and particularly the deepening of interdependencies, this gap is narrowing, and in the international community and the civil society of many countries a cosmopolitan sentiment has been growing. The 'hegemonic wars' and 'hegemonic intoxication' that had dominated European international politics since classical antiquity appear to be drawing to an end (cf. Elias, 2009, cited in Linklater, 2012). As Linklater observes, Elias argued that one of the central questions in world politics is whether societies with different civilising processes and conceptions of appropriate levels of restraint in foreign affairs can undergo a collective learning process in which peoples become more attuned to one another over greater distances.

---

[11] See Pearson (2006) for a discussion of these persistent visions of mass destruction.

For Elias, relations between states, like relations between individuals, have been evolving towards a more cosmopolitan, universalistic, and species-wide outlook driven by globalisation. His earlier emphasis on interdependency also anticipated modern network and social capital theories of human interaction and dependency, and he conceived humans as undergoing fundamental change as socialisation adapts to the change wrought by these civilising processes:

> The image of the human being as a 'closed personality' is here replaced by the image of the human being as an 'open personality' who possesses a greater or lesser degree of relative (but never absolute and total) autonomy *vis-à-vis* other people and who is, in fact fundamentally oriented toward and dependent on other people throughout his life. The network of interdependencies among human beings is what binds them together. Such interdependencies are the nexus of what here is called the figuration, a structure of mutually oriented and dependent people. (Elias, 1939/2012, p. 525)

Pinker (2011) discussed this fundamental change in the personality structures of Western populations as the result of the unfolding impact of the Enlightenment and convergence among the 'common threads in the Pacification Process, the Civilizing Process, the Humanitarian Revolution, the Long Peace, the New Peace and the Rights Revolution. Each should represent a way in which predation, dominance, revenge, sadism or ideology has been overpowered by self-control, empathy, morality or reason' (p. 672). We can see how among the virtues of modernity in the digital age, the shift in the threshold of repugnancy has reduced our tolerance for violence, along with the expansion of 'gentle commerce', travel and mobility, literacy and general education. A universal empirical finding is that the females of our species contribute a small share of the overall burden of violence inflicted upon humanity. It is not surprising that in its various forms feminisation has increased our repugnance for violence and that 'direct political empowerment, the deflation of manly honour, the promotion of marriage on women's terms, the right of girls to be born, and women's control over their own reproduction – have been forces in the decline in violence' (Pinker, 2011, p. 688).

Discussing questions of determinism, free will, human aggression, and violence but also imagination and creativity, Laborit (1983) remarked that discovering the laws of gravity did not free us from gravity but gave us the opportunity to use these laws to our advantage (e.g. in aeronautics). In this book we have tried to distinguish between value judgements and statements of facts, not to belittle the importance of normative judgements, on the contrary, but to signal the need for logical consistency if we want these normative judgements to lead to our desired goals, that is, to what, as a species, we would deem to be to our advantage. We think that, like us, most human beings make the assumption (i.e. normative judgement) that peace, pleasure, happiness, and the survival of our species are good and war, suffering, despair, and extinction are bad. In the same vein, discovering the laws of the development of humanity will probably not free us from these laws but give us the opportunity to use them to our advantage. Given that humanity had not yet reached a state when it was free from the threat of wars and other forms of violence, Elias ended his book *The Civilizing Process* by quoting Holbach: *'la civilisation... n'est pas encore terminée'* (Elias, 1939/2012, p. 490).

The particular salience of the civilising and decivilising processes in any given society offers a diagnosis for understanding the kinds of interventions that will aid pacification and enable those processes to transform individuals and their societies. Our quest for survival therefore entails the strengthening of pacification and other civilising processes, such that the emergence of world governance, centralised in some respects and decentralised in others, could be a plausible end point.

Appendix: Historical data

This section provides the archival reference of the various primary historical documents consulted for this work, by location. The codes GGI and RSC indicate the number of the box where the documents are kept at the *Archives Nationales d'Outre-Mer*.

BIBLIOTHÈQUE NATIONALE DE FRANCE (BNF), PARIS

Bulletins de Police Criminelle, 1936–40 : cote 4-JO-774

ARCHIVES NATIONALES D'OUTRE-MER (ANOM), AIX EN PROVENCE

GGI 10202	organisation de la justice au Cambodge
GGI 17198	organisation de la police judiciaire and administrative, 1911
GGI 64262	rapports politiques trimestriels, 1916
GGI 64264	rapports politiques trimestriels, 1920
GGI 64265	rapports politiques trimestriels, 1921
GGI 64280	rapports politiques mensuels, 1936–7
GGI 64281	rapports politiques mensuels, 1936–7
GGI 64394	statistiques des affaires des tribunaux, 1890
GGI 65448	notes mensuelles sur les évènements politiques et l'activité révolutionnaire, 1936
GGI 65449	notes mensuelles sur les évènements politiques et l'activité révolutionnaire, 1937
	rapport annuel du Service de la Sûreté, 1937
	rapport mensuel, Septembre 1937
GGI 65789	juridiction française et cambodgienne: conflit, 1935
GGI 65840	tribunaux résidentiels, 1927–39
GGI 65841	tribunaux résidentiels Kampong Cham, 1939
GGI 65850	juridiction indigène, 1938
GGI 65855	commissions criminelles, 1929–38
GGI 65902	fonctionnement de la gendarmerie, 1934
RSC 209	résidence de Battambang, rapports politiques, 1918–19
RSC 218	rapport police/ Sûreté, 1929–30
RSC 230	Garde indochinoise, 1944–5
RSC 237	rapports politiques, 1911–12

	extraits des rapports politiques destinés au Deuxième Bureau, Kratie, 1911
	extraits des rapports de province, Kampot, 1911
	extraits des rapports de province, Prey Veng, 1911
	rapport politique et économique du territoire de Battambang, 1912
RSC 239	justice, 1895–1907
RSC 242	rapports mensuels de la résidence de Kampong Cham, 1932–40
RSC 243	rapports politiques, 1905
	crimes et délits, Kampot, Kampong Thom, Kampong Speu, 1905
RSC 257	rapport politiques, 1897–1906
RSC 263	rapports mensuels, 1905–9
	rapport annuel, 1909
	extraits des rapports des résidents, April 1909
	rapports annuels, 1940–1
RSC 266	rapports mensuels de la résidence de Kampot, 1935–40
RSC 270	rapports mensuels de la résidence de Kampong Chhnang, 1934–9
RSC 289	rapports politiques des provinces, 1942
RSC 321	prisons, 1924–34
RSC 329	rapports mensuels de la résidence de Kampong Speu, 1934–40
RSC 336	rapports d'inspection des provinces
	rapports d'inspections des prisons
RSC 338	rapports d'inspection de la résidence de Kampong Thom, 1932–7
RSC343	rapport d'inspection, juin 1939
	rapports d'inspection de la résidence de Kampong Chnnang, 1932–9
RSC 346	rapports d'inspection de la résidence de Siem Reap, 1932–7
RSC 347	rapports d'inspection de la résidence de Kompong Thom, 1942–4
RSC 350	rapport d'inspection, mars 1940
	rapports d'inspection de la résidence de Kampong Speu, 1940–4
RSC 352	rapports d'inspection de la résidence de Kampong Chnnang, 1942–4
RSC 354	rapports d'inspection de la résidence de Siem Reap, 1942–3
RSC 409	rapports mensuels du gouverneur de Siem Reap, 1936–9
	rapports d'inspection de la résidence de Siem Reap, 1934–40
RSC 421	rapports politiques, 1933–4
RSC 422	rapport annuel, résidence de Stung Treng, 1934–5
RSC 427	rapports politiques, 1933–4
RSC 430	rapports politiques, 1913–16
RSC 431	rapports politiques, 1917–20
RSC 460	lutte contre la piraterie, 1933
RSC 468	prisons, 1933
RSC 475	rapports politiques, 1921–5
	minutes des rapports trimestriels, 1920–5
	inspections des forces de police
RSC 647	extraits des rapports annuels au Résident Supérieur
RSC 674	rapport annuel de la résidence de Kampong Cham, 1942–3
RSC 675	rapports annuels sur l'exercice du protectorat, 1942–3
RSC 676	rapports annuels des résidences de Kampot, Kampong Chnnang, Kampong Cham, et Kampong Speu

338　Appendix

RSC 688	Garde Indigène
RSC 691	rapports politiques, 1910
	rapport provincial pour le Deuxième Bureau, 1910
RSC 692	rapports annuels des résidences provinciales au Résident Supérieur, 1939–40
RSC 926	correspondance du tribunal de Kampong Thom, 1918
RSC 927	correspondance du tribunal de Kampong Thom, 1920–3

BIBLIOTHÈQUE DES ARCHIVES D'OUTRE-MER (BIB AOM), AIX EN PROVENCE

BIB AOM A/1017 Annuaire Statistique de l'Indochine, 1913–48
BIB AOM A/1048 Annuaire Statistique de l'Indochine, 1937–57

NATIONAL ARCHIVES OF CAMBODIA (NAC), PHNOM PENH

Rapports du Ministère de la Justice, 1927–34 and 1936–42
Bulletins de Police Criminelle, 1947–55

NATIONAL LIBRARY OF CAMBODIA (NLC), PHNOM PENH

Rapports de mortalité dans les hôpitaux, 1958–65
Cahiers du Sangkum, janvier–avril 1959
Cahiers du Sangkum, janvier–février 1961
Cahiers du Sangkum, avril 1961
Cahiers du Sangkum, mai 1962–avril 1963

References

Abuza, Z. (1993). The Khmer Rouge quest for economic independence. *Asian Survey*, *33*(10), 1010–21.
Adams, B. (2001, November 23). Demobilizations' house of mirrors. *Phnom Penh Post*. Retrieved from www.phnompenhpost.com/national/demobilizations-house-mirrors
Adams, B. (2007, July 28). Cambodia: July 1997: Shock and aftermath. *Phnom Penh Post*. Retrieved from www.phnompenhpost.com/national/july-1997-shock-and-aftermath
Akers, R. L. (2009). *Social learning and social structure: A general theory of crime and deviance*. New Brunswick, NJ: Transaction Publishers.
Albritton, R. B. (2004). Cambodia in 2003: On the road to democratic consolidation. *Asian Survey*, *44*(1), 102–9.
Aldrich, R. (1996). *A history of French overseas expansion*. Basingstoke, England: Macmillan.
Archer, D., & Gartner, R. (1976). Violent acts and violent times: A comparative approach to post-war homicide rates. *American Sociological Review*, *41*, 937–63.
Arquilla, J. (2009). Realities of war: Global development, growing destructiveness and the coming of a new Dark Age? *Third World Quarterly*, *30*(1), 69–80.
Athens, L. (1992). *The creation of dangerous violent criminals*. Champaign: University of Illinois Press.
AusAID. (2001). *Cambodian criminal justice assistance project: Feasibility study phase II* (Unpublished report). AusAID, Canberra, Australia.
Australian Institute of Criminology. (2012). *Australian crime: Facts and figures 2011*. Canberra, Australia: Author.
Avineri, S. (1968). *Karl Marx on colonialism and modernization: His dispatches and other wrtings on China, India, Mexico, the Middle East, and North Africa*. New York, NY: Doubleday.
Bandura, A. (1999). Moral disengagement in the perpetration of inhumanities. *Personality and Social Psychology Review*, 3193–209.
Barnes, B. (2001). The macro/micro problem and the problem of structure and agency. In G. Ritzer & B. Smart (Eds.), *Handbook of social theory* (pp. 339–52). London, United Kingdom: Sage.
Bartlett, R. (2000). *England under the Norman and Angevin kings 1075–1225*. Oxford, England: Oxford University Press.
Batz, Lt. (1931). Historique de l'occupation militaire du Cambodge par les troupes françaises de 1855–1910. *Bulletin de la Societe des Etudes Indochinoises de Saigon*, 3–4.

Bauman, Z. (1989). *Modernity and the Holocaust.* Ithaca, NY: Cornell University Press.
Bauman, Z. (1993). *Postmodern ethics.* Oxford, England: Blackwell.
Baumeister, R. F. (1997). *Evil: Inside human violence and cruelty.* New York, NY: Holt.
Bauzon, L. (1991). *A comparative study of peasant unrest in Southeast Asia.* Singapore: Southeast Asian Studies Program, Institute of Southeast Asian Studies.
Beang, P., & Cougill, W. (2006). *Vanished stories from Cambodia's new people under Democratic Kampuchea.* Phnom Penh: Documentation Center of Cambodia.
Beaudonnet, L. (1998). La Gendarmerie d'Indochine: de l'ère des amiraux au coup de force japonais. *Revue Historique des Armées, 4,* 26–40.
Becker, E. (1984). Kampuchea in 1983: Further from peace. *Asian Survey, 24,* 37–48.
Becker, E. (1986). *When the war was over: Cambodia and the Khmer Rouge revolution.* New York, NY: Simon and Schuster.
Becker, H. (1963). *Outsiders: Studies in the sociology of deviance.* New York, NY: Free Press.
Bekaert, J. (1997). *Cambodian diary: Tales of a divided nation 1983–1986* (vol. 1). Bangkok, Thailand: White Lotus Press.
Bérard, D. (1989). *Des Français au Cambodge: Anthologie.* Phnom Penh, Cambodia: Espace Bayon.
Beresford, B. (2005). Redistributing profit and loss: The new economics of the market and social welfare. *Critical Social Policy, 25*(4), 464–82.
Bizot, F. (2004). *The gate.* London, England: Vintage. (Original work published 2000)
Black, D. (1976). *The behavior of law.* New York, NY: Academic Press.
Black, D. (1983). Crime as social control. *American Sociological Review, 48,* 34–45.
Black, D. (1993). La Mobilisation du Droit: Autobiographie d'un Concept (The mobilization of law: Autobiography of a concept). In A.-J. Arnaud (Dir.), *Dictionnaire Encyclopédique de Théorie et de Sociologie de Droit* (pp. 376–78). Paris, France: Librairie, Générale de Droit et de Jurisprudence.
Blaney D. L., & Inayatullah, N. (2010). *Savage economics: Wealth, poverty and the temporal walls of capitalism.* London, England: Routledge.
Bollen, K. A. (1983). World system position, dependency and political democracy. *American Sociological Review, 48,* 468–79.
Boreham, K., & Hobbs, H. (2011, December 22). Justice denied for Cambodia. *East Asia Forum.* Retrieved from www.eastasiaforum.org/2011/12/22/justice-denied-for-cambodia/
Boua, C. (1983). Observation of the Heng Samrin government, 1980–1982. In D. Chandler & B. Kiernan (Eds.), *Revolution and its aftermath in Kampuchea: Eight essays* (pp. 259–71). New Haven, CT: Yale University Press.
Boua, C. (1994, September 9). Tide must be turned on oldest profession. *Phnom Penh Post.* Retrieved from www.phnompenhpost.com/national/tide-must-be-turned-oldest-profession
Braithwaite, J. (1989). *Crime, shame, and reintegration.* Cambridge, England: Cambridge University Press.
Braithwaite, J. (1991). Poverty, power, white collar crime and the paradoxes of criminological theory. *Australian and New Zealand Journal of Criminology, 24,* 40–56.
Braithwaite, J., Braithwaite, V., Cookson, M., & Dunn, L. (2010). *Anomie and violence.* Canberra, Australia: ANU E-Press.
Braithwaite, J., & Pettit, P. (1990). *Not just deserts: A republican theory of criminal justice.* Oxford, England: Clarendon Press.

Brinkley, J. (2009, March/April). Cambodia's curse: Struggling to shed the Khmer Rouge's legacy. *Foreign Affairs*, 88111–122. Retrieved from www.foreignaffairs.com/articles/64833/joel-brinkley/cambodias-curse

Brinkley, J. (2011). *Cambodia's curse: The modern history of a troubled land.* Collingwood, Victoria, Australia: Black Inc.

Broadhurst, R. (2002). Lethal violence, crime and state formation in Cambodia. *Australian and New Zealand Journal of Criminology, 35*(1), 1–26.

Broadhurst, R. (2006). Lethal violence, crime, and political change in Cambodia. In A. Croissant, B. Martin, & S. Kneip (Eds.), *The politics of death: Political violence in Southeast Asia* (pp. 343–78). Muenster, Germany: Lit Verlag.

Broadhurst, R., & Bouhours, T. (2009). Policing in Cambodia: Legitimacy in the making? *Policing and Society, 19*, 174–90.

Broadhurst, R., & Keo, C. (2011). Cambodia: A criminal justice system in transition. In C. Smith, S. Zhang, & R. Barbaret (Eds.), *International handbook of criminology* (pp. 338–48). New York, NY: Routledge.

Broadhurst, R., Keo, C., & Bouhours, T. (2013). Cambodia: Criminal justice in a post-conflict society. In B. Hebenton, S.Y. Shou, & J. Liu (Eds.), *Asian handbook of criminology* (pp. 167–82). New York, NY: Springer.

Brocheux, P., & Hémery, D. (1995). *Indochine: La colonisation ambiguë (1858–1954).* Paris, France: La Découverte.

Brown, F. Z. (1992). Cambodia in 1991: An uncertain peace. *Asian Survey, 32*(1), 88–96.

Burger, J. M. (2009). Replicating Milgram: Would people still obey today? *American Psychologist, 64*, 1–11.

Cambodian Acid Survivors Charity. (2010). *Breaking the silence: Addressing acid attacks in Cambodia.* Phnom Penh, Cambodia: Author.

Cambodian League for the Promotion and Defense of Human Rights. (2009). *Prison conditions in Cambodia 2008: Women in prison.* Phnom Penh, Cambodia: Author.

Cambodian Mine Action Centre. (2010). *Ten years achievement and perspective.* Phnom Penh, Cambodia: Author.

Cardozo, B. L., Blanton, C., Zalewski, T., Tor, S., McDonald, L., Lavelle, J., . . . Mollica, R. (2012). Mental health survey among landmine survivors in Siem Reap province, Cambodia. *Medicine, Conflict and Survival, 28*, 161–81.

Carney, T. (1989). Organization of power. In K. D. Jackson (Ed.), *Cambodia 1975–1978: Rendezvous with death.* Princeton, NJ: Princeton University Press.

Chanda, N. (1986). *Brother enemy: The war after the war.* San Diego, CA: Harcourt.

Chanda, N. (1987). Cambodia in 1986: Beginning to tire. *Asian Survey, 27*(1), 115–24.

Chanda, N. (1988). Cambodia in 1987: Sihanouk on center stage. *Asian Survey, 28*, 105–15.

Chandler, D. P. (1974). *Cambodia before the French: Politics in a tributary kingdom, 1794–1848* (PhD dissertation). University of Michigan, Ann Harbor.

Chandler, D. P. (1975). An anti-Vietnamese rebellion in early nineteenth century Cambodia: Pre-colonial imperialism and a pre-nationalist response. *Journal of Southeast Asian Studies, 6*, 16–24.

Chandler, D. P. (1991). *The tragedy of Cambodian history.* New Haven, CT: Yale University Press.

Chandler, D. P. (1992). *Brother Number One.* Melbourne, Australia: Westview Press.

Chandler, D. P. (1999). *Voices from S-21: Terror and history in Pol Pot's secret prison*. Berkeley: University of California Press.
Chandler, D. P. (2008). *A history of Cambodia* (4th ed.). Boulder, CO: Westview Press.
Chandler, D. P. (2010). Cambodia in 2009: Plus c'est la même chose. *Asian Survey, 50*, 228–34.
Christie, N. (1977). Conflicts as property. *British Journal of Criminology, 17*, 1–15.
Ciorciari, J., & Chhang, Y. (2005). Documenting the crimes of Democratic Kampuchea. In J. Ramji & B. Van Schaak (Eds.), *Bringing the Khmer Rouge to justice: Prosecuting mass violence before the Cambodian courts* (pp. 226–7). London, England: Mellin Press.
Coates, K. J. (2005). *Cambodia now: Life in the wake of war*. Jefferson, NC: McFarland.
Cohen, S. (1993). Human rights and crimes of the state: The culture of denial. *Australian and New Zealand Journal of Criminology, 26*(2), 97–115.
Cole, J. H., & Gramajo, A. M. (2009). Homicide rates in a cross-section of countries: Evidence and interpretations. *Population and Development Review, 35*, 749–76.
Collard, P. (1925). *Cambodge et Cambodgiens: Métamorphose du royaume Khmer par une méthode française de protectorat*. Paris, France: Ams Pr. (Reprinted Cederock Phnom Penh 2001)
Cooney, M. (1997). From war to tyranny: Lethal conflict and the state. *American Sociological Review, 62*(2), 316–38.
Cooney, M. (2003). The privatization of violence. *Criminology, 41*, 1377–406.
Currie, E. (1991). Crime in the market society: From bad to worse in the nineties. *Dissent, 38*, 254–9.
Danish Centre for Human Rights. (2001). *The police in Cambodia: Project assessment report – Cambodia*. Copenhagen: Author.
Daufès, E. (1933). *La Garde Indigène de l'Indochine, de sa création à nos jours*. Avignon, France: imprimerie Seguin.
de Beer, D. (2005). *Workshop on the promotion of the United Nations study on nonproliferation and disarmament education*. Disarmament Education in the SALW Programme of EU ASAC. Bali, Indonesia, 21–22 December 2005. Retrieved from www.eu-asac.org/media_library/reports/051222.pdf
Debré, F. (1976). *Cambodge: La révolution de la forêt*. Paris, France: Flammarion.
de Jong, J. T. V. M., Komproe, I. H., Van Ommeren, M., El Masri, M., Araya, M., Khaled, N., . . . Somasundaram, D. (2001). Lifetime events and posttraumatic stress disorder in 4 post-conflict settings. *Journal of the American Medical Association, 286*, 555–62.
Delvert, J. (1961). *Le paysan Cambodgien [The Cambodian peasant]*. Paris, France: Mouton & Co.
de Swaan, A. (2001). Dyscivilization, mass extermination and the state. *Theory, Culture and Society, 18*, 265–76.
Doyle, S. E. (2012, October). City of water: Architecture, urbanism and the floods of Phnom Penh. *Nakhara Journal of Environmental Design and Planning*. Retrieved from www.academia.edu/2502352/City_of_Water_Architecture_Urbanism_and_the_Floods_of_Phnom_Penh
Dubois, V., Tonglet, R., Hoyois, P., Sunbaunat, K., Roussaux, J.-P., & Hauff, E. (2004). Household survey of psychiatric morbidity in Cambodia. *International Journal of Social Psychiatry, 50*(2), 174–85.

Dumont, H. (2006). Le crime de génocide: Construction d'un paradigme pour la criminologie, la philosophie et le droit pénal. *Criminologie, 39*(2), 3–22.
Dunlop, N. (2005). *The last executioner.* New York, NY: Walker.
Durkheim, E. (1950). *The rules of sociological method.* Glencoe, IL: Free Press.
Durkheim, E. (1964). *The division of labor in society.* New York, NY: Free Press. (Original work published 1893)
Dy, K. (2007). *A history of Democratic Kampuchea.* Phnom Penh: Documentation Center of Cambodia.
Ear, S. (2009). The political economy of aid and regime legitimacy in Cambodia. In O. Joakim & M. Lilja (Eds.), *Beyond democracy in Cambodia: Political reconstruction in a post-conflict society* (pp. 151–88). Copenhagen: Nordic Institute of Asian Studies.
Easterly, W., Gatti, R., & Kurlat, S. (2006). Development, democracy, and mass killings. *Journal of Economic Growth, 11,* 129–56.
Ebihara, M. (2002). Memories of the Pol Pot era in a Cambodian village. In J. Ledgerwoord (Ed.), *Cambodia emerges from the past: Eight essays* (pp. 91–108). DeKalb: Northern Illinois University Southeast Asia Publications.
Eckberg, D. L. (1995). Estimates of early twentieth-century U.S. homicide rates: An econometric forecasting approach. *Demography, 32,* 1–16.
Edwards, P. (2007). *Cambodge: The cultivation of a nation, 1860–1945.* Honolulu: University of Hawaii Press.
Eiland, M. (1985). Kampuchea in 1984: Yet further from peace. *Asian Survey, 25,* 106–13.
Eisner, M. (2001). Modernization, self-control and lethal violence: The long-term dynamics of European homicide rates in theoretical perspective. *British Journal of Criminology, 41,* 618–38.
Eisner, M. (2003). Long-term historical trends in violent crime. *Crime and Justice: A Review of Research, 30,* 83–142.
Eisner, M. (2008). Modernity strikes back? A historical perspective on the latest increase in inter-personal violence (1960–1990). *International Journal of Conflict and Violence, 2*(2), 288–316.
Elias, N. (1994). *The civilizing process.* Oxford, England: Blackwell. (Original work published 1939)
Elias, N. (1994). *Reflections on a life.* Cambridge, England: Polity Press.
Elias, N. (2012). *On the process of civilisation* (E. Jephcott, Trans.; S. Mennell, E. Dunning, J. Goudsblom, & R. Kilminster, Eds.). Dublin, Ireland: UCD Press. (Original work published 1939)
Ennis, T. E. (1936). *French policy and development in Indo-China.* Chicago, IL: University of Chicago Press.
Erikson, K. (1966). *Wayward Puritans.* New York, NY: Wiley.
Etcheson, C. (1984). *The rise and demise of Democratic Kampuchea,* Boulder, CO: Westview.
European Union's Assistance on Curbing Small Arms and Light Weapons in the Kingdom of Cambodia. (2003). *Final report on weapons in exchange for development project in 4 districts in Preah Vihear province.* Phnom Penh: Author. Retrieved from eu-asac.org/programme/weapons_collection.php
Fein, H. (1993). Revolutionary and anti-revolutionary genocides: A comparison of state murders in Democratic Kampuchea, 1975 to 1979, and in Indonesia, 1965 to 1966. *Comparative Studies in Society and History, 35*(4), 796–823.

Fein, H. (2000). Civil wars and genocide: Paths and circles. *Human Rights Review, 1*, 49–61.

Felices-Luna, M. (2012). Introduction à l'issue spéciale sur la violence politique et les conflits armés. *Criminologie, 45*(1), 5–9.

Fletcher, J. (1997). *Violence and civilization: An introduction to the work of Norbert Elias*. Cambridge, England: Polity.

Forest, A. (1980). *Le Cambodge et la colonisation française: Histoire d'une colonisation sans heurts (1897–1920)*. Paris, France: Éditions L'Harmattan.

Foucault, M. (1977). *Discipline and punish*. Harmondsworth, United Kingdom: Penguin Harmondsworth.

Frieson, K. (1992). *The impact of revolution on Cambodian peasants: 1970–1975* (PhD dissertation). Monash University, Ann Arbor, MI. UMI Dissertation Services.

Frieson, K. (2011). No longer a 'happy balance': The decline of female status in Khmer village culture. In J. Marston (Ed.), *Anthropology and community in Cambodia: Reflections on the work of May Ebihara* (pp. 171–88). Melbourne, Australia: Monash Asia Institute.

Frings, V. (1994). Cambodia after decollectivization (1989–1992). *Journal of Contemporary Asia, 24*(1), 49–66.

Frings, V. (1997). Rewriting Cambodian history to 'adapt' it to a new political context: The Kampuchean People's Revolutionary Party's historiography (1979–1991). *Modern Asian Studies, 31*, 807–46.

Fuller, T. (1999, June 7). Fraud alleged at mine-clearance center. *New York Times*. Retrieved from www.nytimes.com/1999/06/07/news/07iht-cambo.2.t.html

Fulu, E., Warner, X., Miedema, S., Jewkes, R., Roselli, T., & Lang, J. (2013). *Why do some men use violence against women and how can we prevent it? Quantitative findings from the United Nations Multi-country Study on Men and Violence in Asia and the Pacific*. Bangkok, Thailand: UNDP, UNFPA, UN Women, and UNV.

Gambetta, D. (1996). *The Sicilian Mafia: The business of private protection*. Cambridge, MA: Harvard University Press.

Garland, D. (1990). *Punishment and modern society: A study in social theory*. Chicago, IL: University of Chicago Press.

Gatrell, V. A. C. (1990). Crime, authority and the policeman-state. In F. M. L. Thompson (Ed.), *The Cambridge social history of Britain 1750–1950* (pp. 243–310). Cambridge, England: Cambridge University Press.

Gender and Development for Cambodia. (2003). *Paupers and princelings: Youth attitudes toward gangs, violence, rape, drugs and theft*. Phnom Penh: Author.

Gerlach, C. (2006). Extremely violent societies: An alternative to the concept of genocide. *Journal of Genocide Research, 8*(4), 455–71.

Gilboa, A. (1998). *Off the rails in Phnom Penh: Into the dark heart of guns, girls, and ganja*. Bangkok, Thailand: Asia Books.

Goldhagen, D. J. (2009). *Worse than war: Genocide, eliminationism and the ongoing assault on humanity*. New York, NY: Public Affairs.

Gordon, B. K. (1965). Cambodia: Where foreign policy counts. *Asian Survey, 5*(9), 433–48.

Gordon, B. K., & Young, K. (1970). Cambodia: Following the leader. *Asian Survey, 10*(2), 169–76.

Gordon, B. K., & Young, K. (1971). The Khmer Republic: That was the Cambodia that was. *Asian Survey, 11*, 26–40.

Gottesman, E. (2003). *Cambodia after the Khmer Rouge: Inside the politics of nation building*. New Haven, CT: Yale University Press.

Goudsblom, J. (1992). *Fire and civilization*. London, England: Allen Lane/Penguin.

Goudsblom, J. (1994, April 7–8). *The theory of the civilizing process and its discontents*. Paper voor de Sectie Figuratiesociologie van de Zesde Sociaal-Wetenschappelijke Studiedagen Amsterdam.

Grabosky, P. N. (1974). Patterns of criminality in New South Wales, 1788–1973. *Australian and New Zealand Journal of Criminology, 7*, 215–29.

Greenberg, D. F. (2003). Long-term trends in crimes of violence (comment on Cooney, 2003). *Criminology, 44*, 1407–18.

Guérin, M. (2008). *Paysans de la forêt à l'époque coloniale: La pacification des aborigènes des hautes terres du Cambodge (1863–1940)*. In *Bibliothèque d'Histoire Rurale, Vol. 10*. Caen, France: Association d'Histoire des Sociétés Rurales/ Presses Universitaires de Rennes.

Guérin, M. (2012). Khmer peasants and land access in Kompong Thom Province in the 1930s. *Journal of Southeast Asian Studies, 43*, 441–62.

Gurr, T. R. (1981). Historical trends in violent crime: A critical review of the evidence. *Crime and Justice, 3*, 295–353.

Hagan, J., & Pederson, R. D. (Eds.). (1995). *Crime and inequality*. Stanford, CA: Stanford University Press.

Hagan, J., & Rymond-Richmond, W. (2009). *Darfur and the crime of genocide*. New York, NY: Cambridge University Press.

Hagan, J., Rymond-Richmond, W., & Parker, P. (2005). The criminology of genocide: The death and rape of Darfur. *Criminology, 43*, 525–61.

Haney, C., Banks, W. C., & Zimbardo, P. G. (1973). Study of prisoners and guards in a simulated prison. *Naval Research Reviews, 9*, 1–17.

Hansen, A. (2008). Gaps in the world: Violence, harm and suffering in Khmer ethical narratives. In A. R. Hansen & J. Ledgerwood (Eds.), *At the edge of the forest: Essays on Cambodia, history and narrative in honor of David Chandler*. Ithaca, NY: Cornell University Southeast Asia Program Press.

Hasselskog, M. (2009). (Re)creating local political legitimacy through governance intervention? In O. Joakim & M. Lilja (Eds.), *Beyond democracy in Cambodia: Political reconstruction in a post-conflict society* (pp. 189–223). Copenhagen, Denmark: Nordic Institute of Asian Studies.

Heder, S. R. (1980). *Kampuchean occupation and resistance* (Asian Studies Monographs No. 027). Bangkok, Thailand: Institute of Asian Studies, Chulalongkorn University.

Heder, S. R., & Ledgerwood, J. (Eds.). (1996). *Propaganda, politics and violence in Cambodia*. Armonk, NY: M.E. Sharpe.

Heming, J. (1970). *The conquest of the Incas*. New York, NY: Harcourt, Brace and Jovanovich.

Hill, H., & Menon, J. (2013). Cambodia: Rapid growth with weak institutions. *Asian Economic Policy Review, 8*, 46–65.

Hill, H., Menon, J., & Sophal, C. (2010, July 31). Globalisation with weak institutions: Cambodia. *East Asia Forum*. Retrieved from www.eastasiaforum.org/2010/07/31/globalisation-with-weak-institutions-cambodia/

Him, C. (2000). *Growing up under the Khmer Rouge*. New York, NY: W. W. Norton.

Hinton, A. L. (1998). Why did you kill?: The Cambodian genocide and the dark side of face and honor. *Journal of Asian Studies, 57*, 93–122.

Hinton, A. L. (2002). The dark side of modernity: Toward an anthropology of genocide. In A. L. Hinton (Ed.), *Annihilating difference: The anthropology of genocide* (pp. 1–33). Berkeley: University of California Press.
Hinton, A. L. (2005). *Why did they kill? Cambodia in the shadow of genocide.* Berkeley: University of California Press.
Hinton, A. L. (2012). Critical genocide studies. *Genocide and Prevention, 7,* 4–15.
Hinton, D. E., Hinton, A. L., Pich, V., Loeum, J. R., & Pollack, M. H. (2009). Nightmares among Cambodian refugees: The breaching of concentric ontological security. *Culture, Medicine and Psychiatry, 33*(2), 219–65.
Hobsbawm, E. (1959). *Primitive rebels: Studies in archaic forms of social movement in the 19th and 20th centuries.* Manchester, England: Manchester University Press.
Hobsbawm, E. (1969). *Bandits.* London, England: Weidenfeld and Nicolson.
Hughes, C. (2003a, Summer). Phnom Penh: Beautification and corruption. *IIAS Newsletter, 31.* Retrieved from www.iias.nl/iiasn/31/index.html
Hughes, C. (2003b). *The political economy of Cambodia's transition. 1991–2000.* London, England: Routledge.
Hughes, C. (2006). The politics of gifts: Tradition and regimentation in contemporary Cambodia. *Journal of Southeast Asian Studies, 37,* 469–89.
Hughes, C. (2009). Reconstructing legitimate political authority through elections? In O. Joakim & M. Lilja (Eds.), *Beyond democracy in Cambodia: Political reconstruction in a post-conflict society* (pp. 31–69). Copenhagen, Denmark: Nordic Institute of Asian Studies.
Hughes, J. (2012). Norbert Elias and the habits of good sociology. *Human Figurations, 2,* 1. Retrieved from http://hdl.handle.net/2027/spo.11217607.0002.107
Indochina Research Limited. (2005). *Violence against women: A baseline survey, final report.* Phnom Penh, Cambodia: Author.
Indochina Research Limited. (2009). *Violence against women: 2009 follow up survey.* Phnom Penh, Cambodia: Author.
International Monetary Fund. (2013). *World economic outlook: Hopes, realities, risk.* Washington, DC: Author.
Jackson, K. D. (1989). Intellectual origins of the Khmer Rouge. In K. D. Jackson (Ed.), *Cambodia 1975–1978: Rendezvous with death.* Princeton, NJ: Princeton University Press.
Jennar, R. M. (1995). *Les clés du Cambodge.* Paris, France: Maisonneuve et Larose.
Jennar, R. M. (2010). *Trente ans depuis Pol Pot: Le Cambodge de 1979 à 2009.* Paris, France: L'Harmattan.
Johnson, D. T., & Zimring, F. E. (2009). *The next frontier: National development, political change, and the death penalty in Asia.* New York, NY: Oxford University Press.
Johnson, E. A., & Monkkonen, E. H. (Eds.). (1996). *The civilization of crime: Violence in town and country since the Middle Ages.* Chicago: University of Illinois Press.
Johnson, H., Ollus, N., & Nevala, S. (2008). *Violence against women: An international perspective.* New York, NY: Springer.
Jordens, J. (1996). Persecution of Cambodia's ethnic Vietnamese communities during and since the UNTAC period. In S. R. Heder & J. Ledgerwood (Eds.), *Propaganda, politics, and violence in Cambodia: Democratic transition under United Nations peace-keeping* (pp. 134–58). Armonk, NY: M. E. Sharpe.

Júnior, D. P., & Muniz, J. (2006). 'Stop or I'll call the police!' The idea of police, or the effects of police encounters over time. *British Journal of Criminology*, *46*, 234–57.
Kamm, H. (2011). *Cambodia: Report from a stricken land*. New York, NY: Arcade Publishing.
Kane, S. (2007). *Dictionnaire des khmers rouges*. Paris, France: Aux Lieux d'être.
Karstedt, S. (2003). Legacies of a culture of inequality: The Janus face of crime in post-communist countries. *Crime, Law, and Social Change*, *40*, 295–320.
Karstedt, S. (2006). Democracy, values, and violence: Paradoxes, tension, and comparative advantages of liberal inclusion. *Annals of the American Academy of Political and Social Science*, *605*, 50–81.
Katz, J. (1988). *Seductions of crime: Moral and sensual attractions of doing evil*. New York, NY: Basic Books.
Keo, C. (2014). *Human trafficking in Cambodia*. London, England: Routledge.
Keo, C., Bouhours, T., Broadhurst, R., & Bouhours, B. (2014). Human trafficking and moral panic in Cambodia. *Annals of the American Academy of Political and Social Science*, *653*(1), 202–23.
Keo, C., Broadhurst, R., & Bouhours, T. (2011). Inside the Cambodian correctional system. *British Journal of Community Justice*, *8*, 7–22.
Kiernan, B. (2004). *How Pol Pot came to power: Colonialism, nationalism, and communism in Cambodia, 1930–1975* (2nd ed.). New Haven, CT: Yale University Press.
Kiernan, B. (2007). *Blood and soil*. New Haven, CT: Yale University Press.
Kiernan, B. (2008). *The Pol Pot regime: Race, power and genocide in Cambodia under the Khmer Rouge, 1975–1979* (3rd ed.). New Haven, CT: Yale University Press.
Kiernan, B., & Boua, C. (1982). *Peasants and politics in Kampuchea, 1942–1981*. London, England: Zed Books.
Kiernan, B., & Owen, T. (2006, October). Bombs over Cambodia: New information reveals that Cambodia was bombed far more heavily than previously believed. *The Walrus*. Retrieved from http://thewalrus.ca/2006-10-history/
Kipling, R. (1940). *Rudyard Kipling's verse: Definitive edition*. New York, NY: Doubleday.
Kirk, D. (1971). Cambodia's economic crisis. *Asian Survey*, *11*, 238–55.
Kirk, D. (1975). Cambodia 1974: Government on trial. *Asian Survey*, *15*, 53–60.
Krohn, M. D. (1978). A Durkheimian analysis of international crime rates. *Social Forces*, *57*, 654.
Kyne, P. (1999, May 14). Fraud at CMAC widespread. *Phnom Penh Post*. Retrieved from www.phnompenhpost.com/national/fraud-cmac-widespread
Kyne, P. (2000, March 31). CMAC spends money like rich kids. *Phnom Penh Post*. Retrieved from www.phnompenhpost.com/national/cmac-spends-money-rich-kids
Laborit, H. (1983). *La colombe assassinée*. Paris, France: Grasset and Fasquelle.
Laborit, H. (1986). *L'inhibition de l'action* (2nd ed.). Paris, France: Masson.
LaFree, G. A. (1999). Summary and review of cross-national comparative studies of homicide. In M. D. Smith & M. A. Zahn (Eds.), *Homicide: A sourcebook of social research* (pp. 125–45). London, England: Sage.
Landmine & Cluster Munition Monitor. (2014). Cambodia: Mine action. Retrieved from www.the-monitor.org/index.php/cp/display/region_profiles/theme/3324
Langran, I. V. (2000). Cambodia in 1999: Year of hope. *Asian Survey*, *40*(1), 25–31.

Langran, I. V. (2001). Cambodia in 2000: New hopes are challenged. *Asian Survey*, *41*(1), 156–63.
Lavoix, H. (2007, November 4). Scholarly review: Cambodia. *Online Encyclopedia of Mass Violence*. Retrieved from www.massviolence.org/Article?id_article=50
Le Billon, P. (2002). Logging in muddy waters: The politics of forest exploitation in Cambodia. *Critical Asian Studies*, *34*(4), 536–86.
Leclère, A. (1975). *Histoire du Cambodge depuis le 1er siècle de notre ère*. Paris, France: P. Gerthner. (Original work published 1914)
Ledgerwood, J. (1998). Rural development in Cambodia: The view from the village. In F. Brown & D. Timberman (Eds.), *Cambodia and the international community: The quest for peace, development, and democracy* (pp. 127–47). New York, NY: Asia Society.
Ledgerwood, J. (Ed.). (2002). *Cambodia emerges from the past: Eight essays*. DeKalb: Northern Illinois University Center for Southeast Asian Studies.
Ledgerwood, J., & Un, K. (2002). Introduction. In J. Ledgerwood (Ed.), *Cambodia emerges from the past* (pp. 1–15). DeKalb: Northern Illinois University Center for Southeast Asian Studies.
Ledgerwood, J., & Vijghen, J. (2002). Decision making in Khmer villages. In J. Ledgerwood (Ed.), *Cambodia emerges from the past: Eight essays* (pp. 109–150). DeKalb: Northern Illinois University Center for Southeast Asian Publications.
Leifer, M. (1963). Cambodia: In search of neutrality. *Asian Survey*, *3*, 55–60.
Leifer, M. (1967). Cambodia: The limits of diplomacy. *Asian Survey*, *7*, 69–73.
Leifer, M. (1981). Kampuchea in 1980: The politics of attrition. *Asian Survey*, *21*, 93–101.
Leman-Langlois, S. (2006). The 'megacrime', legitimacy, legality and obedience. *Criminologie*, *39*, 23–37.
Lilja, M. (2009). Globalization, women's political participation and the politics of legitimacy and reconstruction in Cambodia. In O. Joakim & M. Lilja (Eds.), *Beyond democracy in Cambodia: Political reconstruction in a post-conflict society* (pp. 136–50). Copenhagen, Denmark: Nordic Institute of Asian Studies.
Lilja, M., & Ojendal, J. (2009). The never ending hunt for political legitimacy in a post-conflict context: Cambodia: A 'hybrid' democracy'. In O. Joakim & M. Lilja (Eds.), *Beyond democracy in Cambodia: Political reconstruction in a post-conflict society* (pp. 297–312). Copenhagen, Denmark: Nordic Institute of Asian Studies.
Linklater, A. (2011). *The problem of harm in world politics: Theoretical investigations*. Cambridge, England: Cambridge University Press.
Linklater, A. (2012). Long term patterns of change in human interconnectedness: A view from international relations. *Human Figurations*, *1*(1). Retrieved from http://hdl.handle.net/2027/spo.11217607.0001.104
Liwerant, S. (2007). Mass murder: Discussing criminological perspectives. *Journal of International Criminal Justice*, *5*, 917–39.
Liwerant, S. (2012). Voices of war violence and ways of interpretation: Which echoes? *Criminologie*, *45*, 11–20.
Lizee, P. P. (1996). Cambodia in 1995: From hope to despair. *Asian Survey*, *36*, 83–8.
Lizee, P. P. (1997). Cambodia in 1996: Of tigers, crocodiles and doves. *Asian Survey*, *37*, 65–71.

Locard, H. (2013). *Pourquoi les Khmers Rouges [Why the Khmer Rouge]*. Paris, France: Éditions Vendémiaire.

Lovibond, S. H., Mithiran, & Adams, W. G. (1979). The effects of three experimental prison environments on the behaviour of non-convict volunteer subjects. *Australian Psychologist, 14*, 273–87.

Loyle, C. E. (2009). Why men participate: A review of perpetrator research on the Rwandan genocide. *Journal of African Conflicts and Peace Studies, 1*(2), 26–42.

Luciolli, E. (1988). *Le mur de bamboo: le Cambodge après Pol Pot. R. Deforges Médecins sans frontières, Diffusion*. Paris, France: A. Michel.

Maier-Katkin, D., Mears, D., & Bernard, T. J. (2009). Towards a criminology of crimes against humanity. *Theoretical Criminology, 13*, 227–55.

Malešević, S. (2013). Forms of brutality: Towards a historical sociology of violence. *European Journal of Social Theory*, 1–19. doi:10.1177/1368431013476524

Malešević, S., & Ryan, K. (2012). The disfigured ontology of figurational sociology: Norbet Elias and the question of violence. *Critical Sociology, 39*, 165–81.

Marston, J. (1997). *Cambodia 1991–94: Hierarchy, neutrality and etiquettes of discourse* (Unpublished doctoral dissertation). University of Washington, Seattle.

Marston, J. (2002). Democratic Kampuchea and the idea of modernity. In J. Ledgerwood (Ed.), *Cambodia emerges from the past: Eight essays* (pp. 38–59). DeKalb: Northern Illinois University Center for Southeast Asian Publications.

Martin, M. (1994). *Cambodia: A shattered society*. Berkeley: University of California Press. (Original work published in French in 1989)

Mathieson, T. (1984). *Defences of the weak: A study of a Norwegian correctional institution*. London, England: Tavistock.

Matza, D. (1964). *Delinquency and drift*. New York, NY: Wiley.

McGrew, L. (2009). Re-establishing legitimacy through the extraordinary chambers in the courts of Cambodia. In O. Joakim & M. Lilja (Eds.), *Beyond democracy in Cambodia: Political reconstruction in a post-conflict society* (pp. 250–96). Copenhagen, Denmark: Nordic Institute of Asian Studies.

Mennell, S. (1990a). Decivilising processes: Theoretical significance and some lines for research. *International Sociology, 5*(2), 205–23.

Mennell, S. (1990b). The globalisation of human society as a very long-term social process: Elias's theory. *Theory, Culture and Society, 7*(3), 359–71.

Mennell, S., & Goudsblom, J. (1997). Civilizing processes – myth or reality? A comment on Duerr's critique of Elias. *Comparative Studies in Society and History, 39*, 729–33.

Merton, R. K. (1949). *Social theory and social structure*. New York, NY: Free Press. (Original work published 1938)

Messner, S. F. (1982). Societal development, social equality, and homicide: A cross-national test of a Durkheimian model. *Social Forces, 61*(1), 225–40.

Messner, S. F., Liu, J., & Karstedt, S. (2008). Economic reform and crime in contemporary urban China: Paradoxes of a planned transition. In J. R. Logan (Ed.), *Urban China in transition* (pp. 271–93). Oxford, England: Blackwell's.

Messner, S. F., & Rosenfeld, R. (2000). Market dominance, crime and globalization. In S. Karstedt & K. Bussmann (Eds.), *Social dynamics of crime and control: New theories for a world in transition*. Oxford, England: Hart Publishing.

Messner, S. F., Thome, H., & Rosenfeld, R. (2008). Institutions, anomie, and violent crime: Clarifying and elaborating institutional anomie theory. *International Journal of Conflict and Violence*, 2(2), 163–81.

Meyer, C. (1971). *Derrière le Sourire Khmer*. Paris, France: Plon Publishers.

Meyer, C. (1985). *La vie quotidienne des français en Indochine, 1860–1910*. Paris, France: Hachette.

Mikaelian, G. (2009). *La royauté d'Oudong. Réformes institutionnelles et crise du pouvoir dans le royaume khmer du XVIIe siècle*. Paris, France: Presses Universitaires de la Sorbonne.

Milgram, S. (1963). Behavioural study of obedience. *Journal of Abnormal and Social Psychology*, 67, 371–8.

Milgram, S. (1974). *Obedience to authority: An experimental view*. New York, NY: HarperCollins.

Mollica, R. F., Brooks, R., Tor, S., Lopes-Cardozo, B., & Silove, D. (2014). The enduring mental health impact of mass violence: A community comparison study of Cambodian civilians living in Cambodia and Thailand. *International Journal of Social Psychiatry*, 60(1), 6–20.

Monkkonen, E. H. (2001). Estimating the accuracy of historic homicide rates: New York City and Los Angeles. *Social Science History*, 25, 53–66.

Moorthy, B., & Saroeun, B. (1998, September 18). Corpses in saffron? Death toll climbs to 18. *Phnom Penh Post*. Retrieved from www.phnompenhpost.com/national/corpses-saffron-death-toll-climbs-18

Morlat, P. (1995). *Les affaires politiques de l'Indochine, 1895–1923 les grands commis, du savoir au pouvoir*. Paris, France: Harmattan Press.

Morris, P. K., & Graycar, A. (2011). Homicide through a different lens. *British Journal of Criminology*, 51, 823–38.

Mouzos, J. (2003). *Homicide in the course of other crime in Australia* (Trends and Issues in Crime and Criminal Justice No. 252). Canberra: Australian Institute of Criminology.

Muller, G. (2006). *Colonial Cambodia's 'bad Frenchman': The rise of French rule and the life of Thomas Caraman 1840–87*. London, England: Routledge.

Mysliwiec, E. (1988). *Punishing the poor: The international isolation of Kampuchea*. Oxford, England: Oxfam.

Nathan, A. J. (2003). Authoritarian resilience. *Journal of Democracy*, 14, 6–17.

National Institute of Public Health, National Institute of Statistics, & ORC Macro. (2006). *Cambodia demographic and health survey 2005*. Phnom Penh, Cambodia: Author.

National Institute of Statistics. (2004). *Cambodia socio-economic survey 2004*. Phnom Penh, Cambodia: National Institute of Statistics, Ministry of Planning.

National Institute of Statistics. (2009). *Cambodia socio-economic survey 2009*. Phnom Penh, Cambodia: National Institute of Statistics, Ministry of Planning.

National Institute of Statistics, Directorate General for Health, & ICF Macro. (2011). *Cambodia demographic and health survey 2010*. Phnom Penh: Author.

National Institute of Statistics, Directorate General for Health, & ORC Macro. (2001). *Cambodia demographic and health survey 2000*. Phnom Penh, Cambodia: Author.

National Police Commissariat. (2009). *The 2008 report on the situation and the operations to maintain security and social order, and the plan of action for 2009*

of the National Police Force of Cambodia. Phnom Penh, Cambodia: Ministry of Interior.
Nelson, E., & Zimmerman, C. (1996, August). *Household survey on domestic violence in Cambodia.* Phnom Penh, Cambodia: Ministry of Women's Affairs and the Project against Domestic Violence.
Neopolitan, J. L. (1997). Homicides in developing nations: Results of research using a large and representative sample. *International Journal of Offender Therapy and Comparative Criminology, 41*, 358–74.
Neuman, W. L., & Berger, R. J. (1988). Competing perspectives on cross-national crime: An evaluation of theory and evidence. *Sociological Quarterly, 29*, 281–313.
O'Donnell, I. (2005). Lethal violence in Ireland, 1841 to 2003: Famine, celibacy and parental pacification. *British Journal of Criminology, 45*(5), 671–95.
Ojendal, J., & Lilja, M. (2009). Beyond democracy in Cambodia: Political reconstruction in a post-conflict society. In O. Joakim & M. Lilja (Eds.), *Beyond democracy in Cambodia: Political reconstruction in a post-conflict society* (pp. 1–31). Copenhagen, Denmark: Nordic Institute of Asian Studies.
Ojendal, J., & Ou, S. (2013). From friction to hybridity in Cambodia: 20 years of unfinished peacebuilding. *Peacebuilding and Development.* doi:10.1080/21647259
Olusanya, O. (2013). A macro-micro integrated theoretical model of mass participation in genocide. *British Journal of Criminology, 53*(5), 843–63.
Ortega, S. T., Corzine, J., Burnett, C., & Poyer, T. (1992). Modernization, age structure, and regional context: A cross-national study of crime. *Sociological Spectrum, 12*, 257–77.
Osborne, M. (1969). *The French presence in Cochinchina and Cambodia: Rule and response (1859–1905).* Ithaca, NY: Cornell University Press.
Osborne, M. (1973). *Politics and power in Cambodia: The Sihanouk years.* Sydney, Australia: Longman.
Osborne, M. (1979). *Before Kampuchea: Preludes to tragedy.* Sydney, Australia: Allen and Unwin.
Osborne, M. (1994). *Sihanouk, Prince of Light, Prince of Darkness.* Bangkok, Thailand: Silkworm.
Ovesen, J., Trankell, I.-B., & Ojendal, J. (1996). *When every household is and island – social organization and power structure in rural Cambodia* (Uppsala Research Reports in Cultural Anthropology). Uppsala, Sweden: Department of Cultural Anthropology, Uppsala University.
Pearson, S. (2006). *The end of the world: From revelation to eco-disaster.* New York, NY: Carroll & Graf.
Peou, S. (1998). Cambodia in 1997: Back to square one. *Asian Survey, 38*(1), 69–74.
Peou, S. (1999). Cambodia in 1998: From despair to hope. *Asian Survey, 39*(1), 20–6.
Peou, S. (2000). *Change and regime change in Cambodia: Toward democracy?* London, England: St. Martin's.
Peou, S. (2006). Consolidation or crisis of democracy? Cambodia's parliamentary elections in 2003 and beyond. In A. Croissant, B. Martin, & S. Kneip (Eds.), *The politics of death: Political violence in Southeast Asia* (pp. 41–83). Muenster, Germany: Lit Verlag.
Phandara, Y. (1982). *Retour à Phnom Penh: Le Cambodge du génocide à la colonisation.* Paris, France: A.-M. Metailie.

Picq, L. (1989). *Beyond the horizon: Five years with the Khmer Rouge.* London, England: St. Martin's.

Pinker, S. (2011). *The better angels of our nature: Why violence has declined.* New York, NY: Viking.

Pomonti, J.-C., & Thion, S. (1971). *Des courtisans aux partisans. Essai sur la crise cambodgienne.* Paris, France: Gallimard.

Ponchaud, F. (1978). *Cambodia: Year Zero.* New York, NY: Henry Holt.

Ponchaud, F. (1989). Social change in the vortex of revolution. In K. Jackson (Ed.), *Cambodia 1975–1978: Rendez vous with death* (pp. 151–77). Princeton, NJ: Princeton University Press.

Pou, S. (1977). *Etudes sur le Ramakerti (XVIè–XVIIè siècles).* Paris: Ecole Française d'Extrême Orient.

Powell, R. (2013). The theoretical concept of the 'civilising offensive' (*Beschavingsoffensief*): Notes on its origins and uses. *Human Figurations, 2*(2). Retrieved from http://hdl.handle.net/2027/spo.11217607.0002.203

Pridemore, W. A., & Kim, S. W. (2006). Democratization and political change as threats to collective sentiments: Testing Durkheim in Russia. *Annals of the American Academy of Political and Social Science, 605*(1), 82–103.

Quinlan, D., Boyle, D., & Street, N. (2013, October 25). CNRP rally ends peacefully. *Phnom Penh Post.* Retrieved from www.phnompenhpost.com/video/cnrp-rally-ends-peacefully

Quinn, K. M. (1978). Cambodia 1977: Internal consolidation and external expansion. *Asian Survey, 17*, 43–54.

Quinn, K. M. (1989). The pattern and scope of violence. In K. D. Jackson (Ed.), *Cambodia 1975–1978: Rendezvous with death.* Princeton, NJ: Princeton University Press.

Raffin, A. (2005). *Youth mobilization in Vichy Indochina and its legacies: 1940 to 1970.* Lanham, MD: Lexington Books.

Reddi, V. M. (1970). *A history of the Cambodian independence movement, 1863–1955* (2nd ed.). Tirupati, India: Sri Venkateswara University.

Regaud, N. (1992). *Le Cambodge dans la Tourmente: Le Troisieme Conflit Indochinois, 1978–1991.* Paris, France: L'Harmattan.

Rhodes, R. (2002). *Masters of death: The SS-Einsatzgruppen and the invention of the Holocaust.* New York, NY: Vintage

Roberts, D. W. (2001). *Political transition in Cambodia 1991–99: Power, elitism and democracy.* New York, NY: St. Martin's.

Robins, N. A., & Jones, A. (Eds.). (2009). *Genocides by the oppressed: Subaltern genocide in theory and practice.* Bloomington: Indiana University Press.

Ros, C. (1993). *La République Khmère (1970–1975).* Paris, France: L'Harmattan.

Roth, R. (2009). *American homicide.* Cambridge, MA: Belknap Press of Harvard University Press.

Rummel, R. J. (1994). *Death by government.* New Brunswick, NJ: Transaction Publishers.

Sandy, L. (2006). Sex work in Cambodia: Beyond the voluntary/forced dichotomy. *Asian and Pacific Migration Journal, 15*, 449–69.

Saroeun, B., & Chaumeau, C. (1998, May 22). Negotiators' killings explained. *Phnom Penh Post.* Retrieved from www.phnompenhpost.com/national/negotiators-killings-explained

Saroeun, B., & Eckardt, J. (1998, September 18). CPP demos: The empire strikes back. *Phnom Penh Post*. Retrieved from www.phnompenhpost.com/national/cpp-demos-empire-strikes-back

Saroeun, B., & Grainger, M. (1998, September 12). Lundy's police act after Tea Banh refusal. *Phnom Penh Post*. Retrieved from www.phnompenhpost.com/national/lundys-police-act-after-tea-banh-refusal

Scalabrino, C. (1989). *Affaires cambodgiennes 1979–1989* (Coll. Asie-débat 2). Paris, France: L'Harmattan.

Scherrer, C. P. (1999). Toward a theory of modern genocide: Comparative genocide research: Definition, criteria, typologies, cases, key elements, patterns and voids. *Journal of Genocide Research*, 1(1), 13–23.

Scott, J. C. (1985). *Weapons of the weak: Everyday forms of peasant resistance*. New Haven, CT: Yale University Press.

Sharpe, J. A. (1996). *Crime in early modern England*. London, England: Pearson.

Shaw, C., & McKay, H. (1942). *Juvenile delinquency and urban areas*. Chicago, IL: University of Chicago Press.

Shawcross, W. (1979). *Sideshow: Kissinger, Nixon, and the destruction of Cambodia*. New York, NY: Simon and Schuster.

Shawcross, W. (1984). *The quality of mercy: Cambodia, holocaust and modern conscience*. London, England: André Deutsch.

Shelley, L. I. (1981). *Crime and modernization: The impact of industrialization and urbanization on crime*. Carbondale: Southern Illinois University Press.

Short, P. (2004). *Pol Pot: The history of a nightmare*. London, England: John Murray.

Sihanouk, N. (1980). *War and hope: The case of Cambodia*. New York, NY: Random House.

Slocomb, M. (2002). Forestry policy and practices of the People's Republic of Kampuchea, 1979–1989. *Asian Survey*, 42(5), 772–93.

Slocomb, M. (2010). *An economic history of Cambodia in the twentieth century*. Singapore: NUS.

Smith, R. M. (1961). Cambodia's neutrality and the Laotian crisis. *Asian Survey*, 1(5), 17–24.

Smith, R. M. (1968). Cambodia: Between Scylla and Charybdis. *Asian Survey*, 8, 72–9.

Sok, K. (1991). *Le Cambodge entre le Siam et le Viêtnam*. Paris, France: Adrien-Maisonneuve, Ecole française d'Extrême-Orient.

Sokha, C. (2013, November 18). Eyeing KRT's legacy, future. *Phnom Penh Post*. Retrieved from www.phnompenhpost.com/national/eyeing-krt's-legacy-future

Sonis, J., Gibson, J. L., de Jong, J. T., Field, N. P., Hean, S., & Komproe, I. (2009). Probable posttraumatic stress disorder and disability in Cambodia: Associations with perceived justice, desire for revenge, and attitudes toward the Khmer Rouge trials. *Journal American Medical Association*, 302, 527–36.

Sorn, S. (1995). *L'évolution de la société cambodgienne entre les deux guerres mondiales (1919–1939)* (Unpublished PhD dissertation). University of Paris, France.

Souyris-Rolland, A. (1950). Les pirates du Cambodge. *Bulletin de la Société des Etudes Indochinoises*, 25(4), 307–13.

Spierenburg, P. (2006). Democracy came too early: A tentative explanation for the problem of American homicide. *American Historical Review*, *111*, 104–14.
Spierenburg, P. (2008). *A history of murder: Personal violence in Europe from the Middle Ages to the Present*. Cambridge, England: Polity.
Springer, S. D. (2011). Articulated neo-liberalism: The specificity of patronage, kleptocracy, and violence in Cambodia's neoliberalization. *Environment and Planning*, *43*, 2554–70.
Starr, S. (2007). Extraordinary crimes at ordinary times: International justice beyond crisis situations. *Northwestern University Law Review Online*, *101*, 1257–314.
Steinberg, D. J. (1959). *Cambodia: Its people, its society, its culture*. New Haven, CT: HRAF Press.
Steinfatt, T. M. (2011). Sex trafficking in Cambodia: Fabricated numbers versus empirical evidence. *Crime, Law and social change*, *56*(5), 443–62.
Stickley, A., & Makinen, I. H. (2005). Homicide in the Russian Empire and Soviet Union: Continuity or change? *British Journal of Criminology*, *45*, 647–70.
Stone, L. (1983). Interpersonal violence in English society, 1300–1980. *Past and Present*, *101*, 22–33.
Suong, S. (2013). *Itinéraire d'un intellectuel Khmer Rouge*. Paris, France: Cerf.
Surtees, R. (2003). Rape and sexual transgression in Cambodian society. In L. Manderson & L. R. Bennett (Eds.), *Violence against women in Asian societies* (pp. 93–113). London, England: Routledge.
Sykes, G. M., & Matza, D. (1957). Techniques of neutralization: A theory of delinquency. *American Sociological Review*, *22*, 664–70.
Szaz, Z. M. (1955). Cambodia's foreign policy. *Far Eastern Survey*, *XXIV*, 151–8.
Taboulet, G. (1956). *La geste française en Indochine: Histoire par les textes de la France en Indochine des origines à 1914*. Paris, France: Adrien-Maisonneuve.
Tanner, S. (2006). Le génocide à l'épreuve des massacres de masse contemporains: Vers une rupture paradigmatique? [Genocide put to the test in light of contemporary mass massacres: Towards a paradigmatic rupture]. *Criminologie*, *39*, 39–58.
Tanner, S. (2012). De la sécurité privée à l'armée de destruction massive: La «bande armée» et la criminalité de masse. *Criminologie*, *45*(1), 29–49.
Terry, F. (2002). *Condemned to repeat? The paradox of humanitarian aid*. Ithaca, NY: Cornell University Press.
Thayer, C. A. (1994). *The Vietnam People's Army under Đổi Mới*. (Institute of Southeast Asian Studies No. 7). Singapore: Institute of Southeast Asian Studies.
Thion, S. (1993). *Watching Cambodia*. Bangkok, Thailand: White Lotus.
Thomas, R. (1978). *L'évolution économique du Cambodge, 1900–1940* (PhD dissertation). Université de Paris VII, France.
Thome, H. (2001). Explaining long term trends in violent crime. *Crime, Histoire and Sociétés* [Crime History and Societies], *5*, 69–86.
Thome, H. (2007). Explaining the long-term trend in violent crime: A heuristic scheme and some methodological considerations. *International Journal of Conflict and Violence*, *1*(2), 185–202.
Thompson, L. C. (2010). *Refugee workers in the Indochina exodus: 1975–1982*. Jefferson, NC: McFarland.
Tifft, L., & Sullivan, D. (1980). *The struggle to be human: Crime, criminology, and anarchism*. Orkney, Scotland: Cienfuegos Press.

Tilly, C. (1985). War making and state making as organized crime. In P. B. Evans, D. Rueschemeyer, & T. Skocpol (Eds.), *Bringing the state back in* (pp. 169–91). Cambridge, England: Cambridge University Press.

Timberlake, M., & Williams, K. R. (1984). Dependence, political exclusion, and government repression: Some cross-national evidence. *American Sociological Review, 49*, 141–146.

Titthara, M., & Channyda, C. (2008, August 29). Students drive a booming business at Phnom Penh's Internet cafes. *Phnom Penh Post*. Retrieved from www.phnompenhpost.com/national/students-drive-booming-business-phnom-penhs-internet-cafes

Tittle, C. R. (1995). *Control balance: Toward a general theory of deviance*. Boulder, CO: Westview.

Toby, J. (1957). Social disorganization and stake in conformity: Complementary factors in the predatory behavior of hoodlums. *Journal of Criminal Law and Criminology, 48*(1), 12–17.

Tully, J. (1996). *Cambodia under the Tricolour: King Sisowath and the 'mission civilisatrice', 1904–1927*. Clayton, Victoria, Australia: Monash Asia Institute.

Tully, J. (2002). *France on the Mekong: A history of the Protectorate in Cambodia, 1863–1953*. Lanham, MD: University Press of America.

Um, K. (1990). Cambodia in 1989: Still talking but no settlement. *Asian Survey, 30*, 96–104.

Um, K. (1994). Cambodia in 1993: Year Zero plus one. *Asian Survey, 34*, 72–81.

Um, K. (1995). Cambodia in 1994: The year of transition. *Asian Survey, 35*, 76–83.

Un, K., & Ledgerwood J. (2002). Cambodia in 2001: Towards democratic consolidation? *Asian Survey, 42*, 100–7.

Un, K., & Ledgerwood J. (2003). Cambodia in 2002: Decentralization and its effects on party politics. *Asian Survey, 43*, 113–19.

United Nations Office on Drugs and Crime. (2010). *The globalization of crime: A transnational organized crime threat assessment* (United Nations publication No. E.10.IV.6). Vienna, Austria: Author.

United Nations Office on Drugs and Crime. (2011). *Global study on homicide: Trends, context, data*. New York, NY: Author.

United Nations Special Representative of the Secretary General for Human Rights in Cambodia. (2002, June). *Street retribution in Cambodia*. Retrieved from http://cambodia.ohchr.org/WebDOCs/DocReports/2-Thematic-Reports/Thematic_CMB06062002E.pdf

van der Kroef, J. M. (1979). From 'Democratic Kampuchea' to 'People's Republic'. *Asian Survey, 19*, 731–50.

van der Kroef, J. M. (1984). Kampuchea: Protracted conflict, suspended compromise. *Asian Survey, 24*, 314–34.

van der Kroef, J. M. (1991). Cambodia in 1990: The elusive peace. *Asian Survey, 31*, 94–102.

van Dijk, J., van Kesteren, J., & Smit, P. (2007). *Criminal victimisation in international perspective: Key findings from the 2004–2005 ICVS and EU ICS*. The Hague: Ministry of Justice, WODC.

van Krieken, R. (1998). *Norbert Elias* (Key Sociologists series). London, England: Routledge.

van Krieken, R. (2001). Norbert Elias and process sociology. In G. Ritzer & B. Smart, (Eds.), *The handbook of social theory* (pp. 353–67). London, England: Sage.
van Krieken, R. (2005). Occidental self-understanding and the Elias-Duerr dispute: 'Thick' versus 'thin' conceptions of human subjectivity and civilization'. *Modern Greek Studies, 13*, 273–81.
Varese, F. (2011). *Mafias on the move: How organized crime conquers new territories.* Princeton, NJ: Princeton University Press.
Vickery, M. (1982). Looking back at Cambodia [1945–1974]. In B. Kiernan & C. Boua (Eds.), *Peasants and politics in Kampuchea 1942–1981* (pp. 89–113). London, England: Zed Press.
Vickery, M. (1984). *Cambodia 1975–1982.* Sydney, Australia: Allen and Unwin.
Vickery, M. (1986). *Kampuchea – economics, politics and society.* London, England: Pinter/Rienner.
Von Clausewitz, C. (1968). *On war* (J. J. Graham, Trans., A. Rapoport, Ed.). Hardmondsworth, England: Penguin. (Original work published 1832)
Wacquant, L. (1999). *Les Prisons de la misère.* Paris, France: Editions Raisons d'agir.
Wallerstein, I. (1984). *The politics of the world-economy: The states, the movements and the civilizations.* Cambridge, England: Cambridge University Press.
Wallerstein, I. (1989). *The modern world-system, Vol. III: The second great expansion of the capitalist world-economy, 1730–1840's.* San Diego, CA: Academic Press.
Weitzer, R. (2011). Sex trafficking and the sex industry: The need for evidence-based theory and legislation. *Journal of Criminal Law and Criminology, 101*, 1337–70.
Whittock, M. (2009). *A brief history of life in the Middle Ages.* London, England: Constable and Robinson.
Widyono, B. (2008). *Dancing in shadows: Sihanouk, the Khmer Rouge, and the United Nations in Cambodia.* Lanham, MD: Rowman and Littlefield.
Wille, C. (2006a). *How many weapons are there in Cambodia?* (Working Paper 4). Geneva, Switzerland: Small Arms Survey, Graduate Institute of International Studies.
Wille, C. (2006b). Stabilizing Cambodia: Small arms control and security sector reform. In *Small Arms Survey 2006: Unfinished business* (pp. 119–39). Geneva, Switzerland: Small Arms Survey, Graduate Institute of International Studies. Retrieved from www.smallarmssurvey.org/publications/by-type/yearbook/small-arms-survey-2006.html
Wilson, J. Q., & Kelling, G. (1982, March). Broken windows: The police and neighborhood safety. *Atlantic Monthly*, 29–38.
Winton, M. A. (2011). Violentization theory and genocide. *Homicide Studies, 15*, 363–81.
World Travel and Tourism Council. (2013). *Travel and tourism economic impact 2013: Cambodia.* London, England: Author.
Yang, J. (2012). *Tombstone: The great Chinese famine, 1958–1962.* London, England: Macmillan.
Zhang, S. X. (2009). Beyond the 'Natasha' story: A review and critique of current research on sex trafficking. *Global Crime, 10*, 178–95.
Zinoman, P. (2001). *The colonial Bastille: A history of imprisonment in Vietnam, 1862–1940.* Berkeley: University of California Press.

Zucker, E. (2011). Trust and distrust in a highland Khmer community after thirty years of war. In J. A. Marston (Ed.), *Anthropology and community in Cambodia: Reflections on the work of May Ebihara* (Monash Papers on Southeast Asia Vol. 70, pp. 79–104). Caulfield, Victoria, Australia: Monash University Press.

Index

1916 affair, 49–52
  consequences of, 53, 76
  impact on police, 93, 95, 107

Achar Sva, 38, 54
achieved justice, 285, 286. *See also* vigilante justice
Angkar. *See* Communist Party of Kampuchea
anomie/anomic
  and change, 26, 206, 220, 318, 323
  characteristics of, 35, 128, 131, 135, 144, 167, 243, 246
  and crime, 24, 27, 145, 269, 273
  definition, 21, 212
  institutional anomie theory, 27, 323
  process-induced (developmental), 21, 22, 24, 27, 56, 74, 294, 306
  structural (chronic), 22, 24, 27, 56, 74, 316, 323
  and violence, 5, 142, 146, 278, 332
anti-colonial struggle, 118, 128, 129, 132, 137, 143, 144, 145, 146, 154, 295
  homicides during, 141–7
Archer and Gartner, 5, 244, 306. *See also* legitimation of violence

bamboo wall, 231
banditry
  characteristics of, 55–9, 72, 116, 119, 288, 292
  control of, 62, 63, 76–9, 80, 92, 93, 95, 99, 114, 120
  data on, 54, 66–7, 102, 118
  and guerilla, 172, 228, 247, 292
  offenders, 57–9, 72, 116
  and rebellión, 40
  social. *See* social bandits
  targets of, 59, 73, 88, 120
  trends, 1920 to independence, 108–10, 114, 115, 116, 118–19, 135, 143
  trends, post-independence, 155, 166, 233, 251, 276, 327
  trends, prior to 1920, 59–60, 67, 68–72
  and uprisings, 44, 45, 144, 146
Bardez affair, 100, 112
base people, 192–3, 195, 201, 203. *See also* new people
beautification, 281, 283–4, 321
biopsychosociological theory, 11, 13, 18
Bokor scandal, 113
bombing, American, 141, 160, 168, 176, 182, 227
BPC. *See Bulletins de Police Criminelle*
bribery. *See* corruption
Brother
  Number One. *See* Pol Pot
  Number Two. *See* Nuon Chea
Bulletins de Police Criminelle
  data and coding, 102–3, 115, 117, 128, 141–2, 145

Caldwell, Malcolm, 223
Cambodian Socio-Economic Survey, 249, 255, 273, 290, 291
centrifugal forces, 14, 15, 17, 279, 332
centripetal forces, 14, 15, 17, 22, 279
Chinese, the
  as target of crime, 49, 50, 51, 59, 65, 70, 73–4, 120
  as victims of the KR, 188, 200
civilising mission, 16, 28, 35, 37, 47, 321, 325. *See also* civilising offensive
civilising offensive, 16, 321, 322, 323, 324. *See also* civilising mission; *mission civilisatrice*
Cold War, 139, 228, 229, 239
  and support for KR, 224, 225, 229–30
collective conscience, 23, 241, 242, 317
collectivisation
  under DK, 187, 195, 196, 202, 205, 222
collectivism, 20, 24, 28, 243
Communist Party of Kampuchea, 165, 171, 173, 183, 187, 196, 203
  ideology, 187, 194–7, 204–6

358

Index

training by, 216, 222
and violence, 171, 187, 190, 193, 200–2, 206
Cooney, Mark. *See also* privatisation of violence
   on the development of the state, 4, 22, 26, 305
corruption. *See also* elite crime; kleptocracy
   control of, 76, 84, 85, 88, 290, 304, 321, 329
   of police, 289, 290, 298, 299
   during Protectorate, 36, 50, 55, 61, 63, 75–6, 83, 89, 101, 138
   resurfacing during PRK, 226, 233, 235, 237, 241
   during RGC, 255, 258, 260, 261, 283, 300, 313, 327, 328, 330
   during *Sangkum*, 151, 152, 161–3, 164, 166–9, 173
Corruption Perception Index, 262, 329
CPK. *See* Communist Party of Kampuchea
crime, definition of, 9–10
cult of antiquity, 107, 133, 147

death toll under KR, 188–9, 192, 194, 230, 232
decivilisation, 2, 17, 187, 219, 222, 318. *See also* decivilising process
democide, 169, 182, 183, 219, 230
differential association theory, 209, 210, 211
displacement, of crime, 70, 284
domestic violence
   attitude to, 309, 310, 312–13
   characteristics of, 122, 266, 267, 268, 296, 297
   trends, 308–10, 319
Duch, xi, 105, 192, 248
Durkheim, Emile, 19–25, 124, 241, 291, 316–17

ECCC. *See* Extraordinary Chambers in the Court of Cambodia
Eisner, Manual, 4, 5, 14–15
Elias, Norbert
   theory of the civilising process, 2, 14, 15–17, 22, 318, 322, 328, 332, 335
elimination contests, 18, 246, 279, 281, 282, 293, 318, 326
elite crime, 61, 75, 76, 255, 260–3, 323. *See also* corruption; kleptocracy
extrajudicial killings
   post-1992, 286–7, 289, 298
   during Protectorate, 63, 77, 289
Extraordinary Chambers in the Court of Cambodia, 248, 324

Franco-Thai war, 130–1

full rights people. *See* base people
functionalist approaches, 4, 25

Garde Indigène, 77, 92, 93, 98, 110
   size of, 52, 92, 93, 96, 107–8, 129
gendarmerie, 93–4, 129, 287
genocide, 177–9, 184, 189, 200, 206, 228, 249
   and criminology, 207, 209, 212, 215
ghosting, 238, 261
Great Insurrection, the, 40–3, 85, 92
Gurr, Ted, 3, 25, 32, 68, 74

Heng, Samrin, 204, 227, 237, 239
highlanders' rebellion
   first, 47–9, 66, 76, 94
   second and third, 114, 171–2
Hinton, Alexander, 207, 243, 311
   on revenge, 216, 217, 242, 317
Hobsbawm, Eric, 38, 55, 56, 58, 137. *See also* social bandits
homicide
   and anti-colonial struggle, 141–7
   characteristics of, 69, 74, 121–2, 142–3, 267–8, 295
   data on, 66–7, 102–4, 118, 128, 141, 249–50
   historical studies of, 3–5, 14, 22, 25
   trends in Cambodia, 7
   trends post-DK, 244, 250–2, 253, 276
   trends up to end of World War II, 67, 68, 108, 110, 114, 121
   trends, independence to DK, 154, 166, 169, 174, 188
honour
   and crime/violence, 20, 25, 217, 268, 334
   contest, 124, 217, 280, 293
Hou Youn, 152, 163, 165, 171, 172, 175
Hun Sen
   and corruption, 238
   post-1998, 324, 326, 328
   pre-1998, 204, 227, 228, 235, 247
hybrid state, 150, 325, 326, 327

Ieng Sary, 164, 183, 194, 203, 204, 228, 247, 248
independence struggle. *See* anti-colonial struggle
individualisation of violence. *See* privatisation of violence
individualism, 20, 22, 25, 199
   egoistic, 20, 24, 27, 28, 316
   moral, 20, 23, 24, 27, 316, 317
   under the KR, 199, 221, 243
Indochina War, Second, 33, 150, 160

insurrection
and banditry, 59, 60, 142, 144, 233
interdependence
chains of, 14, 16, 20, 299–304, 318, 319, 326
in Cambodia, 182, 219, 221, 246, 318–21, 326, 330, 332
in Elias's theory, 2, 14, 15, 17, 20, 24, 299
interdependency. *See* interdependence
intimate partner violence. *See* domestic violence
Issaraks, 137–40, 144–7, 155, 156, 181, 200, 220

justice system, 89–91, 124, 209, 295, 304

Karstedt, Suzanne, 25
Khieu Samphan
at the ECCC, 249
post-DK, 227
during *Sangkum*, 152, 163, 164, 172
Khmer Serei, 156, 158, 161, 232, 234
Khmerism. *See also* khmérité
khmérité, 107, 193. *See also* nationalism, Khmer
King Monivong, 128, 129, 130
King Norodom, 36, 38, 40, 42, 43, 49
kleptocracy, 163, 235–8, 327

Laborit, Henri, 11, 334
landmines, 258–9, 262
legitimation of violence, 5, 26, 305–6
legitimisation of violence. *See* legitimation of violence
Lon Nol, 134, 148, 157, 160, 166, 169, 170, 177, 185, 186, 194

Malesevic, Sinisa and Ryan, Kevin, 17, 18, 19
Marx, Karl, 15, 28–30, 91, 148, 322
megacrimes, 16, 192, 204, 218
and criminology, 207–18
mekhum
as target of banditry, 73, 88, 93
policing function of, 87, 88, 94, 120
Messner, Steven and Rosenfeld, Richard, 27
Messner, Steven, *et al.*, 21, 22, 23, 29, 317
millenarian. *See* millenarianism
millenarianism
under the KR, 195, 204
under Lon Nol, 185
under Protectorate, 37, 38, 41, 43, 56
mission civilisatrice, 28, 37, 147. *See also* civilising mission; civilising offensive
modernisation
definition, 11, 19

modernisation and crime
general theories of, 3, 20, 21, 22, 23, 24, 26, 28, 291
during Protectorate, 99, 116, 121, 264, 265
under the RGC, 273–6, 278–9, 284, 293, 298, 313, 318–21
monopolisation of violence
and crime/violence, 318–21, 332
in Elias's theory, 14–16, 18, 20, 30
post-independence, 168, 181
during Protectorate, 80, 81
under Protectorate, 89, 124
under the RGC, 279–99, 313, 316

nationalism, Khmer, 100, 107, 132–3, 135, 147, 164, 330. *See also* khmérité
neutralisation, 215, 217, 219
techniques of, 209, 210–12, 214
new people, 188, 192–3, 195, 199, 201, 216, 221. *See also* base people
Nuon Chea, 140, 189, 195, 248, 249

obedience
as explanation of violence, 206, 211, 213–14
old people. *See* base people

pacification
and crime/violence, 319, 321, 332, 334, 335
in Elias's theory, 17, 22, 246, 280
of the Highlands, 47–9, 114
under the RGC, 323, 325–8
People's Army of Vietnam, 203, 224, 226, 230, 232
Pinker, Steven
on decline in violence, 2, 18
on interdependency, 23, 299, 334
on obedience, 212, 214
refutation of, 18–19
Pol Pot, 137, 141, 148, 164, 186, 194, 195, 197, 199, 203, 204, 222, 228, 234, 248
police force
confidence in, 290–1, 298
crime by, 286–90, 298
policing
modern, 240–1, 285, 286, 298, 299
during Protectorate, 62, 63, 76–9, 91–9. *See also Garde Indigène*; *Sûreté, police de la*
political violence, 4, 10, 30, 292, 314, 327
post-1993, 248, 258–60, 281, 300
pre-1993, 239, 250, 265
Pou Kombo, 38–40
Poulo Condor, 90, 125, 134
Prince Sivotha, 40, 41
Prince Yuthevong, 136

Index

prison
  conditions, 269, 289
  rate of imprisonment, 123, 126, 129–30, 252
  S-21, 192, 206
  simulation, 213
privatisation of violence, 26, 117, 291, 293–8
prostitution
  post-DK, 234, 240, 255, 269
  pre-DK, 115, 162, 163, 168, 169
psychogenesis
  and crime/violence, 3, 25, 318, 322
  in Elias's theory, 2, 5, 13, 16, 24, 30, 331
purges, 141, 195, 239
  under DK, 192, 200, 202, 203, 204
  as a tool of control, 197, 221, 236

rape
  cases of, 42, 47, 228, 233, 240, 260
  characteristics of, 267, 268–9, 288
  trends in, 108, 155, 166, 241, 258, 276, 309
rational choice theory, 209, 210
refugees
  after DK, 229, 231–3, 255
  in Phnom Penh, 167, 194, 323
  from Vietnam, 169, 176
revenge
  disproportionate, 185, 216
  after DK, 234, 242, 285
  during DK, 205, 219, 223
  and homicide, 267, 268, 278
  in Khmer culture, 182, 216, 317
  in premodern societies, 291, 317, 334
  during Protectorate, 57, 62, 75, 78, 121
  by Sihanouk, 184–5
  subaltern, 193, 198, 204
  by Vietnamese, 178–9
revolt of the parasols, 131–2

S-21. *See* prison
Samlaut rebellion, 169–71, 175
securitisation, 281, 284
Sena Ouch, 46–7, 74
sensitisation to violence
  as a process of civilisation, 25, 26, 318–21
  in Cambodia, 80, 304–13, 316, 317, 326, 332
  in Elias's theory, 16, 30, 181
sensitivity to violence. *See* sensitisation to violence
sentencing
  data, 104, 125
  trends, 65, 89, 123, 125–6, 129, 239

sex trade, 269–70. *See also* prostitution
sexual assault. *See* rape
sexual violence. *See* rape
Shelley, Louise, 26, 117, 244, 273, 279
slave trade, 37, 47, 61. *See also* slavery
slavery, 80, 83, 84. *See also* slave trade
social bandits, 38, 41, 55–7, 58. *See also* Hobsbawm
social cohesion, 242, 243
social control
  changing mode of, 20, 23, 298
  and crime/violence, 25, 146, 209, 304, 318
  formal, 124, 280, 294, 318
  informal, 318
social solidarity, 20–1, 23, 24, 218, 242
  mechanical, 21, 294
  organic, 21, 23, 24, 27
sociogenesis
  and crime/violence, 25, 318–21
  in Elias's theory, 2, 13, 16, 24, 30, 319
Son Ngoc Minh, 132
Son Ngoc Thanh, 131, 132, 134, 135, 140, 156, 159
Son Sen, 164, 192, 194
sorcery, 62, 72, 121, 185, 277, 278
Sûreté, Police de la, 96, 97, 98, 99, 105, 129

Ta Mok, 140, 194, 199, 228, 232
torture
  post-independence, 160, 239, 243, 262, 289
  pre-independence, 35, 48, 90, 91, 105
trafficking
  drug, 10, 261
  human, 262, 269, 270

UNICVS. *See* United Nations International Crime Victims Survey
United Nations International Crime Victims Survey, 249, 252, 255, 257, 266, 273, 289, 290, 291
United Nations Transitional Authority in Cambodia. *See* UNTAC
UNTAC, 246–7
  and civilising processes, 306, 316, 323, 324, 325
  and crime, 255, 260, 261, 268, 288
urbanisation and crime, 19, 26, 30. *See also* Shelley, Louise
  in Cambodia, 117, 145, 244, 271–6, 323

Vichy regime, 107, 128–30, 131, 133
vigilante justice, 262, 285, 289

violence
  definition, 9
violentisation, 208, 215–16, 218, 219, 220

weapon
  collection, 281, 282–3, 306–7
  use in banditry, 59, 72, 74, 79, 119
  use post-1998, 268, 277

Weber, Max, 5, 13, 18, 25, 332
Winton, Mark, 208, 215. *See also* violentisation
witchcraft. *See* sorcery

xenophobia, 73, 107, 173, 176–9, 324, 330

year zero, 5, 6, 194

Lightning Source UK Ltd.
Milton Keynes UK
UKHW022052170719
346372UK00017B/281/P

Welcome

This book is to help you
your way through doing, o

People don't realise the time and ettort
it takes to get these jobs planned and
prepared before you actually make a start.

You are not alone my friend.

Keep going, stay strong.
Do not be swayed in your procrastination!

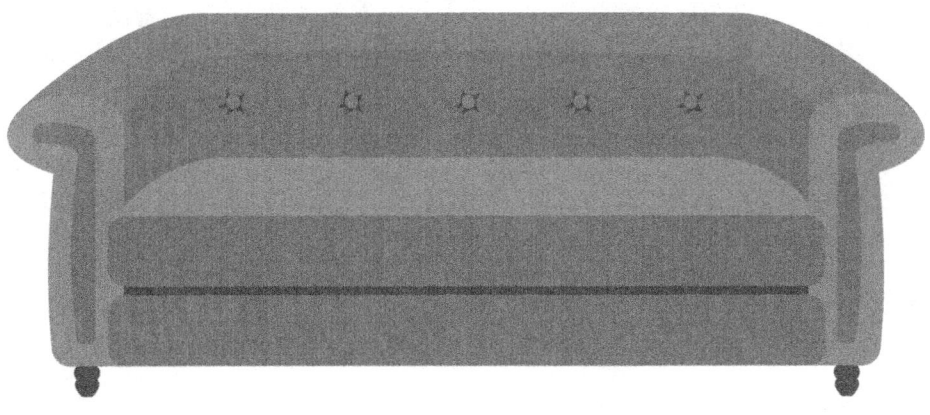

- The No. 1 reason for NOT doing a task!

- Do not put yourself or others at any risk

- Use the correct tool for the job

- Do not cut corners

- Get an expert in – there is a reason (usually) why they are expensive!

- If in doubt seek advice, or wait until everyone has forgotten about it, then pretend it didn't need doing!

EMERGENCY DETAILS

CARPENTER _____

PLUMBER _____

ELECTRICIAN _____

BUILDER _____

LOCKSMITH _____

GARDENER _____

PLASTERER _____

THE ELECTRICAL FUSE BOX IS LOCATED _____

THE WATER STOP-COCK IS LOCATED _____

THE FIRST AID KIT IS LOCATED _____

THE TWIRLY THING FOR THE CENTRAL HEATING IS _____

EMERGENCY CHECKLIST

For use during any DIY-related incident, misunderstanding, or household uproar

1. Initial Assessment

☐ Do I smell burning?
☐ Is anything leaking that wasn't leaking before?
☐ Is there blood? (Mine? Someone else's?)
☐ Did I just say "uh-oh" out loud?

2. Say Something That Sounds Professional

Choose one and say it firmly:
☐ "It's a settling crack."
☐ "This is just a pilot hole."
☐ "This part always looks weird at first."
☐ "I'm letting the sealant cure before phase two."
☐ "This is actually a feature, not a fault."

3. Immediate Cover-Up Actions

☐ Place a cardboard box over the affected area.
☐ Rearrange furniture "for a change."
☐ Tape up the mess with duct tape and say "Temporary fix."
☐ Dim the lights. Drastically.
☐ Start vacuuming—this will confuse everyone.

EMERGENCY CHECKLIST

4. Strategic Blame Transfer

Select your scapegoat:
- ☐ Greg (next door) – "His drilling vibrated the wall."
- ☐ The previous owner – "They clearly botched this."
- ☐ The dog – "She was acting weird near the radiator earlier."
- ☐ Cheap tools – "Never trust discount spirit levels."
- ☐ Mercury retrograde – "It's cosmic interference, really."

5. Create the Illusion of Progress

- ☐ Scatter tools. All of them.
- ☐ Smear a little dirt on your hands/forehead.
- ☐ Open a YouTube tutorial on your phone. Loudly.
- ☐ Scribble notes on a post-it: "Check stud integrity"
- ☐ Take a picture of the problem and say "Need to send this to the group chat."

6. Buy Time

Phrases to deploy when questioned:
- ☐ "Can't rush these things."
- ☐ "I'm halfway through a very specific drying cycle."
- ☐ "I'm waiting for a part from Germany."
- ☐ "It's a weekend job. Not this weekend though."
- ☐ "Don't touch it. It's calibrated."

7. Bonus Manoeuvres

- ☐ Offer to "make tea" (flee to kitchen for 20 mins).
- ☐ Suggest you were "doing a dry run."
- ☐ Start a completely unrelated task with gusto.
- ☐ Pull out the safety goggles—no one argues with PPE.
- ☐ Say, "You know who'd be great at this? Your dad."

Table of Contents

Section 1:
Foundations of Avoidance

Section 2:
Strategic Consideration Phase

Section 3:
Tactical Deflection Techniques

Section 4:
Reflection, Celebration & Lies

Section 5:
Tools, Materials & Other Household Terrors

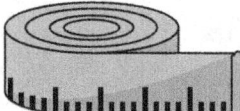

Section 1: Foundations of Avoidance

The Noble Art of Doing Nothing

"To do nothing is sometimes the most effective form of resistance."

- Sir Reginald H. Socketwrench, 1912, noted avoider of responsibility

Section 1: The Noble Art of Doing Nothing

The Case For Inaction

We need to question and re-evaluate this modern obsession with "getting things done."

We need to liberate men from the tyranny of productivity.

We frame inaction not as laziness, but as a refined lifestyle choice.

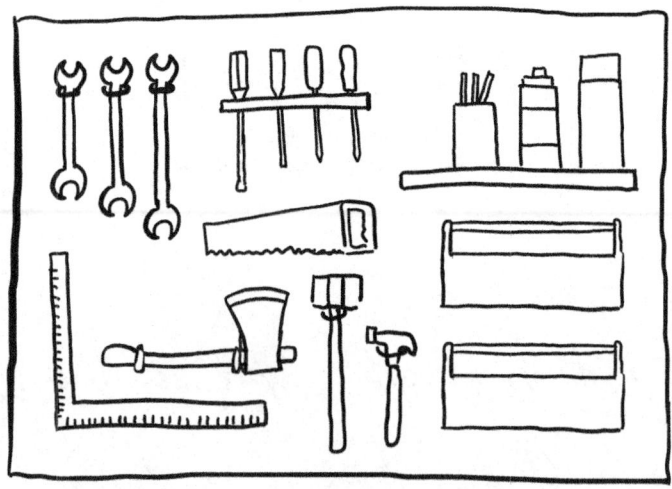

A Rich Heritage of Hesitation

Let us journey through the ages and honour the silent guardians of inaction:

- Cavemen, who wisely avoided DIY by pointing to the sky and saying "storm coming."
- The Ancient Greeks, who invented democracy so they could argue endlessly about which colour grout to use, without ever applying it.
- Medieval knights, whose real quest was for "someone else to fix the drawbridge."

Even during the Industrial Revolution, a time of great invention, there was always that one bloke standing in the corner holding a spanner upside down, nodding thoughtfully, and hoping someone else would take over.

Section 1: The Noble Art of Doing Nothing

Timeline of Honourable Inaction

8000 BC – First wooden frame left leaning against a cave wall for "later."

1287 – First medieval man draws up pergola plans for the castle courtyard. They remain in draft.

1953 – Harold in Kent says he's "about to start" the shed. His son finishes it in 2009.

2021 – You open a DIY YouTube playlist, then fall asleep halfway through the second thumbnail.

History is not made by those who leap into action.

It is made by those who wisely wait... until the moment passes.

The Health Benefits of Doing Absolutely Nothing

DIY is hazardous.
This cannot be overstated.

According to statistics I absolutely haven't made up,
men who avoid DIY live 37% longer,
have better joints,
and almost never trap their fingers in folding ladders.

Risks of Doing Something:
Splinters.
Extreme Tiredness.
Electrocution from that "mystery wire."
Discovering a much bigger problem behind the first problem.
The dreaded "while you're at it…" from your partner.
Dust inhalation.
Paint fume confusion.
Emotional collapse.

Benefits of Doing Nothing:
Peace of mind.
An intact back.
No plaster in your eyebrows.
Time to "observe the problem from multiple angles," ideally seated.

Remember: your body is a temple. DIY is a siege.

Section 1: The Noble Art of Doing Nothing

Mastering the Psychological Edge

It takes immense inner strength to look at a leaking tap and think, "Yes, but is that really my journey?"

Here's how to master your inner zen:

REFRAME THE PRESSURE.

"JUST GET IT DONE TODAY" BECOMES "AM I THE BEST PERSON FOR THIS LONG-TERM CHALLENGE?"

SIT BY THE PROBLEM. BECOME ONE WITH IT.

BONUS: OVER TIME, OTHERS WILL EITHER FIX IT OR LEARN TO LIVE WITH IT.

AVOID EYE CONTACT WITH THE TOOLBOX.

ITS PRESENCE IS SYMBOLIC, NOT INSTRUCTIONAL.

 # Time to take stock

Section 1: The Noble Art of Doing Nothing

Mastering the Psychological Edge

The Meditation of the Untouched Tool

Spend five minutes a day looking at your tools...

...simply acknowledge them.

Let go of expectation.

Let go of action.

Let go of reaching for the hammer that's definitely too small for the job anyway.

They are clean, pristine and pure why get them dirty?

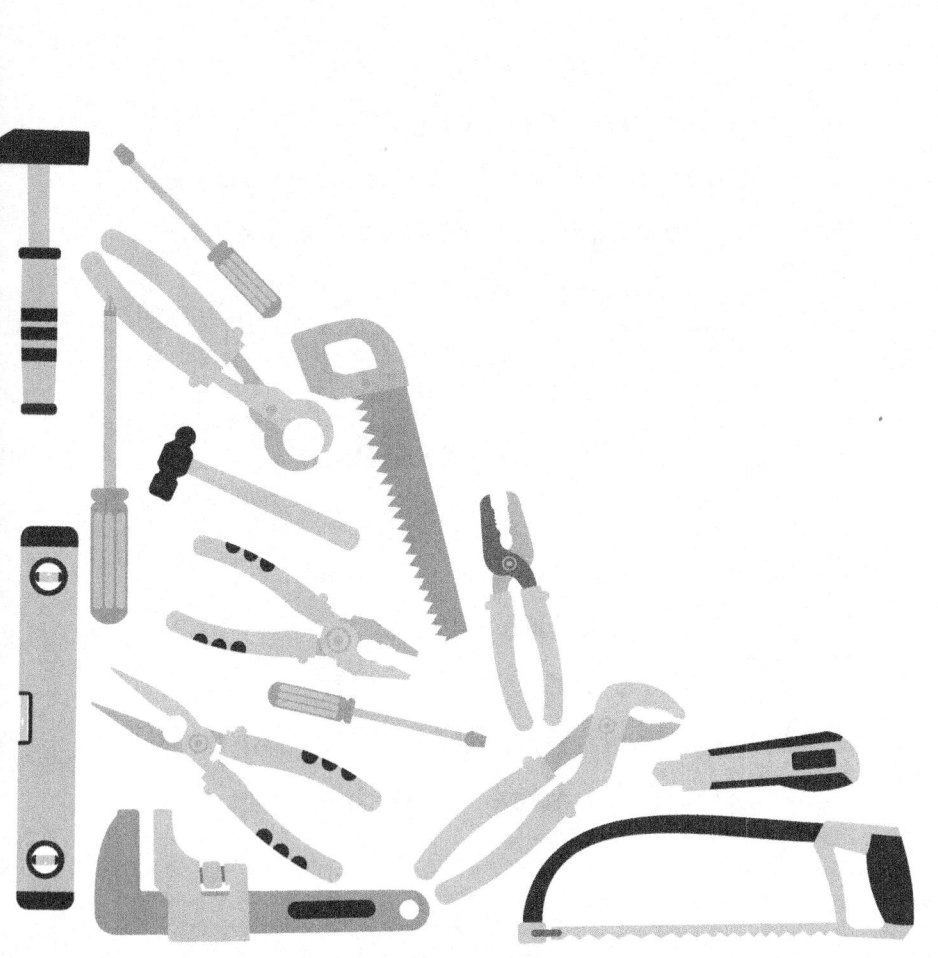

Section 1: The Noble Art of Doing Nothing

This book will help you develop the Advanced Techniques for Appearing Busy While Doing Nothing

The secret isn't in what you do,
but what you appear to be
on the verge of doing.

🔧 The Walkabout

Carry a single tool
(ideally a spirit level or socket wrench)
and walk slowly around the area in question.
Occasionally grunt. Look at the ceiling.
Then go make tea.

The List Shuffle

Write lists.
Cross one thing off.
Add it back again with a different title.
Refer to "Phase 2" in passing.

Check List

Section 1: The Noble Art of Doing Nothing

This book will help you develop the Advanced Techniques for Appearing Busy While Doing Nothing

The Folder of Eternal Planning

Create a folder labelled
"Kitchen Project – Critical Path."
Fill it with printed templates, a diagram of a tap,
and a takeaway menu.
Occasionally leave it on the kitchen table.

 The Mid-Thought Stare

Stand still in front of the problem
with furrowed brows.
People will think you're deep in calculation.
You're not. You're wondering what's in the fridge.

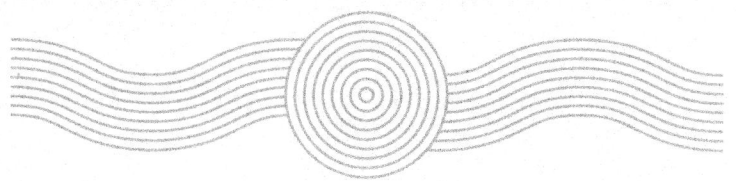

Section 1: The Noble Art of Doing Nothing

The Glory of the Undone

**The beauty of the unfinished job
is that it is still full of potential.
Once you do it, it becomes
"something you should've done differently."
Leave it undone, and it remains:**

> **A concept
> An idea
> A dream not yet
> corrupted by action**

>>> **Every unscrewed shelf,
every unassembled flat-pack box
is a monument to imagination.** <<<

You've already done far more than expected
by reading this chapter.
In fact, you've done so much doing-nothing,
you may wish to lie down.

There is no need to rush into Section 2.
You've earned the right to digest this wisdom slowly.
Maybe over a long weekend.
Or next month.
Or after a good rest.

Just remember:
doing nothing, with intention, is doing something.

Avoid boldly. Rest heroically. Delay with pride.

- The No. 1 reason for NOT doing a task!

- Do not put yourself or others at any risk

- Use the correct tool for the job

- Do not cut corners

- Get an expert in – there is a reason (usually) why they are expensive!

- If in doubt seek advice, or wait until everyone has forgotten about it, then pretend it didn't need doing!

Section 2:

Strategic Consideration Phase

"To do nothing is sometimes the most effective form of resistance."

– Sir Reginald H. Socketwrench, 1912, noted avoider of responsibility

Risk Assessments are essential for even the Simplest Tasks

You may be tempted to hang a picture.

STOP

First, conduct a full Risk Assessment (See later in the book!)

Hazards to document include:

- Trip hazards and whip-lash from the tape measure you'll never use.

- Emotional distress from discovering the frame is 2 degrees off.

- Structural collapse of the entire wall due to one misplaced nail.

- Interpersonal tension from the phrase 'Its fine' (its not).

Use official language like:
Risk of minor injury due to unforeseen oscillations in wall stability.

Once you've filled in your Risk Matrix and laminated it, take a break. Maybe even the week.

Section 2: Strategic Consideration Phase

SWOT Analysis: Strategic Waiting Over Time

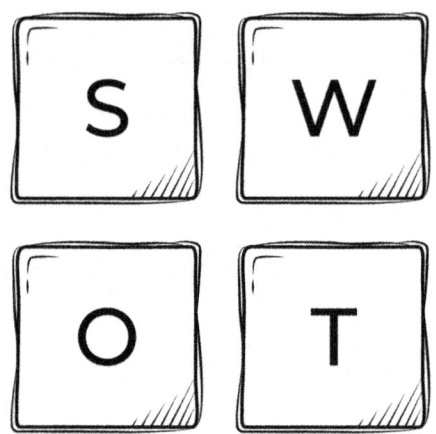

 **Why act, when you can analyse?**

Before replacing a lightbulb, build a full SWOT analysis:

Strengths: You can Google it. You own a stepladder.

Weaknesses: You don't want to. Its buried under clutter.

Opportunities: Someone else might do it.

Threats: Electrocution. Setting a precedent of success.

Conclusion: You need to stop
Waiting builds character.
Strategic Waiting Over Time.

Tools You'll Never Own but Might Mention in Conversation

While you'll never operate a rotary multi-tool, its vital to name-drop convincingly:

- "You'd need a Fein MultiMaster for that."

- "I was going to sand with a random orbital, but the grain..."

- "Ever tried a Japanese pull saw? Totally different."

Pro Tip: Keep a tool catalogue open on your phone. Occasionally swipe and nod.

Section 2: Strategic Consideration Phase

The Myth of the Perfect Time

 There is no such thing as the perfect time to do DIY.

Common myths:
- I can't paint until the humidity drops.

- We should wait until after Christmas. Or Easter. Or May.

- Mercurys in retrograde. Not good for flat-pack assembly.

Become so attuned to the mythical perfect moment that you never start anything.

Don't forget

- The No. 1 reason for NOT doing a task!

- Do not put yourself or others at any risk

- Use the correct tool for the job

- Do not cut corners

- Get an expert in – there is a reason (usually) why they are expensive!

- If in doubt seek advice, or wait until everyone has forgotten about it, then pretend it didn't need doing!

How to talk your way out of accepting a task....

- *I will need to plan it carefully (walk away)*
- *What a great idea (walk away - fast)*
- *I'll need some new tools!*
- *No problem, once the weather improves*
- *No problem, when it is a bit cooler*
- *No problem, when it is a bit warmer*
- *There is a lot of safety to consider (walk away)*
- *I will need to do a Risk Assessment first!*
- *I will need to research the best approach*
- *I know a better way which I will look into*
- *It will cost a lot of money, but if YOU think it is important...*
- *Yes, that is a good idea, let me find my book and write it down (walk away)*
- *Yes, I have time in (see calendar for acceptable months next year)*
- *No problem. I will enrol on a course to do it properly (don't enrol on a course - just watch a short Youtube video)*

Section 3:

Tactical Deflection Techniques

"The secret to Tactical Deflection isn't saying no — it's saying 'Hmm, interesting... let me just check something,' and disappearing for three days."

Section 3: Tactical Deflection Techniques

8. The Science of Excuses

We begin with a truth:
No man really wants to spend a weekend trapped with a paint brush.

Deep down, most would rather watch an out-of-date documentary about steam engines than attempt to fix a dripping tap.

Enter the hero of DIY resistance:

Evolutionary Background

From the ancient hunter-gatherer who "couldn't build the shelter because he was tracking a very fast antelope," to today's man who "would have painted the fence but the weather app said a chance of drizzle," excuses have kept generations of men alive, out of trouble, and unpaint-splattered.

Categories of Excuse:

The Technical Misdirection
"The Allen key's the wrong size, love. Can't risk damaging the bolts."

The Existential Quandary
"What even is a load-bearing wall?"

The Philosophical Delay
"I've been thinking about it a lot. It's important to approach this from the right headspace."

The Sacrificial Scapegoat
"I was about to start, but your dad borrowed the drill again."

The Health & Safety Hazard
"I could do it today, but I think I might be coming down with something. I don't want to faint mid-shelving."

TIP:
Rotate excuses regularly. Like sourdough, if overused they go stale.

Section 3: Tactical Deflection Techniques

Delegation as a Virtue

Some see delegation as avoidance. You, however, will soon see it as a masterstroke of masculine leadership. Real leaders don't hammer — they enable.

What Would a Roman General Do?

He'd say: "Centurion, fetch the spade." He wouldn't dig. Why? Because he had vision. Because he could inspire others to act. Because he valued not hurting his back.

So, why should you ruin a perfectly good Saturday afternoon trying to remove grout when there's a teenager in the house desperate for screen-free time and character development?

Delegation as a Virtue

Who can you delegate to?

Potential Delegate	Rationale You Can Use	Suggested Bribe
Your Children	"It's good for your CV"	Extra screen time
Your Neighbour	"You're so good at this"	Beer
A Professional	"This deserves a *real* expert"	Money, sadly
Mavis	"I don't want to get in your way"	Compliment sandwich

Delegation as a Virtue

Your delegation Notes:

Potential Delegate	Rationale You Can Use	Suggested Bribe

Engagement and Communication Techniques

While deflection is tactical, communication is strategic.
You must be equipped with phrases
and responses that sound reasonable,
vaguely progressive, and slightly apologetic.

Tactical deflection isn't laziness
— it's an art form.
It's leadership wrapped in domesticity.
It's the noble dance between "I could do that"
and "it's probably best if someone else does."

So, as you sip your third coffee while staring
thoughtfully at the flat-pack instructions
(still in the box), remember:

You are not avoiding DIY.
You are preserving the integrity of the
household... by not making it worse.

Section 3: Tactical Deflection Techniques

Engagement and Communication Techniques

Tried And Tested Suggestions
(With Great Power Comes Great Responsibility...)

The Postponement Pledge™
"Let's wait until we've really researched all the options."
(Hint: never define when that ends.)

The Suggestive Empowerment Technique
"You're so good at choosing colours. Maybe you could pick the tiles while I... put the kettle on?"

Engagement and Communication Techniques

Tried And Tested Suggestions
(With Great Power Comes Great Responsibility...)

The Consultation Loophole
"I've put a call in to Dave — you remember Dave?
— he knows someone who's done this sort of thing before.
We should wait and see what he says."

The Feigned Complexity Gambit
"It's more complicated than it looks.
The support beam might need checking.
I think we'd need to hire someone with one of those infrared... things."

THE BIG STUFF

I will need to address the following tasks in the next 5 years or so, no messing!!

-
-
-
-

Notes

EMERGENCY CHECKLIST

For use during any DIY-related incident, misunderstanding, or household uproar

1. Initial Assessment

- ☐ Do I smell burning?
- ☐ Is anything leaking that wasn't leaking before?
- ☐ Is there blood? (Mine? Someone else's?)
- ☐ Did I just say "uh-oh" out loud?

2. Say Something That Sounds Professional

Choose one and say it firmly:
- ☐ "It's a settling crack."
- ☐ "This is just a pilot hole."
- ☐ "This part always looks weird at first."
- ☐ "I'm letting the sealant cure before phase two."
- ☐ "This is actually a feature, not a fault."

3. Immediate Cover-Up Actions

- ☐ Place a cardboard box over the affected area.
- ☐ Rearrange furniture "for a change."
- ☐ Tape up the mess with duct tape and say "Temporary fix."
- ☐ Dim the lights. Drastically.
- ☐ Start vacuuming—this will confuse everyone.

EMERGENCY CHECKLIST

4. Strategic Blame Transfer

Select your scapegoat:
- ☐ Greg (next door) – "His drilling vibrated the wall."
- ☐ The previous owner – "They clearly botched this."
- ☐ The dog – "She was acting weird near the radiator earlier."
- ☐ Cheap tools – "Never trust discount spirit levels."
- ☐ Mercury retrograde – "It's cosmic interference, really."

5. Create the Illusion of Progress

- ☐ Scatter tools. All of them.
- ☐ Smear a little dirt on your hands/forehead.
- ☐ Open a YouTube tutorial on your phone. Loudly.
- ☐ Scribble notes on a post-it: "Check stud integrity"
- ☐ Take a picture of the problem and say "Need to send this to the group chat."

6. Buy Time

Phrases to deploy when questioned:
- ☐ "Can't rush these things."
- ☐ "I'm halfway through a very specific drying cycle."
- ☐ "I'm waiting for a part from Germany."
- ☐ "It's a weekend job. Not this weekend though."
- ☐ "Don't touch it. It's calibrated."

7. Bonus Manoeuvres

- ☐ Offer to "make tea" (flee to kitchen for 20 mins).
- ☐ Suggest you were "doing a dry run."
- ☐ Start a completely unrelated task with gusto.
- ☐ Pull out the safety goggles—no one argues with PPE.
- ☐ Say, "You know who'd be great at this? Your dad."

Section 4:

Reflection, Celebration & Lies

"Every great DIY journey ends with either a finished shelf or a completely fabricated story of why it was never meant to be finished."
— Stan, philosopher of the half-done

The Post-Project Review (That No One Asked For)

You've survived. Maybe.
The tools are scattered like emotional debris.
You're covered in dust, there's a faint smell of burnt plastic, and someone's asking, "Was it meant to do that?"

Now is the time for reflection.
Not honest reflection, of course — that would imply learning.
No, this is the time for selective memory, strategic justification, and tactical misdirection.

Use our Post-Project Reflection Form
(That No One Will Ever Use) to grade yourself on a scale of:

"I Meant To Do That"

"Structurally Ambiguous"

"Look, It Works If You Don't Touch It"

"We Don't Talk About The Shed Anymore"

Stan says: "I mark every project 10/10, mainly to boost morale, and Mavis can't prove anything."

Section 4: Reflection, Celebration & Lies

Celebration: The Unsung Rituals

**You did something...
Or at least started something.
That's enough reason for a victory lap.**

Approved Post-DIY Celebrations:

Standing heroically with one foot on the toolbox

Dramatically washing your hands for 9 minutes like a surgeon

Telling your mate down the pub, "It's all about the prep"

Show your partner the "Before" photo (leave out the "After")

Cracking open a beer you absolutely earned

Don't forget the DIY Hero's Certificate of Triumph.
You can award it to yourself for:

"Creative Bodging Under Pressure"
"Using the Right Tool for the Wrong Reason"
"Avoiding Injury Through Inaction"

"You hammered what exactly, into what exactly?"

DIY HERO'S CERTIFICATE OF TRIUMPH

THIS CERTIFIES THAT

_____

- Creative Bodging Under Pressure
- Using the Right Tool for the Wrong Reason
- Avoiding Injury Through Inaction

Signed

Section 4: Reflection, Celebration & Lies

Lies We Tell Ourselves (and Others)

The truth is a bit like your spirit level — best ignored if it contradicts the narrative.

Here are some certified lies you're now permitted to repeat:

"I read the instructions but they were wrong."

"I just need a part they don't make anymore."

"It's a prototype."

"Honestly, it's better this way."

"It's not broken — it's resting."

POST-PROJECT REFLECTION FORM

FOR INTERNAL USE ONLY (I.E., YOUR EGO)
FORM 4A - VERSION 0.1 (STILL IN DRAFT)

PROJECT NAME: _____
(E.G., OPERATION WOBBLY SHELF, MILDLY AMBITIOUS DECKING, THE GREAT TILE INCIDENT)

START DATE: ___ / ___ / ___   PROJECTED COMPLETION DATE:
                                  [ ] SAME DAY   [ ] WITHIN THE MONTH   [ ] SUBJECT TO CLIMATE

ACTUAL COMPLETION DATE: ___ / ___ / ___   [ ] STILL PENDING

.PERSONAL ASSESSMENT
PLEASE RATE YOUR PERFORMANCE IN THE FOLLOWING AREAS:

Category	Rating (Tick One)
Planning & Preparation	[ ] Printed something [ ] Made notes [ ] Winged it gloriously
Tool Familiarity	[ ] Totally confident [ ] YouTubed it [ ] Used a spoon again
Structural Soundness	[ ] Rock solid [ ] Slight flex [ ] Will collapse when judged
Time Management	[ ] On schedule [ ] Lost 3 weekends [ ] Time is a construct
Stress Management	[ ] Zen monk [ ] Mildly snappy [ ] Shouted at the ladder
Communication with Partner	[ ] Harmonious [ ] Passive-aggressive [ ] Divorce imminent
Final Outcome	[ ] Functional [ ] Functional(ish) [ ] Artistic reinterpretation

INVENTORY & CASUALTIES

Please indicate the number of the following:
Tools lost: ____
Screws left over: ____
Injuries sustained: ____
Arguments sparked: ____
"Let's call a professional" moments: ____
Number of times you used the phrase: "That'll do." ____

LESSONS (ALLEGEDLY) LEARNED

[ ] Next time, I'll measure first
[ ] Spirit levels are not optional
[ ] Maybe I do need a workbench
[ ] MDF isn't indestructible
[ ] I'm better at delegating
[ ] I regret everything

NEXT STEPS

[ ] Retell story at every social event
[ ] Submit for "DIY Hero of the Year" award
[ ] Cover it with a rug
[ ] Let Mavis think you planned it that way
[ ] Move house

"It was supposed to be a shelf, but became a journey of self-discovery involving metric screws, betrayal, and a plumber named Stanislav..."

WHAT TO SAY WHEN YOU'VE NAILED THE WRONG THING

AH YES, THAT CRUCIAL MOMENT WHEN THE NAIL GOES THROUGH THE TABLE, THE WALL STUD, OR WORSE, YOUR OWN THUMB. PANIC IS NATURAL, BUT WORDS MATTER.

RECOMMENDED LINES:

- "THAT WAS JUST A TEST NAIL."
- "STRUCTURALLY, THIS IMPROVES THE INTEGRITY OF THE HOUSE."
- "THIS IS WHAT'S KNOWN AS 'FRENCH JOINERY.' LOOK IT UP."
- "IT'S PART OF MY NEW ABSTRACT CARPENTRY SERIES."

PRO TIP: SPEAK WITH CALM AUTHORITY AND GENTLY STROKE YOUR CHIN WHILE NODDING.
EVEN IF YOU'VE JUST FASTENED THE TV BRACKET TO THE RADIATOR.

JOB WELL DONE!

HOW TO HIDE EVIDENCE BEFORE SHE GETS HOME
THIS IS NOT ABOUT DECEPTION, IT'S ABOUT PRESERVING DOMESTIC HARMONY.

WHEN THINGS GO CATASTROPHICALLY WRONG, CONCEALMENT IS YOUR FIRST LINE OF DEFENCE.

EMERGENCY ACTIONS:

- ALWAYS KEEP A DECORATIVE THROW NEARBY, IT CAN COVER A HOLE, A SPILL, OR A SMOULDERING POWER TOOL.

- CREATE "TEMPORARY WORKS ZONES" USING CONES, TAPE, AND A CLIPBOARD. THE MORE OFFICIAL IT LOOKS, THE LESS LIKELY SHE'LL ASK.

- A LAUNDRY BASKET CAN HIDE ANYTHING FROM BROKEN TOOLS TO CRACKED TILES. JUST SAY YOU'RE "DOING A SORT-THROUGH."

- SPRAY FEBREZE LIBERALLY TO HIDE THE SMELL OF SCORCHED MDF OR PANIC SWEAT.

ADVANCED TIP: PLACE AN AMAZON DELIVERY BOX OVER THE DAMAGED AREA. IT'LL TAKE DAYS BEFORE ANYONE DARES MOVE IT.

WHICH NEIGHBOUR TO BLAME (AND HOW)

SOMETIMES, THE BEST DEFENCE IS A FICTIONAL OFFENCE. BLAMING YOURSELF IS BRAVE. BLAMING GREG NEXT DOOR IS STRATEGIC.

BLAME TEMPLATES:

"PRETTY SURE THE DAMAGE STARTED WHEN DAVE NEXT DOOR DRILLED THAT SATELLITE DISH BRACKET."

"OUR ELECTRICS ARE WEIRD—PETE SAID THEY'RE ALL LINKED THROUGH HIS SHED SOMEHOW."

"YOU REMEMBER JANE FROM NO. 5? HER CAT CAME IN HERE AND CHEWED THE WIRES."

EXECUTION:

SAY IT CASUALLY, WHILE SIPPING TEA, LOOKING CONFUSED BUT NOT GUILTY. BONUS POINTS IF YOU TEXT THE NEIGHBOUR SOMETHING VAGUE LIKE, "EVERYTHING OKAY YOUR END? JUST CHECKING..."

CREATING THE ILLUSION OF PROGRESS WITH DUST AND MESS

THERE ARE DAYS WHEN YOU'VE DONE NOTHING, BUT IT LOOKS LIKE YOU'VE BEEN TO WAR WITH THE PLUMBING GODS. THAT'S THE ILLUSION YOU NEED.

VISUAL CUES OF "PROGRESS":
SPRINKLE LIGHT DUST (NOT MUD—IT CLUMPS) AROUND KEY TOOLS.

SCATTER A FEW SCREWS AND WASHERS RANDOMLY, ESPECIALLY NEAR ANYTHING BROKEN. THIS SUGGESTS "ASSESSMENT PHASE."

LEAVE AN OPEN INSTRUCTION MANUAL ON A TABLE, IDEALLY WITH SCRIBBLED NOTES. BONUS POINTS FOR HIGHLIGHTERS.

SMUDGE YOUR CHEEK WITH A BIT OF CHARCOAL OR GROUT, AND SIGH LOUDLY.

NARRATIVE SUPPORT:
"IT'S ALL BEHIND-THE-SCENES STUFF RIGHT NOW."
"WAITING FOR SOME COMPOUND TO CURE..."
"I'M IN PHASE TWO OF PREP—CAN'T RUSH THIS SORT OF THING."

Section 5:

Tools, Materials & Other Household Terrors

The Tools You Do Own... and Why You Shouldn't Trust Them

*Ah yes, the "toolbox."...
Or as we call it, The Cluster of Dubious Inventions.*

Inside:
- *A rusty adjustable spanner (no longer adjusts).*
- *Four screwdrivers, none the right size.*
- *One lone Allen key — from a flat-pack chair you broke in 2013.*
- *A tape measure that only retracts when it feels like it.*

This section celebrates the heroic optimism of owning tools while deeply mistrusting their motives.

We include tips like:
Never use a tool you can't pronounce properly.
If it sparks and it's not Christmas, stop.

Section 5: Tools, Materials & Other Household Terrors

Choosing Materials Based on What's in the Garage
Why shop for materials when you already have:

- A roll of leftover carpet (circa 1997).

- A mysterious plank (origin unknown, possibly sacred).

- Five half-empty tins of paint (four labelled "white" but none matching).

- This chapter introduces the principle of Creative Reuse (i.e., bodging with enthusiasm). You'll find inspiration for using:
- Shower curtain rings as light fittings.
- Old tea towels as insulation.
- Gaffer tape as an emotional crutch.

The Principle of Creative Reuse
(i.e. Bodging With Enthusiasm)

Welcome, fellow innovator, to the noble tradition of making do with whatever's lying around. Why buy things when your shed, attic, glovebox, and possibly that drawer in the kitchen labelled "Bits" are already brimming with... potential?

Creative Reuse is the cornerstone of the amateur DIY philosophy. It's not about cutting corners — it's about enthusiastically galloping around them while waving a broken broom handle and declaring, "That'll do!"

Let's dive into some of the foundational pillars of this noble craft:

Section 5: Tools, Materials & Other Household Terrors

1. The Law of Substitution

Can't find the right part? Simply find something that's the same shape-ish.

- Lost a washer? Use a 2p coin.
- Missing a doorstop? Tennis ball. Preferably one you've stepped on barefoot in the middle of the night.
- No rubber grip for that spanner? One of Mavis's old hairbands. She'll never notice. Unless she does. Then deny everything.

This approach is 37% problem-solving and 63% blind optimism.

2. The Sacred Box or Drawer of Bits

Every home has one.
Usually in a Kitchen Drawer or a box stored in the garage, loft, or "somewhere in the utility room under the ironing board,". This hallowed container holds:

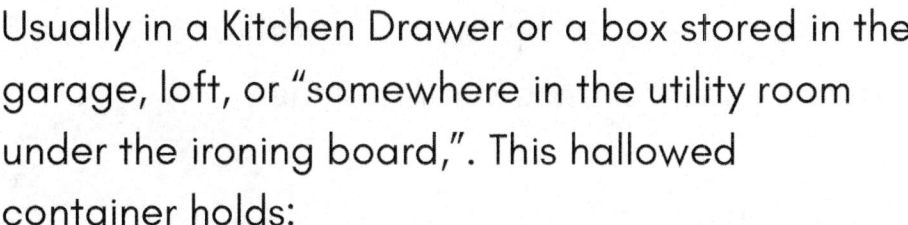

- 33 unmatched screws
- A single weird hinge
- A few random springs from an unidentified source
- A plastic thingy that might be important
- 2 door keys that have no known door
- Two IKEA hex keys (identical, and yet neither quite right)

This is your DIY treasure chest.
Never throw it away.
 Never organise it.
Occasionally shake it
to hear the sound of possibility.

Section 5: Tools, Materials & Other Household Terrors

3. Function Over Form...

In the world of Creative Reuse, beauty is secondary. Stability? Tertiary. What matters is that the thing stays up, holds together, or at least doesn't collapse during dinner.

Examples:

- A curtain rod supported by two garden trowels and a heavy sigh.
- A bookshelf made from cinder blocks and hope.
- The porch held up by an old fridge (yes, it's technically "structural recycling").

Remember:
If it works
and no one dies,
it's a win.

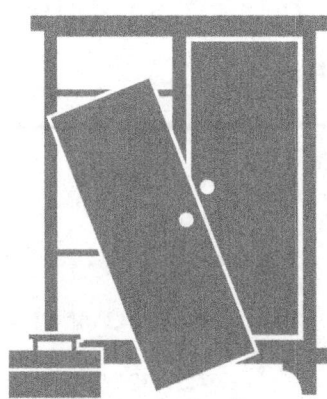

4. Naming the Creation

True artists name their work.
So too must the DIY bodger.

Examples:

- "The Shelf of Slight Regret"
- "Operation: That'll Do, Pig"
- "The Leaning Coat Rack of (insert county here)"

Naming your masterpiece elevates it
from "half-job" to "bespoke installation."

5. The Confidence Multiplier

No matter how questionable the solution, present it with swagger.

Try:

"Yeah, I could've used standard fixings, but I prefer a more sustainable, adaptive reuse methodology."

Or:

"It's industrial-chic. Very Brooklyn."

Confidence. It's 90% of the DIY game.
(The other 10% is apologising afterwards.)

Section 5: Tools, Materials & Other Household Terrors

Final Word

Creative Reuse isn't failure.
It's resourceful genius wrapped
in duct tape and whispered excuses.
It's environmentally friendly (ish),
budget-conscious (allegedly),
and oddly satisfying.

**So go on. Salvage that pallet.
Frame your shelf with curtain rail offcuts.
Hang your tools from an old belt.**

Because in this house, we don't waste.
We improvise.
We repurpose.
We bodgify.

POST-PROJECT REFLECTION FORM

FOR INTERNAL USE ONLY (I.E., YOUR EGO)
FORM 4A - VERSION 0.1 (STILL IN DRAFT)

PROJECT NAME: _____
(E.G., OPERATION WOBBLY SHELF, MILDLY AMBITIOUS DECKING, THE GREAT TILE INCIDENT)

START DATE: ____ / ____ / ____   PROJECTED COMPLETION DATE:
[ ] SAME DAY   [ ] WITHIN THE MONTH   [ ] SUBJECT TO CLIMATE

ACTUAL COMPLETION DATE: ____ / ____ / ____   [ ] STILL PENDING

PERSONAL ASSESSMENT
PLEASE RATE YOUR PERFORMANCE IN THE FOLLOWING AREAS:

Category	Rating (Tick One)
Planning & Preparation	[ ] Printed something [ ] Made notes [ ] Winged it gloriously
Tool Familiarity	[ ] Totally confident [ ] YouTubed it [ ] Used a spoon again
Structural Soundness	[ ] Rock solid [ ] Slight flex [ ] Will collapse when judged
Time Management	[ ] On schedule [ ] Lost 3 weekends [ ] Time is a construct
Stress Management	[ ] Zen monk [ ] Mildly snappy [ ] Shouted at the ladder
Communication with Partner	[ ] Harmonious [ ] Passive-aggressive [ ] Divorce imminent
Final Outcome	[ ] Functional [ ] Functional(ish) [ ] Artistic reinterpretation

INVENTORY & CASUALTIES

Please indicate the number of the following:
Tools lost: ____
Screws left over: ____
Injuries sustained: ____
Arguments sparked: ____
"Let's call a professional" moments: ____
Number of times you used the phrase: "That'll do." ____

LESSONS (ALLEGEDLY) LEARNED

[ ] Next time, I'll measure first
[ ] Spirit levels are not optional
[ ] Maybe I do need a workbench
[ ] MDF isn't indestructible
[ ] I'm better at delegating
[ ] I regret everything

NEXT STEPS

[ ] Retell story at every social event
[ ] Submit for "DIY Hero of the Year" award
[ ] Cover it with a rug
[ ] Let Mavis think you planned it that way
[ ] Move house

POST-PROJECT REFLECTION FORM

FOR INTERNAL USE ONLY (I.E., YOUR EGO)
FORM 4A - VERSION 0.1 (STILL IN DRAFT)

PROJECT NAME: _____
(E.G., OPERATION WOBBLY SHELF, MILDLY AMBITIOUS DECKING, THE GREAT TILE INCIDENT)

START DATE: ___ / ___ / ___   PROJECTED COMPLETION DATE:
                                [ ] SAME DAY [ ] WITHIN THE MONTH [ ] SUBJECT TO CLIMATE

ACTUAL COMPLETION DATE: ___ / ___ / ___   [ ] STILL PENDING

PERSONAL ASSESSMENT
PLEASE RATE YOUR PERFORMANCE IN THE FOLLOWING AREAS:

Category	Rating (Tick One)
Planning & Preparation	[ ] Printed something [ ] Made notes [ ] Winged it gloriously
Tool Familiarity	[ ] Totally confident [ ] YouTubed it [ ] Used a spoon again
Structural Soundness	[ ] Rock solid [ ] Slight flex [ ] Will collapse when judged
Time Management	[ ] On schedule [ ] Lost 3 weekends [ ] Time is a construct
Stress Management	[ ] Zen monk [ ] Mildly snappy [ ] Shouted at the ladder
Communication with Partner	[ ] Harmonious [ ] Passive-aggressive [ ] Divorce imminent
Final Outcome	[ ] Functional [ ] Functional(ish) [ ] Artistic reinterpretation

INVENTORY & CASUALTIES

Please indicate the number of the following:
Tools lost: ____
Screws left over: ____
Injuries sustained: ____
Arguments sparked: ____
"Let's call a professional" moments: ____
Number of times you used the phrase:
"That'll do." ____

LESSONS (ALLEGEDLY) LEARNED

[ ] Next time, I'll measure first
[ ] Spirit levels are not optional
[ ] Maybe I do need a workbench
[ ] MDF isn't indestructible
[ ] I'm better at delegating
[ ] I regret everything

NEXT STEPS

[ ] Retell story at every social event
[ ] Submit for "DIY Hero of the Year" award
[ ] Cover it with a rug
[ ] Let Mavis think you planned it that way
[ ] Move house

SPECIAL FEATURE

HBM
The Secret Brotherhood of Harry Black Maskers

"If it can't be fixed with masking tape... you're not using enough."

Move over screwdrivers, take a seat pliers — it's time to bow before the true miracle of DIY: Masking Tape.

APPLIES TO ALL MASKING / DUCT TAPE

Often overlooked. Frequently misapplied.
Rarely understood. But always present.
Introducing: The Secret Brotherhood of Harry Black Maskers,
those who know that when all else fails,
a few carefully applied strips of tacky glory
can suggest professionalism,
even if the reality is closer to panic patchwork.

SPECIAL FEATURE
HBM

*HBM isn't a formal organisation.
It's a state of mind. If you've ever:*

- *Masked a crack instead of filling it,*
- *Reinforced a chair leg like it's heading into battle,*
- *Or sealed a draughty window with enough tape to mummify Tutankhamun...*

You are already a member.

The 7 Sacred Uses of all Masking Tape (Ranked by Legitimacy)

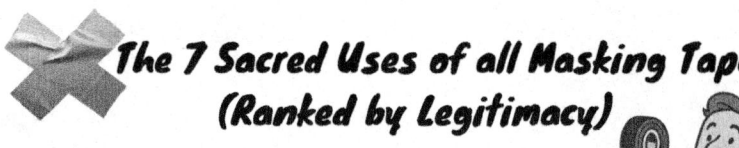

- **Actually Masking Things (Rare)**
  Used properly to edge off painting work. Almost noble.
- **Labelling Random Jars in the Garage**
  What does "Screws: maybe" even mean?
- **Temporarily Holding Stuff While You "Go Get the Real Fixings"**
  Spoiler: this is the fix.
- **Bandaging a Finger in Crisis**
  First aid? No. But it's tight and sticks to hair like a spiteful ex.
- **Attaching One Object to Another Object That Shouldn't Be Attached**
  E.g., spatula + electric whisk = DIY concrete mixer.
- **Preventing Conversations About "Doing It Properly"**
  If Mavis can't see the problem, there is no problem.
- **Art Installation / Modern Sculpture / Evidence of Panic**
  Common in rental properties.

SPECIAL FEATURE
HBM

Brotherhood Rituals (Observed but Never Admitted)

The Silent Tug Test:
Pulling at it gently to see if it holds... then pretending that was intentional when it falls off.

The Diagonal Strip of Shame:
That one bit of tape that peels off and flaps forever in judgement.

The "Looks Fine from a Distance" Doctrine:
3ft away = perfection.

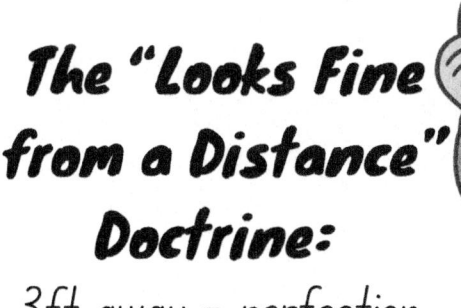

Tape Type	Use Case	Actual Outcome
Masking Tape	Gentle hold, painting	Peels itself off in 2 hours.
Duct Tape	Apocalypse survival	Peels paint, finger skin, and relationships.
Electrical Tape	Anything involving electricity (theoretically)	Melted into the appliance forever.
Double-sided Tape	Hanging things with optimism	Object remains airborne for 7 minutes.

SPECIAL FEATURE

HBM

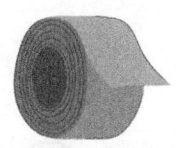 

FINAL WORD FROM HBM HEADQUARTERS

"Measure twice, cut once, tape forever."

Masking tape isn't just a tool.
It's a lifestyle.
A philosophy.
A very thin lie told with confidence.

So go on. Wrap it. Reinforce it. Pretend it's holding everything together.

CERTIFICATE OF MEMBERSHIP

SECRET BROTHERHOOD OF HARRY BLACK MASKERS

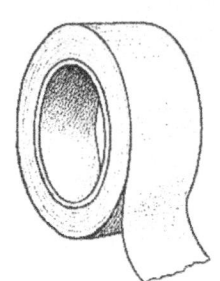

"If it can't be fixed with masking tape... you're not using enough."

THIS CERTIFIES THAT

is henceforth recognized as a master of improvisational repair and craftsmanship through the avid application of masking tape.

- The No. 1 reason for NOT doing a task!

- Do not put yourself or others at any risk

- Use the correct tool for the job

- Do not cut corners

- Get an expert in – there is a reason (usually) why they are expensive!

- If in doubt seek advice, or wait until everyone has forgotten about it, then pretend it didn't need doing!

THE BIG STUFF

I will need to address the following tasks in the next 5 years or so, no messing!!

THINGS TO DO

GOOD
THINGS
TAKE
TIME

OK
YOU CAN MAKE A LIST...

1.

2.

3.

4.

5.

6.

...BUT DOES IT REALLY NEED TO BE DONE?

IMPORTANT!

POST-PROJECT REFLECTION FORM

FOR INTERNAL USE ONLY (I.E., YOUR EGO)
FORM 4A - VERSION 0.1 (STILL IN DRAFT)

PROJECT NAME: _____
(E.G., OPERATION WOBBLY SHELF, MILDLY AMBITIOUS DECKING, THE GREAT TILE INCIDENT)

START DATE: ___ / ___ / ___   PROJECTED COMPLETION DATE:
                                [ ] SAME DAY [ ] WITHIN THE MONTH [ ] SUBJECT TO CLIMATE

ACTUAL COMPLETION DATE: ___ / ___ / ___   [ ] STILL PENDING

PERSONAL ASSESSMENT
PLEASE RATE YOUR PERFORMANCE IN THE FOLLOWING AREAS:

Category	Rating (Tick One)
Planning & Preparation	[ ] Printed something [ ] Made notes [ ] Winged it gloriously
Tool Familiarity	[ ] Totally confident [ ] YouTubed it [ ] Used a spoon again
Structural Soundness	[ ] Rock solid [ ] Slight flex [ ] Will collapse when judged
Time Management	[ ] On schedule [ ] Lost 3 weekends [ ] Time is a construct
Stress Management	[ ] Zen monk [ ] Mildly snappy [ ] Shouted at the ladder
Communication with Partner	[ ] Harmonious [ ] Passive-aggressive [ ] Divorce imminent
Final Outcome	[ ] Functional [ ] Functional(ish) [ ] Artistic reinterpretation

INVENTORY & CASUALTIES

Please indicate the number of the following:
Tools lost: ____
Screws left over: ____
Injuries sustained: ____
Arguments sparked: ____
"Let's call a professional" moments: ____
Number of times you used the phrase: "That'll do." ____

LESSONS (ALLEGEDLY) LEARNED

[ ] Next time, I'll measure first
[ ] Spirit levels are not optional
[ ] Maybe I do need a workbench
[ ] MDF isn't indestructible
[ ] I'm better at delegating
[ ] I regret everything

NEXT STEPS

[ ] Retell story at every social event
[ ] Submit for "DIY Hero of the Year" award
[ ] Cover it with a rug
[ ] Let Mavis think you planned it that way
[ ] Move house

Careful planning takes time!
Not to be rushed.

"If you don't have a plan, you plan to fail"

(also showing someone your plan usually stops them bothering you for a while!!)

A YEAR AT A GLANCE
(DOESN'T SAY WHICH YEAR!)

JANUARY

FEBRUARY

MARCH

APRIL

MAY

JUNE

JULY

AUGUST

SEPTEMBER

OCTOBER

NOVEMBER

DECEMBER

REMEMBER
YOU MUST PACE YOUR TASKS

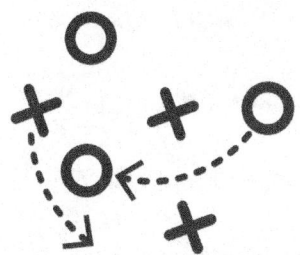

TOMORROW

NEXT WEEK

NEXT MONTH

Next Year

RECOMMENDED!

I will need to plan it carefully (walk away)

What a great idea (walk away - fast)

I'll need to get some new tools first!

No problem, once the weather improves

No problem, when it is a bit cooler

No problem, when it is a bit warmer

There is a lot of safety to consider (walk away)

I will need to do a Risk Assessment first!

I will need to research the best approach

I know a better way which I will look into

It will cost a lot of money,
but if YOU think it is important...

Yes, that is a good idea,
let me find my book and write it down (walk away)

Yes, I have time in
(see calendar for acceptable months next year)

No problem. I will enrol on a course to do it properly
(don't enrol on a course - just watch a short Youtube video)

DIY RISK ASSESSMENT FORM

FOR INTERNAL USE ONLY (I.E., YOUR EGO).
FORM 5A – VERSION 0.1 (STILL IN DRAFT)

PPROJECT TITLE:
"THE THING MY PARTNER ASKED ME TO FIX (EVENTUALLY)"

DATE:
☐ TODAY ☐ TOMORROW ☑ "LET'S NOT RUSH THESE THINGS"

ASSESSMENT CONDUCTED BY:
☐ ME
☐ NOT ME
☑ SOMEONE WITH MORE EXPERIENCE, IDEALLY A NEIGHBOUR

TASK DESCRIPTION

Describe the DIY task:

"Replace the thing with the other thing using... what do you call it... the twisty rod thing."

Potential Hazard	Likelihood	Severity	Mitigation Strategy
Hurting self with tool	High	Medium	Use tool box as decoy, do nothing
Confusing instruction manual	Certain	Existential	Blame poor translation, ignore entirely
Argument with partner	High	High	Nod enthusiastically, say "on it, babe!"
Getting distracted by kettle/TV/dog	Guaranteed	Low	Embrace distraction, declare "break"
Actually finishing the task	Very Low	Unknown	Not a current concern

DIY RISK ASSESSMENT FORM (PART 2)

COMPETENCE & TRAINING

Do you have experience in this task?
- ☐ Yes
- ☐ No
- ☑ Let's be honest, not really

Have you watched a YouTube tutorial?
- ☐ Yes
- ☑ Watched 3 mins, skipped to end
- ☐ Thought about watching one

REQUIRED TOOLS (TICK WHAT YOU PRETEND TO USE)

- ☐ Hammer
- ☐ Drill
- ☐ Level
- ☑ Coffee mug
- ☐ Masking Tape (HBM-approved)
- ☑ Pencil (mainly for chewing)
- ☐ Vague sense of initiative

EMERGENCY PREPAREDNESS

Who to contact if it all goes wrong:
- ☐ Local tradesperson
- ☑ Father-in-law
- ☐ Neighbour called Dave
- ☐ Emergency biscuit tin

First aid kit location:
- ☑ Somewhere behind the Christmas decorations
- ☐ Just rub it with tea

FINAL ASSESSMENT

- ☐ Task is safe and I am prepared
- ☐ Task is dangerous but I'm brave
- ☑ Task is terrifying, best leave it until next weekend

Signed: _____ (under duress)

Witnessed by: _____ (eye roll implied)

DESIGN GRIDS
FOR YOUR INTENSE
PLANNING STAGES

REMEMBER:

**PROPER
PLANNING
TAKES
TIME!**

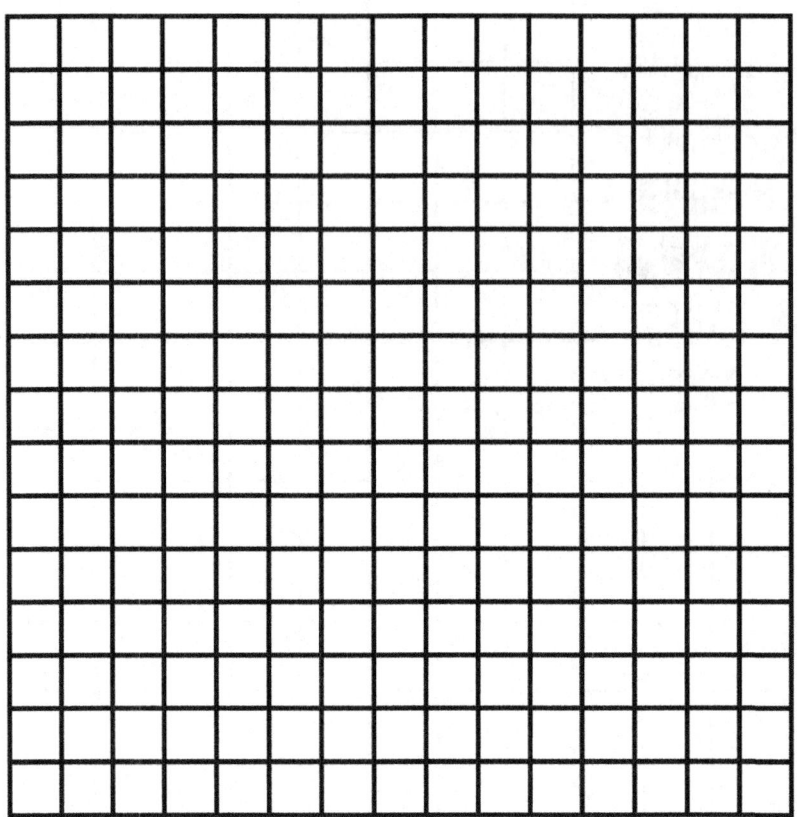

PRIOR
PLANNING
PREVENTS
POOR
PERFORMANCE

REMEMBER SAFETY
& USE THE RIGHT TOOLS!

DO NOT RUSH INTO THESE SORT OF THINGS!

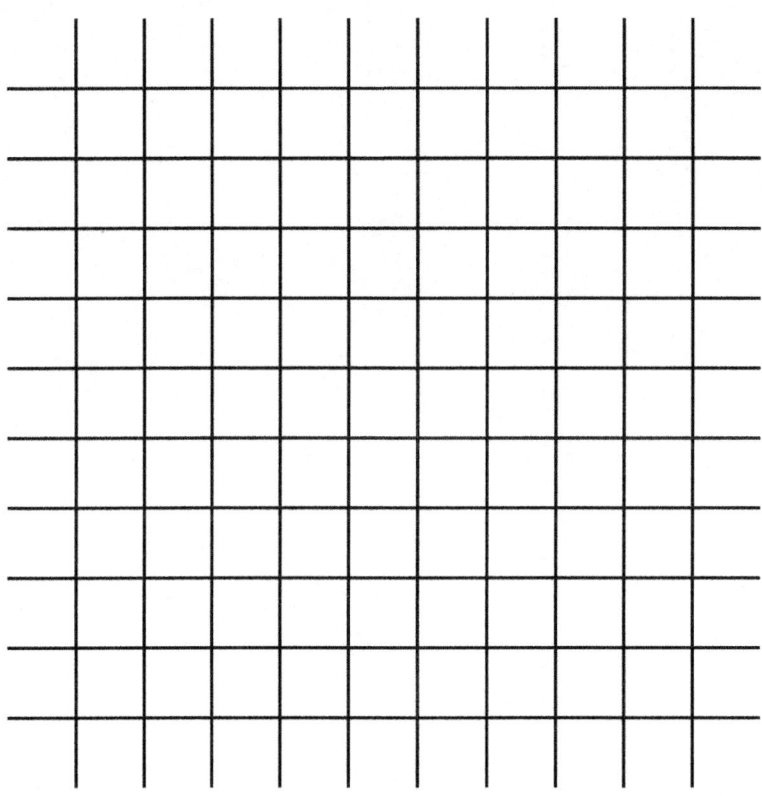

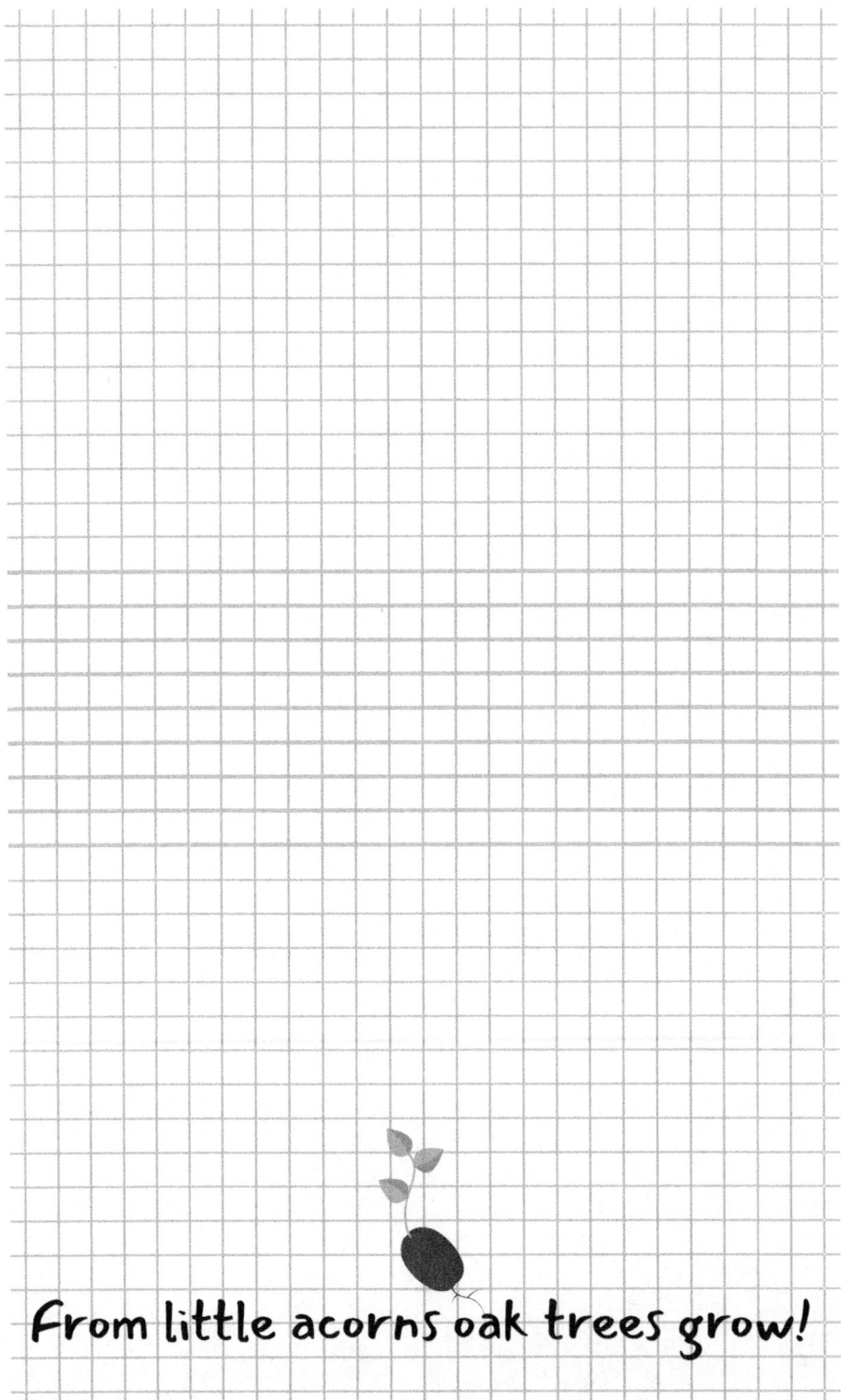

From little acorns oak trees grow!

- I will need to plan it carefully (walk away)
- What a great idea (walk away - fast)
- I'll need some new tools!
- No problem, once the weather improves
- No problem, when it is a bit cooler
- No problem, when it is a bit warmer
- There is a lot of safety to consider (walk away)
- I will need to do a Risk Assessment first!
- I will need to research the best approach
- I know a better way which I will look into
- It will cost a lot of money, but if YOU think it is important...
- Yes, that is a good idea, let me find my book and write it down (walk away)
- Yes, I have time in (see calendar for acceptable months next year)
- No problem. I will enrol on a course to do it properly
  (don't enrol on a course - just watch a short online video)

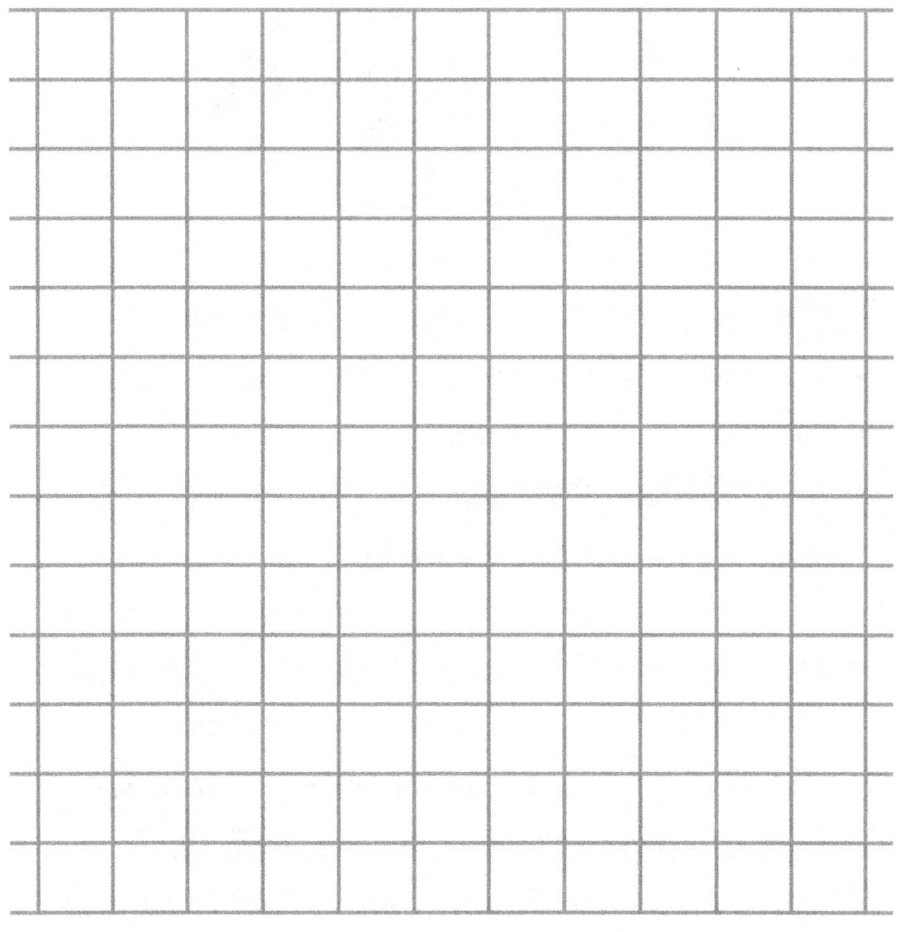

Have you considered everything?

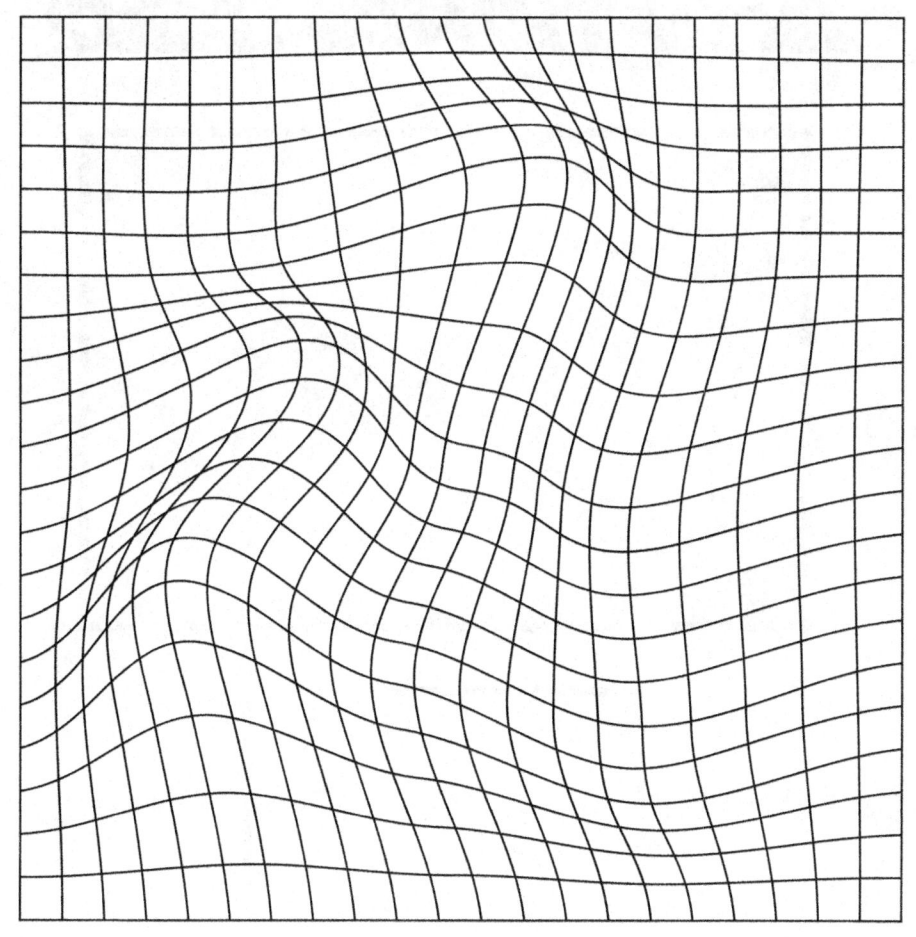

Have you really considered everything?

LET'S NOT RUSH INTO THINGS HERE!

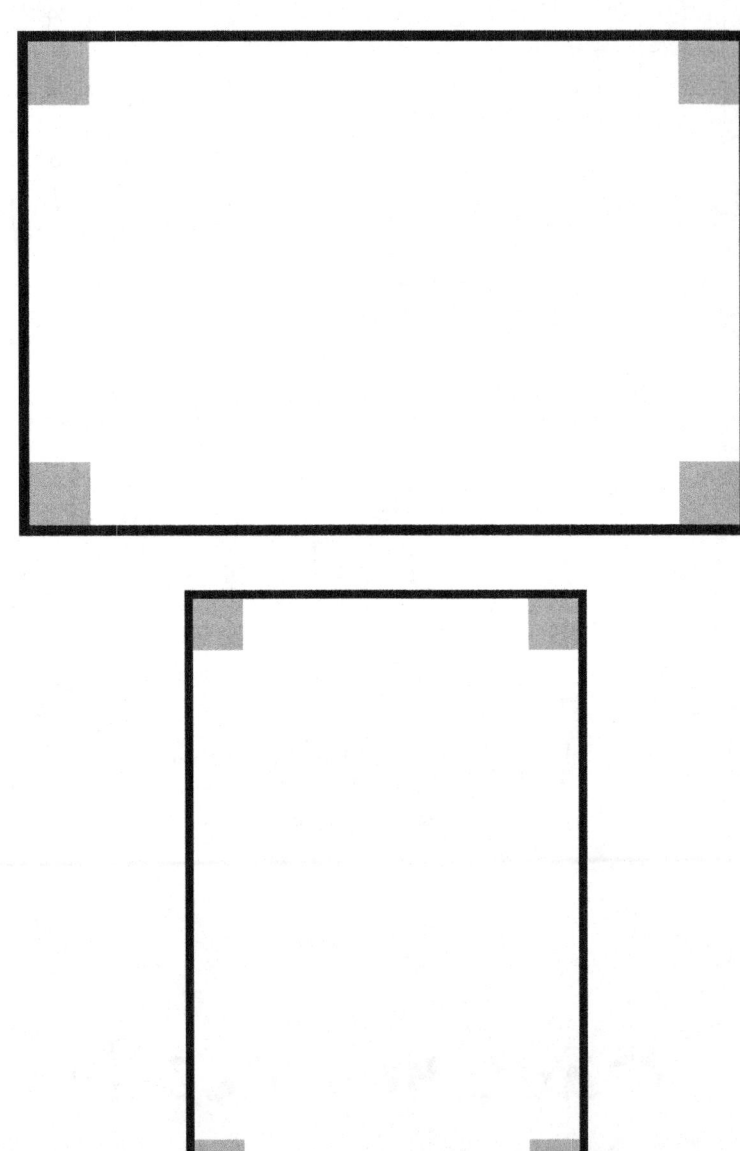

DESIGN GRIDS FOR YOUR INTENSE PLANNING STAGES

REMEMBER:
PROPER PLANNING TAKES TIME!

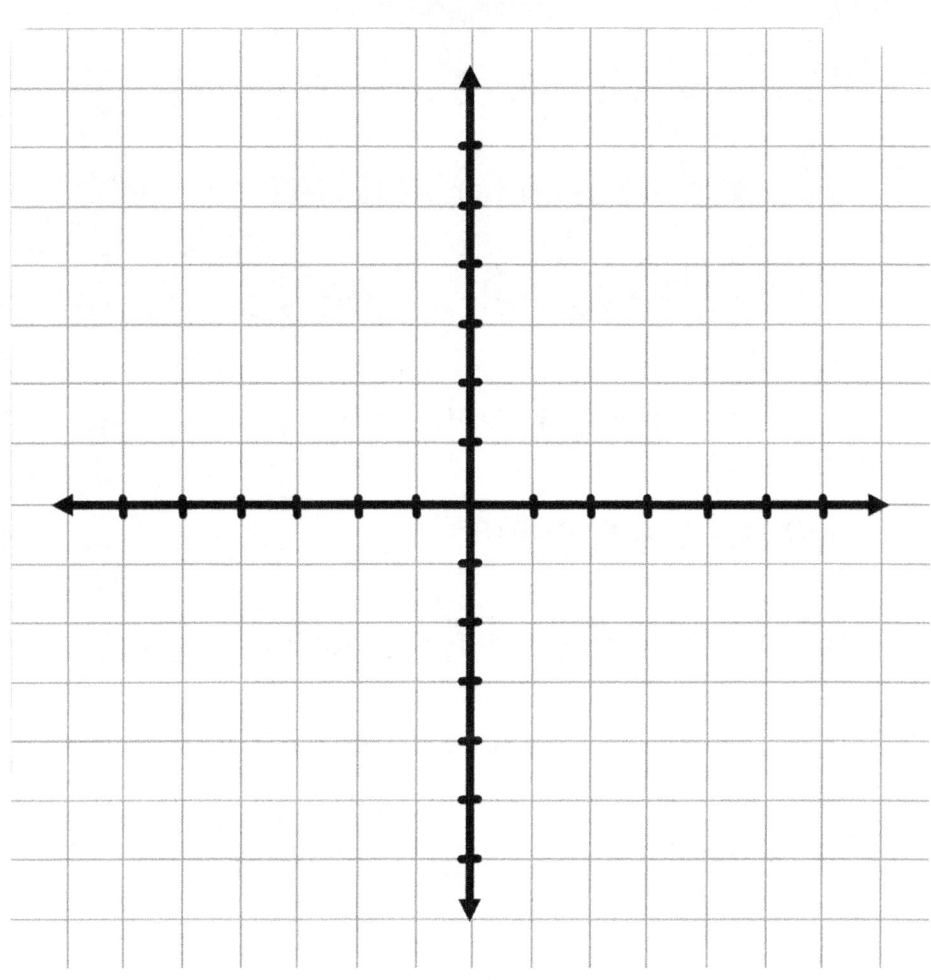

- The No. 1 reason for NOT doing a task!

- Do not put yourself or others at any risk

- Use the correct tool for the job

- Do not cut corners

- Get an expert in – there is a reason (usually) why they are expensive!

- If in doubt seek advice, or wait until everyone has forgotten about it, then pretend it didn't need doing!

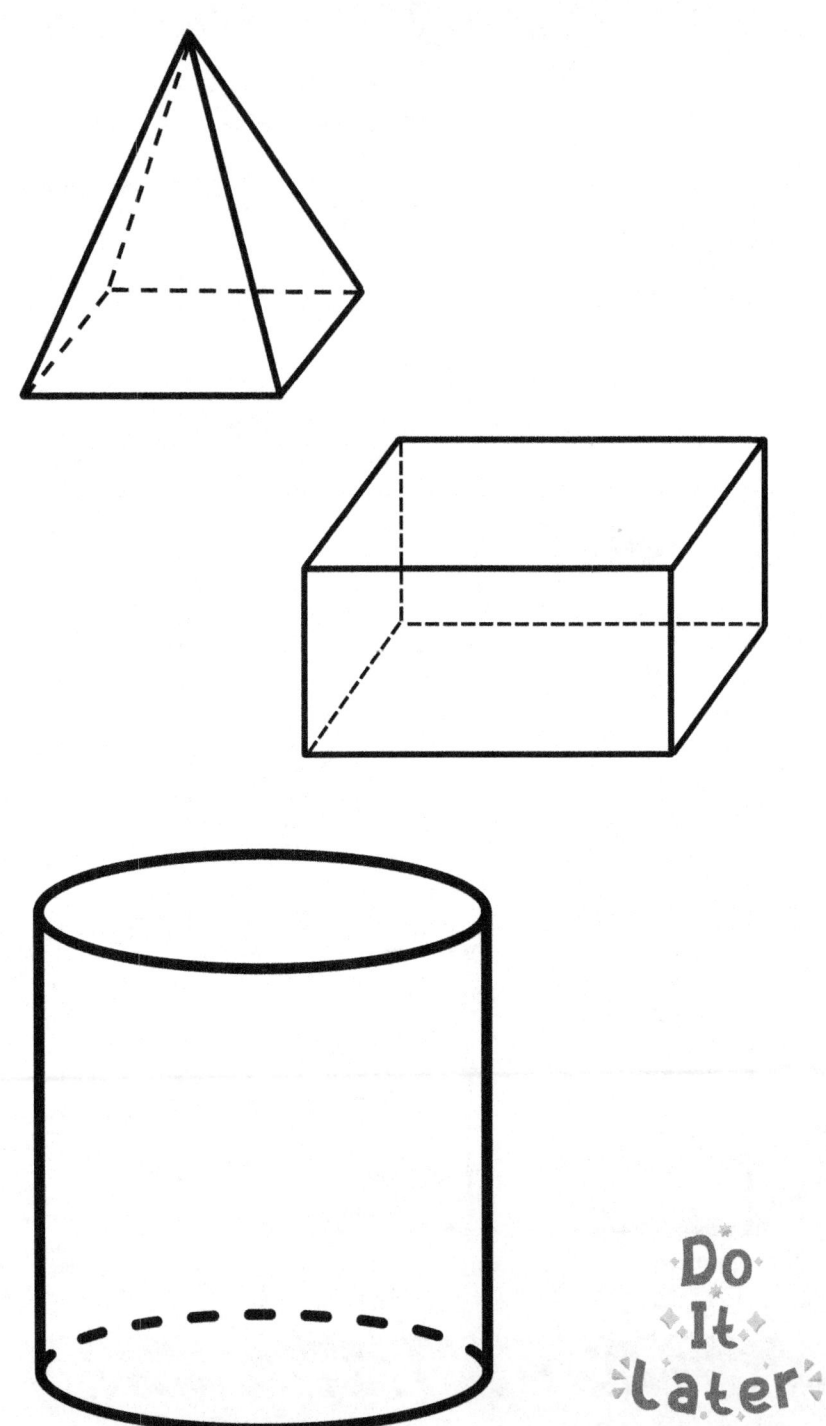

> MINIMIZE ANY RISK TO
YOURSELF & OTHERS!

CONSIDER STUFF CAREFULLY <

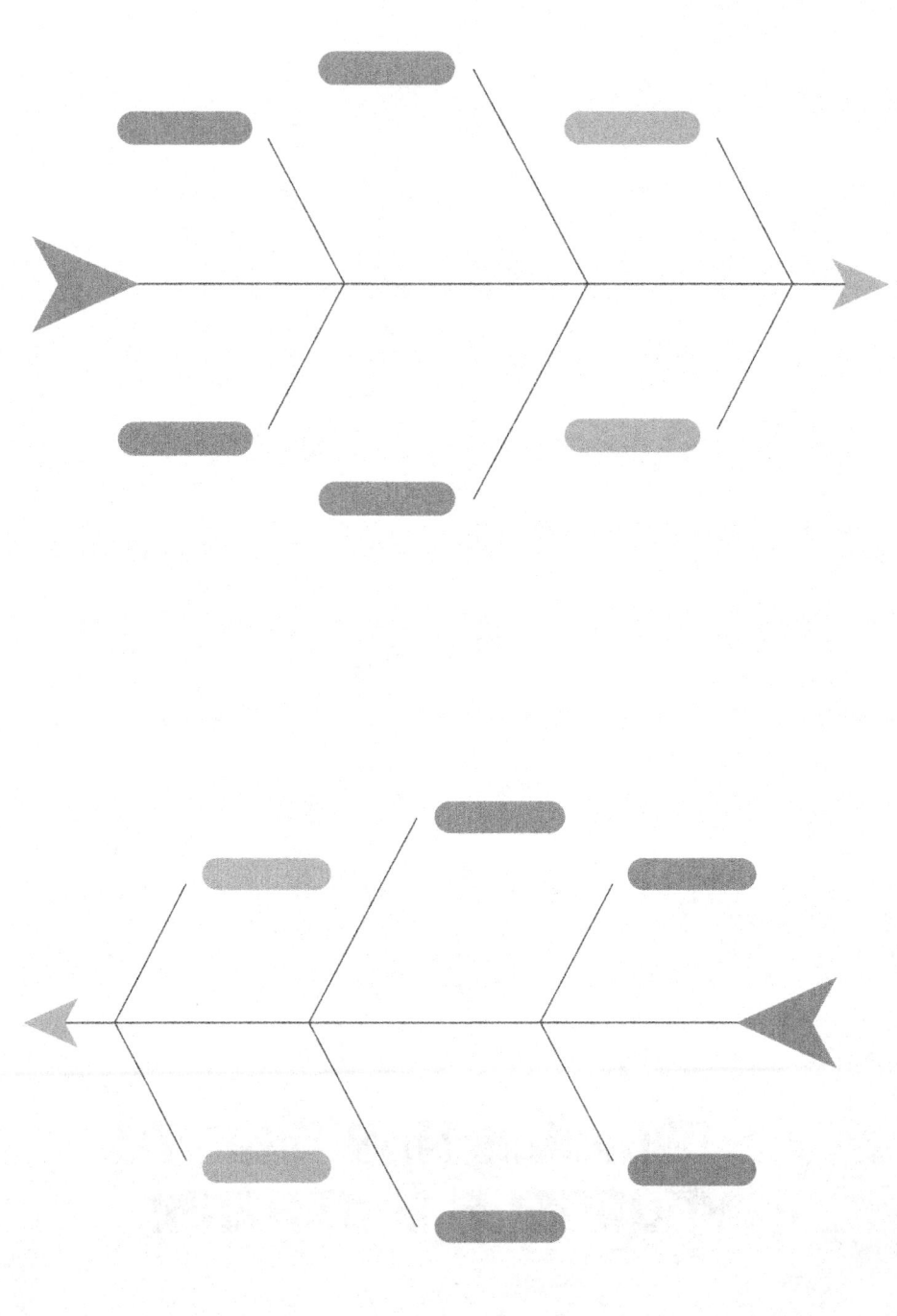

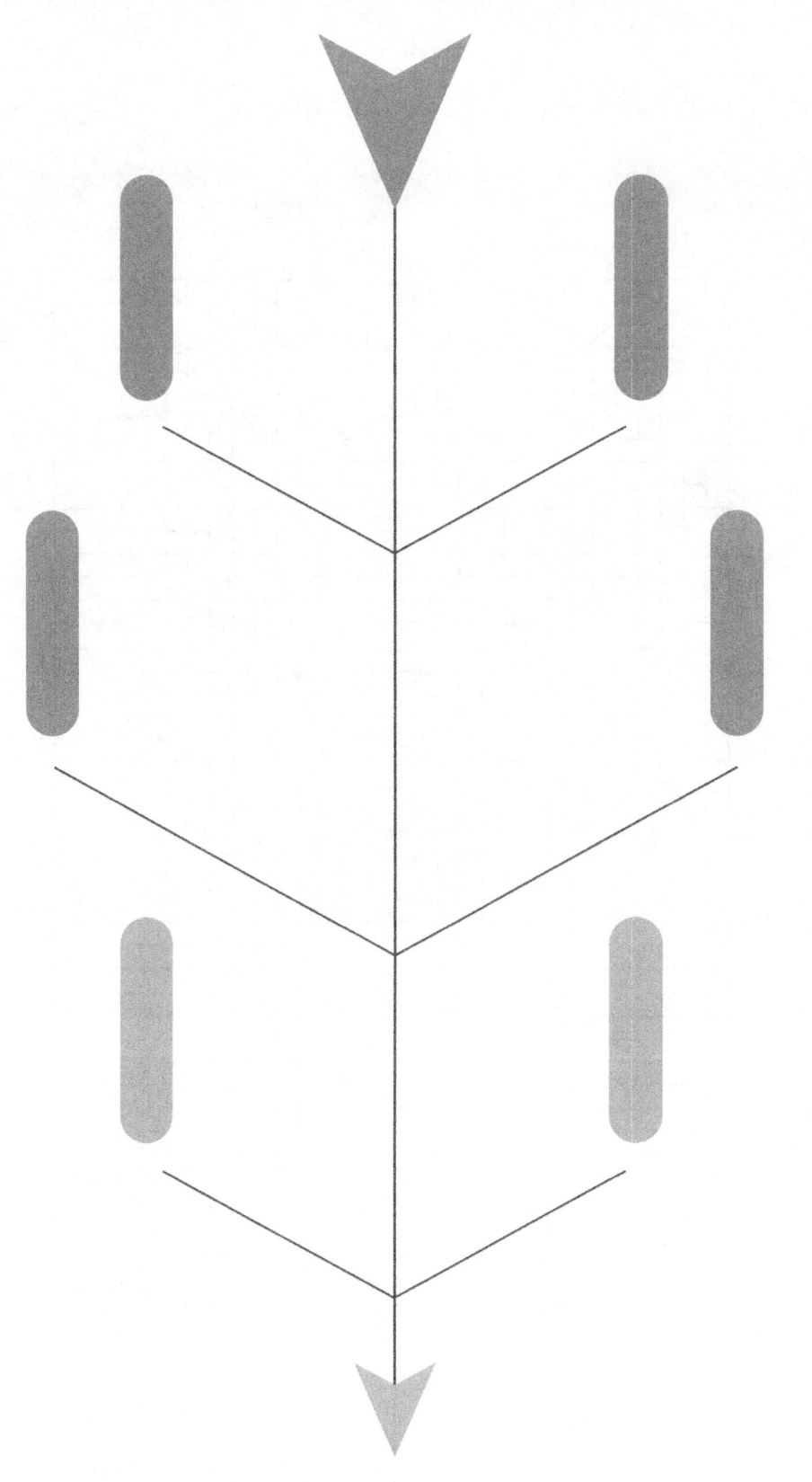

REMEMBER SAFETY & USING THE RIGHT TOOLS!

DO NOT RUSH INTO THESE SORT OF THINGS!

Garden design
(if you really have to!)

Garden design
(if you really have to!)

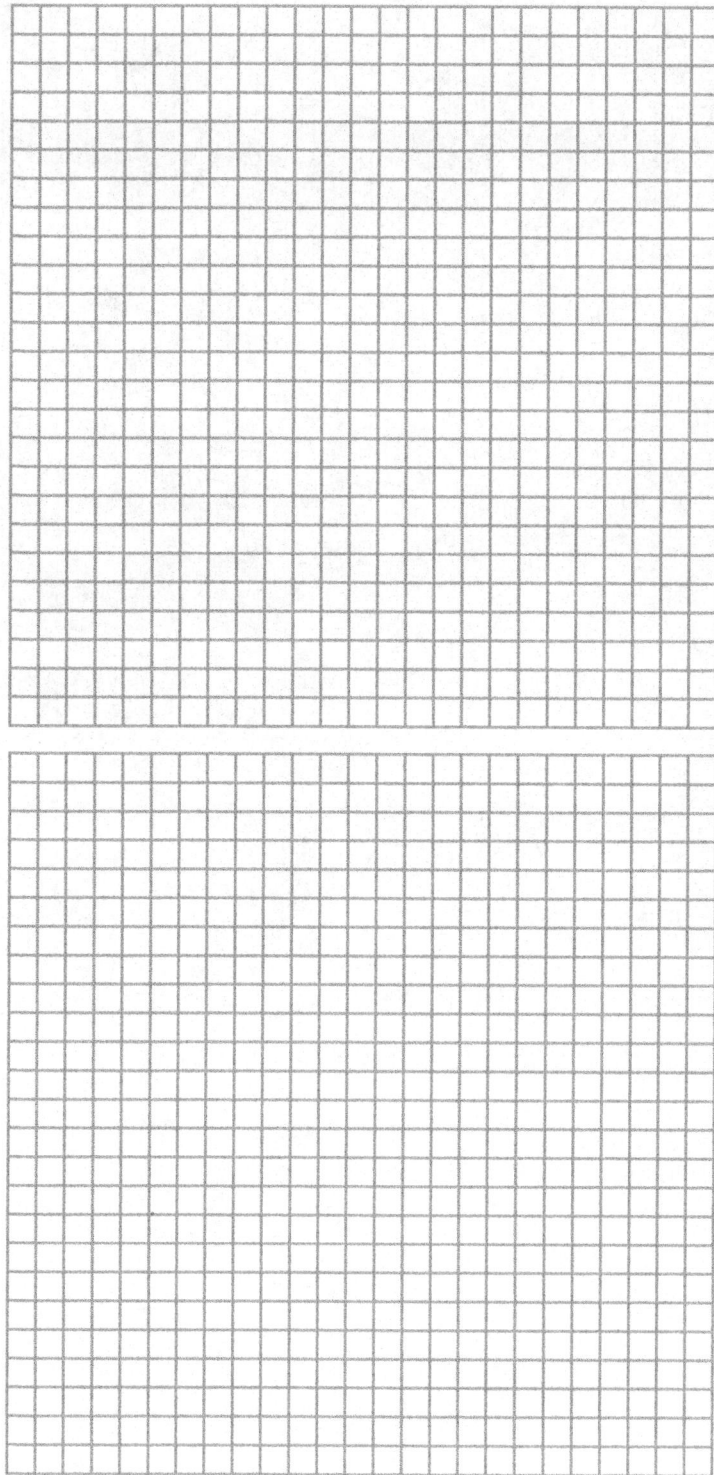

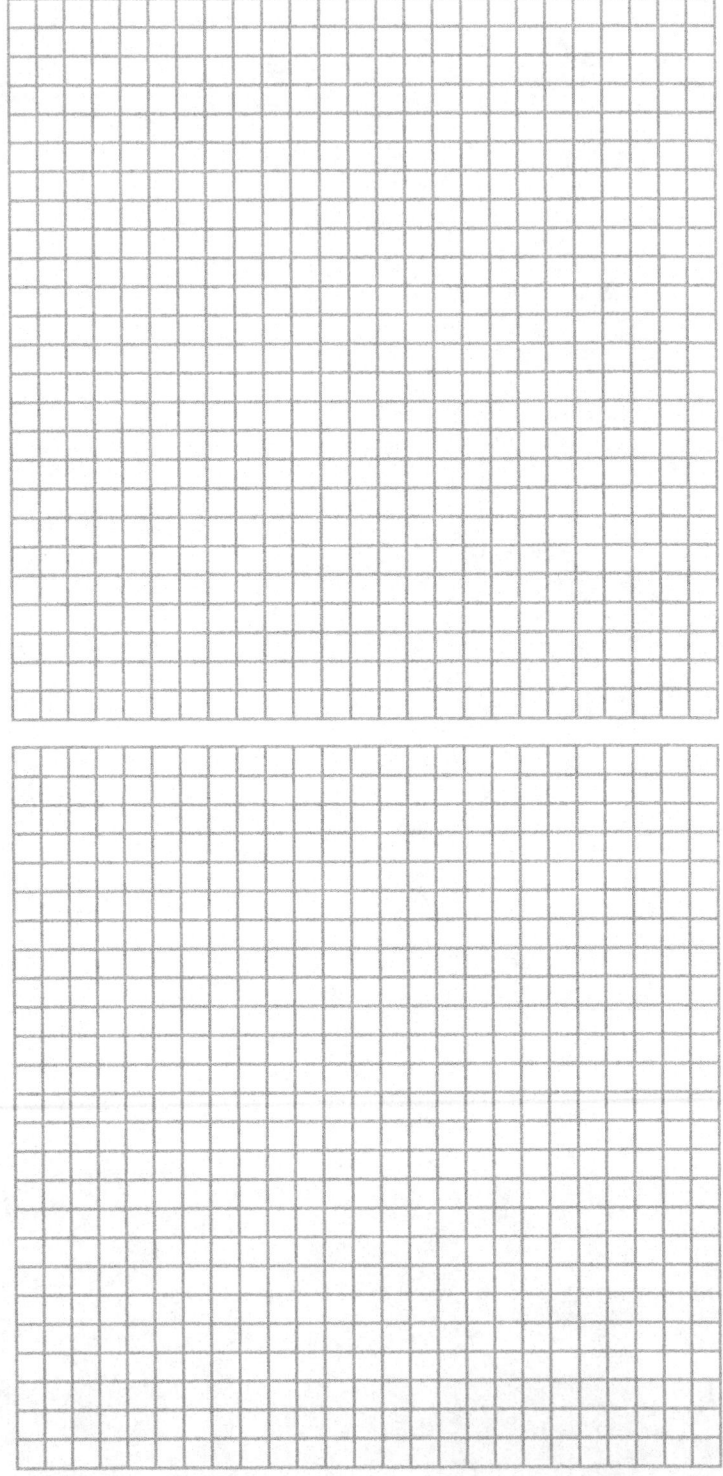

GARDEN DESIGN
(IF YOU REALLY HAVE TO!)

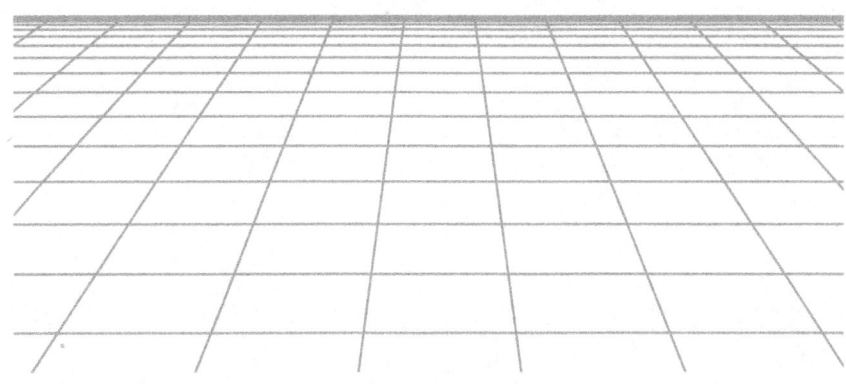

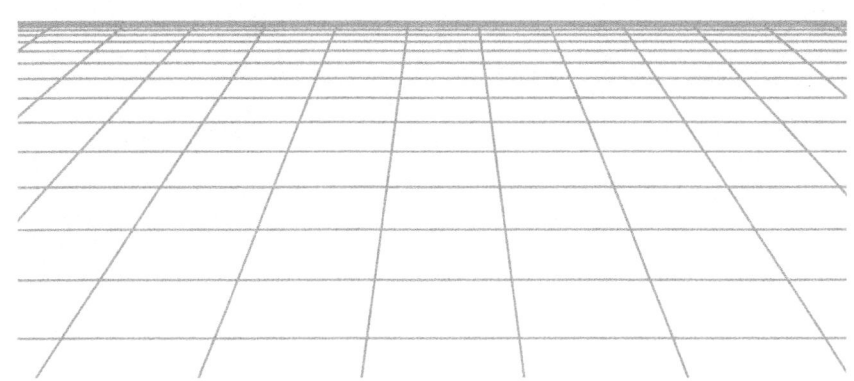

Weeds have feelings too!

GARDEN DESIGN
(IF YOU REALLY HAVE TO!)

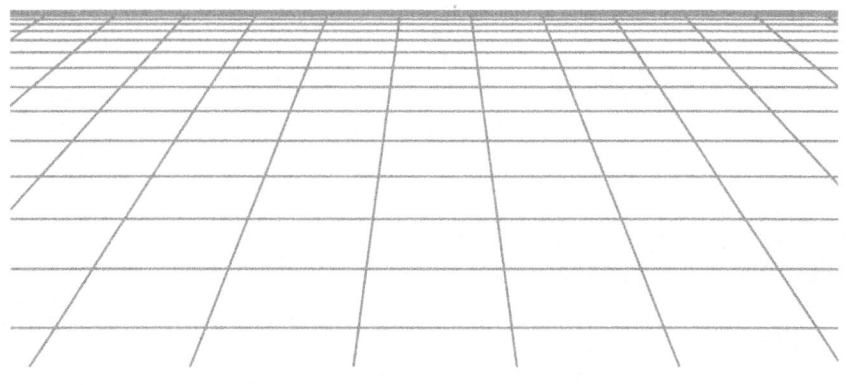

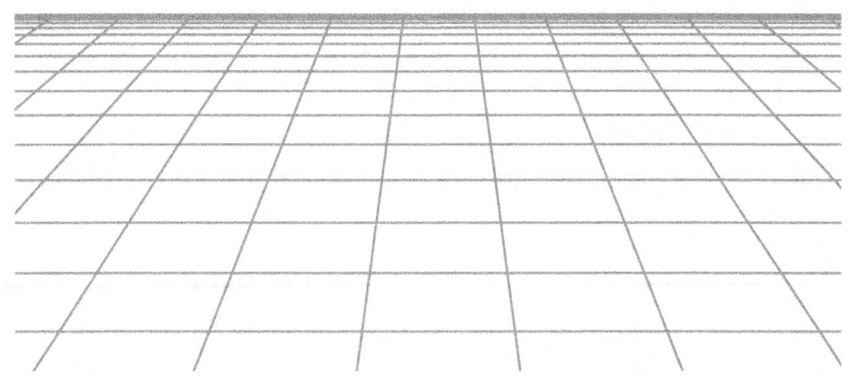

Weeds have feelings too!

Garden design

Garden design

No!
You do not need a water feature!
...too much hassle!

PATIO DESIGNER
(I'D LEAVE IT IF I WAS YOU!)

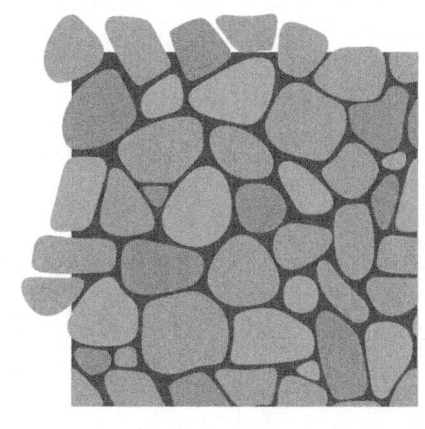
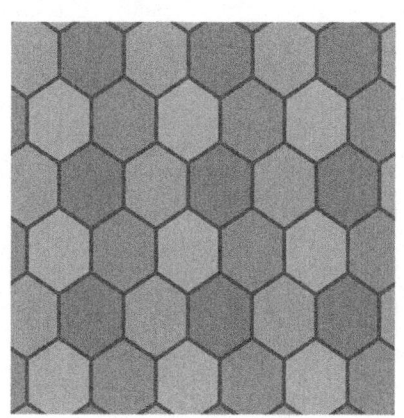

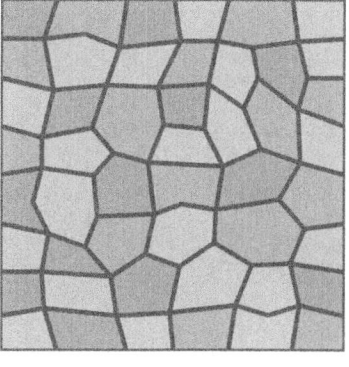

PATIO DESIGNER

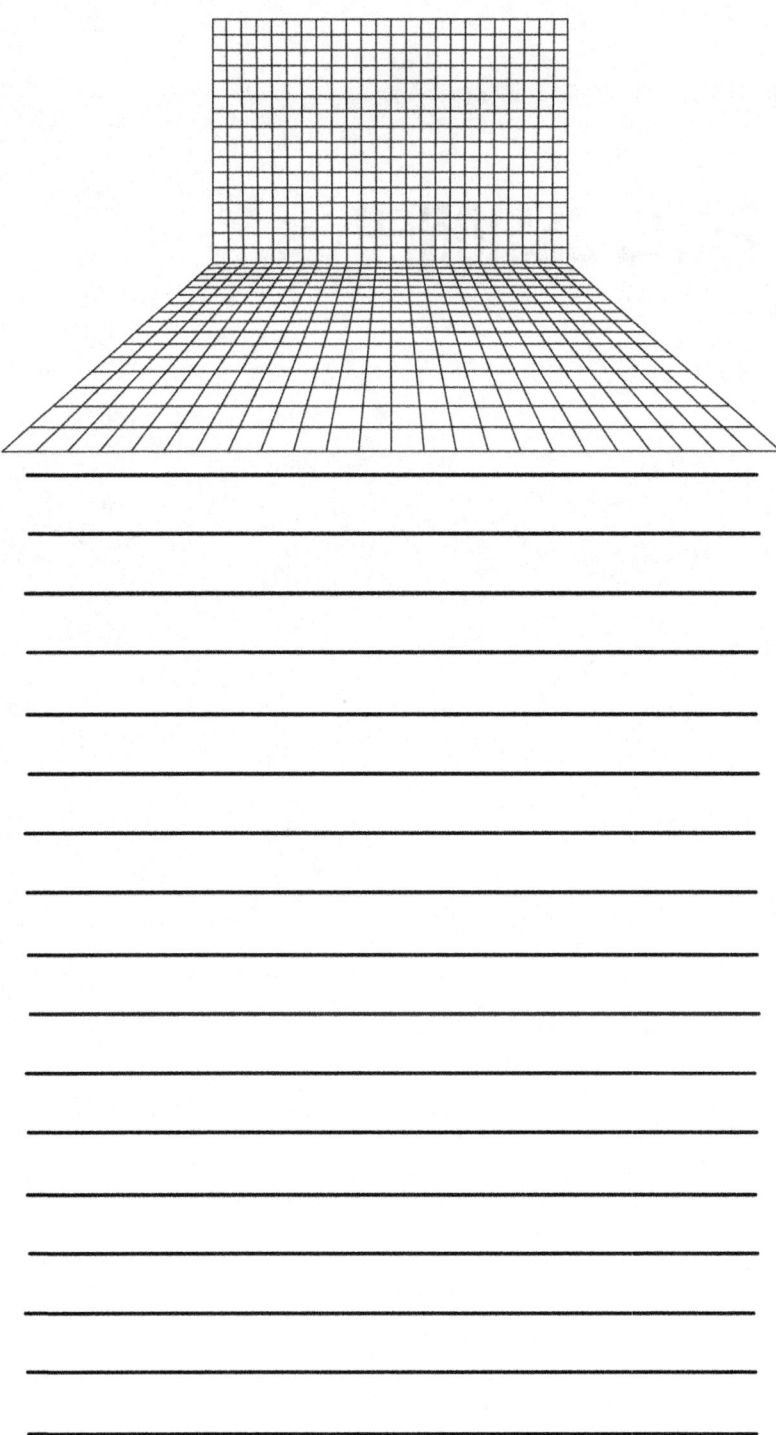

PATIO DESIGNER

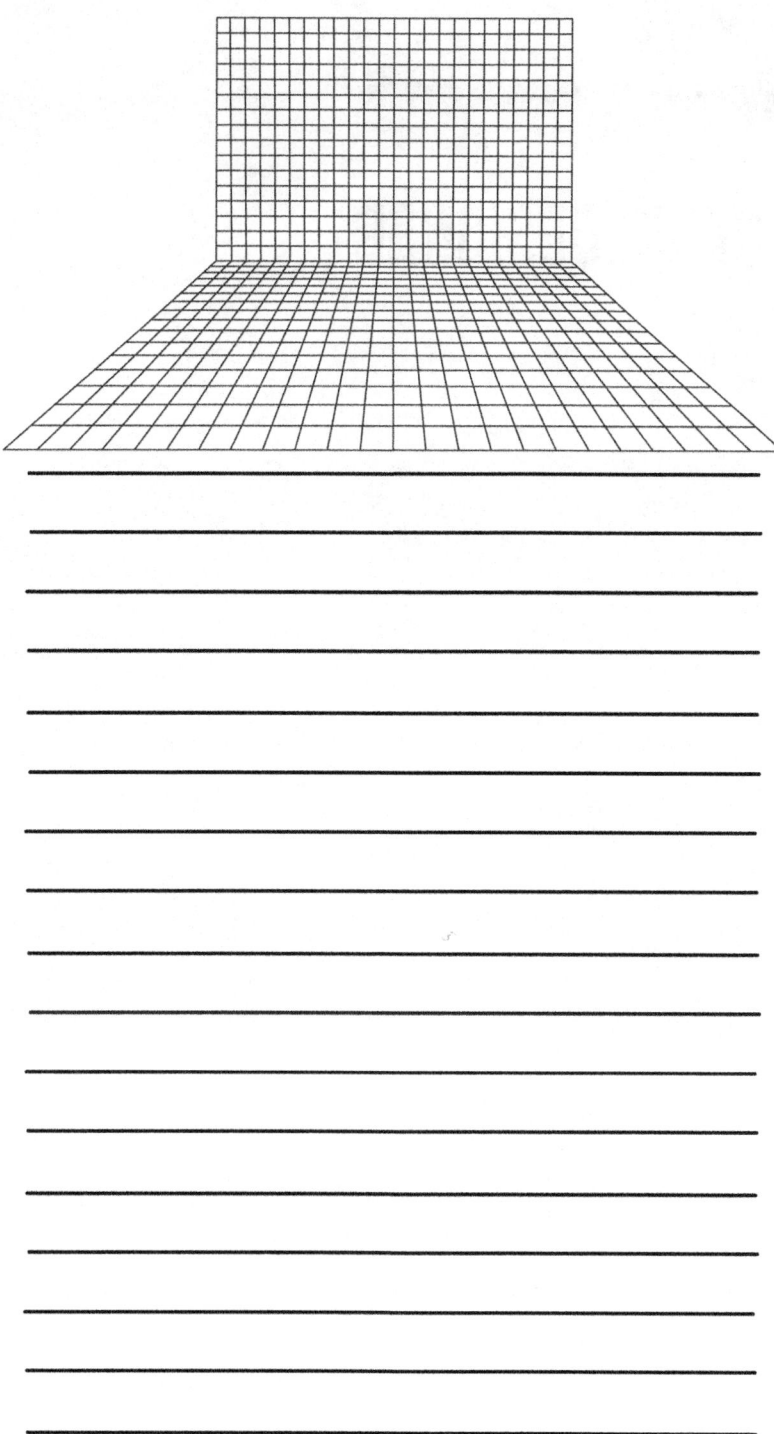

PATIO DESIGNER

VERY IMPORTANT PROJECT

SERIOUS STUFF HERE

PROJECT NAME:

_____

TARGET DATE (NON BINDING):

_____

DIY RISK ASSESSMENT FORM

FOR INTERNAL USE ONLY (I.E., YOUR EGO).
FORM 5A – VERSION 0.1 (STILL IN DRAFT)

PPROJECT TITLE:
"THE THING MY PARTNER ASKED ME TO FIX (EVENTUALLY)"

DATE:
☐ TODAY   ☐ TOMORROW   ☑ "LET'S NOT RUSH THESE THINGS"

ASSESSMENT CONDUCTED BY:
☐ ME
☐ NOT ME
☑ SOMEONE WITH MORE EXPERIENCE, IDEALLY A NEIGHBOUR

TASK DESCRIPTION

Describe the DIY task:

"Replace the thing with the other thing using... what do you call it... the twisty rod thing."

Potential Hazard	Likelihood	Severity	Mitigation Strategy
Hurting self with tool	High	Medium	Use tool box as decoy, do nothing
Confusing instruction manual	Certain	Existential	Blame poor translation, ignore entirely
Argument with partner	High	High	Nod enthusiastically, say "on it, babe!"
Getting distracted by kettle/TV/dog	Guaranteed	Low	Embrace distraction, declare "break"
Actually finishing the task	Very Low	Unknown	Not a current concern

DIY RISK ASSESSMENT FORM (PART 2)

COMPETENCE & TRAINING

Do you have experience in this task?
☐ Yes
☐ No
☑ Let's be honest, not really

Have you watched a YouTube tutorial?

☐ Yes
☑ Watched 3 mins, skipped to end
☐ Thought about watching one

REQUIRED TOOLS (TICK WHAT YOU PRETEND TO USE)

☐ Hammer
☐ Drill
☐ Level
☑ Coffee mug
☐ Masking Tape (HBM-approved)
☑ Pencil (mainly for chewing)
☐ Vague sense of initiative

EMERGENCY PREPAREDNESS

Who to contact if it all goes wrong:
☐ Local tradesperson
☑ Father-in-law
☐ Neighbour called Dave
☐ Emergency biscuit tin

First aid kit location:
☑ Somewhere behind the Christmas decorations
☐ Just rub it with tea

FINAL ASSESSMENT

☐ Task is safe and I am prepared
☐ Task is dangerous but I'm brave
☑ Task is terrifying, best leave it until next weekend

Signed: _____ (under duress)

Witnessed by: _____ (eye roll implied)

PROJECT DESCRIPTION

SAFETY

TOOLS

PROJECT PREPARATION

PROJECT STEPS

PROJECT NOTES

PROJECT NOTES

PROJECT NOTES

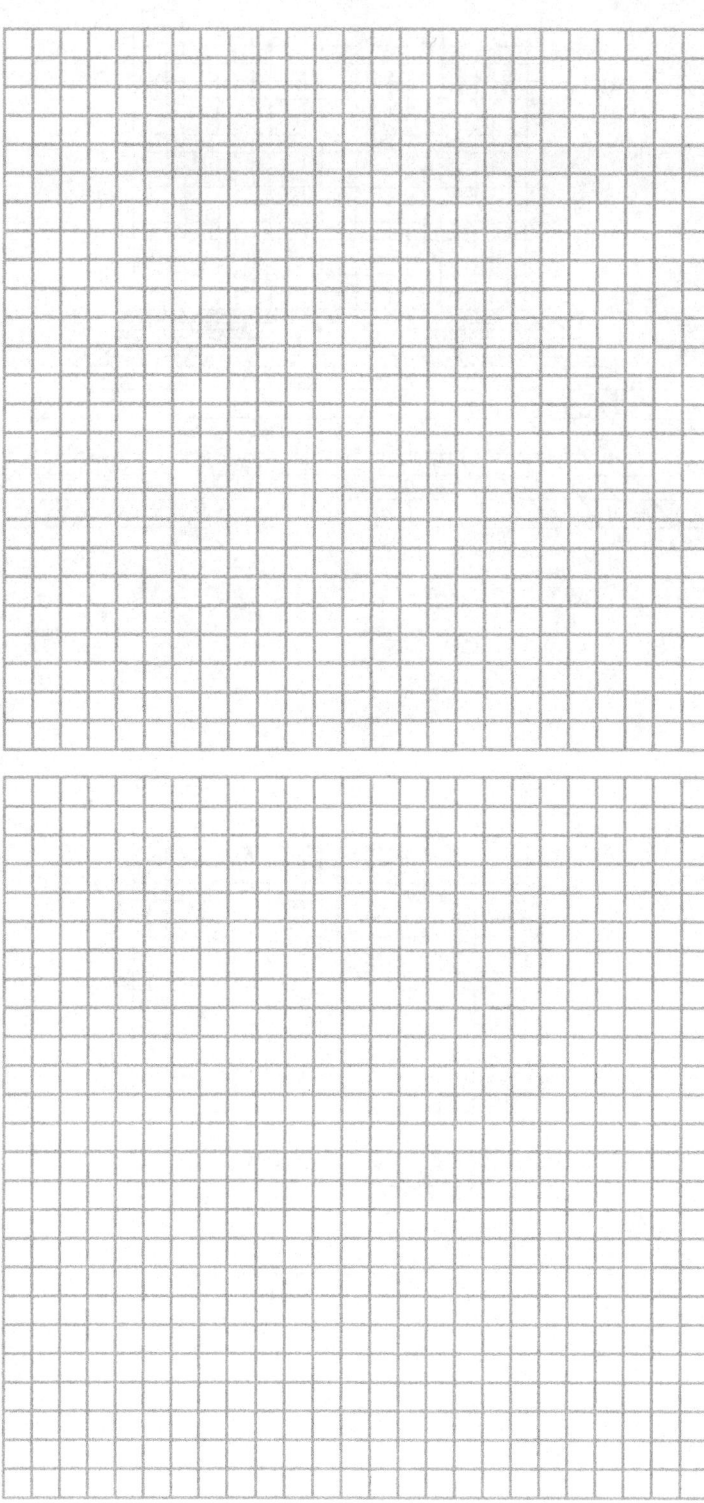

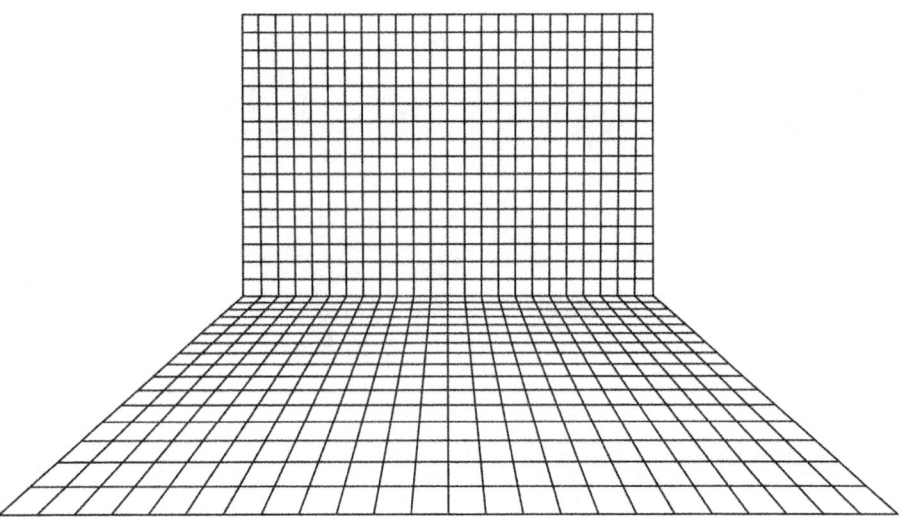

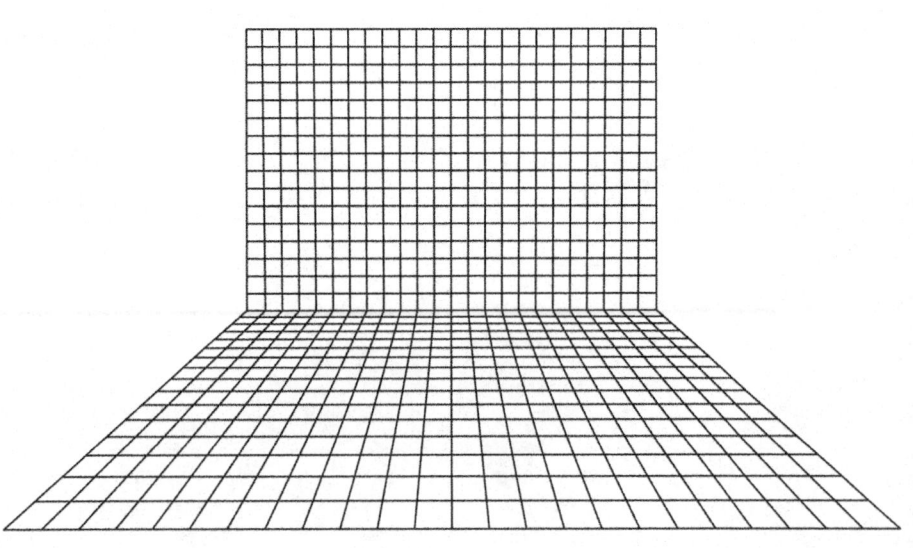

POST-PROJECT REFLECTION FORM

FOR INTERNAL USE ONLY (I.E., YOUR EGO)
FORM 4A - VERSION 0.1 (STILL IN DRAFT)

PROJECT NAME: _____
(E.G., OPERATION WOBBLY SHELF, MILDLY AMBITIOUS DECKING, THE GREAT TILE INCIDENT)

START DATE: ___ / ___ / ___

PROJECTED COMPLETION DATE:
[ ] SAME DAY [ ] WITHIN THE MONTH [ ] SUBJECT TO CLIMATE

ACTUAL COMPLETION DATE: ___ / ___ / ___   [ ] STILL PENDING

PERSONAL ASSESSMENT
PLEASE RATE YOUR PERFORMANCE IN THE FOLLOWING AREAS:

Category	Rating (Tick One)
Planning & Preparation	[ ] Printed something [ ] Made notes [ ] Winged it gloriously
Tool Familiarity	[ ] Totally confident [ ] YouTubed it [ ] Used a spoon again
Structural Soundness	[ ] Rock solid [ ] Slight flex [ ] Will collapse when judged
Time Management	[ ] On schedule [ ] Lost 3 weekends [ ] Time is a construct
Stress Management	[ ] Zen monk [ ] Mildly snappy [ ] Shouted at the ladder
Communication with Partner	[ ] Harmonious [ ] Passive-aggressive [ ] Divorce imminent
Final Outcome	[ ] Functional [ ] Functional(ish) [ ] Artistic reinterpretation

INVENTORY & CASUALTIES

Please indicate the number of the following:
Tools lost: ____
Screws left over: ____
Injuries sustained: ____
Arguments sparked: ____
"Let's call a professional" moments: ____
Number of times you used the phrase: "That'll do." ____

LESSONS (ALLEGEDLY) LEARNED

[ ] Next time, I'll measure first
[ ] Spirit levels are not optional
[ ] Maybe I do need a workbench
[ ] MDF isn't indestructible
[ ] I'm better at delegating
[ ] I regret everything

NEXT STEPS

[ ] Retell story at every social event
[ ] Submit for "DIY Hero of the Year" award
[ ] Cover it with a rug
[ ] Let Mavis think you planned it that way
[ ] Move house

POST-PROJECT REFLECTION FORM

FOR INTERNAL USE ONLY (I.E., YOUR EGO)
FORM 4A - VERSION 0.1 (STILL IN DRAFT)

PROJECT NAME: _____
(E.G., OPERATION WOBBLY SHELF, MILDLY AMBITIOUS DECKING, THE GREAT TILE INCIDENT)

START DATE: ___ / ___ / ___   PROJECTED COMPLETION DATE:
[ ] SAME DAY   [ ] WITHIN THE MONTH   [ ] SUBJECT TO CLIMATE

ACTUAL COMPLETION DATE: ___ / ___ / ___   [ ] STILL PENDING

PERSONAL ASSESSMENT
PLEASE RATE YOUR PERFORMANCE IN THE FOLLOWING AREAS:

Category	Rating (Tick One)
Planning & Preparation	[ ] Printed something [ ] Made notes [ ] Winged it gloriously
Tool Familiarity	[ ] Totally confident [ ] YouTubed it [ ] Used a spoon again
Structural Soundness	[ ] Rock solid [ ] Slight flex [ ] Will collapse when judged
Time Management	[ ] On schedule [ ] Lost 3 weekends [ ] Time is a construct
Stress Management	[ ] Zen monk [ ] Mildly snappy [ ] Shouted at the ladder
Communication with Partner	[ ] Harmonious [ ] Passive-aggressive [ ] Divorce imminent
Final Outcome	[ ] Functional [ ] Functional(ish) [ ] Artistic reinterpretation

INVENTORY & CASUALTIES

Please indicate the number of the following:
Tools lost: ____
Screws left over: ____
Injuries sustained: ____
Arguments sparked: ____
"Let's call a professional" moments: ____
Number of times you used the phrase: "That'll do." ____

LESSONS (ALLEGEDLY) LEARNED

[ ] Next time, I'll measure first
[ ] Spirit levels are not optional
[ ] Maybe I do need a workbench
[ ] MDF isn't indestructible
[ ] I'm better at delegating
[ ] I regret everything

NEXT STEPS

[ ] Retell story at every social event
[ ] Submit for "DIY Hero of the Year" award
[ ] Cover it with a rug
[ ] Let Mavis think you planned it that way
[ ] Move house

VERY IMPORTANT PROJECT

SERIOUS STUFF HERE

PROJECT NAME:

_____

TARGET DATE (NON BINDING):

_____

PROJECT DESCRIPTION

_____

_____

_____

_____

_____

SAFETY

_____

_____

_____

_____

_____

TOOLS

PROJECT PREPARATION

PROJECT STEPS

PROJECT NOTES

PROJECT NOTES

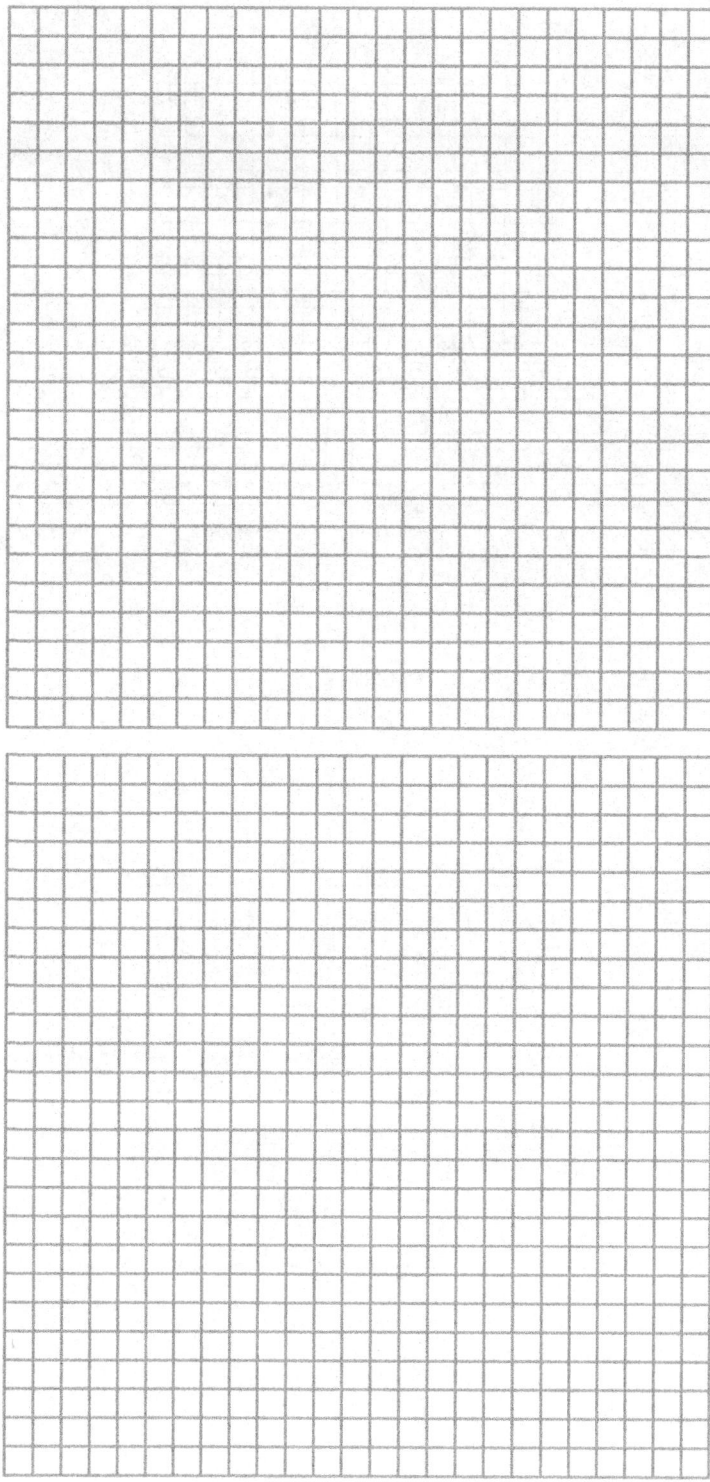

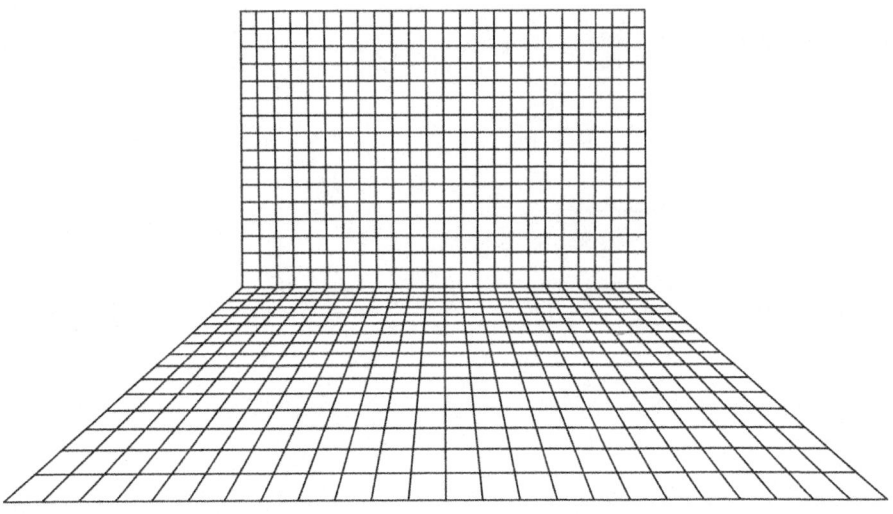
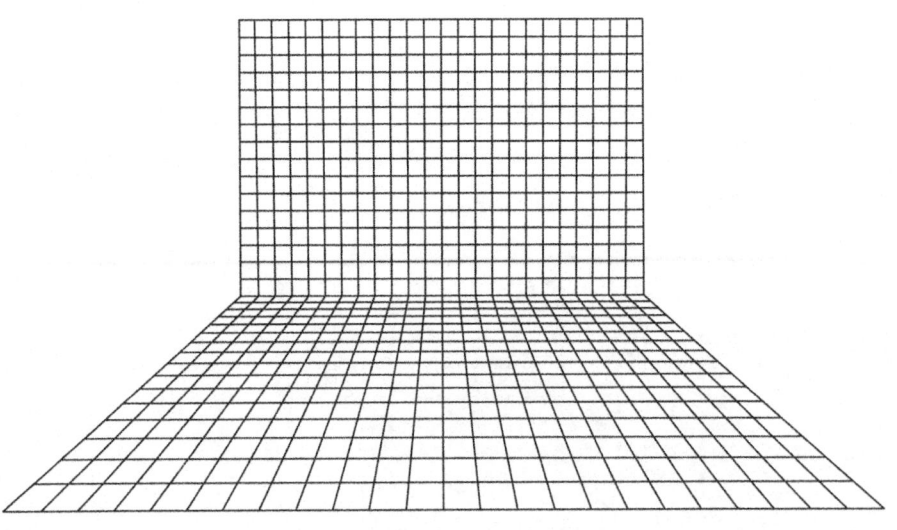

BASK IN THE GLORY OF A JOB WELL DONE!

POST-PROJECT REFLECTION FORM

FOR INTERNAL USE ONLY (I.E., YOUR EGO)
FORM 4A - VERSION 0.1 (STILL IN DRAFT)

PROJECT NAME: _____
(E.G., OPERATION WOBBLY SHELF, MILDLY AMBITIOUS DECKING, THE GREAT TILE INCIDENT)

START DATE: ____ / ____ / ____   PROJECTED COMPLETION DATE:
[ ] SAME DAY [ ] WITHIN THE MONTH [ ] SUBJECT TO CLIMATE

ACTUAL COMPLETION DATE: ____ / ____ / ____   [ ] STILL PENDING

PERSONAL ASSESSMENT
PLEASE RATE YOUR PERFORMANCE IN THE FOLLOWING AREAS:

Category	Rating (Tick One)
Planning & Preparation	[ ] Printed something [ ] Made notes [ ] Winged it gloriously
Tool Familiarity	[ ] Totally confident [ ] YouTubed it [ ] Used a spoon again
Structural Soundness	[ ] Rock solid [ ] Slight flex [ ] Will collapse when judged
Time Management	[ ] On schedule [ ] Lost 3 weekends [ ] Time is a construct
Stress Management	[ ] Zen monk [ ] Mildly snappy [ ] Shouted at the ladder
Communication with Partner	[ ] Harmonious [ ] Passive-aggressive [ ] Divorce imminent
Final Outcome	[ ] Functional [ ] Functional(ish) [ ] Artistic reinterpretation

INVENTORY & CASUALTIES

Please indicate the number of the following:
Tools lost: ____
Screws left over: ____
Injuries sustained: ____
Arguments sparked: ____
"Let's call a professional" moments: ____
Number of times you used the phrase: "That'll do." ____

LESSONS (ALLEGEDLY) LEARNED

[ ] Next time, I'll measure first
[ ] Spirit levels are not optional
[ ] Maybe I do need a workbench
[ ] MDF isn't indestructible
[ ] I'm better at delegating
[ ] I regret everything

NEXT STEPS

[ ] Retell story at every social event
[ ] Submit for "DIY Hero of the Year" award
[ ] Cover it with a rug
[ ] Let Mavis think you planned it that way
[ ] Move house

POST-PROJECT REFLECTION FORM

FOR INTERNAL USE ONLY (I.E., YOUR EGO)
FORM 4A - VERSION 0.1 (STILL IN DRAFT)

PROJECT NAME: _____
(E.G., OPERATION WOBBLY SHELF, MILDLY AMBITIOUS DECKING, THE GREAT TILE INCIDENT)

START DATE: ___ / ___ / ___ PROJECTED COMPLETION DATE:
[ ] SAME DAY   [ ] WITHIN THE MONTH   [ ] SUBJECT TO CLIMATE

ACTUAL COMPLETION DATE: ___ / ___ / ___   [ ] STILL PENDING

PERSONAL ASSESSMENT
PLEASE RATE YOUR PERFORMANCE IN THE FOLLOWING AREAS:

Category	Rating (Tick One)
Planning & Preparation	[ ] Printed something [ ] Made notes [ ] Winged it gloriously
Tool Familiarity	[ ] Totally confident [ ] YouTubed it [ ] Used a spoon again
Structural Soundness	[ ] Rock solid [ ] Slight flex [ ] Will collapse when judged
Time Management	[ ] On schedule [ ] Lost 3 weekends [ ] Time is a construct
Stress Management	[ ] Zen monk [ ] Mildly snappy [ ] Shouted at the ladder
Communication with Partner	[ ] Harmonious [ ] Passive-aggressive [ ] Divorce imminent
Final Outcome	[ ] Functional [ ] Functional(ish) [ ] Artistic reinterpretation

INVENTORY & CASUALTIES

Please indicate the number of the following:
Tools lost: ____
Screws left over: ____
Injuries sustained: ____
Arguments sparked: ____
"Let's call a professional" moments: ____
Number of times you used the phrase: "That'll do." ____

LESSONS (ALLEGEDLY) LEARNED

[ ] Next time, I'll measure first
[ ] Spirit levels are not optional
[ ] Maybe I do need a workbench
[ ] MDF isn't indestructible
[ ] I'm better at delegating
[ ] I regret everything

NEXT STEPS

[ ] Retell story at every social event
[ ] Submit for "DIY Hero of the Year" award
[ ] Cover it with a rug
[ ] Let Mavis think you planned it that way
[ ] Move house

DIY RISK ASSESSMENT FORM

FOR INTERNAL USE ONLY (I.E., YOUR EGO).
FORM 5A – VERSION 0.1 (STILL IN DRAFT)

PPROJECT TITLE:
"THE THING MY PARTNER ASKED ME TO FIX (EVENTUALLY)"

DATE:
☐ TODAY   ☐ TOMORROW   ☒ "LET'S NOT RUSH THESE THINGS"

ASSESSMENT CONDUCTED BY:
☐ ME
☐ NOT ME
☒ SOMEONE WITH MORE EXPERIENCE, IDEALLY A NEIGHBOUR

TASK DESCRIPTION

Describe the DIY task:

"Replace the thing with the other thing using... what do you call it... the twisty rod thing."

Potential Hazard	Likelihood	Severity	Mitigation Strategy
Hurting self with tool	High	Medium	Use tool box as decoy, do nothing
Confusing instruction manual	Certain	Existential	Blame poor translation, ignore entirely
Argument with partner	High	High	Nod enthusiastically, say "on it, babe!"
Getting distracted by kettle/TV/dog	Guaranteed	Low	Embrace distraction, declare "break"
Actually finishing the task	Very Low	Unknown	Not a current concern

DIY RISK ASSESSMENT FORM (PART 2)

COMPETENCE & TRAINING

Do you have experience in this task?
☐ Yes
☐ No
☑ Let's be honest, not really

Have you watched a YouTube tutorial?

☐ Yes
☑ Watched 3 mins, skipped to end
☐ Thought about watching one

REQUIRED TOOLS (TICK WHAT YOU PRETEND TO USE)

☐ Hammer
☐ Drill
☐ Level
☑ Coffee mug
☐ Masking Tape (HBM-approved)
☑ Pencil (mainly for chewing)
☐ Vague sense of initiative

EMERGENCY PREPAREDNESS

Who to contact if it all goes wrong:
☐ Local tradesperson
☑ Father-in-law
☐ Neighbour called Dave
☐ Emergency biscuit tin

First aid kit location:
☑ Somewhere behind the Christmas decorations
☐ Just rub it with tea

FINAL ASSESSMENT

☐ Task is safe and I am prepared
☐ Task is dangerous but I'm brave
☑ Task is terrifying, best leave it until next weekend

Signed: _____ (under duress)

Witnessed by: _____ (eye roll implied)

Printed in Dunstable, United Kingdom